Gerry Frank's

WHERE TO:

Find It
Buy It
Eat It
in
New York

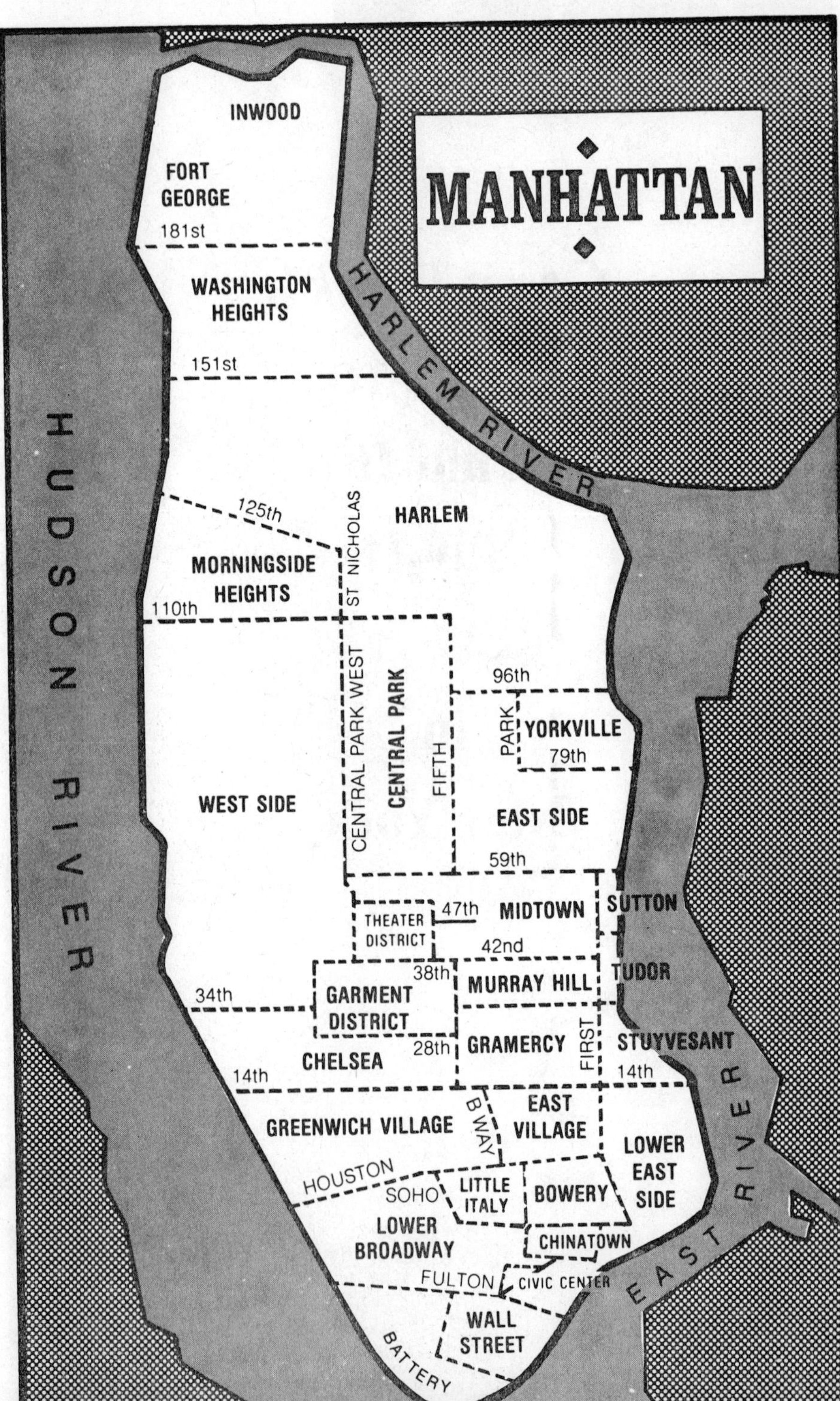
MANHATTAN
INWOOD
FORT GEORGE
181st
WASHINGTON HEIGHTS
151st
HARLEM RIVER
HUDSON RIVER
125th
ST NICHOLAS
HARLEM
MORNINGSIDE HEIGHTS
110th
CENTRAL PARK WEST
CENTRAL PARK
FIFTH
96th
PARK
YORKVILLE
79th
WEST SIDE
EAST SIDE
59th
47th
THEATER DISTRICT
MIDTOWN
SUTTON
42nd
38th
MURRAY HILL
TUDOR
34th
GARMENT DISTRICT
28th
GRAMERCY
FIRST
STUYVESANT
CHELSEA
14th
14th
B WAY
EAST VILLAGE
GREENWICH VILLAGE
LOWER EAST SIDE
HOUSTON
SOHO
LITTLE ITALY
BOWERY
LOWER BROADWAY
CHINATOWN
FULTON
CIVIC CENTER
EAST RIVER
WALL STREET
BATTERY

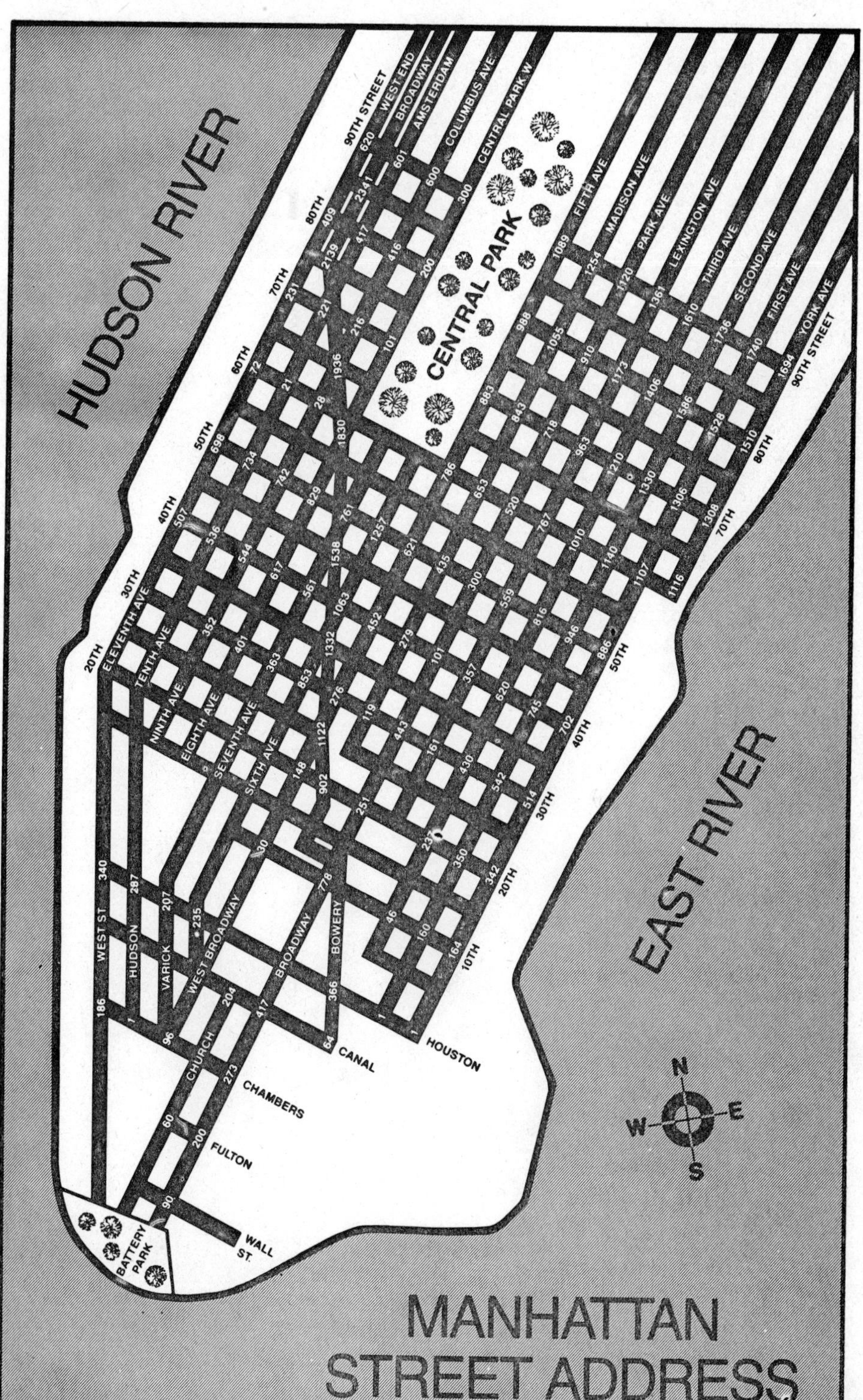

HUDSON RIVER
EAST RIVER
CENTRAL PARK
BATTERY PARK
MANHATTAN
STREET ADDRESS
N
S
E
W
WEST END
BROADWAY
AMSTERDAM
COLUMBUS AVE
CENTRAL PARK W
FIFTH AVE
MADISON AVE
PARK AVE
LEXINGTON AVE
THIRD AVE
SECOND AVE
FIRST AVE
YORK AVE
90TH STREET
ELEVENTH AVE
TENTH AVE
NINTH AVE
EIGHTH AVE
SEVENTH AVE
SIXTH AVE
WEST ST
HUDSON
VARICK
WEST BROADWAY
BROADWAY
BOWERY
CHURCH
CANAL
HOUSTON
CHAMBERS
FULTON
WALL ST.

Gerry Frank's

WHERE TO:

Find It
Buy It
Eat It
in
New York

For additional copies, write or call:
Gerry's Frankly Speaking
P.O. Box 2225
Salem, Oregon 97308
(503) 585-8411

Gerry Frank's
Where to Find It, Buy It, Eat It
in New York

Printed in the United States of America
Library of Congress Catalog Card Number: 80-7802
ISBN: 0-9612578-3-0
First Edition 1980
Second Printing 1980
Second Edition 1981
Second Printing 1981
Third Printing 1982
Third Edition 1983
Second Printing 1984
Third Printing 1984
Fourth Edition 1985
Second Printing 1986

Foreword

Thank you! You are now reading one of more than 125,000 copies of this book that are in print. Little did I think that what started as a hobby some 10 years ago would turn out to be the number-one best-selling complete guide to New York. What fun it has been, especially for two reasons: first, because someone from Oregon is writing about the Big Apple (how many times have I been asked how a guy from the other side of America can know so much about Manhattan?); and second, because some of those same snooty publishers who wouldn't give me the time of day when I showed them the manuscript for the first edition now want to publish this book. Where were they when I needed them? Now I don't; I am publishing it myself. So I owe *you,* the readers, the thanks. You have made it all possible, and I am very grateful.

This is the fourth edition. Since New York changes very rapidly, particularly the restaurants, I am constantly on the go, month in and month out, collecting new places, updating reviews of stores, services, food shops, et cetera, that have changed in one way or another. A completely new and revised edition is published every two years. Every review from previous editions that is included has been checked and updated where necessary. Over 300 new restaurants, stores, services, and food shops have been included in this volume, and a new section of special tours of all kinds has been prepared for both New York residents and visitors. A completely new, exclusive list of the best taste treats and the most valuable shopping hints for Manhattan is also presented for your pleasure.

Hearing from readers is one of the real treats of this business. I have had the pleasure of visiting with literally hundreds of you in bookstores, fairs, meetings, and the like. Many others have called or written with suggestions or evaluations of their own (particularly on the eating places). This input is very valuable. I hope you will continue to contact me at P.O. Box 2225, Salem, Oregon 97308, or by phone at 503-585-8411. What a thrill it is when a reader says, "You made my trip to New York," or "I found the best bargain of my life at that H.B.A. Fur store you suggested," or "That dinner at Primavera was the finest Italian dinner I have ever had." When a New York authority like Malcolm Forbes took the time to say some nice things, such as the quote on the front cover, I felt that all the work had definitely been worthwhile. And when jaded New Yorkers tell me that I've helped them find treasures they hadn't known about before, it is a very special pleasure, indeed. Of course, some readers don't agree with my selections or omissions. So be it. I think it was Voltaire who said, "When everyone is thinking the same way, no one is thinking very much."

It is important for you to note that no one pays to be included in this book. The selections are all mine, personally, and except for a few of the women's services, I have visited every place listed in this book. Many establishments now ask to be included. I check out all of them myself; many are not selected. No one featured here has editorial control over their write-up. A number of proprietors don't like what I've said about their establishments. Too bad. Many have changed or improved as a result of criticism here. Charivari, for example, toned down their background music in response to my review. But a lot have not: Barney's still makes the customer and salesperson go through almost as much paperwork as the Pentagon for every purchase that is made.

There is one person who deserves special credit for her help: Esther Benovitz. She knows New York City, inside and out, like no one else. Her expertise has been an invaluable asset in the compilation and presentation of the information in this edition. Special thanks also must go to a number of other people who have contributed their help in a variety of different ways: Cheryl Johnson, Brant Mewborn, LaVelle Blum, Rhonna Bassett, Mary and Con Paulson, Carol Gutmann, Rosalyn Friedman, Jeryme English, and Carolyn Levock. Cheryl Johnson has been particularly helpful in many technical aspects of compiling this volume.

Contents

V. WHERE TO FIND IT: NEW YORK'S BEST SERVICES

I. The World's Greatest City

Introduction

The Big Apple. New York, New York. "If I can make it there, I'll make it anywhere," croons Frank Sinatra, and suddenly that glorious Manhattan skyline looms before you, and the realization hits you—"Hey, I'm really in New York now."

This realization occurs to tourists flying over the city, to motorists coming into the tunnels from the New Jersey side, to serious businessmen lunching atop one of the city's buildings, and even to jaded natives elbowing their way through the streets. It matters not a bit that they've seen New York on TV, in movies, and in real life as often as they've seen a morning newspaper. Sooner or later, there's a moment when just being there is overwhelming, and you want to say, "This is it! This is New York!"

So just what is this New York? Geographically, New York City encompasses five boroughs and nearly 8 million people. But when people say "New York," they're usually refering to the island of Manhattan. And yet it is a great deal more. New York's educational TV station and football teams are based in New Jersey. The two baseball teams are in the Bronx and Queens, respectively, and the New York Aquarium is in Brooklyn.

Philosophically, New York is as Sinatra says it is. It's the pinnacle for umpteen professions and industries (Park Avenue doctors, Wall Street executives, Madison Avenue ad men, Upper West Side yuppies, Seventh Avenue garment manufacturers, and media and showbiz personalities—the list is endless). Virtually every possible financial enterprise and type of commerce is centered in New York, and each supports a myriad of auxiliary businesses. But Manhattan is an island, and its limited size influences the lifestyles of its residents again and again. Yes, the variety and novelty add to the vitality of the city, but when space is limited, only the best survive. And that is true at every level of city activity. In New York, it may be easier to find esoteric places like a copper retinning establishment, a natural herbist, a stained-glass repairing operation, or half a dozen Chinese pasta factories, but not even a city of 8 million is going to come up with enough customers for a product that's not the best.

A large percentage of Manhattan is residential (a fact that is a surprise to non-New Yorkers), and that percentage is increasing as neighborhoods that were formerly industrial or had degenerated into slums are reclaimed by urban homesteading. But there is always a mad scramble for space and apartments, and New Yorkers, never known for their stability anyway, think nothing of moving from neighborhood to neighborhood. In the first edition, I ventured the opinion that there probably wasn't a 30 year old in Manhattan who was still residing in a non-rent controlled or non-co-op apartment in which he or she had been born. No one has challenged that statement in five years. What this means is that Manhattan is an island of transients. They moved to Manhattan, and they move around a lot within Manhattan. So, that notorious New York coldness is not so much a lack of civility as it is a response to the fact that your neighbor may not be your neighbor in six months, and even if they're around for three years, the occasion to meet may never arise.

There's a flip side to this. New Yorkers are a proud and feisty breed, but they will readily accept anyone who loosens up and appreciates them. Sharing a cab, getting trapped in an elevator, going to the same show, or living on the same block are all valid reasons for friendship. No one cares a lot about roots. If you want to call yourself a New Yorker, you are one. Accents don't matter, either. People from Boise, Idaho, or Bensonhurst, Brooklyn, have the same claims on being a quintessential New Yorker. We are a nation of immigrants, and New York, the home of Ellis Island and the Statue of Liberty, has been the flagship for 400 years. Each immigrant group has left its imprint on the city and made it what it is today.

New York began at the lower end of Manhattan known as the Battery, and there are still reminders there of the original Dutch settlement of New Amsterdam. Streets are tiny, winding, and narrow. The world-renowned Wall Street, no wider than a suburban driveway, takes its name from the wall erected in 1653 to guard the northern frontier of the Dutch community. It is mind-boggling to stand on Wall Street and realize that all of New York once existed only south of that point. (City Hall, for example, has an ornate facade facing downtown and a plain brownstone front facing uptown. When it was built, not many people ever saw the uptown side.) The tip of Manhattan has remained a center of commerce, banking, and industry. It is here that the federal, state, and municipal government offices are located, adjacent to the financial capital of the world. But even down there, Battery Park City is now housing new residents, and Pathmark has opened a supermarket within sight of corporate dining halls.

Getting to the City

These days, most tourists travel to New York City by air, touching down at either La Guardia, Kennedy, or Newark airports. While LaGuardia and Kennedy are within the city limits proper, Newark is probably the closest to Manhattan. Newark, located in New Jersey, is grossly underused and therefore underserviced as well. The situation has improved since Peoplexpress made the formerly incomplete Terminal C its headquarters, but that economy airline's passengers are not known for generating limo and car services. So Newark remains the poorest in ground transportation and convenience. All three airports are serviced by rental cars, express buses, taxis, and group limousines. There are some variations at each, so we will discuss them separately.

Kennedy International Airport is the busiest and furthest from Manhattan. Chances are that an international flight will be out of Kennedy.

Buses—The Carey Coach Company is the most venerable of the bus services. They have recently upgraded the service, and it is now much more convenient from each airport. The bus stops at the baggage-claim area of each terminal and goes to 125 Park Avenue (41st St, opposite Grand Central Terminal) or the Port Authority Bus Terminal (Eighth Ave at 42nd St, on the West Side). There are also connecting buses between all three airports, although the Newark route is a little convoluted. There is a recording for Carey information (718-632-0500), or for information in general, call 1-800-AIR-RIDE, which is Port Authority information. They are very helpful. Even cheaper than Carey is the much-lauded J.F.K. Express, the "Train to the Plane." Call 718-858-7272 to make sure it is in operation. It is one of the best deals in town, if you don't have a lot of baggage. Periodically, there are movements to cancel it, since it is hardly used by anyone other than airport personnel, who know a good deal when they see one. The trains are clean, swift, and very safe, and make seven stops in Manhattan every 20 minutes between 5:30 a.m. and 12:50 a.m. everyday. Pick up points (for a shuttle that takes passengers to the train at the Howard Beach Station) are clearly marked outside each terminal. And speaking of Howard Beach, there is a still cheaper way of taking a train from Kennedy into Manhattan. The A train stops at Howard Beach and then goes back to the city (or to Far Rockaway). Passengers may catch the "Train to the Plane" shuttle bus to Howard

Beach for double the regular subway fare and then take the A train rather than the special express. In addition to being half the price of the express, the A connects with regular subway stops, making it more accessible than the express. Those are the advantages. The disadvantages are that we are not talking about a great deal of money either way; the A route is longer in time; and the express runs on the A tracks, so all of the stops on the express can be duplicated on the A. Besides, I wouldn't recommend that any visitor's introduction to the city be a plunge into the regular subway system. There is one other really cheap way of getting to the airport which involves a subway-bus hookup. The IND subway line to Queens (the E or the F) stops at Union Turnpike, about 20 minutes out of Manhattan. Upstairs at that stop, the Green Bus Line's Q-10 (718-995-4700) travels to Kennedy Airport. The cost is a token's worth each for the bus and subway, and many of the passengers are airline staff members.

Taxis—At each airport, taxis are carefully organized and regulated. Taxis are called from taxi queues and dispatched by officials. *Never accept an offer from someone who says they'll help get you a cab.* It is unnecessary. The airports are also experimenting with group share-a-ride cabs. This is the only place within the city where this practice is legal; at all other times, the number of passengers or stops has no effect on taxi fare. In this case, though, the fare is shared and reduced. Of course, you can arrange an informal agreement with a fellow traveler to share a cab with you. But the share-a-ride service has the advantage of an official rate set before the fare has to be paid.

Car Service—In addition to private services called in advance, there are quasi-group limo rides. One is Fugazy Share A Ride, which is very difficult to track down. (I was given 15 phone numbers, including the executive offices. It was there that I was told, "There are a lot of stupid people who work for this company." Unfortunately, even that person didn't know how Share A Ride worked. I tell you all of this so you shouldn't think the life of a guidebook writer is easy! Fugazy has just been bought by Metromedia, so maybe the picture will clear up.) Abbey's Transportation (718-361-9092) is a world apart. (They must be number two, because they certainly try harder!) Trips are organized from transportation desks at each terminal between 7 a.m. and 11 p.m. If there is no desk, look for an Abbey's phone. The price is only slightly more than the "Train to the Plane" and would be the optimum choice for those with a lot of luggage. For the return trip, Abbey's stops at all the major hotels. This can add to travel time, so make allowances.

LaGuardia Airport is closer to Manhattan than Kennedy, and it is the airport most used for domestic travel. The shuttles and regional airlines operate out of LaGuardia. The ground transportation is similar to that at Kennedy.

Buses—Here, too, Carey operates an express bus (718-632-0500). It runs every 15 minutes from each baggage claim area to 125 Park Avenue or the Port Authority bus terminal. Return service runs from those locations to each individual terminal. While there is no "Train to the Plane" to LaGuardia, it is possible to get there by public transportation. It's not terribly swift, convenient, or easy, but it is cheap. The Triboro Coach #Q.33 (718-335-1000) stops at the Roosevelt Avenue I.N.D. subway station in Queens and goes to LaGuardia. That same station is also the IRT line's #7 train's 74th Street stop. It's a classic example of the nonmeshing of the early subway lines, so getting from one train to the other is a long trek. (The I.R.T. at that point isn't even a subway; it's an elevated line.) However, either line is convenient for catching the Q.33, and the trip from there to the airport is very quick. Many of the airline employees who live in Manhattan take this route. When in doubt, follow them, although here, too, I would hesitate to recommend this route on your first trip to the city.

Taxis—The story is exactly the same as at J.F.K., although proximity to the city can make the tab half the price. Taxis line up in order, and each rider takes a cab by turn. Unlike Manhattan in the rain, there is no problem in getting a cab at the airport, but know your destination and adopt an attitude that says you know where you are going. Also, it is permissible to ask the dispatcher or cabbie for a rough idea of what the trip will cost. They should be able to predict the fare within a dollar or two. If the meter differs drastically from the estimate, or you're told the only way to reach Manhattan is through a scenic tour of all five boroughs, you've been had. (If you need to register a complaint, the number for the Taxi and Limousine Commission is 869-4110, ext: 866 for non-medallion cabs and 869-4513 or 382-9301 for medallion cabs; the address is 221 W 41st St, NY, NY 10036.) And here's a hint: a good cabbie can get to Manhattan toll-free via the 59th Street bridge. Many cabbies will take the Queens-Midtown tunnel, which incurs a toll cost and adds the mileage between 34th Street and 59th Street to your destination. That's still not bad, and it may even be a good choice if traffic is heavy or if your destination is midtown or further downtown. However, under no circumstances should you end up on the Tri-Borough bridge, unless you're staying with someone who lives in upper Manhattan; most hotels are in midtown.

Car Service—At LaGuardia, the Fugazy and Abbey folks operate services identical to those from Kennedy. However, the Port Authority and the Taxi Dispatch Service have a joint share-a-ride program, which applies to LaGuardia alone. Specially marked dispatch areas are the meeting points for people who are willing to share a cab (and costs) to points in Manhattan below 96th Street. It runs virtually all the time except (for some unknown reason) Saturdays and the wee hours of the morning. It's only a dollar or two more than the Carey bus, and the service is door to door.

Newark Airport is the stepsister of airports in the Metropolitan area. For one thing, it is not in the city or even in the state of New York. So the city authorities have no control (I'd even go so far as to say they have no interest) in Newark's transportation. The Port Authority is by name a bi-state agency, but for the longest time, there were inequities there as well. Recently, things have improved drastically. A large part of that improvement can be credited to the growth of the economy airlines, who, having been closed out of J.F.K. and LaGuardia, were forced to set up shop at Newark. Then, too, both of the former airports are vastly overcrowded, and many patrons (both corporate and individual) opt for the no-hassle, relative calm that Newark offers. As a result, ground transportation has improved as well.

Buses—Transport of New Jersey runs an express bus every 15 minutes from Newark to the Port Authority bus terminal at 42nd Street and Eighth Avenue. (From 1 a.m. to 5 a.m., the schedule slows to every half hour.) The fare is the lowest of all the bus services, and remember, Newark is the closest of the airports. The Carey Bus Company's counterpart in New Jersey is the Olympic Trails Bus Company (201-589-6513 or 212-964-6233). For the same fare as the TNJ bus, Olympic stops at the World Trade Center, the outside of the East Side Airlines Terminal (the building is now closed, but the bus stop remains, check to make sure this stop is in use) at 38th Street and First Avenue, and Park Avenue and 41st Street. (The latter is the same 125 Park Avenue where Carey stops.) These are also the pickup points, and the bus runs every 20 minutes. There is a public transportation method for going from Newark to New York as well. However, as the current charge for the Olympic and TNJ buses is only four dollars, it hardly seems worth it. But here it is: The #62 TNJ bus stops outside terminals A, B, and C (but *not* the North Terminal) at Newark Airport. It is a local bus that goes through Newark and terminates at Newark's (not New York's) Penn Station. From there, it is possible to get into N.Y. via the P.A.T.H. (Port Authority Trans-Hudson) train. The P.A.T.H. goes to the World Trade Center, but it is possible to change trains in Jersey City at New Jersey's Journal Square for a 33rd Street Manhattan terminus. That doesn't seem to be worth saving two bucks. For a bit more money, you can take the Airlink bus (also run by TNJ), which runs from all four terminals directly to Newark's Penn Station. There are better alternatives, but the point is that travel from Newark is very reasonable.

Taxis—The economic angle changes when you deal with taxis. Until quite recently, the fare *from* New York to Newark (N.Y. cabbies aren't allowed to make pickups in New Jersey) was twice the meter rate plus tolls. That has been changed to a flat $10 plus tolls over the meter fare. This is still not remotely in the reasonable class unless there are several people in the party. Since cabs charge by the mile and not by the number of passengers, and bus fares are determined by the exact opposite, several people dividing one fare can make a taxi actually cheaper than a bus.

Car Service—Our friends at Abbey's have a Newark Aiport/ N.Y. Minibus Service. They are not alone, since their successful service has spawned competitors. It runs from 8 a.m. to midnight and operates from all of the terminals to the midtown hotels. The price is currently about $11 from Newark to a hotel. The advantages are that the service is door to door, and the price is reasonable. Finally, there are car services and limousines from various points in the city. Several are listed under Taxicabs and Limousines in "Services," and I would venture that you haven't a chance of getting one to come out to the airport to pick you up if they have no prior relationship with you. For that reason, most of them should be used to return to the airport, and for that, several are excellent. (The scene often changes rapidly here. Don't count on any unless you have a firm reservation.)

So that's it, in a rather large nutshell. Welcome to New York!

Getting Around in the City

Travel within the city (and Manhattan in particular) involves four basic modes of transportation: car (taxi), subway, bus, and shank's mare. There are some more grandiose ideas such as hydroplanes, ferries, and movable sidewalks, but for the most part, the former four are the formal means of transportation.

Cars—New York is decidedly not a convenient city for automobiles. There is no place to legally park on a midtown street during business hours. Garage fees are exorbitant, and hotels often charge as much to park a car as it costs to rent a small room. Compounding all that is the delightful institution of alternate-side-of-the-street parking. Ostensibly, its purpose is to clear the streets for street cleaning. Natives, or indeed anyone who has ever seen a New York City street, know better. While custom allows certain neighborhoods to double-and-triple-park on the "good" side, the people who benefit most from alternate-side-of-the-street parking are the enterprising individuals who make arrangements to move and park the cars of their regular customers. But most Manhattanites never use a car within the island. Its primary purpose is to transport its owner to summer and weekend homes and airports.

Taxis—Taxis in New York are carefully regulated and controlled, but the situation is still a mess. The easiest thing to know is a rider's rights, and the hardest thing is to get them enforced. (By the way, all the jokes about not being able to get a cab in New York in the rain are true. You can't.) Perhaps this is the best place to start using New York assertiveness. There are three kinds of cabs. Medallion cabs are the only ones to display medallions on their hoods, call numbers on their roof lights, and yellow exteriors. They are also the only ones allowed to cruise for passengers, and they must agree to go anywhere in the city. In New York, there are no fare zones or fees for extra passengers, pets, or luggage, although only checker cabs (the larger ones with the checkered band around the middle) are allowed to take more than four passengers. Fleet cabs (usually the ones with advertisements on their roofs) impose a surcharge of 50¢ for after-8 p.m. fares. Passengers may request several stops and pickups while in the cab, for which a driver cannot make an additional charge or start the meter anew. There are also minor rights, such as the right to pick the music, smoking or nonsmoking conditions, and even conversation. If you feel that any of these rights are seriously violated, register your complaints with the Taxi and Limousine Commission. Incidentally, each cabbie must clearly display his name and license number. There are also gypsy cabs, best explained by the slogan of one, "We're not yellow, we go anywhere." This is true, but they also have varying degrees of regulation (try applying a standard to a car that will "go anywhere") and insurance. I don't recommend them, and officially, they are not allowed to cruise in Manhattan for passengers. In the rain, sometimes the officials become color-blind as do desparate passengers. Usually it works out, because most gypsy cabs have meters and livery licenses. I'd still rather get wet. Finally, there are car and limousine services. I have listed them separately under "Services," but they can only answer calls made in advance. The price is usually higher, although renting a car and driver for a specific period of time (if there are going to be a lot of stops) may work out better than taking a series of cabs.

Subways and Buses—First, a little history. The subways started as independent, privately run lines, and thus there wasn't much meshing or even civic interest in the lines. Stations were laid out with an eye toward economics rather than future city growth or convenience, and whole sections of the city are very poorly served with minimal local stops. With the exception of the 42nd Street shuttle and the Canarsie and Flushing lines, it is also impossible to go crosstown on one line. Use exact change or tokens, which can be purchased at booths in subway stations. For schedule information, call 718-330-1234. If it's hopelessly busy (not an unusual situation), call 218-330-4660, the MTA's public-relations office. Both the buses and subways run 24 hours, seven days a week. Bus stops are clearly marked, usually at two to four block intervals, and each stop should have a route map posted as well.

Walking—At one point, the cover of this book was going to be a worn-out shoe, which accumulated its mileage on scouting trips around the city. I still think it's the best way to get around. There's nothing like a walk in New York, but here's some advice to high-heel fans: wear running shoes if you plan to do much serious walking. Don't worry about looking silly. Manhattan businesswomen wear Nikes and Adidas while walking to work. They carry their dress shoes in their bags. And one day on the streets will convince you of the sensibleness of that ploy.

New York is laid out, more or less, in a grid-iron pattern. Avenues run north-south, and numbered streets run east-west, with Fifth Avenue dividing east from west. In the geographical center is Central Park, where it's possible to forget that you're in New York City.

But the early settlers didn't use the grid-iron idea. South of Fourth Street, there isn't a street or avenue that runs straight, let alone one that's numbered. They turn, twist, vanish, and reappear. This would be manageable if we were talking about a single neighborhood, but this area happens to include Wall Street, City Hall, Chinatown, Little Italy, the Lower East Side, SoHo, the Bowery, and the Village.

Above 14th Street, order returns, except for Broadway, which makes two almost 45-degree angles on its route north. Heading cross-town from the East River, you get First Avenue (where the land widens, there are York and East End Avenues uptown, and Avenues, A, B, and C downtown), Second Avenue, Third Avenue, Lexington Avenue, Park Avenue (fed by Fourth Avenue, south of 14th Street; Park Avenue South is Park Avenue south of 32nd Street), Madison Avenue, Fifth Avenue, and Sixth Avenue (New Yorkers call it Sixth Avenue; officials and hicks call it Avenue of the Americas). After Sixth Avenue comes Seventh Avenue, Eighth Avenue (which becomes Central Park West at Columbus Circle, where Broadway dissects it at 59th Street), Ninth Avenue (which becomes Columbus when Broadway crosses *it* at 66th Street), Tenth Avenue (which becomes Amsterdam Avenue at 63rd Street). Then Broadway, at 72nd Street, heads north, between Amsterdam and West End Avenues (the latter is Eleventh, below 63rd Street). If you're still following all of this, at 107th Street, Broadway merges with West End Avenue, which becomes Broadway.

Key to Manhattan Addresses

To determine the approximate cross street for addresses located on the avenues, try the following formula. Cancel the last figure of the house number. Divide the remainder by two and add the key number below. The result is approximately the nearest cross street.

Ave A, B, C, D .... Add 3
1st and 2nd Ave .... Add 3
3rd Ave .... Add 9 or 10
4th Ave (Park Ave South) .... Add 8
5th Ave
  Up to 200 .... Add 13
  Up to 400 .... Add 16
  Up to 600 .... Add 18
  Up to 775 .... Add 20
  From 775 to 1286
    Cancel last figure and subtract 18
  Up to 1500 .... Add 45
  Above 2000 .... Add 24
Ave of the Americas .... Subt 12 or 13
7th Ave .... Add 12
  Above 110th St .... Add 20
8th Ave .... Add 9 or 10
9th Ave .... Add 13
10th Ave .... Add 14
11th Ave .... Add 15
Amsterdam Ave .... Add 59 or 60
Audubon Ave .... Add 165
Broadway .... Up to 750 is below 8th St
  756 to 846 .... Subt 29
  847 to 953 .... Subt 25
  Above 953 .... Subt 31
Columbus Ave .... Add 59 or 60
Convent Ave .... Add 127
Ft. Washington Ave .... Add 158
Lenox Ave .... Add 110
Lexington Ave .... Add 22
Madison Ave .... Add 26
Manhattan Ave .... Add 100
Park Ave .... Add 34 or 35
St. Nicholas Ave .... Add 110
West End Ave .... Add 59 or 60
Central Park West
  Divide House Number by 10 and add 60
Riverside Drive
  Divide by 10 and add 72

To determine which avenue is nearest to a street address, use the following chart. Example: 356 W 34th St is located between 8th and 9th Avenues.

East Side
1 at 5th Ave
101 at Park or 4th Ave
201 at 3rd Ave
301 at 2nd Ave
401 at 1st Ave
501 at York Ave or Ave A
601 at Ave B

West Side
1 at 5th Ave
101 at 6th Ave (Lenox Ave north of 110th St)
201 at 7th Ave
301 at 8th Ave
401 at 9th Ave (Columbus Ave north of 59th St)
501 at 10th Ave (Amsterdam Ave north of 59th St)
601 at 11th Ave (West End Ave north of 59th St)

Where to Find It

Unlike almost any other city, New York's merchants, be they wholesale or retail, clump together in districts. The city has dozens of such areas, and shoppers instinctively flock to them first. The boundaries change, sometimes slowly by expansion or by loss of popularity for the stores' products, and sometimes so rapidly that whole districts, which have existed in the same place for years, up and move in less than six months. The electronics area around the World Trade Center gave way for that edifice in record time. The used-books area around Cooper Square is another that has slowly faded away. Starting from lower Manhattan, here are the shopping districts of the city.

Fish: The Fulton Fish Market, across from the South Street Seaport, is the source of nearly every fish or seafood item in the metropolitan area, if not the Eastern Seaboard. If you want it fresh, six a.m. is considered a late time to shop, and the fishmongers preparing for the A&P are not about to discuss the virtue of the day's flounder catch. But the price is right. They sell to the general public, and there are a series of tours and lectures that imply they are doing *something* to upgrade their image, if not their smell. The Clams on the Halfshell tour (call 962-1608) at dawn is sold out months in advance.

Junk: The Canal Street area, which borders the financial district and SoHo, is a bargain hunter's dream. In front of the stores are bins full of everything from rusty nails to used raincoats, but the neighborhood specialty is hardware and household items. The scene resembles nothing so much as last year's rummage sale, but those who do rummage through the merchandise can unearth great finds.

Kitchenware, Lighting and Restaurant Supplies: Starting at the Bowery and Houston Street and walking north to Cooper Square, you'll want to ignore the neighborhood denizens and concentrate on professional kitchenware. Everything from Garland stoves to specialized light bulbs can be had here for laughable fractions of the usual retail prices. Most of the "local color" is too busy sleeping it off to bother shoppers, but do come with a partner.

Books: In the old days, Cooper Square was book country. Today, the Strand and Barnes and Noble's original store are two of the vestiges of the old-, used-, and rare-book venue. The rest have moved uptown and become antiquarians (read expensive).

Appliances, Fashions, Housewares: And I could add sheer madness to that list. Where else but the place that throbs like an international bazaar—the Lower East Side. Don't miss it!

Discounted Men's Wear: Walk up and down the buildings on Fifth Avenue between 18th, 19th, and 20th Streets. The usual cry is, "I got two suits for less than I usually spend on one."

Flowers: From 26th Street through 30th Street and from Sixth Avenue to Seventh Avenue, business is blooming. Most of the flower merchants are open for early-morning wholesale only. But the normal business day sees plant accessories, pots, baskets, planters, and artificial flowers sold to all. Note: Several wholesalers are moving to new quarters in College Point, Queens.

Fur: The area around Seventh Avenue, between 27th Street and 30th Street, could pass for an outpost of the Yukon. Manufacturers, wholesalers, distributors, and showrooms burrow into these three blocks, and many of the operations run a retail business that puts Macy's to shame.

Feathers, Beads, and Trimmings: An auxiliary to the garment district, the area off Sixth Avenue in the upper twenties offers flowers, bows, and buckles. There are probably more beads and bangles on 28th Street than in all of Ohio.

Women's Clothing: The Garment Center, Seventh Avenue, Fashion Avenue—each term is synonymous, and each one says it all. From 35th Street to 39th Street and from Broadway to Seventh Avenue, there is only one industry—the wholesale dressing of America's women. There's nothing quite like it.

Hats and Fabrics: These may seem like strange bedfellows, but both of these Garment Center accessories can be found in the upper thirties and lower forties between Sixth and Seventh Avenue.

Handbags: The thirties off Fifth Avenue. For some reason, few of these stores are on ground level, but on the higher floors, wholesale and retail handbag operations abound.

Furniture: The fraternal headquarters of the furniture industry (not the manufacturing plants) are on Lexington Avenue between 29th Street and 33rd Street. The buildings in this area house either official dealers and showrooms or such accessory industries as upholsterers, cooperative showrooms, or clearance centers. Note, however, that this is not the interior-design center. The D&D Building (Decoration and Design) is located at 979 Third Avenue, and it is not usually open to the public.

Photographic Supplies: It may not be a coincidence that the photographic supply sources of the East Coast are located in the lower thirties between Seventh Avenue and Broadway, next to the Garment Center, whose showrooms display fashion photographs of their models and products.

Theater: Even out-of-towners know the streets of the theater district, because of the plays and songs that have made them famous. For instance: "Give my regards to Broadway," or "Come and meet those dancing feet on the avenue I'm taking you to, 42nd Street." Now that I've got you singing, let me give you a quick update. The real theater district today is a bit further uptown and decidedly on the west side of Broadway—basically, 44th Street to 51st Street. And don't forget the TKTS (reduced-price tickets) booth in Duffy Square.

Diamonds: 47th Street between Fifth Avenue and Sixth Avenue is the diamond district. They don't give samples.

Musical Equipment: Classical sheet music and piano stores are located around Carnegie Hall (57th Street and Seventh Avenue). Other instruments, acoustic and electronic, are found in the shops clustered on the block between Sixth Avenue and Seventh Avenue on West 48th Street.

Boutiques: Madison Avenue. The shops on ground level are all boutiques. Higher up are the offices of the nation's most powerful advertising firms.

Museums: Museum Row may be known as the longest mile to those who don't love museums. But between 70th Street and 103rd Street on Fifth Avenue stand the Frick Collection, the Guggenheim, the Metropolitan, the Jewish Museum, the Cooper-Hewitt, and the Museum of the City of New York.

Thrift Shops: Third Avenue in the upper east seventies, all of the east eighties, and part of the east nineties is "resale country." Note the neighborhood. The Salvation Army outposts are elsewhere; the merchandise on Third Avenue is high class.

After this list, it should be apparent that in New York it is possible to buy virtually anything at wholesale prices. New Yorkers, even those who exclusively shop Bloomie's, have a subconscious awareness of this fact at all times. So how is it possible that the world's largest store (not to mention close to a million others) are also located in the city? Because price isn't everything. While researching this book, we constantly searched for places that were distinctive and offered something special. For lack of a better word, we call it value and define it as an offering of service, uniqueness, style, and price. If an establishment has all of these qualities, so much the better, but shopping in New York always assumes that they are obtainable—and expected. Yes, New Yorkers expect service. If they don't get it, they can always go next door or down the street or elsewhere . . . and they do.

The places included in this volume qualify on as many of those points as possible. Once in a while, uniqueness or a good price will triumph over service (ever visit the Lower East Side?), but it's usually an equitable trade off. And when one shops in New York, bear in mind that this is all to be expected.

Finally, relax. New York may be big, but it really is a friendly hometown. New Yorkers delight in sharing their city to the point of believing that it belongs to anyone who wants to claim it. Don't stop strangers and ask for the best spot to stow a wad of money, but a typical New York scene is a bellboy with a heavy Spanish accent proudly giving directions to the best cheap restaurant in midtown to a couple from Iowa. Only in New York is "Indian Jewish" or "Cuban Italian" cuisine a common option. Members of every ethnic group live in New York in great numbers, but whatever nationalism is exhibited it is usually "New York" first and native land second. The famous, the simple, the rich, the poor—they all live together in New York. Jackie Onassis lives in Manhattan. So does Greta Garbo. No one cares. Odds are that someone famous crosses the path of a New Yorker everyday. The average New York kid thinks nothing of having been on television or going to the opera, the Philharmonic, the ballet, or Broadway. It's all part of living in New York. And that brings us full circle. That average New York kid will grow up to rush through the streets of New York in part of the bustle that makes the city what it is. And one day he'll look up and notice the skyline and say, "This is incredible. This is New York. And I'm here."

Manhattan at Night

As the song says, New York is the city that never sleeps. (That's also been adopted as the slogan of Citibank.) A good percentage of the population works the swing shift (No, they're not all ladies of the evening!), and an even larger percentage uses the late and early hours to recover from the nine-to-five grind. The subways and buses run all night, though irregularly, so I would recommend taking cabs. And remember, as Ann Landers (I think) once said,

"Any kind of trouble you could get into at night could just as easily happen in daylight." In any event, where else but New York City could you get a haircut at 1 a.m., eat a fresh bagel an hour later, then browse through rare records for an hour or so before meeting someone for a game of tennis at 4:15 a.m., and buy a newspaper on the way home?

What follows is really only a partial list. I am omitting the nightclub scene and operating on the assumption that you're looking for "normal" activities that you just happen to need after dark.

Animal Services—*The Animal Medical Center* (510 E 62nd St, 838-8100) This would be my first choice, day or night. These people are the best. Rates are higher at night, but they are open 24 hours and will deal with any emergency.

Bagels and Bakeries

Bagel Corner (Seventh Ave Arcade in Penn Station, 695-9261)

Bagels on the Square (7 Carmine St, 691-3041) Whole meals can be made for takeout.

Donut Pub (203 W 14th St, 929-0126)

H&H Bagels (2239 Broadway, 799-9680)

Clothing—*Jeff Kint* (117 W Broadway, 431-8043) The hours here are as wild as the clothes. Most days, except Monday, the shop doesn't open until noon and remains open until 1 a.m.

Emergencies—Ambulance/Fire/Police. 911 is the emergency number in New York. A call will notify the police, who will summon an ambulance authorized to go to the nearest hospital.

Florists—*Rialto Florists* (707 Lexington Ave at 57th St, 688-3234)

Food—(Takeout)

Alamari Candy Store (218 W 42nd St, 764-9085)

Alhadei Grocery Store (210 W 42nd St, 391-8376) You can even comparison-shop at 4 a.m.!

Big Boy Delicatessen (510 Sixth Ave, 255-5644)

Cathedral Market (2853 Broadway, 662-7535)

Delion Grocery (729 Broadway at Waverly Place, 260-3759)

88th Street Market (1566 Third Ave at 88th St, 722-5360)

Georgetown Delicatessen (596 Ninth Ave, 265-5390) No, I have no idea why it's named that, but it is open 24 hours.

Grand Union (130 Bleecker St, 475-8873; 350 E 86th St, 535-2417) These two stores are part of an East Coast supermarket chain. They close at midnight on Saturday and reopen on Sunday from 8-7.

Hillside Market (1428 Lexington Ave at 93rd St, 876-5880)

Pathmark (410 W 207th St, 569-0600; 227 Cherry St, Pike Slip, 227-8988)

Sims Deli (494 Sixth Ave near 12th St, 243-6611) There are half a dozen Sims around town. All keep late hours, but this is the only one open all night.

696 Deli (696 Third Ave, 490-7115)
Smilers Food Stores
—413 Park Ave S (at 29th St), 684-5175
—686 Third Ave (at 43rd St), 682-6940
—766 Third Ave (at 47th St), 753-0781
—924 Third Ave (at 56th St), 935-9170
—106 Seventh Ave South, 242-1889
—726 Eighth Ave (at 45th St), 221-2750
—637 Ninth Ave (at 45th St), 582-5550
—850 Seventh Ave (at 55th St), 757-5871
—469 Lexington Ave (at 45th St), 986-5120
White Mark Delicatessen (373 Sixth Ave, 741-3768)

Food—*(Eat in)*
Brasserie (100 E 53rd St, 751-4840)
Burger King
—1165 Sixth Ave (at 45th St), 575-9137 — Thurs, Fri, Sat
—1557 Broadway (at 47th St), 391-0890 — 24 hrs
—957 Eighth Ave (at 57th St), 582-4492 — 24 hrs
Charlie's Pizza (140 E 58th St, 752-3747)
College Inn Restaurant (2896 Broadway at 96th St, 663-0257)
Cooper Square Restaurant (87 Second Ave at Fifth St, 420-8050)
Green Kitchen (1477 First Ave at 77th St, 988-4163)
Hot Diggity (140 Eighth Ave, 807-8781) Open till 3 a.m. Fri, Sat
Night Birds (92 Second Ave at Fifth St, 254-4747)
Richoux of London (1373 Sixth Ave at 55th St, 265-3090)
Thanos Restaurant (888 Eighth Ave at 52nd St, 586-4980)
Tramway Coffee House (1143 Second Ave at 60th St, 758-7017)
Village Inn (169 Bleecker St, 533-0823)
(See also under "Restaurants")

Fruits and Vegetables
Eden Farm
—549 Hudson St, 242-3069
—154 W 14th St, 255-5960
—252 Third Ave, 228-9406
Empire Fruits & Vegetables (200 W 96th, 866-9337)
Green Village Food & Vegetable
—468 Sixth Ave, 255-4728
—127 Fourth Ave, 475-2729
—241 Bleecker St, 989-8268
—177 Bleecker St, 982-5888

Games
Bowlmor Lanes (110 University Place, 255-8188) Daily: 10-3 or 4 a.m.
Backgammon, Chess & Games Club (212 W 72nd St, 874-8299)

Hair

Heads & Tales (36 St Marks Pl, 677-9125) Mon-Fri: 11:30 a.m.-midnight; Sat: 11-7; Sun: 12-6

Larry Matthews Beauty Salon (536 Madison Ave at 54th St, 246-6100) Mon-Sat: 7 a.m.-10 p.m.; Sun: 9-5

Neither of these is really quite 24 hours a day, but why quibble?

Health Clubs

Parc Swim & Health Club (363 W 56th St, 586-3675)

Polygym (428 E 75th St, 628-6969)

Newsstands—Many are open 24 hours. This is a partial list of newsstands in neighborhoods where there are likely to be a few people around.

—Broadway at 72nd, 79th, 94th, 96th, and 104th St
—First Ave at 65th and 86th St
—Second Ave at St. Marks Place, 50th and 53rd St
—Third Ave at St. Marks Place and 54th St
—Lexington Ave at 64th and 89th St
—Sixth Ave at Eighth and 48th St
—Seventh Ave South and Sheridan Square
—Eighth Ave at 41st St (Port Authority Bus Terminal), 23rd, 42nd, and 46th St

Pharmacy—*Kaufman Pharmacy* (Lexington Ave at 50th St, 755-2266)

Post Offices—The main post office at 33rd Street and Eighth Avenue (971-7176) is open 24 hours a day with limited service for packages. With the exception of registered mail, all other postal services are available. This is also the place to be at midnight of the day for filing for such events as the New York Marathon, popular rock concerts, and income tax. (I'll bet that's the first time those have been linked in one sentence.) The Church Street Station (90 Church St) and Grand Central Station (Lexington at 45th St) have vending machines for stamps available at all times.

Records

Tower Records stores are open until midnight (692 Broadway, 505-1500 and Fourth St and Lafayette, 505-1505)

Bleecker Bob's Golden Oldies (179 MacDougal St, 475-9677)

Sights

Empire State Building Observatory (350 Fifth Ave at 34th St) Tickets sold till 11:25 p.m.

II. Where To Eat It: New York's Restaurants

Of all the sections in this book, the restaurant listings provoke the most comment. I guess that is natural, as we all must eat and we all do not have to buy a new fur coat. I want to emphasize that the opinions are mine alone, and just like you, my feelings can be affected by the wrong waiter or the chef's night off. I have now visited over 1200 restaurants in Manhattan of every description, small and large, cheap and expensive, in every area, with dozens of different types of cuisines, so I feel that I can pretty well review them in a manner that will allow you to choose the best value for your dollar in whatever type of meal you are looking for. I evaluate the ambiance, the service, the cleanliness, the pricing, and all the other little things that, put together, make for a pleasant and satisfying dining experience.

For this volume, I have dropped a number of listings featured in previous editions. Some have gone out of business, some have gone downhill, and others don't measure up to places that I have recently reviewed. I don't rate them with stars or the like. If an eating spot is included, then I believe it is worth visiting. This edition includes nearly 100 new listings. Separate lists single out some places I don't think are worthy of your time, and still other lists offer choices in a number of different categories. I do not pretend to be a wine expert, therefore no mention is made of drinks. I do not pretend to be a gourmet, either. Also, remember that restaurants can change overnight. These descriptions were accurate when this edition went to press. I'd be pleased, as always, to get your comments or criticisms of my choices, or your suggestions of places that might be included in later editions.

Inexpensive generally means a full-course meal for less than $14; moderate, up to $29; and expensive, above $29 (all without drinks, for one person). The following abbreviations indicate credit facilities: AE (American Express), CB (Carte Blanche), DC (Diner's

Club), MC (Mastercard), VISA. Almost all establishments will take traveler's checks. The average tip should be 15 percent of the tab, more if the service is special, less if the opposite is true. Remember, you are under no obligation to tip at all, if the experience is an unsatisfactory one. You may specify how much is to go to the captain and how much to the waiter. In my opinion, maitre d's are usually a pain in the neck, and their outstretched palms should be greased only in the most unusual circumstances or when you really want to make a lasting impression in a certain restaurant for return visits. You can also save a bit by leaving your coats locked in your car, or, if possible, take them to the table with you. This business of buying back your coats every time you eat out is ridiculous.

Some things to look out for when dining out in Manhattan:

1. When making reservations (and always try to do this), be sure to give yourself a few minutes leeway on time of arrival, so that if you are late, your table will be held. Getting a taxi at dinner time on a Friday evening when it is raining is practically impossible.
2. Don't let them play the "wait in the bar" game. If you have made proper reservations, you are entitled to be seated. Even if your entire party has not arrived, ask to be seated. What difference should it make if some of the guests arrive a few minutes later?
3. Be leery of (a) restaurants on top of buildings (the view in most cases is better than the food); (b) restaurants with dirty menus and crossed-out prices; (c) restaurants with lots of signs and reviews in the window (look at the date, the reviewer, and the publication); (d) restaurants that are very dark (how would the place look in the daylight?); and (e) restaurants with dirty, smelly restrooms (what must the kitchen look like?).

Over 200 of the Best Eating Places in New York in Every Category

(Full reviews of the top choices from these lists may be found on subsequent pages.)

Best for eating in a garden: Terrace Restaurant (400 W 119th St); Raphael (33 W 54th St); Julia (226 W 79th St); Gordon's (38 McDougal St); Barbetta (321 W 46th St); Le Paris Bistro (48 Barrow St); Tavern on the Green (Central Park at W 67th St); Giordano (409 W 39th St); Ye Waverly Inn (16 Bank St); Lion's Rock (316 E 77th St)

Best for health foods: Au Natural (Second Ave and 55th St); Greener Pastures (117 E 60th St); Food Workshop (424 W 43rd St)

Best for late dining: Cafe Luxembourg (200 W 70th St); Carnegie Deli (854 Seventh Ave); Central Falls (478 W Broadway); Odeon (145 W Broadway); Jim McMullen's (1341 Third Ave); Primavera (1578 First Ave); Pig Heaven (1540 Second Ave); Christo's (143 E 49th St)

Best for dessert: Peppermint Park (1225 First Ave); Palm Court (Plaza Hotel); Agora (1550 Third Ave); Cafe Della Palma (327 Columbus Ave); Serendipity (225 E 60th St); Sarabeth's (412 Amsterdam Ave); Old Fashioned Mr. Jennings (12 W 55th St)

Best for breakfast: Good Enough to Eat (Amsterdam Ave at 80th St); Thomas St. Inn (8 Thomas St); Rumpelmeyers (50 Central Park S); Empire Diner (210 10th Ave); Les Delices Guy Pascal (2241 Broadway, 1231 Madison Ave, 939 First Ave); Bagel (170 W Fourth St); Mary Elizabeth's (6 E 37th St); Moondance Diner (80 Sixth Ave)

Most romantic: One If By Land, Two If By Sea (17 Barrow St); L'Endroit (208 E 52nd St); Vanessa (289 Bleecker St); Roxanne's (158 Eighth Ave)

Best for tea: Algonquin Hotel (59 W 44th St); Palm Court (Plaza Hotel); Carlyle Hotel Gallery (983 Madison Ave); Serendipity (225 E 60th St); Mayfair Regent Hotel Lounge (610 Park Ave); Helmsley Palace Hotel (455 Madison Ave); Pierre Hotel Rotunda Room (Fifth Ave and 61st St)

Best sidewalk cafes: Maxwell's Plum (First Ave at 64th St); Da Silvano (260 Sixth Ave); Jane Street Seafood (31 Eighth Ave); Ruelles (321 Columbus Ave); American Festival Cafe (Rockefeller Center)

Vintage New York: Palm Court (Plaza Hotel, white collar); Frank's (431 W 14th St, blue collar)

24-hour restaurants: (see also "Manhattan at Night") 103 Second Ave at Sixth St; Brasserie (100 E 53rd St); Burger King (1165 Sixth Ave, 1557 Broadway, 975 Eighth Ave); Caffe Reggio (119 MacDougal St); College Inn Restaurant (2896 Broadway); Green Kitchen (1477 First Ave); Market Diner (256 West St); Richoux of London (1373 Sixth Ave); Thanos (888 Eighth Ave); Tramway Coffee House (1143 Second Ave); Village Inn (169 Bleecker St)

For expense accounts: La Tulipe (104 W 13th St); Le Cygne (53 E 54th St); Le Cirque (58 E 65th St); Chanterelle (89 Grand St); Quilted Giraffe (955 Second Ave); Manhattan Ocean Club (57 W 58th St); Petrossian (182 W 58th St)

Best for kids: Peppermint Park (1225 First Ave); Serendipity (225 E 60th St); Tavern on the Green (Central Park at W 67th St);

Agora (1550 Third Ave); Jackson Hole Hamburgers (232 E 64th St); South Street Seaport (second floor)

Best for teenagers: Hard Rock Cafe (221 W 57th St); Maxwell's Plum (First Ave at 64th St); Pizza Piazza (785 Broadway); Tony Roma's (400 E 57th St, 450 Sixth Ave)

Best for Sunday dining: Bistro Bordeaux (407 Eighth Ave); Cafe Luxembourg (200 W 70th St); Canton (377 W 125th St); Capsouto Fréres (451 Washington St); Coach House (110 Waverly Pl); Da Silvano (260 Sixth Ave); Jim McMullen's (1341 Third Ave); John Clancy's (181 W 10th St); Mme. Romaine De Lyon (29 E 61st St); Maxwell's Plum (First Ave at 64th St); La Metairie (189 W 10th St); Post House (28 E 63rd St); Primavera (1578 First Ave); Russian Tea Room (150 W 57th St); La Tulipe (104 W 13th St)

Best diner fare: Moondance Diner (80 Sixth Ave)

Best for value: Food (127 Prince St); Il Vagabondo (351 E 62nd St); Cafe 58 (232 E 58th St)

Best for food and suds: Manhattan Brewing Co. (40 Thompson St); McSorley's Old Ale House (15 E Seventh St); Landmark Tavern (626 11th Ave)

Best celebrity watching: Jams (154 E 79th St); La Grenouille (3 E 52nd St); Cafe Luxembourg (200 W 70th St); Russian Tea Room (150 W 57th St); Le Cirque (58 E 65th St); "21" (21 W 52nd St); Ecco (124 Chambers St); Four Seasons (99 E 52nd St); Elio's (1621 Second Ave)

Best for light lunch: Pie in the Sky (173 Third Ave)

Most intimate: La Metairie (189 W 10th St); Il Bocconcino (168 Sullivan St); Grove St. Cafe (53 Grove St); La Colombe D'Or (134 E 26th St); La Petite Ferme (973 Lexington Ave)

Most nostalgic: Rainbow Room (Rockefeller Plaza)

Best business lunch: Westfall's (251 E 50th St)

Most historic: Landmark Tavern (626 11th Ave)

Snootiest: Pearl's (38 W 48th St); SoHo Charcuterie (195 Spring St); Jockey Club (380 Madison Ave); Water Club (500 E 30th St); "21" (21 W 52nd St); Le Cirque (58 E 65th St)

Most unusual nouvelle cuisine: Grove Street Cafe (53 Grove St)

Most personal touch: Roxanne's (158 Eighth Ave)

Best family feeling: Rene Pujol (321 W 51st St); Table D'Hote (44 E 92nd St)

Best service: Les Pleiades (20 E 76th St)

Best sandwiches: Katz's Delicatessen (205 E Houston St)

Best brunch: Grand Hyatt (42nd St at Grand Central—the best in New York); Tavern on the Green (Central Park at W 67th St); Gordon's (38 McDougal St); Berry's (180 Spring St); Vanessa (289 Bleecker St); Windows on the World (1 World Trade

Center); Palm Court (Plaza Hotel); River Cafe (1 Water St, Brooklyn); Central Falls (478 W Broadway); Landmark Tavern (626 11th Ave)

Best delis: Second Avenue Deli (156 Second Ave); Katz's Deli (205 E Houston St); Carnegie Deli (854 Seventh Ave)

Most exquisite surroundings: Helmsley Palace Restaurants (455 Madison Ave)

Undiscovered good bets: Toscana (246 E 54th St); Vanessa (289 Bleecker St); Elmer's (1034 Second Ave)

Best for Texas style: Yellow Rose Cafe (450 Amsterdam Ave)

Best Jewish food: Bernstein's on Essex (135 Essex St); Lou G. Siegel (209 W 38th St); Ratner's (138 Delancey St)

Best views (Skyline, from below): River Cafe (1 Water St, Brooklyn)

Best views (Skyline, from above): Rainbow Room (Rockefeller Plaza); Windows on the World (1 World Trade Center); Top of the Park (Gulf & Western Plaza)

Best views (Central Park): Tavern on the Green (Central Park at W 67th St)

Best fountain: Old Fashioned Mr. Jennings (12 W 55th St)

Best barbecue: Smokey's (230 Ninth Ave, 685 Amsterdam Ave, 310 Third Ave)

Most feminine: La Grenouille (3 E 52nd St)

Most macho: Palm (837 Second Ave); Jake's (801 Second Ave)

Best coffeehouse: Ruelle's (321 Columbus Ave)

Friendliest place in town: Black Sheep (342 W 11th St)

Noisiest: Ernie's (2150 Broadway)

Best for Particular Foods

Omelets: Mme. Romaine De Lyon (29 E 61 St)

Game: Ottomanelli's (1549 York Ave)

Hamburgers: Jackson Hole (232 E 64th St); Corner Bistro (331 W Fourth St); Hamburger Harry's (157 Chambers St)

Sushi: Hatsuhana (17 E 48th St)

Pizza: Ray's Famous (465 Ave of Americas); John's Pizzeria (278 Bleecker St); Pizza Piazza (785 Broadway)

French toast: Berry's (180 Spring St)

Steak: Christ Cella (160 E 46th St); Post House (28 E 63rd St); Palm (837 Second Ave)

Seafood: Wilkinson's (1573 York Ave); Oyster Bar & Restaurant (Grand Central Station); Pesca (23 E 22nd St); Gloucester House (37 E 50th St); Le Régence (Hotel Plaza Athénée — 37 E 64th St)

Roast beef: Adam's Rib (23 E 74th St)
Fried chicken: La Louisiana (132 Lexington Ave); Yellow Rose Cafe (450 Amsterdam Ave)
Soup: La Bonne Soupe (48 W 55th St)
Ribs: Tony Roma's (400 E 57th St, 450 Sixth Ave); Smokey's (230 Ninth Ave, 685 Amsterdam Ave, 310 Third Ave); Wylie's (891 First Ave)
Brioche: Cafe Europa (347 E 54th St)
Wrapped foods: Wrapsody (73 Thompson St)
Southern: Memphis (329 Columbus Ave)
Vegetarian: Levanna's (148 W 67th St); Greener Pastures (117 E 60th St)

Best by New York Areas

TriBeCa: Ecco (124 Chambers St); Acute Cafe (110 W Broadway); Scaramouche Bistro (157 Duane St)
Near Madison Square Garden: Bistro Bordeaux (407 Eighth Ave)
For Renewing Strength while Shopping Bloomingdale's: Contrapunto (1009 Third Ave)
Midtown: La Fondue (43 W 55th St); Lavin's (23 W 39th St); La Cote Basque (5 E 55th St)
Wall Street Area: Delmonico's (56 Beaver St)
Garment District: Woods (148 W 37th St)
Theater District: Les Pyrenees (251 W 51st St); Lattanzi (361 W 46th St); Cafe 43 (147 W 43rd St)
Near Lincoln Center: Ginger Man (51 W 64th St)
SoHo: Central Falls (478 W Broadway); J.S. Vandam (150 Varick St); Greene St. Cafe (101 Greene St); Food (127 Prince St)
Little Italy: Grotto Azzurra (387 Broome St)
Chinatown: Bo Bo (20½ Pell St); Canton (377 W 125th St); Hwa Yuan (40 E Broadway)
Murray Hill: La Louisiana (132 Lexington Ave); Mon Paris (111 E 29th St)
Village: La Ripaille (605 Hudson St); Black Sheep (342 W 11th St); Village Green (531 Hudson St); Coach House (110 Waverly Pl); K.O. (99 Bank St); Zinno (126 W 13th St); One If by Land, Two If by Sea (17 Barrow St)
Upper West Side: Cafe Luxembourg (200 W 70th); Terrace (400 W 119th St); Cafe Della Palma (327 Columbus Ave); Dobson's (341 Columbus Ave); West Side Storey (700 Columbus Ave); Amsterdam's Bar & Rotisserie (428 Amsterdam Ave); Memphis (329 Columbus Ave)
Spanish Harlem: Rao's (455 E 114th St)
Chelsea: Roxanne's (158 Eighth Ave)
Gramercy Park: Woods Gramercy (24 E 21st St)
Upper East Side: Wilkinson's (1573 York Ave); Primavera (1578 First Ave); Diva (306 E 81st St); An American Place (969 Lexington Ave)

Best by Types of Cuisine

Afghan: Pamir (1423 Second Ave)
Belgian: Le St. Jean Des Pres (112 Duane St)
Brazilian: Amazonas (492 Broome St)
Cambodian: Indochine (430 Lafayette St)
Chinese: Tse Yang (34 E 51st St); Canton (45 Division St.); Sun Hop Shing Tea House (21 Mott St)
Continental: Vienna '79 (35 E 60th St)
Cuban: Victor's (240 Columbus Ave, 236 W 52nd St)
Czechoslovakian: Ruc (312 E 72nd St)
Danish: Old Denmark (133 E 65th St)
English: Tracy's (127 Lexington Ave); Covent Garden (133 W 13th St); Bull & Bear (Waldorf-Astoria Hotel)
French: La Reserve (4 W 49th St); Lutece (249 E 50th St); Le Cirque (58 E 65th St); Le Cygne (55 E 54th St); Cafe 58 (232 E 58th St, bistro); Black Sheep (342 W 11th St, bistro); Capsouto Fréres (451 Washington St); Le Zinc (139 Duane St, bistro); Mon Paris (111 E 29th St); La Tulipe (104 W 13th St)
German: There aren't any.
Hungarian: Csarda (1477 Second Ave)
Indian: Darbar (44 W 56th St)
Indonesian: Tamu (340 W Broadway)
Italian: Primavera (1578 First Ave); Parioli Romanissimo (24 E 81st St); Trattoria Da Alfredo (90 Bank St)
Japanese: Nippon (155 E 52nd St); Kitcho (22 W 46th St); Mitsukoshi (461 Park Ave)
Mediterranean: Andree's (354 E 75th St)
Mexican: Cafe Marimba (1115 Third Ave); Rosa Mexicana (1063 First Ave)
Polish: Christine's Coffee Shop (208 First Ave)
Russian: Russian Tea Room (150 W 57th St)
Spanish: El Faro (823 Greenwich St); Meson Madrid (1394 York Ave)
Swiss: Chalet Suisse (6 E 48th St)
Thai: Bangkok House (1485 First Ave)
Vietnamese: Saigon (60 Mulberry St)

"Don't Bother" Restaurants

Beware the Mob Instinct! Someone gives a restaurant a rave review. All of a sudden, it's the "in" place, and the line forms at the nearest phone booth for reservations. It must be good, if so-and-so said so. The restaurant personnel also think they are good, because people are begging to get in. The place is successfully launched—or is it? A good example, in my opinion, of what too much hype can do is the relatively new Positano, an Italian swinger at 250 Park Avenue South. This place got off to a roaring start; I wonder how long that will last, if my experience was any example. Reservations? Mine were made eight days in advance. When I arrived, there was no record of it. Ambiance? Attractive enough, a two-level room with a noise level beyond belief. Personnel? Young, eager, and inexperienced, with the most unattractive uniforms you can imagine. (They look like the ones worn by the cleaning ladies in the public lavatories in Rome.) Food? Very mediocre, no excitement in either flavor or presentation. Breadbasket? Cold and uninteresting. To top it off, my check was nearly doubled, a mistake *I* found and for which the waitress made no apology. ("That's what happens when you use a calculator," she offered lamely.) When the owner was confronted with all this, his condescending and mildly disinterested response was offensive. Beware the sheep. They don't always go in the right direction.

There are tens of thousands of restaurants located in every corner of Manhattan; some come and go as quickly as the seasons. Listed here are some rather well-known eating establishments that I don't feel represent true value for what you will have to pay. Some are not recommended because of poor food, others lack in service or atmosphere, and others suffer from inflated pricing. You can't say you weren't warned!

Angelo of Mulberry St.: The president obviously got special treatment.
Aubergine: The waiters need a traffic cop.
Barclay-Intercontinental: An overpriced weekend buffet.
Cafe Reginette: They flunked every course.
Cajun: It ain't New Orleans.
Capriccio: Don't waste your lire.
Carolina: "Nothing could be finer" wasn't written here.
Catch of the Sea: The fish aren't biting.
Chatfield's: An amateur production.
Chez Pascal: Color me gray.
Coho's: Don't drop your anchor here.
Del Barone: It's a long way to Rome.
De Marco: Forgettable.
Devon House: Nothing to get excited about.
Felidia: The reputation is better than the product.
Gotham Bar & Grill: Only a good press agent.
Healthworks: They lost their touch.
Huberts: They don't know how to spell *s-e-r-v-i-c-e.*
Il Nido: It's pretty — period.
Jack's Nest: Jack's soul has disappeared.
Jams: Trivial pursuit.
Jockey Club: It never got out of the starting gate.

La Cascade: Outrageous pricing.
La Cocotte: Dullsville.
La Gauloise: Francly disappointing.
La Recolte: Pretentious. Pricey. Poor.
Le Chambertin: Des Moines special.
Le Clodenis: A dollhouse, not for serious eating.
Leopard: The unattractive atmosphere spoils the palate.
Le Perigord: Fading.
LeVeau D'Or: Don't bother if you aren't a regular.
Luchow's: It's not what you remembered.
Mamma Leone's: Mamma must not spend much time in the kitchen.
Maurice: Undersized portions and oversized tabs.
Mr. Chow: Let's buy him a new wok.
New York Deli: It should have stayed an automat.
Orsini's: A *Women's Wear Daily* myth.
Palatine: The Padre should visit his kitchen more often.
Paradis: They haven't read Emily Post.
Pearl's: The pearl's luster has faded.
Positano: Success has gone to their heads.
Rare Form: Needs to be a bit better done.
Romeo Salta: Wherefore art thou Romeo?
Sardi's: My childhood memories have been ruined.
Shun Lee Dynasty: The chopsticks are wearing thin.
Sign of the Dove: Only if you're taking pictures.
S.P.Q.R.: An insult to Rome.
Sylvia's: It isn't worth the trip to Harlem.
Tennessee Mountain: Tony Roma gave them a ribbing.
Terrace Five: Don Trump, have you really eaten here?
Water Club: The view is *extra*ordinary; the food just plain ordinary.

Alphabetical Listing

Where the Wheelers Deal

ABE'S
1290 Third Ave
861-6600
Daily: 5:15-midnight
Major credit cards
Moderate

Lots of folks have visions of New York being a place where big deals are made. And indeed, many a business deal has probably been settled over dinner at Abe's Steak House, a smallish, attractive bistro on the East Side. There is nothing unusual about the menu; there are the usual appetizers, soups, and salads. However, the chicken liver sauté is rather special, the beef is exceptional, the extra-thick double-rib lamb chops are superb, and the old-fashioned Romanian steak is worth a try. The fried shrimps in Abe's batter are also very good, as is the roast duckling with wild rice. Other tasty showcase items are the roast prime ribs of beef au jus and the prime sirloin steak. If you're like me, you'll go for the trimmings. Abe's cottage-fried potatoes, potato skins, fried zucchini, or fried broccoli are great. A suggestion for a dinner party of two: the combination platter of cottage-fried potatoes, potato pancakes, onion rings, and zucchini. There is nothing too special about about the desserts—just the usual ice cream and cheesecake.

A Cute Place

ACUTE CAFE
110 W Broadway
349-5566
Mon-Sat: 12:30-12:30
Major credit cards
Moderate

You will remember that one of the more interesting areas in New York City is TriBeCa, the *triangle below Canal Street.* One of the best places to eat in this area is the Acute Cafe. There is an airy, pleasant dining room with a large bar, fresh flowers, and a sunken center area that can be used for larger gatherings. I would advise you to visit at noon when you could enjoy a delicious quiche or salad. In the latter category, I would recommend the seafood salad served in a lobster shell, or the Caesar salad. For hot entrees, the chicken breast sautéed with a light mustard sauce or any of the fish entrees are excellent. (The fish is brought in fresh each morning.) The scallops and leeks with wild rice is another house specialty. The breads are excellent, and by all means try the superb herb garlic butter — it's unusual and delicious! There are homemade desserts, including a special coffee ice cream, great tarts, strawberries (in season) with Grand Marnier sauce, or real Italian profiteroles smothered with absolutely the best chocolate sauce I've ever tasted. The price-fixed dinner includes your choice of appetizers, entrees, and a green salad. Besides the aforementioned excellent fish, I would recommend the breast and thigh of Long Island duckling or the medallions of veal with mushroom sauce. The *pièce de résistance* is the feuillete de fruits de mer (poached seafood in puff pastry with a light champagne sauce).

Something to Beef About

ADAM'S RIB
23 E 74th St
535-2112
Mon-Fri: noon-3, 4:30-11; Sat: 4:30-11; Sun: 4:30-10
Major credit cards, personal checks
Moderate

The menu of this attractive, wood-paneled restaurant in the Volney condo states that it's a simple restaurant run by one man whose philosophy is "serving the best always." Mr. Nicholas succeeds. The menu is basic, but what they do, they do very well, indeed. And the place is always busy. Even the atmosphere is appetizing—initimate, warm, and friendly. I particularly recommend it for Sunday evening dinner; it just fits that kind of an occasion. You begin with a delicious loaf of warm homemade bread that you slice at the table. The salads are exceptionally good, and the Adam's Rib (one full rib thick) or the Eve's Rib (just a bit smaller)—served with Yorkshire pudding, a horseradish sauce, and fresh broiled mushrooms—is star quality. For the non-beef eater, there's a selection of roast duckling, South African lobster tails, and several breast-of-chicken dishes, broiled filet of sole, or an excellent shrimp on a skewer. A very good Caesar salad, an Idaho baked potato, or gently fried zucchini are also available. And the Swiss chocolate pie can put a crowning touch on a very satisfying dinner. I like everything about this place. The staff makes you feel at home, while serving you excellent food at a very reasonable price.

Fountain and Fashion

AGORA
1550 Third Ave (at 87th St)
369-6983
Mon-Thurs: 10-11:30; Fri, Sat: 11:30-1 a.m.;
Sun: noon-11:30
Major credit cards
Moderate

Agora is one of the few shops in the city that can be all things to all people. In fact, Agora—which is really at least three shops in one—has drawn accolades in each of its undertakings, and that is rare indeed. The largest section of the store is a ladies' boutique—a boutique that can keep any woman who wants to be well dressed at the least expense occupied for hours. Agora also has a very attractive men's store, with many designer labels at reasonable prices. The selection is amazingly complete for a relatively small space, and the careful shopper can secure some of the area's best fashion buys. All this leads us to the third section of the store. Agora's ice-cream parlor and soda fountain were originally created in 1896 for a Haverstraw, New York, shop. George and Paul Gorra, Agora's owners (the name Agora means marketplace in Greek, and they say the similarity in names is just a coincidence), discovered it in 1971 and had it moved to New York. Nostalgia and furniture fans will get a kick out of the fountain, with its mahogany cabinets and woodwork, onyx columns (trimmed with 14-karat gold leaf), and awesome counter space. But for the child of any age, the best of Agora's features has to be what that soda fountain dispenses. Their ice cream is super, and it is served in all the best 1890 configurations. The Gorras have re-created recipes as well as a soda fountain. Their *large* sundaes are a sight to behold, and the local favorite—egg creams—comes in 25 flavors. If you're feeling whimsical, you might try the pound cake, ice cream, and hot fudge dessert they call the "Flatiron Building." It's named for the Flatiron Building, which was constructed in a wedge shape. All in all, Agora has something for everyone. Don't miss it.

Traditional Mongul Fare

AKBAR
475 Park Ave (at 57th St)
838-1717
Mon-Sat: 11:30-2:45, 5:30-10:45; Sun: 5:30-10:45
Major credit cards
Moderate

There are so many ethnic restaurants in New York that you can find nearly every type of cuisine there is. Akbar features northern Indian food, specializing in muglai cooking. This cuisine is not too hot or too oily. The specialties from the Indian clay oven are delicious and varied, from tandoori chicken marinated in yogurt to sheesh kebab (minced lamb with onion). Fresh from the oven are the breads—the round whole wheat chapati, a layered whole wheat stuffed with potatoes (aloo paratha), and a puffed, deep-fried one (poori). You could make a meal from these alone. An excellent selection of vegetarian entrees is also offered: homemade cheese with green peas, cottage cheese with spinach, or cauliflower and potatoes cooked in spices. If none of the above appeal to you, there are several unusual rice dishes and such traditional delicacies as lamb marinated in yogurt and spices and cooked in cream sauce. Desserts here are nothing special, but the hospitality and authenticity of the dishes *are* special.

A Healthy Hotel Harvest

AMERICAN HARVEST
Vista International Hotel
3 World Trade Center
938-9100
Mon-Fri: 7 a.m.-9:30 a.m., 12-2:30, 6-10; Sat: 6-10
Major credit cards
Moderate to expensive

I usually don't get excited about dining in hotel restaurants, because they are usually more convenient than they are excellent. But this one is a bit different. Hilton International has done an excellent job. The décor is Early American, with items displayed from local museums. The restaurant is divided into three areas, and the tables are arranged far enough apart to create a very comfortable and pleasant dining experience. The menu changes, as the name implies, with each month's harvest. The vegetable or produce that is featured during a specific month is prepared in a variety of ways. Order from an extensive à la carte menu or select dinner at a fixed price with appetizer, soup, main course, a choice of three of the freshest vegetables, plus salad, dessert, and beverage. Actually, the fixed-price dinner is the best value. One particular month's selections featured excellent spring asparagus fixed with smoked salmon, and another with American caviar cream sauce. Also available was aspagarus bisque soup. A typical selection of vegetables includes carrots, spring squash, cauliflower and buttered herb crumbs, sweet and sour beets, broccoli buds with cashew nuts, and new potatoes with dill—quite an offering! For the main course, the seafoods are excellent. Sea trout, Florida pompano, and butterflied shrimp are among the best selections. I also recommend the stuffed lamb chops and the excellent steaks. Save some room for the dessert trolley! It's magnificent, laden with chocolate cheesecake, chocolate layer cake, maple date pecan pie, maple mousse loaf, et cetera—all made in the hotel. The American Harvest is a delightful place to bring guests; it's well worth the trip downtown.

Red, White, and Pricey

AN AMERICAN PLACE
969 Lexington Ave
517-7660
Mon-Sat: 6-11
Major credit cards
Expensive

You're going to really pay for a price-fixed dinner at this small, delightful spot, but it sure will be worth it. The chef is also the owner, so you can understand why everything is done to perfection. For cold appetizers, the lobster and fresh Florida frog-leg salad or the terrine of smoked fish with caviar is excellent; for hot appetizers, the Willipa Bay oysters or the fresh pasta with baked California goat cheese is delicious. Lawrence Forgione does a superb job with the entrees, especially the New York duck foie gras sauté, the breast of wild mallard duck, or the grilled striped bass. The latter is served with Oregon white truffles. The breadbasket is unusual; make sure you try the pepper bread. There is a big dessert selection. I'd suggest the apple pan dowdy, strawberry shortcake, or bread pudding. The waiters here complement the meal by being exceedingly well informed. For refined dining at its best, An American Place is a flag-waving choice.

A Cruise on the Mediterranean

ANDREE'S MEDITERRANEAN CUISINE
354 E 74th St
249-6619
Tues-Sat: 6:30-9:30
No credit cards
Moderate to expensive

Andree and Charlie have created a charming, intimate restaurant with an emphasis on Mediterranean cuisine. Everything except the bread is done in-house, and the results are tasty, indeed. You can choose from an à la carte menu, whose prices seem a little high, or opt for a price-fixed dinner with four courses, which is a much better deal. Visualize some of these interesting appetizers: spinach and cheese puffs, stuffed wheat shells, stuffed grape leaves, falafel, or a delicious salmon mousse. For entrees, there is a choice of duck with green peppercorns; rack of lamb; a superb fresh Cornish game hen stuffed with pine nuts, raisins, and bulgur; couscous; moussaka (beef or meatless); and several fish dishes. The most unusual dessert is the sensational pistachio baklava. After a tasty dinner like this, a Mideastern fruit salad (khochaf) is very enjoyable. For coffee drinkers, there is a special Mideastern version. The house will also prepare mousse-stuffed filet of sole, bouillabaisse, or striped bass, if such special orders are given at least a day in advance. This intimate restaurant should please the palate of anyone who wants to cruise the Mediterranean without getting seasick.

The Best Little Warehouse in Chelsea

ARTIE'S WAREHOUSE RESTAURANT
539 W 21st St
989-9500
Sun-Thurs: 5-10:30; Fri: 5-11; Sat: 5-11:30
Major credit cards
Moderate

Some folks have told me that they are always interested in really out-of-the-way places. Well, this one surely falls into that category. Artie's Warehouse Restaurant is located in a warehouse district, and it's actually part of a working warehouse. For a friendly greeting, prompt and efficient service, and good food at reasonable prices, I haven't found too many that beat it. And it certainly is different! Artie himself is a frustrated piano player, who entertains and table-hops. And he keeps a steady eye on the help; they're right on the job, providing informed, courteous service. Start with fried wontons or steamed fish in a bag. Then go on to one of the daily special entrees of veal, chicken or fish, or an Oriental offering. I can heartily recommend the spareribs or the shrimp scampi. If you're a vegetarian, there is even a special sautéed vegetable plate. All the entrees are served with a salad, baked potato or rice, and a fresh vegetable. And be sure to save room for the great homemade desserts. What an offering! Chocolate or orange cheesecake, Häagen Dazs ice cream, chocolate silk pie, chocolate fudge cake, lemon mousse, chocolate mousse, pecan pie and even marzipan-apricot cake. What a spot for relaxing and enjoying a leisure dinner, topped off with such exotic drinks as Amaretto coffee, an Irish Float, a Tipsy Monk, or an Angel Cloud. You'll have to go there to find out exactly what they are! There are a dozen different coffees on the menu. Dinner in a warehouse? Sure, and you don't even have to wear your overalls.

For a Pretheater Dinner

BARBETTA
321 W 46th St (at Ninth Ave)
246-9171
Mon-Sat: noon-2, 5-11:30
Major credit cards
Moderate to expensive

This is an elegant restaurant with Piemontese cuisine; Piemonte is located in the northern part of Italy, and the cuisine reflects that charming part of the country. You can dine here in European elegance. It is one of New York's oldest restaurants still owned by the family that founded it, and the family has been here for nearly eight decades. One of the special attractions about Barbetta is the very attractive garden setting available during summer. There is a before-the-theater dinner menu, which offers a choice of a fish specialty, baby salmon, fresh dover sole, calf's brains, and a number of other selections served expeditiously to allow you to make the opening curtain. If you have more time and can enjoy a leisure dinner, think about the minestrone soup, almost a meal in itself, the ravioli that is made by hand, or a fabulous mushroom salad. Barbetta specializes in fish or game dishes that vary daily. If you're lucky enough to find squab on the menu, by all means take advantage of it. Other selections include veal kidneys, beef braised in red wine with polenta, or a delicious sirloin of beef. Desserts include several chocolate offerings and an assortment of cooked fruits, as well as one of the best creme caramels in the city. To be in business in the highly competitive restaurant field for such a long time, Barbetta's has to be doing something right, and they are.

A Quick Kosher Deli Lunch

BERNSTEIN-ON-ESSEX
135 Essex St
473-3900
Sun-Thurs: 9 a.m.-1a.m.; Fri: 8-one hour before sunset;
Sat: two hours after sunset-3 a.m.; closed Jewish holidays
Major credit cards
Moderate

You can't leave New York City without visiting Bernstein-on-Essex. It's a New York institution. The place is noisy, the aroma is wonderful, and the selection is outrageous. Their pastrami (hickory smoked) is world famous. Bernstein's has authentic kosher Chinese food as a specialty. They process all of their own meats, from the slaughter to the finished product. They also do all the cooking and smoking on the premises, using their own recipes. The sandwich selections are as good as the titles. How about "Schmulka's Choice"—roast beef, turkey, and tongue, Bermuda onion, and cole slaw? Bernstein's is located on the Lower East Side, and is subject to the quirks of the neighborhood, which is evident in the surly service. But this is one case in which the pluses (the food) definitely outweigh the minuses (the service).

For a Special Sunday Brunch

BERRY'S
180 Spring St (near Thompson St)
226-4394
Tues-Sun: 11:30-3:30 p.m., 5:30-11:30 p.m.;
Fri, Sat: 11:30-3:30 p.m., 5:30-midnight; Sun: 11-4
Major credit cards
Moderate

Coming here for Sunday brunch seems to be a tradition, not just for visitors, but for New Yorkers. Housed in a cozy, crowded, noisy, dark room, Berry's is the place where everyone eats with their friends. If there are problems in the world, you'd never know it from spending a few hours in this well-run restaurant. Your mouth will water as delicious, light omelets (ham, cheese, mushroom), calf's liver sauté, smoked Nova Scotia salmon, or Belgian waffles are placed in front of you. For the weight-conscious, how about a "Sunday salad," their own special combination? I must mention the chocolate desserts, which are extraordinary for a small restaurant. Save room for the double chocolate layer cake.

Simply Delicious, In or Out

BETWEEN THE BREAD

141 E 56th St
888-0449
Mon-Fri: 8 a.m.-8:30 p.m.; Sat: 9-4

145 W 55th St
581-1189
Mon-Fri: 8-9

No credit cards
Inexpensive

Between the Bread is an unusual charcuterie, serving a variety of healthy and appetizing dishes, as well as providing a delivery and catering service and good packaged products for sale. It is an antiseptically clean restaurant, with white walls, white tile, butcher block, and glass. You can eat at a counter or a table. The menu covers a wide assortment of sandwiches, from the familiar (a three-cheese sandwich) to the unusual (tofu and cashew salad). Salads run the gamut from pasta with fresh vegetables to broccoli and tenderloin. The fresh fruit salad with cottage cheese is *really* fresh. Several seafood salads are also available. Among the specials are quiche, steamed vegetables with melted cheese, and baked potatoes. A good selection of desserts is attractively displayed. One of the highlights is the enormous selection of oversized homemade muffins, baked daily. What a variety! There's fresh bran and honey, apple cinnamon, apricot, pineapple, carrot, banana, chocolate chip, strawberry, peanut butter, coconut, peach, and ginger pear, just to name a few. Also available is a large selection of delicious homemade, old-fashioned cookies.

A First Avenue Institution

BILLY'S

948 First Ave
355-8920
Mon-Fri: noon-3, 5-11:30; Sat, Sun: 5-11:30
Major credit cards
Moderate

If you like old-fashioned setups, complete with white tiled floors, checkered tablecloths, and a busy bar right in the center of the dining area, then Billy's is your kind of place. Established in 1870, this bustling pub-restaurant is a First Avenue institution, where the food is just as inviting as the atmosphere. No menus, just a blackboard listing steaks, scallops, chops, hamburgers, and the like. All are well-prepared, large portions accompanied by fair French fries or non-foil-wrapped baked potatoes. Cole slaw is served when you are seated. Oh, yes. The waiters are vintage New York. For example, when a party of four arrives, they'll ask, "Do you all wish to sit together?" But they are all efficient, pleasant guys. A word about the bread. The ethnic mix of the Big Apple makes for exceptional talent in baking, and you can take advantage of these fine breads at many restaurants like Billy's. And desserts? Well, the ice cream is creamy and delicious and comes in large portions, but I wonder, why can't this type of eatery provide any better choices than ice cream and the ever-present cheesecake?

When You're Going to the Garden

BISTRO-BORDEAUX
407 Eighth Ave
594-6305
Mon-Fri: 12-3, 5-10:30; Sat: 5-11
Major credit cards
Moderate

It's not easy to find a pleasant, reliable spot to eat in the Madison Square Garden area. Bistro-Bordeaux, a delightful French restaurant, is a very satisfactory place for either a pre-Garden or after-Garden meal. Alan and Gerard (one's in the front and one's in the kitchen), who have had lots of experience in various New York restaurants, have put together an unpretentious, homey bistro with tasty and well-prepared food at reasonable prices. I was struck by how anxious they and their help are to provide for their guests. If there are any complaints, it's that the portions are too big. This is one place you can be sure you won't go away hungry. Escargots, paté, smoked salmon—all are available for starters, along with fresh artichokes and fresh asparagus, if in season. The filet mignon is done to perfection, the grilled sole and grilled chicken are both delicious, and the escalope de veau is really special. The vegetables have a home-cooked appeal. Desserts seemed a bit expensive to me in comparison with the rest of the dinner, but the quality is certainly there. Of all the desserts (and there are nearly a dozen), the creme caramel was the best. Instead of spending your hard-earned money on junk food places in and around Madison Square Garden, I suggest this bistro as a handy and satisfying place to go.

This One Is No Black Sheep

BLACK SHEEP RESTAURANT AND CHARCUTERIE
342 W 11th St
242-1010
Mon-Thurs: 6-11; Fri, Sat: 6-12; Sun: 12-4
Major credit cards
Moderate

The Black Sheep is a cozy, unpretentious two-room establishment in the Village that serves a six-course feast for which the price of the entree includes the entire dinner. And you can even eat by fireside! You can start with a platter of fresh vegetables accompanied by a tasty sauce, then go on to a choice of soups, a French country paté, and an excellent choice of entrees, followed by a green salad and a selection from the desert table. Entrees include grilled striped bass, a provencal fish stew, sautéed scallops and mushrooms, and a very tasty roast leg of lamb. Pleasant music plays in the background, and the dinner is served by extremely friendly, accommodating help. As a matter of fact, I don't know of many places where the staff is as gracious and as hospitable. There are many daily specials, so be sure you get the full run-down from your well-informed waiter. The desserts are all homemade. Thanks to some chiding in former editions of this book, management has speeded up the service a bit.

Chinese Food on a Budget

BO BO (TOONG LAI SHOON)
20-1/2 Pell St
267-8373
Sun-Thurs: noon-11; Fri, Sat: noon-midnight
Major credit cards
Inexpensive

If it's an inexpensive Chinese restaurant you're looking for, you can't do better than Bo Bo's. It's truly vintage Oriental (no atmosphere), the food is special, and the price is right. There are all kinds of Peking and Hunan delicacies, besides an assortment of the usual beef, chicken, shrimp, and pork dishes. Bo Bo's specialty is noodles and fried rice. You get a choice of beef, chicken, pork, baby shrimp, or a 10-ingredient fried rice. The help is pleasant and accommodating, and you might strike up an interesting conversation with the Chinese family eating next to you.

Blimey! The Taste Buds Dictate Some English Fare

BULL AND BEAR
301 Lexington Ave (Waldorf-Astoria Hotel)
872-4900
Daily: 11:30-12:30 a.m.
Major credit cards
Expensive

The Bull and Bear in the Waldorf-Astoria is as close to London as you can get in Manhattan. It has been recently remodeled and is most attractive. The bar is very popular; it has a certain dignified charm. The meal is good, the service professional, and the atmosphere appealing. If a huge hunk of roast beef or some lamb chops make your mouth water, this is the place to go. Excellent seafood is also available. The place exudes solid English tradition and a clublike atmosphere, but the "club" is more an Englishman's club than an American's. No one was ever burned from too much warmth here. And here's a bit of New York trivia. The Waldorf is built over the tracks of Grand Central Station. If you look to where the Waldorf meets the sidewalk, you will see that they do *not,* in fact, meet at all. The hotel does not rest on the ground but upon piles.

An "Old Money" Favorite

CAFE ARGENTEUIL
253 E 52nd St
753-9273
Mon-Fri: noon-3, 6-10:30; Sat: 6-11
Major credit cards
Expensive

The atmosphere here is up-scale European; the clientele is decidedly "old money." Once inside, the food and the service are great. Fresh celery is placed at each table, knowledgeable captains give sensible advice, and the evening gets more pleasant with each passing course. An assortment of patés and baked clams and smoked salmon will get you off to a good start. You can follow that with a cream of vegetable soup or a crisp fresh salad. Dover sole or the salmon in the fish department are good entree possibilities, but my favorite is the roast chicken. No one does it better. If your tastes are a bit more exotic, try the sweetbreads, quail or pigeon. And watch the way the captains fix your dish—what artists! Top it all off with strawberries Romanoff, accompanied by a selection of delicious pastries and cookies.

After the Opera

CAFE DELLA PALMA
327 Columbus Ave
496-2727
Mon-Thurs: noon-midnight; Fri, Sat: noon-2 a.m.
Major credit cards
Moderate

So you have to drag your husband to the opera? Well, make a deal with him: tell him that if he'll take you to Lincoln Center, you'll take him to Cafe Della Palma. I assure you that both of you will come out winners; he'll love this place. The gelato, sorbetto, salads, and cappuccinos are superb. Just listen to the descriptions of some of the offerings: an assortment of cream-based gelatos with fresh chantilly cream and chocolate shavings topped with vanilla wafers, a parfait of fresh fruit gelato with whipped cream, or a combination of cremolati, sorbetto, and creamy vanilla gelato topped with chantilly cream, fresh strawberries, guava, kiwi, and vanilla wafers. The gelato is only 2.5 percent butter content, low in calories, and so creamy it absolutely melts in your mouth. (You can tell I've been hooked!) If all this is not enough, there are sandwiches and salads as well. Try stepping up to the showcase as you walk in; the assortment of gelatos will dazzle you. Brent Varner, the manager, is right on the job, making sure everything is 100 percent professional.

For Not-So-Big Spenders

CAFE DES SPORTS
329 W 51st St
581-1283, 974-9052
Mon-Fri: noon-3, 5-11; Sat, Sun: 5-11
AE
Inexpensive

This is a cozy spot, with an intensely loyal following developed over a period of 25 years of serving good, wholesome food in generous amounts at a reasonable price. The selections change daily, depending on what is available from the marketplaces. I have found the homemade sausage and the London broil to be exceptionally good values. Blue jeans and your most comfortable house dress are perfectly acceptable here. You'll smile along with the hospitable personnel, especially when they hand you a very realistic tab for a most satisfying meal.

A Bit of Old Europe

CAFE EUROPA & LA BRIOCHE
347 E 54th St
755-0160
Mon-Fri: 12-2:30, 5:30-11; Sat: 5:30-11
Major credit cards
Moderate

A charming cafe. It gives you the feeling that you're walking in from the streets of Paris or Munich. I recommend it for either lunch or dinner. For lunch, you might be interested in the imperial sandwich (steak tartare with caviar, icy vodka, and beer), but my choice is the chicken brioche with fresh tarragon, celery, carrots, and mushrooms. It's a hefty portion and just right for a delightful lunch. The brioche offerings change from time to time, variously featuring curried beef, veal marengo, or shrimp and mushroom. The menu is varied for dinner, with entree selections ranging from chicken breast to beef stroganoff to filet of beef Wellington. There is a large selection of desserts, from chocolate mousse to lemon Bavarian cream or bananas with rum. I'd suggest you try the pineapple carrot cake or the Valencia orange cake, both unusual and delicious. Another dessert alternative would be the French, English, or Italian cheese selection served with fruit or nuts. There is an interesting combination of European and Oriental personnel in the kitchen and out front. It all adds up to a most pleasant dining experience.

One of the Best Values in New York

CAFE 58
232 E 58th St (at Second Ave)
758-5665
Mon-Sat: noon-midnight; Sun: 5-11
Major credit cards
Moderate

Cafe 58 is an unusually good bistro; it's small, cozy yet attractively decorated, with personal attention from management and waiters. The place has a very large following, so it would be wise to make reservations, although it is not necessary. Complete dinners include appetizers or soup, a main course, and a dessert at very reasonable prices. The hors d'oeuvre selection is large, including coquille St. Jacques, and Little Neck clams. Here you will find a large selection of entrees, from broiled striped bass to frog legs, duck, and chicken. The rack of lamb and the bouillabaisse are both reasonably priced for a New York restaurant, and are extremely tasty. Pig's feet is a specialty here. I couldn't think of a spot I would recommend more highly for a very nice dinner—and you won't have to sell the family jewels to pay the bill.

The Big Apple at Its Best

CAFE 43
147 W 43rd St
869-4200
Mon-Fri: 12-3, 5-12; Sat: 5-12
Major credit cards
Moderate

In any city other than New York, Cafe 43 would be a sensation. It's just because there are so many attractive and well-run spots in the Big Apple that we take professionalism for granted, and Cafe

43 *is* professional. Although wine is a speciality here, the service and food are first class, also. The location is particularly convenient for before- or after-theater meals. The old-fashioned tile floor, huge ceiling fans, and etched-glass dividers lend a particularly attractive background to really fine food at sensible prices. A five-course table d'hôte dinner is available, with three glasses of wine from their special wine bar included. I found the sautéed shrimp with oranges and broccoli a very tasty starter. Sea scallops glazed with curry sauce, and the clams and oysters on the half shell, were also excellent. For entrees, the selections run the gamut from burgers to sweetbreads, with duck, pheasant, chicken, steak, or salmon in between. The garnishes are tasty and unusual. By now you know I love profiteroles (theirs rate five stars), but you can also get rid of your frustrations while enjoying sweet-potato pie, apple and praline parfait, or any of their delicious homemade sorbets and ice creams.

Bon Mots for Cuisine Extraordinaire

CAFE LAVANDOU
134 E 61st St.
838-7987
Mon-Sat: 12-2:30, 6-10:30
Major credit cards
Moderate to expensive

Word-of-mouth is the best advertising, and this small, attractive French charmer is getting a lot of good press. Cafe Lavandou is always busy, so don't come at the last minute. Reservations are always necessary. It's so crowded (the tables are too close together) that you might expect service to be rushed, but it's not. The staff is perfectly supervised, and the food presentation is superior. Begin with a paté, smoked salmon, quenelles, or escargots. All the soups are very good; my favorite is the poisson Marseillaise. Each of the entrees is worth a try, and the veal and lamb dishes are especially good. The quail stuffed with foie gras, the rack of lamb, and the breast of pheasant are extraordinary. I get hungry just writing about them! Save room for the marvelous desserts, especially la bombe aux trois couleurs maison and le gateau delice du chef. You'll soon see why most of Cafe Lavandou's patrons are regulars.

Din and In

CAFE LUXEMBOURG
200 W 70th St
873-7411
Mon-Fri: 5:30-1:30; Sat: 12-3, 5:30-1:30;
Sun: 11-3, 5:30-1:30
Major credit cards
Moderate

If atmosphere doesn't mean too much to you, Cafe Luxembourg could be your place. Physically, it is anything but attractive: the dining room is ugly, the tile on the walls adds little, and the tables are too close together. However, the food is excellent, and the prices are right. It's no wonder the place is so busy. For appetizers, try the poached oysters in champagne sauce, the chicken-liver terrine, or the country salad with chicory, roquefort cheese, and garlic croutons and bacon. Go on to the cassoulet, a casserole of pork, duck, white beans, garlic sausage, and tomato sauce, or the sliced breast of duckling salad with pickled turnips, lettuce, and raspberry vinegar sauce. The grilled Coho salmon is done to perfection by executive chef Patrick Clark. For dessert, try the white and dark chocolate mousse in chocolate sauce, or the Luxembourg banana sundae. An annoying policy here is that they don't seat you until everyone in your party arrives. But all in all, you can't do much better for a great meal, if you don't mind the tasteless surroundings and the noise.

Nouveau Mexicana

CAFE MARIMBA
1115 Third Ave
935-1161
Mon-Sat: 6-1; Sun: 5-12
AE, DC
Moderate

Mexican cuisine has become very popular in Manhattan, with new spots opening regularly. Cafe Marimba is one of the best of the new breed; it is busy, noisy, and friendly. The atmosphere is early Arizona. The personnel are harried and preoccupied, but the kitchen is capable of some really delicious dishes. Try not to sit around the wall; the tile seating ledge is very attractive, but it isn't the most comfortable on a not-too-well padded posterior. Great openers include fajitas (grilled steak with tortillas, salsa, and guacamole) or queso fundido (casserole of melted mozzarella cheese with your choice of jalapeno chilis, seafood, or chorizo). Forget the salads, and save room for a marvelous grilled rack of lamb (in a Mexican restaurant!), or chicken enchiladas baked in soft tortillas, or a fresh filet of mesquite-grilled fish wrapped in corn husks. A caloric dessert selection (all homemade) changes regularly. You'll find delicious sorbets and ice creams, double-chocolate-vanilla cake, chocolate crepes, and a fine selection of coffees.

Color Me Delicious

CAFE UN DEUX TROIS
123 W 44th St
354-4148
Mon-Fri: noon-midnight; Sat, Sun: 5-midnight
AE
Moderate

Paper tablecloths and napkins may seem like a stingy way to dress a restaurant table, but at this bustling cafe, there's a reason. Two reasons, in fact. One is that it helps keep the tab down. The other is to provide drawing paper; crayons are furnished on every table. Doodling helps pass the time, and isn't it something you've always wanted to do since you were a kid? The surroundings (an old hotel lobby) are plain, and the location is handy if you're going to the theater. Service is very prompt and friendly, and prices are moderate. Though the menu is limited, each item is handled with obvious attention to quality and taste. Begin with a hearty onion soup, salade nicoise, or paté de canard. Seafood en papillote is an excellent selection, or perhaps you'd prefer a steak or sole meuniere. Finish with sliced fruit! For some reason, this spot is popular with the big names in the recording industry and with young people. Maybe aspiring singers will be able to make the deal of their lives over a cup of cappucino at Cafe Un Deux Trois. I hope so!

Fish and Vegetables, Kosher Style

CALDRON
306 E Sixth St
473-9543
Sun-Thurs: 12:30-11
No credit cards
Inexpensive

You step from an East Village street into a small, narrow, immaculately clean restaurant. Cards on the bulletin board reflect the divergent views of the neighborhood and the Caldron's owners. (The latter are followers of the Chasidic Jewish Lubavitch Rabbi.) The menu is almost entirely vegetables and fish, tempura style. In fact, it seems that everything is tempura. In keeping with the owner's religious beliefs, all the fish—and other ingredients—are kosher. The restaurant sells only kosher and chemical-free products. It's probably the only place that makes absolutely sure that all of its products are 100 percent vegetarian. And the prices are very, very reasonable.

Cantonese Home Cooking

CANTON
45 Division St
226-9173
Wed-Thurs: 12-10; Fri, Sat: 12-11; Sun: 12-10
No credit cards
Moderate

For those in the know, Canton has been a favorite spot for some time. Why? The place is clean, and the personnel are friendly and very polite, but most of all, unlike so many Chinese restaurants, the cooking is done on an individual basis. It's almost like stepping into the kitchen of a Chinese family. Visit with the waiter and tell him the kind of Cantonese delicacies you wish to have. You will be delighted with the results! I would suggest the butterfly shrimp, the diced chicken with Chinese vegetables and mushrooms, or the fried young squab done Chinese style. All the seafood is fresh and exceptionally tasty. So, gather up a group of friends for a special Chinese treat. You'll be pleased with the quality of your food *and* the moderate bill.

Mother's Boys

CAPSOUTO FRÈRES
451 Washington St
966-4900
Sun: noon-5, 6-midnight; Mon: 6-12 a.m.;
Tues-Fri: noon-5, 6 p.m.-1 a.m.;
Sat: noon-5, 6 p.m.-2 a.m.
Major credit cards
Moderate

At Capsouto Frères, three brothers and their mother team up to run a restaurant, and they do it with flair. The setting is an 1891 landmark warehouse. The atmosphere is casual, with ceiling fans, wooden tables, and the like. The menu is classic French, and the price is right. By all means, start with the French onion soup. It tastes like Mama Capsouto just made it herself. For entrees, I would suggest the sautéed fresh red snapper or roast duckling bigarrade. There are also some lighter dishes like the vegetarian plate, the steak sandwich, and the sensational salmon and cream cheese sandwich. The gateau au chocolat is number one for dessert. A touch of nouvelle cuisine, a dash of bistro atmosphere, and a large helping of friendliness is the recipe for success here.

A Dawn-to-Dawn Deli

CARNEGIE DELICATESSEN AND RESTAURANT
854 Seventh Ave (at 55th St)
757-2245
Daily: 6:40 a.m.-4 a.m.
No credit cards
Moderate

There's no city on earth with delis like New York's, and the Carnegie is one of the best. Its location in the middle of the hotel district makes it perfect for midnight snacks. Everything is made on the premises, and Carnegie offers free delivery at any time between 7 a.m. and 3 a.m., if you're within a five-block radius. Where to start? Your favorite Jewish mother didn't make chicken soup better than the Carnegie's homemade variety. It's practically worth getting sick for! It comes with matzo balls, garden noodles, fresh rice or fresh, homemade kreplach, or real homemade kasha. And there's more. Great blintzes. Open sandwhiches, hot and delicious. Ten different deli and egg sandwiches. A very juicy burger with all the trimmings. Lots of fish dishes. A choice of egg dishes unequaled in New York. Salads. Side orders of everything from hot baked potatoes to potato pancakes. Outrageous cheesecake topped with strawberries, blueberries, pineapple, cherries, or plain. Desserts from A to Z—even Jello.

It Will Moisten Your Appetite

CENTRAL FALLS
478 W Broadway
475-3333
Mon-Sat: noon to 2 a.m.; Sun: 11:30-2 a.m.
AE, DC
Moderate

With a name like Central Falls, I'm not sure what I expected! But Central Falls serves very good food, and your palate will tell you that it is far above average, and the selection is different enough to be interesting. For example, you might start dinner with steamed artichokes with lemon butter, grilled chicken livers wrapped in bacon and served with tamari and watercress, or a smoked mozzarella salad with beets, braised leeks, tomatoes, lemon and oil. My recommendation for the main course would be the baked chicken breast with prosciutto and gruyère, broiled loin lamb chops in a house mustard sauce, or green and white fettucine with leeks, prosciutto, and mushrooms served in a light cream sauce. The baked potatoes are excellent, garnished with cheddar, bacon, and chives, and the deep-fried onion rings are above average. The desserts are expensive but worth it. The chocolate mocha roll cake is a winner, as is the hazelnut cheesecake. My favorite brand of ice cream, Frusen Gladje, is also on the menu.

A Luncheon Institution

CHALET SUISSE
6 E 48th St
355-0855
Mon-Fri: noon-2:30, 5-9:30
Major credit cards
Moderate

When a place is packed every day, you know that something good is going on. And indeed, Chalet Suisse has all the right elements: a small but interesting space, pleasant and accommodating help, a handy midtown location, and hearty food at a reasonable price. You'll find such Swiss offerings as cheese and onion pie, bundnerschinken, veal à la Suisse, and bratwurst. For less Alpine taste buds, there's English sole amandine, breaded veal cutlet (very good), or a refreshing shrimp salad. By all means, save room for such desserts as chocolate fondue, kirschtorte, or Swiss apple tart. I could come here just for dessert! Chalet Suisse has been a New York institution for many years. If it maintains its current standards of operation, it will continue to be for a long time to come.

A Good Thing in a Small Package

CHANTERELLE
89 Grand St (at Greene St)
966-6960
Tues-Sat: 6:30-10:30
Major credit cards
Expensive

Even if you've never been to SoHo, make plans (a good time ahead) to visit this first-rate, simple but elegant charmer. The neighborhood is as dismal and ordinary as the restaurant is exciting and classy. The front is capably managed by Karen Waltuck, while the back is covered by her marine biologist husband, David. The small (10 tables) Georgian dining room is filled with the famous and near-famous, artists and designers who have made it and some who haven't, as well as with people who just like good food. Karen really mothers you. Be prepared for a leisurely two-hour dinner. The very special menu changes every week, and the staff that serves you is intent upon making your evening romantic or filling—whatever you came for. Of course, you pay for all this, but because the bills are handwritten and presented in discreet folders, the bite isn't quite as painful. (The dinner is price fixed.) Your appetizer selection could include squab or lobster bisque. Of the entrees, perhaps soft-shell crabs, poached chicken, red snapper, or sauté of lamb would be good (all vary according to what's in season). The salads are refreshing, the cheese assortment first-rate, the desserts (raspberry sherbet with eau de vie, homemade ice cream, or orange tart) light enough to go with the entrees.

Eclectic Dining

CHELSEA PLACE
147 Eighth Ave (bet 17th and 18th St)
924-8413
Mon-Fri: noon-3, 5:30-11:30; Sat: 5-11:45; Sun: 5-11
Major credit cards
Moderate

Chelsea Place is different—very different. I think the exact word is *eclectic*. The interior designer must have ended up 25th in a class of 25, but the chef finished first with honors. You won't be impressed by the neighborhood or the rather disheveled antique shop through which you enter. A door at the rear of the shop takes you into a noisy, crowded, smoke-filled bar, where the biggest challenge is elbowing through without Gertrude spilling her trays of drinks on you, or getting tangled up with today's answer to Ginger Rogers and Fred Astaire as they wheel around the tiny dance floor. Up some stairs and through another room, you enter what looks like a maiden aunt's room, circa 1929: hanging plants, a strange collection of pictures, mismatched chairs, water fountains, ceiling fans—you name it, it's here. But you didn't come to Chelsea Place for the décor; you come for the Italian food. And it's excellent. The menu includes traditional fare: baked manicotti, scampi alla Romana, and scaloppini francese. But don't look at the menu. Instead, listen to your waiter recite the list of daily specials, which include fish, poultry, and meat served with first-class vegetables. I recommend this eatery as a very unusual dining experience. It may look like its been put together by the Marx Brothers, but the culinary satisfaction is strictly first-rate.

Happy Days Are Here Again

CHEZ NAPOLEON
365 W 50th St
265-6980
Mon-Thurs: 12-2:30, 5-10:30; Fri: 12-2:30, 5-11; Sat: 5-11
Major credit cards
Inexpensive to moderate

With all the problems of daily life, it's fun to go to a place where the atmosphere is cheerful. Chez Napoleon is that kind of place. The lady who owns it greets you like a long lost friend and seats you in a small, clean dining area. It's an old house—warm and cozy and obviously a neighborhood favorite for many years. The cooking is dependable and hearty, and although the portions are small, you'll be satisfied. My top recommendations from the large menu are coquille St. Jacques, bouillabaisse (only served on weekends), rabbit with mustard sauce, broiled sea scallops, and sweetbreads. Many of the desserts are homemade. But the big plus here is the freshness of the dishes and the gracious feeling of "We're glad to have you."

Let's Have a Steak Dinner Tonight

CHRIST CELLA
160 E 46th St (at Lexington Ave)
697-2479
Mon-Fri: noon-10:30; Sat: 5-10:45
Major credit cards
Expensive

New York has an abundance of steakhouses (there are almost as many as there are Chinese restaurants), so for one to stand out from the rest, it has to offer something special. A steak is a steak, I suspect, but Christ Cella serves one of the best. They also serve a variety of fresh seafood every day, as well as chops, hamburgers, and roast beef. It's expensive, and the atmosphere isn't all that great, but the food is excellent. You'll see lots of interesting people, and the waiters are truly professional—so professional they don't even give you a menu. At Christ Cella, you'll have yourself a tasty no-nonsense meal and a hefty bill. Jackets and ties, please.

Vintage New York

CHRISTO'S
143 E 49th St
355-2695
Mon-Fri: noon-2 a.m.; Sat, Sun: 4:30 p.m.-2 a.m.
Major credit cards
Moderate

Seventh Avenue fashion designers might get indigestion here, but most everybody else should find Christo's an interesting, convenient, pleasant place to dine. Double-knit suits and plump bleached blondes are in abundance, and the place is full of supersalesmen making superdeals at high noon. It is vintage New York, with the atmosphere complementing all the activity: the walls are hung with pictures of the famous and not-so-famous people who have dined at Christo's and are friends of the management. In the evening, it's a mixture of locals and New York visitors; all are eating very hearty food, well-prepared in sizable portions at a reasonable price. You might start with excellent homemade soup; if you have a cold, you can even try some chicken consommé with matzo balls. The house specialties include pan-fried veal steak, beef à la stroganoff, boneless capon, and steak tartar. Lots of veal items are featured, plus the usual entrees from the broiler and a fair selection of seafood. I'd stick to the veal or the beef. Christo's is open very late, so it's an excellent place to come for an after-theater meal. And everyone is very congenial; you might meet some rather interesting new people at the busy bar.

Leon Is a Great Coach

COACH HOUSE
110 Waverly Pl
777-0303, 777-0349
Tues-Sat: 5:30-10:30; Sun: 4:30-9:30; closed Aug
Major credit cards
Expensive

When you're at the top, people shoot at you, and Leon Lianides knows this only too well. There seems to be an ongoing love-hate relationship with this restaurant. Some of New York's food critics give the Coach House a very bad rating, but I have always been one of their strong supporters. I've dined here dozens of times, and each time I have found the food to be absolutely superb. The atmosphere is warm and the service excellent. As I have indicated, you have to pay a price for all of this, and men must wear a coat and necktie, but isn't it fun to get all dressed up once in a while? I can say without fear of equivocation, that if you have a bowl of their black bean soup, the rack of lamb, and a piece of their famous chocolate cake, you'll be glowing for days afterward. Of course, dozens of other equally delicious dishes are available. For years, this place has been a favorite dining spot for thousands of New Yorkers, and as long as Leon is on the job himself and overseeing his establishment with his perfectionist eyes, it will continue to be a winner.

Important Imported Pastas

CONTRAPUNTO
1009 Third Ave
751-8616
Mon-Sat: 12-11:30; Sun: 4-10
Major credit cards
Moderate

The thing that struck me first about Contrapunto was the airiness and lightness of the dining room. It is located on the second floor of a busy corner building across the street from Bloomingdale's, with full-length windows allowing a view of the activity on Third Avenue. It is a delightful place for a delicious and different Italian lunch. For appetizers, you might have a salad of Belgian onions, radishes, and mushrooms with a walnut-oil dressing, or another delicious salad of smoked scamorza cheese, buffalo-milk mozzarella, tomato, and red onion. The pastas are unique. On the imported side, there is the angel-hair pasta with imported dried red tomato, fresh artichokes, mushrooms, chives and aged parmesan cheese, or another delicious angel-hair pasta with clams, shallots, leeks, and Japanese basil. For the fresh pasta, I recommend the pasta squares with crab meat, white wine, fresh mushrooms, or an unusual thin pasta with sweet red pepper, zucchini, eggplant, and tomato. All the portions are a good size, and you will be impressed with the quality. If there is one drawback, it is that service is very slow; don't come here if you have an appointment within the hour. This place advertises itself as a pasta, wine, and gelati house, and it is just that. Be sure and save room for dessert. The chocolate cake is absolutely sinful, and I recommend that you try the chocolate, praline, or strawberry gelati.

English Flavor and Yankee Seasoning

COVENT GARDEN
133 W 13th St
675-0020
Tues-Fri, Sun: 12-3, 5-11; Sat: 5-11
Major credit cards
Moderate

The best way to describe Covent Garden is to think of a restaurant that serves the kind of food you'd expect to find in the home of a dear friend who has made a special effort to fix dinner for you. You are greeted heartily by the proprietor, who, by the way, comes from the ready-to-wear fashion world. You are seated by a gracious hostess at a table with fresh flowers in a well-appointed dining room, or you may find yourself in a semi-outdoor setting, which is equally attractive and comfortable. The food is wholesome and plentiful; your waiter is attentive and efficient. My only complaint is that the entree plate is too crowded to be appetizing. The Covent Garden salad, their specialty, or the vegetarian salad, are both tasty. The real treats are any of the old English dishes, such as Cornish pastry with cubed beef, potato, spices, and garden vegetables; steak and kidney pie; shepherd's pie; or the very tender, nongreasy fish and chips. I would also recommend the bouillabaisse or the sole francese, a filet of sole dipped in batter. The boneless chicken breast or the veal picatta are your best choices in the meat area. It is unusual to find really good stuffed potatoes in a restaurant; I heartily recommend the ones here. The desserts are nothing to write home about, but I would like to call your attention to the coffees—Irish, Swiss, and Jamaican—all great toppers to an excellent meal. The proprietor is personally interested in maintaining a high-quality restaurant, and his attention to the little details certainly makes it just that.

Passage to India

DARBAR
44 W 56th St
4-DARBAR
Mon-Fri: noon-3, 5:30-11; Sat, Sun: 12:30-2, 5:30-11
Major credit cards
Moderate

It's a joy to walk into a very appealing and well-designed restaurant, where the tables are separated by partitions and one can really have a private conversation. Darbar is such a spot, and all of the staff wait on you in a quick and respectful manner, at the same time providing truly informed and efficient service and presenting fresh and attractive Indian dishes. A wonderful start for your meal would be the murgh pakoras, tender pieces of chicken sautéed in yogurt and Indian spices and batter fried. Specialties from the charcoal clay oven are sizable in selection: lobster, chicken, prawns, and lamb. My favorite is the tandoori prawns. By all means, try some of the Indian breads. A real taste treat is the vegetarian paratha, unleavened whole wheat bread filled with vegetables and baked in the tandoor with butter. Rice dishes are excellent, and the desserts are exceptionally good. The chocolate cinnamon ice cream is worth the visit in itself. There is a buffet lunch daily.

Pasta Perfection

DA SILVANO
260 Sixth Ave (at Houston St)
982-2343
Mon-Fri: noon-3, 6-11:30; Sat: 6-midnight; Sun: 6-11
No credit cards
Moderate

This small northern Italian restaurant, housed in a Village storefront, has a simple menu, and with a few exceptions, the dishes are handled with taste and talent. Forget the meat and concentrate on the pasta and antipasto, like the lightly breaded, grilled shrimp. The choices are superb. Try tortellini alla panna (tortellini with heavy cream, parmesan cheese, and butter) and spaghettini puttanesca (chunks of tomato, garlic, black olive, capers, and anchovies). Cannelloni Silvano is another winner: homemade rolled noodles, stuffed with ricotta and spinach and covered with a light bechamel sauce and cheese. Prices are very reasonable. That, combined with the casual service and the décor—green plants against brick walls—make dining here a pleasant experience.

Olde Tyme

DELMONICO'S
56 Beaver St
422-4747
Mon-Fri: 7:30-10 a.m., 12-3, 5-8:30
Major credit cards
Moderate to expensive

Those who are familiar with the Wall Street area already know about Delmonico's; it has been a tradition for decades and is still a class act. The elegant furnishings and the polite service add up to near perfection well-honed from years of experience. Whether you're here for a "what's new in the market lunch" or for a social dinner, I heartily recommend this consistent, established institution. It's hard to pick out only a few specialties, but I would suggest the swordfish; the marvelous filet of sole glazed with white wine, mushrooms, and tomatoes; the boneless breast of chicken in brandy mustard sauce; or the mixed grill Delmonico (which consists of lamb chop, filet mignon, liver, and bacon). All of these should be at the top of anybody's list. And bitter chocolate with vanilla sauce is the Delmonico dessert showpiece.

Divine

DIVINO
1556 Second Ave (at 80th St)
861-1096
Mon-Sat: noon-3, 5-midnight; Sun: 2-10:30
Major credit cards
Moderate

Divino is a professional Northern Italian restaurant—professional service, professional cooking, professional supervision. It's always a thrill to watch a well-trained team in action, and Divino has one of the best in town. The owner is on the job, and the place is orchestrated with the baton of a master. The moment you enter (better make reservations), you see the vista of the Italian garden-like setting and an attractive and unusual bowl of relishes on the bar. Every sight and sense is a happy one, and each dish is served piping hot when it should be, or chilled if that is called for. And there's plenty of good, hot, fresh Italian bread. For starters, try baked clams or raw beef with green sauce. Or if it's a cold evening, the tortellini in brado (meat-filled pasta in broth) is a winner. And what a selection of pasta! Pasta stuffed with meat, spinach, and cheese; Genovese-style pasta in garlic and basil sauce; and pasta and seafood. Steamed clams or Italian-style bouillabaisse or scampi with tarragon are featured, but my choice is the stuffed breast of veal, one of the best dishes I've tasted anywhere. All entrees are served with fresh vegetables. And if you like strawberries, you'll enjoy the desserts; otherwise, forget it.

Go West, Young Man!

DOBSON'S
341 Columbus Ave (at 76th St)
362-0100
Sun-Thurs: 11:30 a.m.-12:30 a.m.; Fri, Sat: 11:30 a.m.-1:30 a.m.
Major credit cards
Moderate

While out exploring the Upper West Side, you can't go wrong if you stop by Dobson's. This is not gourmet dining, but the menu runs the gamut: soups, very tasty salads, a cheese and fruit board, a nice variety of omelets, broiled sole or trout, hamburgers, and quiches. Dobson's also features a better-than-average brunch. You can have your choice of eggs Benedict, or eggs any style with ham, bacon, or sausage, Nova Scotia salmon, omelets, quiches, or even French toast. The portions are adequate, the quality very good, and the ambiance appealing. The service is prompt and efficient, and the price is certainly right. Don't forget to look at their list of daily specials.

All I Want Are Some Noodles

DOSANKO
(various locations)
No credit cards
Inexpensive

Shops dispensing pasta are among the fastest-growing shops in the city, but Dosanko's noodles have an exotic twist: theirs are Japanese. Larmen is a steaming bowl of Japanese soup and noodles garnished with pieces of beef or pork and freshly sautéed vegetables. This is the specialty of the house, and the prices are very reasonable. Dosanko advertises itself as the "World's Finest Noodle Shop," and as brash as that may sound, it certainly has to be *one* of the best, especially if you like larmen. Other dishes include Japanese dumplings with seasoned ground pork and a bowl of crispy fried noodles and beef smothered in sautéed vegetables. There isn't a great deal of atmosphere, but watching the noodles being prepared is interesting.

Napoleon's à la Italia

ECCO
124 Chambers St
227-7074
Mon-Fri: 12-3, 5-11:30; Sat-Sun: 5-11:30
Major credit cards
Moderate

How unusual to find a really tasty and professional spot in the middle of Chambers Street in TriBeCa! Ecco is one of those places where the owner sees to it that things are done correctly. There is an old-fashioned bar as you enter, and you can even eat there. Although the dining area is small, it gives the impression of being a spacious room. And all of it is absolutely spotless. In my opinion, Ecco serves the best Italian food in TriBeCa; the added bonus is that you might see some well-known faces there. You might be eating with the stars! The antipasto from the buffet is attractive and delicious with such choices as sea scallops baked with capers, clams, shrimp, artichokes, mozzarella, and many other interesting nibbles. Then on to the choices of a typical Italian menu with spaghetti, fettuccine, tortellini—and most anything else your heart desires. Swordfish is one of the things they prepare particularly well. The double-cut veal chops are also delicious. And the breast of chicken with white wine, peas, prosciutto, and mushrooms is at the top of my list, along with the calf's liver sautéed with white wine and onions. Don't miss the Napoleon for dessert. I've tasted Napoleons in a lot of places, and without equivocation the offering at Ecco is one of the very best. You are probably amused at a chocolate lover making this suggestion for dessert; I realize not everyone likes chocolate like your author!

When You're Not Trying to Impress . . .

ELMER'S
1034 Second Ave
751-8020
Sun-Thurs: 12-11; Fri, Sat: 12-12
Major credit cards
Moderate

If it's just good food you're looking for, and if an "in" place doesn't make that much difference, then I would certainly recommend Elmer's for a hearty dinner. The location used to be part of El Morocco; the signs of the former ownership are still apparent in the familiar zebra pattern on the chairs. The bar is a meeting place for neighborhood regulars and high rollers of one kind or another. The atmosphere is strictly masculine, with dark-wood interior; the help is the mature no-nonsense type. It is a treat to be greeted by a maitre d' who knows why he is there! Attractive iced munchies are immediately served along with an interesting breadbasket and real old-time New York unsalted butter, a rarity these days. Elmer's Salad is a winner, a combination of various greens, avocado, and vegetables. Although a number of usual meat dishes such as a steak and chops are available, I would suggest the chicken breast done with just enough lemon to make it tasty. Plates are served really hot or chilled as they should be. The cottage fried potatoes accompanying the entrees are a winner. The desserts are very ho-hum, so concentrate on the rest of the meal.

A Jewel

ERMINIA
250 E 83rd St
879-4284
Daily: 5-11
AE
Moderate

The Trastevere operation now has four branches, and Erminia, the smallest, is really the jewel in the crown. It has about a dozen tables in a most pleasant, informal, and rather rustic atmosphere—

just right for a leisurely intimate dinner. I found it an absolutely charming spot with helpful personnel and outstanding food. But on to the menu . . . Try the artichokes cooked in olive oil or the fresh baked oysters with mushrooms to start. In the pasta category, you can't go wrong with the tender dumplings with potatoes and tomatoes or the large noodles with ricotta cheese. The number of entrees are limited and all are grilled, but they are tasty and served with delicious vegetables. There is grilled chicken, various seafood items on a skewer, a special fish dish, and lamb or veal chops. The dessert selections vary daily. I found the tartufo (ice cream and a cherry covered with chocolate) to be supreme.

Noisy Noshing

ERNIE'S
2150 Broadway (at 75th St)
496-1588
Sun-Thurs: 12-3:30, 5:30-12; Fri, Sat: 12-3:30, 5:30-1
Major credit cards
Moderate

Some people like noise with their food—I'm not one of them. But for those who really want to be part of the action, I recommend Ernie's. It is a busy, informal spot on the Upper West Side that resembles a college dining room. The brick walls are unfinished, there are paper tablecloths, and the attire is shirt sleeve. But there is no question that the food is good, the portions adequate, the help polite. If you're in the mood to be with the swingers, head in this direction. The menu is Italian. Among the excellent and reasonably priced starters are fresh mushrooms in balsamic vinaigrette, chilled shrimp sausage, and a delicious chilled roast veal breast with cheese. For something a bit more substantial, you might try one of the individual pizzas, like duck sausage and leeks with fresh sage, fresh wild mushroom, and my favorite, artichoke with bacon and tomato. Other entrees include grilled baby chicken with garlic, grilled marinated leg of lamb, or pork chops with garlic and herbs. The roasted potatoes and grilled Tuscan garlic bread are two things that you don't want to miss, and the very light and delicious chocolate soufflé cake is another.

Yummy Yogurt Plus

EVERYTHING YOGURT
One Coenties Slip (opposite 55 Water St)
635-3800
Mon-Fri: 6 a.m.-6:30 p.m.; Sat: 10-4
No credit cards
Moderate

If you're doing business or working in the Wall Street area, here's a spot I really recommend. The selection is sensational, and much attention is given to displaying the healthy-looking food. These people are obviously professionals. I would suggest their mixed vegie salad with broccoli, cauliflower, zucchini, yellow squash, carrots, red cabbage, and green pepper—what a bowl! To go with it is a whole assortment of dressings and garnishes. There are cold pasta salads, whole-wheat crust quiches, hot casseroles, and crepes like their spinach roulade. This delicious dish is a mixture of mild cheese, mushrooms, and herbs rolled in spinach with rice pilaf and topped with cherry tomatoes. The soups are all homemade, and the sandwiches are very special. An unusual choice are the croissant sandwiches filled with tuna, chicken, or egg salad. There are also a number of low-calorie platters and, of course, yogurt, yogurt, yogurt! Their yogurt sundaes have about every possible topping, and you can mix the yogurt with fresh fruit. Not only is this a great spot for lunch, but if you're in the neighborhood early enough, they offer a healthy, varied, delicious breakfast menu. I particularly recommend the orange-juice cocktail—orange juice, frozen yogurt, milk, and honey.

Food and Then Some . . .

FOOD
127 Prince St
(no phone)
Mon-Wed: noon-10; Thurs-Sat: 12-11; Sun: 11:30-4:30
No credit cards
Inexpensive

I recommend Food without qualification. For a while, it was a very small "in" spot in the SoHo neighborhood. But it became so popular that it had to expand. Service is cafeteria style, and what a selection: great salads, soups, sandwiches, and desserts—all homemade and many of them vegetarian. The portions are enormous. Substantial entrees are also available, as well as outstanding dessert selections. If you're looking for good, hearty food at sensible prices, this is the place.

1, 2, 3, Go!

FOUR FIVE SIX (SAY ENG LOOK)
2 Bowery
964-5853
Sun-Thurs: 11:30 a.m.-11 p.m.; Fri, Sat: 11:30 a.m.-midnight
No credit cards
Inexpensive to moderate

A good find in Chinatown! Four Five Six, like most Chinese restaurants, has an extensive menu featuring dozens of Shanghai-style dishes in addition to a sizable number of Cantonese offerings. The Shanghai-style listings include the usual appetizers, cold cuts, soups, meat, and seafood offerings. I'd recommend the fried chicken Shanghai style, the shrimp with bean cake, the sea cucumber with shrimp seed, and the pork with bamboo shoots in brown sauce. Other winners are dried sautéed string beans in spiced sauce, the scallops with crab meat or spiced sauce, stewed pork with bean curd sheet, and crab meat and abalone with baby corn. Warning! Make sure you are seated upstairs. The ventilation downstairs is not good, and the smells from the kitchen are overwhelming.

Quality

FOUR SEASONS
99 E 52nd St
754-9494
Mon-Sat: noon-1:45, 5-11:30
Major credit cards
Expensive

What's special about this magnificent restaurant? A spectacular setting around a pool. A huge, airy, spacious atmosphere. Tables far enough apart to allow the most intimate conversations. A menu that changes with the seasons. A staff that's thoroughly professional out front and in the kitchen. A marvelous selection of beautifully prepared vegetables, great sauces and dressings, fresh fish, superbly cooked meat, and fabulous desserts. The chocolate velvet cake is a real treat. Individual soufflés in coffee cups are something special. And the wine selection is just about the best in New York, I'm told. This may be the closest you'll get to a meal at the White House, and you'll pay for it. But, unlike many expensive restaurants, Four Seasons is worth it. If you want a quick or less expensive meal, the bar-grill is also a winner.

You'll "Beef" at This One!

FRANK'S
431 W 14th St
243-1349
Mon-Thurs: 4 a.m.-3 p.m., 5-10 p.m.;
Fri: 4 a.m.-3 p.m., 5-11 p.m.;
Sat: 5-11 p.m.
Major credit cards
Moderate

At breakfast and lunch, this old-time spot is crowded with nearby butchers, with blood on their aprons and large stomachs to fill. If that doesn't bother you, come on down early. But dinner is really the best at Frank's, operated by five members of the Molinari family, the third generation in a business started in 1912. Reservations are difficult, especially on weekends (a week in advance is necessary), since they can take care of only 65 people. When cloths come out on the tables for dinner, the family chef (well trained at the now-defunct Brussels Restaurant) will offer you superb prime ribs of beef, fresh fish, great steaks, and pasta. The neighborhood is seamy, the desserts are ho-hum, and the ambiance is Pittsburgh diner, but the food is absolutely top drawer.

A Lincoln Center Possibility

GINGER MAN
51 W 64th St
399-2358
Daily: 11:30 a.m.-midnight
Major credit cards
Moderate

It's become a hackneyed observation that restaurants around Lincoln Center are not very good, and I have to agree. The Ginger Man is extolled by some and vilified by others, but I find that they *can* do a good job. If I'd attended a performance at Lincoln Center and wanted a conventional meal, then I'd give the Ginger Man a chance—but not otherwise. The place looks as though it were put together by a committee; the dining rooms are labyrinthine. The service is harried but pleasant. The menu is nothing fancy, but I happen to be a potato-skin lover, and I recommend theirs for an appetizer. The salads are adequate and delicious. Grilled shrimp curry is a specialty. The rack of lamb is a truly superb dish, and I defy anyone to find a better one anywhere in New York (except, possibly, at the Coach House). Dessert offerings are heavy on the calories. But one night I tried the Tobler double-chocolate, chocolate chip ice cream, and it was worth every calorie. Give the Ginger Man a try. If your expectations aren't too high, you won't be disappointed.

Practice Makes Perfect

GIORDANO
409 W 39th St
947-9811
Mon-Thurs: 12-11; Fri, Sat: 12-12
Major credit cards
Moderate

When a restaurant has been in the same family for 25 years, you know they have fine-tuned the establishment. The Creglia family runs a first-rate operation at Giordano. An attractive bar greets you with trays of appetizers available during the cocktail hour. There are several pleasant dining areas as well as an outdoor patio. The cuisine is Northern Italian. Delicious pasta includes a wonderful fettuccine al fungetto, tortellini alla panna, fettuccine alfredo, or linguine al sugo. For entrees, I'd suggest the langostine alla mugnaia, an excellent seafood dish, or the calf's liver alla veneziana. A side order of fried zucchini or eggplant parmigiana tops off a superb meal. Although the food is excellent, I was most impressed with how comforting it is to have old-time waiters taking care of you; they sure know what they're doing. For no-nonsense Italian food at a reasonable price, you can't beat Giordano.

Rapture of the Deep

GLOUCESTER HOUSE
37 E 50th St (at Park Ave)
755-7394
Mon-Fri: noon-2:30, 5:30-10; Sat, Sun: noon-10
Major credit cards
Expensive

This is probably the best seafood house in Manhattan; it's certainly one of the most expensive. First impressions are good: the restaurant is spacious and shipshape, with wooden tables, superb homemade biscuits, an à la carte menu only, and even a printed timetable of seasonal fish. There are nine oyster, five clam, three mussel, three shrimp, two crab, and five bisque and chowder choices. Those are the appetizers. For entrees, there are lobster, crab, shrimp, broiled fish, pompano, salmon, swordfish, sole, turbot, trout, frog's legs, scallops, soft-shell crab, shad and shad roe, and smelt. The shrimp roasted in garlic butter, lemon-broiled sole fillet, and the crab meat and lobster au gratin are especially good. The smelt, available in winter, are worth a visit in themselves (they come sautéed, broiled, or fried). French-fried onion rings and zucchini chips are delicious side orders. Specialties of the house include finnan haddock (smoked cod), red snapper, and fried sautéed oysters. The lobster, although very well presented (with corn on the cob), is outrageously expensive. Be warned, though, that the gentlemen in your party must wear jackets and ties, and be prepared for unpleasant, supercilious help. Have your wallet stuffed with the largest bills printed. The place is never crowded, and you can understand why. But don't pass it up if seafood is your thing and price is no object.

Inspired to Sin

GORDON'S
38 McDougal St (at Prince St)
475-7500
Tues-Thurs: 12-3, 6-11; Fri: 12-3, 6-12; Sat: 12-4, 6-12; Sun: 12-4, 5-10
AE, DC
Moderate

Gordon's is really three eating places in one: a publike front room with big picture windows overlooking the Village, a back room done in a bright modern manner, and an attractive open-air garden in the rear for summer dining. I was struck by the friendliness of the establishment, the cozy atmosphere, and the no-nonsense menu. This is not gourmet fare, but it certainly is the kind of place you will enjoy and want to come back to time and time again. My first visit was in the midst of the "blizzard of 1983." I couldn't imagine a more picturesque place to watch such an event. The food? Great! Unusual starters include poached spinach and ricotta dumplings or toasted Italian bread brushed with garlic and olive oil. Entree selections run the gamut from grilled game hen to pork chops with rosemary and sautéed calf's liver. Homemade chocolate truffle cake or almond cake will top off a very satisfying meal.

Oysters at the Station

GRAND CENTRAL OYSTER BAR AND RESTAURANT
Grand Central Station (lower level)
490-6650
Mon-Fri: 11:30-9:30
Major credit cards
Moderate

If you are a native New Yorker, you know about the half-century institution that is the Old Oyster Bar at Grand Central; it was once popular with commuters and residents. A midtown institution that was neglected for years, it is now restored and doing nicely, thank you. (They serve over 2,000 folks a day!) Located in the caverns of Grand Central, it is attractive, the young help most accommodating, and the drain on the pocketbook minimal. The menu boasts more than 90 seafood items (new, fresh entrees daily), six different kinds of oysters, super oyster stew and clam chowder (both kinds), and oyster pan roast.

Not Just for Vegetarians

GREENER PASTURES
117 E 60th St
355-3214
Mon-Thurs, Sat: noon-9:30; Fri, Sun: noon-8:30
No credit cards
Moderate

Before Bloomingdale's opened its salad bar, chic and vegetarian shoppers frequently dashed out for a quick lunch in the back room of Greener Pastures. The closely spaced, narrow tables filled the tiny rooms, and patrons frequently found themselves sharing tables, utensils, and condiments. Fortunately, after years of cramped existence, owner Jerry Singer finally expanded his restaurant. The atmosphere is still laid-back and informal, but now there is a picture window that looks out onto a backyard garden—a garden on 60th Street! Terra cotta floors, brick walls, and natural wood complete the décor. But one doesn't select a restaurant for its décor, and here it is only a pleasant background for excellent natural foods. All selections are vegetarian and kosher. The latter leads to some interesting variations. Most noticeable is the absence of gelatin and the use of kosher cheese, which can make a familiar dish very different. You can also get blintzes and sour cream and vegetarian chopped liver and fresh fish. They're not bad, but try the salads (they vary according to the availability of ingredients), the vegetables (Japanese style), or the quiches, which are truly magnificent.

Light, Melodic Dining

GREENE STREET CAFE
101 Greene St
925-2415
Mon-Sun: 6-midnight; Sun: 12-4
Major credit cards
Moderate

Housed in a large, renovated building (in this case, a former garage), Greene Street Cafe features entertainment in the late evening. Earlier in the day, activity centers around a very busy bar and a dining area filled with dozens of tables arranged theater style. (The chairs are midget-sized: diners with long legs should go elsewhere. David Utz, the chair designer, needs to go back to the drawing board.) Though this restaurant relies on atmosphere, its popularity owes a lot to its food and drink departments. Selections are somewhat limited: heavy on the fruit, vegetable, and seafood offerings, all done quite nicely. Start with the asparagus soup or tartar of salmon. For desserts, try the apple tart, black velvet cake, or the macademian nut cake. Next door is the Greene Street Kitchen and Bar, supposedly the world's largest wine bar (over 125 varieties).

A Grotta with Gusto

GROTTA AZZURRA
387 Broome St
226-9283
Tues-Thurs: 12-11; Fri: 12-12; Sat: 12-12:30; Sun: 12-11
No credit cards
Moderate

Grotta Azzurra is an institution and rightly so. If you're looking for a hearty Italian atmosphere (in a basement) with old-time waiters serving food with conviction (if not flair), this is the place to go. The menu is enormous; every possible Italian dish is available. The portions are large, the ingredients top quality, and the ambiance acceptable. The Grotta is perfect, if all you have in mind is good food without worrying about the formalities of eating out.

A Well-Kept Secret

GROVE STREET CAFE
53 Grove St
924-9501
Tues-Sat: 6-10:30
No credit cards
Moderate

Shhh! Keep this a secret! It would be a shame to spoil such a cozy, unpretentious spot. The place has only about a dozen tables, you bring your own wine, and the menu is limited, but what they do they sure do well. The best appetizer, and one which I felt was worth the visit in itself, was the shrimp-stuffed artichoke with egg-yolk vinaigrette. A tastier dish you can't imagine. You might also try the galantine of chicken with pork, veal, and pistachio, or a sauté of bay scallops with snow peas, mushrooms, and sherry. It's an unusual combination, but it turns out well. For the main course, there is a fresh fish dish each day, a delicious boneless breast of chicken, and lamb ratatouille. No credit cards and no cigar or pipe smoking here. There is a very pleasant atmosphere and truly delicious food in a rather out-of-the way location.

The Back Room at the Macaroni Factory

GUIDO'S
511 Ninth Ave (at W 39th St)
244-9314
Mon-Fri: 12-3, 5-11; Sat: 5-11
No credit cards
Inexpensive

You might ask yourself what a nice person like you would be doing in the middle of Ninth Avenue having lunch in the back room of a macaroni factory? Well, this is no usual back room and no usual macaroni factory. Up front, as you walk in, you'll see a display of 23 brands of macaroni. That was the origins of the business, but now it's just a sideline. The real draw is the smallish restaurant in the back, which is as busy as Times Square. Tom Scarola is the fifth-generation family member who runs this unusual spot. Whether you're here for lunch or dinner, make sure you have a reservation; you might even rub shoulders with Olivia Newton-John, Robert de Niro, or other celebrities. If not in person, their pictures (along with the blue checkered tablecloths and wine bottles on the ceiling) help create a special atmosphere at Guido's. You don't want to miss the shrimp francese, the veal sorrentino, or the house specialty, chicken al la guido. The pastas are all freshly made, authentic, inexpensive, and delicious. Finish with spumoni or rum cake, and you will have had a marvelous meal. Lunch specials include four different chicken, veal, and shrimp entrees, as well as linguine or spaghetti with all the trimmings.

Veddy British

HARVEY'S CHELSEA RESTAURANT
108 W 18th St (at Sixth Ave)
243-5644
Mon-Thurs, Sun: noon-midnight; Fri, Sat: noon-1 a.m.
No credit cards
Moderate

Since 1890, this has been a New York favorite. The atmosphere hasn't changed that much in nearly a century. It is still a charming and warm establishment. It's a place for relaxed eating, convivial conversation, and good fellowship. Everything is cooked to order, so your meal may take a bit of time. How about trying an unusual salad? It's called the German Snack Platter, and it consists of sliced knockwurst, German cheese, cherry tomatoes, and pretzels, and it's almost a meal in itself. A specialty of the house is two bratwurst sausages served with potato salad, pickles, and hot mustard. (Their potato salad is definitely not the usual bland variety.) Another great dish is the shepherd's pie: chopped beef and lamb sautéed with herb spices and topped with rosettes of mashed potatoes, peas, and carrots. Along with the English atmosphere goes a fish-and-chips dish served with malt vinegar as well as tartar sauce and a great prime rib. And if you're not going dancing, try the stuffed shrimp scampi, a combination of shrimp and crab meat in garlic butter. Also, don't pass up the pecan pie served with fresh whipped cream. Sinful Sunday brunch is fun here, too. Chelsea is becoming a more and more interesting place for browsing, shopping, and dining, and Harvey's is one of the landmarks of the area.

Sensational Sushi

HATSUHANA
17 E 48th St
355-3345
Mon-Fri: 11:45-2:30, 5:30-9:30; Sat, Sun: 5-9:30
Major credit cards
Moderate

Hatsuhana has deservedly become known as the best sushi house in Manhattan. One can sit at a table or at the bar and get equal attention from the informed help. It always pleases me to see so many Japanese men and women eating here; one knows, then, that the food is authentic. There are several dozen choice appetizers, including such oddities as broiled eel in cucumber wrap, steamed egg custard with shrimp, fish and vegetables, squid mixed with Japanese apricots, or even chopped fatty tuna with aged soybeans. Next, try the salmon teriyaki (which is fresh salmon grilled with fresh teriyaki sauce) or any number of tuna or sushi dishes best described by the personnel. Forget about the desserts, and concentrate on the exotic offerings for your meal.

A Seafood Paradise

HISAE WEST
20 W 72nd St
787-5656
Mon-Sat: 5-midnight; Sun: 4-11
Major credit cards
Moderate

This place is for health nuts. It's the spot for dinner or late supper when you've hopped on the scale and that little indicator goes too far to the right, or after that size 12 dress feels more comfortable than the size 10 you've been wearing. You might try the Chinese broccoli in oyster sauce or the cold watercress in sesame dressing, or how about the scallop chowder? Hisae West's specialty is seafood. There are all kinds of vegetarian dishes, as well as steak, filet mignon, and Long Island duckling. A good sushi bar is also available. Note: Hisae's serves only freshly ground water-processed coffee. Top the meal off with Hisae's chocolate cake made with hazelnut flour and honey instead of sugar.

Hot Stuff

HWA YUAN
40 E Broadway
966-5534, 966-5535
Daily: 12-10
Major credit cards
Inexpensive

Szechuan cooking is a big thing in New York, and some of the best places are old-time Chinese restaurants that aren't fancy but sure know how to cook. One of these is Hwa Yuan, located in not the best area, but an extremely popular place with the local inhabitants. If hot stuff is your bag, I would recommend the Chinese cabbage, shredded beef with hot green peppers, "chunked" chicken with hot sauce, or the hot-spiced sautéed kidney. In the seafood category, the hot-spiced shrimp is a winner! Hwa Yuan has little if any atmosphere and few of the nicer amenities, but you'll be assured of an authentic Chinese meal.

A Toscano Lunch

IL CANTINORI
32 E 10th St
673-6044
Mon-Thurs: 12-3, 6-11:30; Fri: 12-3, 6-12; Sat: 6-12; Sun: 5-11
Major credit cards
Moderate

Il Cantinori bills itself as a "Ristorante Toscano," and Toscan-style cooking is done to perfection at this rather pleasant spot, which I recommend for lunch. The fresh bean soup with peasant bread or the shrimp grilled Toscan style is a good way to start, followed by ravioli alla fiorentina, a delicious combination of ricotta cheese and spinach dumplings served with Toscan sauce. Another delicious pasta is the spaghettini alla rustica, a pasta sautéed with tomatoes and garlic. For a lighter lunch, try the red-lettuce salad with fresh oranges. Good dessert choices include biscuits with egg custard or a delicious cream bain Marie style. The bread is fresh and delicious, the waiters professional, the place spotless; I would say this is a first-class place for a business meeting.

Quality Comes Through

IL MONELLO
1460 Second Ave
535-9310
Mon-Sat: 12-3, 5-12
Major credit cards
Moderate to expensive

If you can put up with snotty, disinterested captains who are looking the other way when you're talking to them and who are really not very concerned with what you're there for, you can have a very pleasant dining experience at this classy, Upper East Side Italian restaurant. The room is warm and inviting, and the quality of the food and the presentation excellent. This is definitely *not* the place to go for intimate sweet talk or a highly sensitive political or business discussion; it's crowded, and the tables are within eavesdropping distance. Instead, concentrate on your palate. You might do well by starting with broiled scampi or mussels in tomato sauce or spinach in broth. By all means have the angel-hair pasta; it is done to perfection. Take note of the delicious breaded rack of veal or the chicken with prosciutto and cheese. The dessert cart is laden with good things like English trifles, zabaglione, or strawberries *flambé*. Each day of the week a special is offered. One of the outstanding offerings is on Friday: mixed seafood in broth.

Solidly Italian

IL MULINO
86 W Third St (at Thompson St)
673-3783
Mon-Fri: 12-3, 5-11:30; Sat: 5-11:30
AE
Moderate

It's amazing how many good Italian restaurants have sprung up all over the city. This one, in the Village, is making a name for itself with good, solid Italian cooking—not fancy but well worth the very reasonable tab. The usual offerings are available for starters: spaghetti, fettuccine Alfredo, or scampi, along with a number of other tasty treats. For entrees, they specialize in veal, and what a selection—veal sautéed in cream and champagne, veal sautéed in lemon and butter, veal sautéed with sage and prosciutto, breaded veal chops, rolled veal braised in wine, veal sautéed in wine, veal sautéed with mushrooms, and on and on. I'd stick to the veal, although there are chicken and beef selections. Portions are sizable, the atmosphere is pleasant, the service is prompt, friendly, and efficient, and the tab won't give you nightmares.

Doing What They Do Best

IL VAGABONDO
351 E 62nd St
832-9221
Mon-Fri: 12-3, 5:30-12; Sat, Sun: 5:30-12
Major credit cards
Inexpensive

One of the major airlines advertises "doing what we do best." It could just as well be the motto of this bustling, inexpensive restaurant, which has been a favorite with knowledgeable New Yorkers for over 20 years. The atmosphere is strictly old-time, complete with checkered tablecloths, four busy rooms, and an even busier bar. No menus are offered; the pleasant but harried waiters reel off the regular items and the daily specials. Depending on when you go, you may have spaghetti or ravioli, an absolutely marvelous minestrone soup, chicken parmesan, prime rib steak, or sliced beef. I would also heartily recommend the Friday scampi or lobster special. There is no pretense in this place. It is a great spot for office parties and for guys and gals with slim pocketbooks. Be sure to take a look at the way the kitchen is set up, and on the way out, go past the butcher shop (which Il Vagabondo also owns) just down the street; you can see why the quality of the meat is so high. You won't see Jackie O. or Halston here, but you'll see happy faces, compliments of a delicious meal and the extremely reasonable bill. Save room for the Bocce Ball dessert—other places call it tartufo—it's great. They are the only restaurant in New York with an indoor bocce court.

Burger Master

JACKSON HOLE WYOMING BURGERS
232 E 64th St (other locations are not as good)
371-7187
Mon-Sat: 10:30-1 a.m.; Sun: 12-12
No credit cards
Inexpensive

You might think a burger is a burger is a burger, but having tasted them all around the city, I can say that these are the best. Each one weighs in at seven juicy and delicious ounces. And there are all types of hamburgers, as well as great coffee and French fries. All ingredients here are fresh. Jackson Hole is certainly not fancy, but who needs a fancy place when all you want is a good sandwich: a pizza burger, an alpine burger, maybe an English burger, or even a Baldouney burger (mushrooms, fried onions, and American cheese). Another attraction is the late closing hours; you can stop by to get rid of bedtime hunger pangs. If your partner can't face a burger, the omelets are tasty—and don't miss the French-fried onion rings. P.S. The desserts are homemade.

Macho Munching

JAKE'S
801 Second Ave
687-5320
Mon-Sat: 12-4, 5:30-11:30
Major credit cards
Moderate to expensive

Jake's could become to men what LaGrenouille is to women. Every aspect of this spot is very masculine: the atmosphere, the service, the menu. Not that women don't enjoy this place; they do, indeed. The breadbasket is unusual and delicious, which is always a good sign, and an excellent relish dish is presented. If you can raise your voice above the din, get the waiter to bring you Jake's special cole-slaw salad, a magificent red-cabbage presentation. The veal dishes are particularly well done; I would put the veal piccata at the top of the list. Other selections I would recommend include delicious stir-fried chicken with pecans, red peppers, scallions, and fresh vegetables, the rack of spring lamb chops, and the usual assortment of steak and roast beef dishes. Jake's is a Palm without the rudeness! It is *very* busy here, and reservations are a must. It is definitely *not* a dessert house.

Seafood with an Oriental Accent

JANICE'S FISH PLACE
570 Hudson St (at W 11th St)
243-4212
Mon-Fri: 6-11; Sat: 5-12; Sun: 12-4, 5-11
Major credit cards
Moderate

I can't remember ever being impressed with a seafood restaurant that prepares ocean delicacies with a Chinese flavor, but Janice's is something special. The enclosed patio gives you a good view of the passers-by, and the blackboard shows the fresh specialty of the day. A particularly nice touch is the bean sprout dish and other munchies placed on your table when you sit down. Unusual appetizers include sautéed bean sprouts with nuts and raisins, special scallop chowder, and scungilli vinaigrette. As for the entrees, I found the shrimp sautéed with fresh Oriental vegetables, the swordfish teriyaki, and the whole steamed sea bass to be the winners. Healthfood lovers should try the fresh mixed vegetables cooked Oriental style with ginger or sautéed and topped with melted cheese.

Southern Comfort

JEZEBEL
630 Ninth Ave
582-1045
Mon-Sat: 6-11:30
AE
Moderate

It's hard to describe what Jezebel looks like. It's a cross between a New Orleans brothel (I guess), a vintage clothing and artifacts store, and an old Southern town's best place to eat. All of this adds up to an unusual mix, but if it's food from Dixieland you want, this is the place to go. You might begin with the sautéed chicken livers or garlic shrimps and go on to spicy honey chicken, smothered Southern chicken, shrimp creole, baked ham with orange wine sauce and raisins, or delicious smothered pork chops. The selection of vegetables is most unusual and good, including black-eyed peas, rutabaga turnips, yams, grits, and fried okra. Finish with sweet potato pie, obviously the specialty of the house. The portions are generous, indeed. The service is slow, but it's worth the waiting. It is a little hard to tell the help from the customers because of the way they dress, and they seem more interested in chatting with the customers than serving them!

A Model "In"

JIM McMULLEN'S
1341 Third Ave
861-4700
Daily: 11:30-1:45 a.m.
AE
Moderate

I'm always a bit suspicious of a restaurant where the waiting line moves with irregular motion, and this is one spot where that happens. If the maitre d' or Jim McMullen knows you, or if your name is a well-known one, the wait is short. Otherwise, it's ridiculous. But people do wait, I guess, not only because it is chic to see and be seen here, but because the food is good and the prices are certainly right. Jim was a model, and the place is a favorite hangout for well-known faces—and for those who hope to be. The menu is unimaginative, with the usual appetizers, ranging from barley soup to clams on the half shell. But I found the chicken pot pie worth the visit in itself. There is a good selection of fish dishes, including poached salmon and several steak offerings. The chocolate brownie pie is an A-1 dessert, and the hot fudge sundae is not the usual ice-cream store variety. An attractive selection for supper served after 11 p.m. includes popular sandwiches and salads at bargain prices. There is also a private dining room (seating 30-50 guests) available for lunch or dinner. If you don't mind being a statistic, you will enjoy the glamour of this place. Bring along Nancy and Henry Kissinger, though, if you're in a hurry.

Good Ole Joe's

JOE'S
79 MacDougal St
473-8834
Wed-Mon: noon-11:30
Major credit cards
Moderate

There is no shortage of Italian restaurants in New York; I sometimes think there are more here than in Rome! And they come in all grades—most are mediocre, a few very good, a handful superb. Joe's belongs in the very good category, not only for the quality of the food but also for the value given your dining dollar. Joe himself is on the job, as he has been for several decades, imparting Old-World charm to this small Village establishment. His staff are also experienced, efficient, no-nonsense old-timers. Spaghetti (in six different ways), baked ziti, linguini or homemade egg noodles are all excellent starters. I'd stick to the veal scaloppine (fixed five different ways), the veal chops or veal cutlets for entrees. Shrimps and clams are featured, and the breast of chicken alla parmigiana is a winner. My favorite meal here is cannelloni along with the great Italian bread and a very fresh salad "alla Joe's." A perfect meal at a tiny price. If the name of this place was Valentino's instead of Joe's, you'd pay double!

A Good Fish Story

JOHN CLANCY'S
181 W 10th St
242-7350
Mon-Sat: 5:30-11:30; Sun: 5-11
Major credit cards
Moderate

Although this rather elegant place is a little bit stuffy, they do an exceptional job with a rather limited seafood menu. Forget about the delay in getting a table even when there is no crowd. Forget about the affectation of the help. Concentrate instead on some of the really good, hot appetizers like mushrooms stuffed with crab or broiled clams with herbed butter. A specialty of the house is Fisherman's Stew, a hefty brew that is well done. Other favorites (all served on a skewer) include shrimp, sea scallops, and swordfish. Shrimp seems to be the star attraction, and it's available sautéed with garlic butter, with jalapeno chillies, or in mustard dill sauce. Dover sole is available, but I think it's overpriced. The desserts are very special, homemade and delicious. For a change, try the English trifle. If it's chocolate you want, try the roulade.

54, Not 57, Varieties!

JOHN'S PIZZERIA
278 Bleecker St
243-1680
Mon-Thurs 11:30 a.m.-11:30 p.m.;
Fri, Sat: 11:30 a.m.-12:30 p.m.;
Sun: 12-11:30 p.m.
No credit cards
Inexpensive

Why is it that most pizzerias are called Joe's or John's or Jack's or Jimmy's? Couldn't we have a Priscilla's or Penelope's pizzeria? The boss here isn't even named John— he's Pete Castellotti, a.k.a. the Baron of Bleecker Street. Pete offers 54—count 'em—varieties of pizza, from just cheese and tomatoes to a gourmet extravaganza of cheese, tomatoes, anchovies, sausage, peppers, meatballs, onions, and mushrooms. If spaghetti or cheese ravioli or manicotti (all homemade) are your preference, this is also the place for you. The manicotti filled with ricotta and mozzarella cheese, covered with plain tomato sauce, and served with great Italian bread will make even your Uncle Menachem a believer. The surroundings are shabby, the menus are shabby, the plates are shabby, and the neighborhood is shabby, *but* the pizzas are perfection.

Bring Your Earplugs

J.S. VANDAM
150 Varick St
929-7466
Sun-Thurs: 7 p.m.-12:30 a.m.; Fri, Sat: 7 p.m.-3 a.m.
Major credit cards
Moderate

J.S. Vandam is quite an unusual place—and one of the noisiest restaurants I've even been in. The bartender is a musician, and he seems to feel that if he wants to be entertained, everybody else in the place should be, too. But the music is awful, to put it midly. And J.S. Vandam is certainly not exactly in the mainstream of things. It's located downtown, just above Canal Street. The tables are not fancy; as a matter of fact, they use paper tablecloths. And they must have the most unusual and oddest-looking personnel I've every seen in a restaurant. However—and it's a big however—the food is really excellent. I'm not exaggerating when I say it's worth all the negatives, because you get an excellent meal at a very reasonable tab. For starters, try the steamed mussels, smoked salmon, or snails, and then go on perhaps to the marinated lamb steak, sea scallops, pheasant, or duck. The dishes are served warm, and the vegetables are well cooked. The lemon tarte or the chocolate mousseline cake are the best dessert suggestions.

A Garden of Delights

JULIA
226 W 79th St
787-1511
Daily: 12-4, 5:30-12
Major credit cards
Moderate

Julia is a charming spot, particularly in nice weather when one can eat in a covered garden with the sun or stars in full view. But even in nasty weather, the setting is pleasant, with the food matching the atmosphere. If you can't eat in the garden, there is a pleasant dining area upstairs. Another nice thing about Julia's is that they are open seven days a week for lunch, brunch, dinner, and supper. Moreover, the service is polite, efficient, and unobtrusive. By all means, start with Julia's Soup, a chicken soup with meatballs, vegetables, and croutons. It's tasty, not too fattening, and a good value. Next, ask for cold tortellini salad (cheese tortellini with tomatoes and red onions). Of course, if you're in a seafood mood, try the smoked trout and salmon salad. The charcoal grilled meats, especially the lamb chops or chicken breast, are worth a try. For dessert, I'd pass up the usual and ask for coffee toffee pie. It's delicious and worth every calorie.

The Biggest Sandwich in Town

KATZ'S DELICATESSEN
205 E Houston St (at Ludlow St)
254-2246
Sun-Thurs: 7-11 p.m.; Fri, Sat: 7-1 a.m.
No credit cards
Inexpensive

When you are down on the Lower East Side and need an extra big bite, try Katz's Delicatessen. It is a super place with some of the biggest and best sandwiches in town. The atmosphere goes along with the great food, and the prices are reasonable. You can go right up to the counter and order (it is fun watching the no-nonsense operators slicing and fixing), or sit at a table where a well-worn waiter will take excellent care of you. Try the dill pickles and the sauerkraut along with your sandwich, and I guarantee even Rolaids will not diminish the memories of one of New York's great institutions. Katz's is a perfect way to sample the unique ambiance of Lower East Side establishments. When you wait at a table for an hour, or discover that the salt, pepper, and napkin containers are empty and the ketchup is missing, you'll know what I mean.

Hot Rocks

KITCHO
22 W 46th St
575-8880
Mon-Fri: noon-2:30, 6-10:30; Sun: 5-10:30
AE, DC
Moderate

In Japanese, *kitcho* means good omen, and I'm sure you'll find your dinner to be just that. This is one of the better Oriental restaurants in Manhattan: you can tell by the fact that most of the patrons are Japanese. Like many Chinese and Japanese restaurants, the décor and atmosphere are nothing special—clean and functional, but not much more. The charm lies in the delicious Japanese food. Start with ishi yaki, a hot rock in an attractive container, upon which you cook your own shrimp, squid, or beef. The aroma is tantalizing, the results spectacular. Other delicious appetizers include boiled spinach with sesame sauce, fried bean curd, and red caviar with grated white radish. The usual tempura or teriyake (beef, pork, chichen, or fish) are available; another favorite is yaki-tori, broiled chicken and scallions on a skewer. Rice (in many forms) tastes better in this setting than at home, and the sushi is a real winner.

German Food, Great Cakes, and Pastries

KLEINE KONDITOREI
234 E 86th St
737-7130
Sun-Thurs: 10 a.m.-midnight; Fri, Sat: 10 a.m.-1 a.m.
AE, DC
Moderate

If you're in the mood for sauerbraten and potato dumplings and red cabbage, wiener schnitzel, or an outrageously calorie-laden linzer torte, try Kleine Konditorei. It is one of the very few German restaurants worth visiting in New York; the cakes and pastries would do credit to the fine little pastry shops you find in Munich. East 86th Street is one of New York's most colorful areas, and a walk around the neighborhood (which you'll need after a stop here) is interesting. I'd recommend Kleine Konditorei for an after-the-show visit, or for a special lunch when a golden-brown German pancake sounds just right. There is also a bakery section for takeout.

At Last! A Sensibly Priced Steakhouse

K.O.'S
99 Bank St
243-0561
Tues-Thurs, Sun: 6-10:30; Fri, Sat: 6-11:30
Major credit cards
Moderate

CLOSED

In my opinion, New York's better steakhouses are grossly overpriced, but here is one in the Village that is both attractive and reasonable. The atmosphere is pleasant, the tables are sensibly spaced apart, and the young help, though not very professional, are accommodating. Try the smoked salmon or the zucchini frittata. Stick to the steaks for the main course, filet mignon or the porterhouse, since the other offerings are not all that great. As a potato lover, I would recommend the home fries or the stuffed double-baked potato. The inevitable cheesecake is offered for dessert. Or you might try the créme brulée instead. K.O.'s is a very popular spot, so reservations should be made in advance.

A Bowl of Soup, a Loaf of Bread, and Thou

LA BONNE SOUPE
48 W 55th St (at Fifth Ave)
586-7650
Daily: 11:30-midnight
AE
Moderate

If you just want some soup or an omelet with wine and dessert, this is certainly the spot. The onion soup is the one that made Les Halles famous. They even suggest that you sniff it like fine brandy before eating. But don't expect a fancy restaurant here; it is a place for lighter fare, and the surroundings are plain. Keep to the specialties of the house, and if you are like me, a hot bowl of soup (I'll take vegetable) with some French bread is just about the best thing going. (Their vegetable offering is called Créme Andalouse.) La Bonne Soupe is particularly handy if you're doing some shopping and want a quick bite.

Eating with the High and Mighty

LA CARAVELLE
33 W 55th St (at Fifth Ave)
586-4252
Mon-Sat: noon-2:30, 6-10:30; closed Aug
Major credit cards
Expensive

La Caravelle is a snooty restaurant, but it has delicious food. It's one of those places where, if they know you, you'll get a good place near the front. If they don't, you'll still get great food, but the scenery won't be as pleasant. The service is always professional, and it should be at the prices they charge. The hors d'oeuvres are a gourmet's delight, ranging from foie gras des landes to cherrystones, bluepoints, or quenelles Lyonnaise. Entrees for lunch include sole, veal, and excellent steak and chicken items, plus some daily specialties. The desserts are among the best in New York, and the cheese selection is superior. For dinner, you'll find almost everything: Little Neck clams, beluga caviar, great smoked salmon, and—if you really want something out of this world—le cote de veau Caravelle or le poussin Poele au beurre d'estragon. For dessert, I recommended les crêpes ma pomme or le soufflé glace aux abricots (ice cream soufflé with apricots)—both are super! A meal at La Caravelle is a gastronomical experience for gourmets and for those who like to boast about "the last great place I had dinner." There is also a special price-fixed pretheater dinner.

An Old Favorite

LA COLOMBE D'OR
134 E 26th St
689-0666
Mon-Fri: 12-2:30, 6-10:30; Sat: 6-11
Major credit cards
Moderate

It's easy to see why La Colombe d'Or is always busy. They provide well-prepared meals at a reasonable price. The place has an intimate French provincial atmosphere, and the service is prompt and efficient. Take note of this spot, since there are not too many good eating establishments in this part of town. I'd suggest the super bouillabaisse maison for a very good lunch dish. I also recommend the pastas. For dinner, you might start with ratatouille (vegetable stew) or the snails in Roquefort sauce. Then go on to the roast chicken with black olives, chopped tomatoes, and garlic. A superb dish. The roasted squab, however, is not done too well. Gateau Victoire, their chocolate cake, is first rate. One of the nicest features is the number of specialty coffees offered with liqueur and fresh whipped cream. There is coffee with cognac, triple sec, calvados or even cafe morello (cappuccino), kahlua, whipped cream, chocolate shavings, orange rindlets . . . *wow*! Let's start with coffee and dessert for a change! My hat is off to chef Richard Steffann; he does a good job. Make reservations well in advance.

A Special Evening on the Town

LA COTE BASQUE
5 E 55th St
688-6525
Mon-Sat: noon-2:30, 6-10:30
Major credit cards
Expensive

La Cote Basque is a superb restaurant. The Beautiful People flock to this restaurant for fine French food, and if you're a gourmet, this is a spot you won't want to miss. The people watching is as enthralling as the food is treméndous. But be prepared, if the location of your table means something to you. They take care of the regulars first. And the elegant murals and flowers are matched by the elegant guests. Once in a while, we are all tempted to try some spectacular dish that we can't buy in the frozen-food section of the supermarket or make at home. This is the place to go (with a very full wallet or the company credit card) when you have this desire. Specialties of the house include pepper steak, Dover sole, and quail. The appetizers, especially the smoked salmon, are among the best in the city.

A Snacker's Delight

LA FONDUE
43 W 55th St
581-0820
Mon-Thurs: 11:45-midnight; Fri, Sat: 11:45-12:30 a.m.;
Sun: 11:45-11 p.m.
No credit cards
Inexpensive

You know a restaurant is good when it's always crowded, and La Fondue is always busy. This is certainly not the place for leisurely, intimate dining, but it's a great spot for a quick snack, a good lunch, a no-frills dinner, or an after-theater repast. My favorites for starters include onion soup, cheddar-cheese soup, or Swedish green-pea soup—all very well made and very filling. The specialty of the house for light snacks is a cheese and sausage board, featuring a great variety of imported cheeses and sausages from Denmark, Poland, the Netherlands, Spain, Norway, Austria, Switzerland, Germany, Italy, Hungary, and almost any other place you could think of. This attractive offering includes salad, bread, and relishes. You can also have fun with a prime filet mignon fondue, or a genuine imported Swiss cheese fondue. For heartier dining, try the cheeseburgers, the boned breast of chicken, the cheese omelet, a very hefty chef's salad, a variety of quiches, or the sirloin steak. There's even a Continental Cheese Tour, in which you get a fine selection of the native cheeses, plus bread, fresh fruit, and crackers. I'd also recommend the Swiss chocolate fondue with fruit and fruit bread for dessert, or perhaps the banana fruit bread, rum raisin ice cream, and chocolate fondue sauce. This is a number-one spot, where your stomach will be satisfied and your pocketbook treated kindly.

A Fresh Flower Paradise

LA GRENOUILLE
3 E 52nd St (at Fifth Ave)
752-1495
Mon-Fri: noon-2:30, 6-11:30
AE, DC
Expensive

La Grenouille is one of those special places that one really has to see to believe. It is impossible to describe. The beautiful fresh flowers are but a clue to a unique, not-to-be-forgotten dining experience. The food is just as great as the atmosphere, and although the prices are high, it is worth every penny. The celebrity watching adds to the fun. The French menu is complete, the staff professional. Be sure to try their cold hors d'oeuvres; they are a specialty of the house, as are the clams and the Bayonne ham. Don't miss the soufflés for dessert—they are superb. The tables are very close together, but what difference does it make when the people at your elbows are so interesting?

Try This Before Theater

LA GRILLADE
845 Eighth Ave (at 51st St)
265-1610
Mon-Fri: noon-3, 5-11:30; Sat, Sun: 5-11:30
Major credit cards
Moderate

If you don't mind an average-looking place with good food that's not going to set you back a lot of bucks, try La Grillade. There isn't much atmosphere; however, everything is very tasty. It's a great spot if you're going to take in a movie, or if you just want to get out of your apartment or hotel room for a while. At lunch, the place is crowded, and a wait is usually in order. In the evening, it is a bit more relaxed, but the staff always seems to have time to take care of you. The lamb chops are super, and the vegetables taste as good as the ones that used to be prepared in my family store's luncheon room back in Oregon. Ask your waiter what he suggests, then loosen your belt and go to it.

Cajun Cooking with Style

LA LOUISIANA
132 Lexington Ave
686-3959
Mon-Thurs: 6-11; Fri, Sat: 6-12
AE, DC
Moderate

There are a number of reasons to visit this restaurant, not the least of them being the talent and hospitality of Alene and Abe, the "directors" who also run Texarkana. And I was pleased to learn that Alene once worked at Salishan, our premier coastal resort in Oregon, which is known for grace and quality. The place is small (about 50 diners can be served) but very busy, because of the moderate prices as much as the great food. The menu has a Cajun accent, evident in selections like the fresh Louisiana catfish, or the boudin—a spicy sausage appetizer of pork, scallions, and rice. All the seafood is fresh, and there are superb crab cakes and even crawfish. The soups are great, the bread assortment is interesting, and all desserts are baked on the premises. That rum pecan pie is *something*, especially if you enjoy it with some strong Louisiana chicory coffee. The best dish of all is the Southern fried chicken. My taste buds' memory went back to the chicken served by "Badger," the only black man (at the time) in Gearhart, a small coastal town in Oregon; his fried chicken has been what I consider to be the epitome of the dish since I was five years old. La Louisiana's chicken is the best I've found since Badger's. For experiencing polite, friendly service in an establishment where personal attention to detail is not a lost art, you must try this restaurant.

Cozy, Simple, and Tasty

LA METAIRIE
189 W 10th St (bet W Fourth and Bleecker St)
989-0343
Daily: 6-11
No credit cards
Moderate

La Metairie has built its reputation through a succession of individual owners, who have given tender, loving care to this tiny hole-in-the-wall in the Village. The menu changes every three months. I'd suggest you call ahead to see if your favorite is being featured that day, be it tripe, or rabbit with mustard sauce, or bouillabaisse. The room accommodates only 22 people, the tables are close together, and the atmosphere extremely cozy and friendly. How they can operate in a thimble-size kitchen and produce such tasty morsels is a mystery, but the owners are carrying on a quality tradition.

A Landmark Sunday Lunch

LANDMARK TAVERN
626 11th Ave (at 46th St)
757-8595
Sun-Thurs: noon-midnight; Fri, Sat: noon-1 a.m.
No credit cards
Inexpensive

What to do and where to go for lunch on Sunday? The larger hotels advertise extravagant buffets that range from excellent-plus (Grand Hyatt) to pretty awful (Barclay Inter-Continental). And many smaller restaurants have look-alike brunches, with the usual selection (omelets, eggs, sausages, etc.) and very little imagination. So, I suggest you get out your strolling shoes and proceed to the Landmark Tavern, a New York institution since 1865. The usual brunch items are indeed available (at very nominal prices), but you also have the options of such house specialties as shepherd's pie (ground lamb sautéed with herbs), roast leg of lamb (delicious!), or English-style fish and chips. To accompany your selection is Landmark's homemade (every hour) soda bread served with imported jams and marmalade. Some of the desserts are also homemade; the chocolate cake, pecan pie, and carrot cake are all above average. Of course, Sunday is not the only time to enjoy this three-story historic dining spot. (The top floor is available for banquets.) Drop in for their daily regular dinners, which include sandwich platters, a variety of salads, omelets, fresh seafood, steaks, and roast prime ribs of beef. The bar is friendly, the help is harried, the atmosphere reeks of nostalgia, and the food is a bargain. Take it in after church next Sunday.

Intimate and Delicious

LA PETITE FERME
973 Lexington Ave (at 70th St)
249-3272
Mon-Sat: 6-10:30
Major credit cards
Moderate

La Petite Ferme was a very small spot down in the Village the first time I visited it. It has since grown to be a larger, fancier place on Lexington Avenue. The atmosphere is still intimate, and the same sort of menu (printed on a blackboard) is available to a large group of faithful customers. As the seating is quite limited, calling for reservations is a good idea. Without them, it is easier to get in during the early part of the dinner hour. The cuisine is French country style, and the three or four featured entree selections are all tastefully prepared, whether it's poached bass, veal, sole, or whatever. I have to give high marks to their vegetables, because they don't overcook them. There is an attractive garden downstairs, and although the service is a little confusing (the kitchen is upstairs), the help manages to do a very satisfactory job.

A French Masterpiece

LA RESERVE
4 W 49th St
247-2993
Mon-Sat: 12-3, 5:30-11
Major credit cards
Expensive

Jean Louis is a master, and La Reserve reflects the master's superb touch in every respect. The pink-and-green décor is restful and flattering, the chef is a culinary purist, the service by the captains and waiters has been tuned like a fine musical instrument, and the result is an exceptionally delicious symphony. A pretheater dinner at a reasonable price is available, as well as private-party facilities in their banquet room. Each dish is a masterpiece! Mousse of chicken liver served with walnuts, fresh marinated salmon or duckling terrine are on a par with—or better than—any French restaurant in town. And their artichoke is presented with each leaf taken off and arranged on a plate like a flower. Now try that the next time you are entertaining! On to the lobster cream soup and then red snapper or roasted duck or veal medallion. Better yet, let Jean Louis order for you, as there are always seasonal specials. To finish if off: le chariots de patisseries "La Reserve"! Turn up the music!

Smallness Is Betterness

LA RIPAILLE
605 Hudson St
255-4406
Mon-Sat: 6-11:30
Major credit cards
Moderate

There's a new menu every night at this small Parisian-style cafe. Inasmuch as you're going to get different offerings every time, call ahead to see what's available. I found it to be a cozy spot for an informal dinner. The tables are rickety, but the chef puts his heart into every dish. It is certainly worth a visit. Most entrees are done to perfection, the seafood is always fresh (seafood in puff pastry is a specialty), and they do an excellent job with their chicken dishes. White chocolate is a house favorite; at least half of the dessert offerings use chocolate as an ingredient. Proudly displayed at the front of the room are rave notices from a number of New York gourmets. If they want, they can add mine, too.

A Prize Flower

LA TULIPE
104 W 13th St
691-8860
Tues-Sun: 6:30-10
Major credit cards
Expensive

The rules for getting a table at this small restaurant are unnecessarily annoying (answering machines and specified call-back hours), and the service is slow. But La Tulipe is worth it all: the food is sensational. It's French as its best—innovative and light fare, with great sauces, and each plate is a work of art. Let me describe the desserts first! You know by now that I'm a dessert nut. All pastries, sherbets, and ice creams are made on the premises. The best is called La Tulipe Javanaise, a creamy coffee ice cream with chocolate sauce in a flower-shaped pastry shell. Magnificent! And there's an apple tart, a floating island with hazelnuts, an apricot soufflé, a hazelnut meringue, and a layered chocolate cake with chocolate tiles. Enough? Okay, let's get back to the basics. Start with the zucchini fritters or the mussel soup with saffron—they're very special. Then proceed to the red snapper, the sautéed chicken, or the grilled sliced squab. I'm partial to the rack of lamb with garlic crumbs and tomato; however, the braised sweetbreads are equally good. The condescending manner of the management is annoying, but you can be sure you'll have a professionally prepared meal. Also, prices are on the high side, and portions are not large. I have a feeling that they're trying to create an "it's hard to get a reservation" reputation, but don't get discouraged and keep trying, even if you have to tell 'em that Ed Koch or Liz Taylor will be in your party.

Going in Style

LAURENT
111 E 56th St (at Park Ave)
753-2729
Mon-Sat: noon-3, 6-10:30; Sun: 5-10:30
AE, DC
Expensive

Laurent serves excellent food, beautifully prepared and presented (their fruit tart is a work of art) by waiters in black tie. It's a quiet, elegant restaurant patronized by quiet, elegantly dressed diners—the sort of place to go for an intimate dinner *à deux*, or for discussing business over a lobster. The sort of restaurant, in short, that is favored by executives with company credit cards. The menu changes daily, according to the season's best produce. Thus, in spring, soft-shell crabs are offered, while later on, shad and shad roe are found on the menu. Year-round favorites are duckling served with orange sauce, and steak au poivre flambé a l'Armagnac. There are three private dining rooms, and the restaurant's wine cellars stock over 30,000 bottles of wine, including those vintages old and rare enough to satisfy discriminating palates. Quite a place!

A Midtown Menu

LAVIN'S
23 W 39th St
921-1288
Mon-Fri: noon-3, 5-midnight; Sat: 6-midnight
Major credit cards
Moderate

Lavin's started the trend toward New American cuisine, and they have been successful ever since. They combine prompt service and moderate prices with a warm atmosphere and very polite personnel. It is a particularly convenient place for a midtown lunch or a pretheater dinner. I'd suggest you start with the salad of garden rows, which is made with carrots, tomatoes, broccoli, radishes, green beans, and the like, or the walnut or veal and apricot paté. Or perhaps you'd like the delicious warm chicken salad. Their mesquite grilled chicken, the grilled veal chop, or grilled calf's liver are other winners. A number of pastas are available, the best being linguini with shrimp and bay scallops. An added feature is the cruvinet, a wine dispenser that offers wine by the taste or the glass.

A Bagel Sandwich

LE BAGEL CHATEAU
1026 Third Ave (at 61st St)
755-5473
Daily: 7:30 a.m.- 10 p.m.
No credit cards
Inexpensive

If you just want something light, try a bagel sandwich. At Le Bagel Chateau—which is a pretty pretentious name for a sandwich shop—you can order a simple toasted bagel or the works. "Everything on a bagel" is the motto here, and that means anything from the standard cream cheese and lox to roast beef, turkey, corned beef, egg salad, or any combination you want. The ambiance isn't the greatest, but the prices are decent and the food is tasty. Le Bagel Chateau will also do catering—nothing fancy, but good and hearty.

A Neighborly Delight

LE BIARRITZ
325 W 57th St (at Ninth Ave)
757-2390
Mon-Fri: noon-3, 5-10:30; Sat: noon-3, 5-midnight
Major credit cards
Moderate

This is the kind of homey place where the busboy "lets" you keep the used knife from the first course to use with the entree. But then, you don't come here for professional service or fancy trimmings. New York is full of "neighborhood" restaurants, and Le Biarritz is one of the best in that category. It seems like home every evening as the regulars take most of the seats in this smallish, warm eatery. The place has been in the same location and in the same hands for over 18 years. If you're like me, gleaming copper makes any eating establishment look inviting, and here you can see a first-rate collection of beautiful French copper cooking and serving pieces. You might be in the mood for escargots to start, and they know how to prepare them well. Or maybe some real French onion soup or quiche Lorraine. You can't go wrong with either. Entrees range from frog legs provencale to boeuf Bourguignonne to filet de sole Veronique. The menu includes all kinds of chicken, lamb, beef, veal, and fish dishes, all served with fresh vegetables. Although there are no unusual desserts, each is homemade and very tasty. The reasonably priced dinner includes soup, salad, and a choice of dessert. I recommend Le Biarritz if you are going to a Broadway show or an event in the Coliseum and Lincoln Center area.

The Boss Is in the Kitchen

LE BISTROQUET
90 Bedford St
242-8309
Sun-Thurs: 5-11; Fri, Sat: 5-11:30
Major credit cards
Moderate

It's always a good sign when the owner of a restaurant is in the kitchen, where he or she can personally supervise what's going on. This is true at Le Bistroquet, a small restaurant in the Village that is warm and friendly to the point of being laid back. I would especially recommend the mousses (salmon or crab meat) for hors d'oeuvres. The garlic shrimp is also worth a try. The showpiece dish is Spanish paella, a Spanish seafood casserole of mussels, clams, scallops, lobster, shrimp, and chicken cooked in saffron rice. Another featured item is the chicken bistroquet, a breast of chicken cooked in Madeira wine and with mushrooms baked in pastry and served with rice. All the desserts are homemade; the apple cake and chocolate torte are very special. At Le Bistroquet, the portions are generous, the service is unobtrusive and informed. The only negative feature are the paper napkins. Mr. Owner, with such delicious food and such a pleasant atmosphere, couldn't you splurge for some decent linen?

Class à la Mode

LE BOEUF A LA MODE
539 E 81st St
650-9664
Tues-Sun: 5:30-11
Major credit cards
Moderate

This is an unheralded spot on the Upper East Side, which the regulars know of and love and the rest of the city has never even heard of. The setting is intimate, warm, and well done, with fresh flowers at each table; the help, with the exception of the hostess, is talented, friendly, and efficient; and the food is very good. I particularly noted how well-groomed the clientele looked. The menu is typically French; the appetizers are a feast in themselves. How about smoked salmon, oysters, snails, or clams? The entrees range from sirloin steak to grilled chicken. All are served with a wonderful soup and vegetables. You may choose from a great selection of desserts, including chocolate mousse, creme caramel, and delicious French pastries. The price of the entree determines the tab on the whole four-course dinner.

Another Classic French Beauty

LE CIRQUE
58 E 65th St (at Park Ave)
794-9292
Mon-Sat: noon-2:30, 6-10
AE, DC
Expensive

Le Cirque has great food, with tremendously talented people in the kitchen and haughty ones out front. It is one of those spots you can always count on for excellent food, if you can stand the cool reception you may get if your name doesn't appear in the *Women's Wear Daily* gossip column. The menu features both French and Italian dishes, with veal dishes, duck, and spaghetti primavera as some of the specialties. The rack of lamb takes forever to prepare, but it is delicious. Take along your credit card (the necessary cash would be bulky) and your appetite—both will be well served in this attractive spot.

A Marvelous Restaurant

LE CYGNE
55 E 54th St
759-5941
Mon-Thurs: noon-2, 6-10; Fri: noon-2; Sat: 6-11
Major credit cards
Expensive

A most appealing ambiance combined with a very professional kitchen is really all that needs to be said about Le Cygne. This spot is one that you will not want to miss, but make sure it's saved for a great occasion or when you're dining on an expense account. The whole setting is comfortable, relaxing, and appealing. How about Maine scallops in a wine and saffron sauce or perhaps artichoke hearts with sweetbreads, mushrooms, and truffle sauce to begin the meal? And what a selection for the main course! Frog legs sautéed in garlic butter, snails with wild mushrooms, braised squab with olives, mushrooms and artichokes, breast of duck in honey-vinegar sauce, or an absolutely sensational braised sweetbread with Chanterelle mushrooms. Meals run a hefty price-fixed tab, but it's well worth it. There are specialties of the house everyday, and private dining facilities are available.

Ladies' Choice

L'ENDROIT
208 E 52nd St
PL9-7373
Mon-Fri: 12-2:45, 6-10; Sat: 6-10
Major credit cards
Moderately expensive

You're in the doghouse with your wife. It's your secretary's birthday. You want a really nice place to "take the girls" to lunch. Well, L'Endroit is that place (*l'endroit* is French for "the place"). An oasis of pink and calm in bustling midtown, this is a little-known room charmingly appointed in superb taste: classic chairs, striking paintings, classy stemware, gorgeous fresh flowers. It's a spot the ladies will love, especially for lunch, but dinners there are also a treat. The luncheon menu offers such excitement as marinated rolls of sand dabs in a bed of steamed vegetables, or slices of beef tenderloin as appetizers, pastas, soups (like a great Les Halles-style onion soup), on to sautéed calf's liver, legs of duck, fresh fish, and Le Saucisson Habille de Jour Fete (the king of the French charcuterie, wrapped in veal loin sliced over linguini, with creamed and grated parmesan sauce). Wow! Additional offerings at dinner might include escargots or salmon with capers for the first course, and lobster tails, loin of lamb in puff pastry, or steaks to follow. Homemade English trifle or cheesecake will top off a spectacular meal. Service is helpful and unobtrusive; you'll want to stretch out this meal, because the atmosphere is so pleasant.

Park Avenue Splendor

LE PERIGORD PARK
575 Park Ave
752-0050
Mon-Fri: noon-3, 6-12; Sat: 6-12
Major credit cards
Expensive

An old favorite, always a reliable family friend, Le Perigord Park offers a pleasant dining experience in a sedate, mellow atmosphere. You will pay mightly for the very professional service, the beautiful appointments, and the highly capable kitchen, but it's worth the hefty tab. Willy Krause deserves his many honors. Diners love to take as much time as possible having the captains describe every entree, but at the prices asked, it surely is a reasonable request. Want to really splurge right from the start? Well, the caviar and the foie gras de Mr. Grimaud are unequaled in Manhattan. More down to earth in price and substance are the delicious clams, smoked salmon, or the garlic-drenched snails. Coquille St. Jacques, turbot soufflé, sautéed chicken, medallions of veal, roast duck, and roast pigeon are but a few of the mouth-watering, sensationally prepared entrees. And the seasonings, sauces, and vegetables are just simply grand. It ends there. The desserts are nothing to travel for. Instead, at these prices, buy a ticket to Salem, Oregon, and visit Gerry Frank's Konditorei. Sure, I have to get a plug in for my own dessert shop. If I do say so myself, the extravagant cakes featured are without equal. My partner, Barney Rogers, and I promise to take special care of you, filling you up with super rich dark chocolate blackout cake, or refreshingly delightful lemon cake. Enough of this commercial.

The Best of Paris

LE REGENCE
37 E 64th St
734-9100
Daily: 12-2:30, 6-10:30
Major credit cards
Expensive

Hotel Plaza Athénée is well known in Paris; now there is a New York version—not quite like the original, but still very nice. You'll want to see the hotel, but the winner is the restaurant, a real class act. Not only is the setting understated and immensely attractive, but the tables are even far enough apart to have a private conversation. The presentation is outstanding, and the food is superb! One of the most impressive points of Le Regence is that the personnel are not impressed with their own importance. The waiters and maitre d' are pleasantly accommodating, hard-working, and well-informed. Other expensive New York restaurants, take note; it can be done. This spot is suitable for either lunch or dinner. You can't go wrong with any of the selections, but a few favorites stand out. Since it is mainly a seafood house, I strongly recommend the Dover sole filets in champagne sauce, the grilled fish salmon, and the braised striped bass in a marvelous wine sauce. The luncheon salads are magnificent; a real treat is the sliced chicken breast salad with hazel nuts. It's so inviting to look at, you hate to eat it! Even mundane French-fried potatoes are done to perfection. Desserts are rather ordinary fare; in as much as the price tag is of the expense-account variety, spend it on the entree and you won't go wrong.

Out-of-the-Way Romance

LE SAINT JEAN DES PRES
112 Duane St
608-2332
Mon-Fri: 12-3, 6-11; Sat: 6-12; Sun: 12-4
Major credit cards
Moderate to expensive

In my opinion, this is one of the most beautiful restaurants in New York, and well it should be, because it was designed by the same folks responsible for sister restaurants in Brussels. My only fear is that the out-of-the-way location in New York City may make its survival difficult. It is particularly unhandy for lunch, but for a leisurely dinner you can't pick a more delightful spot. It is large, airy, and attractively furnished, and the staff is friendly, if a little bit amateurish. To begin with, try the seafood salad or tomato stuffed with shrimp, or perhaps a warm appetizer like the poached egg with spinach or the scampi salad with basil. For the main course, the fish is particularly good. The Belgian-style lobster waterzooie and the sole meuniere are particularly tasty. If you're a party of two and both of you are beef lovers, the prime rib roast for two is excellent, but it does take extra time. Save a corner for the homemade desserts! If you can find your way to this place, you won't be disappointed. Romance is in the air here, for sure.

Eating at a Snail's Pace, or Faster If You Want . . .

L'ESCARGOT
47 W 55th St
245-4266
Mon-Sat: 12-3, 5-11:30
Major credit cards
Moderate

In the midst of the major hotel area in New York, it is good to find a restaurant that offers a wide choice of entrees, good service paced according to your needs, and reasonable prices. L'Escargot does all of these things very well. It's not haute cuisine, but it's good French cooking. For appetizers, you'll find everything from quiche to clams to herring in sour cream or Danish caviar. Of course, the house specialty is escargot. It is served three different ways, each one delicious and worth a visit in itself. For entrees, again there is a choice of escargots prepared a number of different ways, two of the best being with fettucini or fricassee. Other entrees (the price also includes appetizer, dessert, and beverage) I would recommend are the grilled striped bass, sautéed frog legs, calf's liver with avocado, an excellent grilled filet mignon, and the shrimp provencale. And what desserts! Try the Black Forest cake, creme caramel, crepes suzette, or the strawberries Romanoff. There is also a fine selection of cheese. I was impressed with the friendly atmosphere and the outstandingly varied selections. For those who are entertaining and not sure of the likes and dislikes of their guests, this would be an excellent place to go. In addition, L'Escargot has a facility called the Tapestry Room for private parties of almost any size.

Polite, Pretty, Prompt, and Professional

LES PLEIADES
20 E 76th St
535-7230
Mon-Sat: 12-3, 5:30-11
Major credit cards
Moderate to expensive

Wow! What a well-organized restaurant this is! It's obvious that the folks here know the ins and outs of the business, and it's another case of the management being on the job. I have seldom encountered a restaurant with better trained, more courteous personnel. From the time you call to make the reservation to your goodbye at the door, your host, captain, waiter, and busboy—everyone—give the impression that they know what they're doing and that they're pleased to serve you. The clientele are strictly Upper East Side matrons and their aging husbands, or perhaps their middle-aged sons and daughters taking the "old folks" out to dinner. But what a nice, comfortable place to do so! The food is excellent, the atmosphere is charming, and the entire evening can be a most satisfactory experience. Many of the hors d'oeuvres are displayed at an attractive table near the entrance, and the choices are numerous: coquilles au safran, sardines a l'Huile, le saumon fume, a great lobster salad, and on and on. For entrees, try the coquilles St. Jacques with white wine and saffron, or the frogs' legs sautéed with garlic. Specialties of the house include sweetbreads, rack of Lamb and broiled Dover sole. If you feel really hungry, tell them at the start that you'd like one of their soufflés for dessert—either the Grand Marnier soufflé or the chocolate soufflé.

Vegetarian Eclectic

LEVANA'S
148 W 67th St (bet Broadway and Amsterdam Ave)
877-8457
Sun-Thurs: noon-11; Sat: 8 p.m.-2 a.m.;
closed Sat night in summer
AE
Moderate

Lavana's interior design won the grand prize from *Interior Design* magazine, and its strictly vegetarian fare (they do have fish) has won similar accolades. Despite this, I find the indirect lighting, grid-work tables, hard benches, and folding chairs highly uncomfortable, and I'm only grateful that the food reviews are more trustworthy. There are always several fish dishes prepared in a healthy (nonfried) manner, and there's an equal number of salads. Owner Sol Kirschaenbaum, who is always on the premises (sometimes even babysitting his children) favors Morrocan and European cuisines, although the restaurant is vegetarian and kosher. It makes for some interesting combinations. And yet the mixture works. The bakery products are light, fluffy, and delicious. (Levana's used to be a bakery as well. Nowadays, it concentrates on the newly expanded restaurant and its catering services.) The bread is underwhelming (not healthy enough?), but the desserts are outstanding. And the pasta dishes almost don't make you feel guilty. After all, it's healthy!

La Mixture

LE ZINC
139 Duane St
732-1226
Mon-Thurs: 6:30-12:30; Fri, Sat: 6:30-1; Sun: 6-11
AE
Moderate

The neighborhood is somewhat seedy. The atmosphere is somewhat French bistro and somewhat turn-of-the-century American frontier. The help is somewhat Oriental, somewhat French, and somewhat Yankee. The clientele is also somewhat mixed—three-piece suits rub elbows with short sleeves, pantsuits, and "anything goes" outfits. And amazingly, it all works. Le Zinc is noisy, busy, and harried, but the continental menu is very good, indeed. Try the cream of celery soup or the salad with goat cheese or the snails to start. For the main course, I recommend smoked salmon, duck, or the house specialty, chicken with black mushrooms. As in most French restaurants, the lamb chops are excellent; they also do a great job with the steaks. The desserts are homemade. In my opinion, it's worth the visit just to have the chocolate profiteroles — absolutely sensational!

A Classy Italian Lunch

L'HOSTARIA DEL BONGUSTAIO
108 E 60th St (at Park Ave)
751-3530
Mon-Fri: 12-3, 5:30-10; Sat: 5:30-10
Major credit cards
Moderate to expensive

A welcome addition to the Upper East Side scene is L'Hostaria, a classy Italian dining room that is both attractive in décor and in food presentation. Their selection of pasta is excellent. You might try the spaghetti with vegetables, fettuccine with salmon, rigatoni with five cheeses, or tortellini with cream sauce. In the meat department, besides the excellent veal dishes, I'd suggest the breast of chicken with artichokes or the delicious loin of pork sautéed in wines. On the seafood side, the fish stew Italian style and the Dover sole are my recommendations. Forget the shrimp—it is not one of their strong points. An unusually good vegetable selection includes peas and prosciutto, fried artichokes, and sautéed mushrooms. I was not impressed with the desserts, but I was impressed with the professionalism of the operation. The waiters were mature, service was prompt, and the rooms and table settings were attractive. If you are going to make the midday meal your major one of the day, I would say this is a good place for it.

Pastrami in the Garment District

LOU G. SIEGEL
209 W 38th St
921-4433
Sun-Thurs: 11:30-9; Fri: 11:30-3 p.m.
Major credit cards
Moderate

Lou G. Siegel's has been around longer than most New Yorkers can remember. It opened the doors in 1917, and customers have been pushing through them ever since. Its reputation—of which it is well aware ("The best-known kosher restaurant in the world," says Siegel's Eddie Share)—is based mostly on their cold cuts, especially the pastrami. Workers in the garment district fill the place during lunch and dinner hours. Remember that, and try to schedule your visit to Siegel's as an early lunch or a supper.

The Grande Dame

LUTECE
249 E 50th St (at Third Ave)
752-2225
Tues-Fri: noon-1:45, 6-9:30; Mon, Sat: 6-9:30
AE, CB, MC
Expensive

The standard by which so many of the restaurants in Manhattan are judged is Lutece. It is so high tone that there aren't even prices on the menu. Almost every restaurant guide lists it as #1. I'm not sure it's that, but certainly the chefs are masters, and the service is impeccable. The owner, Andre Soltner, has received many awards, and they're well deserved. Lutece is housed in a former brownstone that's tastefully decorated with handsome furnishings and tableware. An inside garden at the back adds to the charm. The restaurant also features three great *S's*—soups, snails, and sauces. All are about the best in New York. But be prepared for less than great service if they don't know you. Nonetheless, you can't beat Lutece. And at their prices, see if you can take home the beautiful menu as a souvenir!

Super Heroes

MANGANARO'S HERO BOY
492 Ninth Ave (bet 37th and 38th St)
947-7325
Mon-Sat: 6 a.m.-7:30 p.m.
Moderate

Hero sandwiches (also known as po' boys) are sold everywhere, but Manganaro's has the best. Eggs, peppers, meat, cheese, eggplant—you name it. Manganaro's will put the ingredients of your choice between two pieces of thick, chewy Italian bread. Talk about a meal in a sandwich! These heroes will soothe the hunger pangs of the most serious eater. Manganaro's also serves cooked Italian food, but nothing to write home about, compared to the heroes. Stick with the sandwiches, and if you're having a party, get one of their six-foot heroes, a colossal snack that will feed 40 nibblers or 10 hungry people. It includes 15 pounds of goodies on 7 pounds of bread! If you need help, ask Jimmy Dell'Orto, a man who knows his sandwiches. Take out and delivery is also available.

A Classy Brew

MANHATTAN BREWING COMPANY
40-42 Thompson St (at Broome St)
219-9250
Tues-Sun: 11:30-1 a.m.
Inexpensive

Manhattan, particularly Yorkville, has historically been beer-brewing country. And for 300 years, the city boasted at least one, and often several, local brands that were nationwide favorites. The last brewery closed in Brooklyn in 1976. (That was F&M Shaefer. Here's a trivia question: besides Rheingold and Knickerbocker, how many other New York brands can you name?) The reasons are economic. It just wasn't feasible to support small local brands. But no one said that to Robert D'Adonna and Richard Wrigley when they formed the Manhattan Brewing Company, and perhaps D'Adonna's Brooklyn origins made him wax nostalgic for the city's suds. (Wrigley is from London, though, so he's not too susceptible to American nostalgia.) In any event, they converted a Con Ed substation in SoHo (how typically New York!) into a brewery and taproom, and nowadays it is once again possible to down a hometown brew at a hometown bar in the old hometown. Because of Wrigley, the Manhattan brew is made English style in both its beers and ales. The kegs, however, are being delivered to restaurants in horse-drawn drays, which has to be a decidedly New York advertising touch. And the taproom is almost a must-see tourist attraction, regardless of how one feels about the beer. Its three levels overlook six gigantic imported brewing kettles, which are massive and impressive. And they're in working order and use. For those who like to down their beer with a little carbohydrate, the taproom has a clam and oyster bar as well as some great meat pies and sandwiches from the visible kitchen. But the big virtue still is vat-fresh beer. And don't overlook the view from the upstairs lounge. Thank you, Manhattan Brewing, for returning beer to Manhattan.

Steaks and American Express

MANHATTAN CAFE
First Ave (at 64th St)
888-6556
Daily: 12-11
Major credit cards
Moderate to expensive

New York does not have all that many classy steakhouses, although several have opened in recent years. Manhattan Cafe is one of them and it is indeed an attractive, pleasant place to dine. For starters, you'd especially enjoy the shrimp, the lump of crab meat, or even the overpriced Scotch salmon. The steaks are large and delicious, as are the lamb chops and prime rib. Even the seafood, especially the filet of sole, is worth trying. A number of veal dishes are available, with the veal piccata being particularly good. Accompany your choice with the excellent cottage fried potatoes. For dessert, the tartufo equals any I've tasted in Italy (except for Tre Scalini's in Rome), and the cheesecake absolutely melts in your mouth. This polished establishment is an excellent place for business accounts! The only drawback I see here are that the seats are woefully uncomfortable. Has management ever sat in them?

David's Delicious Market

MANHATTAN MARKET
1016 Second Ave (bet 53rd and 54th St)
752-1400
Mon-Fri: 11:45-3, 5:30-11:30; Sat: 6-midnight; Sun: 11-3:30
Major credit cards
Moderate

The Manhattan Market is a popular spot because of its convenient midtown setting and its varied and generally well-done cuisine. The menu changes everyday, and they pride themselves in having particularly fresh ingredients. And one of the advantages is that you don't have to get dressed up to have a really first-class meal. They usually have good chicken dishes, like broiled boneless breast of chicken with fresh tomatoes or pecan-breaded chicken breast with sour-cream mustard sauce. Or you might try the sautéed calf's liver with bacon, onions, and sherry vinegar. A special bistro or club menu is also available. David is a well-known quality name in food in New York, and here you can find David's French bread, David's cake, David's ice cream, David's sundaes, and of course David's famous cookies. (That could be because David Liederman owns this establishment.) If you want something other than his dessert "label," you might try the homemade chocolate sweetness cake, which is a favorite of mine. Top it all off with chocolate-mint coffee or the Market's special coffee with amaretto, apricot brandy, and whipped cream. You'll go home feeling fuller, fitter, and fatter.

A Costly Yet Delicious Fishing Trip

MANHATTAN OCEAN CLUB
57 W 58th St
371-7777
Mon-Fri: 12-11:30; Sat, Sun: 5-11:30
Major credit cards
Expensive

I've often been asked to recommend a good seafood restaurant in the major hotel district near Central Park. I finally found a relatively new one, which is open every day for lunch and dinner. It's a handy spot around the corner from the Plaza Hotel and near the Essex House, Parker Meridien, Salisbury, and Wyndham hotels. There are two pleasant, very clean dining-room levels, and there's a novel twist—a wire container on each table that prevents the condiments from falling off the attractive wooden tables and also serves as a holder for large dishes. They even furnish a scratch pad for those who get a bright idea in the middle of a seafood salad. Service is prompt and efficient, the help informed, the portions huge, and they are served on attractive china. There's just one major drawback: the prices are outrageously high. For appetizers, I would suggest the lemon pepper shrimp, stone crabs (in season), or the mussels. Then try the broiled shellfish, Maryland crab cakes, or the delicious seafood salad. You are provided with a listing of fresh fish dishes dependent on the season—lemon sole, Dover sole, striped bass, pompano, swordfish, salmon, and many others. The vegetables accompanying the main course are well prepared as are the desserts, all homemade. In the latter category, they have a great chocolate mousse, and the Ocean Club cake is also very good. For something a little less filling, try the hot deep-dish apple with vanilla sauce. This place is a winner—if you are on an expense account.

To Market, to Market

MARKET PLACE
5 World Trade Center (Main Concourse)
938-1155
Mon-Fri: 11:30-2:30, 5-10; Sat: 5-10
Major credit cards
Moderate

It's crowded and noisy, with a profusion of good things to eat, but the Market Place is definitely worth the lines, background noise, and slightly chaotic atmosphere you'll have to endure. Don't miss the Market Place if you're in lower Manhattan, and think seriously about it even if it means a trip downtown. Each day's market dictates the menu: there are fresh vegetables and fruit, bread straight out of the oven, and fish caught just hours before being served. Specialty counters offer salads, sandwiches, baked goods, chicken, seafood, and hamburgers that are to McDonald's what a Cadillac is to a jeep. You take your choices to cafe tables, relax, and enjoy the food—and the spectacle. For those who prefer a more formal meal, there are dining rooms serving the same fare, at slightly elevated prices.

The Village Fish Lady

MARYLOU'S
21 W Ninth St
533-0012
Mon-Thurs: 11:45-3, 5:30-1; Fri: 11:45-3, 5:30-2;
Sat: 5:30-2 a.m.; Sun: 12-4, 5:30-10:45
Major credit cards
Moderate

Marylou has her own fish store in the Village, so it's only natural that she should want to see her own product served in an appealing manner. She has done just that at Marylou's, also in the Village. There are several rooms—some with fireplaces, some with books—all very cozy. Not-too-close tables help set the stage for a very pleasant meal. For starters, there's quite a selection of fish dishes, including cold mussel salad, shrimp Bangkok, smoked trout and great soups. The entree menu is large, including many things other than fish, although they are the specialties. Of particular note are the broiled filet of sole, the seafood brochette, the trout almondine and mesquite-grilled jumbo shrimp. Inasmuch as Marylou has a number of special fresh fish items in her market, the menu reflects these daily specials. Before you order, make sure you ask about them. For those not wanting fish, the chicken pot pie is scrumptious, and the steak Madagascar equally good. All the entrees are served with rice or potatoes and a vegetable. And here we go again! Save some room for the double chocolate cake. Other offerings include Marylou's chocolate mousse, a very special lemon mousse, and chocolate nut roll like Mother used to make. I was very impressed with the efficient and friendly, but not overbearing, help, the reasonable prices, and the truly delicious food. This is definitely one of the Village's better spots.

There's No Place Like It Back Home

MAXWELL'S PLUM
1181 First Ave (at 64th St)
628-2100
Mon-Thurs: noon-12:20 a.m.; Fri, Sat: noon-1:20 a.m.; Sun: 11 a.m.-12:20 a.m.
Major credit cards
Moderate to expensive

It has to be one of the busiest places in New York and one of the largest, but they still do a good job and feature an extensive menu. With this selection and the fun of seeing everything from a six-year-old's birthday party with balloons to the Rolls-Royce set from Park Avenue, you shouldn't miss this attractively decorated Tiffany-era spot. Special compliments go to Warner LeRoy, who runs quite an establishment. It is best to call for reservations and ask for the back room. Talk to the very accommodating Werner Mair, if there are any problems. What to order? Anything your heart desires, but you'll be so busy looking around that the food will seem secondary. By the way, the breadbasket is superb. Although its reputation as a singles pickup spot has diminished a bit, Maxwell's Plum is still quite a swinging establishment.

Sawdust and Suds

McSORLEY'S OLD ALE HOUSE
15 E Seventh St (east of Third Ave)
473-8800
Mon-Fri: 11-midnight; Sat: noon-midnight; Sun: 1-midnight
No credit cards
Inexpensive

If it's color you want, you've got to visit one of the original (1854) pubs of New York called McSorley's Old Ale House. Abe Lincoln, the Roosevelts, and John Kennedy all have guzzled here. It's certainly not on the beaten track, but the atmosphere is terrific, and the ale is great. The sawdust on the floor completes the picture of a spot where you can take your drinking buddy for an unusual treat in Manhattan. And now, after all these years, women are welcome. One can conjure up visions of all the good times spent in this unique watering hole. It completely lacks the pretentiousness of so many New York eating places. The menu is limited and is actually secondary. Hearty sandwiches, cheese platters, and burgers are available. Put on your jeans, take a stroll down to old New York, and listen while you sip. Everyone in the place is a character—except you, of course.

Chattanooga Chew-Chew

MEMPHIS
329 Columbus Ave
496-1840
Mon-Fri: 6-12; Sat: 12:30-3:30, 6-12: Sun: 12:30-3:30, 6-10
AE, MC, VISA
Moderate

Don't waste another minute getting here, if (1) you like Southern-style food, (2) you don't mind being a part of a mob scene, and (3) if you're *really* hungry. Memphis is a winner in all categories. The setting is what's left of an old hotel lobby, complete with gothic columns, an old-time stairway leading to additional balcony seats, and the oddest looking light fixtures this side of a space-adventure movie. The folks here—especially Steve, the maitre d'—are anxious to please, and the waiters deserve a better-than-average tip, since they haul your plates up two or three flights of stairs from the basement kitchen. And the food: *sensational.* The best baby back ribs I've ever tasted. Great jambalaya, a pot full of chicken, Cajun rice, and seafood servings hefty enough to feed two. Blackened redfish or como salmon that melt in your mouth. Outstanding authentic Southern-fried chicken with old-fashioned mashed potatoes and gravy. Wash these down with Dixie beer! All desserts—goodies like sweet potato and pecan pie, chocolate-almond cake, black-bottom pie, and carrot cake—are made on the premises. The height of being "in": there is no name on the front of the restaurant, just some numbers. If it maintains the quality with which it has made such a promising start, no name will ever be necessary; everyone will know how to get to Memphis.

Si, Senor!

MESON MADRID
1394 York Ave (at 74th St)
772-7007
Mon-Thurs: 5-11; Fri, Sat: 5-12; Sun: 3-10
Major credit cards
Moderate

Meson Madrid presents a very attractive setting for a Spanish restaurant. Pleasant background music welcomes you, as do some of the nicest and most attentive personnel I've come in contact with in New York. In my opinion, this is the best Spanish restaurant in Manhattan. If you like asparagus, their asparagus vinaigrette is superb; as a matter of fact, it's the best vinaigrette dressing I've ever tasted. And this also goes for their salad dressing—absolutely delicious! For hot appetizers, you might try the garlic shrimp or the Spanish sausages, and I can also heartily recommend the black bean soup. Paellas are the featured item. They have two versions, one with all seafood and the other with chicken, sausage, and seafood. You can't go wrong with the broiled lobster, the lobster stuffed with crab meat, the filet of sole almondine, or the seafood in casserole, which is one of the house specialties. A good selection of poultry and meats are available, with veal cordon bleu and the tournedos chef among the best. All the dishes are served with vegetables and potatoes, and the seafood dishes are served with rice. Every meal that I have had here has been served warm and has been visually appealing. In keeping with the Spanish tradition, you'll probably want to have a relaxed dinner; you might want to accompany your dessert with some Spanish coffee.

An Outstanding Salad Interval

MISS K'S DELI
118 Madison Ave
689-2250
Daily: 24 hours
No credit cards
Inexpensive

There is no atmosphere in this place, which is essentially a combination deli/grocery. But there is absolutely the best salad-bar selection I've seen in a long time. You can choose from dozens of items, all very attractive and fresh. You pay by the pound! There is an adequate upstairs dining area, and if you want something a little heavier, there are hot sandwiches and Italian dishes available.

The Best Omelets

MME. ROMAINE DE LYON
29 E 61st St (at Madison Ave)
758-2422
Daily: 11 a.m.-3 p.m., 5 p.m.-10 p.m.
AE, DC, VISA
Moderate

Mme. Romaine has moved across the street and added some new things to the menu, but essentially it is still an omelet house. As a matter of fact, they are supposed to have about 600 omelets as their specialty, and no one does them better. This operation is run by a brother-sister team. The brother is talented, accommodating, and professional. His sister, the hostess, could do with a little training in how customers should be treated and how to smile; nevertheless, if you're in the mood for a light lunch or dinner, this is the place to go. If omelets are not your bag, you might try the chef salad or the smoked salmon, and at dinner time, duck, chicken, calf's liver, and veal dishes are available.

Unpretentious and Delicious

MON PARIS
111 E 29th St (at Lexington Ave)
683-4255, 684-9411
Mon-Fri: noon-2:45, 5:30-10:30; Sat: 5:30-10:30
AE, VISA, MC
Moderate

Mon Paris is not that well known, but the food is uniformly good, and the price is right. It's an undistinguished-looking neighborhood restaurant that is always busy. The snails are excellent, and so is the filet de boeuf. Their potatoes are worth a visit in themselves. Since the location (for a French restaurant) is offbeat, the savings are passed along to the well-fed customers. Delicious lobster costs less than at most restaurants. It is best to call for a reservation, and if my experience is any indication, Mon Paris could be habit forming.

Dinner in the Diner

MOONDANCE DINER
Sixth Ave at Grand St
226-1191
Mon-Fri: 8:30 a.m.-midnight; Sat, Sun: 9:30 a.m.-midnight
No credit cards
Inexpensive

Remember that old song: "Dinner in the diner, nothing could be finer." Well, of course it *could* be finer than the Moondance, but it surely would cost you a heck of a lot more, and I'm not sure the quality would be any better. Larry Panish, a graduate of the Culinary Institute of America, turned an old greasy-spoon diner into a spotless, efficient operation that serves absolutely first-class "simple" food at a price anyone can afford. There is the usual counter and about a dozen tables; what isn't usual is the great taste of wholesome salads and sandwiches for lunch and the gourmet-style chicken, steak, veal, or what-have-you for dinner. The help is extra polite, the plates are balanced and attractive, and Larry is in the kitchen several nights a week to make sure things are running smoothly. Specialties include great onion rings, outstanding chili, and homemade apple pie. Daily specials are listed on the blackboard, and carry-out orders are available. Drop by for breakfast, and you'll be starting the day out right!

Premiere Pasta

NANNI AL VALLETTO
133 E 61st St (at Lexington Ave)
838-3939
Mon-Fri: noon-3, 5:30-11:30; Sat: 5:30-11:30
Major credit cards
Moderate to expensive

I'd suggest Nanni for one special reason: pasta! You can't go wrong—any kind you order will be something special. This multilevel restaurant is not terribly attractive, but it does have a pleasant, friendly atmosphere, and the service is exceptionally good. The menu features a large choice of appetizers, fish, game, fresh vegetables, and several dozen Italian specialties, including scaloppina alla francese, filetto di bue alla griglia, and saltinbocca alla romana. You are not going to leave this place hungry, or with a full wallet, but it's worth visiting a spot where those helping you are obviously eager to please and where they do one thing *very* well.

Veally Good

NICOLA'S
146 E 84th St
249-9850
Daily: 6-12:30
No credit cards
Moderate

First, a few basics: (1) Make sure this is the only place you're going to eat today, because portions are more than adequate; (2) bring cash, because they don't take credit cards; (3) it sure helps if you like veal, because they have more than half a dozen veal dishes (all delicious) on the menu. Let's start with the veal: veal scallopine with mushrooms, piccata, emiliana, pizzaiola, veal parmigiana, veal Milanese, paillarde of veal, or broiled veal chops. They sure know how to fix'em. As a matter of fact, the other dishes fade into the background in comparison, except for such seafood dishes as the sautéed lobster pescatore and the broiled scallops. Home fried potatoes or hash browns make a nice addition, and a good selection of vegetables are usually available. If it's strictly Italian fare you're looking for, of course there is also tortellini, cannelloni, fettucine, manicotti, or just about anything Italian your heart desires. Backing up just a bit, I'd opt for the clam dishes as starters: clams on the half shell, clams casino, or mussels marinieri. They do them well. The Italian bread is some of the very best. As a matter of fact, I have filled up on just their delicious bread and butter—it's that good.

Danish Delicacies

OLD DENMARK
133 E 65th St (at Lexington Ave)
744-2533
Mon-Sat: 9-5:30
No credit cards
Moderate

Old Denmark is really a gourmet food shop, but it is also a good spot to go for a light, quick, inexpensive, and different kind of lunch. And if you are keen on Scandinavian food items, this is a place to stock up. While you're there, have an informal lunch. There is no menu, but you have your choice of a number of assorted salads and appetizers, tasty breads, and cakes. Old Denmark is very handy when you are out shopping and don't want anything too heavy. The personnel is particularly helpful. And with all the emphasis on calories these days, this choice is one that won't make the scales tip in the wrong direction the next morning.

He Keeps You Young Forever

OLD FASHIONED MR. JENNINGS
12 W 55th St
582-2238
Mon-Fri: 11-9; Sat: 11-7
No credit cards
Moderate

Great guy Lou Jennings is a New York institution. At Hick's Fountain and later at Bonwit's, he developed a loyal and classy following who loved his rich desserts, his frantic pace, and his great storehouse of stories and well-meaning put-downs. Now Lou is holding forth at his own ice cream and sandwich parlor right in the midst of all those mink-clad matrons who get their special kicks from Old Fashioned Mr. Jennings' fudge extreme (homemade pound cake, with ice cream and chocolate fudge) rather than from their chubby, balding hubbies at home. Don't miss this spot for a great sandwich at noon (broiled corned beef hash with cabbage slaw on toasted open roll, or cottage cheese, watercress, and tomato on wheat bread), a tasty salad after shopping (strawberry jello with peach halves, fruit dressing, and cottage cheese), or a sensational (the very best) soda, "extreme" sundae, or obscene pastry. If you really want to have fun, ask Lou (he's always on the job) to fix one of his outrageous ice cream concoctions. The heck with calories; let's live for a change.

Dinner à Deux

ONE IF BY LAND, TWO IF BY SEA
17 Barrow St (bet Seventh Ave and W Fourth St)
228-0822
Sun-Thurs: 5:30-midnight; Fri, Sat: 5:30-1
Major credit cards
Expensive

It's a bit of a challenge finding this place, but what a reward when you do! The building that was once Aaron Burr's old carriage house is truly unique, with a warm, friendly atmosphere. One If by Land is especially popular with young people, who appreciate the romantic ambiance, as well as the extraordinarily good food. Make reservations before coming down, and allow yourself enough time to find Barrow Street (one of the Village's charming but exasperating side streets) and the restaurant (there's no sign out front), so that you'll have a few minutes to enjoy a drink at the spacious bar by the fireplace. The place has been recently remodeled, and is more attractive than ever. Try to get a table on the balcony level; it's especially romantic. As for dinner, you can't miss. Crab claws, shrimp, snails, beef Wellington, and spinach salad are all good, and for dessert there's a chocolate ganache that one member of the staff described as "just plain sinful!"

You'll Win with This Game . . .

OTTOMANELLI BROS.
439 E 82nd St (at York Ave)
744-9600
Mon-Sat: 5-11; Sun: 4-10
Major credit cards
Moderate

This small but interesting, two-level steak-and-wild game house is a true delight. The atmosphere is friendly, help is accommodating, and for a steakhouse it is a remarkably personal operation. Be sure to try one of the unusual salads! I'd suggest their own Caesar salad or a great mango, crab, shrimp, pineapple, apple, and kiwi combination. Another delicious starter is the Potpourri Ottomanelli, pieces of quail, pheasant, and venison served with "wild game" sauce. If meat is what you're looking for, the prime rib (on weekends) is outstanding, or try the baby loin lamb chops or sirloin steak. All are excellent as they should be, since Ottomanelli has its own meat shop. The wild game is the real speciality here, and boneless partridge filet, Long Island duck, or breast of fresh squab with steamed spinach and wine sauce are recommended. Finish the evening with a marvelous lemon mousse pie or apple walnut crumb pie, and you will have had yourself a very special dining experience.

Easy on the Pocketbook, Satisfying to the Tummy

OYSTER HOUSE
306 E 49th St
371-7976
Mon-Sat: 11-11
Major credit cards
Moderate

What a joy to find a seafood house that combines an attractive atmosphere, excellent service, and good food with a price structure that's reasonable. The Oyster House is just such a place. It's worth the visit even if you just have a bowl of their Manhattan or New England clam chowder; I can say without fear of contradiction that it's one of the very best served in the city. The specialty here is broiled seafood with offerings of sole, flounder, scrod, bass, red snapper, salmon, halibut, shrimp, scallops, trout, and swordfish—take your pick. There are several fried seafood dishes also available, along with a surf-and-turf combination. Hot hors d'oeuvres are offered daily during the cocktail hour. A special tip of the hat to the extremely accommodating personnel; if they keep up this type of service, this place will be one of New York's true winners.

Seafood without Frills

PADDY'S CLAM HOUSE
367 Seventh Ave
244-1040
Mon-Sat: 11-9; 11-10
Major credit cards
Moderate

Paddy's Clam House has decent prices for fresh seafood that's simply prepared. You won't find any fancy sauces or experimental cuisine at Paddy's, but you will find a good shrimp cocktail and lobster at a price that's as reasonable as you'll get in Manhattan. Service is fast, courteous, and professional. Atmosphere? Ambiance? Think of the Dairy Queen at high noon on a busy day. You want romance? Not here. But there is a certain rough-hewn charm in the old-fashioned pub, and Paddy's has been a New York institution since 1898.

Big Steaks and Big Lobsters

PALM
837 Second Ave (at 44th St)
687-2953

PALM TOO
840 Second Ave (at 44th St)
697-5198

Mon-Fri: noon-11:30; Sat: 5-11:30
Major credit cards
Expensive

Steak and lobster lovers in Manhattan have a special place in their hearts for the Palm and Palm Too. These two restaurants are located across the street from each other, and both have much the same atmosphere. The waiters will tell you what's available—there is no printed menu. They're noted for huge and delicious steaks, chops, and lobsters, but don't miss the Palm fries—homemade potato chips. They're the best. Or try a combination order of fries and great onion rings. It's an earthy spot, so I wouldn't get too dressed up. There is sawdust on the floor, thick tobacco and grease smoke in the air, and outrageous caricatures on the dirty walls. You are only part of the passing scene to the indolent waiters, but come early (it's usually crowded) and enjoy the good bread, an excellent salad, and the expensive entrees. You won't forget it.

A Pleasant Taste of Afghanistan

PAMIR
1437 Second Ave (bet 74th and 75th St)
734-3791
Daily: 5:30-11
MC, VISA
Inexpensive

You probably don't have Afghanistan at the top of your list of places to visit, but this Afghan restaurant is definitely one that should be. The room is small, the personnel refreshingly low-key, modest, and friendly, and the food different enough to make an evening here a novel experience. Turnovers are an Afghan specialty, and Pamir offers several: one stuffed with scallions, herbs, and spices; another stuffed with potato, ground beef, and spices. If you like extra-spicy food (like that served in the native country), they will gladly oblige, but you needn't worry, if that is not to your liking. And the Afghan bread! It's great, and you get it with each entree. Lamb is the order of the day: seasoned lamb with rice, almonds, and pistachios; chunks of lamb in an onion- and garlic-flavored spinach sauce; lamb and eggplant cooked with tomatoes, onions, and spices; lamb on a skewer, marinated in spices; lamb chops broiled on a skewer—all worth a try. The best choice, however, is pamir kabab: four different kinds of kabab on skewers, broiled with vegetables and served with brown rice. Several vegetarian dishes are also available. The one that took my fancy was Chalaw Kadu, spiced sautéed pumpkin topped with yogurt and served with spiced white rice. Eat heartily from the start, because the desserts are zilch. The folks here are so unpretentious, the desire to please so sincere, the prices so modest, that this has to be one of the better ethnic-restaurant choices.

Lamborghini Style

PARIOLI ROMANISSIMO
24 E 81st St
288-2391
Tues-Sat: 6-11:30
AE, DC
Expensive

When you pay these prices, you want some class and some great food. You get both in abundance at Parioli's new Upper East Side location. Outstandingly helpful personnel serve you in a rather intimate room (or garden area) on tables appointed with Tiffany-style china, glassware, and silver. Save your appetite even if you must pass up the Macadamian nuts at the bar! Instead, feast upon scampis or some delicious pastas like trevette or fettuccine alfredo. Appetizer selections change with every season. And what a selection of veal dishes. Each one is a treat in itself. Choose from sautéed veal, breaded veal chops, rolled veal scalloppine, filet of veal, or rack of veal. Of course, chicken, beef, and steak dishes are also offered, with superbly done (and very expensive) vegetables as side orders. The zabaglione is marvelous, and the chocolate cake—a bittersweet and brownie delight—is not only sinful, it's downright exciting!

A Tasty Pub

PARNELL'S
350 E 53rd St
753-1761
Sun-Thurs: noon-midnight; Fri, Sat: noon-1 a.m.
Major credit cards
Moderate

I'm always impressed when I see a lot of shirt-sleeved workers enjoying a hearty meal. Most of them know where value and good food are, just as truck drivers do when they're on the road. If you look at the bar area (where you can also eat), you'll see Parnell's is a popular place with those in the know in midtown. The place is small (just over a dozen tables) and features a limited menu with almost everything done to perfection. I would suggest this spot for lunch; you'll want to come early since the place fills up in a hurry. Specialties include excellent burgers, shrimp scampi with rice, spinach quiche, and sliced beefsteak on toast. Blackboard specials are offered everyday, and the service is strictly the neighborhood coffee-shop variety—very friendly and helpful. Make special note of the ribs of beef on Saturday night; they are always a sellout.

Sweet Thoughts

PEPPERMINT PARK CAFE AND BAKERY
1225 First Ave (bet 66th and 67th St)
288-5054 (cafe); 879-9484 (candy)
Mon-Thurs: 10-midnight; Fri: 10-1 a.m.; Sat: 10-2 a.m.
Sun: 11 a.m.-midnight
No credit cards
Moderate

There are a number of excellent reasons to visit Peppermint Park: if you want a light meal, if you're a dessert lover, if you want to eat after a show, if you've got the kids with you, or if you simply prefer informal restaurants with carnival-like atmospheres. For sustenance, there are fantastic crepes, like the Crepe Train Robbery (creamed spinach with your choice of sharp cheddar or Roquefort), or Crepe Canaveral—they say it blasts your spirits into orbit. Another good combination: fresh mushrooms, sautéed onions, melted Gruyère, and blended herbs. Several dessert crepes are also available, like the one with maple syrup, melted butter, and powdered sugar. All kinds of Belgian waffle concoctions are featured, as well as a few quiches. The big news here, though, is the fantastic selection of homemade ice creams (from mocha chip—number one for me—to rum raisin and black raspberry), several sherbets and sorbets, overflowing banana splits, really thick shakes, yogurts, a selection of 10 (yes, 10) toppings—among them, walnuts in syrup, crushed cherries, and hot butterscotch—and an array of pastries, cakes, and cookies you won't believe, all made with fresh eggs. Also on the dessert list: Bavarian cream éclair, baba au rhum, cannoli, bittersweet chocolate fudge cake, pecan pie, Italian cheesecake, and Zuppa Inglese (sponge cake layered with chocolate and vanilla custard). As you stagger out, shelf after shelf of every conceivable kind of candy will remind you that you have just visited the place that heaven must be modeled after.

Jewels from the Deep

PESCA
23 E 22nd St
533-2293
Mon-Fri: 12-3, 6-11; Sat, Sun: 12-3, 6-11
AE
Moderate

Not just another seafood restaurant, Pesca is an enchantingly warm, colorful, friendly establishment featuring one of the most imaginative seafood menus I have ever encountered. And the taste is as good as the presentation. How about unusual pastas? Start with seafood risotto (rice simmered in fish stock) or seafood lasagna (prepared with spinach noodles, shrimp, scallops, and fish fillets). Other delicious openers include steamed mussels or Louisiana seafood gumbo with sausage. The sky is the limit for entrees. There is lemon sole baked in parchment, or cioppino (with lobster, shrimp, mussels, clams, and scallops in a red wine sauce) and boned whole brook trout. The accompanying vegetables are done to perfection. A very popular side dish is the deep-fried zucchini spears. The menu even states that pipe and cigar smoking are not permitted! This nice feature—along with gorgeous floral bouquets spectacularly illuminated around the room and a hostess who just oozes friendliness—creates a very special ambiance that goes well with a superb dinner.

Heavenly Treats

PIE IN THE SKY
194 Third Ave
505-5454
Sun-Thurs: 9 a.m.-10 p.m.; Fri, Sat: 9 a.m.-1 a.m.
VISA, MC
Moderate

Meeting a friend for lunch? Looking for a spot for afternoon tea and goodies? Looking for a modest place for a wholesome dinner? Well, you can't go wrong at Pie in the Sky, a takeout shop with a most attractive cafe dining room in the back. The carry-out listings include a wonderful array of salads, quiches, and desserts and a variety of chicken dishes. If you're here for a sit-down meal, I would strongly suggest the chicken pot pie made with all white meat, one of the best pies in New York. The steamed vegetable platter—fresh vegetables with lemon butter, curry sauce, or sherried soy sauce—is another excellent choice. The salads are first class, particularly the charcuterie platter with chicken hazelnut paté, country paté, Black Forest ham, cheese, and potatoes. If you are a chili con carne fan, their version is excellent—spicy but not overly so. Be sure to save room for dessert, and before you decide, go to the counter and take a look at the marvelous selection of pastries.

Man-Sized Portions with Italian Flavoring

PIETRO'S
232 E 43rd St
682-9760
Mon-Fri: noon-2:30, 5:30-10:30; Sat: 5:30-10:30
Closed Sat from June to Oct
AE, Pietro's charge
Expensive

Pietro's Restaurant is a steakhouse with Northern Italian cuisine; everything is cooked to order. The menu features steaks and chops, seafood, chicken, and an enormous selection of veal. Tell your companion not to bother getting dressed up. Bring your appetite, though, as the portions are huge! Although steaks are the best known of Pietro's dishes, you will also find eight kinds of chicken dishes and ten different veal selections (marsala, cacciatore, scallopini, piccata, francaise, etc.). And for meat-and-potato lovers, there are eight different potato dishes. Prices border on the expensive, and the service is boisterous, but you'll get your money's worth of good food.

This Little Piggie Went to Peking

PIG HEAVEN
1540 Second Ave (bet 80th and 81st St)
PIG-4333
Daily: noon-midnight
AE, DC
Moderate

Well, this is a unique one! The look is French country, the food is Chinese delicious, the pigs are everywhere. You'd never know you were in a Chinese restaurant, judging from the wood-covered walls and the fresh flowers. This is one of David K's operations; he owns and operates a number of different types of Chinese eating spots in Manhattan. The menu offers many hot/cold pig dishes, the best of which are the spring rolls and steamed little dumplings in a basket. The barbecued spare ribs are also super. Other winners include three-glass chicken, beef with snow peas, and flattened shrimp in shells with hot pepper sauce. A number of dishes are very spicy, so be prepared. You can look in through a glass window at the kitchen and see the various items being prepared for both in-house consumption and orders to go. And hallelujah! Finally, someone got smart about the dessert selections in a Chinese restaurant. Instead of the unappetizing selection offered in most, here you can enjoy American apple pie, Peking snow balls, and a sensational frozen praline mousse. I wonder what Chairman Mao would have said about a banana split in a Chinese restaurant! I hate to end on a negative note, but even Confucius would get a mild case of indigestion from the restaurant's awful music.

A Gastronomic Trip to Italy

PINOCCHIO
170 E 81st St
650-1513, 879-0752
Tues-Sun: 5:30-10:30; closed some weeks in summer
No credit cards
Moderate

Pinocchio is off the beaten path: a small and inexpensive restaurant that serves the kind of Italian food that Geppetto's grandmother used to make. You won't find the menu limited to spaghetti and pizza. Pinocchio specializes in regional Italian cooking, and if you're puzzled about what to order, the friendly waiters are happy to advise. And, unlike too many restaurants, families are welcome here, perhaps because it's a family-run place. (Sal Petrillo and his four children do the honors.) Small parties are also treated well. What a difference a little personal attention can make! Some of the classier restaurants downtown could learn a lesson from Pinocchio's staff.

Pizza in the Deep

PIZZA PIAZZA
785 Broadway (at 10th St)
505-0977
Daily: noon-midnight
Major credit cards
Inexpensive

Does deep-dish pizza sound good to you? If so, get off to Pizza Piazza in a hurry. Their pizza comes in three sizes, all made to order and absolutely chockablock full of cheeses, vegetables, and meats. All are prepared without any preservatives. If you're a crust lover like I am, you'll definitely love these. The pizzas are served piping hot, and they look as good as they taste. There is a choice of over a dozen possibilities, from chicken Mexicana and shrimp creole to Piazza pepperoni and the ultimate Piazza special, which includes tomato sauce, meatballs, peppers, mushrooms, pepperoni, sausage, onions, tomatoes, zucchini, broccoli, and three cheeses. Get the picture? Forget about the burgers and chili; concentrate on the absolutely super specialty of the house. If you have any room left for dessert, you might ask for the Bailey's Bombe: coffee ice cream with Irish cream liqueur and chocolate coffee beans.

Handy and Classy

PLAZA HOTEL OYSTER BAR
59th St at Fifth Ave
546-5340
Mon-Sat: 11:30-1 a.m.; Sun: noon-1 a.m.
Major credit cards
Moderate

The Oyster Bar at the Plaza is open most of the time, and it's a good place to visit when you don't want to leave the hotel (if you happen to be lucky enough to be staying at the Plaza), or if you are just in the area and you don't want a fancy restaurant. The tables are rather close together; it is more fun to sit at the bar, where the personnel are extremely friendly and efficient. The tableware is particularly attractive, and all the dishes are served with class. A wide variety of seafood dishes, hot and cold, are offered. The clam chowder (both varieties) and the salads are exceptional. Be sure to inspect the desserts on the cart.

Posthaste!

POST HOUSE
28 E 63rd St
935-2888
Mon-Thurs: 12-11; Fri: 12-12;
Sat: 5:30-12; Sun: 5:30-11
Major credit cards
Moderate to expensive

The best way to describe the Post House would be as a social and politically "in" hangout on East 63rd Street that serves excellent food in comfortable surroundings. The guest list usually includes many well-known names and easily recognizable faces. They are attracted, of course, by the fact that this spot has been written up favorably in the gossip columns. Hors d'oeuvres like crab-meat cocktail, lobster cocktail, and stone crabs are available in season, but the major draws are the steaks and lobsters. Prices for the latter two are definitely not in the moderate category; ditto for lamb chops. However, the quality is excellent, and the cottage fries, fried zucchini, hashed browns, and onion rings are superb. Save room for the hot deep-dish apple betty with vanilla sauce, and if you can walk out of the place under your own steam after all this, you're doing well! The Post House is not as earthy as the Palm or as masculine as Christ Cella, but it is really a fitting spot to take your favorite lady for a hearty dining experience at a top New York steakhouse.

She's a Prime Donna

PRIMA DONNA
508 E 58th St
PL3-5400
Daily: 11:30 a.m.-2 a.m.
Major credit cards
Moderate

Here is a busy new Italian beauty right in the heart of the city, and it's large enough to be important yet small enough to serve tasty food. There are several different rooms; the front one filled with beautiful people and the back one giving the feeling you've been relegated to Siberia. However, the back room does allow you to view the ovens and enjoy the mouth-watering aroma. For a delicious lunch, I would suggest one of the eight-inch pizzas from the wood-burning ovens; both the Tartufi d'Alba with white truffles, cream, and fontina and the legumi with mixed fresh vegetables sprinkled with pignoli nuts are delicious. Other suggestions would be the fresh figs and peppers or the quill-shaped pasta with fresh vegetables in season. You can't go wrong with the homemade duck sausage and the marinated swordfish with honey-mustard sauce. You are certainly on display if seated in the front room of this place, but for satisfactory food, a handy location, and an affordable price, it is a winner. Recent reviews have made them sharpen their act.

Nicola's Masterpiece

PRIMAVERA
1578 First Ave (at 82nd St)
861-8608
Daily: 5:30-midnight
Major credit cards
Expensive

So many times an establishment reflects a proprietor's personality and talents; nowhere is this more apparent than at Primavera. Were I to mention one place that is an absolute must if Italian cuisine is what you want, Primavera would be that place! Owner Nicola Civetta is the epitome of class. He knows how to greet you, how to make you feel at home, and how to present a superb Italian meal. The restaurant has recently moved a few doors north to a very cozy, warm, and attractive setting. Don't go if you're in a hurry, though. This place is for relaxed dining. I could wax eloquently with descriptions of the dishes, but enough said: you can't go wrong no matter what you order. Let Nicola order for you, as there are specials everyday. To top it all off, they have one of the most beautiful desserts anywhere, a gorgeous platter of seasonal fruit that is more like a painting than something to eat. Primavera is always busy, so reservations are a must. Tell Nicola I sent you. If this is not as good as any place at which you've dined in Italy, I'd be very surprised.

Tender, Loving Dinner

QUILTED GIRAFFE
955 Second Ave (at 50th St)
753-5355
Mon-Fri: 5:45-10:30
Major credit cards
Expensive

We all have our favorite animals, and I've always been fascinated with the giraffe because it is so unusual, haughty, and rare. Well, I can say much the same thing about this restaurant; it is indeed unusual and rare and can be a bit haughty. When a restaurant reaches the four-star category, it has to be good, and the Quilted Giraffe is just that. Susan and Barry Wine and kitchen director Noel Comess have put together a superb dining spot. With its excellent reputation, there are times the place can be a little overbearing, but just brush that aside, because the price-fixed dinner (believe me, it's not inexpensive) is something you'll long remember. You'll have to plan some time ahead as reservations are not always easy to get at the last minute. The dishes are unusual, to say the least. Try the Japanese tuna with potato pancake and horseradish, or the sweetbreads and duck livers with bacon and cabbage. Their smoked salmon with risotto is pure heaven. Or think about these entrees: rare breast of duck with celery root and fennel, grilled Norwegian salmon with mustard, or veal medallions with onions and vinegar. Each one is presented in a kingly manner. You can follow all this with a fabulous selection of cheese, and go on to a dessert selection that would do justice to any world-class restaurant. There's spice cake with warm pear and carmel sauce, pecan squares served warm with whipped cream, apple tarts with cinnamon ice cream (absolutely delicious), or fresh fruit sorbets in cranberry soup. You can even try their "grand dessert," which features samples of many of the offerings. I could make a whole meal of just that. Barry and Susan are to be congratulated. They set out to carve a special niche in Manhattan dining, and they've succeeded in doing it in spades.

Good Food, Good View, Good Music

RAINBOW ROOM
30 Rockefeller Plaza (RCA Building)
757-9090
Mon: 5-10; Tues-Sat: 5-12:30; Sun: 11:30-3, 5-10
Major credit cards
Moderate to expensive

The Rainbow Room has been the scene for great occasions in New York for decades. This isn't surprising, considering the dramatic setting and excellent food. Although I've often said that dining in the sky can be less than satisfactory, this place is the exception. Whether you go for a nostaglic evening or whether this is your first time in Manhattan, you will have a great evening at the Rainbow Room. The specialty here is French and Italian cuisine. Some entrees worth considering are the beef Wellington, broiled salmon steak, or the medallions of veal. There is also a reasonably priced pretheater dinner. If you go later in the evening, you can dance to the big band sound (every night except Monday) while enjoying an outstanding meal. The service is very attentive; they manage to make you feel you are the most important guest they have ever had. For out-of-town visitors, it could well be the highlight of their time in the Big Apple. Young people will love it, too.

An Adventure in Spanish Harlem

RAO'S
455 E 114th St
534-9625
Mon-Fri: 6:30-11
No credit cards
Inexpensive

What are you doing for dinner three months from tonight? Sound ridiculous? Not really, if you want to go to Rao's, an intimate, old-time (1896) Italian-type restaurant run by an aunt and an uncle in the kitchen and nephew Frank out front. The regulars know it, and the place is crowded all the time for two very good reasons: the food is great, and the prices are ridiculously low. Don't walk, but don't take your car either. Take a taxi and get out right in front of the restaurant. When you're ready to leave, have Frank call a local taxi service to pick you up and deliver you to your home or hotel. (A sizable tip to the driver will be necessary for this.) Frank is a gregarious and charming host who makes you feel right at home; he'll even sit with you at your table while you order. Be prepared for leisurely dining; while you're waiting, enjoy the excellent bread and warm atmosphere (even what looks like last year's Christmas decorations are still hanging over the bar). Among the offerings that are especially tasty, I enjoyed the pasta and piselli (with peas). The veal marsala or veal piccata are excellent choices, as well as any number of shrimp dishes. Believe it or not, the Southern fried chicken is absolutely superb; it would be my number-one choice. Don't miss this spot in Spanish Harlem. The wait is worth it!

Saucy SoHo Supper

RAOUL'S
180 Prince St
966-3518
Sun-Thurs: 6:30-11:30; Fri, Sat: 6:30-12
AE, MC, Visa
Moderate

A few years ago, nobody went to SoHo for a meal. Today, there are dozens of reasonably good restaurants in the area, and Raoul's is one of the best. The place surely isn't very fancy or even attractive; it was an old saloon. There are paper table coverings and ugly walls covered with a mishmash of posters, pictures, and calendars of every description. No menu is presented. You read the day's choices on a blackboard. The bistro atmosphere is neighborly, friendly, and intimate (about 100 seats), the prices moderate, and the service attentive. The clientele's attire runs the gamut from jeans to mink. Snails out of the shell (with mushrooms, brown sauce, heavy cream, cognac, and garlic) makes a good starter. Excellent seafood entrees include grilled salmon, and a filet of sole in white wine sauce. From time to time, a thin-sliced liver (again in white wine), brown sauce, and bacon is offered, as well as delicious sweetbreads with calvados cream sauce and small cut apples or veal kidneys with mustard sauce. (All of Raoul's sauces are above average.) Fresh fruit tarts or creme caramel will complete an excellent meal. Sometimes an almost black chocolate cake (spiked with a bit of Grand Marnier) is offered.

Delicious Pizza by the Slice

(THE FAMOUS) RAY'S PIZZA OF GREENWICH VILLAGE
465 Sixth Ave (at 11th St)
243-2253
Daily: 11 a.m.-2 a.m.; Fri, Sat: 11 a.m.-3 a.m.
No credit cards
Inexpensive

There are an untold number of pizzerias in New York, and you can smell many of them blocks away! But none of them is really too distinguished, except a special place called Ray's Pizza located in the Village. It's a busy parlor, serving over 2,000 customers a day. The pizzas are super. Because Ray's is so busy, you don't have to worry about the slice being stale; they will even reheat it for you. Of course, you can buy a whole pizza. And why not try one of the Sicilian squares or one of the Neapolitan wedges for a change? Unusual toppings are available, and I guarantee this place is the ultimate for the pizza crowd in the Big Apple. They even offer the "Famous Slice," a slice of pizza with *all* the toppings on it! But just a hint: come early, or you'll have a good opportunity to make new friends in the long waiting line. In nice weather, you can eat outside, seated on a carpet on the sidewalk.

All in the Family

RENÉ PUJOL
321 W 51st St
246-3023
Mon-Fri: noon-3, 5-11:30; Sat: 5-11:30
Major credit cards
Moderate

This very attractive French restaurant is an ideal spot for a pretheater dinner. It's always busy, and it's obvious that a large number of the customers are regular patrons, which always speaks well for a restaurant. One of the reasons this is such a successful operation is because it's a family enterprise. The owner is on the job, and his son-in-law is the chef. The restaurant is composed of two warmly decorated, cozy, and comfortable rooms. There are private party rooms upstairs in this old brownstone, and they are attractive, too. The menu is vintage French. There is a nice dish of paté waiting for you at the table. It might be fun to start in with the vichyssoise, or perhaps quiche Lorraine. For entrees, I'd suggest the poached salmon, the poached turbot, duck, boeuf bourguignon, or if there are two of you, maybe a chateaubriand. Every dish is beautifully presented, and to me, that's half the fun of dining. I can personally vouch for all the desserts. They're homemade; each one is better than the last. Try the crêpes suzettes, chocolate mousse, or the peach Melba.

The Skyline's the Limit

RIVER CAFE
One Water St (Brooklyn)
(718) 522-5200
Mon-Thurs: 12-2:30, 6:30-11; Fri: 12-2:30, 7-11:30;
Sat: 12-2:30, 7-11:30; Sun: 12-2:30, 6:30-11
AE, DC
Moderately expensive

By including this restaurant, I'm breaking a promise I made to myself and to you that I'd include only Manhattan businesses. I have to make one exception here. The River Cafe isn't *in* Manhattan; it's in Brooklyn, but it *overlooks* Manhattan. And that's the reason to come here. The view from the window tables (be *sure* to ask for one) is fantastic, awesome, unequaled, romantic—you name it. There's no other skyline like it in the world. Just across the East River, in the shadow of the Brooklyn Bridge, the River Cafe is an extremely popular place. Be sure to call at least a week in advance to make reservations. There's no point in describing the dishes in detail, since you'll be looking out the window more than down at your plate. Most of the items on the menu are keyed to a geographic theme. The lamb and game dishes are particularly good. This is a true, Yankee, flag-waving restaurant that's proud of its American cuisine. And desserts, different each evening, are uniformly rich and fresh. You won't forget to hold hands at this romantic spot—once you've made the trek across the bridge.

Yum, Yum!

ROMA NOVA
166 E 33rd St
683-8027
Mon-Fri: 12-3, 5-11; Sat: 5-11
Major credit cards
Moderate

New York is full of Italian restaurants, some very fancy and expensive and some not so fancy and inexpensive. This one is right in the middle, pleasant but not overdone, excellent food without being overpriced, friendly service without being obsequious. All in all, Roma Nova is a good value. The selections are what you'd expect from an Italian menu. The pollo dei castelli (chicken with artichokes and mushrooms) is light, tasty, and absolutely delicious. Another excellent choice is the medallions of veal sautéed in vernaccia. My seafood choice is the red snapper in bay leaves. If you've examined other write-ups in this section, you know by now that Tartufo (ice cream around a cherry and coated with chocolate) is a favorite of mine. Now, there are Tartufos and there are Tartufos, but the Tartufo at Roma Nova is superb. If that doesn't appeal to you, how about the strawberries in vinegar?

Small and Romantic

ROXANNE'S
158 Eighth Ave
741-2455
Daily: 6-11
Major credit cards
Moderate

This is an intimate, personal type of restaurant, where Roxanne Betesh herself obviously makes the place tick. You'd never expect to find a classy place in this neighborhood; forget the outside and come in to experience a really fine dining event. The mussels in coconut cream or the salad of warm shrimp or the ballontine of chicken are all unusual, delicious starters. Duck, one of the specialties of the house, is served in two courses: duck breast entree with Sechuan orange-peel sauce and sweet and sour eggplant, preceded by an appetizer of herb-stuffed duck leg. Other delicious entrees are the loin of veal with carmelized onions and garlic spinach, or the sweetbreads with cognac pepper sauce and glazed leeks. Save some room for the cinnamon chocolate ice cream with chocolate fudge sauce, or the cold orange soufflé with caramel sauce. Everything is done with class and perfection. The service is almost overpowering as so much help is available, but everyone is accommodating. Roxanne's is small and romantic; I would strongly suggest you make reservations in ample time.

Sandwiches on the Park

RUMPELMAYER'S
50 Central Park S
755-5800
Daily: 7 a.m.-12:30
Major credit cards
Moderate

Rumpelmayer's is just the place for breakfast or a quick sandwich at noon, when you're in the Central Park area. It's New York at its best, justly famous for both location and quality. I like to sit at the small counter inside,, where the sandwiches and fountain items are excellently prepared by old-timers who know what they are doing. One of my favorites is the St. Moritz sandwich, which includes ham, sliced turkey, Swiss cheese, lettuce, tomatoes, and Russian dressing on rye bread. And, if you'd like something really unusual, how about Rumpelmayer's Delight—turkey, tongue, and Nova Scotia salmon, crisp lettuce, and sliced tomato on toast? There are a number of afternoon tea suggestions and caloric sundaes and ice cream sodas any time of the day. In summer, the outside tables are great for people watching.

From Russia with Love

THE RUSSIAN TEA ROOM
150 W 57th St (at Seventh Ave)
265-0947
Mon-Fri: 11:30 a.m.-12:30 a.m.; Sat, Sun: 11-12:30 a.m.
Major credit cards
Moderate

The Russian Tea Room is a popular place with Manhattan socialites and showbiz people. Warren Beatty has a table here, as do many Broadway and Hollywood producers, directors, writers, and actors (among them Mel Brooks, Woody Allen, Cheryl Ladd, and Neil Simon). Unless you specially request a table in the main room (sort of a celebrity's Grand Central Station), you'll be seated in Siberia, way back from the line of action. Assuming you're coming here to fill your mouth as well as your eyes, note that the specialties on the à la carte menu are eggplant à la Russe, blinchiki with cheese and sour cream, and shashlik Caucasian. Or there's hot and cold borscht, cream of spinach soup, caviar, and meats grilled with a Russian flair. And check out the décor! It's kitsch with class. Any other restaurant looking like this would be laughed out of business, but the Tea Room's an institution.

All-American Dining

RUSTY'S
1271 Third Ave
861-4518
Mon-Fri: noon-3, 4:30-1 a.m.; Sat, Sun: noon-4, 4:30-2 a.m.
Major credit cards
Moderate

There is only one way to describe this restaurant: it's all-American. The menu is all-American, the help is all-American, the customers are all-American. It is as red, white, and blue as apple pie. Don't get too dressed up to come here, or you'll feel out of place. A great starter is the Grand Slam Salad, made up of everything you could put in a salad bowl: ham, cheese, tomato, black olives,, cucumbers, shrimp, eggs, et cetera. You name it, it's there. The French onion soup is another winner. The specialty of the house is the rack of ribs: whole baby back ribs marinated and cooked with barbecue sauce. Other winning entrees are the seafood New Orleans, a blend of lobster, shrimp, clams, mussels, and scallops simmered in red wine, garlic, tomatoes, and a special seafood sauce; or the Louisiana chili topped with onion, mild cheddar cheese, and grilled franks. All entrees are served to you with bayou rice. The portions are for hearty eaters. (This could be why the place is always filled.) And the desserts are all baked on the premises. Note to Rusty's: take the foil off of your baked potatoes.

Scare up the Waiters

SCARAMOUCHE
157 Duane St
964-2206
Mon-Sat: 6-10:30
Major credit cards
Moderate

It's always a shame when the ingredients of a restaurant don't quite work together. Scaramouche is a perfect example. The kitchen serves outstanding food, *but* the meal is spoiled by careless, unprofessional front-room help who are not trained properly. The loud music only compounds the problem. But if you can put all of this aside, you'll enjoy this spotless bistro, because you can't beat the corn and oyster chowder or the sweetbreads in puff pastry. The dandelion green and mushroom salad is excellent; in fact, it is one of the best salads I've ever had. For the main course, try their filet of salmon, the grilled breast of duck, or the grilled breast of chicken with oyster and tarragon butter—all absolute winners! The dessert portions are large and caloric.

Mama's "K" Rations

SECOND AVENUE KOSHER DELICATESSEN
156 Second Ave (at 10th St)
677-0606
Daily: 5:30 a.m.-11:30 p.m.
No credit cards
Inexpensive

You've heard of the great New York delicatessens; now you should try one of the really authentic ones located in a historic area of the city, the East Village. From the traditional K's like knishes,

Kasha varnishkes (egg barley with mushrooms), and Kugel to boiled beef or chicken in the pot (with noodles, carrots, and matzo balls), no one does it quite like the Lebewohl family. The selections are enormous: homemade soups, three-decker sandwiches (the tongue or the hot corned beef is sensational), deli platters, complete dinners—you name it, they've got it. (No breakfasts are available.) The smell is overwhelmingly appetizing, the atmosphere is "Jewish mother caring," and they don't mind if you want to take your meal with you instead of enjoying the colorful back room. Don't leave without trying their chopped liver or the warm apple strudel. Then break out the Alka-Seltzer.

Oh, Calcutta!

SHEZAN
8 W 58th St (off Fifth Ave)
371-1414
Mon-Fri: noon-2:30, 6-11; Sat: 6-11
Major credit cards
Moderate

Shezan specializes in Indian and Pakistani cuisine, and it's one of the best restaurants of its kind in Manhattan. The casual service, the unusual and excellent food, and the peaceful atmosphere make Shezan a special place. The staff is pleasant and helpful to diners, and will explain unusual-sounding items on the menu. The kitchen is conscientious in preparing the food as it has been prepared for centuries. Curry dishes (a bit hot) and some excellent vegetable offerings are available. The wheat bread, fresh always, is baked every day in a tandoor, a clay oven similar to the ones used in Asia, and the sheesh-kabab is barbecued according to the old tradition. One of the best dishes, chicken tikka, is cooked over charcoal in the clay oven until meltingly tender. And it's not too hot for Western taste buds. Be sure to try their special ice cream, *kulfi.*

For Big Eaters

SMITH & WOLLENSKY
797 Third Avenue
753-1530
Mon-Fri: noon-midnight; Sat, Sun: 5-midnight
Major credit cards
Moderate to moderately expensive

This is a big place for big appetites. If you have teenagers or some college friends whom you want to treat to a special meal, can't think of a better place. Fancy and elite, it is not. Hearty, fun, and satisfying, it is. It has two floors of facilities, nicely divided to give it a comfortable and rather masculine atmosphere. There is no shortage of help; lots of bright, young men eager to help you—a bit of a contrast to the older, disinterested waiters at the Palm and Palm Too. The bread is varied, tasty, and warm. The lobster cocktail, though expensive, is the best in New York. The big sellers among the entrees are the steaks, prime ribs of beef, lamp chops, and lobster. On the side, you don't want to miss the cottage fries, onion rings, and fried zucchini. And just a word for the baked potatoes: they don't use foil—*three cheers!* About the desserts—the pignola nut cake is super, and the hot deep-dish apple pie with vanilla sauce can top off a great dinner.

They'll Stick to Your Ribs

SMOKEY'S REAL PIT BAR-B-Q
230 Ninth Ave (at 24th St)
924-8181

685 Amsterdam Ave (at 93rd St)
865-2900

310 Third Ave (bet 23rd and 24th St)
674-3000

Mon-Fri: 11-11; Sat, Sun: noon-11
No credit cards
Inexpensive

New York's not famous for its barbecue houses; in fact, there are few good ones. Josh Lewin realized this, and opened Smokey's, an unpretentious, small, self-service barbecue house where the emphasis is on ribs. And what ribs! Josh serves over 1,500 slabs of ribs each week. Every rib is smothered with Smokey's original sauce (medium or—beware—hot). Warning: load up on Wash 'n' Dries before coming here, 'cause you'll be covered from ear to ear if you really delve into these delicious pieces of meat. The menu includes not only barbecue ribs, but barbecue chicken, a combo dish, Texas-style beef, and Southern-style pork sandwiches. For side dishes, the tiny 'taters and cole slaw are delicious, and the homemade chili is of champion caliber. For dessert, try the famous icebox cake, or Key lime or pecan pie. Josh prides himself on the fact that everything's homemade. You may want to take your order home; they'll gladly pack it. Smokey's also does catering.

Not So-So in SoHo

SOHO CHARCUTERIE
195 Spring St (at Sullivan St)
226-3545
Tues-Fri: noon-3:30, 6-11; Sat: 11:30-4, 6-11;
Sun: 10:30-4 (brunch, by reservation)
Major credit cards
Moderate

An unusually interesting spot in SoHo is the SoHo Charcuterie, a gourmet deli in front and an attractive restaurant in the rear. One can get a quick and wholesome lunch (to eat in or take out) at the clean and inviting counter, or be seated in the candle-lit modern dining room. The menu includes many unusual items, such as crepes filled with smoked chicken, walnuts, and apples with madeira sauce; swordfish with red pepper sauce; duck and mango stuffed fried wontons with spicy chinese walnuts; or slices of duck breast with pears. The Sunday brunch is different and tasty. Prices are fair, service is friendly and not rushed, and the whole operation is professional. There is also a catering service.

Dim Sum Wonders

SUN HOP SHING TEA HOUSE
21 Mott St
267-2729
Daily: 7:30 a.m.-8:30 p.m.
No credit cards
Inexpensive

This teahouse is not fancy or classy. But you know it's a good place to get food when you see the locals lined up ten deep to "eat in" or "take out." I would especially recommend the garlic spare ribs, chicken or duck feet, fried shrimp balls, mushrooms with shrimp, beef balls or turnip cake. Of course, there are other specialties, including Chinese-style chow mein with all sorts of possibilities: shredded chicken, fresh pork, shrimp, or mixed vegetables. But the specialty here is dim-sum, and you can't get better.

Fresh Seafood on Fulton Street

SWEET'S
2 Fulton St
344-9189
Mon-Fri: 11:30-8:30
AE, MC, VISA
Moderate

Sweet's is the oldest seafood restaurant in the city (since 1842), and its tables are usually jammed with loyal patrons of many years standing. The proud owner, Lea Lake, is a second-generation Sweet's proprietor, her father having bought the restaurant from Abraham Sweet in 1917. James Lake maintained the Sweet tradition, and the reasons for its longevity are obvious to anyone who visits the place, though the rather recent remodeling destroyed much of the old atmosphere. The clientele—who, incidentally, often stand outside waiting for table space—include movie stars, Broadway actors, politicians (City Hall is within walking distance), and other loyal followers. Either the freshness of the fish (caught that day) or the experience of all those days of seafood cooking has made Sweet's one of the best seafood restaurants in town. The rock fish is outstanding. It is very popular with the Wall Street types at noon, so be sure to go early, or the wait will seem intolerable. No reservations are taken. Sweet's is about the only really interesting restaurant in the South Street Seaport area.

Family-Style Hideaway on 92nd Street

TABLE D'HOTE
44 E 92nd St
348-8125
Tues-Sat: 6-9:30
No credit cards
Moderate

Here are the rules:

(1) You must call, leave a message on the machine, and tell them how many are in your party and when you want to dine.

(2) They call back and tell you whether they have space, ask that you confirm the day of the booking, and read you the menu.

And what do you experience? An absolutely delightful four-course, home-cooked meal at a reasonable price, served in an unpretentious storefront cafe at a leisurely pace by the friendly, charming owners. The tables, chairs, and china are definitely mix and unmatch, but you won't care a bit. It's part of the charm. The menu changes weekly; each of the four entrees seems like it just came from your mother's kitchen. For a delicious casual meal where substance is more important than sytle, try this little-known winner. Table d'Hote can only take care of about 25 guests, so you best book your table early.

A Visit to Fantasyland

TAVERN ON THE GREEN
Central Park at W 67th St
873-3200
Mon-Fri: noon-4, 5:30-1 a.m.; Sat, Sun: 10-4, 5-1 a.m.
Major credit cards
Moderate to expensive

It is hard to describe the beauty of Tavern on the Green. It has to be one of the most magnificent eating spots in the world. Warner LeRoy, who made Maxwell's Plum famous, has done it again with a place that is impeccably appointed. There are several unusual rooms, but when you go, be sure you ask for reservations in the Crystal Room. Looking out at the illuminated trees, no matter what kind of dinner you have, will provide a memorable experience. The Continental menu is large and uneven—sometimes the food is great and other times mediocre. The staff has its ups and downs, too, but the place is so exotic that you should go at least once to see this mass-production palace. The prices are generally reasonable, so don't hesitate to make this a family occasion. Kids will find an adequate selection of burgers and the like. For a gourmet experience, no; for an experience in food fantasyland, definitely yes. A Tavern gift store full of gourmet items is a recent addition.

Rooftop Style

TERRACE
400 W 119th St
666-9490
Tues-Thurs: noon-2:30, 6-10; Fri: noon-2:30, 6-10:30;
Sat: 6-10:30
Major credit cards
Moderate

You'll have to go a bit out of your way to visit the Terrace Restaurant, but I assure you it's well worth the time. The Terrace is located on the roof of a Columbia University building, providing a superb view of Manhattan. Try to reserve a table by the window. In the evening, it's absolutely enchanting. You'll be impressed by the classy atmosphere, the beautiful table settings (attractive china, candlelight, and a single red rose), and the soft dinner music. The tables are spaced nicely apart, giving one a chance to talk confidentially. Indeed, if there's one word that describes this operation, it's *style.* The Terrace has it in spades! The food is as good as the atmosphere. Specialties include fresh game in season and an outstanding selection of fresh seafood. Don't miss the homemade pasta with wild mushrooms or the New Zealand mussels! The desserts are made in house. Special services include free valet parking.

Delicious Productivity

TONY ROMA'S—A PLACE FOR RIBS
400 E 57th St 456 Sixth Ave
308-0200 505-7000

Mon-Sat: 11 a.m.-4 a.m.; Sun: 4-4
Major credit cards
Inexpensive

The "big wheels" in production in this country could take a lesson from Tony Roma's, "A Place for Ribs." It's a part of a national restaurant chain with two noisy, bustling spots in Manhattan. They sure know what they're doing; the turnover is so fast that they hardly sweep away the paper menu place mats before the next folks are seated. And what kind of folks come here? You name them, they're here—in high-fashion designer gowns and in blue jeans; young and old; thin and fat. In short, anyone who's attracted by fast, tasty, inexpensive barbecued food. Featured are superb barbecued baby back ribs, a combination barbecued chicken and rib platter, and barbecued chicken by itself. Each of these dishes is served with not-very-good French fries and reasonably good cole slaw. Also available is filet mignon on a skewer, their own hamburger called a Romaburger, and a variety of daily specials, salads, and the like. Really sensational is their loaf of onion rings, and it is indeed a loaf—not the usual greasy variety, but a crisp filling side dish. Unless you're awfully hungry, a half order should do nicely. Potato skins and chicken fingers are featured, as well as a special children's menu.

Easy on the Lire

TOSCANA
246 E 54th St
371-8144
Mon-Thurs: noon-3, 5:30-10:30; Fri: noon-3, 5:30-11;
Sat: 5:30-11
Major credit cards
Moderate

When you can combine excellent Northern Italian cooking and a clean, classy, and intimate atmosphere with very friendly service, you're ahead of the game. Toscana fits this description. They could charge twice as much for their meals, and it still would be a value. You can't go wrong with any of the selections. My favorites include tortellini alla massimo, shrimp allo spumante, lemon chicken, and striped bass. Of course, you could also have beef or steak, or they'd be glad to concoct a special Italian selection of your choice. The vegetables are fresh and delicious, the salads first class. The cooking features very light sauces, so you don't go away stuffed. The folks really seem happy to have you here, and go out of their way to be helpful. I don't understand why this spot has not received more attention. I'd put it right at the top of the "must"list.

Good Things in a Small Package

TRASTEVERE
309 E 83rd St
734-6343
Daily: 5:30-11
AE
Moderate

This is one of my favorites. The atmosphere reminds one of the Italian countryside; it's very small (about a dozen tables), and the décor shows little glamour. But the food preparation is just as professional as the atmosphere is not. The brochette of cheese and prosciutto with anchovy sauce, the mussels in light tomato sauce, the pasta la spaghettini and vegetables, or the fettucine with peas, prosciutto, mushroom, and cream—all are sensational! Also first-rate are sizable offerings of various chicken dishes, the rack of veal breaded with tomato salad on top, and the filet of sole with mushrooms, scallions, and wine. And be sure to save a bit of room for the Napoleon dessert or the chocolate cartufel. You can tell a lot about a restaurant by the little things, and these people obviously know what they are doing. The glassware literally gleams, the bread is warm and delicious, the vegetables are fresh, and their seasonings have just the right amount of garlic to be tasty but not offensive. And the waiters are well informed and friendly. It's a good idea to call early for reservations, since the place is always busy. The Lattanzi family has opened three additional restaurants: Trastevere 84 (155 E 84th St), Erminia (250 E 83rd St), and Lattanzi (361 W 46th St).

Viva Italiano!

TRATTORIA DA ALFREDO
90 Bank St (at Hudson St)
929-4400
Mon, Wed-Sat: noon-2, 6-10; Sun: 5-9
No credit cards
Moderate

What a popular place this is! Folks line up before the doors even open; when they do, customers literally dash for one of the approximately 40 seats. Dinner reservations are absolutely necessary—and don't be late; they'll give away your table if you're more than a few minutes tardy. Is the food worth this? Well, about 120 people per evening (three seatings) think so, and the owners claim they turn down hundreds of reservations a day. Even if that's exaggerated, the food *is* exceptional. The atmosphere (an ugly floor and wooden tables) isn't special, but come here anyway. The food won't disappoint you. What to eat? Start with carciofo alla Romano or zucchini ripieni del Genovese. You can't go wrong with the cannelloni del Bolognese or the spaghettini alla puttanesca. How about cacciucco di pesce dei livornesi? The salads (eight varieties) are superb, prices are modest, and the Italian coffee is the best. This place is a real bargain, if you don't mind making plans far in advance.

To Pasta the Time of Day

TRATTORIA PINO
981 Third Ave
688-3817
Daily: noon-11
Major credit cards
Inexpensive

You've just come out of Bloomingdale's, and it's three in the afternoon. You're hungry and tired. Go across the steet to a good pizza place called Trattoria Pino. The pizzas are as unusual as the pasta sauces. Most have tomato sauce and a variety of other ingredients such as goat cheese, mozzarella, sausage, fresh egg, ham, and mushroom. Pastas include fettucine with broccoli aglio e olio, lasagna, spaghetti, ravioli, and insalata di pasta fredda (pasta, tuna, and olive)—29 pasta specialties in all. Entrees feature veal, mushroom, and chicken dishes, all served with spaghetti. Try garlic bread with these combinations, unless you have a date later. A very complete dessert selection includes assorted pastries, cheesecake and ice cream, spumoni, tortini, peach melba, and banana split. Takeout service is available. An added treat is that you might be served by a soon-to-be Broadway stage star!

A Beaut!

TSE YANG
34 E 51st St
688-5447
Daily: noon to midnight
Major credit cards
Expensive

This is a class act. The location adds to the elegance; it is right next door to the Helmsley Palace Hotel. The restaurant is well done: understated, comfortably spacious, and airy. The knowledgeable and polite help make the dining experience a pleasant one. Don't come for the usual Chinese items—splurge! Try the Pekinese hot-sour soup for a starter, or the Tse Yang fresh smoked salmon. Selections for entrees include a half-dozen each of seafood, fowl, and meat dishes. I found the Szechuan-style lobster and the Jade Phoenix giant shrimp to be the best offerings in the seafood area. Roast duck served Peking style would be an excellent choice in the fowl category. There are at least two winners in the meat area: Szechuan-style beef or the Tse Yang beef filet. The usual rice and noodles are available for those who feel the entree portions are not adequate. Not being a rice fan, I found I could do without that. The typical Chinese desserts are not the greatest, but Tse Yang does have a fine selection of fresh fruit. I find this satisfying after a Chinese dinner. If you are going with several in your party, Tse Yang offers a Shanghai-style and Peking-style dinner with at least eight courses. This is extravagant but good!

A Tasty Hunting Ground

UZIE'S
1442 Third Ave (at 82nd St)
744-8020
Mon-Sat: 6-12:30; Sun: noon-3:30, 6-12:30
Major credit cards
Moderate

If you're single and over 29, this is an excellent place for you to enjoy a good meal and meet someone who might make your evening more interesting. The bar at Uzie's is a favorite for singles with wandering eyes, and the place is a popular watering hole for trendy Upper East Siders who crave Italian food but don't know where Little Italy is. Uzie's really does a good job with a somewhat sanitized menu. The place is an attractive, warm, two-room, dining saloon, where well-seasoned Italian specialties are served without pretense. I'd skip the first course and settle on tasty veal dishes (they have at least five) or a fresh fish dish that may be the day's special. There are 13 pasta dishes available. And there's a real plus for this restaurant: they have no freezer, so everything *must* be fresh. And it tastes fresh. The vegetables are crisp, not overcooked, and delicious. The bread is true Italian: fresh, warm, and scrumptious when loaded with New York unsalted butter. Cappuccino mousse pie, fresh berries with cold Zabaglione sauce, or white mousse cake will add a few calories to your dinner—and taste pretty darn good. The brunch menu is unusually complete. Your check will not equal the national debt, and who knows, this evening might also be the start of something beautiful.

Good Taste

VANESSA
289 Bleecker St (at Seventh Ave)
243-4225
Daily: 6-midnight
Major credit cards
Moderate

You may have trouble finding Vanessa, because its name isn't posted outside. (I'm told that the building is a historic landmark, which once even served as a funeral home.) But once you get inside, the fresh flowers, the comfortable setting, and particularly the attractive lighting make dining here most pleasant. I find that really bright lighting is unattractive and not very soothing, and that really dim lighting makes it too difficult to see the menu or the food. This place is a nice compromise between the two. Vanessa means good taste: good taste in the way it is decorated, good taste in the way the food is presented. Goat cheese is very much "in" at this time, and an excellent roasted goat cheese salad is offered here. Or you might try the warm duck salad with vegetables and vinaigrette dressing. All the pastas are delicious, and the beef Vanessa served in light honey sauce is another winner. Be sure to leave room for dessert. I heartily recommend the chocolate mousse or Vanessa's chocolate cake. You'll get good value for your hard-earned bucks at this one.

Hijack Preparation

VICTOR'S CAFE

240 Columbus Ave (at 71st St)	236 W 52nd St
595-8599	586-7714

Daily: 10:30 a.m.-1 a.m.
Major credit cards
Inexpensive

Cuban cuisine is quite popular, and most New Yorkers will agree that the best eating in this category is to be found at Victor's Cafes. There are such entrees as roast pig and baked rice, stuffed pot roast, shredded beef, and roast leg of pork. The fried beef, garlic, and smothered onions is one of the most popular house specialties. Special seafood combinations are also available; my favorite is the breaded red snapper with white rice, black beans, and fried bananas. If you're a rice lover, try some of the fine Cuban rice dishes: paella, seafood and rice, yellow rice with Spanish sausages, and fried rice with ham and shrimp. For the light eater, there are various sandwiches: a Cuban corn tamale platter, fried green or ripe bananas, and eggs and omelets Cuban-style. A party room is also available. Victor does catering, and all of their pastries are homemade. The place is always busy, but the waiters take time to lead you through the unfamiliar menu, if you so desire. I haven't seen Fidel there, but I'm confident that if he came to New York, this would be his number-one stop!

Interlude in Vienna

VIENNA 79
33 E 60th St (at Park Ave)
758-1051
Mon-Fri: noon-2:30, 5:30-10; Sat: noon-11
Major credit cards
Expensive

There were two Vienna restaurants for a time, but operations have been consolidated in this one location, a very warm and attractive room. Management properly took some criticisms to heart, and thankfully, the glow of romantic Vienna (one of my favorite cities) is being rekindled. Follow the example of the Viennese, and save room for pastries and desserts when you're considering the menu. The selections are delicious; ice cream and sherbert with fresh fruit, cream strudel with vanilla sauce, raspberry puree with cream (very tasty), crepes with chestnut puree and whipped cream, and Sacher torte made from the recipe used by the famous Hotel Sacher in Vienna. It's worth every calorie. Among the appetizers, try the smoked fillet of trout with horseradish sauce or the sea scallops in orange sauce. And what's the point of having an ordinary entree at a Viennese restaurant? Don't. Try the Viennese beef cutlet with onions or Viennese boiled beef with chives and horseradish (another Hotel Sacher favorite). The wiener schnitzel is just as good as that of Vienna's Hotel Imperial, and that's saying a great deal, for it is one of the world's great hotels. I'm not going to tell you what the *grunerhauptelsalat* is. If you can order it without tripping over your tongue, the waiter will probably give it to you free. Anyway, it's darn good.

A Real New York Adventure

VILLAGE GREEN
531 Hudson St
255-1650
Tues-Fri: 5:30-11; Sat: 5:30-midnight
Major credit cards
Moderate

The mood of this romantic spot—especially at night, with its attractive, well-appointed candlelit tables—can't help but stimulate both taste buds and conversation. Everything is done with class and finesse: the staff is young but well trained and helpful, the noise level tolerable, and the tables far enough apart so you aren't hearing your neighbor's stock-market troubles. You can start with shrimp, snails, paté, oysters, or mushrooms. All the entrees are served with fresh vegetables, and the selection includes at least four fish dishes (the scallops in cream sauce are a specialty), steaks, veal, lamb, duck, and chicken. Name your choice, and there is a beautifully presented, well-seasoned entree ready for you. If you're like me, after a heavy meal, fresh fruit tastes awfully good. It is always available here. Of course, other desserts are also featured. I think you'll leave this Village spot well-satisfied with both price and quality, and you'll feel you have visited a restaurant with a real New York touch.

A Cadillac for Lunch

WESTFALL
251 E 50th St
644-9555
Mon-Fri: 12-12
Major credit cards
Moderate

So many times I am asked where one can get a good reasonably priced, nonfancy lunch in midtown. Well, I found one! The name is Westfall, which is advertised as an American bar and restaurant. The setting is nice enough: brick walls and inexpensive furnishings. The menu: tasty food, reasonable prices, large portions. By all means, try the "Cadillac" for the lunch entree. It is ground steak with bacon and cheese on a sesame roll. You've never tasted better! The French fries served with it are of the nongreasy variety. Other possibilities include the Westfall salad (fresh vegetables, chicken breast and prosciutto on mixed greens), or the very tasty grilled breast of chicken—and save room for the homemade sorbets for dessert. Westfall is as busy as the dickens during noon time, so be sure and make reservations.

Bountiful Breakfast and Scrumptious Salads

WEST SIDE STORY
700 Columbus Ave (at W 95th St)
749-1900
Daily: 7:30 a.m.-11 p.m.
No credit cards
Moderate

This is not a fancy place, but if you're out to get a wholesome, satisfying, delicious, and inexpensive meal, it's worth the visit. The breakfast plates include French toast and flapjacks with delicious whipped butter and Vermont maple syrup. Walnut apple flapjacks are the specialty of the house. You also have your choice of Vermont cheddar cheese omelets; country cream cheese and parsley omelets; herb omelets; ham, green pepper, and onion omelets; or nova and cream cheese omelets. All the eggs and omelets are served with home fries and toast; you can also get sweet breakfast pastries. (If you're not an early riser, you'll be happy to note that breakfast is served late.) The salads are equally great. The West Side Chef's Salad is a delicious combination of cold meats and cheeses, bean sprouts, cherry tomatoes, seasonal vegetables, herbs, and an artichoke heart—and you won't believe the very moderate price! Equally good is the spinach salad, or the West Side Sampler, a variety of delicatessen salads with deli meats and imported cheeses. There's even a seasonal fruit salad, if you like. All the salad bowls are served with fresh bread and whipped butter. And what a selection of sandwiches! You name it, and they'll make it! You also have your choice of breads. Hot dishes include quiche, grilled hamburgers, a fried-chicken basket, chili, hot roast beef, or hot turkey. And the small fry can dine for pennies (almost!) on frankfurters and beans, or spaghetti and meatballs. It's easy to see why this is such a popular spot for quick dining.

For Vegetarians

WHOLE GRAIN RESTAURANT
7 W 19th St
206-7518
Mon-Sat: 11:30-9:30
No credit cards
Inexpensive

The health kick is still in full swing, and even if you're not a committed natural-foods devotee, there are many times one feels that a vegetarian meal would just fit the bill. I'd like to suggest this nonfancy place that does a good job with a relatively light menu.

Whole Grain uses organically grown food and filtered water. Best choices for starters include miso soup, seaweed, sauerkraut, beans, or broccoli. For entrees: soba in miso broth, tempeh burger with onions, and apiral strogonoff are all worth trying. You get your choice of a vegetable, rice, or seaweed with your selection. Also, there are fresh-squeezed vegetable juices available and some truly unusual, delicious teas. The desserts, although hearty, aren't devoid of calories. The walnut cream pie and tofu cheesecake are the best. Most of the dishes are available to take out.

In the Pink of the Blue

WILKINSON'S
1573 York Ave
535-5454
Mon-Fri: 6-10; Sat: 6-11; Sun: 6-9
Major credit cards
Moderate to expensive

Everything looks good at Wilkinson's! The people look good because the lighting is very flattering. The pink tones make the diners look as though they've just returned from a holiday in the sun. The food looks good because it really is! This is a delightful, intimate seafood cafe that does not pretend to be everything to everybody, but does particularly well with a somewhat limited menu. The appetizer dishes are unique. My favorite is the spinach roulade with smoked trout. For an entree, don't miss the crab strudel with leek purée. Other possibilities are the broiled swordfish or the tuna with tomato sauce. As a thoughtful gesture, no cigars or pipes are allowed in the main dining area, so you can totally enjoy the delicious desserts, the best of which is the black-and-white chocolate cake or the cranberry tart.

Just for the View

WINDOWS ON THE WORLD
1 World Trade Center
938-1111
Mon-Fri: 5-10; Sat: 12-3, 5-10; Sun: noon-7:30
Major credit cards
Expensive

Windows on the World, on top of the World Trade Center, features one of the most spectacular views in all the world! It's worth going up just to see the great panorama from the 107th floor. (Don't go in jeans.) You need reservations for the restaurant, but I recommend that you don't stay for dinner—the food is not all that great. If you do decide to eat, I suggest the grand buffet table on weekends, which is attractive and reasonably priced. There is a super dessert selection that includes chocolate pastry cake, mocha layer cake, coconut layer cake, strawberry compote, and rum-glazed savarin with orange sauce! Or you might have cocktails and some hors d'oeuvres in the Hors d'Oeuvrerie (open Mon-Sat: 3 p.m.-12:45 a.m.; Sun: 4-9). Try the coconut-fried shrimp or baked sesame clams—just the thing to get your evening started. Music and dancing start at 7:30 p.m. On Sundays, dancing starts at 4 p.m. and continues until 9 p.m. Also available is the Cellar in the Sky, where a preset menu (which changes every two weeks) features a seven-course dinner with five wines at an appropriate high-in-the-sky price.

In and Out of the Woods

WOODS
148 W 37th St
564-7340
Mon-Fri: 11:45-3, 5:15-9:30

24 E 21st St
505-5252
Mon-Fri: 12-3, 5:30-11; Sat: 5:30-11;
Sun: 12-4, 5:30-11

718 Madison Ave
688-1126
Mon-Sat: 12-3:30, 5:30-9:30

Major credit cards
Moderate

Woods has been very successful, featuring new American cuisine in attractive surroundings at good locations for a reasonable price. Particularly convenient is the Woods on West 37th Street, the original of the group. So popular was this place (one of the few good dining spots in the garment district) that two more restaurants and a carry-out service have been added. Steamed vegetable platters, pastas, fresh fish, and homemade desserts (their chocolate mocca roulade is worth coming out of the woods for) are always available. The entire menu at each location changes every season. "Out-of-the Woods" takeout (564-7348) features sandwiches, hot and cold platters, and desserts, including homemade ice creams. Delivery is available for some really great lunches, with a good choice of entrees.

An Indoor Picnic

WYLIE'S RIBS & COMPANY
891 First Ave
751-0700
Mon-Sun: 11:30-1:00 a.m.
Major credit cards
Moderate

Finding a convenient, pleasant, not-too-crowded spot that serves great food at a reasonable price is not always easy. But I have one such place for you. That is, if you like Texas-style barbecued chicken and ribs, just like picnic fare. Wylie's is the best in this department, featuring ample platters of the tastiest, crispiest back ribs you have ever gotten all over your fingers—and some of the tenderest Northern fried chicken available. I'd suggest the combination dish served with excellent steak fries and cole slaw. Of course, there's more available, like half-pound burgers, barbecued beef sandwiches, salads, chili, omelets, and very special brick onion loaf. The dinner menu is much the same, although it leans more toward steak and fish in addition to their famous ribs. The atmosphere is informal, the service efficient. Early evening hours are the least hectic. I heartily recommend this one, especially if you have young people in tow.

The Chinese "Kee" to Saving Calories

WONG KEE
113 Mott St
226-9018
Daily: 11-10
No credit cards
Inexpensive

Wong Kee was suggested to me by a well-traveled Chinese gourmand, and I certainly go along with his evaluation. It is one of Chinatown's best! Some specific chef's suggestions include: steak served with Chinese broccoli and snow peas, a seafood delight (Chinese vegetables mixed with fish cake, fresh squid, shrimp, and snow peas), and Wong Kee spicy pork mixed with black bean, fresh garlic, and a little hot pepper. Also, a special dish called Tip Par Ngau (cuts of sirloin steak sautéed Cantonese style with a great sauce and served with pan-fried onions) is a real winner! Wong Kee is not fancy or sophisticated. The waiters don't smile, and you won't get your picture taken for *Women's Wear Daily*, but if you're hankering for some excellent Chinese food and you don't want to get dressed up, head in this direction. Wong Kee serves no desserts, so your calorie counter will be most appreciative.

Deep in the Heart of Amsterdam Avenue

YELLOW ROSE CAFE
450 Amsterdam Ave
595-8760
Mon-Fri: 11-11; Sat, Sun: 10-3, 4-12
No credit cards
Inexpensive

Barbara Clifford of Fort Worth, Texas, has transplanted Texas-style chicken-fried steak, Southern-fried chicken, smothered pork chops and El Paso cheese enchiladas to Manhattan in her 12-table cafe. Accompanied by buttermilk biscuits, red chili, real mashed potatoes, and home-grown vegetables from her father's garden in Texas, Barbara's portions are huge, delicious, and incredibly inexpensive. The cafe is cactus filled, homey and very busy. Strawberry shortcake, pecan pie, or sweet potato pie will top off a great meal during the week or a hearty country brunch on weekends.

Male Order

YE OLDE CHOP HOUSE
111 Broadway
732-6166
Mon-Thurs: 11:30 a.m.-7:30 p.m.; Fri: 11:30 a.m.-3 p.m.
Major credit cards
Moderate

A restaurant established in 1800 and kept in the same family for three-quarters of a century just has to set some kind of a record in New York. It's easy to see why, because Ye Olde Chop House is indeed a unique spot. I'd suggest this one if you want to take a couple of friends for lunch in the Wall Street area. The atmosphere is strictly macho, particularly at the bar. But ladies would not feel unwelcome among all this talk about athletic enterprises and big financial dealings. As you enter, you step downstairs into old English-style surroundings. If you don't stand at the bar, you are seated at cozy wooden tables. The place is very busy at noon. The hosts are not the most pleasant during rush hours, but they will take care of you. Game is a house specialty, and you can have your choice of entrees of broiled venison steak, broiled half pheasant, broiled whole partridge, or broiled whole partridge, or broiled whole quail. All of these are served with a baked sweet potato and currant jelly. Other entrees include an assorted seafood plate, Long Island bay scallops, a broiled English mixed grill, and a first-class steak tartare. Dessert selection includes various fresh fruits (even cultivated blueberries), and apple, pecan, blueberry, or Nesselrode pie, as well as the usual ice creams.

CLOSED

Chicken in the Pot

YE WAVERLY INN
16 Bank St
929-4377
Mon-Thurs: 10:45-2, 5:15-10; Fri, Sat: 10:45-2, 5:15-11; Sun: 12-3, 4:30-9
Major credit cards
Moderate

I spent the majority of my college days studying at Cambridge University in England, where one of the real joys was the chance to get away from terrible college food and visit the inns and pubs throughout the Cambridge area. English food at best is not very fancy, but the pubs do have atmosphere, and they do some things quite well. There is an old-time spot in the Village called *Ye Waverly Inn,* a picturesque pub of sorts in confined quarters, which dates from the early part of the century, and it reminds me of the Cambridge spots. There are four rooms and an outside eating area with adequate but uncomfortable furnishings, but the atmosphere is truly delightful. One is certain the food is good, because the place is always crowded and there are a number of famous folk who dine there. If all this is not reason enough to go to the Inn, their chicken pot pie should be. It is absolutely one of the best I have ever eaten. Other possibilities would be the sautéed calf's liver, barbecued rack of ribs, boiled beef and horseradish sauce, or the boneless chicken breast. You can precede the main course with fresh fruit and cheese, French-fried eggplant, or a delicious fresh vegetable marinade. For the light eater, I'd suggest the smoked brook trout or the quiche and Waldorf salad. The dessert selection is excellent, especially the tasty pecan pie. I can see why legions of Village regulars flock here; you will, too, whenever you have a craving for chicken pot pie.

"F" in Class, "A" in Food

YUN LUCK RICE SHOPPE
17 Doyer (near Pell St)
571-1375
Daily: noon-11
Inexpensive

Yun Luck's food brings back the best memories of Hong Kong. The selection is enormous: 13 different kinds of soup, including "kitchen sink" soup with won tons, 7 beef dishes, 9 pork ones, and 5 kinds of fried rice. House specialties include hong shu yu (whole sea bass fried in butter, topped with shredded pork, bamboo shoots, water chestnuts, and Chinese vegetables) and mushroom shrimp kew (jumbo shrimps fried in batter with star mushrooms in oyster sauce). The niceties of service and presentation are nonexistent here. But you'll find good food at prices that won't even put a dent in your pocketbook.

North of the Border

ZAPATA's
330 E 53rd St
223-9408
Mon-Fri: noon-3, 5-11; Sat, Sun: 5-11
Major credit cards
Inexpensive

I'll be the first to admit that I'm not a great Mexican food fan and that most of the New York Mexican restaurants are not all that great. However, Zapata's is the exception. Not only does it have an attractive atmosphere—a brick wall, dimly lit tables, Mexican music, and the like—but it is small enough to allow the authentic Mexican kitchen to do a very responsible job, and the personnel fit right into the picture. They are helpful in describing to the uninitiated just what each Mexican dish really is. You don't have to order only hot dishes; they serve them any way you like. The appetizers include guacamole, nachos, or black bean soup. Then there are such Mexican specialties as chicken or beef tacos, chicken, beef, or cheese enchiladas, chicken or beef tostadas, beef or chicken burritos, or maybe even chicken or steak Mexican-style. All the Mexican specialties include a portion of refried beans and rice. The Mexican desserts are just so-so. I'd use up my appetite on the specialties, such as tacos al carbon, soft tacos filled with filet mignon slices. The thing that really makes Zapata's so good is the way they are able to combine just the right ingredients to give you the Mexican flavor without overdoing it. Their chef is superb. To make the evening complete, you might want to try a Mexican drink, and Zapata's provides a sizable variety.

A Pro Shop

ZINNO
126 W 13th St
924-5182
Mon-Fri: 12-2:30, 4:30-10:30; Sat: 4:30-11:30;
Sun: 4:30-10:30
Major credit cards
Moderate

If you're looking for a truly professional, well-run no-nonsense establishment where you can have an excellent Italian dinner, get right down to Zinno's, a multiroom restaurant with a well-scrubbed Italian look. It's easy to see why business is always good; you sure get your money's worth. In late evenings, there is even jazz to accompany your dinner. The chef hails from Tuscany, and he cooks in the Tuscan style. The baked clams alla Zinno with Canadian bacon, green peppers, shallots, and herbs is a superb first course, as are the mussels steamed in white wine, butter, garlic, and parsley. If pasta is in your thoughts, I would certainly recommend the linguini frutti di mare done with clams, shrimp, and red snapper. It's worth a visit in itself! You can't go wrong with the sautéed squid (Calamari Luciana), the veal scaloppine, or a double-cut veal chop sautéed with wine and fresh mushrooms. If you choose this latter entree, skip the first course—it's a full dinner itself! There's nothing special about the desserts, so fill up with the delicious pasta and entrees. Being a person who likes to see any operation run efficiently, I must compliment the ladies and gentlemen here. They are superbly trained. Some higher-priced establishments could well take a lesson from them.

III. Where To Find It: Fun, Ideas, And Activities, The Best Of New York For Residents And Visitors

Discovering New York

ADVENTURE ON A SHOESTRING
300 W 53rd St
265-2663

Started as a lark over two decades ago, Adventure on a Shoestring has blossomed into the perfect city tour. Its title is self-explanatory: it promises and delivers an offbeat look at New York, at a price that's easy on your wallet. How do they do it? There's an annual membership fee that entitles members to discount rates on each trip. Advance notice of trips is published in a newsletter that is sent to nonmembers who request it. Tourists and nonmembers can join the tours at a higher rate, but it's worth it. You'll see a New York that even New Yorkers seldom see: Broadway show rehearsals (the real *Chorus Line*), the crime lab of the New York Police Department, the Fulton Fish Market, and breakfast tours of New York hotel kitchens. There's an average of 15 tours per month, and the people who participate are hopelessly in love with New York—if not before, then after the tour.

BACKSTAGE ON BROADWAY
228 W 47th St (suite 346)
575-8065

This tour offers a look at a Broadway that regular theater patrons miss. The tour is reasonably priced, with reduced rates for children and senior citizens, and includes an explanation of how a play is technically produced. The lecture is illustrated by taking you backstage. Often, you'll get a chance to meet and chat with theater people; stage managers, actors, and technical designers describe what they do as you're guided among the props and sets. You'll get a full understanding of how a play develops, from script to opening night. Reservations are required; this gives you a chance to learn, in advance, who will be your guide. It is an excellent tour.

BEHIND THE SCENES AT THE WALDORF
c/o Waldorf Astoria Food and Beverage Department
301 Park Ave
872-4770

The Waldorf has developed its own mystique over the years, and even people hurrying by are impressed as they catch a glimpse of the lobby. Now, you can see how the Waldorf's staff makes this legendary hotel what it is, from the lobby to the kitchen. If the art-deco elegance isn't enough, the tour grandly concludes with lunch in Peacock Alley, one of the hotel's famous dining rooms. You must have reservations, the price is reasonable, and they require groups to be at least 15 strong. (You might try to join a group already scheduled.) Monday nights at 7:15 (so students can find on-street parking), Harriet Lembeck offers a 10-week wine program with an optional four-week extension that deals with spirits. Students sample 12 wines per night and receive a highly prized certificate upon completion (and supposedly no hangover the next day).

CIRCLE LINE TOURS
Pier 83 (at W 43rd St)
563-3200
Daily: April thru mid-Nov

The Circle Line boats cruise Manhattan's waters for three hours. Along the way, sights are pointed out and explained. Unless there's a snowstorm, you can count on having a pleasant trip. Cynics who are too blasé to be moved by the city skyline (and you'd have to be pretty hard-nosed) amuse themselves by listening for mistakes in the guide's pat spiel and loudly correcting him. Keep an ear cocked for a New York-wise skeptic.

COUNTRY CYCLING TOURS
140 W 83rd St (bet Columbus and Amsterdam Ave)
874-5151
Mon-Fri: 9:30 a.m.-5:00 p.m.; Sat: noon-5 p.m.

Country Cycling runs cycling tours that range from quiet one-day rides in areas around the city to two-week tours of Europe. Tours are geared to the cyclers' ability, be they neophytes or professionals. They even provide round-trip transportation to and from the city for those who require it, as well as bike rentals. In season (i.e., nice weather), tours leave every weekend morning at 8:30 and return by 6 in the afternoon, touring the environs of the city (but very seldom in Manhattan proper). Country Cycling can also arrange group tours, customized tours, and specific treks for visitors with specific interests. Arlene Brooks, one of the directors (the others are her husband, Gerry, and Peter and Sherry Goldstein), claims that one cycling experience almost always invites another. It's certainly more invigorating than a taxi ride! They have also just opened a Country Cycling store that offers bicycle touring clothes and accessories.

DAILEY-THORP CULTURAL TOURS

Park Tower S
315 W 57th St (bet Eighth and Ninth Ave)
307-1555
Mon-Fri: 9:30-5:30

Dailey-Thorp works with the Metropolitan Opera Guild, organizing cultural tours around the world. At their home base in New York, Dailey-Thorp offers special tour packages of the Met, which are each limited to 25 guests. Most of the tours center around weekends, the exceptions being the opening night and opening week of the opera season. They include hotel accommodations (usually at the Westbury), center orchestra seats at the opera, transportation, meals, and a tour guide who also guides the participants through other cultural sites, such as the Museum of Modern Art. There are similar arrangements for the New York City Opera, the New York Philharmonic, and Carnegie Hall. And for New Yorkers who wish to expand their horizons, there are East Coast, North America, and worldwide opera-based tours. You could sing an aria about the smoothness and efficiency of this operation.

"DISCOVER NEW YORK"

Grand Central Station
457 Madison Ave
935-3960

Every Wednesday at 12:30, the Municipal Art Society sponsors a free tour of Grand Central Station. Participants meet under the Kodak and Chemical Bank Commuter Express signs inside the terminal. The one-hour tour is free (yes, free), and it is conducted by a guide wearing a red "Discover New York" T-shirt. The Grand Central Station tour is run throughout the year, but in the spring and summer, the Society runs other tours of historic areas and buildings on weekends. The tours take three hours, and there is a nominal charge, but history buffs will find the expense (in time and money) well worth it. No reservations are needed.

FULTON FISH MARKET TOURS

South Street at Fulton
962-1608

The Fulton Fish Market is the second largest such market in the world (the largest is in Japan) and has served the entire Eastern

Seaboard from the same location since 1837. Despite repeated attempts to clean up, modernize, or otherwise improve the market (including one act of God in 1936, when the market built in 1907 fell into the East River), it still operates with the same traditions and unwritten law. Part of that tradition is that the market will tolerate retail customers if they are unobtrusive (this means not asking for *one* anchovy filleted), pay cash, and keep the market's hours. The buyers arrive by 3 a.m. and depart by 6 a.m. By 8 the market is virtually closed, so the best time for individual customers is about 5 a.m. to 8 a.m.

GRACIE MANSION TOUR

East End Ave at 88th St
570-4751
Wed: 10-4; every hour in spring and summer

The tour of the newly renovated mayor's home only began in recent years, and since it's the first time in history that Hizzoner's home has been open to the public, business is brisk. Reservations may be obtained by writing or calling the tour director. Since the tour is only held one day a week, an out-of-towner doesn't have much of a chance to catch one of the hourly tours, but it's worth a try if you're good at planning ahead. Gracie Mansion remains (as it was when the Gracie family owned it) one of the choicest parcels of real estate on the Upper East Side. The view of the East River and the Fire Boat Station is terrific, and the house itself is magnificent.

GREENWICH VILLAGE WALKING TOUR

Tour daily: 10 a.m.
675-3213
8-9:30 a.m. for reservations

Maggie Kenyon offers several tours of the Village, including tours tailored to special-interest groups. Multilingual guides are available (advance notice is needed) at no extra charge for a daytime walking tour, or a tour that includes dinner and a show at a Village nightspot. The latter tours include an off-Broadway show, followed by visits to Village restaurants, cafes, or nightclubs. Most of this you could do on your own, but the "Village by Night" packages include an hour-long walking tour that's really interesting.

LOU SINGER TOURS

130 St. Edwards St
Brooklyn, NY 11021
Mon-Fri: 875-9084 (evenings only)

Lou Singer is a New Yorker who shares his city with others in his off hours. Though there isn't a city resident who won't do the same, there is hardly a one who can do it as well and as knowledgeably as Lou. There are currently half a dozen theme tours that Lou offers to groups, whenever enough people show interest. The most popular is "Noshing in New York," which is a gastronomic tour of the best places for light snacks in downtown Manhattan and Brooklyn. Singer claims that it's the gastronomic equivalent of a trip around the world. (Those who have taken it seldom manage more than a burp of agreement.) Singer also offers historic tours, house tours, an "on the trail of Tiffany" tour, and a detailed examination of the Upper West Side's history. Finally, he will tailor a day-long trek to individual interests, with enough advance notice. One of these tours leaves almost every week, so call Singer and find out what he's up to. You might want to tag along.

NBC TOURS

30 Rockefeller Center
664-4444
Mon-Sat: 10-4

NBC Tours were once led, at various times, by David Hartman, Ted Koppel, Ken Howard, and Gene Rayburn, when they were just NBC pages. Part of the thrill of this tour is the chance to meet some future star, as well as the possibility of running into a current one in the hallways. The one-hour tour leaves every half-hour between 10 a.m. and 4 p.m. The tour explores the studios of NBC with a visit to the famous Studio 8H. It was once the home base for Arturo Toscanini and his orchestra, and since then it has been the site of *Saturday Night Live* and all national-election coverage. There are also stops at a replica of the *Tonight Show* set, with a chance for the audience to play host, announcer, and audience (other studios are viewed behind plexiglass). There's even lots of background information on how the television industry produces shows. The tours were revived a few years ago after a six-year hiatus and have proved so popular that there are frequently long waits for a tour. Reservations are advised, and no one under six years old is accepted. Be warned also that those under ten I've spoken to have been *under*whelmed by the whole thing.

OLD MERCHANT'S HOUSE

29 E Fourth St
777-1089
Sun: 1-4

If you love restored Victorian homes, don't miss this one. It took 11 years to fix it up, it's staffed by volunteers, and it's magnificent. Joseph and Caroline Roberto are the volunteer caretakers, and they treat the house (and you) with dignified warmth, as if the owners had just stepped out for a Sunday ride. The house is still being restored; if you visit, they'll likely express apologies for not having fixed the fireplaces yet. But they're working on them.

PETREL

825-1976
Departures: (May to October) Mon-Fri: noon, 1, 5:30, 7:30; Thurs, Fri: 9:30 p.m.-11 p.m. (moonlight sail)

When the *Petrel* was owned by the Coast Guard, President John Kennedy coveted it as a presidential sailboat, and Captain Nick van Nes still gets offers from corporate presidents down to office boys who cast a longing eye on the ship. During fair weather, the *Petrel* sails on 45-minute tours, starting at noon; there are also two-hour cruises on Mondays and back-to-back ones on weekends. Reservations for this little-known but popular cruise are recommended. By the way, although van Nes is at the helm, the *Petrel* is operated by the city's Department of Parks and Recreation. He couldn't take those offers if he wanted to.

SCHAPIRO'S HOUSE OF KOSHER WINES TOUR

126 Rivington St (at Essex St)
674-4404
Sun: 11-4 every hour (tours)
Sun-Thurs: 9-6; Fri: 9-3; closed Jewish holidays (winery)

The side streets of the Lower East Side house two kosher wineries. Remnants of the days when all of the Jewish sacramental wines used in North America came from a three-block area, they have survived in nondescript storefronts. However, behind the storefronts are centuries-old vats, deep cellars, and incredible modern-day varieties in wines. All of them are kosher, but the sticky sweet Concord grape wines have now been joined by chablis, tokays, sauternes, sherries, and champagnes. Schapiro's now conducts tours that are open to the public, and offers a free complete course in wine-making, a tour of the tanks and vats, and as much wine-tasting as the visitor cares to try. Best of all, under a new law, kosher wineries (which are closed on Saturday) are open Sunday and can sell wine as well as dispense it to those on tour. The tour is interesting as much for the glimpse of what goes on behind the storefronts and in caverns beneath the city streets, as it is for its information about wine-making. It is one more fascinating place to visit on a Sunday on the Lower East Side, and it and the Kedem Winery on Ludlow Street are the only places in the city where one can buy wine on a Sunday. It was also here that a life-long Oregon resident stood beneath the streets of the Lower East Side and learned that his state's berries are so well known that they are used exclusively in their wines. Now, that was news!

SHORT LINE TOURS

166 W 46th St
354-4740

The conventional bus tour of the city that Short Line offers is anything but conventional. For one thing, there is not one but eight different tour itineraries, and the line utilizes bus, boat, helicopter, and horse and buggy to see it all. Along the way, tourists can visit Harlem, Grant's Tomb, the United Nations, the Empire State Building, Chinatown, the Statue of Liberty, the South Street Seaport, the World Trade Center, and much, much more. Of course, that requires all eight tours (some of which are combinations of single tours already) and probably much more time than the average tourist has, but there is no better way to get a well-documented orientation to the city. All tours leave from the Times Square headquarters and range from two hours to the all-day Big Apple Tour. Though they are more frequent in warm weather, they run all year. Incidentally, jaded New Yorkers *never* try this. One trip can make a visitor more knowledgeable than the natives . . . and you can do it in the lap of luxury from the glass-roofed, air-conditioned buses.

VIEWPOINT INTERNATIONAL

1414 Sixth Ave (at 58th St)
355-1055
Mon-Fri: 9:30-6

V.P.I.'s aim is to supply events, programs, and tours of New York "from a fresh point of view." Most of their clients are corporate—or at least institutional—but the actual relationship is usually one-on-one with a V.I.P. or convention delegate. Partners Margaret Gins, Allyn Simmons, and Bill Harris (talented creator of all those slick coffee-table books on New York) coordinated all aspects of the Congressional Medal of Honor Society, a five-day meeting in New York, culminating with a luncheon for President Reagan and the joint chiefs of staff. So, they can arrange an entire convention or a miniconference down to soup, nuts, and accommodations, and then escort an unexpected spouse on a grand tour of the city, complete with native-language guides. Other clients book Viewpoint for unique settings or parties: the Mysterious Bookshop has used them for a mystery party; a husband arranged to have his wife "kidnapped" and escorted to her own surprise party; and corporate parties have been arranged everywhere from the Metropolitan Museum of Art to a fishing boat. Still other services include tours of the city with an emphasis on personal interests, complete convention or tour arrangements, and personalized attention to tourists. Finally, this organization differentiates itself from similar groups (there aren't many, and fewer still are competent) by living up to its name. With connections in cities throughout the country and a working relationship with travel agents throughout the world, Viewpoint can map out a trip to New York from start to finish and make it a really singular experience.

Specialized New York

BEAUTIFUL LADY

The ladies' magazines are forever promoting a "New York Makeover." So, not surprisingly, many women come to the city to achieve a new look. What is surprising is that the cost can range from virtually zero to "zoop-de-do." From the following list, it should be possible to pick out desired services *and* please the pocketbook. (Note: I am only briefly touching upon places listed in the "Beauty Services" section.) Most prices are omitted because they change rapidly. The following suggestions are designed for a specific day.

Beauty Checkers at Henri Bendel (10 W 57th St, 247-2829) This gets everyone's vote for best *paid* makeover in town. For a reasonable amount, Beauty Checkers offers a makeover using the client's own cosmetics. (Most of the other salons push their own brands.) What's ironic is that Beauty Checkers' own products are as good a bargain as their makeover.

Christine Valmy (153 W 57th St, 767 Fifth Ave, 752-0303) The complete day (including lunch) features makeup, eyebrow care, body waxing, massages, nail treatments, and facials, as well as an introduction to the Valmy product line. The day can also be ordered in segments and is priced accordingly. For fractions of the price, though, Valmy has a training center (260 Fifth Ave, 581-1520) you might want to consider. Students offer facials and vegetable peels. There is also waxing and some skin treatments for dirt-cheap prices. The one-hour session requires an appointment a few days in advance; these sessions are currently scheduled for 10 a.m., 11:30 a.m., 2 and 4 p.m.

Clairol Test Center and Consumer Product Evaluation (345 Park Ave, 546-2715 for the Test Center, 546-2716 for the Product Center) The merits of Clairol are praised elsewhere in this book. The Research Center, in addition to offering a free styling for using Clairol appliances, also offers a free makeup consultation. Hard to beat!

Elizabeth Arden (691 Fifth Ave, 407-7900) Behind the world-famous Red Door, beauty treatments can take a whole day or any portion thereof. The whole day "Main Chance" procedure—which is the works, including a light lunch—is not inexpensive. The department stores run Red Door Seminars for makeup about twice a year for modest amounts, and the fee is applicable to any Elizabeth Arden purchase. But read on; you can do better.

Georgette Klinger (501 Madison Ave, 838-3200) This establishment offers a two-hour facial and makeup session at a good price. A half day includes a facial, a body massage *or* scalp treatment.

The full day adds a haircut, styling, lunch, and makeup lesson. Georgette Klinger serves both men and women — and a very famous clientele at that!

L'Oreal Technical Center (530 Fifth Ave, 840-3900) L'Oreal runs a program requiring attendance for half a day every three to four weeks. In exchange, the tester experiments with various L'Oreal products and receives a free coloring, set, and blow drying. Sometimes there are permanent waves as well.

Louis-Guy D (41 E 57th St, 753-6077) Despite the toney address and model-heavy clientele, Louis-Guy D is the beauty-conscious consumer's best freind. After a haircut, clients have the option of using the self-styling bar to style and blow-dry their hair personally. There is a discount for using that service, but the real bonus is that a member of the staff will offer help and tips for achieving the salon look in your own home.

Tomo N Tomo (299 E 60th St, 753-9640) Tomo N Tomo's specialty is hair coloring, but they also do makeovers, including hair styling and makeup lessons. It's a favorite for models and soap-opera stars because of its bargain prices.

Check out the beauty section in this book for places that offer free haircuts in exchange for your cooperation in their training sessions. Since the cheapest regular haircut in town probably runs around $35, don't be hasty in ruling out the training institutes. Incidentally, the pros pick up their beauty supplies from *William Pahl* (232 W St, 265-6083). Not only do they carry professional equipment and supplies, they offer advice and the best prices in town.

BOOK LOVERS' TREAT

New York is book country, and New Yorkers are readers. They read on buses, on the trains, standing in lines, and even at concerts and sporting events. Bookstores are as numerous as bars in some sections of the city, and even if a store specializes in a particular type of book (no matter how esoteric), the store usually has a rival. Would you believe there are two stores specializing in books on royalty? I couldn't possibly list all the bookstores in the city, but here is a representative sampling of the city's book highlights.

For general book browsing, there are several stores with branches around town. Both B. Dalton and Walden books have a wide selection in every field, with an emphasis on local interests. Barnes & Noble has similar offers and features good discount prices on all its books, with even better prices on closeouts, odd lots, and older best sellers.

Uptown, *Murder Ink,* (271 W 87th St) was one of the first mystery bookshops. Others are *Mysterious Book Shop* (129 W 56th St) and *Foul Play* (10 Eighth Ave). These shops take their interest in the field beyond the mere selling of books. They sponsor "mystery weekends," field trips, and tea parties that patrons can attend. Also uptown in *Eeyore's* (2252 Broadway and 1066 Madison Ave), the definitive children's book shop. There are free story hours here on weekends and one day during the week.

Midtown has several fine bookstores, offering, for the most part, service and specialization as opposed to bargain prices. But where else in the world can so many such specialized fields be found? *E. Weyhe* (794 Lexington Ave) is a prime example of this. Almost the definitive art store since its founding in 1923, Weyhe supported both the arts and artists. Over the years, the line between the two blurred to the extent that E. Weyhe now runs an art gallery as well as a bookstore at this location. Another excellent midtown art bookstore is *Hacker* (54 W 57th St). Here, too, the specialty is books *on* the arts rather than arty books for coffee tables, but Hacker's definition of the arts is quite wide. There are excellent sections on costumes and architecture as well. Both E. Weyhe and Hacker carry rare and antique art books, as do most of the specialized bookstores. The best specialist in rare books, however, is *J. N. Bartfield* (45 W 57th St, second floor). There are several other reputable dealers, but Bartfield is the source par excellence, especially when it comes to old maps, western prints, and American paintings. But the housekeeping!

Visitors both to and from the city could benefit from a visit to the *Complete Traveller* (199 Madison Ave). This shop is remarkable for stocking every kind of literature on travel and travelers. Some of its best customers are people who travel vicariously and never actually leave the city.

Travel across town to the *McGraw-Hill Building* (1221 Sixth Ave) and its bookstore on the lower mezzanine opposite the New York Experience. Of course, it carries all McGraw-Hill publications along with a sizable number of others, but the real forte here is technical and computer studies. This is probably the definitive store for those subjects.

The fastest-growing field of book specialization is probably theater arts. The legendary *Gotham Book Mart* (41 W 47th St) stands in a class by itself. It shouldn't be missed. The Gotham carries poetry, literature, and art titles as well as books on theater. Then there is the ultramodern, ultrasleek *Drama Bookshop* (723 Seventh Ave). It has one of the finest collections of musical scores, libretti, arrangements, scripts, and plays in the world.

Down in the Village, the historic home of New York poets, the *Phoenix Book Shop* (22 Jones St) is dedicated to poetry, naturally enough. It's most noted for rare and first editions of 20th-century poets. While that is the shop's principal interest, there is also a good collection of out-of-print poetry and other 20th-century literary and dramatic milestones.

Finally, the best for last: if there is only limited time and money, the only "must" stop is the *Strand* (828 Broadway). Part of the charm is that it has no charm. Looking as though it hasn't been cleaned in decades, the dirt and dust are scattered daily by shipments of brand-new books, which are all sold at half price. Downstairs, older best sellers are consigned to stacks that wind around the basement; on the main level, books are shelved by topic and scarcity. Although there is no better place anywhere for bargains, the Strand is often the only place you can find certain books at any price.

CHILDREN IN MANHATTAN

Giving a Party

Send *out* the clowns! They, along with the magicians, bakers, and pony rides are already routine to the blasé guests at New York birthday parties. With a whole city to chose from and such eye-openers as the Statue of Liberty and the United Nations, mere spots on the hometown landscape, it's hard to impress a kid's friends with unique settings. For that matter, sometimes the party's guest list is impressive enough to make the pages of *The New York Times.* So what *do* you do with these kids?

For starters, location makes a big difference in the plans. Is this party going to be "in" or "out"? If "out," is location an integral part of the party (such as renting the *Petrel*), or is it merely an "out" because there's not enough room at home for an "in" party?

"In" parties require outstanding entertainment. Linda Kaye's Birthday Bakers, Party Makers started out this way and ended up as an ongoing business. Those who don't want the headache can try Kaye or half a dozen professional party planners who will organize the whole shebang down to the straws. All sorts of entertainers can be hired for a kid's party (and yes, *those* can be hired for a more adult party, too). A few ideas of people and things available for birthday parties are professional team athletes, ventriloquists, character artists, parapsychologists, pantomimes, computer portrait artists, T-shirt makers, balloon sculpturists, glassblowers, handwriting analysists, robots, pinball machines, pizza bakers, and, of course, don't rule out using video equipment and filming your own party and/or showing a first-run movie. It will cost less than taking the crew to the movies.

For "out" birthday parties, the city is the party giver's oyster. Where to start? Well, let time and the budget decide. Although the instinct may be to ship the darlings off on a day-long Circle Line cruise to Poughkeepsie, reason would suggest a shorter party time. Similarly, we have been going under the assumption that this is a knock-their-socks-off party. Of course, I would be the last person in the world to encourage such an annual event. Pin the Tail on the Donkey has always gone well enough with ice cream and birthday cake, in my opinion. Nevertheless, here are some other possibilities for city parties:

1. *Champion's Sports Club* (1160 Fifth Ave, 427-3800) This venerable sports facility has turned its knack and programming for sports-minded youngsters into totally organized birthday parties for jocks. The party begins when the Champion minibus picks up each child and takes him to participate in a team sport. (The exact game depends upon season, age, and interest.) Champion's leaders organize the entire three-hour-or-so shebang, and refreshments can be provided (for an additional charge, of course) or be sent from the host's home.

2. *Chateau Stables* (608 W 48th St, 246-0520) Will organize and run a hayride.

3. *Children's Museum of Manhattan* (314 W 54th St, 765-5904) On Tuesday and Friday afternoons from 2:30-5:00, the museum will rent out the premises for private birthday parties. The fee includes a tour of the museum and the services of counselors who direct the guests in some crafts project. Refreshments can be brought from home or provided by the museum for an additional fee. (That can include guests baking the birthday cake.)

4. *Cottage Marionette Theater* (Central Park at 81st St and West Drive, 988-9093) The theater offers puppet shows suitable for children aged four to eight on Saturdays only, from November to June. Advantages include very reasonable prices and a "bring your own food" policy, which can really keep costs down.

5. *Crossroads Sightseeing Tours* (701 Seventh Ave, 581-2828) Will arrange a tour of New York that can be tailor-made to individual interests.

6. *East Side Tennis* (177 E 84th St, 472-9114) The good news is that food can be brought in. More good news is that the regular courts, practice courts, and even group instruction are available for birthday parties almost anytime. The bad news is the price. They think it's a big bargain. Maybe it is for tennis, but for a birthday party?

7. *Fourth Wall Repertory Company, Truck and Warehouse Theatre* (79 E Fourth St, 254-5060) Don't you like the name? How could it be bad? On weekends, from October to June, a rock & roll space odyssey, with audience participation and costumes, schedules

performances for children and welcomes birthday parties. The show seems to touch all bases and appeals to children from age four on up to adults. Private food supplies and parties are allowed, and group discounts are offered.

8. *Jeremy's Place* (905 Madison Ave, 628-1414) Jeremy Sage is the New York kids party entertainer extraordinaire. He is particularly phenomenal because, although he has performed all over, he manages to make each show different. He proved so successful that he opened his own "party room" atop his shop, Diversions. Now do-it-yourselfers as well as the very wealthy can spread the Sage image around. Jeremy's Place can be rented sans Jeremy but with a party coordinator. Cake, juice, paper goods, and Jeremy's presence require additional charges. The costs can mount rapidly, but if there's one ultimate kids' party, this is it.

9. *Little People's Company* (Courtyard Playhouse, 39 Grove St, 765-9540) On weekend afternoons, from September to June at 1:30 p.m. and 3:00 p.m., this playhouse performs children's stories with some audience participation for the three-to-eight age group. They have no objection to your serving birthday cake and refreshments either before the early show or after the late one.

10. *Madison Square Garden Bowling Center* (4 Pennsylvania Plaza, 563-8160) The really birthday-crazed could actually rent the Garden or any portion thereof. I'm not going to recommend that possibility, but if you're hankering to be able to say that you once had a birthday party at Madison Square Garden, then rent the bowling alley. The fee includes two games and shoes, on weekdays from nine to four. Cake and refreshments can be brought in or ordered at the snack bar.

11. *Magic Townhouse* (1026 Third Ave, 722-1165) Great ideas for kids of all ages.

12. *Manhattan Gymnastics* (415 E 73rd St, 737-2016) One hour of gymnastic activity is provided for children over four on Saturday afternoons from September to June. Afterward, private party food can be served. It's cheaper, but not as comprehensive as Champion's.

13. *Midtown Tennis* (341 Eighth Ave, 989-8572) The situation, though not the price, is similar to that at East Side Tennis, in that here, too, one can bring in food and rent courts. The difference is that at Midtown, only courts can be rented, as opposed to practice alleys and instructors. For the lazy, the revelers can move down to the McDonald's at the same address.

14. *Mostly Magic* (55 Carmine St, 924-1472) On weekend afternoons, Mostly Magic turns its nightclub into a private birthday party for hire. The theater seats 65, and the fee includes an hour-long magic show, cake and ice cream, balloon favors, and all you can drink in the soft-drink category.

15. *Museum of the City of New York* (Fifth Ave at 103rd St, 534-1672) One of the first museums to go into the party business, the Museum of the City of New York still does it best. The party offers a complete museum tour and ends in the "Please Touch" room, where the museum supplies cake and ice cream Tuesday through Fridays, from October to June, at 3 p.m. They like small groups and the six-to-twelve age range. On weekends, there are puppet shows for the three-to-nine-year-old crowd at 1:30 p.m., Saturdays. On alternate Sundays, there are concerts at 3 p.m. for the six-to-twelve-year-old crowd. Refreshments after the show *cannot* be had in the museum at this time.

16. *Origami Center of America* (31 Union Square, 255-6469) An exotic change of pace is the show at 2 p.m., from November to May. Parties of a minimum of 25 are treated to either a puppet show or an hour of instruction in Origami. It depends upon the age of the group. They will provide refreshments.

17. *Penny Jones and Company Puppets* (Greenwich Music School, 46 Barrow St, 924-4589) Year round there are two performances for three to eight year olds, on Sundays at 1:30 p.m. and 3 p.m. The show includes audience participation, and the big advantage is that the school insists you arrange for your own refreshments. This is one of the most accommodating places in town.

18. Roxy Roller Rink (515 W 18th St, 691-3113) This very popular place with the disco skating crowd is also a good bet for birthday skating parties, if the kids can skate. The rink will take care of nearly everything. A flat fee per child covers party invitations, unlimited skating time, skate rental, the pinball room, and a clown-waiter who will dispense a hot dog and soda to each participant. Goodies include discounts with future visits, and clowns and instructors can be rented by the hour. The only thing Roxy will not provide is the actual birthday cake, but it might be too hard to track down the whirling kids to eat it, anyway. If you *do* catch them, Roxy will allow the serving of a home-brought cake.

19. *Sky Rink* (450 W 33rd St, 695-6556) Another place for athletic activity, Sky Rink is available Wednesday, Thursday, Friday, Saturday mornings, and Sunday afternoons for parties for kids age nine and up. The admission charge includes lunch and balloons, but does not include skates or birthday cake, which can make this an expensive party.

20. *Sutton Gym* (Lancaster Hotel, 22 E 38th St, 684-5833) Really active children who can't seem to sit still can have their energy channeled into constructive gymnastics at Sutton Gym, which offers a one-hour activity lesson on weekend afternoons. The Gym will supply instructors, equipment, and a table. The rest of the party is up to the parent.

21. *Thirteenth Street Theatre* (50 W 13th St, 675-6677) There

are two reasonably priced shows for children here on weekend afternoons at 1 p.m. and 3 p.m. There's a group discount, too. Either before or after the performance, which is geared to four to eight year olds and involves audience participation in a musical of children's stories, home-brought refreshments can be served to the party at a very nominal fee. For this age group, this may be the most reasonable option.

Finally, here are some locations for parties, that provide, in varying degrees, little more than the room. If the fee is modest and/or the home quarters really crammed, this may be the ticket. Of course, all of the suggestions for "in" parties can be held at these "out" locations as well, and those that follow border on the unusual.

1. *American Stanhope Hotel* (995 Fifth Ave, 288-5800) The American Stanhope's location and décor make it a classic and a first choice for museum lovers. There are three party rooms that can be rented for fairly nominal fees, but the hotel charges additionally for refreshments, dinner, drinks, and/or entertainment. The final tab may well equal one of the all-inclusive types of activities.

2. *Automat* (Horn & Hardart, 977 Eighth Ave, 846-9036; executive offices, 265-6000) Once there were automats everywhere in the city, and the high spot of a kid's trip to New York was getting his lunch by dropping nickles into the slots. Well, the automats are all but gone, and nickels won't come close to buying lunch, but with advance notice, the Automat's party rooms can be rented out and the food presented to guests through the windows as in the days of yore. The snobs in the group will think of this as chic "slumming," and the honest ones will own up to loving it.

3. *Autopub* (Fifth Ave at 59th St, 832-3232) In the General Motors building, this restaurant is often overlooked as a party source. The guests sit back in the cockpits of old cars, watch movies, and get served lunch or dinner.

4. *Gimbels East* (125 E 86th St, 348-2300, ext. 316) Gimbels East has always tried to be a community-minded store, and their rental fee for their banquet room proves this. The fee is downright cheap, and if Gimbels caters the party, it is absorbed in the food cost. Even if food is brought from home, that fee includes the room, table, and chairs, but not cake, balloons, party favors, or entertainment. Then again, if you forget something, you can always run into the store and buy it.

5. *The Petrel* (South Street Seaport) The *Petrel* can be rented during the day and on weekends for a two-hour cruise. The fee, which does not include the refreshments and cake, can be substantial. But it certainly qualifies as a knock-their-socks-off party.

Shopping

Shopping with kids in the city can be a lot of fun. (Yes, I've done it!) The limits are really more geographical than monetary, since travel time is the only thing that precludes doing it all. I am going to divide this tour into three locations—West Side, East Side, and downtown, *way* downtown. But the subway runs to all three areas, and the intrepid shouldn't hesitate to cover it all.

I probably shouldn't start here (ice cream for breakfast?), but a visit to *Rumpelmayer's* (50 Central Park South) is a must. The way they serve kids is a novel in itself, and the ice-cream treats are legendary.

For some serious shopping, try *Greenstone and Cie* (422 Columbus Ave), where the tyke in the next aisle is likely to be the offspring of a celebrity. Less likely is that the Greenstone and Cie wardrobe can be duplicated anywhere else. The clothes are unique, trendy, and for the most part, imported designs.

Dressed à la Columbus Avenue, it's time to shop Columbus Avenue style. *Last Wound-Up* (290 Columbus Ave) may be the quintessential Columbus Avenue shop. It's trendy, whimsical, and a throwback to childhood fun. The store carries almost anything that winds up (naturally), with a special emphasis on music boxes. The well-to-do can browse through the antique boxes, and the shopkeeper doesn't get upset at the sight of pint-sized patrons tampering with the items. Those on tighter budgets can still bring home a souvenir marching soldier or train.

Speaking of trains, the model-railroad industry's terminal is on West 45th Street. This isn't strictly kids' stuff; these guys are serious about miniature trains. Two of the best stores are *Red Caboose* (16 W 45th St) and its neighbor, *Train Shop* (the basement at 23 W 45th St).

For fun and games (and wars, too), the *Compleat Strategist* has an outpost at 320 West 57th Street, as well as the original fort at 11 East 33rd Street. Both stores show evidence of their origins as a military-game store. But nowadays there's much more, and the staff is particularly expert at guiding players to the best games.

Straddling the East-West dividing line is *F.A.O. Schwarz* (745 Fifth Ave). What can be said about this world-famous institution except that it deserves a visit but probably not much more? (Surprised you, huh?) The store is legendary, overpriced, and understaffed, and there isn't much point in subjecting the kids to the enticing items at Schwarz' exalted prices.

Now that we've crossed over to the East Side, visit *Muppet Stuff* (833 Lexington Ave). In a city of Only Hearts and Snoopy's Place, Muppet Stuff is the very best of the superspecialized novelty boutiques, and it's a lot of fun. Muppet Stuff carries everything from T-shirts to life-sized stuffed replicas of its idols and namesakes.

One of my favorite stores is *Jan's Hobby Shop* (1431A York Ave), in part because of what it carries, but mostly because of the story behind it. Jan's was a neighborhood hobby shop when owner Fred Hutchins was a neighborhood kid. He spent so much time and money there that his parents bought the store. Fred is the best source in town for models, showcases, and dioramas, and Jan's is still the best source in town for hobbies and modeling equipment. Meanwhile, the combination of store and owner exude a neighborly ambiance in one of the ritziest neighborhoods in town.

For refueling, the East Side offers a choice of locales. In no particular order, I recommend *Jackson Hole Hamburgers* (232 E 64th St) for the definitive all-American kids' food; *Serendipity 3* (225 E 60th St) for dinner in general but ice cream in particular; *Maxwell's Plum* for dinner in elegance; and *Horn and Hardart's* only remaining automat (200 E 42nd St) for the exact opposite of Maxwell's Plum. It's hard to believe the clientele of those two establishments share the same planet, let alone the same city! For dessert at any time of the day, a favorite is *Peppermint Park* (1225 First Ave). It's a winner for all except calorie watchers.

Finally, it's time to head downtown. The *South Street Seaport* deserves a day unto itself. So does the *Strand Bookstore* (828 Broadway) and its branch at the Seaport. One of my favorite things to do is to shop the Lower East Side, particularly on Sunday. Surprisingly, it can be an excellent destination for kids as well. I would hold onto them tightly down there, though. Perhaps, it's not so surprising. After all, just gastronomically speaking, what other age group would dance cartwheels at finding fresh pickles and pastrami, discount candy, and bagels, bialeys, and rolls, all within a three-block area? In fact, what other group could digest that combination?

After that, shove your way up Orchard Street to take advantage of bargains for all kinds of clothing. Even the higher prices will be much less than retail, and the kids have that innate eye for picking out the stores which carry the "right" stuff. To watch that instinct in action is worth the whole outing.

Touring

Although New York doesn't come to mind as quickly as Disneyland as the destination for a children's holiday, there are those who think of the city as the best playground in the world. And the resources of the city are such that fans of particular areas of interest can find not only the most and the biggest in their fields but often the best. Junior city residents can attend school at Juilliard for music, La Guardia High School (the heir to both the famous Music and Art and Performing Arts, the school of *Fame* fame), Bronx High School of Science (the source of more Nobel Prize winners than any other American institution), Brooklyn Technical High School, and scores more, including John W. Brown School of Maritime Trades, which actually administers a ship.

When school lets out, young talents take to the city to continue their education, and the city meets the challenge. The artistic child can choose from the city's museums (almost all of them have children's programs and classes), dozens of art classes taught by masters, or such schools as the Art Students League.

The theater arts are equally well represented. Take your child to a matinee on Broadway with tickets from TKTS, the discount ticket service in Duffy Square. Even a New York kid gets stars in his eyes from a trip to Broadway to see a play up close. There are even half a dozen revue programs run by and for kids. And don't miss the costume institution at the Metropolitan Museum, or the Museum of Broadcasting where parent and child can enjoy an old television program together, or the Library of Performing Arts at Lincoln Center. Within the Library, there are all sorts of programs, and often complete tapes of sellout performances can be obtained. At Lincoln Center, in addition to the scheduled concerts and events (the winter holiday performances of *The Nutcracker* are virtually childhood traditions), there are backstage tours, special school performances, and even open rehearsals.

For the sports lover, Madison Square Garden is the home of the New York Knicks basketball team and the New York Rangers ice hockey team. For most of the spring, the Ringling Bros. and Barnum and Bailey circus is in residence there between games. Baseball at Yankee and Shea Stadiums can be found in the Bronx and Queens, respectively, and football is across the river in New Jersey, though no one likes to admit that both New York teams are no longer in the state.

The individual-sports enthusiast can rent a bicycle or rowboat in Central Park. For that matter, one can do almost *anything* in Central Park, and it isn't all untenable. The park offers fishing, a carousel, horseback riding (Claremont Riding Academy), ice skating, model-boat sailing, free Shakespearean plays in the summer, concerts, pony rides, a zoo, roller skating, story telling, and puppet and marionette shows. Most information can be obtained at the Dairy (65th St near Fifth Ave, 397-3156). One new program is available at Belvedere Castle. The restored castle (79th St off the Great Lawn next to the Shakespearean theater) now offers free programs on weekends. Reservations can be made by calling either the Dairy or 360-3476.

The museum-minded child is not a creature I've ever come

across, but New York's idea of a museum is not a stodgy cliché. Every special-interest museum features an homage to its history. So while the "biggies," particularly the Museum of Natural History, the Museum of the City of New York, and maybe even MOMA, have excellent children's programs, Manhattan alone is home to museums on American Crafts (44 W 53rd St, 397-0630; 77 W 45th St, 397-0605), Energy (145 E 14th St, 460-6244), Fire Departments (104 Duane St, 570-4230; note: their hospitality for small children is not exactly consistent, the Hayden Planetarium (W 79th St and Central Park W, 873-1300), the *Intrepid,* a former naval aircraft carrier cum Air Sea Space Museum (Pier 86 at 46th St, 245-2533), and the Children's Museum of Manhattan (314 W 59th St, 765-5904), which is in a class by itself, existing only to entertain children.

Nautical enthusiasts can ride the Staten Island Ferry ad nauseum (yes, people do get seasick on it), hang around the South Street Seaport, or book a ride on either the Circle Line (Pier 83 at W 43rd St, 563-3200), the *Petrel* (Battery Park and South Ferry, 825-1976) or the *Pioneer* (the South Street Seaport, Pier 16, 699-9400). The latter two book rapidly, so reservations are a must.

And then there are the tours for kids that adults can map out themselves. One of my favorites is a day in Rockefeller Center. Start at the New York Experience (1221 Sixth Ave, 869-0345), then try Radio City, and if in season, go ice skating in the Rockefeller Center rink. If not, have lunch there anyway. There are a number of new restaurants. The kids will love it. Then, again depending on the season, explore the windows on Fifth Avenue, check out the Children's Museum of Manhattan, the tour of NBC Studios (which only got a ho-hum from the kids I took), or the Rockefeller Center tour at 30 Rockefeller Center (which did considerably better with my panel), or head up to Central Park. It doesn't sound like much, but it's the makings of several days' outings, and it's all within a 10-block area.

Another tour could take in the South Street Seaport downtown (lots of fast-food places), and those who manage to finish that in one day can add the Fire Department Museum and/or the World Trade Center to the intinerary. Incidentally, most kids seem to prefer the Empire State Building to the World Trade Center, despite the fact that the latter is officially taller.

Which brings us to the third children's tour: the Razzle Dazzle New York Tourist Trap tour. Start at the Empire State Building. Downstairs, near the ticket booth for the Observatory, is the Guiness Book of World Records Exhibit, which is as good as the view upstairs. From there, walk up 34th Street to Macy's, "the world's largest store," and let the kids loose. No matter what their passion, Macy's has a department for it, and it won't set you back a bundle.

Then, cross town to 42nd Street and the East River for a visit of the United Nations (another place not receptive to small children, but worth it nevertheless). Be sure to tell the kids that they have left the country and are on international territory!

Finally, find the crosstown bus, or better yet, the subway shuttle at 42nd Street. Although that will require more walking, you get to see the grandeur of Grand Central Station and travel on the only automated subway ever put into operation. It's at least 20 years old, but the idea never went much further. Sort of like the shuttle itself! In any event, get to the Hudson River at 43rd Street and take the Circle Line cruise around Manhattan. That tour will point out anything else that might be of interest.

ETHNIC DELIGHTS EXPERIENCES

Grab the Alka-Seltzer! We are about to embark on an ethnic tour of New York, and in this city (as with mothers everywhere), ethnic pride is most apparent in the food. The only advantage New York has is that most nationalities are settled in particular areas, so that takeout bakeries and restaurants are all within easy walking distance. Come to think of it, that's not an advantage. You won't even get a chance to walk off the calories. The following groups call the city home:

Black—In Manhattan, Harlem is synonymous with black life and culture. (Historically, it hasn't been all that long, but tell that to any non-New Yorker! Everyone's heard of Harlem). There are all sorts of choices here. Among the best are the following:

Better Crust Bakers (2380 Seventh Ave) is renown for its sweet potato pie, bread pudding, and brownies. Its location on "Strivers Row," the classiest two streets in Harlem, is also noteworthy.

Sylvia's (328 Lenox Ave.) has been cited on national television for the best soul food in New York. I'd question that, but I'm not an authority.

The Pink Teacup (42 Grove St, off Bleecker St) is in the Village, not Harlem. But it is the typical small, big-city, out-of-the-way find that's known to connoisseurs. The ambiance (pink walls with old fashioned oil-clothed tables) is modest at most, but the soul food has been recommended by scores of celebrities. Best of all, they are open almost continuously, except on Mondays. And how can you resist the name?

Chinese—Chinatown here we come! The area is the backyard of the financial district and the front yard of the Lower East Side. Key streets are Mott, Canal, and Pell. Unlike other ethnic areas, Chinatown is still as well populated and authentic as it was first settled. The best Chinese restaurant in Chinatown is *Canton* (45 Division

St). Uptown, *Tse Yang* (34 E 51st St) serves a similar quality meal at much higher prices. Do it yourselfers can get all the ingredients at either *Kam Kuo Food* (7 Mott St) or *Kam Man Food Products* (200 Canal St). Desserts are the speciality of *Chinatown Ice Cream Factory* (65 Bayard St).

French—There is no French Quarter per se in New York City. But uptown, almost every good restaurant has French pretensions, as does every gourmet emporium. (Why does French mean expensive?) One of the definitive French restaurants is *Le Cirque* (58 E 65th St). Another beauty is *La Reserve* (4 W 49th St).

German—The historic German stronghold in New York is Yorkville, centered around 86th Street between Second and Third Avenues. It was settled by brewery owners and workers, and the area had more rathskellers and konditoreis than all of the rest of the East Coast. The neighborhood has since been infused with Hungarians and Ukranians and most recently with yuppies.

Bremen House (220 E 86th St) is all of Germany in one store. There is everthing from takeout food to beer steins.

Schaller and Weber (1654 Second Ave) offers ethnic cuts of meat and delicatessen, a word that originated in Germany.

The Black Forest Pastry Shop (342 E 11th St.) is not in Yorkville, but it has great bakery products.

Orwasher's (308 E 78th St) offers breads as good as that made in the old country. Orwasher is not strictly German, but it's the best there is.

Kleine Konditorei (234 E 86th St) has everything from sweets, such as kuchen, linzer tortes, and strudel, to such main dishes as beef goulash. Upstairs, there's a restaurant for authentic dining out.

Luchow's (1633 Broadway), in New York German tradition, Luchow's is always hosting some kind of "fest." It's an interesting mixture of German and New Yorkese! It doesn't always come off very well, however.

Greek—The "old" Greeks in New York lived in Chelsea and were the original ethnics on Ninth Avenue, helping to make the annual Ninth Avenue festival the cornucopia it is. Recent Greek political refugees have moved into Queens and Washington Heights. The stores with generations-old reputations are consequently in Chelsea.

Kossos Brothers (570 Ninth Ave) is an all-encompassing Greek supermarket, owned since 1935, by two Greek brothers. It stocks feta cheese by the barrel, Greek caviar spread, and enough olives and stuffed grape leaves to cater a wedding.

International Groceries and Meat Market (529 Ninth Ave) fills you in on what you might miss at Kassos Brothers. Note the name, though. International speaks worldwide foodstuffs, albeit with a Greek accent.

Poseidon Confectionery (629 Ninth Ave) is more than a Greek bakery; it's a chamber of commerce. Generations of Poseidon family members have dispensed culture, culinary suggestions, and folklore, along with filo, baklava, and spanakopitas.

The Pantheon (689 Eighth Ave) is one of the oldest and best Greek restaurants in town. The proof: look at all the Greeks in the dinnertime line.

Hungarian—Yorkville is Hungarian country, too.

Two of the best Hungarian grocery stores have cute names, and both are probably the ethnic equivalent of Zabar's. They are *Paprikas Weiss* (1546 Second Ave) and *Lekvar by the Barrel* (1577 First Ave). Lekvar is prune butter. Don't knock it till you've . . .

The Hungarian Meat Center (1592 Second Ave) is as good an indication as any of what a butcher shop in Budapest is like, but the countermen speak more English than most of their customers. A Hungarian delicacy is the goose liver.

Paul's Charcuterie & Patisserie (235 E 57th St) is ostensibly Czech, but the cuisine is quite possibly Hungarian.

Surprisingly, the best Hungarian restaurant in town may be the very commercial *Hungaria* in the Citicorp Center (Lexington Ave at 53rd St). The food is excellent, and the atmosphere authentic.

Indian—Asian Indians, as opposed to American Indians, have settled in large numbers all across New York. But their marketplace is the high twenties from Lexington Avenue to Fifth Avenue. Perhaps because of the cuisine, the chief advantage of the Indian influx has been the availability of fresh, plentiful, exotic spices. (Even the Hungarians buy Indian paprika!) Two such spices stores are *Kalustyan* (123 Lexington Ave) and *Foods of India* (120 Lexington Ave). The latter also stocks large amounts of foodstuffs as well.

Annapurna (108 Lexington Ave) is both a restaurant and food store. *Raga* (57 W 48th St), while out of that area, is an excellent restaurant, with first-class help and prices.

Tandoor (40 E 49th St), also out of that neighborhood, is the place Indians go to for tandoori cooking.

Shezan (8 W 58th St) is another non-neighborhood restaurant, which specializes in pricey Indian and Pakistani cuisine.

Italian—Little Italy is the area at Grand Street that is not the Lower East Side and the area at Mulberry Street that is not Chinatown. The stores and shops resemble Italy, and the San Gennaro festival in September has capacity crowds on the sidewalks. All of the older stores still dispense original recipes, and the specter of the World Trade Center looks like a mirage next to the three-story buildings and hanging bolognas. Among the best are:

Alleva Dairy (188 Grand St) specializes in homemade cheese. The place is simply incredible.

Italian Food Center (186 Grand St) is a mini-supermarket that maximizes all kinds of Italian foodstuff. There is smoked meat, groceries, bread, and much more.

Parisi Bakery (198 Mott St) is the source for authentic Italian bread that comes in intriguing shapes and configurations and dotted with all sorts of cheeses and meats.

Todaro Brothers (557 Second Ave) is a full-service Italian grocery store, which ships nationwide. There are cheeses, meats, pastas, risottas, coffee, candies, herbs, condiments, cakes, and gourmet items.

Little Italy has "cafes" rather than restaurants. Two of the classics are *Terrara's* (195 Grand St) and *Caffe Roma* (385 Broome St). The latter also has pastries for over-the-counter consumption.

The best Italian restaurant is uptown. That's *Primavera* (1570 First Ave), where the service is as classy as the food.

Aside from Little Italy, the next best spot for the Italian kitchen is probably Ninth Avenue. *The Grosseria* (488 Ninth Ave) bills itself as the country's biggest Italian grocery store, and it is. Next door, *Manganaro's Hero Boy* (492 Ninth Ave) claims to be able to produce the world's biggest hero. Italian delicatessen here is simple but excellent.

Japanese—The Japanese community in New York is fairly new. Most are executives here on extended business terms. Despite this, sushi bars have invaded the neighborhoods, and the *Hotel Kitano* (66 Park Ave) is a Japanese-owned-and-managed hotel, which takes care of the needs of Japanese travelers.

Katagiri & Company (224 E 59th St) has been dispensing Japanese foodstuffs for almost 80 years.

Hatsuhana (17 E 48th St) offers the best sushi in the city.

Dosanko shops all over town offer the best larmen noodles. In fact, Dosanko has made larmen noodles as ubiquitous as tofu.

For dining out, *Nippon* (145 E 52nd St) and its branch, *Hyo Tan Nippon* (119 E 59th St), are highly recommended. It was one of the first Japanese restaurants in the city and deserves its venerable reputation.

Jewish—The Lower East Side is the historical Jewish center. But because kosher cuisine is a religious tenent and not merely a cultural reminder of home, kosher establishments can be found wherever Jews congregate in the city. The New York variation on this theme is that there are kosher Chinese, kosher pizza, kosher vegetarian, and even kosher Indian restaurants. What there is a decided lack of, ironically, are the good old celery-soda-and-belching-sandwich delicatessens that served side orders of chicken soup. So while the dietary laws may be observed, the cultural cuisine seems to be a victim of dietary consciousness.

Groceries in Jewish cuisine are assigned to specific stores: pickles from *Guss/Hollander* (35 Essex St) and *Fulton Market* (South Street Seaport); knishes from *Yonah Schimmel* (137 E Houston St and 1275 Lexington Ave); bagels from *H & H* (2239 Broadway); lox from *Zabar's* (2245 Broadway) or *Russ and Daughters* (179 E Houston St); baked goods (and atmosphere) from *Gertel's* (53 Hester St); and wine from *Schapiro's* (126 Rivington St).

For dining out, there is a wide spectrum of choices. The only spot capable of still recalling the traditional meals of the Lower East Side is *Sammy's Roumanian Jewish Restaurant* (157 Chrystie St). It's a remnant from the days when the East Village was the home of Yiddish theater. Its cuisine, while not kosher, is a throwback to the days when seltzer and alka-seltzer were passed out to patrons along with the flanken and pastrami. Virtually every other Jewish restaurant in the city has either eased up on the grease or invoked accents of a different cuisine to entertain the diners.

Bernstein-On-Essex (135 Essex St) is the originator of kosher Chinese food. Its pastrami is unexcelled.

The Caldron (308 E Sixth St) is vegetarian, Japanese, and Kosher.

Greener Pastures (117 E 60th St) is vegetarian and operated by Indians.

Katz's (205 E Houston) is not kosher deli, but its atmosphere is typical Lower East Side Jewish. Check out the varieties of sausage.

La Difference (Madison Avenue at 45th St, in the Roosevelt Hotel) is a kosher French restaurant so fancy-shmantsy that many of its diners don't know of its kosher credentials.

Levana's (148 W 67th St) is Moroccan and kosher vegetarian.

Lou G. Siegel (209 W 38th St) is the veritable grandfather of kosher restaurants. Its cuisine is the kind grandma would serve to garment center executives: chicken soup, boiled beef, kreplach, and pastrami. But it's served by proper waiters on linen tablecloths.

Ratner's (138 Delancey St) is the all-dairy source of every Jewish waiter joke ever told. In the 70 years or so of its existence, Ratner's has seldom had a waiter who looks younger than the restaurant. They are experts at ignoring patrons. When orders are finally taken, the waiters will often "offer" their opinions. But it's a wonder they stop at the table at all.

Latin American—There are distinctive Latin American areas in the city, but the pervasiveness of the Hispanic populace has managed to spread Spanish foods into neighborhood grocery stores (bodegas) and gourmet emporiums. El Barrio, from East 102nd Street to East 125th Street, is the longtime home of the Puerto Rican population. And La Marqueta, the marketplace under the railroad between East 111th Street and 116th on Park Avenue, provides all of the ethnic food for that population. "Little Brazil," centered around West 46th Street off Fifth Avenue, is mostly a commercial enclave. It's been in the making since the early 1950s, but Brazilians don't live there. They just eat and trade there.

The Brazilian Coffee Restaurant (45 W 46th St) has a deceptive name. It is the oldest native restaurant outside Brazil, and its specialty is the national dish *feijoada.* And it *is* a restaurant, not a coffeehouse.

For authentic Latin American foodstuffs, nothing beats *Casa Moneo* (210 W 14th St). One Mexican-born friend buys things here and ships them home to Mexico.

For Mexican takeout food, *Anita's Chili Parlor* (287 Columbus Ave) and her offshoot, *Rocking Horse Cafe* (224 Columbus Ave) have been dispensing chili to New Yorkers for a decade.

One of the best Mexican restaurants in the city is *Zapata* (330 E 53rd St), which offers proof that there is some real chili cooking in New York. And for purer *español,* there's *Meson Madrid* (1394 York Ave). The latter speaks with a regal Madrid accent.

Russian—The Russian presence in New York runs the gamut from "Little Odessa" in Brighton Beach, Brooklyn, populated by recent Russian emigrés, to the imposing Soviet delegation compound in Riverdale in the Bronx. (There is also a Russian enclave in Glen Cove, Long Island, that made national headlines for strained community relations.) Consequently, the Russian community in New York may be even more diverse than that in the U.S.S.R. There are historical as well as political and religious divisions here: white Russians, Communists, Czarists (yes, indeedy!), government officials, and political and religious refugees.

Russian groceries are best found in Brooklyn. But the best takeout food (particularly borscht) is at *A la Russe* (315 W 54th St).

The Russian Tea Room (150 W 57th St), "slightly to the left of Carnegie Hall," is synonymous with New York City. It played a prominent role in *Tootsie* and many other movies, and the clientele at lunch is predominantly showbiz. The menu is authentic Russian right down to the Strawberries Romanoff. That gives a good clue to its political leanings, too.

The Russian Bear (139 E 56th St) also seems frozen in old-time Russia. Founded in 1908, the Bear features food that is some of the most authentic this side of the Iron Curtain—and maybe *that* side, too.

Scandinavian—The Scandinavian presence in the city is neither distinct nor new in Manhattan. (There is a "Little Scandinavia" in Brooklyn.) But there are some very fine establishments, particularly for food to go.

Old Denmark (133 E 65th St) is a smorgasbord of a shop. There's a restaurant, a gourmet shop, and, in the kitchen, a catering service. They do a little bit of everything.

Nyborg Nelson (153 E 53rd St, Citicorp Center) is primarily a Swedish delicatessen, but there is a whole lot more. Despite the Citicorp Center location and trendy patrons, the store is authenitc enough for the natives.

Swiss—Swiss cuisine in the city is pretty neutral. But there is one outstanding restaurant, the *Chalet Suisse* (6 E 48th St).

Ukranian—The Ukranian community in the East Village is one of the oldest and most entrenched in the city. The early settlers were refugees from Czarist Russia. Later infusions came after World War I, with the German and Russian Occupations. This kept the community alive, but the 1980s gentrification of the East Village directly threatens Ukranian strongholds. Right now, though, there are still strong influences in the neighborhood stores.

Kurowycky's (124 First Ave) may be the best meat market in the city. Its owner, Jaroslav (Jeri) Kurowycky, is an American-born community activist who dispenses communal and ethnic pride along with the best sausages and hams in the city.

There are several restaurants, although the best one, the Ukrainan Restaurant, burned along with the Ukranian National Home on Second Avenue. It might relocate. If so, try it. In the meantime, try *Leshko Coffee Shop* (111 Avenue A) or *Veselka Coffee Shop* (144 Second Ave). Both are much closer to being restaurants than coffee shops.

EXTRAVAGANCE, PURE AND SIMPLE

Okay. The company is paying, you won the lottery, or the oil well just came up behind the tomatoes. Or perhaps just once you want to live really well. All right, then, here are some suggestions on how to do it.

For starters, there are some trappings of wealth that are useless in this city. Porsches may make a statement in California, but in New York they would be a bit ridiculous. You would not want to risk either driving or parking an expensive sports car anywhere in Manhattan. So, the optimal mode of transportation for New York City is livery. Maybe a rented limo, but definitely livery. For the best, rent a Rolls from *Cooper Classics* (132 Perry St). The most popular ones seem to be those previously used by rock stars.

As for food . . . A couple of years ago it was all the rage to see which establishment could charge absolutely the most for the absolutely gaudiest pig-out. But when the Palace (it is no more) entered the fray, the entire concept became too gross for even the most extreme status seekers. Today, while no one will say New York dining is cheap (or even reasonable), price doesn't really determine the quality of a meal.

The same is true for dry goods. Almost every item can be gotten at a discount in the city. The differential is service and availability. So even if money is no object, that money will not provide an extravagant purchase so much as first-class service. Now, let's *spend* the day.

You could start pampering yourself from the bottom up with shoes from *Susan Bennis/Warren Edwards* (440 Park Ave). For good measure, check out *Maud Frizon's* stylish and luxurious footwear (49 E 57th St) as well. While in the neighborhood, smaller women should browse *Henri Bendel* (10 W 57th St), while the men could pick up a new wardrobe at *Andre Oliver* (34 E 57th St). Wait, though, for *Burberry's* (9 E 57th St) to buy the best rainwear. While the meter is ticking, stop at *James Robinson* (15 E 57th St) for a few antique trinkets to remember the day by. Don't worry if the Victorian silver service won't fit into the limo. They'll be happy to send it to you. Then, by all means, stop at *Tiffany* (727 Fifth Ave) for a few more elegant baubles, some gifts to take home, and some socially correct stationery. You might also breeze through *Trump Tower* (57th St and Fifth Ave). They won't grovel at your feet, but a couple of bullion bricks might get their attention.

Lunch at *Le Grenouille* (3 E 52nd St) for a good satisfying meal with super atmosphere. (See what I mean about the limo? So far we've gone less than six blocks.) Again, this is the best that money can buy without being more money than buy.

Stop at *Aaron Faber* (666 Fifth Ave) for a magnificent antique watch that will make the most modern one seem déclassé. Then make your way through the locked doors of *Prastesi* (829 Madison Ave) to find the world's finest linens. Your heirs will thank you for whatever you purchase there; it will last that long. As a personal indulgence, pick out a soft, fluffy, several-inches-thick bathrobe in your favorite color. You can always use it as a pillow!

Grab some ice cream at *Le Glacier* (1022 Madison at 78th St), and then stop at *Caviateria* (29 E 60th St) for the ingredients for a late-night snack of guess what. Not for you the Zabar's/Macy's price wars! Then Rolls on over to *Sylvia Pines Uniquities* (1102 Lexington Ave) for an antique bag. Next stop: *H.B.A. Furs* (350 Seventh Ave). He has designer labels so the finest in furs can be gathered here at good prices—as if you cared! Tell the chauffeur to head downtown for some jade from *Jim Chan* (3 Elizabeth St), before dropping in on *Nicole* (19 Fulton St) to place orders for a few dozen handmade sweaters. Head back uptown for dinner at *Lutece* (249 E 50th St). Generously grease lots of palms if this is a first visit. For good measure, make sure they get a glimpse of the Rolls and all the goodies in it, or glance impatiently and dramatically at your antique watch from Aaron Faber. After dinner, it's "Home, James!" and time to snuggle in your Prastesi linens and nibble on that caviar.

All in all, a day well spent!

FIRST TIME IN NEW YORK

First timers in the city need a sampling of a little bit of everything. Some tourist razzmatazz, some authentic flavoring, and a healthy dash of the really unique. For me, all of these things require shopping. So here is my list, in no particular order. If you want to merely sight-see, skip this list and board the Circle Line. Then again, why would you be reading this if that's the way you feel?

1. *Broadway*—No trip to the city would be complete without a visit to the Great White Way. Try TKTS for bargain tickets, but to really "do" Broadway, try for the Backstage of Broadway tour (575-8065). I would recommend this for even the most casual visitor, but theater buffs and budding thespians can't afford to miss it.

2. *The Cloisters*—A branch of the Metropolitan Museum, the Cloisters on the north end of Fort Tryon Park overlooks the Hudson River and the park, with spectacular views and the pristine atmosphere of a medieval monastery. The Cloisters was assembled from over 7,000 pieces of four basic European monasteries by George Grey Barnard, a sculptor. With the help of John D. Rockefeller, who donated part of the collection and the land on both sides of the Hudson to ensure a clear view, the complete building was created to incorporate the authentic medieval architecture in a more modern building. The overall effect is that of a trip to Europe, and the treasures therein are of museum quality.

3. *The Empire State Building*—Perhaps it is its midtown location that makes me prefer the Empire State Building to the World Trade Center. Neither is the tallest building in the world, but there's so much more to see from the Empire State Building, and the amenities are better, too. Apparently, I'm not alone in my feelings. Statistically, the Empire State Building draws more visitors than any other site in the city.

4. *The Museum of Natural History and Hayden Planetarium*—I'm sticking my neck out here, but if there's time for only one museum, this is the one that will tell you you're in New York. Of course, if you have time for others, don't miss the Metropolitan and the Museum of Modern Art.

5. *The Museum of the City of New York*—Some would put MOMA or the Metropolitan on this list. Then again, some would deem every museum in the city a must-see for first timers. I am not a museum fan, and my list is perhaps on the short side. But this institution is truly a wonder, and it has the right attitude toward its patrons, as evidenced by its "Please Touch" room and its availability as a place for birthday parties.

6. *The New York Experience*—There is no better orientation to the city. This multidimensional movie explains the city's past and present and points out its highlights. Its location in Rockefeller Center puts it within easy walking distance of the Radio City, NBC, and RCA tours, the ice-skating rink, the diamond district, Broadway theater, and Times Square.

7. *The New York Public Library at 42nd St*—It is quite simply awesome, and it's another institution most natives overlook. There are special rooms for American History, magazines and periodicals, charts and maps, and card catalogs (although most of the cards are on computer). Anyone can call a book up from the stacks, and the ongoing restoration has uncovered architectural glories that have been hidden for years. Incidentally, the two monumental lions out front were nicknamed Patience and Fortitude by Mayor LaGuardia in the 1930s. That's an acid-test question of New Yorkese.

8. *Lincoln Center*—A must for culture lovers, but even philistines can spend a day here. In season, don't miss the performances of *The Nutcracker* or "The Mostly Mozart" festival. At other times, try the "Backstage at the Met" tour open rehearsals of the Philharmonic, and the Library of Performing Arts. Or just enjoy the glorious Chagall tapestries at the opera house.

9. *Radio City*—For sheer entertainment and the world-famous Rockettes. And if the art-deco atmosphere leads to a hankering for more, check out the Chrysler and the Empire State Buildings. The Chrysler is the smaller tower further uptown at 200 Park Avenue.

10. *Rockefeller Center*—While in the neighborhood, explore Rockefeller Center. Don't miss the skating rink, the under-building concourse, Radio City, or one of the tours (either NBC, Rockefeller Center, or Radio City). Around holiday time, catch the glow of the Rockefeller Center Christmas tree, a tradition that started when the workmen topped out the center itself with a tree when it was being built. The spirit has remained contagious for 50 years.

11. *South Street Seaport*—This is a personal favorite. Just as the Cloisters seem like a disjointed experience in time and location, so does the Seaport. Isn't it interesting that two of the essential New York experiences are not about the New York of today and in fact achieve their uniqueness by seeming to have nothing to do with the hubbub of the city?

12. *Statue of Liberty, Ellis Island, Staten Island Ferry*—Enjoy the city by leaving it and surveying the view from the harbor. When the Lady and Ellis Island are restored, they will be among the most dramatic in town.

13. *The United Nations*—Not just an "only in New York" experience, the U.N. is an "only in the world" site. How can you miss it? There are guided tours available in each of the U.N.'s official languages or perhaps a dozen more. The open sessions are free.

14. *World Trade Center*—How can you miss the city's tallest buildings and the second tallest building in the world?

Some of the quintessential New York shopping experiences would include the garment center; Tender Buttons, for a truly specialized shop; Zabar's, for the best in gourmet without being conspicuous consumption; Welcome to New York City, for a true New York City welcome in a typical New York location; Job Lot Trading, for the experience of push-cart shopping and ambiance; and H&H Hot Bagels for the ultimate New York snack.

Finally, New York exists on its stomach. The must dining experiences for me would be breakfast at the Helmsley Palace Hotel, lunch at the Carnegie Deli (especially if they're in the midst of a pastrami war), and dinner at the Post House. Those are all midtown locations. If your first trek takes you elsewhere, don't hesitate to try the recommended local fare.

FIX UP THE APARTMENT

The moment has come. You've decided to put down roots and become a full-fledged New Yorker! Whether this means you have found the greatest job in the city that you'll never, ever leave, or you've realized that housing being what it is, you and your living quarters are going to be together until retirement, the main way you put down roots in this city is to fix up the apartment you already have. The place you call home may be a tenement, a SoHo loft, a sublet Fifth Avenue co-op, or the back of some great aunt in Florida's West End Avenue apartment. It matters not. If you're shopping for bathroom tile, then you're somebody who's staying!

You can try all or part of this tour. My hunch is that if the time has arrived, you'll need it all. One further note: this guide is strictly for do-it-yourselfers. Those who want or need help can hire professionals by contacting the American Society of Interior Designers (421-8765) for member recommendations, the Fashion Interior Designers (421-8765) also for member recommendations, or the Fashion Institute of Technology. The latter has the top school of interior design in the city, and has students and graduates on file for reasonably priced consultations.

Start with the renowned Bloomingdale's model rooms. Of course, no one actually buys the complete model room. But there are no displays like them anywhere, and they are a great source for the best ideas in interior design. Now on to fundamentals.

Pintchik (278 Third Ave) is one of the best stops for one of the very best selections of wall covering at a discount. *Wallpaper Mart* (187 Lexington Ave) is the grandfather discount wall-and-floor-covering store in Manhattan. But both of these stores can be slightly overwhelming for novice decorators. A more personal touch can be found at *Shelia's Wallstyles* (281 Grand St). That's personal as in one-on-one assistance, as well as customized screen printing, color coding, and matching fabric. Shelia can put together an entirely coordinated room and do it at the lowest prices in town. One of the largest flooring dealers in the city is *A.B.C. Carpet Company* (881 Broadway). The place is cavernous, and that doesn't include the basement, which carries sale and remnant rolls. For elegant rugs, check out both the *A.B.C. Rug Center* and *Momeni* (79 Madison Ave). The welcome is less than overwhelming, but the wholesale prices for quality Oriental rugs will make up for the lack of warmth.

With the floors and walls done, it's time to furnish. For a general look, my first choice would be *New York Furniture Center* (41 E 31st St). They have *everything*, and it would be an excellent starting place for those first setting up an apartment.

French Country Antiques (35 E 10th St) provides just that. They are accommodating, and with their help an entire house can become a perfect French Country home.

Shine up that home with a few pieces of brass from the *Brass Loft* (20 Greene St) or a statement in brass from *A Parable's Tail* (172 Ninth Ave). If you have the space, pick out both a bed and a table.

And don't forget the bathroom. *The Elegant John* (812 Lexington Ave) can turn the apartment's busiest yet most overlooked room into . . . well, an elegant one. The options are remarkable.

For kitchen appliances, such as Garland stoves or Sub-Zero refrigerators, start on the Bowery. Stop in at *Just Bulbs* (938 Broadway), strictly for fun. After ogling thousands of different bulbs, you'll wonder how anyone can spruce up a house without changing the bulbs. *Bowery Lighting* (132 Bowery), *Harem Lites* (139 Bowery), or *New York Ceiling Fan* (620 Broadway) carry all kinds of lighting fixtures.

For more kitchen appliances, I recommend *Bondy Export Company* (40 Canal St) or *Uncle Steve* (343 Canal St) for the best prices. And nearby, visit *Kaufman Electrical Appliances* (365 Grand St) for major or minor kitchen appliances. Chaim Kaufman is a wiz at fitting the best appliances into New York apartments. You can round out the kitchen décor with accessories from *Carole Stupell.* Then set the new table and tablecloth with china and crystal from *Lanac Sales* (73 Canal St) and silver from *Eastern Silver* (54 Canal St), both down on the Lower East Side.

Finally, also in this neighborhood, shop for your linens, sheets, and blankets at *Ezra Cohen* (307 Grand St) and the sundry items that every household needs at *D.F. Sanders* (386 W Broadway). They can make a dish drain a work of art; indeed, they offer it in a dozen colors. Don't make this your first stop on your refurbishing rounds, or you might be tempted to furnish every room with housewares items. Not a bad idea, but it will never make the Bloomingdale's model room!

GERRY FRANK'S LOWER EAST SIDE

Part bazaar, part wholesale market, part teeming immigrant headquarters, part historically entrenched ethnic capital, and so much more, the Lower East Side defies description. It seems to be a world of its own, with its own rules, morés, sense of time, and way of life. Nonetheless, if I had to pick just one destination in New York, this would be it. It is like no experience anywhere else.

First, a little background. The area has no physical boundaries because, again, it is always changing. Historically, it was the first stop for immigrants after Ellis Island. But around the turn of the century, various ethnic groups carved out territories and gave rise to the Jewish Lower East Side, Little Italy, Chinatown, and the Ukrainian East Village. While these boundaries ebbed and flowed as later refugees displaced the original inhabitants, many of those early groups never gave up their sections of the neighborhood. So today, almost 100 years later, it is possible to sample ethnic delights from half a dozen nations within a three-block area. What's more, this isn't Disney World's Epcot Center; this is the real thing. Sociologists often even study the Lower East Side for original authentic culture long gone from the mother country.

From a shopper's point of view, the Lower East Side mainly involves the Jewish area. (The others come into play when we discuss food.) And what goes on there operates on its own standards, which need some translation.

Take, for example, the operating hours. Despite the fact that several of the stores boast *Aqui Se Habla Español* signs, the neighborhood still runs on Orthodox Jewish Standard Time. This means no Saturdays, early Friday closings in the winter, all Jewish holidays off, a jam-packed Sunday, and a relaxed attitude toward official hours. So what if the sign says "Open at 10"? Maybe it's too hot today, so they'll open at noon. And if at 4:30 p.m., no one is in the store (or sometimes even if there is), it's closing time. This is especially true during the week. The day seldom starts before 11 a.m. and is usually long over by 5 p.m., even in the summer. But it's no posh job. Standing behind a counter just one Sunday can create candidates for a long-term rest cure. Since that's the day most of the business is conducted, the lackadaisical attitude during the rest of the week is understandable.

Then there's the matter of business: this is not retail America. Stores tend to be very old, very small, and very dingy. It's almost a matter of pride to pay no attention to your setting. Lack of space is coped with by hanging merchandise from the ceilings, out the front door, and from other merchandise. Many of the stores display "wholesale only" signs, and the way the merchants down here manage to get first-class merchandise, often before the uptown stores, and sell it at a good discount is expected but never explained. Most of the "wholesale only" signs can be ignored, as can a good portion of the stores, especially those dangling merchandise outside. There's a reason why they leave it outside! Follow our list, and you won't get ripped off or chased away.

Finally, we come to the topic of amenities and manners: expect none. You may be surprised, but probably not. The theory seems to be that politeness, information, and saleshelp went out with the public restrooms. If you want a good price, you must understand that there are certain sacrifices to be made. On the Lower East Side, that sacrifice borders on the loss of human dignity. Pushing, shoving, and brassiness are the rule—and that's among the customers! The worst offenders are the natives, pseudo natives (his grandfather once passed through), and little old ladies. The latter even have their own anthem. "My next" means it's *her* turn. It is most often shouted from a doorway over the heads and bodies of the 25 people who really are next. The merchants aren't much better. Asking for help on the part of a customer implies weakness. Due partially to the limited display space, you're supposed to know what you want before you take up a merchant's precious time. (This holds true for restaurants and waiters, too.) A nod in your direction means it's your turn. Miss it, and the "my next" lady has already been served. While some merchants now accept credit cards, cash is still the operative currency.

Why bother, then? Because there is nothing like it. The fashions are the best, the price for virtually everything (even pickles) is drastically discounted, and dozens of things are sold that are unavailable elsewhere at any price. The latest Lower East Side trend seems to be the stocking of designer labels, particularly designer shoes. But that doesn't preclude silver, religious articles, children's clothing, books, and hundreds of food outlets (there's even a Baskin & Robbins) to supply the neighborhood pastime of noshing while shopping. Among my favorites, the following are exceptional. For a full day's trip, I would include any establishment listed elsewhere in this book, but I shall briefly list what I think are the essentials. Details can be found under the actual categories.

On Sunday, the Lower East Side *is* Orchard Street, and its status is acknowledged by the fact that the street is closed to traffic to accommodate the push of the crowds. Starting from the bottom (near Canal):

Leslie's Bootery (36 and 65 Orchard St) was one of the first of the designer-shoe outlets. It carries very stylish footwear for both men and women. I asked why they have two stores a block apart. The answer: "Because Orchard Street has lots and lots of business." That's a good introduction to shopping here.

Charles Weiss & Sons (38 Orchard St) For ladies lingerie. I once saw a salesman personally demonstrate a bra here. That was during the week, of course!

A.W. Kaufman (73 Orchard St) For undergarments and hosiery for the rest of the family.

Louis Chock (74 Orchard St) Ditto. Kaufman is newer, I think. The crowds are at Chock.

Forman's (82 Orchard St) For name-brand, off-the-rack designer women's clothing. The Forman name is so trustworthy that Forman's has become a mini-emporium. Forman's Petite (78 Orchard St) offers everything the exclusive boutiques uptown do but at a discount. The Forman's at 92 Orchard is dedicated to coats, and at 94 Orchard the "good" names graduate into true designer fashions. The main store at 82 Orchard is a prime source for Liz Claiborne, while 94 Orchard handles Pringle cashmere sweaters, Nipon Boutique, and Ralph Lauren. You get the idea.

Carry On Luggage (97 Orchard St) is the definitive luggage shop. If it doesn't work out, Bettinger's is nearby at 80 Rivington Street.

Lace Up Shoes, (110 Orchard St), across Delancey Street is another designer-shoe source. Very high fashion and almost entirely women's.

Fine & Klein (119 Orchard St) is the definitive handbag, attaché case, and leather goods store. I'd call it the best in the world.

Samuel Beckenstein (118 Orchard St, 125 Orchard St) is another emporium. But this one is veritably old, unlike the cloths, woolens, and fabrics that it carries. Beckenstein's is the source for virtually any kind of fabric and is often the only hope of interior decorators, home sewers, and even professional couturiers. It started as a pushcart dispensing woolens for men's suits, and it still has one of the finest departments for that alone.

A. Altman (182 Orchard St) is legendary for its tiny store, first-class women's garments, and top labels, as well as its discount prices. There are other branches around town, but why miss the thrill of standing outside in the middle of Orchard Street begging for the opportunity to be let in?

M. Friedlich (196 Orchard St) is the first choice for women who wear French and Italian sportswear and knits.

After Orchard Street, Grand Street is the next "must" stop. Primarily for household needs, there are several excellent stops.

Harris Levy (278 Grand St) has virtually every linen and domestic item. So does *Ezra Cohen* (307 Grand St). The latter is probably the best source for sheets, both current and discontinued, and *that* doesn't cover the custom departments, commode covers, matching towels, and bathroom rugs.

J. Schachter (115 Allen St), across the street, is the place where the down coverlet was born. (It had another name in another language when the great-grandparents brought it to Schachter for repair.) They also coordinate entire bedroom suites.

Sheila's Wallpaper (273 Grand St) was the first wallpaper shop in the area and is still the best. Most of Sheila's customers are suburban homemakers seeking the total look.

Kaufman Electrical Appliances (365 Grand St) is one of several shops dispensing small and large electrical items and appliances, dishes, pens, and cameras at great discounts. They also carry merchandise adapted for use abroad. Others are *Bondy* (40 Canal St) and *Dembitzer Bros.* (5 Essex St).

Next door to Kaufman is *Kossar's Bialystoker Bakery* (367 Grand St). Stop in for a bite to tide you over till the next spot.

Hollander Pickles (35 Essex St) is the first of three pickle stores on one block. I think it's the best, but if the line is long or a price war is going on, try one of the competitors. One of my very best New York stories is about a very dignified group of Oregon friends conducting a pickle-tasting contest in the middle of Essex Street.

A long way down the block and around the corner from the pickles is *Gertel's* (53 Hester St). There is a quasi-coffee shop beside the bakery counters here, so the tired can sit for a bite to eat *if* they're aggressive enough to grab a table. Lower East Side manners are *de rigeur* here, too. While waiting for a chance to order the best chocolate blackout cake in the city, it's also possible to garner the latest shopping hints. (Try boarding a plane loaded with blackout cake and pickles. I did.)

Eastern Silver (54 Canal St) shouldn't be missed, although geographically it could have been the first spot on the tour. Climb the stairs of the nondescript building and enter a gleaming world of shiny silver. The small store has virtually anything imaginable in sterling and very little that isn't, at great savings.

Back on the other end of town, Orchard Street ends at Houston, and that's where gastronomic heaven begins. (That's for those who can stomach blackout cake and pickles.)

Yonah Schimmel (137 E Houston St) is the furthest west. The knish factory is better in reputation than taste, but no politican or bona fide tourist would miss it.

Moishe's Bakery (181 E Houston St) is a better choice. The breads are great—Old World, moist, dark, and delicious.

Russ & Daughters, next door (179 E Houston St), is just the place for getting appetizers to serve with Moishe's bread. The lox is a natural with a bagel, but there's much, much more.

Finally, *Katz's Delicatessen* (205 E Houston St), on the corner at Ludlow Street, can serve the meal to top off a day of the unusual and the reasonable. The deli is fresh, choice, and very economical. And by now, the surly service, lack of amenities, and communal ketchup should be second nature to you.

MAN'S DAY: TAKING CARE OF NUMBER ONE

New York is a great man's town; there is no place on earth that can provide the same diversity of activity, whether it's working, eating, shopping, or just plain having fun. How about taking a day off to just take care of number one? Here are a few suggestions.

Start off the day by getting an excellent haircut and shampoo from Emil at *James of the Plaza Barber Shop* (Plaza Hotel). Then think about outfitting the body. Go by *Saint Laurie* (897 Broadway) to get some of the best clothing buys in the city, or if you're into designer names, head toward *Barney's* (111 Seventh Ave). It's a zoo, but they have everything. Some of the best values in shirts are at *The Custom Shop,* which has branches all over town; accessorize them with terrific buys from *Heritage Neckwear* (194 Allen St). You'll pay one-third of what the department stores charge. How about a new pair of shoes? Try *Anbar* (93 Reade St) for discount prices, or *Vogel Boots & Shoes* (19 Howard St) if you really want to splurge. Finish off your wardrobe shopping with a classy new raincoat from *Norman Lawrence* (475 Fifth Ave), some off-price and off-duty jeans from *Alaska Fashions* (41 Orchard St), and a classic sweater from *A. Peter Pushbottom* (1157 Second Ave).

If you're into gadgets like I am, don't miss *Brookstone* at the South Street Seaport or Herald Square. It's a gadget hunter's dream house. *Forty-seventh Street Photo* (115 W 45th St, 67 W 47th St, 38 E 19th St) can provide the camera you've been looking for, and go by *Orpheus Remarkable Recordings* (1047 Lexington Ave) for some great new compact digital discs.

Your sporting-goods needs can be taken care of at *Paragon* (867 Broadway) or *Eastern Mountain Sports* (18 W 61st St). And to make your face irresistible to the little lady, check out *Caswell-Massey* (518 Lexington Ave); they've been making guys look and smell better since 1752. Pipe broken? Treat yourself to a new one from the *Connoisseur Pipe Shop* (51 W 40th St). For an unusual lark, go by the *Fire Department Museum* (104 Duane St) to see a unique collection of old fire trucks. And by the time you've done all this, a great massage would be the best way to get ready for a sensational evening. Call Ron Filippi (758-7134), and he'll come over to your home or hotel.

Oh yes, you'll have to feed yourself well to get through a day like this. I'd suggest you start out with a hearty (and inexpensive) breakfast at the *Moondance Diner* (80 Sixth Ave), have lunch at old-time *Delmonico's* (56 Beaver St) or the *Oyster Bar* at Grand Central Station, go by *Zabar's* (2245 Broadway) to pick up some tasty treats to bring home, have dinner at *Ottomanelli's* (439 E 82nd St), and after taking your one and only dancing at the *St. Regis Hotel* (Fifth Ave and 55th St), go by *Cafe Della Palma* (327 Columbus Ave) for some of the most outrageous Italian gelati outside of Rome. What a way to go!

SOHO: ANOTHER WORLD

By definition, what's exciting about SoHo can't be captured on the printed page. The area that started as a bohemian artist's retreat now has tour buses and Madison Avenue branches. SoHo today is less avant-garde, but it's also cleaner and safer.

SoHo was originally the manufacturing backyard of the city. When the city grew, most of the factories and plants moved out of town, but it really wasn't until the 1970s that the huge lofts and empty industrial canyons were renovated and appropriated for residential use. That the city seemed to skip over SoHo, despite its proximity to the Village and the financial district, would be surprising, except that aside from their sheer magnitude, the machine-orientated spaces were decidedly uninviting for human habitation. Furthermore, the area had no services. No laundromats, no dry cleaners, no grocery stores, and certainly no place to "send out" to for food. Consequently, some of the area's oldest retailers are food merchants or "basics" providers. Tamala Design With Bagel is a classic example. Here's a clothing shop that felt it necessary to feed its customers. And in fact, it was so successful at it that the shop spawned a full-fledged catering service.

When the trendy boutiques moved in, they signaled that the neighborhood was undergoing yet another change. SoHo today is where the Village was in the 1950s and 1960s in status and tourism. But there remains much more than a smidgen of homage to the artists who first settled the area. So today it is possible to find the very best art galleries in a two-block area, alongside boutiques better than Madison Avenue's, and then toast your shopping success at some of the least expensive restaurants in town. So here's SoHo:

Gallery goers will have to visit during the week; nearly all galleries are closed on Sunday, although unknown artists have street showings on Sunday. Among the best galleries are:

A.I.R. (63 Crosby St) A gallery devoted to the art work of women. It is a nonprofit cooperative.

Mary Boone/Michael Werner (417 W Broadway) One of the brightest and biggest lights on the gallery scene, Mary Boone is said to be the new Leo Castelli. (He's not so old, but Mary is in her thirties.) They sometimes do joint showings, and a showing at either gallery is as "in" as you can get.

Leo Castelli (420 W Broadway; 142 Green St), *Castelli Graphics* (43 W 61 St; 4 E 77 St), *Sonnabend Tapes and Films* (142 Green St) Even if the name means nothing, the sheer number of locations should give a hint that Castelli's is the "pop" of all art in SoHo. Castelli made his name during the pop-art craze. Today, he's big enough to be uptown, downtown, East Side, and West Side. He has been called the most influential art dealer alive. Ileana Sonnabend, his ex-wife, has her own gallery (420 W Broadway) and lends her name to Castelli's tape and film gallery.

Paula Cooper (155 Wooster) Cooper opened SoHo's first gallery in 1968. That vision is still evident in her selection of artists and sculpture. The gallery emphasizes the latter as well as prints and unusual media.

O.K. Harris (383 W Broadway) This place is legendary. Perhaps the largest gallery in SoHo, it's still not large enough to display all that it wants to. Owner Ivan Karp trained under Leo Castelli uptown, but came to SoHo shortly after Paula Cooper. Hyper-realism has been synonymous from the beginning with O.K. Harris (a fictional namesake, whose portrait reflects his gambling tendencies).

Nancy Hoffman Gallery (429 W Broadway) There's no real game plan here. Mixed media is the operative word. Nancy Hoffman mixes eras, periods, styles, and materials as well. The one unifying theme is that it's contemporary. Other than that, almost anything goes.

Edward Thorp Gallery (419 W Broadway) Thorp is almost a native of SoHo, although he comes from Santa Barbara. He has eschewed the popular patron-pleasing route, and instead has exhibited local artists consistently. Short of getting invited into a struggling artist's loft, this is the best way to see what the artist population is doing. Thorp—and SoHo—are already old enough to have exhibited and sold some real discoveries.

After the galleries, it's time to turn yourself into a work of art. Several SoHo stores literally have created artistic works to be worn. *Artwear* (409 W Broadway) is the prototype of these shops. Clothing stores abound, and all hawk the distinctive SoHo look. It can be vintage: *Harriet Love* (472 W Broadway) is another pioneer; she started out in the Village. *The Antique Boutique* (712 Broadway) is the largest and best vintage-clothing store in the city. It can be designer: *Betsey Johnson* (130 Thompson St) started uptown, came to SoHo, and now has branches back uptown. *Dianne B* (426 W Broadway) is another example; the SoHo branch now calls the tune for her older Madison Avenue store. Or it can be totally SoHo. *Parachute* (121 Wooster St) will outfit a SoHo wardrobe. *Macondo* (150 Spring St) is definitive SoHo. Its wares are made of expensive silks and hand-decorated fabrics, and the price tags are nothing a starving artist could afford. But they're unique, attention getting, and kind of timeless. They look like either they were just marked down at the thrift shop, or the designer just finished taking the pins out.

La Rue Des Reves (139 Spring St) is a proponent of the new wave of SoHo merchandising. The clothing is sleek and trendy, but it can also be worn uptown, although it would take guts.

Manufacturers Shoe Outlet (527 Broadway) may be the most difficult place in town to track down, but it keeps SoHo hours and has sensational buys for the whole family.

Even the housewares and home furnishings stores are different in SoHo. *D.F. Sanders* (386 W Broadway) would be an old-fashioned hardware store in Iowa, but here it sells high-tech door knobs, lacquered dinnerware, portable closets, and all kinds of weird gadgets. It seems that while nearly everything Sanders sells is utilitarian, none of it is the usual. For example, have you ever seen a watch that runs counter-clockwise?

Think Big (390 W Broadway) and *Niedermaier Display* (435 Hudson St) are the places to go for giant Crayola crayons and Campbell soup cans. It's kind of overpowering in the showroom, but a single giant item makes a distinctive decorating statement at home. A top seller is the baseball-glove loveseat.

Wooden Furniture (508 Canal St) is one of my favorite places. Kipp and Margot Osborne custom-make Shaker-style furniture.

Urban Archaeology (137 Spring St) is the place to go for oak doors, salvaged barber poles, wooden Indians, and much more. This may be the Grandma's attic of New York City.

And finally we get to food.

The raw ingredients (or in some cases the gourmet, imported ingredients) for dinner can be purchased on Prince Street. West

Broadway seems to be for boutiques; Prince is for food.

Vesuvio Bakery (160 Prince St) was in SoHo long before it was called SoHo. Owner Tony Napolito is the unofficial mayor of the area, and his tall tales and lore are the second reason to go there. The first is some of the finest Italian Bread and sugar-free cakes around.

Dean & DeLuca (121 Prince St) melds the best of the new and old neighborhood. Giorgio DeLuca owned an Italian cheese shop for years. The shop was updated, and today Dean & DeLuca is the neighborhood's answer to Zabar's uptown.

Almost next door is the inconspicuous *Food* (127 Prince St), which serves just that. It's the best value and best meal in town. There is a nod to health food. Try Food's soups with a sandwich. Much better than nouvelle cuisine. Health food fans should also try *Whole Foods in SoHo* (117 Prince St). The *Prince Street Bar* (125 Prince St) looks like a high-school gym on dance night and serves a compatible meal. There are hamburgers as well as Indonesian dishes. (Why? Don't ask. This is SoHo. Maybe it was an Indonesian High School.)

The SoHo Wine Bar (422 W Broadway) offers light snacks and brunch on weekends, along with an excellent selection of wines and alcoholic beverages. After a day of wandering the galleries, it's possible to rest here and never even notice that the rest of the neighborhood is a little strange.

Raoul's (180 Prince St) is such a successful bistro that it spawned its own specialty butcher shop. The menu is continental and delicious. It is also justifiably famous.

Finally, the *Cupping Room Cafe* (359 W Broadway) is a skylighted restaurant in what was formerly a coffee warehouse. True to its origins, the cafe serves superb coffees and teas, but the brunches, light snacks, and desserts aren't bad either.

Notice that the emphasis is on "light." That pretty much holds true for SoHo in general. It won't strain your pocketbook or your brain, but it sure is fun.

SOUTH STREET SEAPORT

The South Street Seaport is, at once, one of the city's oldest and newest places. In 1611, just two years after Henry Hudson first sailed into the harbor, Dutch trading ships had already begun to create the greatest port in the world. Yet just a few decades ago, the Seaport was so rundown, it was all but abandoned. Even its heyday as a slum (brought on by the switch from sail to steam power) was over 100 years ago.

In 1967, a small group began the South Street Seaport Museum and tried to alert sponsors and historians to the magnitude of the

Seaport. A real boost to their plans arrived with the Bicentennial, when New York celebrated with a "Tall Ship" extravaganza, which allowed the boardings of ships docked at the Seaport, their historic home. Suddenly, an area known solely to contemporary New Yorkers for the Fulton Fish Market, and perhaps the restaurant *Sweets,* became, as one brochure put it, "New York's Newest Place to Be."

The actual Seaport wasn't completely reopened until the fall of 1983, and there are still ongoing changes and additions. The Seaport now consists of several sections. A ticket for all or parts of it can be purchased at the Seaport Gallery (213 Water St), the Visitor's Center (14 Fulton St), or the Pilot House (piers 15 and 16) where the ships are docked. Of course, some of it is completely free. The various sections may appeal to different groups, but the Seaport as a whole is smashing and surely my number-one "must see" attraction in the city.

The Ships—There are usually at least three ships in port, as well as three other smaller vessels. The *Peking* is perhaps the best known of these (the premier party for Yves St. Laurent's Opium perfume was held on the *Peking*). One of the largest existing sailing ships, it is almost completely restored, and it's an education in itself. The *Wavertree* is in the process of restoration and offers a healthy appreciation for what has been done to the *Peking,* as well as a view of the life aboard a 19th-century masted sailing ship. The *Wavertree* operated as a barge in one of the bleaker periods of its existence. The *Ambrose Light Ship,* a floating lighthouse, is now permanently docked at pier 16, and since it is the most recently retired ship, it is most accurate in its portrayal of life aboard a ship. (The cast-iron stove has railings around it, which kept pots from sliding, and overhead bars for the cook to grasp so he wouldn't slide as well.) Other ships include the *Lettie Giltoward* (which is dwarfed by the *Wavertree*; it puts the *Wavertree* and *Peking* in perspective), the *Aqua,* the *Major General Hart,* and the *Pioneer,* which take lunchtime cruises and minicruises.

The *Seaport Experience* (from 11 a.m. daily) This 50-minute multimedia show truly appeals to all ages. It traces the history of the Seaport, as well as commerce in the Northeast. During its course, the audience experiences fires, sea storms, the Fulton Fish Market's heyday, and even vibrating chairs (or so it seems). The show was put together by Rusty Russell, who also did "The New York Experience." Children seem to enjoy it. It is a trifle long and disjointed, but it's hard to lose interest when a ship's mast is falling in front of you. The least expensive way to see it is with a combination ticket.

The Fulton Market—The original Fulton Market was built in 1822. The restored three-story building was developed by the Rouse

Company. (Rouse seems to delight in redoing older city commerce centers. He redid Baltimore's Harbor, and is now creating a similar historic district in Pittsburgh.) The object is to renew the mixture of commerce, business, and pleasure that the Seaport once enjoyed, so the first floor looks like an indoor forum for the city's best outdoor vendors. Guss' pickles has a spot, so does Zaro's bread and a coffee outlet. Upstairs on the second floor, kids and Wall Streeters at lunchtime can devour anything from frozen yogurt to pastrami sandwiches, and *that* doesn't begin to cover the fast-food potato skin or lobster places. There are also several restaurants (the Coho is one, but it isn't very good) for more formal dining.

Shopping at the Fulton Market can take up the entire day . . . there are so many booths and things to see. The best is *A & D Mercantile* on the first floor. What a place! Gifts and surprises and neat things galore. And are they nice people! There are also the ships and adjuncts of the Seaport Museum on Schermerhorn Row and "Museum Block" (Fulton and Water Streets). Here the effort has been to restore the area with compatible small retailers, who market wares that are either indicative of the Seaport's heyday and/or simpatico with contemporary browsers. All of the wares are whimsical and usually reasonable.

Browne & Company is a prime example of this. A stationery company with roots in the original Seaport, Browne has both a modern shop and an homage to old-fashioned printing techniques at one location. Visitors can select postcards, stationery, and souvenirs from the vast selection out front, or enroll for printing classes or guided tours in the back. (Every Valentine's Day, some local television station "discovers" a Browne & Company handmade Valentine's Day card as the most romantic gift in town.)

Geppeto's Toys is another charmer; their clothing, imported from Europe, is first class.

The Seaport Gallery on Museum Block, next door to the Seaport Theater, and the largest store on Water Street, is an ongoing exhibit of the Seaport and its history. Run like an art gallery, it is also partially a museum. Visitors are encouraged to browse, and there is always one major theme on exhibit.

Around the Seaport, *Sweets,* the oldest restaurant in the city, and *Sloppy Louie's* take advantage of their location and offer some of the freshest seafood in town.

Some of the original tenants at the Fulton Market and other areas have experienced financial problems, because the city had trouble reorienting itself to the Seaport and the current layout is not conducive to bad-weather browsing. But the latter problem has been surmounted. A huge new red steel-and-glass pavilion housing over 100 stores and restaurants is the latest addition to the area. It is located just south of the Brooklyn Bridge.

IV. Where To Eat It: New York's Best Food Shops (Eat In Or Take Out)

Over 100 of the Best Taste Treats in Manhattan

An Exclusive List

Best all-around food and kitchen extravaganza in the world: Zabar's (2245 Broadway)
Hand-dipped chocolate pretzels, cookies, etc.: Evelyn's Chocolates (4 John St and 9A Beaver St)
Chicken-in-the-pot: Fine & Schapiro (138 W 72nd St)
Chinese barbecue items: Quon Jan Meat Products (79 Chrystie St)
Linzer torte: T.A.S.T.E. Sensations (412 E Ninth St)
Homemade mozzarella and ricotta: Russo & Son Dairy Products (344 E 11th St)
Fresh Jersey eggs: (72 E Seventh St; Thursday only, 7-5:30)
SemiFreddi: Gran Gelato (1614 Third Ave)
Hot dogs: Hotdiggity (140 Eighth Ave)
Afghan bread: (764 Ninth Ave)
Cannoli: Caffe Vivaldi (32 Jones St)
Triple-chocolate ice cream: Minter's Ice Cream Kitchen (551 Hudson St)
Open-faced sandwiches: Fledermaus (34 Water St)
Eggplant salad: Juliana (891 Eighth Ave)
Marzipan: Elk Candy Co. (240 E 86th St)
Pecan-pie cookies: Plumbridge (30 E 67th St)
Malt whiskeys: SoHo Wines & Spirits (461 W Broadway)
Pepper biscuits: Vesuvio Bakery (160 Prince St)
Fresh coffee: Porto Rico Importing Co. (201 Bleecker St)
Calzones: Little Italy Gourmet Pizza (65 Vanderbilt Ave and other locations)

Cheesecake: Grossinger's Home Bakery (337 Columbus Ave)
Chocolate chip cookies: Mrs. Field's (Bloomingdale's; 86th St and Broadway; and other locations)
Truffles: Andras (1226 Madison Ave)
Chocolate and orange mousse cake: David Glass Cakes at Fisher & Levy (1026 Second Ave)
Apple tart: Quatorze (240 14th St)
Chicken salad: As You Like It (120 Hudson St)
Tomato soup: Sarabeth's Kitchen (412 Amsterdam Ave, 1295 Madison Ave)
Tuna salad: Todaro Bros. (555 Second Ave)
Rum-pecan pie: A Sweet Place (301 E 91st St)
Deep-dish apple pie: Chelsea Baking Co. (259 W 19th St)
Ice cream mud pie: N.Y. Ice and Chocolate (113 Seventh Ave S., 17 Barrow St)
Diet ice cream: Gelato Modo (Broadway and 97th St, Columbus Ave and 82nd St)
Ukranian dumplings (pierogi): Hladun's of New York (102 E Seventh St)
Chocolate mousse pie: Montana Bakery (231 E Ninth St)
Vinegars: Marketplace (54 W 74th St)
Texas chili: As You Like It (120 Hudson St)
Ravioli: Piemonte Homemade Ravioli Co. (190 Grand St)
Blackout cake: Gertel's (53 Hester St)
Gourmet appetizers: Russ & Daughters (179 E Houston St)
Corned beef sandwich: Carnegie Deli (55th St & Seventh Ave)
Ton katsu: Obento Delight (152 Seventh Ave S)
Black-bottom ice cream pie: Steve's (444 Sixth Ave and 286 Columbus Ave)
Split pea soup: Balducci's (424 Sixth Ave)
Vegetable soup: Country Host (1435 Lexington Ave)
Snow pea salad: Artichoke (968 Second Ave)
Borscht: A La Russe Catering (315 W 54th St)
Great spinach roulade: Fisher & Levy (1026 Second Ave)
Chinese noodles: Yat Gaw Min Co. (100 Reade St)
Lasagna: The Green Noodle (313 Columbus Ave)
Japanese food: Katagiri (224 E 59th St)
Grilled chicken: Rainbow Chicken (2801 Broadway at 108th St)
Muffins: Between the Bread (141 E 56th St, 145 W 55th St)
Authentic N.Y. egg cream: Dave's Corner Restaurant (Broadway and Canal St)
French sausage: P. Carnevale and Son (631 Ninth Ave)
Cheese selection: Cheese of All Nations (153 Chambers St)
Baklava: Alleva Dairy (188 Grand St)
Greek spinach pies: Poseidon Bakery (629 Ninth Ave)

Dim sum: China Royal (17 Division St)
Picnic baskets: In A Basket (226 E 83rd St)
Milk-fed veal: Ottomanelli's (281 Bleecker St)
Chili: Anita's Chili Parlor (287 Columbus Ave)
Salmon mousse: Silver Palate (274 Columbus Ave)
Scandinavian food: Old Denmark (133 E 65th St)
Fresh fish: South Seas Seafood (call 966-2340)
Cold cuts: Bremen House (220 E 86th St)
Homemade baked ham: Kurowycky's (124 First Ave)
Preserves (and all-around fine store): Dean & Deluca (121 Prince St)
Natural Dates: Gillies 1840 (160 Bleecker St)
Pickles: Hollander/Guss Pickles (35 Essex St, South Street Seaport)
Fresh fruit: Balducci's (424 Sixth Ave)
Gaspe salmon: Russ & Daughters (179 E Houston St)
Cornbread: Moishe's Bakery (181 E Houston St; 115 Second Ave)
Bagels: H & H Bagels (80th St and Broadway)
Raisin pumpernickel bread: Orwasher's (308 E 78th St)
Chocolates: Manon (872 Madison Ave)
Healthy veggies: Country Life (48 Trinity Place)
Seafood frittata: Chelsea Foods (198 Eighth Ave)
Smoked chicken salad: Donald Sacks (120 Prince St)
Pita bread: Pitaria (230 Thompson St)
Beluga caviar: Iron Gate (424 W 54th St)
Mince pie: As You Like It (120 Hudson St)
Tabbouleh: Benny's (321½ Amsterdam Ave; 37 Seventh Ave)
Fruits and vegetables: Fairway (2127 Broadway)
Cranberry relish: Artichoke (968 Second Ave)
Montasio cheese: Todaro Bros. (555 Second Ave)
Stuffed cabbage: Kalinka (1067 Madison Ave)
Delicious cake: Les Delices Guy Pascal (123 Madison Ave; 939 First Ave)
"Stick to your ribs" barbecue items: Macy's (Herald Square)
Giant chocolate truffle: Chocolatier (Hotel Pierre, Fifth Ave and 61st St)
Rigo cake: Louis Lichtman (532 Amsterdam Ave)
Paté: Les Trois Petits Cochons (17 E 13th St)
Scones: Mangia (54 W 56th St)
Smoked fish: M. Schacht Co. (99 Second Ave)
Spices: H. Roth & Son (1577 First Ave)
Beef bourguignonne: Philippe (1202 Lexington Ave)
Hungarian pastries: Budapest Pastries (207 E 84th St)
Combination fruit cheesecake: Eileen's Cheese Cake (17 Cleveland Pl)

Croissants: Paris Croissant (609 Madison Ave; 1776 Broadway; and other locations)
Chocolate ganache: Fledermaus (34 Water St; 35 E 60th St)
Chocolate roulade: Out of the Woods (24 E 21st St)
Marquise au chocolat: As You Like It (120 Hudson St)
Tiramisu: Balducci's (424 Sixth Ave)
Praline ice-cream cake: Grossinger's (337 Columbus Ave; 570 Columbus Ave)
Milanese Italian fruit cake: Bleecker Street Pastry (245 Bleecker St)

Bakery Goods

A. ORWASHER BAKERY

308 E 78th St (near Second Ave)
288-6569
Mon-Sat: 7-7

This family business has been in existence for over 50 years, and many of their breads are family recipes handed down from father to son. You'll find Old World breads that used to exist in the local immigrant bakeries and have become extremely rare. Over 30 varieties are always available. Hearth-baked in brick ovens, made with natural ingredients, the breads come in a marvelous array of shapes—triple twists, cornucopias, and hearts, just to name a few. (I've seen their ovens; they're the real thing.) Be sure to sample the onion boards and cinnamon raisin bread (a Saturday special) and the challah, available on Fridays. It is almost as good as the home-baked variety. Best of all is their raisin pumpernickel, which comes in small rolls or loaves. When warm, it is moist, delicious, and sensational. Orwasher also sells coffee, tea, and bread and butter condiments, as well as professional bread-making ingredients that are difficult to find. A baking school is conducted three times a year by Orwasher, using ingredients from their shop.

A. ZITO AND SON'S BAKERY

259 Bleecker St (bet Sixth and Seventh Ave)
929-6139
Mon-Sat: 6 a.m.-6:30 p.m.; Sun: 6-2

Those in the know, know Zito's. They flock here at sunrise to buy bread straight from the oven. Among Zito's fans are Frank Sinatra and numerous Village residents. They love Zito's because the bread crust is crunchy perfection, a sharp contrast to the soft, delicate inside. Two of the best sellers are the whole wheat loaves and the Sicilian loaf. Anthony John Zito is proudest of the house specialties: Italian, whole wheat, and white breads. The latter two come in sizes of 4, 7, and 13 ounces.

BLACK FOREST PASTRY SHOP

117 First Ave (at 11th St)
254-8181
Mon-Fri: 8-8; Sat: 8-7

The incredible delicacies here are made by the hand of European-trained owner P. Fuss, a master of all sorts of creations. His house specialties are made from recipes from all over Europe. There are quiche Lorraine, layer cakes, fruit tarts (including a house specialty, walnut tart), cheesecake, diplomat mocha and chocolate cream, chocolate mousse, Black Forest (of course), and apple crumb cakes. And that's only a partial listing.

BONTE PATISSERIE

1316 Third Ave (bet 75th and 76th St)
535-2360
Mon-Sat: 9-6:30; closed Aug

Mrs. Bonte serves a delicious line of pastries and cakes. The style is decidedly European—French, at that—but the taste has earned universal appreciation. The pastry is flaky smooth, the chocolates creamy satin, and the croissants and éclairs—well, they're perfection. Mrs. Bonte personally supervises, and everything sold here bears her hallmark—that of a tremendously accomplished pastry chef. And her husband is just as talented.

BREAD SHOP

3139 Broadway (at La Salle St)
666-4343
Daily: 8-8; closed July 4th, Aug

This tiny, out-of-the-way bakery, under the tracks at 123rd Street, supplies some of the best handmade, untainted-by-preservatives bread in the city. Their customers are mostly local stores and New York's better food shops (Jefferson Market is one), but if you arrive between 10 a.m. and 3 p.m., one of the house specialties will be available fresh from the oven. (A gastronomic treat unique to New York is walking into the neighborhood bagel shop and sampling "whatever's hot.") Jenny Buchanan and Jim Fitzer, who run the shop, are big on healthy breads and natural ingredients, so the bread here is not only delicious but good for you.

COLETTE'S FRENCH PASTRY

1136 Third Ave (bet 66th and 67th St)
988-2605
Tues-Sat: 8-5:45

Some of the best restaurants in the city buy cakes from Colette's, knowing that the French pastry made and sold here is unexcelled. Because of the enormous restaurant trade, their retail selection is somewhat limited, and advance calls are recommended for special orders. A mail-order following (they ship anywhere within the United States) developed from former New Yorkers and from tourists who sampled Colette's wares and couldn't go home without proof to show the neighbors. Sometimes mail order is the only way to get a taste of the trianon (a dark, heavy chocolate) or pain des genes almond cakes. The limited repertoire also includes quiches and a few French entrees that can be eaten in the store.

COUNTRY EPICURE

1896 Broadway (at 63rd St)
245-3444
Mon-Fri: 8-8; Sat, Sun: 9-8

This patisserie, located across the street from Lincoln Center, turns out the finest tortes, cakes, and pies as consistently as the arts complex stages productions. The "Country" in its name can only refer to the "old country," since Country Epicure's accents are European, if not worldwide. They boast of using the finest ingredients garnered from around the world and old-fashioned techniques, which eschew assembly-line methods in favor of individual, hand-worked pastries. The taste is sensational, and the people here possess Old World charm. After taking in a Lincoln Center afternoon performance, this should be your first stop toward an impromptu feast on the grounds (sidewalks). Or you can stop by before an evening performance and sink back into your seat with some of New York's greatest natural-ingredient pastries in a bag on your lap. Bravo, Country Epicure!

CREATIVE CAKES

400 E 74th St (at First Ave)
794-9811
Tues-Fri: 8-5; Sat: 9-11

Stephanie Crookston was a 27-year-old ad copywriter when she traded in her typewriter for baking pans and began to turn out custom-made cakes from a store not much bigger than her former office cubicle. Due to Crookston's personal charm—and in no small part to her creativity and baking ability—Creative Cakes soon had a client list that was only slightly less impressive than its roster of cake patterns. (It's the patterns that are ingenious; the cakes are all fudgy chocolate with frosted buttercream icing.) Creative Cakes has made a tennis-racquet cake for Arthur Ashe, an open book with an airplane atop it for Erica Jong, portraits in cake for honorees, a sneakers cake, and—the one closest to Crookston's heart—a full-scale monopoly board. Speaking of close to Crookston's heart, she has retired yet again. This time it's to spend more time with her three children. But she is still the creative spirit at Creative Cakes, and the cakes are as good as ever. Prices are not remotely cheap, but the smallest cake feeds 12 to 15 people. At that rate and with that much creativity, it may well be a bargain. I wonder what Stephanie's kids eat for dessert.

DELICES LA COTE BASQUE

1032 Lexington Ave (bet 73rd and 74th St)
535-3311
Daily: 7:30-7

Albert Spalter presides over this restaurant and pastry shop, which has a Basque Spanish accent. The pastries are the drawing card, and you don't have to be Spanish to enjoy them. A spinoff of La Cote Basque, this shop was opened to specialize in La Cote Basque's pastries and hors d'oeuvres. It has an expertise that has been heretofore unlauded in the hors d'oeuvres field. Many of the offerings can be heated at home and adapted to any menu, from cocktail tidbits to the main course of a full meal. Try, in particular, the tourte au jambon et fromage or the garlic sausage saucis sone en croute. The latter could make a whole brunch when served with proper accompaniments. There are tables available for on-the-spot snacks, but since it's become a very popular place, don't expect to find a seat.

EROTIC BAKER

246 E 51st St	73 W 83rd St
752-9790	362-7557
Mon-Sat: 11-7	Tues-Thurs: 11-7; Fri, Sat: 11-8; Sun: 12-6

What is the Erotic Baker doing in these pages? Well, the fact is, there's some redeeming social value to the wares of this X-rated bakery chain. Each shop stocks a standard amount of cookies, cakes, and pastries, all of which are available to customers who want to buy something on the spot. But the mainstay of the business is in made-to-order cakes and confections that are created for special occasions and fantasies. The staff claims everything at the Erotic Baker is tastefully done, and samples certainly taste delicious. But if your taste doesn't lean to the risqué, Creative Cakes is still an alternative, right? Not necessarily. Some occasions demand the services of the Erotic Baker. There was the time that someone put a mannequin in the private washroom of a young store executive. The young man opened the door, saw the feminine figure, and politely backed out to face a grinning staff that had assembled at the door. *I* was the young man, and I would have enjoyed it twice as much if the mannequin had at least been edible. Don't take your mother-in-law here!

FERRARA PASTRIES
195 Grand St (bet Mott and Mulberry St)
226-6150
Daily: 8 a.m.-midnight

With branches in Milan and Montreal, Ferrara is truly international in scope. This big store in Little Italy is probably one of the largest (geographically speaking) "little grocery stores" in the world. Undoubtedly, the business must deal in wholesale importing and several other business ventures, but it is easy (and nice) to believe that the sheer perfection of their confections and groceries can support the whole business. Certainly, the atmosphere here would never reveal that this is anything but a very efficiently run Italian grocery store. Their Old World caffe (sic) is famous for its 21 varieties of pastries, ice creams, and coffee.

FUNG WONG BAKERY
30 Mott St
267-4037
Daily: 8:30-8:30

Fung Wong is the real thing, and everyone from the local Chinatown residents to the city's gourmands extol its virtues. The pastries and baked goods are traditional, authentic, and downright delicious; flavor is not compromised to appeal to Western taste. The bakery features a tremendous variety (enough so that Fung Wong wholesales all over town and to some of the best Chinese restaurants), as well as the distinction of being the oldest and largest "real" Chinese bakery. In survey after survey, Fung Wong is rated number one, and a visit is the surest way to see why.

G&M PASTRIES
1006 Madison Ave (bet 77th and 78th St)
288-4424
Tues-Sat: 8-7; Sun, Mon: 8-6

In a neighborhood where everything is chic, elegant, and classic, G&M survives on a reputation as a small immigrant bake shop, which happens to turn out pastry that can best be described as homemade in style. Carlo Gattnig, an Austrian immigrant, started G&M in 1958. These days he still supervises son Frank's management of the business, and the two generations working together help to maintain the homey family shop. The fare can best be described as the kind of sampling any local apartment building would produce. There are accents of Jewish, Italian, French, and German, in addition to Gattnig's native Austrian, in the doughnuts, tortes, Danish, marzipan, and creamy cakes.

GERTELS

53 Hester St
982-3250
Sun-Thurs: 7-6; Fri: 7-3:30

The customers who come here are almost evenly divided between those who call this place Ger-tells (accent on the last syllable) and those who call it Girtils (as in girdles), but all agree that the cakes and breads at this store are among the best in New York. Locals go for the traditional babkas, strudels, and kuchens, but I found the chocolate rolls and chiffon blackout cake to be outstanding. For those who want to sample the wares, there are tables where customers can enjoy baked goods, coffee, or a light lunch. From the regular inhabitants of these tables, one can glean the choicest shopping tidbits on the Lower East Side. A final tip: every Thursday and Friday, Gertels makes a potato kugel that is unexcelled. People have come all the way from California for a Thursday kugel. During a slow week, you can occasionally find one left over on a Sunday. It's good then, too.

GINDI

935 Broadway (bet 21st and 22nd St)
677-0844
Mon-Fri: 9-7:30; Sat: 11-7; closed Sat in summer

Where to start? Well, Gindi is the only bake shop in the city with Dacquoise in six flavors. Any *one* is simply scrumptious. Then there are the other desserts. The truffle-mousse cake is everything those caloric-heavy, sinfully good names imply. (Isn't it enough to be a truffle cake? It has to be a mousse cake as well?) Simple is the operative word here, even if it is at odds with the cuisine. Gindi is in the Madison Square area. (Home of the first, but not the second and third Madison Square Gardens. So don't go looking for it after a ball game.) This is not exactly Fifth Avenue European pastry country or even gourmet chocolate land. Yet Gindi turns out cheesecakes, specialized chocolate desserts, fruit tarts, and pies with a minimum of fuss and price. The flavor speaks for itself. And those who travel down to the neighborhood to sample these joys can do so at the sparse tables and chairs set up at the back of the shop. Madison Square has never been so close to heaven, and since it's so far from everything else, Gindi is a welcome oasis, particularly when shopping for men's suits in the area.

GLASER'S BAKE SHOP

1670 First Ave (bet 87th and 88th St)
289-2562
Tues-Sat: 7-7; Sun: 7-4
Closed July and half of Aug

If it's Sunday, it won't be hard to find Glaser's: the line frequently spills outside as people queue up to buy one of the Glaser family's fresh cakes or baked goods. And one isn't enough. Customers always walk out with both arms full of bulging packages. The Glasers run their shop as a family business, and pride themselves on their cakes and breads, especially wedding cakes. Come here for great cakes and cookies; try the chocolate chip ones. And unless you want to walk a few blocks over to Orwasher's, buy a loaf or two of bread.

GROSSINGER'S HOME BAKERY
337 Columbus Ave (bet 75th and 76th St)
362-8672, 362-8627
Tues-Sat: 7 a.m.-8 p.m.; Sun: 7-6

570 Columbus Ave (at 88th St)
874-6996
Tues-Sat: 8-6; Sun: 9-5

Grossinger's was Grossinger's on Columbus Avenue when Columbus Avenue was just a street on the West Side and not *the* Columbus Avenue. In those days, circa 1935, it was just a darn good neighborhood bakery. That hasn't changed (though the neighborhood certainly has), but nowadays the major drawing card (aside from being a business on the avenue that's more than ten years old) is its ice cream cakes and cheescakes. They are simply delicious and would be notable anywhere. But in a place where the natives snack on ice cream for breakfast, lunch, and dinner, it's really something for Grossinger's ice cream cakes to be the dessert of your choice. If your mother could make them, this is what she would make. Not incidentally; the cheesecake rivals Miss Grimble's, and other pastries are the mainstay of a business that has survived on this trendy avenue and can afford the new rents.

HABEY'S COOKIES
73 W 83rd St (at Columbus Ave)
787-7644
Mon-Sat: 10-8 p.m.; Sun: noon-6

Just what New York needed — another cookie shop. Right? Fortunately, no one said that to John L. Haber (formerly of North Carolina) and his partner Betsey Roberts (from Tennessee) when they combined their names and investments and started Habey's Cookies in 1983. Within a year, Habey's products were sold in over 100 stores around the country, and the amount of cookies sold over the counter is almost uncountable. What makes this all the more amazing is that Habey's headquarters are hardly conducive to over-the-counter, impulse, or even deliberate sales. The store is below ground level (*basement* may be too refined a word), past a locked gate, and then down a hallway. Lesser things have discouraged lesser cookie lovers. On the other hand, that location and those statistics attest to the greatness of Habey's products. All of the items are handmade, using natural ingredients, such as all-butter wafers. There isn't a tremendous variety, precisely because the partners wish to maintain quality control and they base their wafers, biscuits, and cookies on Southern traditions and recipes. Some are very exotic for New Yorkers, such as the cheese biscuit made with brown rice, cracked wheat, and cayenne pepper. I wouldn't try it with Manhattan clam chowder! In any case, imagine the amount of business Habey's would have if they were easy to find.

H&H BAGEL
2239 Broadway (at 80th St) 1551 Second Ave (at 80th St)
799-9680
24 hours

H&H starts baking fresh bagels at 2 a.m., an hour at which you can get a piping hot bagel without having to wait on H&H's long daytime line. But the biggest plus is that you can satisfy your bagel craving at *any* hour of the day or night at H&H. Another only-in-New-York special.

KOSSAR'S BIALYSTOKER KUCHEN BAKERY
367 Grand St | 510 E 14th St
473-4810, 674-9747 | 674-9578
Daily: 24 hours | Daily: 7 a.m.-9 p.m.

Tradition has it that the bialy derives its name from Bialystoker, where they were first made. Kossar's brought the recipe over from Europe almost a century ago, but the bialys, bagels, horns, and onion boards are as fresh as the latest batch from the oven. The taste is Old-World, and those who have never had one should try these authentic versions first.

LET THEM EAT CAKE
287 Hudson St (at Spring St)
989-4970
Mon-Fri: 8-5

Primarily a wholesale bakery offering gourmet desserts, Let Them Eat Cake is not above offering the house quiches, nut loaves, or cakes to the public. All of them are unusually good, which makes it easy for caterers and restaurants to pass them off as their own. The quiches are made to order and—wonder of wonders!—never frozen. Better still, they are interesting and different, aside from the obligatory quiche Lorraine (perhaps by the 18th edition of this book, the quiche craze will have peaked in New York). In the meantime, try the four cheese, asparagus, and crab-meat varieties. They are among the very best. The cakes and pies reflect the health-food consciousness of the neighborhood. Chelsea carrot cake (from a shop in SoHo) is but one of the examples of this, but any bakery that offers zucchini, date-nut and banana-nut loaves as one quarter of the total offerings from the oven is big on health. In any case, the black velvet chocolate chip fudge cake or the black satin chocolate cake won't do a thing for the waistline, although they'll please the palate. Cakes are available in catering sizes as well as smaller sizes suitable, as they say, for resale. They are also available by the slice for on-the-spot consumption. Perhaps *that's* the best way to pick your favorite.

LOUIS LICHTMAN

532 Amsterdam Ave (at 86th St)
873-2373
Tues-Sat: 8-6:30; Sun: 8-5:30; closed July 15th-Aug 15th

Knowing Louis Lichtman is like having a Hungarian mother who lives and bakes on the Upper West Side. The complete name of the store adds "homemade pastries and strudels," and those lucky enough to have had either a Hungarian mother or a taste of a Lichtman product needs no further introduction to the ability of Hungarian bakers. Those who do need an introduction should come here and ask for several slices of strudel (one would never be enough) or, if "goo" is your fancy, the Rigo Jancsi cake. The latter is a chocolate-whipped cream cake that is pure ambrosia. And there are buttery coffee cakes, danish (which go by other names, but are basically Hungarian-accented danish), decorated cakes, and some marvelous pies. Everything tastes homemade and reflects the experience of a shop that has been in business since 1947. But always, always, the main drawing card is the strudel—crisp yet delicate, fluffy and not soggy. And while everyone has had apple strudel, here's a chance to try some of the more exotic strudel flavors. Tell Mr. Lichtman I sent you.

LUNG FONG CHINESE BAKERY

41 Mott St
233-7447
Daily: 8 a.m.-9 p.m.

English is definitely a foreign language here, but you can place your order simply by pointing to the authentic Chinese cookies and pastries of your choice. Molded cookies are in abundance, as are rice cakes and lots of pastries covered with sesame or lotus seeds—or perhaps it's something else. The truth is, these are not your everyday fortune cookies; they defy description. Nevertheless, it's all authentic, and none of it is ordinary. *Don't* ask how anything tastes, because Lung Fung's explanation is liable to be: "Is good. Is good." And it is.

MARY ELIZABETH
6 E 37th St
683-3018
Mon-Sat: 7-4

Why do proprietors of pastry shops seem to feel that novel names are *de rigueur?* Whatever the answer, there seems to be a correlation between shops with women's names that bear no relationship to their owners and the best baked goods in the business. Mary Elizabeth is really a very masculine restaurant, grill, bar, bakery, and coffee shop. Despite all the extraneous activities, the shop comes in first in the homemade baked goods area, and has even beaten specialty bakeries in taste tests. John Scotto proudly presides over homemade bread, crullers, cookies, cakes, pies, and magnificent doughnuts. All of them are served to customers at the restaurant, but you can also order them to take out. Above all, the doughnuts are the best. Once a Mary Elizabeth product has been tasted, a new fan is born.

MISS GRIMBLE
305 Columbus Ave (bet 74th and 75th St)
362-5531
Tues-Sun: 11-11

Miss Grimble is run by transplanted Texan Sylvia Hirsch, and she just may produce some of the most delicious cheesecakes this side of the Rio Grande. The two house specialties are cheesecake and pecan pie. The cheesecake comes in 7″, 10″, and 12″ sizes, and in vanilla, chocolate marble, chocolate, lemon, orange, rum, raspberry, marble, apricot, strawberry, hazelnut (don't miss it!), and coconut. Concerns about calories, cash, and cholesterol must be left at home. There are also Grimbletcrtes (in orange, rum with pineapple and coconut, or strawberry) and several European specialties. The latter include French chocolate truffles, buche de noel, Sacher torte, and praline au chocolat mocha cake. Miss Grimble is also a restaurant, serving American cuisine.

MOISHE'S BAKERY
181 E Houston St (bet Orchard and Allen St)
475-9624
Sun-Thurs: 7-6; Fri: 7-4

115 Second Ave
505-8555
Sun-Thurs: 7 a.m.-9 p.m.; Fri: 7-5

Jewish bakery specials are legendary, and they are done to perfection at Moishe's. The cornbread is prepared exactly as it was in the old country and as it should be now. The pumpernickel is dark and moist, and the ryes are, well, simply scrumptious. The house specialty is the black Russian pumpernickel, which probably cannot be bested in an old-fashioned bakery in Russia, but by no means should you ignore the cakes and pies. Owners Mordechai and Hymie are charming and eager to please, and they may just have one of the best bakeries in the city. There is the usual complement of bagels, bialys, cakes, and pastries, but most of all try the challah on Thursday and Friday. Moishe produces the best. And the chocolate layer cakes are superb.

PALERMO BAKERY
213 First Ave (bet 12th and 13th St)
254-4139
Mon-Sat: 7-7; Sun: 7-2

A made-in-the-back specialty is featured here each day. One of the best is the pork bread—huge slices of pork inside a delicate dough, topped with a crackling crust. Palermo Bakery routinely produces bread in the most unusual and contorted shapes you can imagine, and they taste wonderful.

PARISI BAKERY
198 Mott St (bet Spring and Kenmare St)
226-6378
Mon-Sat: 8-6; Sun: 8-midnight

The bread's always hot here, because this establishment supplies bread to nearly every restaurant in the neighborhood, as well as uptown eateries. The selection is almost completely French and Italian, but there are many variations, including Sicilian bread in the shapes of dog bones, snakes, eyeglasses, and a lard bread peppered with ham, salami, and roast pork. These exotic loaves are sold for reasonable prices. The cost of a two-foot, one-pound loaf of Italian bread beats the price of the commercial stuff sold in supermarkets.

PATISSERIE LANCIANI
271 W Fourth St (bet Perry and W 11th St)
929-0739

177 Prince St (between Thompson and Sullivan St)
477-2788
Tues-Thurs: 8-11; Fri, Sat: 8-midnight; Sun: 8 a.m.-9 p.m.

Patisserie Lanciani isn't terribly impressive; in fact, it seems a bit pretentious until you get a look at the cakes and pastries. After that sight, even the extensive credentials of Joseph and Madeline Lanciani are superfluous. For those who haven't yet observed the delicacies at Patisserie Lanciani, a quick resumé is in order. For starters, you have certainly seen Joseph's work. While a chief pastry chef at the Plaza (enough of a recommendation in itself), he was the creator of Julie Nixon's wedding cake. He is also a certified expert in spun-sugar creations, and is probably the best pastry baker in the city. Results of this experience can now be sampled firsthand in Lanciani's own shop. The cakes, pastries, tortes, mousses, and breads defy description, and for the impatient, there are tables.

POSEIDON GREEK BAKERY
629 Ninth Ave (bet 44th and 45th St)
757-6173
Tues-Sat: 9-7; Sun: 10-4

Poseidon is a family-run bakery that endlessly and effortlessly produces Greek specialties sought by both Greek nationals and those who wish they were. There's tremendous pride here. When a customer peers over the counter and asks, "What is that?" what usually ensues is a long description, and sometimes even an invitation to take a taste. There is homemade baklava, kataif, trigona, tiropita (cheese pie), spanakopita (spinach pie), sargli, and phyllo. Poseidon was founded in 1922 by super Greek baker Demetrios Anagnostou. Today it is still run by his family—his grandsons, John and Anthony Fable—to the same exacting standards. Poseidon's specialty is phyllo pastry (theirs is world renowned), and any and all Greek specialties using phyllo are turned out here year-round.

STREIT MATZOTH COMPANY
150 Rivington St
475-7000
Sun-Thurs: 8-5

Matzoth, for the uninitiated, is a thin, waferlike square cracker that historically came out of Egypt with Moses and the children of Israel when they had to flee so swiftly that there was no time to let the bread rise. Through the years, matzoth was restricted to the time around Passover, and even when matzoth production became automated, business shut down for a good deal of the year. But not today and not in New York. In a small building with a Puerto Rican mural stretching the length of one side, Streit's Matzoth factory pours forth matzoth throughout the year, pausing only for Saturday, Jewish holidays, and time to clean the machines. Matzoth is a year-round business, supported in part by traditional Jews, but even more so by a cracker-loving public who have discovered that matzoth is pure flour and water, has no preservatives, salt or sugar, and can be consumed on the strictest health diets. The Streit's factory not only gives a peek at the actual production—which is fascinating because it is both mechanized and extremely primitive at the same time—it also sells matzoth to the general public. It is baked in enormous thin sheets that are later broken up.

The matzoth is so fresh that if you ask for a batch that happens to be baking at the moment, they will often break if off the production line for you.

A SWEET PLACE
301 E 91st St (bet First and Second Ave)
860-7100
Daily: 8-6

Elaine Bornstein, A Sweet Place's owner and chef, avows that she "gave blood, sweat, and tears to my wonderful little shop and have seen it grow into something grand." Sentiment aside, it's not Bornstein's personal input that has turned the originally wholesale-only shop into the best sweet shop on the Upper East Side for retail buyers. Not a little bit of the credit goes to super cakes, pies, and desserts and the aromas that drew passers-by into the shop, while Bornstein and company were preparing cherry almond bocco, chocolate rum comfort, pecan pie, chocolate and cheesecake, apple pie, linzertorte, and the like for some of the best restaurants and catering establishments in town. A few years ago, A Sweet Place was created as the retail arm of the previous wholesale operation to accommodate all the neighborhood noses pressed to the glass. But the wonder is still fresh. Customers are floored by the scrumptious confections, and Bornstein is more than a little in awe of the attitude and power of her clientele, who turned her blood, sweat, and tears into the best sweet pastry spot in the neighborhood.

VESUVIO BAKERY
160 Prince St (bet Broadway and Thompson St)
925-8248
Mon-Sat: 7-7

Tony Dapolito was born, bred (no pun intended), and nurtured in the family store in SoHo. In all that time, the family's expertise in baking grew along with the bakery's claim to fame as SoHo's common green. When not manning the ovens, Tony serves stints on the community planning board, and if not involved in either of those activities, he's dispersing SoHo lore to a customer. Visitors who are unaware of Dapolito's status (it doesn't remain a secret long) come for the bread, biscuits, and rolls. They all have a reputation that reaches far beyond SoHo. After all, it isn't every commercial bakery that eschews sugar, shortening, and preservatives and still manages to produce the tastiest Italian bread around. Actually, that too reflects the neighborhood. Try the biscotti, the pepper biscuits, or the whole wheat brick-oven-baked bread. And if you've *any* questions about the bread or SoHo, ask Tony. If there's one man who knows it all, it's Tony Dapolito. He can supply you with a slice of SoHo life, so to speak.

WELL-BRED LOAF
1612 Third Ave (at 90th St)
534-6951
Mon-Fri: 8-8; Sat: 9:30-5: Sun: 9-3

When a bakery has a pun for a name and a motto that says, "Better than home-baked," you know that the business has to be a homey, warm place. And it is. Steve Caccavo got started in the bakery business several years ago by turning out home-baked brownies and cookies for wholesale orders. (His customers include Balducci's Ice Cream Parlor.) The Well-Bred Loaf uses only natural ingredients and spurns preservatives. Steve says, "The recipes we use are those we use at home." In 1977, tired of trying to supply both wholesale and retail customers, Caccavo opened the Well-Bred Loaf on St. Patrick's Day. "That's why we make a delicious Irish soda bread," says Steve. The entire atmosphere maintains the small, homey touch (recipes are credited to whomever created them), and more important, the results truly are delicious. Lines form early for a jar of Judy's Apricot-Cranberry Conserve. (His parner is his ex-wife Judy Glicken.) Though Caccavo touts his cookies, his brownies are close to perfect. Steve personally likes the banana and carrot cakes, but he was able to agree with a customer that the pies ("We peel the apples") are equally good. Their chocolate chip cookies and blondies are some of the best in New York.

YONAH SCHIMMEL
137 E Houston St
477-2858
Daily: 8-6

1275 Lexington Ave
(bet 85th and 85th St)
722-4049
Daily: 8-7

Yonah Schimmel has been selling the perfect knish for so long that his name is legendary, and national magazines have written stories about him. In the days when immigrants were flocking to the East Side, he was already dispensing knishes among the pushcarts. A Yonah Schimmel knish is still a totally unique experience. They do not, incidentally, look or taste anything like the mass-produced things sold in supermarkets, at lunch stands, or at New York ball games. A Yonah Schimmel knish has a very thin, flaky crust—almost like strudel dough—surrounding a hot, moist filling. The best-selling filling is potato, but there is also kasha (buckwheat), spinach, and a half-dozen others, not including meat. Yonah Schimmel is strictly kosher and vegetarian. No two knishes come out exactly alike since each is handmade, but if a particular batch is not up to par, the man behind the counter won't sell it.

Beverages

New York has a bottle law which requires a deposit on all bottles and cans containing soft drinks. Supermarkets have become quite defensive about accepting bottles not sold in their store, and most would just as soon that you forget to return the bottle. In any event, that deposit adds to the cost of the soda, but the city's prices are still pretty cheap compared to the rest of the country. Price wars at the supermarket make them even better, and most of the time they beat the distribution centers. Also, keep an eye peeled for local brands such as C & C and Vintage, which are cheaper than brand names.

91st STREET BEVERAGE CENTER
1770 Second Ave
427-4972
Mon-Sat: 9-6

The 91st Street Beverage Center, run by Hector Borrero, mainly supplies wholesalers and large retail orders, but he's not adverse to serving retail customers. The only reason most orders aren't small is because once you've shlepped up there, you might as well take advantage of the good discount. He guarantees that his prices are at least as low as any supermarket. This doesn't include beverages that are "on sale"— a gimmick sponsored by the bottling companies. Because Borrero's store already offers merchandise at a discount, he doesn't have sales.

SERRANO
351 W 14th St (near Ninth Ave)
243-6559
Mon-Sat: 9-5

Serrano is a wholesale beer and soda distributor, and while they happily deal with retail customers, trust them when they tell you that most of their business is wholesale. For example, there is free delivery. The only hitch is that it's only available to customers who order 25 cases at a time. But that doesn't mean that those who shop in person aren't afforded the same excellent prices and service. For those in the neighborhood, Serrano should be a must for all soda and beer needs. Outside the area, unless there's a great love of lugging bottles, Serrano will probably only be a good bet for parties—large, thirsty parties.

Candy

A personal note (in case it wasn't obvious before): I am a chocolate fanatic. There isn't a chocolate shop in the city I haven't tried. These are the very, very best.

ANDRAS KRON CHOCOLATIER

1226 Madison Ave (bet 88th and 89th St)
289-1851
Mon-Sat: 10-6; Tues-Fri (summer): 10-6

Chocolate Magazine rated Andras' truffles the best in the world. Think of the fun involved in trying to prove them wrong. Andras' unique chocolate molded items taste as good as they look, and with over 200 different molds (and more available on special order), they are the makings of very unique gift baskets. Andras also caters parties with specialty items, and the molded chocolates make great gifts. But don't forget those truffles—I couldn't dispute *Chocolate Magazine.*

CHOCOLATERIE CORNÉ TOISON D'OR

Fifth Ave at 56th St (Trump Tower)
308-4060
Mon-Sat: 10-6:30; Sun: noon-5

Chocolaterie Corné Toison d'Or has been rated as one of the finest in Europe for the nearly 50 years of its existence. In part, that is due to its use of all natural ingredients, in part to the timeliness of its products (Valentine hearts give way to Easter eggs), and in part to 50 different variations on the chocolate theme. But above all, it is known for being delicious. Alvan Lewis imported the Chocolaterie Corné Toison d'Or concept to North America. All of its products are produced in Belgium and imported from Brussels weekly. A typical sampling includes sculptured chocolate shells, cream-blended fillings (which, made without preservatives, will keep for up to three weeks), nut pastes and creme fraiche in vanilla and coffee flavors. All of it is aimed at gourmet chocolate connoisseurs. Apparently, such a market exists, and in America, it's located on Fifth Avenue in the ritzy Trump Tower. How's that for snob appeal?

CHOCOLATES BY M

61 W 62nd St (bet Columbus Ave and Broadway)
307-0777
Mon-Sat: 10:30-7:30; Sun: noon-6

Are you ready for yet another chocolate shop in New York? Apparently, Maimie Lee (the "M") believes you are. The Lincoln Center crowd is certainly ready, because business has been booming ever since Chocolates by M opened. Actually, Ms. M. is not very daring. Europeans have long munched chocolates at concerts, and the West Side is notably short of fine chocolate shops. So much of the stock is geared for instant munching, with tidbits sold by the piece and pound as well as gift boxed. The prices will also munch a hole in your wallet, though Lee insists that a $5 bag should get you through the "Mostly Mozart" concert series. But the purchase price goes to hand-dipped pure chocolate made of only the finest ingredients made fresh daily. For a casual evening, try the chocolate-covered fortune cookie. They're reasonably priced and delicious. For the knock-their-socks-off gift, through, why not go all out and order a box of praline truffles packaged in a Limoges gift box? You couldn't do more.

CHOCOLATE PHOTOS
200 W 57th St
977-4340, 1-800-262-0024
Mon-Fri: 9-6

Victor Syrmis is a successful child psychologist in the city. Perhaps because of his profession, he has a knack for picking out whimsical gifts. So, once when he went shopping for a truly unique chocolate gift for friends, he ended up starting a business for himself. That business is Chocolate Photos, founded on the premise that virtually anything can be created in chocolate and that nothing is as personal as one's own picture. Syrmis (actually his employees) can use a black-and-white photo portrait as a reference and etch the image in chocolate. The process takes about three weeks and isn't cheap, but the end results are 24 pieces of personalized chocolate (complete with inscribed name) and an etching (the one used for imprinting the chocolate) suitable for framing. For those who are adverse to consuming images of their own faces (and I must confess I'm one), Chocolate Photos has a dozen alternative subjects in stock; they also have the ability to transcribe 24-letter messages. I received chocolate covers of the second edition of this guidebook, so I can tell you from personal experience that Dr. Syrmis has hit upon a super gift. They make great calling cards!

ECONOMY CANDY
131 Essex St (at Rivington St)
254-1531
Sun-Fri: 8-5:30

Gourmet store:
108 Rivington St
Daily: 8-5:30

Economy Candy spills its wares over as much of the sidewalk outside its doors as is possible without forcing pedestrains to walk in the gutters. This may be done for lack of space inside, but it's also good for business since a great proportion of their business is spur-of-the-moment purchases. In fact, the shop, with all its jars, bags, and bins, looks as though it's been there forever, and it's hard to imagine that they actually pack it all up every night. But they do. And what they pack up is a magnificent collection of nuts (you must try the cashews), unusual imports, dried fruits, and old-fashioned candies. It doesn't appear terribly appetizing at first glance, but investigation can leave you gazing at one square foot of merchandise for 30 minutes. There's so much crammed into a small area. And the prices are right. Next door at 108 Rivington (Economy Candy is on the corner), they have opened a new gourmet shop carrying the same imported chocolates, halvah, dietetic candies (is there such a thing?), cookies, chocolates, and imported jams. In addition, the gourmet shop carries coffee, spices, mustards, soups, caviars, patés, and other gourmet items.

ELK CANDY COMPANY
240 E 86th St
650-1177
Mon-Sat: 9-6:45; Sun: 11-6:45

Elk Candy Company is a magical kingdom devoted to chocolate in all its glory and assortment. There is a royal selection: every conceivable kind of chocolate can be bought in at least two different forms. It's one sure place to find the old-fashioned European chocolate specialties. Elk Candy is known locally as a haven for the marzipan lover. Think of mazipan in all of the configurations of your childhood fantasies, and you'll find it here. If you don't favor marzipan, then sink into the Florentines—thin chocolate layered over cream, fruit, nuts, honey, butter, and who knows what else. If that's not a hit, the little "Cats' Tongues" chocolate bars are bound to be. It's hard to select a favorite, but the most commonly heard comment is "Gee, I haven't had that in *years*."

LE CHOCOLATIER
2 E 61st St (at Fifth Ave, the Pierre Hotel lobby)
371-2252
Mon-Sat: 10-6; Mon-Sat (July and Aug): 12-5

Le Chocolatier used to be synonymous with Heinz Goldschneider, who simultaneously ran his Le Chocolatier chocolate shop and his Mr. Roberts tailor shop from the same location, upstairs on Lexington Avenue and 64th Street. A few years ago, Goldschneider folded both businesses, and Le Chocolatier emerged, after a 10-month absence, in the lobby of the Pierre Hotel, as part of a Chicago-based corporation, sans Goldschneider. The man is missed, if for nothing as much as his personal touch, but Le Chocolatier's chocolates are as good as ever. They are handmade in this country, according to a Swiss formula. Only natural ingredients are used in their creation, and the taste is unique. In addition, Le Chocolatier makes up party trays, gift baskets, and personalized truffle shapes. But Mr. Roberts, where are you?

LE CHOCOLATIER MANON
872 Madison Ave (bet 71st and 72nd St)
288-8088
Mon-Fri: 10-7; Sat: 10-6;
Sun (bet Thanksgiving and Xmas): noon-5

Le Chocolatier Manon offers some of the city's latest enticements in the imported chocolate line. The tiny store doesn't really need much space, since nearly everything offered is handmade in its Belgian offices and imported weekly to the New York store. But not to worry—this trans-Atlantic transport does nothing to diminish the taste of some of the best chocolates in town. The chocolates are made of all-natural ingredients and contain no preservatives. And since the personnel are not busily engaged in production, they devote all of their time to the selling of chocolate. If the weather isn't too warm, they will air-ship the Manon specialties to lucky recipients. I suggest that you sample them here, and then ship them home.

LI-LAC CANDY SHOP
120 Christopher St (at Bleecker St)
242-7374
Sun-Thurs: 10-7:45; Fri, Sat: 10-9:45

For over 60 years, Li-Lac has been *the* source for chocolate in the Village, and a succession of owners in the last few years has not diminished either their reputation or their chocolates, many of which are still based upon the old-time recipes. The most delicious is Li-Lac's own chocolate fudge, which is made fresh every day. If you tire of the chocolate variety, there is also maple walnut, which is every bit as good. But that doesn't scratch the surface. There are pralines, mousses, French rolls, nuts, dried fruits, hand-dipped chocolates, and much more. But come early. Despite the published hours, they tend to close when sold out. Li-Lac also has a branch in Barney's, the men's department store (Seventh Ave at 17th St.)

NEUCHATEL CHOCOLATES

Plaza Hotel
751-7742
Daily: 10-8

Park Avenue Plaza
(55 E 52nd St)
759-1388
Mon-Fri: 10-6

66 Trinity Pl
227-1712
Mon-Fri: 10-6

1369 Sixth Ave
489-9320
Mon-Fri: 10-7; Sat: 10-6

Anyone who doubts that chocolates have become a class act has only to look at Neuchatel's addresses for verification. Those locations are not the stuff of nickel candy bars (is anything?). As if to prove it, Neuchatel offers a discount for orders of over $1,000. (Yes, you read that right.) And it's easy to earn that discount. The chocolates are prepared by hand with natural ingredients for the finest Swiss chocolate from family recipes. The taste has been likened to velvety silk. There are 60 varieties of chocolate, with the house specialty being handmade truffles. But that shouldn't keep anyone from trying the marzipan and the pralines with fruits or nuts. Neuchatel's origins are Swiss, but perhaps its greatest virtue is that there is no pretension of "flown in daily" routines. Rather, the original recipes are re-created afresh in New York. This is one place where the confection is worth every penny.

PLUMBRIDGE

30 E 67th St
744-6640
Mon-Sat: 10-6

Perhaps because it is located on a side street rather than an avenue, or perhaps because its owners, Douglas, Nanette, and Gregory Petrillo, make this a family business, Plumbridge exudes Old World charm. Though one of the oldest confectionary dispensers in the city, Plumbridge has managed to avoid the current ballyhoo of gourmet chocolate shops and to remain the quiet, staid quality shop it has been since 1883. One of the old-time touches is that Petrillo gives out free samples. Where to start? Savor the pecans spiced with brown sugar and cinnamon that pour forth from the back kitchen several times a day. Then ask for a sample of the dragee chocolate, a concoction of every imaginable ingredient buried beneath a dripping layer of semisweet chocolate. The French mocha nuts are similarly draped and just as good. Plumbridge also dispenses truffles, marzipan, orange peel, dessert fruits, and whipped-cream mints. And don't miss the house specialty—steamed, self-stuffed dried fruits. Even a confirmed chocolate lover has to admire that.

TEUSCHER CHOCOLATES OF SWITZERLAND

25 E 61st St (at Madison Ave)
751-8482
Mon-Sat: 10-6

620 Fifth Ave (Rockefeller Center)
246-4416
Mon-Sat: 10-6

If there were an award for the most elegant of the chocolate shops, first prize would have to go to Teuscher's. Theirs are not just chocolates; they're imported works of art. Barnard and Rochelle Bloom, who own these Teuscher stores, import chocolates once a week from Switzerland. And these chocolates do not end up in penny-candy jars or shopping bags, but in the form of ambrosia like truffles, praline chocolates, mints (shaped like sea creatures), and luscious marzipan. Teuscher chocolates are packed into handmade boxes so stunning they grace many a customer's home. The truffles are almost obscenely good. The champagne truffle is as good as any ever tasted, but that tiny dot of champagne cream in the center lifts it to the super class. The same is true of the cocoa, nougat, buttercrunch, muscat, orange, and almond truffles, each of which has its own little surprise. The almond, for instance, has an entire almond at its core. Truffles are the stars here, but Teuscher's aforementioned marzipan, praline chocolates, and mints are of similar quality.

Cheese

ALLEVA DAIRY
188 Grand St (at Mulberry St)
226-7990
Mon-Sat: 8:30-6; Sun: 8:30-2

Alleva, founded in 1892, is the oldest Italian cheese store in America. Fortunately, their cheese isn't as old as the store; it's made fresh daily. The Alleva family has continuously operated the store since its inception, and maintains the same meticulous high standards. The current owners are Irma ("Aunt Irma") Alleva, a daughter of founder Pina Alleva, and her nephew and grandnephew, both named Robert Alleva. They make over 4,000 pounds of fresh cheeses a week: parmigiano, fraschi, manteche, scamoize, and provole affumicale (which is *not* provoloni; that's another cheese entirely). Mozzarella comes in all sorts of shapes and variations, and the ricotta runs out as fast as it appears. Most recently, Alleva expanded with a smoked-meats and cured-meats section and a few choice Italian groceries. But next to the cheese, the prime attraction is still Aunt Irma and her family; and we've rated her baklava the best in the city.

BEN'S CHEESE SHOP
181 E Houston St (bet Allen and Orchard St)
254-8290
Sun-Fri: 8-6

About half of the varieties of cheese sold here are made in the back of the shop. The locals, who are to cheese shops what truck drivers are to roadside diners, swear by the farmer's cheese in any of its forms. Some favorites include the homemade farmer's cheese embedded with strawberries, scallions, raisins, pineapple, and—my personal preferences—almonds and pistachios. If there is a sprinkling ingredient Ben has not thought of, try one of the other cheeses where undoubtedly the missing element can be found. Don't miss the baked farmer's cheese. Ben's also has fresh pasta.

CHEESE OF ALL NATIONS
153 Chambers St (bet W Broadway and Greenwich St)
964-0024 — 732-0752 (shop)
Mon-Fri: 11:30-3 — Mon-Sat: 8-5:30

Cheese is a full-time business here, but Phil Alpert's passion makes it even more than that. Cheese of All Nations is a gastronomic United Nations, a cheese-of-the-month clubhouse, a wholesale supplier to stores and restaurants, a gourmet catering service, a custom cheese-spread manufacturer, and on and on. In short, cheese is a way of life here. The five floors of the shop are constantly engaged in various aspects of cheese production. The store has a worldwide business that for more than 40 years has created, packaged, and shipped more than 1,000 varieties of cheese. That number makes them claim the distinction of having the world's largest selection of cheese, and the sheer magnitude of it all leaves little room for dispute. There are 66 different kinds of cheese spreads that are listed in the free catalog, and prices for the spreads, as well as everything else, are supposed to be among the city's lowest. Be prepared: the place is *always* crowded!

CHEESE UNLIMITED
249 Ninth Ave (at 24th St)
691-1512
Mon-Sat: 9-5

The atmosphere here is very enjoyable, and the selection of bulk cheese is almost uncountable—over 600 varieties of imported and domestic cheese. Each is carefully chronicled and accompanied by a description of its history and taste. The selection is so vast that all nationalities are pretty well represented.

EAST VILLAGE CHEESE
239 E Ninth St (at Second Ave)
477-2601
Mon-Fri: 9-6:45; Sat: 9-5:45

Murray Greenberg ran Murray's Cheese Shop for 37 years. Then he sold the store to his workers and retired. Well retirement wasn't all he thought it would be,so when Greenberg was offered the chance to manage the tiny East Village Cheese, he jumped at the chance. So here he is at this tiny shop in the East Village, which carries an enormous variety of cheeses. Many are superb, and all are cheap (Greenberg prides himself on his ability to buy and sell the most reasonably priced cheeses as a result of his years in the business). What is missing is the exotic and unusual, although with over 100 possibilities, they're not *all* mundane. This after all is the East Village *not* the Upper East Side. But give it a couple of years, and who knows what Greenberg will be selling!

Chinese

Ten years ago, the only place to get authentic Chinese food ingredients was in Chinatown, on Mott or Mulberry streets. Recently though, a love of Chinese food has swept the city. There has also been an influx of Oriental executive families taking up residence in the city and the discovery by health-food lovers that Chinese food is healthy, both in substance and style. As a result, nearly every large supermarket in any neighborhood in the city has fresh Chinese vegetables available. Bean sprouts are sold alongside green beans and peas in the produce section. For the best and largest variety, however, Chinatown is still the definitive market. Try any of the stores on Mulberry or Mott streets. The only variances among the stores are the staff's ability to communicate in English and their receptiveness to "foreigners." The latter is important because the best culinary delights can be achieved with the right guidance.

CHINESE AMERICAN EMPORIUM

14 Pell St
577-8882
Daily: 9:30-9:30

You can't find a more authentic source for Chinese food than this one, not even in Peking, and the proprietors speak English. What's more, unlike some of their competitors, Bill Ng and his staff are happy to explain what some of the more exotic items are, or to give the exact instructions on how to make your favorite takeout dish at home. Located in Chinatown, the store specializes in the ingredients for Szechuan and Hunan food. But there's an ample selection of Korean food, too, and even Japanese and American goods. The latter are mostly ingredients that don't travel well. Nearly everything else in the shop is imported. Ginseng roots, for example, come from China and Korea, and there are so many varieties you'd never be able to count all the different tastes or catalog all the unfamiliar items. In short, this is a great source for really authentic ingredients for Oriental cooking. Prices are great, the food-stuffs perfect, and the personnel helpful.

CHINESE AMERICAN TRADING COMPANY

91 Mulberry St (at Canal St)
267-5224
Daily: 9-8

If an authentic Chinese dinner is on your menu, there may be no better source than this store in Chinatown. Let it be a warning (or a good sign, depending upon your point of view) that Chinese American Trading boasts that 95 percent of their business is conducted with the Chinese community. In any case, there is an open and friendly attitude here and great care is taken to introduce the wide variety of imported Oriental foodstuffs the store carries. Still it's nice to know that the shop is cognizant of the split tradition its name reflects.

FAMILY GARDEN

329 Third Ave
689-1860, 689-1861
Mon-Fri: 11:30 a.m.-11 p.m.; Sat, Sun: 1 p.m.-11 p.m.; closed Thanksgiving

Family Garden is literally that—a family-run and managed Chinese takeout shop on the Upper East Side, which has proved so successful that after 16 years they opened a restaurant under the same name at 1469 York Ave (535-2900). The clamor for the restaurant is proof enough of the quality of Family Garden's kitchen. Though owner-hostess, Nancy Ku, is Taiwanese, the cuisine features Cantonese, Szechuan, and Hunan style takeout and catering. The restaurant introduced Dim Sum to the Upper East Side. In a neighborhood that may be the takeout food capital of the world, surprisingly few quintessential Chinese takeout places exist. The Upper East Side was weaned on gourmet food, and in order to survive, a dinner-to-go source has to offer quality and taste. Family Garden offers that and more. And if turning on the oven is too much effort (or the hotel doesn't have an oven), there's always the restaurant with the same menu.

KAM MAN FOOD PRODUCTS
200 Canal St (bet Mott and Mulberry St)
571-0330
Daily: 9-9

A trip to Kam Man is cheaper than one to China, and there's very little available there that Kam Man doesn't have here. As the largest Oriental grocery store on this coast, even native Chinese will feel at home in this shop, where you can find every possible ingredient for a Chinese meal. Speaking Chinese is not a requirement for shopping at Kam Man—some of the best English in Chinatown is spoken by the people who work here, and the amenities are totally familiar to those who patronize the city's other gourmet delis and supermarkets. The difference is that at Kam Man the shopping carts wheel past produce displays of water chestnuts, bok choy, winter melon, and tofu; grocery displays of pa pao chai (which is really a conglomeration of Chinese vegetables) and 50 other types of delicacies (shark's fin?); and butcher and fish counters offering ducks, sausages, pork dumplings, and shrimp. Desserts and teas (and *more* teas) round out the selection, and the prices for all of this—even American tangerines and oranges—are the least expensive anywhere.

QUON JAN MEAT PRODUCTS
79 Chrystie St (bet Hester and Grand St)
925-5175
Mon-Sat: 10:30-7:30

William Chan, one of Quon Jan's owners, studied Chinese cooking in Hong Kong, and he devoted two years solely to seasoning and cooking barbecued meats. He is just as meticulous with his staff, making sure that his store is the best Chinese barbecue place in the city. And it is. (*The Daily News* concurs.) Although it is just outside of Chinatown, even by the standards of the ever-expanding borders, Oriental is definitely the theme. English is at such a premium that you'd think Chan was still in Hong Kong; most of the business is conducted either in Chinese or sign language. But sign away. Prices are reasonable, and the taste is authentic and delicious. The best seller is the Mandarin duck, but don't overlook the pork, sausages, or roast chicken. They are all equally excellent and exotic.

YAT GAW MIN COMPANY
100 Reade St (bet Church St and W Broadway)
233-7200
Mon-Fri: 9-4; Sat: 9-3

Yat Gaw Min is a noodle manufacturer. It's heavenly to get these noodles straight from the factory when they are so crisp they snap. Try it. They also speak English here.

Coffee, Tea

BELL-BATES
107 W Broadway (corner Reade St)
267-4300
Mon-Fri: 9:30-6; Sat: 11-5

Bell-Bates is a caffeine emporium, specializing in all matters of teas and coffees for the retail customer. Their selection is extensive, and the prices are competitive. Bell-Bates considers itself a complete food center. It stocks health foods, vitamins, nuts, dried fruits, spices, and gourmet food, along with freshly ground coffees and teas. Ask for Mrs. Sayage. She is marvelous.

CAFFE REGGIO
119 MacDougal St
475-9557
Sun-Thurs: 11 a.m.-2 a.m.; Fri, Sat: 11 a.m.-4 a.m.

The owner of Caffe Reggio claims that cappuccino was introduced to this country by a former owner of the same Caffe Reggio. Could be, but this place has other ties with times past. Over 80 pieces of Italian art fill the cafe, and some of them date back to the Renaissance. (The staff will be happy to identify the more important works.) If that doesn't suit you, they'll tell you about the history of the neighborhood. (Louisa May Alcott lived across the street, near the spot where Jo meets the professor in New York, in *Little Women*.) Enough history. This place wouldn't last two minutes unless the food was good, and in the past 60 years, it's only improved. One of the nicest things in the shop is an espresso machine that stands smack in the middle of the room. Hot beverages, teas, and Italian soft drinks are offered on the menu. This isn't the place you want to go to for a seven-course meal, but it's great for a snack. The management encourages you to eat a pastry with your cappuccino. And nobody minds if you spend hours at the table, nursing one cup.

CAFE ROMA
385 Broome St
226-8413
Daily: 8-midnight

Cafe Roma (Eli-Lilla) serves some of the best espresso this side of the Atlantic. Accompanying the espresso are such traditional Italian dishes as spumone, gelati, cremolate, and granite (lemon ice), as well as super pastries and wedding and birthday cakes. This is one of the Little Italy shops that has a deservedly loyal following. Ask for Buddy Zeccardi. He can spell all the Italian food names, which is as much of an accomplishment as knowing what they are!

CHOCK FULL O'NUTS
All over town

At last count, there were over 50 Chock Full O'Nuts shops around town, practically one on every corner. All of them rest on a tradition of being a place where a person can get a fast, filling, warm meal at prices that are downright cheap. But the real attraction is—and always has been—their coffee. Chock Full O'Nuts is such a fine coffee that it is sold in supermarkets. It is sold at the luncheon counters or as a takeout order.

EMPIRE COFFEE AND TEA COMPANY
486 Ninth Ave (bet 37th and 38th St)
564-1460
Mon-Fri: 9-7; Sat: 9-6

Midtown java lovers have all wandered in here at one time or another, recommended by word of mouth. There is an enormous selection of coffees (56 different beans), decaffeinated coffees, teas, and herbs. Because of the aroma and array of the bins, making solo choices is almost impossible. Empire's personnel are very helpful, but perhaps most helpful of all is a perusal of their free mail-order catalog *before* entering the shop. Making a decision in person is almost impossible. Dave Mottel pointed out that fresh coffee beans or tea leaves are available in bulk, along with fresh peanut butter and spices. Everything is sold loose and can be freshly ground—whether tea, coffee beans or peanuts. Empire also has a small section of appliances.

McNULTY'S TEA AND COFFEE COMPANY
109 Christopher St (bet Bleecker and Hudson St)
242-5351
Mon-Sat: 11-11; Sun: 1-7:30

McNulty's has been supplying choosey New Yorkers with their coffees and teas since 1895. Over the years, they have developed a complete line that includes spice and herb teas and coffee blends ground to order. They have a reputation for personalized, gourmet coffee blends, and they work hard to maintain it. However, that reputation is hard on the pocketbook. Of course, a number of their blends are unique, and the personal service is quite valuable. McNulty's aims to please. They maintain an extensive customer coffee-blend file, and they have a new office service.

M. ROHRS
1692 Second Ave (bet 87th and 88th St)
427-8319
Mon-Fri: 10-6:30; Sat: 9-5

Dennis Smith owned a candy store in Manhattan before he bought M. Rohrs, which was established in 1896. The tradeoff of candy for coffee beans was primarily for better working hours, but Smith is still in residence at the store long before it opens and stays long after it closes. Does he use his coffee to keep him awake? He's not telling. But he is willing to expound on the various types of beans and teas that the store stocks. And his guidance is needed. There are hundreds of varieties of tea, coffee, coffee beans, and honey in the store, as well as accessories. While not a coffee shop, it is possible to get a cup of coffee and sample the wares. And incidentally, despite all that coffee, Smith is one of the most relaxed proprietors in the city. So either he doesn't drink coffee or he's right in saying all the studies on caffeine don't amount to a hill of beans.

PORTO RICO IMPORTING COMPANY
201 Bleecker St
477-5421
Mon-Wed: 9:30-7; Thurs-Sat: 9:30-9; Sun: noon-7

In 1907, Peter Longo's family started a small coffee business in the Village. Primarily importers and wholesalers, they were soon being pressured to serve the local community around them, so they opened a small storefront as well. That storefront gained a reputation for having the best and freshest coffee available, and a loyal band of customers patronized it regularly. Since much of the surrounding neighborhood consisted of Village Italians, the Longo family reciprocated the neighborhood loyalty by specializing in Italian espressos and cappuccinos as well as "health" and medicinal teas. Dispensed along with such teas are folk remedies and advice to help mend whatever ails you. The Village store remains true to its tradition, and Peter added a coffee bar. Now it is possible to sit and sip the various coffees while listening to folklore, or while trying to select the best from the bins. A hint: the inexpensive house blends are every bit as good as some of the more expensive coffees.

SCHAPIRA COFFEE COMPANY
117 W 10th St
675-3733
Mon-Fri: 9-6:30; Sat: 9-5

Schapira, also known as the Flavor Cup Shop, has been run by the same family for over 75 years. Joel and Karl Schapira, who run the business now, will offer advice on tea or coffee selections to any customer who asks. Many coffee shops disdain tea, but Schapira is fair to connoisseurs of both and is equally knowledgeable in either field. So secure are they in both knowledge and reputation that they will happily send you a mail-order price list and tuck in answers to any questions you might have as well. One hint: in either coffee or tea, try Flavor Cup's own brand. Coffees are roasted every morning on the premises and are available in bulk, in bean form or ground to personal specifications. Tea is sold similarly (in bulk or bags). There are also coffee- and tea-brewing accessories.

Catering, Delis, Food To Go

This is one of the largest sections in this book. Its only rival may be the clothing section, and there is a connection. Both are visibly consumed by the indigenous population in vast hungry gulps. Food to go in New York, as perhaps nowhere else, is a staple of everyday life. There are luxury apartments with miniscule, nonfunctional kitchens, and the denizens of same pride themselves on never having to "eat in." At the very least, it would take a lifetime to eat through all the takeout places and restaurants in New York. The following are the best, and they run the gamut from caterers who operate an open kitchen on the side to gourmet emporiums.

AS YOU LIKE IT
120 Hudson St (at N Moore St,
three blocks south of Canal St)
226-6654
Mon-Fri: 10-7:30; Sat: 10-6;
closed Sat in summer and last two weeks before Labor Day

As You Like It was recommended by the folks at Hudson Envelope, *The New Yorker,* and Shakespearian punsters who thought this title for a takeout food-and-catering shop couldn't be beat. We recommend it for its magnificent salads. How, you ask, can a salad be magnificent? It's a good question, but perhaps the name is apt, since As You Like It strikes just the right chord with its patrons by having the freshest and most unusual ingredients. (Add *New York* magazine's accolades; it pronounced Margaret Hess' chicken salad the best ever.) The menu changes with the season, but samples would include Thai-style lamb (remember this is a *salad*), shrimp and wild rice, curried chicken, and a pasta wedding salad. Don't overlook the similarly exotic main courses or the lauded desserts. Some of the center-stage highlights include the brownies, gingerbread, mincemeat pie soaked in champagne, custom cakes and pies, and a steak-and-kidney pie that transcends all categories and descriptions. As You Like It is located in TriBeCa, which is an up-and-coming, but not exactly thriving hot spot. That As You Like It is a raging success at this location is a sure sign that it is one of the very best. In a few years, when TriBeCa becomes the next trendy neighborhood, you probably won't be able to get inside As You Like It's doors. So try it now!

BALDUCCI'S
424 Sixth Ave (at Ninth St)
673-2600
Mon-Sat: 7 a.m.-8:30 p.m.; Sun: 7-6:30

Balducci's really has everything. It's number one in the Village. There are magnificent breads, fresh spices, pates and caviars, coffees, tortes, magnificent cheeses, and super cookies. They specialize in making up baskets (from gift to steamer size), and a good rule of thumb is that anything that would be found in a food basket can be purchased individually and directly here. This shop has those huge, perfect fruits and vegetables that look too good to be true, all sorts of exotic canned foods, international smoked meats, pastas, and interesting appetizers. Balducci's will make up gift baskets for personal picnics as well: baskets that serve up all the very best Balducci's can offer. Either give manager Joe Doria free rein and await a cornucopia of fruits, cheeses, and even fresh game, or tell him exactly what you want for your ideal dinner. Gourmet gluttons should try for the most elaborate and longest hero sandwiches. Three days' notice is required, but last-minute cravings can be satisfied as well. With a bakery, meat market, grocery, and vegetable stand, how can they *not* have the makings of the perfect meal? Ask to meet Nina Balducci. What a charmer! She has her own section of "must-have" food-related items.

BARNEY GREENGRASS

541 Amsterdam Ave (bet 86th and 87th St)
724-4707
Tues-Sat: 8:30-5:45; Sun: 8:30-4
Closed Passover and first three weeks in Aug

Barney Greengrass' name is synonymous with sturgeon to New Yorkers, which is as it should be for a family business located at the same place since 1929. Barney has been succeeded by his son, Moe, and Moe's son, Gary (daughter-in-law Shirley is there, too), but the same quality of gourmet smoked fish is still sold over the neighborhood counters just as it was in Barney's day. The Greengrasses lay claim to the title of "sturgeon king," and there are few who would dispute the title. While sturgeon is king here, Barney Greengrass has a school of other smoked-fish delicacies as well. (And he could found a school on preparing and selling them.) There is Nova Scotia salmon, belly lox, white fish, caviar, and pickled herring in the fish lines. The dairy-deli line (including vegetable cream cheese, homemade salads and borscht, and a smashing Nova Scotia salmon with scrambled eggs and onions) is world reknown. In fact, because so many customers couldn't wait to get home to unwrap their packages, Greengrass started a restaurant next door. Devotees claim that the Greengrass brunch is the example *par excellence* of what brunch should be. And after all, how could it be otherwise when the kitchen, which is just a step away, has been producing the ideal brunch menu for more than 50 years?

BENNIE'S

321-1/2 Amsterdam Ave (at 75th St)
874-3032

37 Seventh Ave
242-5134

First Ave (at 68th St)
Daily: 8 a.m.-1 a.m.; closing hour is earlier in winter

Bennie's was founded by Dr. Bennie, a Lebanese plastic surgeon, with his partner and compatriot, a pediatrician. The result was so successful that a branch has already been added, and the doctors may never go back to medicine. And while a takeout food business wouldn't usually hold a candle to a medical career, here it's a toss-up. And that is a pun; Bennie's specializes in salads. Those salads are among the best anywhere. Homage is paid to the Lebanese origins with the best tabbouleh in the city (it may also be the cheapest) and a plate that speaks with a definite Mideastern and European accent. And the health aspect is not ignored either. Besides three sensational chicken salads, Bennie's boasts of the biggest selection of vegetarian foods in the neighborhood. A prime example of that is the Muda-dara (a salad of rice, onions, and lentils), and it, too, is reasonably priced and excellent. If you see Dr. Bennie, don't be surprised if he tells you business is healthy. Don't be surprised if he doesn't say anything, though. English is not spoken fluently here, but with all these goodies, who cares?

BREADLINE
22 E 13th St
777-3565
Daily: 10-6

When you hear the word *breadline,* you think of a scraggly group of plain people who would be happy with simple basic foods, right? Well, not at Jean-Michel Savoca's Breadline catering service. Scraggly? With a minimum order of $200, this company will give you an "omelet table, individually prepared with various fillings for box lunches and picnic baskets." Simple basics? How about a choice of 20 appetizers, of which only the artichokes and caviar, mixed cheese board, Swiss roll, and one or two others have English names? Plain? How would you like being told that for a sample, you should try their restaurant—Au Diable Des Lombards—at 64 Rue Des Lombards, Paris! Breadline likes to take complete charge of any gathering they cater. Party planning is really the name of the game—*large* party planning at that. They will run a party anywhere and provide as much (or as little) staffing as required. In addition to food, their services can include planning, color coordination, liquor, rentals (from flatwear to tents), flowers, lighting, music, and personnel. Breadline has been praised in print as the best catering service in the city. It was the caterer for Lena Horne's 65th birthday party and now works in conjunction with Chef Paul Bocusse from Lyon on receptions for such clients as Frank Sinatra. Paine Webber, the Statue of Liberty Foundation, and Chase Manhattan, among others, preferred their galas aboard Breadline's exclusive yacht. I think you can forget the deprived image.

BREMEN HOUSE
220 E 86th St (bet Second and Third Ave)
288-5500
Mon-Sat: 9-8; Sun: 10-6

Bremen House has gotten bigger and better. It used to have the finest in imported foods and German delicatessen; now, it has all that and more. There is a fantastic assortment of German merchandise, including the largest selection of German records in America. Also, there are housewares, gifts, cards, books, and German magazines. The balance of the store is still devoted to esoteric and unique foodstuffs from Europe. The highlight remains the fresh-food counters. The baked goods are unrivaled. Between the salads, gourmet foods, ready-to-go items, German deli, and cheese, you have all the ingredients of an incredible meal at one source. That one-stop shopping advantage hasn't escaped Bremen House, which features picnic baskets ready to go, plus a complete menu of prepared foods for parties, as well as a mail-order menu. A final note: the store is squeaky clean. I've walked in at all hours of the day, every day of the week, and there is always someone cleaning, polishing, or buffing something.

CASUAL GRACE
153 Prince St (bet W Broadway and Thompson St)
673-8994
Mon-Fri: 10-6; Sat, Sun: 11-6

If there's a mayor of SoHo, it's Aggie Markowitz, the co-owner of Casual Grace, as well as Tamala Design with Bagel, the store out of which the catering business operates. Aggie identifies herself as "the one with short dark hair behind the counter," and she is an encyclopedia of SoHo life. Aggie also has an unerring merchant's sense and can tell you which stores are unique, which are rip-offs, and which are "for tourists." To my knowledge, she's never been wrong. Samples of the menu can be had at the store. For the most part, it's fare that can be placed on a bagel, but it doesn't preclude roast chicken or roast pork with Swiss cheese. It just leans toward casual brunchiness. Casual Grace takes these things out of the store and into catered situations. The service lives up to its name and displays great versatility. There is no cuisine they can't ape, though they are happiest with buffets and brunches. Cocktail buffets might feature pate-stuffed mushroom caps, antipasto, prosciutto, smoked mozzarella cheese, or quiche. Luncheon has more of the same, plus roast beef or antipasto platters, while dinner offers pot roast, salmon-crabmeat mousse, or vegetable lasagna. All of it is served elegantly and with enough variety to please any guest.

CAVIARTERIA
29 E 60th St
759-7410, 1-800-221-1020
Mon-Sat: 9-6

The main stock-in-trade here is, of course, caviar. Caviarteria operates out of a small store, which is sufficient since most of the business is via mail, phone orders, or part of a vast import and wholesale network. Most of the latter is directly imported by Caviarteria and then shipped to retailers throughout the country. Because of the wholesale business, prices are as reasonable as caviar prices can be, and quality is of the very best. The staff is incredibly friendly and helpful. They know the subtle differences between caviars and will help the customer select what is best for his or her needs. Anything selected can be shipped on ice anywhere, with a safe delivery guaranteed. Caviarteria also stocks smoked fish, cheese, paté de foie gras, hand-dipped chocolates, Scotch salmon, and other delicacies. Rumor has it that the tiny store stocks more than 2,000 such items. For a small sample, the El Magnifico assortment can be ordered. The customer receives 12 monthly selections of goodies.

CELEBRATIONS
242 E 28th St (bet Second and Third Ave)
684-4070
Mon-Fri: 9-5

Celebrations' credo is that any celebration they handle is the best advertisement for their business. And so, a Celebrations party is a celebration. Part of the new wave of all-inclusive party planners (as opposed to the old-line food caterers who did that and nothing else), these people can handle a party from soup to nuts and well beyond. In addition to catering some of the best and most imaginative tables in town, Celebrations offers design services, service people, and floral and decorative arrangements. They delight in being given a free rein with deciding what goes into other people's mouths, and they work best when they can handle the entire party. This means out-of-town clients have to do little more than dial the phone to get a completely catered affair from start to finish.

CHARLOTTE'S
146 Chambers St (bet Greenwich St and W Broadway)
732-7939
Mon-Fri: 9-5

Charlotte's is a unique business that can be all things to all people—as long as the cuisine is Swedish or French. Its menu can accommodate an impromptu crepe for one or a dinner for 700 at the Hilton. Other food merchants patronize Charlotte's as well: Restaurant Associates, Healthworks, Bloomingdale's, and Le Cirque are just a few of their clients (the list reads like a who's who of gastronomic New York). But none of this celebrity detracts from Charlotte's ability to cater to individual customers. In fact, they delight in tailoring gourmet delights to individual requests. To that end, the retail store exists side by side with the catering and wholesale businesses, and all aim to serve the best of French and Swedish *haute cuisine* in any form desired. So there are canapés, cookies, brioches, and crepes for hors d'oeuvres, as well as main courses and feuilletes (a puff pastry), gourmet fish, fish smoked the Swedish way (in a log house), mousses and sauces for entrees, and more desserts than can be counted. All of it comes, fresh, frozen, partially cooked or ready to eat, and all of it meets Charlotte's exacting standards. Chances are that if you do a lot of dining in the city, you've eaten some of Charlotte's cuisine already. But that doesn't mean you should miss a trip to the source.

CHELSEA FOODS

198 Eighth Ave (at 20th St)
691-3948

113 Greenwich Ave
929-8830

Mon-Fri: 9-9; Sat, Sun: 9-6; closed Sun in July and Aug

The West Side has Zabar's, the Village has Balducci's, SoHo has Dean & DeLuca, and now Chelsea has its own gourmet emporium. Established in 1982. Chelsea Foods is certainly the fastest-rising food outpost in the city. And with good reason! Chelsea's owners are neighborhood residents who combine a love of the area with the experience and skills necessary to run a really first-rate establishment. One is a former restaurant owner with talents in visual presentation. Another served an apprenticeship at Glorious Foods, while the third's talents are said to be a "serene attitude." Who knows which is more important? In any case, within two months of its opening, Chelsea Foods expanded its store, cuisine, and talents. A cafe now serves customers, and the menu includes braciola and platters of meats. Catering is also available. Located where Walter's Meat Market was situated, Chelsea Food's 113 Greenwich site is the newest expansion effort. The store incorporated the best of the Walter's Meat Market gastronomic tradition with the sheer good taste and trendiness of Chelsea Foods. The result is an art-deco interior that spews forth food preparation demonstrations, unique fresh breads, salads, soups, pastas, fruit and vegetables, and a sleek meat counter in homage to Walter's.

CHIRPING CHICKEN

350 Amsterdam Ave (at 77th St)
787-6631
Daily: noon-7

2755 Broadway
865-3133
Daily: noon-10:30

1260 Lexington Ave (at 85th St)
517-9888
Daily: 11-10

Okay, partners, New York would never settle for just the Colonel's brand of chicken. You all know that. So the latest entry in the sweepstakes to make takeout chicken unique is Chirping Chicken. Can't say I care much for the name, but its method (avowed to be the first charcoal-broiled chicken in New York) is excellent. Chickens are available either whole or in half, with the standard cole slaw, potato or macaroni salad on the side. The chicken is broiled in Chirping's own homemade sauce and served with pita. That's got to be a New York touch. Downhome chicken with Mideastern bread? It's good enough to make you sing!

COUNTRY HOST

1435 Lexington Ave (at 93rd St)
876-6525 (store), 722-5499 (catering)
Mon-Sat: 9-7; closed at noon Sat in summer

Since 1972, Linda Deme, her husband, and mother-in-law have been manning the counters, ovens, and chafing dishes at Country Host. Between stints at the sink, one of the three has been maintaining a culinary policy that is among the city's best. Country Host is two businesses. The retail store grew out of a bakery and take-home establishment that the Demes supplemented with tidbits from their own and others' kitchens. The bread, for example, includes Country Host's own Irish soda bread, honey country loaf, or cottage bread, as well as the best European breads of Orwasher's line. The foodstuffs that supplement the Demes' menu testify to their good taste. What they can do, they do better than anyone else. This is one of the best one-stop food emporiums in the city. There are cakes, cookies, pastries, savory pies in the English tradition, quiches, gourmet main dishes of continental cuisine, a menu of soups (hot and cold), roasts, casseroles, and such house specialties as paella and coquille St. Jacques. Groceries include farm-fresh eggs, jams, jellies, honey, and a variety of teas and cheeses. For dessert, try the mousse or rice pudding. If you want full European service, Country Host will supply the equipment and personnel for your dinner, too. You don't even have to leave your house to make the arrangements; they'll deliver telephoned orders. But you should visit the shop at least once.

DEAN & DELUCA

121 Prince St
431-1691
Mon-Sat: 10-7; Sun: 10-6

Remember that this is SoHo, where people are interested in good, nourishing, appealing food, as opposed to cucumber sandwiches. Also, understand that Giorgio DeLuca had a cheese store that served the area for many years. Only then, perhaps, can the cornucopia that is Dean & DeLuca be explained. It has been called the Zabar's of SoHo, and it is an apt description. Both rely on a tantalizing display of gourmet items to lure visitors, but each reflects its own neighborhood. Here, the emphasis is on fresh-roasted coffees, patés, cozy dinners for two, and, of course, Giorgio's cheeses. The latter come in more varieties than can be imagined and, to several of those, Dean & DeLuca adds exclusive processing. (Marinated French goat cheese is an example.) Dean & DeLuca pretends that the neighborhood comes to shop for its staples and that the gourmet items are supposedly for special occasions and tourists, but of course that's not quite true. When faced with an array of patés, fresh fruit tarts, and sausages of every possible nationality, how could anyone walk in and just ask for a box of salt? Indeed, even salt comes in eight varieties. What *does* work is the sheer artistry of the food. Everything from the aromas to the displays is enticing, and anyone who browses here is sure to become a customer. This is a fabulous store, well organized, priced right, with outstanding management and super-courteous people.

DONALD BRUCE WHITE CATERING
159 E 64th St
988-8410
Mon-Fri: 1-5 by appointment

Donald Bruce White, if you are New York-social-page-knowledgeable, is *the* catering establishment in the city—the one that has done about every social occasion, coming-out party, and business dinner of any importance in the last who-knows-how-many years. If you've been lost in the wilds of the rest of the country, the name probably conjures up the vision of an impeccable butler serving the perfect candlelight dinner for two—and you wouldn't be far from the truth. Donald Bruce White has ruled the New York catering scene for so long that all the others are merely contenders. He retains his title because, although his menu constantly changes, his set of standards does not. The precision that the waiters, bartenders, and chefs bring to a White dinner is similar to that of a well-mapped military campaign. Nonetheless, his food is sensational and his prices reasonable. Call and ask for Donald Bruce White (yes, he exists in the flesh). He will happily discuss what he can do for any customer. While he won't tell who his other customers are, you'll know when you read the society pages.

ELLEN'S CAFE
270 Broadway
962-1257
Mon-Fri: 6:30 a.m.-7 p.m.; Sat: 6:30 a.m.-5 p.m.

Ellen's Cafe may sound real homey, but it's very cosmopolitan. (New York's mayor is one of its patrons.) Aside from its location (near City Hall), Ellen's menu has something to do with that. Though the menu is simple, it leans toward the gourmet. And rather than dabbling in a little bit of whatever might please the hundreds of different palates around City Hall, Ellen makes her specialties in depth and with variation. So, quiches come in five variations, and salads are either Niçoise, spinach, or chef. In addition, there are egg, tuna, or shrimp salads, but without the green leaves, it's not the kind of salad you'd expect to see at the local salad bar. But no matter. Ellen's salads can be delivered to your office or to any catered affair. For any occasion, order the aforementioned quiches and salads or variations on that theme with ratatouille, brioche or turkey, ham or roast-beef sandwiches. The menu isn't vast, but what Ellen does, Ellen does well. Just ask the mayor! Incidentally, Ellen is Ellen Sturm, a former "Miss Subways," who was instrumental in holding a Miss Subways reunion in 1983. Nowadays, the still striking Ms. Sturm is showing her talents via the extensive bake shop on the premises. She says the house specialty is pecan and chocolate pecan pie.

FAIRWAY
2127 Broadway (at 74th St)
595-1888
Mon-Fri: 8 a.m.-9:45 p.m.; Sat, Sun: 8 a.m.-8:45 p.m.

One of the locals swears that since the advent of Fairway, she never ventures "all the way up" to Zabar's anymore for produce. While it's hard to believe that a 10-block area could be considered such a trek, or that said area could support two such stores, Fairway seems to be making the unbelievable quite likely. Originally a fruit and vegetable purveyor, Fairway was never ordinary. The store maintains its own Long Island farm, the better to ensure getting the very finest fruits and vegetables for its clientele. When the farm is dormant or an item is not indigenous to Long Island, Fairway develops personal relationships with produce dealers who can meet its standards. In recent years, the produce line has been expanded. Fairway now carries a full line of cheese, appetizers, delicatessen, bakery products, coffee, and gourmet items. Many of the cheeses and produce are imported, and Fairway boasts that it has the best selection of both in the city. Certainly, it's worth a visit.

FISHER & LEVY FOOD SHOP
1026 Second Ave (at 54th St)
832-3880
Mon-Fri: 11:30-7; Sat: 10-6;
Sun (Nov-Dec only): noon-5
Mon-Fri (May-Sept): 11:30-8; closed Sat and Sun

The trend toward illustrious names for the proprietors of chic gourmet shops is almost as rampant as the trend for chic gourmet shops. Fisher & Levy qualifies on both counts and merits mention only for the high quality of both criteria. Fisher is Charles Avery Fisher (Chip), as in Avery Fisher of Fisher Electronics and the namesake hall at Lincoln Center. (There are many who don't know that Fisher patris is a real person. Theories on the namesake of Avery Fisher Hall range from two donors; one named Avery, one named Fisher, to both names being acronyms for other things.) Levy is Doug Levy, the erstwhile chef of the Acute Cafe, Dean & Deluca, and the SoHo Charcuterie; in short, some of the trendiest kitchens in town. Together, they are Fisher & Levy, the best corporate caterer in town and one of the best takeout places anywhere. The shiny white store offers everything from a salad counter to packaged goods to food-to-go adequate enough to cater a banquet. It is apparent that corporate catering is their first interest, but the takeout department is at least as varied and deep. The salads are unusual and excellent. Try the tortellini salad, or the duck and Soba or Primavera versions. They, along with the baked goods, are freshly prepared daily. The chocolate Grand Marnier cake is unexcelled. And then there are the sandwiches, brie, Black Forest ham and Passendale, and filet mignon with roasted red peppers and horseradish sauce. But chauvinistic pride forces me to recommend the Oregon cured honey ham. And there's a lot more. So the next time someone tells you Avery Fisher never existed, you can tell them of the whereabouts of this second-generation Avery Fisher.

FINE & SCHAPIRO
138 W 72nd St
877-2874, 877-2721
Sun-Thurs: 8 a.m.-11:30 p.m.; Fri: 8-9;
Sat: 8 a.m.-11:30 a.m.

Ostensibly a kosher delicatessen, Fine & Schapiro offers some of the best dinners for at-home consumption in the city. Perhaps because of their uptown location, perhaps merely as homage to the quality of their foods, they modestly term themselves "the Rolls-Royce of Delicatessens." That description is cited here, only because it is very apt. Fine & Schapiro dispenses a complete line of cold cuts, hot and cold hors d'oeuvres, Chinese delicacies, catering platters, and magnificent sandwiches. Everything that issues from Fine & Schapiro is perfectly cooked and artistically arranged. The sandwiches are masterpieces; it seems a shame to eat them, but the aroma and taste are irresistible.

FRASER MORRIS FINE FOODS
931 Madison Ave (at 74th St)
988-6700
Mon-Sat: 9-6

1264 Third Ave (at 73rd St)
288-7716
Mon-Fri: 8:30-7; Sat: 9-6

Fraser Morris was a gourmet-to-go source eons before the neighborhood knew there was such a thing, and certainly long before the Upper East Side became the center of all such operations. The result was a carriage-trade store offering gourmet delicacies at not inconsiderable prices. With a monopoly on virtually the whole idea, Fraser Morris was the definitive such stop and set the standards for the breed. But the changing neighborhood has wrought changes in Fraser Morris. First, the business moved to a cleaner more modern store, and then, as a sure sign of success, it opened a second branch. These days the gourmet shop still stocks the finest in fruits, cheeses (500 different kinds), candies, chocolates, delicatessen (imported sliced ham and paté de foie gras—not chopped liver!), quiches, canned gourmet items, ice cream, cheesecake, caviar, and coffee beans. You get the idea. There's also a newly enlarged catering department, offering such delicacies as salmon and crown roast of lamb. There's a new bakery department that features fruit tarts, Hungarian pastry, scones, and an international variety of goodies. And finally, for the true gourmet-to-go, there's a sandwich department for impulsive meals. This is an old-time spot that has gracefully and successfully entered the modern age.

GREAT MANHATTAN RIB AND CHICKEN COMPANY
1496 Second Ave (at 78th St)
879-9220
Tues-Sat: 10-10; Sun, Mon: 10-9:30

The Great Manhattan Rib and Chicken Company lives up to its name. The menu is fairly simple; it's basically chicken and ribs, though at dinner they throw in shrimp as well. The chicken is fried or barbecued, and the ribs are, well, ribs. You won't be coming here for roast rack of lamb, but then, no one expects you to. The side dishes are chili beans, potato salad, French fries, or corn muffins, and all of it is as good as it is not fancy. What I like best—next to the taste—is the nomenclature of the items. Yorkville chicken and ribs, Gracie Mansion half chicken (I wouldn't begin to explain *that*), or SoHo shrimp, for example. The downhome feeling here is that of downhome New York! Delivery and takeout are available.

HORN AND HARDART
200 E 42nd St
599-1665
Daily: 6:30 a.m.-10 p.m.

This automat is all that is left of the thriving chain that once boasted 23 automats. It still serves good, nourishing food at the drop of a quarter, dime, or a combination thereof. The kids, of course, shouldn't miss it, and while they are putting coins in slots and watching the food *they* selected appear, the adults can put together a good take-along lunch.

INTERNATIONAL GROCERIES AND MEAT MARKET

529 Ninth Ave (bet 39th and 40th St)
279-5514
Mon-Sat: 8-6

Ninth Avenue is one great wholesale market of international cookery, resplendent with exotic spices. So what would an international market on Ninth Avenue be if not a retailer of exotic spices at wholesale prices? The International Groceries and Meat Market is that, but it is also an excellent source for the rudiments on which to sprinkle the spices. The setup complements the wholesale aspect of the operation. Translated, that means that the neat glass jars that display food in other such places are replaced here by huge, open burlap bags, which may be disconcerting for some. But be willing to sacrifice the frills for some of the best prices in town and the assurance that the turnover is high enough to keep things fresh. The meat market is really something else. It's a gourmet market for aficionados of baby lamb and kid. It comes seasoned, prepared, and even sliced. If you're unsure about what to do with it, ask! Aware that baby lamb and kid are delicacies that many people would just as soon pass up, the butchers here will do anything to win converts. Usually it works, because fresh lamb is indeed a treat.

LA FONTANELLA

1304 Second Ave (bet 68th and 69th St)
988-4778
Mon-Sat: 11-7:30; Sun: 2-7

Nelly de Oppes came from Argentina to open La Fontanella more than 17 years ago. She is a caterer who can take care of any kind of gathering, but she claims that her specialty is intimate, formal dinners. She also likes to do buffets, cocktail parties, afternoon teas, wedding breakfasts, and corporate or club luncheons. The accent on her menu is decidedly Spanish, but she is equally, if not more, expert on French and Italian cuisine. Casseroles, quiches, soups, and empanadas are all available on 24-hour notice for reheating at home. The menu for more formal dinners is extensive and à la carte. La Fontanella doesn't care if you order for two or 2,000. With sufficient advance notice, any combination on the incredible menu can be had. There is even delivery service. Note that La Fontanella is primarily a place for food preparation. The food arrives ready to eat but sans butlers, chefs, candelabra, and chafing dishes. The emphasis is on the food itself, as exemplified by the menu's description of dessert. There are 17 entries for regular desserts, including three kinds of mousses, fruit tarts, and a meringue basket with strawberry and cream fillings. Each is listed by price for four, six, or eight people. The entire menu is too extensive to be given here, but if anything seems to be missing, the host is invited to consult with La Fontanella about other choices. The shop itself is rather nondescript, but the culinary products are positively wondrous. Try a quiche for home consumption (perhaps with a soup, shrimp bisque, or any one of a dozen vegetable dishes) for a good indication of La Fontanella's quality and flavor.

LES TROIS PETITS COCHONS
17 E 13th St (at University Pl)
255-3844
Mon-Sat: 9:30-7

Les Trois Petits Cochons bills itself as "French charcuterie/ catering and wholesale" and operates accordingly. The help is neither friendly nor helpful, but the menu (particularly if one reads French) is self-explanatory, and everything is available by the pound for takeout. Paté is the specialty, and it comes in pheasant, pork with green peppercorns, chicken liver with pistachio and port wine, duck with truffles, and country style. Salads (also sold by the pound) are both interesting and flavorful. Try, for example, the mussels, potato and mayonnaise salad, or the ratatouille—eggplant, zucchini, onions, tomatoes, and red and green peppers. The kitchen will also make up dinners for parties and for picnics to go, with advance notice. Prices and components do not differ from the regular menu. In addition to the paté and the salads, there are excellent French dishes (again sold by the pound) for main courses, and very good quiches. For dessert, try the mousse au chocolat or the creme au caramel. All these delicacies can be ordered for parties, and there is a catering service.

LINDA KAYE'S BIRTHDAYBAKERS, PARTYMAKERS
195 E 76th St (bet Lexington and Third Ave)
288-7112
Mon-Fri: 10-6 by appointment; parties daily

Once upon a time, Linda Kaye hired a baker to entertain at her daughter's sixth birthday party. The guests had such a great time baking the birthday cake that Kaye was soon deluged with calls asking how to hire the baker for their own parties. And once that was done often enough, Kaye was asked for other great ideas for kids' birthday parties. As a mother, she knew immediately that the perfect ingredients for a kid's party had to be one that was perfectly orchestrated (for the parents) and entertaining (for the kids). And so Birthdaybakers, Partymakers was born, and Kaye's innovations continue to keep it at the forefront of birthday-party planners. The basic ideal is still in showcasing of artist bakers who will teach partygoers how to bake and cook as part of the party's entertainment. (Cakes for more mature parties can include dancing girls who pop out from beneath the first edible layer.) The Birthdaybakers party includes everything from the invitations to the loot bags, and Linda Kaye has outfitted a "party room" complete with fireplace and its own kitchen and sound system as a place to use for all manner of parties. But children are nothing if not fickle, so for those crowds who've already baked a cake with Birthdaybakers, there are variations on the theme (robots, clowns, sleep-overs) or entirely new themes that might include bowling, ice skating, roller skating, disco dancing, gymnastics, and softball. And Birthdaybakers has grown up as well. They now do corporate catering and party planning, site location, and press parties.

LORENZO AND MARIA'S KITCHEN
1418 Third Ave (bet 80th and 81st St)
794-1080
Mon-Sat: 9-8

Lorenzo and Maria's Kitchen could belong to any good caterer who could prepare gourmet dishes in low-sodium, vegetarian, Italian or nouvelle cuisine in vast numbers. But since most people don't know anyone like that, Lorenzo and Maria are growing by leaps and bounds. They can do all this and more. Indeed, the menu is almost unlimited. Hors d'oeuvres come hot and cold and with a good 15 varieties within that classification. Entrees made of prime fish, meats, and vegetables form a very long list on which the most mundane items are Yankee pot roast and old-fashioned hamburgers. The accent is Italian, but it doesn't preclude Japanese tempura, Chinese egg rolls, or whole roast suckling pig, Hawaiian style. All of it—from the pimento and anchovy roulade to the whole roast baby lamb to the Peking duck in orange sauce—is prepared for home serving and consumption. They prefer advance notice, but often little miracles are performed with same-day orders. Be warned: they can be very unpleasant.

MANGIA
54 W 56th St (bet Fifth and Sixth Ave)
582-3061
Mon-Fri: 8-7; Sat: 10-6

37 W 46th St (second floor)
869-0404
Mon-Fri: 10-3

Joanna Cottrell and Sasha Muniak are a husband-and-wife team of artists. Joanna worked with food, and Sasha played the violin. Together, they became Mangia, which just may be the best, most epicurean gourmet takeout place on the island of Manhattan. And that's saying a lot. Joanna suggests using Mangia's wares to stock a picnic in Central Park (fortunately, you won't have to carry the brimming basket too far) or to take a couple of meals aboard an airplane to offset airfare. If it's a trans-Atlantic flight, many of the ingredients in your lunch might be on the return trip. Cheeses are flown in weekly from France, Italy, and England. Baked goods are homemade, and are English and Colonial in style. There are more scones, Dundee cakes, and patés than can be counted, and all sandwiches are made with sourdough breads. The fresh salads, like everything else in the store, are brought in or made in the shop daily. Mangia is a joy. It's a super source for an impromptu picnic, and even if it's the middle of a blizzard, Mangia will deliver a $10 minimum order. Mangia is so popular at lunchtime that the 46th Street branch was opened just to accommodate the overflow. There is talk of them expanding to full-time.

M. SCHACHT OF SECOND AVENUE GOURMET DELI

99 Second Ave (at Sixth St)
420-8219
Sun-Fri: 8 a.m.-11:30 p.m.; Sat: 8 a.m.-1:30 a.m.

Aggie Markowitz, part owner of Casual Grace Catering, says that if she were ever on the way to an affair and accidentally dropped the food, she would duck into Schacht's for the replacements. That's heady praise for a food purveyor, and all the more so for a self-professed "old-time Lower East Side appetizing store," which is almost totally unknown outside the neighborhood or among noncaterers. What merits it? Without a doubt, some of the best smoked fish anywhere. But here it is served New York style. The emphasis is on salmon, gourmet deli, and any elegant fish. Schacht's slices it, platters it, smokes it, caters it, and even ships it worldwide. A really unique aspect of the business is a Scotch salmon presented on a board with a knife and instructions for slicing. It makes an impressive gift and a mouth-watering centerpiece. Those lucky enough to be able to drop in on Schacht's can sample all matter of fish, as well as cheeses, caviar, and gourmet delicatessen meat. And all that flavor has finally inspired a takeout counter that serves hot food for on-the-spot consumption.

NEUMAN AND BOGDONOFF

1385 Third Ave (bet 78th and 79th St)
861-0303
Mon-Fri: 8:30-8; Sat: 8:30-7; closed Sat in Aug

Neuman is Paul Neuman, the son of Rosedale Fish Market's owner, and Bogdonoff is Paul's wife, Stacy Bogdonoff. Together, they have married the showpiece salads that distinguished Rosedale from being just another fish store to other elegant dishes, and they've created a stylish and trendy catering firm. With a fresh wholesale source for seafood, the menu frankly admits a bias to fish and fish dishes. So, there's shrimp mousse and smoked trout and some of the best seafood salads in the city. (If you can't get down to Neuman and Bogdonoff, Paul still makes it for the Rosedale store.) But where Rosedale is a fish market cum takeout salad spot, Neuman and Bogdonoff is a caterer with a specialty in seafood. So, the lobster can be accompanied by Cornish hens, ribs, or Paul's special citrus chicken. And vegetarians can pick from a half-dozen vegetable salads or a roasted eggplant in a yummy sauce. In fact, the sauces deserve their own mention. Any fish store maintains a good stock recipe, and Rosedale is no exception. At Neuman and Bogdonoff, stocks of both fish and beef can be purchased as a meal.

PETAK'S
1244 Madison Ave (bet 89th and 90th St)
722-7711
Daily: 7:30 a.m.-8 p.m.

Richard and Robert Petak, third-generation cousins of a family that has owned appetizing businesses in the South Bronx and later New Jersey, have now made the leap to New York, offering the first "appy shop" the Carnegie Hill neighborhood has had in a long time. (As housing has gotten scarcer, Carnegie Hill has emerged as a prime neighborhood. Ten years ago, it was the outskirts of Spanish Harlem.) In any event, no neighborhood could be assessed as truly having arrived without a gourmet takeout shop, and now Petak's (both corporately and personally) fills that need. So there are the "appy" standbys, such as salads, corned beef, pastrami, smoked fish, and all sorts of takeout foods. The store offers full catering or quarter-pound containers of potato salad, as well as gift baskets, picnic hampers, and box lunches. And don't forget the sesame snow peas, baked salmon salad, cheeses, vinegars, oils, preserves, breads, and other staples of gourmet food emporiums. In short, Petak's prepares food as mother never served it, unless mother was a patron of Petak's in the South Bronx or Fairlawn, New Jersey. Incidentally, Marion Burros of *The New York Times* lives nearby, and she personally recommends the asparagus with prosciutto, creamy chicken salad, and the noodle pudding.

PITARIA
230 Thompson St (at Bleecker and W Third St)
473-8847
Daily: 10 a.m.-11 p.m.

Pita, as you know (unless you're from outer Mongolia), is the flat Mideastern bread that looks like a frisbee with a pocket that can be stuffed with almost anything. When it first made its appearance in New York, it was most conventionally stuffed with falafel and salad. But when falafel (and the pita) began to become such common fare that it was sold from carts in midtown Manhattan, pita came into its own. Now it's used everywhere, from vegetarian restaurants to delicatessens. Indeed, entire bakeries have been formed to sell pita. The Pitaria is owned and run by people who cut their teeth on pita in their native lands. They make their own, which is worlds apart from that of the pushcarts, but they have conceded to New York style and stuff it with almost anything. True aficionados buy it fresh and pristine, but don't rule out the Pitaria for a quick, filling meal.

RUSS & DAUGHTERS
179 E Houston St
475-4880
Daily: 8-7

A family business for several generations, Russ & Daughters has been a renowned New York shop since it first opened its doors. There are nuts, dried fruits, paté de foie gras, lake sturgeon, pickled herring, Gaspe salmon sliced and replaced on the skin, and a number of fancy fish dishes, including caviar, smoked fish, sable, and herring. Russ & Daughters has a reputation for serving only the very best. Caviar alone comes in five different varieties, all of which are guaranteed to be sold at the lowest prices. They sell both wholesale and over the counter, and many a Lower East Side shopping trip ends with a stop at Russ & Daughters. Their chocolates are premium quality. They also ship anywhere. And be sure to say hello to Ann and Mark Federman (she is a Russ Daughter); they are super people. If I were to give a five-star rating, this would qualify. The store is clean, high quality, and friendly—what more could you ask?

SARGE'S
548 Third Ave (bet 36th and 37th St)
679-0442
Daily: 24 hours

It ain't fancy, but Sarge's could feed an army. The menu leans toward the burping school of delicatessen, but there's much to be said for the taste, quality, and price. Sarge's can cater everything from a hot dog for takeout to a hot or cold buffet for almost any number of people. Prices are gauged by the amount of people served and by what is served, but there are several package deals, and all of them are remarkably reasonable. Even one of the more expensive buffets—the deluxe smoked-fish version—only runs to about $15 per person, and that includes the cream cheese and bagels, as well as sturgeon, sable, and stuffed smoked whitefish. Sarge's also caters deli and has an excellent selection of cold hors d'oeuvres platters that offer everything from canapes of caviar, sturgeon, and Nova Scotia salmon to shrimp cocktails. And to make the party complete, Sarge's can supply serving pieces, condiments, and serving staff. My favorite is the guy who slices hot pastrami in front of the guests. The carver, cutting board, knife, pastrami, warming oven, and table can all be obtained from Sarge's. The army never had it so good!

SCHALLER & WEBER
1654 Second Ave (bet 85th and 86th St)
879-3047
Mon-Fri: 9-6; Sat: 8-6

Once you've been in this store, the image will stay with you for a long time, because of the sheer magnitude of row after row of cold cuts on display and because, suddenly, the Schaller & Weber trucks seem to be everywhere. The store is simply incredible. It is a Babes in Toyland for delicatessen lovers, and there is not a wall or a nook that is not covered with an assortment of deli meat. They hang from hooks on the walls, are heaped beside scales, and are stacked in the refrigerated display cases. Besides a line of delicatessen items so complete it is hard to believe one store could assemble it, Schaller & Weber also occasionally stocks game and poultry, and they foolishly claim that they are a regular butcher shop as well. Who would buy meat when you can have cold cuts like this? However, if you have the willpower, try the sausage and pork. They will bake it, prepare it, smoke it, or roll it for you, and that's just the beginning.

SILVER PALATE
274 Columbus Ave (near 73rd St)
799-6340
Mon-Fri: 10:30-9:30; Sat, Sun: 10:30-7:30

There are picnic baskets, and then there are *picnic baskets.* The Silver Palate gourmet gift baskets are of a caliber that has prompted stores like Saks Fifth Avenue to feature them in their own gourmet sections. In New York, one can go to the source and have owners Julee Rosso and Sheila Lukins prepare anything from a light picnic lunch to a full-course meal or their Decadent Box. The basket will be filled with such gourmet specialties as mousses, patés, and croissants, and each item is at its peak of perfection. Take a basket from the Silver Palate, and you can picnic with the best of them! Even those elaborate picnics with wine goblets pale beside a picnic basket of salmon mousse or paté de campagne or smoked filet in Roquefort sauce and a chunk of exotic cheese. They pride themselves on the reputation of their shop, a reputation built on the unique takeout baskets and gift packages. Moreover, Silver

Palate offers superb foodstuffs at unusually good prices. They also have a cookbook and a gourmet line.

TODARO BROTHERS
555 Second Ave (bet 30th and 31st St)
532-0633
Mon-Sat: 7:30 a.m.-8:30 p.m.; Sun: 9-6:30

Don't come here if you're ravenous or on a diet, because Todaro carries the very best in imported and domestic gourmet food. Just about everything here is irresistible and will wreak havoc with pocketbook and diet alike. There are patés, jams, cheeses, sausages, and a half-dozen gourmet items, all of top quality. Todaro even stocks fresh French truffles, a delicacy seldom seen this side of a haughty restaurant. And then there are the chocolates. Lucien Todaro imports the very, very best from Europe. Surprisingly, the best of the best comes not from Switzerland, but London: Prestat truffles. Here's your chance to try them, if you've got any room left over from the other gourmet goodies. *The Daily News* rated Todaro's tuna fish salad the best in the city, and our own survey gave them a top award for heros. When a gourmet shop is the best in mundane efforts such as heros and tuna salad, that should be a good indication of the quality of its more exotic items.

WORD OF MOUTH
1012 Lexington Ave (bet 72nd and 73rd St)
734-9483
Mon-Fri: 10:30-7; Sat: 10:30-6; Sun: 11:30-5:30
Closed Sun in Aug

The history of Word of Mouth is actually the gastronomic history of Manhattan—or at least the Upper East side of it. When Christi Finch (an Oregonian—they pop up everywhere!) and Eileen Weinberg opened their original tiny shop in 1976, they were one of the very first establishments to purvey home-style prepared foods for at-home or picnic use. But success was almost instantaneous, and by 1979 the shop had moved around the corner to larger quarters and become incorporated. Today, they enjoy a reputation as one of the finest sources for pasta, soups, vegetable salads, quiches, baked goods, and specialty meat dishes. The aim is still the same, however. Nothing is catered per se (although Word of Mouth does work with caterers or amateur caterers), and everything is geared for at-home consumption. There is no ethnic orientation, though there are worldwide influences, and the style is still home-style cooking that makes use of the very finest ingredients. As Word of Mouth adds staff, they add staff specialties, but the aim is always to make everything look as though it just came from the customer's kitchen—and that kitchen is the kitchen of an epicurian. Try them. It brings back the old-home flavor.

ZABAR'S

2245 Broadway (at 80th St)
787-2000
Sun-Thurs: 8-7:30; Fri: 8-10; Sat: 8-midnight

What can you say about this New York institution? A place whose reputation is such that even its shopping bags are prized and have been spotted around the world? An appetizing store sure enough of its offerings that it engaged in a caviar price war with Macy's? A brunch source that generates Sunday-morning lines hours before the store opens in a city where Sunday morning doesn't begin before nine a.m.? Or a kitchen-appliances source that introduced the Cuisinart to America and discounted it, to boot? There are probably a thousand Zabar's stories. The smoked salmon aficionados swear by the stuff. Cheese lovers claim the selection of 400 kinds is unrivaled anywhere. And there are those who claim *those* departments don't hold a candle to the appy, deli, fish, candy, chocolate, gourmet, food-to-go, or cooking sections. Zabar's isn't a store; it's a way of life, and nearly everything there is the very best there is.

In a city of superlatives, Zabar's is the biggest in the Big Apple. In a typical week, Zabar's ships one ton of coffee and sells another five tons over the counter. That includes 20 different varieties that go in the same shopping bags as 600 pounds of whitefish salad, three tons (yes, tons) of smoked fish, and ten tons of cheese. Saul Zabar cautions that those figures aren't exact: "We sell another ton of smoked fish in the fall." Downstairs, Zabar's sells virtually every gourmet product. There are 50 varieties of salami and an equal number of sausage, more vinegars and mustards then can be counted, cookies, knishes, croissants, and those incredible amounts of smoked fish. Upstairs is kitchen-appliance and paraphernalia country. Prices and selection are the best in New York

And nothing seems to stop those mobs, which have included the likes of Barbara Streisand, Mick Jagger, Jerry Lewis, Art Garfunkel, and Harry Belafonte (they have charge accounts). They and the thousands of other patrons are proof that it's more than status that makes them plow through the mobs and/or wait for hours for breakfast. And all of this started two doors away, when Louis Zabar (Saul and Stanley's father) leased a fish counter in a grocery store in 1934. (This may explain why Zabar's family members seem to be most proud of the hundred or so varieties of fish.) When Louis died, his sons decided to concentrate on prepared foods and consolidated the by-then-expanded Zabar's into a single emporium. In 1964, the youngest Zabar, Eli, left to open E.A.T. on the East Side, and Murray Klein became the third partner on the West Side. It is Klein who is credited with making Zabar's a legend; before, it was merely the best store in the neighborhood. Now it may well be the best in the world. Even the eventual retirement of the three partners hopefully will not change Zabar's.

Fruits, Vegetables

GREENMARKET

World Trade Center
(Grand Concourse)
Thurs

Southbridge Towers
(bet Beekman and Pearl St)
Sat

Gansevoort St (at Hudson St)
Sat

City Hall (Municipal Bldg S)
Fri

102nd St (at Amsterdam Ave)
Fri

St. Mark's Church (Tenth St and Second Ave)
Tues

137th St (at Seventh Ave)
Tues

Office:
130 E 16th St
477-3220

175th St (at Broadway)
Thurs

67th St (bet First and York Ave)
Sat

87th St (bet First and Second Ave)
Sat

Union Square (at 17th and Broadway)
Wed, Sat

Tompkins Square
(Ninth St and Ave A)
Sat

Independence Plaza N
(at Greenwich and Harrison St)
Wed, Sat

77th St (at Columbus Ave)
Sun

Info: 566-0990

The city sponsors these open-air markets (made famous in John McPhee's fine article in *The New Yorker*) in various city neighborhoods. Since there's no overhead, prices are cheaper than a supermarket's, and the produce is sold fresh from the farms by the farmers who grew it. One of Greenmarket's drawbacks, however, is that there are no stockrooms to supplement the farmers' supply. When the truckbeds are empty, the farmers close shop. So you have to get there early. Another problem is that Greenmarket isn't well organized. But for farm-fresh produce at super prices, you have to put up with a little inconvenience. And it's worth it. These markets are A-1. Most are open from early June through November or December, one or two days a week; call ahead for exact hours.

LA MARQUETA

Park Ave (under the tracks from 110th to 116th St)

Tucked under the train tracks in Harlem, this is one of the most fabulous shopping places in the city. La Marqueta is famous, and the early-morning babble of voices here is proof that its customers are not only the local residents of Spanish Harlem. Although the accent is definitely South American, there is nothing that isn't sold here. Each building contains several individual businesses that hawk whatever is fresh and reasonable that day. Lest you think that means 600 booths of Florida oranges, you should know that each building has a few stalls that provide really exotic produce. Some of the latter include chitlins, collard greens, bread fruit, celery root, plantains, and Jamaican spice bread. If you can surmount the language barrier and show some curiosity, the merchants are eager to share recipes with you. It's a friendly, informal place. Once in a while, a squawking chicken can be seen among the stalls of papayas, mangoes, and peppers.

Gift Baskets

SANDLER'S
140 W 55th St (bet Sixth and Seventh Ave)
245-3112
Tues-Fri: 10-8; Mon: 10-6; Sat, Sun: noon-8
843 Sixth Ave (at 29th St)
279-9779
Mon-Fri: 10-6

The original Sandler's was the shop on Sixth Avenue, and the gift baskets still come from there. The uptown shop is larger, but both are a key source for scrumptious candies, delicacies, and some of the best chocolate chip cookies in New York. But Sandler's is best known for its gift baskets, which are the perfect thing for any number of occasions. Those who lack strong willpower should order by phone, because the store's goodies are overwhelmingly tempting.

Health Foods

COUNTRY LIFE
48 Trinity Pl (at Rector St)
480-9142
244 E 51st (at Third St)
980-1480
Mon-Fri: breakfast 7:30-9:30; lunch 11:30-2:30

Note the hours. Country Life, in the heart of the financial district, is open for a scant five hours a day. But scant only describes the time of operation and certainly not the ample portions, friendly atmosphere, and the excellent quality of the menu. All of it is vegeterian and is available for takeout. The buffet is so extraordinary that many of Country Life's customers are meat eaters who are enamoured of one of the best and most efficient eateries in the area. The only caveat is the time. Don't bother coming after two o'clock. In the words of one of the ladies behind the counter, "even by 1:30, most of the selection is gone." And the first moments after the doors open are reminiscent of feeding time at a zoo. No doubt about it—those people are lined up for *something*.

DOWN TO EARTH

33 Seventh Ave (bet 12th and 13th St)
924-2711
Mon-Fri: 9:30-9:30; Sat: 10-7:30; Sun: 12-6

This is probably the Village's most complete, best-run, and most appealing health-food store—at a price. Down to Earth's prices are sky high. If you can pay them, look over the vitamins, packaged health foods, vegetables, frozen meats, cheeses, and sprouts. All are first quality. A new service is takeout sandwiches. They are quite filling and wholesome.

GOOD EARTH FOODS

1334 First Ave (bet 71st and 72nd St)
472-9055
Mon, Wed, Thurs: 10-7; Tues, Fri: 10-8; Sat: 10-6
182 Amsterdam Ave (at 69th St)
496-1616
Mon, Wed: 10-8; Tues, Thurs, Sat: 9:30-7:30; Sun: noon-5

The Good Earth has the reputation of being the finest and best-stocked health-food store in New York—and one of the most expensive. The very helpful and knowledgeable sales personnel will vehemently deny that they are overpriced, but a quick comparison of prices will show that they are, just as surely as a quick visit will confirm their reputation for having the largest and freshest stock. In addition to their enormous selection, the Good Earth offers free parking and delivery anywhere within the city, which surely is further proof that they are not in the reasonable class. On the other hand, one-stop shopping is best done here. Next door to the First Avenue store, the finest of their wares are given a practical demonstration in their natural-food restaurant, Zucchini. There, too, the food is natural, good—and expensive.

SKINNY DIP GOURMET FOODS

1395 Second Ave (bet 72nd and 73rd St)
570-6926
Mon-Fri: noon-7:30; Sat, Sun: by appointment

Ever wonder how salespeople can stand behind taste-bud-tempting counters, hour after hour, without ever taking a nibble? How is it that pizza stands always have the thinnest help in town? And chocolate counters run the pizza stands a close second! Well, Barbara Haroche of Skinny Dip doesn't mind if the whole world knows her secret. In fact, it's great publicity. Everything in her shop just *looks* fattening; the calories are missing. Skinny Dip has a takeout menu that rivals the town's choicest caterer's. The only difference is that Haroche labels each package for calorie content. Skinny Dip doesn't use artificial sugar, just small amounts of the real thing. There is free delivery, as well as special menus for different diets. None of this, however, comes cheap. But if you need help in sticking to a diet, you know where to go. P.S. Some thoughtful hostesses order meals from Skinny Dip for dieting friends.

Hungarian

H. ROTH & SON/LEKVAR BY THE BARREL

1577 First Ave
734-1110, 535-2322
Tues-Sat: 9-6:30

Here, in the section of New York known as Little Hungary, Roth carries things that are rare even in Budapest. Some of the specialties include Kolbasz sausage, smoked pork fat, potato candy made of glucose, and a strudel so thin you could read a newspaper through it. The house specialty is spices, starting, of course, with paprika. H. Roth and Son is universal enough to offer nearly 200 different kinds of spices from all over the world. There is also a complete line of housewares and a cooking school.

PAPRIKAS WEISS, IMPORTERS

1546 Second Ave
288-6117, 288-6903
Mon-Sat: 9-6

Paprikas Weiss started as a poor immigrant who peddled spices to his neighbors. He began importing them, developed a reputation for the best and freshest in Hungarian condiments, and over the years built a large import-export business that deals as much in prepared foods, gourmet utensils, and imported delicacies as it does in the original condiments. Their free catalog, which is accompanied by glowing testimonials from the city's leading food columnists, makes fascinating reading. There are special pans, preparatory utensils, and ingredients for dishes that I have never heard of! I have only one complaint: the store is too commercial. Paprikas is *big* business, and they make the most of it, both in price and publicity. Some prices are imaginatively high (similar products can be found in local supermarkets for much less), and "authentic" dishes receive publicity that is either unwarranted (the dish is not *that* authentic) or undeserved (even authentically made, it just isn't that good). But Paprikas is worth a visit, if only for picking up their catalog.

Ice Cream

ANGELICA
82 Seventh Ave S (corner of Bleecker St)
620-9622
Sun-Thurs: 12-12; Fri, Sat: 12-2 a.m. (April-Oct);
Sun-Thurs: 12-10:30; Fri, Sat: 12-12 (Nov-March)

A great spot for gelati-style ice cream in New York is Angelica. It ain't cheap—a single scoop can cost as much as a half gallon at the supermarket, and the help is anything but angelic—but the flavor and taste sensation is just this side of heaven. An assortment of interesting flavors are available, and the wealthy (or the gelati fanatics) among us can buy it by the pint. Take Angelica goodies home quickly. It doesn't fare well for more than a few days. It is, you might say, as delicate as an angel. This is also a takeout shop, and there are some tables for light dining. The latter features Angelica's exclusive pastry (either their own or made to order), granita (which is Sicilian-style natural fruit ice), and d'Orsoy candy. There is a nightly dinner served promptly at seven for one seating of 19. Needless to say, the setting is intimate.

CHINATOWN ICE CREAM FACTORY
65 Bayard St (at Mott St)
608-4170
Mon-Thurs: noon-11; Fri-Sun: noon-1 a.m.

Despite its name, ice cream is but a small part of the Chinatown Ice Cream Factory's business. William and Philip Seid also turn out T-shirts (they'll accept mail orders), custom-made cakes, exotic teas (try the papaya and chrysanthemum), and terrific almond cookies. The Seids boast that their ice cream is the best available in "regular Chinese and exotic flavors." Doesn't that intrigue you? Ever tried "regular Chinese" ice cream? It happens to be delicious, and it's certainly different. For a unique treat, try their custom-made cakes or ice cream flavors; both will make your party.

MINTER'S ICE CREAM KITCHEN
551 Hudson St (bet W 11th and Perry St)
242-4879
Pier 17 Pavillion
South Street Seaport
Mon-Fri: 11 a.m.-midnight; Sat: noon-1 a.m.;
Sun: noon-midnight

It was inevitable that New York couldn't take its ice cream straight. First, we had "natural" ice cream with Scandanavian names. Then Chipwich and ice cream were being peddled on street corners like so many chestnuts. Then came gelati, and who knows what's next? Well, Minter's knows. From a tiny ancient-looking shop, Minter's Kitchen dispenses the latest ice cream fad: "mixes." (If you come from Boston, you've had it already. Just don't tell that to New Yorkers.) A mix is the combination of any of 16 ice cream flavors with any number of over 20 assorted candies, cookies, fresh fruits, and nuts. It is kneaded on a marble slab and dispensed as ice cream scoops (large and larger), sundaes, milkshakes, malts, and ice cream soda. They claim that there are over a million possible combinations, and the small store has customers who are attempting to prove it. An innovation on all of this is the new "mud pie," which mixes all of this to personal order for group consumption (at least they *hope* more than one person plans to eat it). Minter's bills itself as a kitchen, however, and there are country crafts and gifts for sale. They also serve breakfast. If you're trying to work your way through a million combinations, I suppose you have to start early in the morning.

NEEDLHEIMER'S CAFE
262 W 44th St (bet Eighth Ave and Broadway)
944-7490
Mon-Thurs: 11 a.m.-8 p.m.; Fri, Sat: 11 a.m.-11:30 p.m.
Sun: noon-6 p.m.

In the heart of the theater district, Needlheimer's attracts boffo box office because of its location and excels in light pre- and post-show fare. Center-stage in its productions is the Needlheimer's Fountain Menu, which offers several scores of ice cream treats and confections, all named for past productions at nearby theaters. The script draws on over 20 flavors, the stars of which are the vanilla fudge, chocolate chip, maple walnut, chocolate marshmallow, and coffee, in this reviewer's opinion. Loyal readers will note that for once I've selected something other than just chocolate for outstanding choices, but that can be amended with this suggestion: try these flavors à la mode, or on apple pie, or in these three sensational concoctions: "Stop the World I Want to Get Chocolate," "Choc'latemania," or "The Unsinkable Molly Banana." Each offers more chocolate than can be imagined, and each is delicious. For an encore, Needlheimer's is now offering a light menu featuring stuffed croissants and salads. Bravo!

NEW YORK ICE COMPANY
113 Seventh Ave S (at Ninth St)
741-5061
Mon-Thurs: noon-10; Sat, Sun: noon-midnight

When we went to see New York Ice, we were served by Toni Jackson who at that point was finishing her first week of employment there. If the folks at New York Ice are reading this, they should know that they are well-served by Toni. According to her, New York Ice's products are absolutely the best anywhere. She said that before she got her job she had never heard of the place since they primarily sell to restaurants and hotels. However, a supplier to the Pierre and Ritz banquet halls (among others) must have something going for it, and after sampling the wares she (and all the customers) know what it is. Although a wholesaler, New York Ice dispenses its own freshly made ice cream, ices, and other confections. It is the only source for its desserts, and the demand from neighbors who accidently tasted it (like Toni) was such that they opened a takeout counter and installed one bench. ("I wouldn't call it a seating area," says Toni). So if one is not at a formal dinner, it is still possible to pick up New York Ice's ices in raspberry, coconut, mango, blueberry, chocolate or other flavors. Ice cream comes in carmel with pralines, fudge raisin, chocolate fudge (Toni's favorite), and Mexican vanilla rum. The truffles are $20 a pound, but available in smaller sizes. There are more flavors and confections, though connoisseurs go for the Swiss gum balls and espresso ice cream. And a final word—tomato ice balls. Toni thinks that's kind of gross, too. (It's about the only thing that didn't get a rave review.) But caterers use them to accompany caviar. I guess if you can stomach caviar, you develop a taste for tomato ice balls. Say hello to Toni. By now she may be the manager.

PRAVINIE GOURMET ICE CREAM

27 St. Marks Pl (Eighth St, bet Second and Third Ave)
673-5948
Daily: noon-midnight; weekends: noon-1 a.m.

Pravinie offers "gourmet ice cream" and much, much more, none of which is designed to ease the waistline or the guilt. But the calories are well worth it. Ice cream comes in over 30 exotic flavors, both American and Oriental, and Pravinie is always on the lookout for the latest, sweetest indulgence. So tofutti has arrived here (of course, in unusual-for-tofutti flavors), as have cookies and waffles, and the locals claim that this spot offers the best milk shake in town. Needless to say, their help looks like they never eat the goodies. Or maybe this stuff isn't as fattening as it looks . . .

SERENDIPITY 3

225 E 60th St
838-3531
Mon-Thurs: 11:30 a.m.-midnight; Fri: 11:30 a.m.-1 a.m.;
Sat: 11:30 a.m.-2 a.m.; Sun: noon-midnight

Serendipity 3 has the distinction of being the ultimate "in" trendy spot in the city for 30 years. That's almost a contradiction in terms, but Serendipity has seen generations come and go and has always managed to offer the most trendy items in an environment that reeks of nostalgia. Even when cowboy boots were replaced by trivia games, which were in turn replaced by Michael Jackson jackets, Calvin Holt and Stephen Bruce—the co-owners of Serendipity—continued to serenely serve the best sundaes and fast food in town. Most of all, Serendipity lives up to its name. The tiny restaurant at the back of the ground-floor, two-floor brownstone, has only 32 tables. On Saturday nights and other prime dating times, three times that many people can be seen waiting for a table. While they wait, they browse through the eclectic selection of goodies in the front or the clothing and accessories on the second floor. All of this is done with penny candy, ice cream, and a light menu. Nowadays, with the health conscious among us, that's not a big deal. But Serendipity was just as "in" in the Sixties when it was a much heavier scene. I can't think of another establishment that has been at the forefront for 30 years—or one that has done it by constantly changing while maintaining the nostalgia of an old-fashioned ice-cream parlor.

STEVE'S ICE CREAM
286 Columbus Ave (at 74th St)
874-9348
444 Sixth Ave (at 10th St)
677-4221
Mon-Thurs: noon-midnight; Fri, Sat, Sun: noon-1 a.m.

Steve Herrell's ice cream was a stand-in-line-for-hours success in Somerville, Massachusetts. It received rave reviews when he brought it to New York City under the aegis of Integrated Resources, Inc., which makes the best ice cream this side of the Charles. Ice cream cakes can be custom-made to order, as can almost any kind of ice cream concoction. The sundaes feature homemade whipped cream, hot fudge, and butterscotch topping, as well as made-on-the-premises ice cream created in churns in 55 flavors. Going to Steve's is an experience. They're big on ice cream pies, such as Mix In pie, Oreo pie, Black Bottom pie, chocolate almond pie, all of which offer a choice of ice cream and fixings. In this city, Steve's is big business, and he still has them lining up back in Somerville.

YUM-YUM ICE CREAM
407 Sixth Ave (at Eighth St)
691-5303
Daily: 11:30 a.m.-midnight (summer);
Daily: 11:30 a.m.-11 p.m. (winter)

There is a true story told of a New York student who went home on vacation and stopped at one of the "64 different flavors" local ice cream stores. "Pistachio cone," he said, placing his regular New York order. "There's no such thing as pistachio," replied the ice cream man impatiently. "Yes, there is. I have it at school all the time." "Impossible. I've been selling ice cream for 25 years, and I've never heard of pistachio." The young man, sure that he was in Never-Never Land, ordered a plain vanilla cone and left. To this day, "pistachio ice cream" has become the expression for describing a commonplace event that a skeptic will not accept. It's too bad that the student wasn't able to mail the man a copy of Yum Yum's menu. Not only is pistachio ice cream listed, it even comes as Persian Pistachio. Indeed, the oddest flavor here would be vanilla. Yum Yum prides itself in stocking the unusual in ice cream. In addition to the regular flavors—coffee, butter pecan, strawberry, black raspberry, Swiss chocolate, chocolate chip, and mint chocolate chip—there are some that even this dedicated ice cream lover had not heard of. How about Danish Cheesecake, Brandy Alexander, South Pacific Pineapple, Scotch on the Rocks, Amaretto and Cream, or South American Banana Fudge? Yes, most of the flavors seem to be laced with liqueur, and both name and taste seem to be selected for their exotic nature. Intoxicating!

Indian

ANNAPURNA INDIAN GROCERIES
126 E 28th St
889-7540
Daily: 10-7

Annapurna looks like a large neighborhood grocery store—which it is—but it also functions as an Indian information center for non-Indians and as a home-away-from-home for Indians. Thomas Thoppil runs Annapurna like a school. If you even look curious, you may be bombarded with a series of lectures on the many available varieties of whatever foodstuff is at hand and how to cook it. Thoppil has a talent for translating Indian foods to American tastes and for knowing what will appeal to non-Indians. The store stocks nearly every variety of Indian spices and condiments (with an emphasis on hot, hotter, and hottest) as well as canned goods and fresh vegetables. There is much that is not Indian per se, but the cultural aspects are strictly Indian. There are utensils, films, records, religious posters, and gift items—all of the usual ethnic lore. If you wander in from the street, no matter who you are, it's hard to escape without the full Indian treatment. For the more extravagant (or less adventurous), Annapurna also runs a restaurant at 108 Lexington Avenue. After sampling the fare there, many customers come here to get the ingredients from Mr. Thoppil. Annapurna is also the place to find foodstuffs for English expatriates, such as Woodward's Celebrated Gripe Water and Brooke Bond Tea.

KALPANA

2528 Broadway (at 95th St)
663-4190
Mon-Sat: noon-8

Kalpana is a tiny neighborhood store with an excellent reputation among Indians. Personally, I feel that the reputation may be attributed to its solitary location uptown as much as its quality, since many of the other Indian shops are larger, cleaner, and better stocked. Nonetheless, owners Urmilla and Tony Maharau (Indians by way of Trinidad) are supplying the entire Upper West Side with a wide variety of Indian products. For its size, the store carries an incredible number of canned goods as well as food and spices. Urmilla Maharau's main contribution is giving recipes and instructions for preparing the ingredients the store sells. Kalpana stocks fresh vegetables, too, but most of the emphasis is on stocking what appeals to the polyglot neighborhood. The Trinidadian background adds an interesting accent to many of the already unusual Indian dishes. Kalpana also has a catering service.

K. KALUSTYAN

123 Lexington Ave (bet 28th and 29th St)
685-3451
Daily: 10-7

In 1944, Kalustyan opened as an Indian spice store at its present location. After all this time, Kalustyan is still a great spot. Everything is sold in bins or bales rather than prepackaged containers, and everything is available in bulk or wholesale sizes for retail customers. The difference in cost, flavor, and freshness compared to that of regular grocery stores is extraordinary, and the best indication of the latter two points is a simple whiff of the store's aroma. Kalustyan is not strictly an Indian store, but rather an "Orient export trading corporation" with a specialty in Mideastern as well as Indian items.

Italian

ITALIAN FOOD CENTER

186 Grand St (at Mulberry St)
925-2954
Daily: 8 a.m.-7 p.m.

Joseph De Mattia, the Italian Food Center's proprietor, serves a tantalizing array of Italian foods deserving of his choice location in the heart of Little Italy. The Food Center is truly that: it stocks just about everything in general and Italian foods in particular. There are fresh and cured Italian meats and cheeses, delicious fresh-baked breads, Italian-American cold cuts, Italian salads, delicacies, groceries, and dry goods. If it's Italian, he has it.

Liquor, Wine, Beer

Liquors and wines are price regulated in New York. As a result, there isn't too great a price discrepancy between liquor bought at a local shop or at a large supermarket. Note also that New York does not have "package stores" as do most other states. Liquor can be sold at any store that qualifies for a liquor license. (Qualification usually implies a good bank balance and a clean police record.) Because of the lack of price competition and the red tape involved in getting a liquor license, most liquor for home consumption in New York is sold at stores that deal exclusively in liquor. It is not, however, a state law. For both of the above reasons, liquor stores should be selected for their helpfulness, reliability, variety, and convenience, as opposed to price. The following possess all these characteristics.

ARDSLEY WINES AND SPIRITS
976 Lexington Ave (bet 71st and 72nd St)
249-6650
Mon-Fri: 10-6:30; Sat: 10-6; closed Sat July 4th-Labor Day

Neal Rosenthal runs a shop that is, not surprisingly, heavy on wines and liqueurs and light on the hard stuff. Rosenthal is an expert on wine, and has a vast stock with a good selection of unusual wines and liqueurs. He prides himself on selecting top vintages from vineyards he personally keeps tabs on. The liqueur line stresses cognac, sherries, and special liqueurs. Dessert liqueurs mentioned in the "Living" section of *The New York Times* are almost always in stock here; Rosenthal keeps a finger on the pulse of the trendy. This is a good place for a gift bottle, as well as an excellent source for your own wine cellar.

D. SOKOLIN
178 Madison Ave (bet 33rd and 34th St)
532-5893
Mon-Fri: 9:30-6:30; Sat: 10-5; closed Sat in summer

Sokolin makes our wine list on all points. He is knowledgeable (pamphlets and newsletters put out by the store are signed WM Sokolin, the WM standing for "wine merchant," not William), reasonable (catch the Thursday night sales or bargains available by the case), and extremely convenient. Sokolin has a large import retail business, and innumerable domestic and imported wines are available here; the staff is instantly able to expound the virtues and deficiencies of most of them. Sokolin himself takes a perverse delight in extolling the virtues of cheap, unknown wines at the expense of some of the exalted names. The liquor department is self-service, allowing the knowledgeable staff to concentrate exclusively on wine. Sokolin's attitude, like his merchandise, is totally refreshing.

FAIRFAX LIQUOR

849 Lexington Ave (bet 64th and 65th St)
734-6871
Mon-Sat: 8 a.m.-10 p.m.

Since you can't pick a liquor supplier by price (although Fairfax promises that their markup is the absolute minimum allowed by law—12 percent), you might as well pick one by the company it keeps and the service it offers. You'd be hard-pressed to beat this store on either of those counts. The selection is vast, there's hardly a vintage that's not represented, and the price is guaranteed to be the lowest in town. And Fairfax claims to supply David Rockefeller, Richard Nixon, and Ronald Reagan, among others. If you think that's just a listing of Republicans, Victor Abbandenato at the store says that those are merely the names that first come to mind. He adds: "We're not fussy. We sell to *all* the big people in town." This is the place to go if you want to be able to place a bottle on the table and say, "Oh, the Rockefellers recommend this label."

GARNET LIQUORS

929 Lexington Ave (bet 68th and 69th St)
772-3211 or 800-USA-VINO (out of state)
Mon-Sat: 9-9

Don't you love that "800" number? You'll love Garnet's prices even more. This may be the cheapest place in the city for specialty wines. At least they like to think so. So if you're in the market for champagne, bordeaux, burgundy or imported wines, check out the prices here first. And they're equally good on other wines and liquors. This is a first choice for choice spirits.

MORRELL AND COMPANY

535 Madison Ave (bet 54th and 55th St)
688-9370
Mon-Fri: 9-7:30; Sat: 9-7

Peter J. Morrell, who is charming and educated, owns a small jam-packed store that has every possible type of wine and liqueur. The stock is really overwhelming; since there isn't room for everything in stock to be on display, a good portion is held in the wine cellar. All of it is easily accessible, however, and the Morrell staff is knowledgeable and quite amenable to plucking the right thing from the nonvisible stock. The stock consists of all spirits, including brandy liqueurs and all vintages of wines from rare and old to young and "pop." Morrell and Company is also called the Wine Emporium Ltd., and is the rising star on the wine scene.

PIONEER DISCOUNT LIQUORS

319 Third Ave (at 24th St)
683-3857
Mon-Thurs: 9 a.m.-10 p.m.; Fri, Sat: 9 a.m.-11 p.m.

While some make points on knowledge and helpfulness, Pioneer scores on price and efficient inventories. Scorning frills and luxuries, Pioneer attempts to deliver "the lowest prices in town and a large diversified inventory." Some of the more esoteric vintages and labels are not available here, but if you need a popular brand bottle, it can be had. Because of the prices, Pioneer has a fast turnover, which is another plus.

SOHO WINES AND SPIRITS

461 W Broadway (bet Prince and Houston St)
777-4332
Mon-Sat: 10 a.m.-9 p.m.

Stephen Masullo's father ran a neighborhood liquor store on Spring Street for over 25 years. When his local neighborhood became SoHo, his sons expanded the business and opened a typical SoHo establishment—for wine. The shop is lofty. In fact, it looks more like an art gallery than a wine shop. The various bottles are "tastefully displayed" (Stephen's words), with classical music playing in the background. In addition, every advantage is made of the enormous floor space,and Stephen boasts that SoHo Wines has one of the largest selections of champagnes and wines in New York. Again, in keeping with the neighborhood, SoHo Wines and Spirits offers several unique services. Among them are party planning, wine-cellar advice, and specialty items of interest to the neighborhood. Note that this is *not* a liquor store (as Mr. Masullo Sr.'s is). *This* is a wine shop.

WAVERLY DELI

327 Sixth Ave (at W Third St)
741-1030
Sun-Thurs: 9 a.m.-1 a.m.; Fri, Sat: 9 a.m.-3 a.m.

New York University probably does not think that having a neighborhood deli that's renown for its beer is terribly helpful for the school's image. But there's no helping it: Waverly Deli, in the heart of NYU country, is a beer purveyor *par excellence,* offering over 194 different brands. (This is in a day when the "bottle law" has every other merchant in town cutting down on labels so they don't have to accept them for return.) And Waverly doesn't stop there. There are glasses, steins, T-shirts, and collectibles, all on guess what theme? To wash all the beer down, there are over 60 salads, sandwiches, and the usual grocery items, but you can get those anywhere. The toast here is the beer—and yes, there are those who claim to have gone through all 194 brands. Burp!

WINE & LIQUOR OUTLET
1114 First Ave (at 61st St)
308-1650
Daily: 9 a.m.-11 p.m.

Marc Gouran, Wine & Liquor Outlet's general manager, claims that his is the most complete liquor and wine shop in the city. That's half the reason to shop here. The other half is the excellent discount policy. And with a helpful, knowledgeable staff, Wine & Liquor Outlet may be the best place to shop in the country.

Meat, Poultry

AKRON MEATS
1414 Third Ave
744-1551
Mon-Sat: 9-6

Akron Meats is one of the few places where you can be certain of purchasing excellent prime meat. Quality is superb, which accounts for the long list of prominent customers who remain loyal to the shop. In addition to offering superior meat, occasional game, and other rare items, Akron is a friendly store that offers much in the line of service. Your order can be custom-ground or chopped, and Akron will take orders over the phone. If you're not sure what to do with your purchase, manager Eddie Kohut has a host of suggestions he'll happily share. And the quality of the meat is so high that Akron supplies wholesale orders to restaurants, too.

ARBERANN MEAT MARKET
1378 Lexington Ave (at 91st St)
876-1140
Mon-Sat: 8:30-6:30

This is the shop for people who prefer their bacon and hot dogs nitrate-free. If that's you (and a little editorializing would tell you that it ought to be: anyone who knows what goes into our meat should care), write down the name of this market. It's one of two such sources in the city. They don't cure the meat themselves; it's imported from Connecticut and processed by No-Dime. For those who like to indulge in these products, this market is additive-free. Ralph is a great guy to have wait on you.

BASIOR-SCHWARTZ MEAT PRODUCTS
421-423 W 14th St (bet Ninth and Tenth Ave)
929-5368
Mon-Fri: 5 a.m.-12:30 p.m.

The hours are unusual and the neighborhood is not the best, but Basior-Schwartz is the heart of the wholesale meat district, and that alone is enough to recommend a visit. This is a wholesaler who sells retail customers prime meat, cheese, frozen poultry, and gourmet products at the same prices it charges its regular wholesale customers—hotels and restaurants. Although this has been one of the worst-kept secrets among New York hostesses for years, there have been only minor concessions to the retail trade. The hours are more reasonable than they've been in the past, but the big change has been an additional selection of smoked fish, imported and domestic cheeses, and gourmet items that are obviously geared to individual customers. But the tradition for freshness and quality remains, and the prices are literally fractions of those uptown. Sure, you may have to get up early and lug your purchases home by public transportation (it's difficult to find parking spaces here), but that's a very small price to pay for lower prices. Basior-Schwartz may well be the main source in the city for meats, cheese, gourmet fish, and appetizing prices, and now that they carry eggs, butter, and grocery items, you may not need to patronize a supermarket again.

CAPECCI AND PERNICE PORK STORE
26 Carmine St (at Bleecker St)
675-7942
Tues-Sat: 7-5:30

Before it was discovered by the trendy, Greenwich Village was a small Italian enclave. Many of the stores and residents are holdovers from that period, and, as a result, some of the best Italian foods and meats in the city can be found in Village shops. One of these is Capecci and Pernice, formerly known as Frank's Pork Store. Among the delicacies are the finest prosciutto and salami. The latter is sliced meticulously into hero sandwiches that defy description.

CITY WHOLESALE MEATS
121 E 77th St
879-4241
Mon-Fri: 6 a.m.-3 p.m.

Off the beaten track for wholesale meat, but certainly *on* the track for Upper East Side denizens, City Wholesale Meats Corporation keeps wholesale hours and wholesale prices. There are some concessions to retail customers, i.e., freezer wrapping of individual items, which are priced per pound rather than by the side of beef or whole animal. Consumer-sized portions are available (albeit with substantial minimum orders), and the meat is cut and trimmed for immediate use for individuals rather than institutions. Prices are incredible. It's difficult to quote them because of the fluctuating market, but as we went to print, filet mignon was going for around $4 a pound with a 6 pound to 10 pound minimum order. At those prices, you could have a gourmet dinner for 12 at home for less than eating out for two. And did I mention that they deliver?

DELANCEY LIVE POULTRY MARKET

207 Delancey St
475-9875
Mon-Fri, Sun: 8-5

Delancey's is one of about half a dozen live poultry markets on Manhattan Island. The only complaint customers seem to have is that it takes you a little too close to the live action. Chickens, ducks, geese, and turkeys inhabit crates that are stacked almost everywhere, and occasional stragglers and freedom fighters wander the floor. The actual purchase and dispatch from live animal to food item takes place on that same floor in full view of all assembled. It is not for the weak of stomach, but it is definitely for those who desire the ultimate in fresh poultry.

FAICCO PORK STORE

260 Bleecker St (at Sixth Ave)
243-1974
Tues-Sat: 8-6; Fri: 8-7; Sun: 9-2

Recently remodeled and an Italian institution, Faicco's has delectable dried pepperoni, cuts of pork, and fresh-frying sweet or sour sausage in two varieties. They also sell an equally good cut for barbecue and an oven-ready rolled leg of stuffed pork. The latter, a house specialty, is locally famous. Note Faicco's title, because the shop really specializes in sausage and cold cuts rather than meats. Where there are more sausages and cheeses than can seemingly be counted, there are no white meats, veal, poultry, or lamb—and no steaks. If you're into Italian-style deli, try Faicco's first. And if you're a lazy cook, take home some ready-to-heat chicken rollettes: breast of chicken rolled around cheese and then dipped in a crunchy coating. It's the perfect introduction to Faicco's specialties.

JEFFERSON MARKET

455 Sixth Ave (at 10th St)
675-2277
Mon-Sat: 8 a.m.-9 p.m.; Sun: 9 a.m.-8 p.m.

The Jefferson Market is turning into an emporium. Originally a meat and poultry market, it is evolving into one of those definitive gourmet sources for virtually anything. Jefferson tops virtually every list as a source for meat, steaks, game, and poultry. The seafood was so top-notch that the entire fish department moved into its own store down the street at 449 Sixth Avenue. The store showcases whole fish (as opposed to fillets), but the choices are as exotic and gourmand as ever. The move left more room for the original market's meats, patés (from Les Trois Petits Cochons), naturally aged steaks, and prime meats. All veal is milk-fed plume de veau, a rating prized in gastronomic circles despite recent exposés about the deplorable conditions the animals endure. The produce section has fruits and vegetables that almost seem artificial in their beauty, and their orange juice has been rated the freshest in town. And finally, the service, quality, and prices of all of Jefferson's offerings make the place as much a Renaissance market—being all things to all people—as its namesake president was.

KUROWYCKY MEAT PRODUCTS

124 First Ave (bet Seventh and Eighth St)
477-0344
Mon-Sat: 7-6; closed Mon in July and Aug

Erast Kurowycky came to New York from the Ukraine in 1954. He opened this tiny shop in the same year, and almost immediately it become a home-away-from-home, a mecca, and top-secret bargain spot for the city's Poles, Germans, Hungarians, Russians, Lithuanians, and Ukrainians. Many of these nationalities still harbor centuries-old grudges, but they all come to Kurowycky's where they agree on at least one thing—the meats are the finest and the prices the best available. Erast's son, Jaroslaw ("Jerry"), runs the shop he grew up in, and he maintains the same traditions and recipes his father handed down. Come and taste the thick black bread, sausages, or ham (ask Jerry for a sample). Hams, sausages, meat loaves, and breads are sold ready to eat, as well as in various stages of preparation. There are also condiments, including a homemade Polish mustard, honey (imported directly from Poland), sauerkraut, and a half-dozen other Ukrainian specialities imported or reproduced from the area. On any given day, Kurowycky plays host to native sons coming "home," second generations being introduced to the old-country flavor, and foreigners who want the real stuff. Jerry treats them all courteously and efficiently, and they all come back for more.

M. LOBEL AND SONS

1096 Madison Ave (bet 82nd and 83rd St)
737-1373
Mon-Sat: 9-6; closed Sat in summer

If you read *New York* magazine, you know that Lobel's is the place that (a) has periodic sales on meat and (b) has some of the best cuts of meat in town. Because of Lobel's excellent service and reasonable prices, there are few human carnivores in Manhattan who haven't heard of Lobel's. They have published four meat cookbooks, and the staff is always willing to explain the best use for each cut. It's hard to go wrong here, since the store carries nothing but the best. But it's still nice to be shown the sort of beef most suited to your needs.

OTTOMANELLI'S MEAT MARKET

281 Bleecker St (bet Seventh Ave and Jones St)
675-4217
Mon-Fri: 7:30-6:30; Sat: 7-6

The standard variety here is rare gourmet fare. Among the regular weekly stock are such meats as boar's head, whole baby lambs, game rabbits, and pheasant. This is *not* a place to act young and naive. Quality is good, but being served by the right person can make the difference between a good cut and an excellent cut. Other family members run similar operations in other sections of town, but this is the original store, and it's noteworthy. They gained their reputation by offering full butcher services and a top-notch selection of prime meats, game, prime-aged steaks, and milk-fed veal. The latter is available as prepared Italian roast, chops, and steaks, and its preparation by the Ottomanellis makes it unique. Best of all, they will sell it by the piece for a quick meal at home.

PREMIER VEAL

555 West St (off the erstwhile West Side Hwy,
two blocks south of 14th St)
243-3170
Mon-Fri: 5 a.m.-1 p.m.

Merle Hirschorn served in various jobs in the restaurant business from Albany to Aspen before deciding to join the family wholesale veal distribution center. As a result, he is better attuned to the needs of both wholesale and retail customers than most such distributors or, as he says, he's been on both sides of the counter. This translates to a wholesaler who has a good eye for what sells in restaurants and institutions and who has a business that is friendlier than most to small individual orders. Premier Veal offers veal stew, Italian cutlets, shoulder or leg roasts and veal pockets for stuffing at wholesale prices with no minimum order. Of course, if you're going to make a trip to West Street, it might be economical to make the order as big as possible. And since larger orders receive greater attention, Hirschorn suggests that three or four customers get together to order a few loins. Less than that leaves too much waste and is not profitable for him or the customer. A loin weighing 18 pounds breaks down to 25 or 30 steaks and chops, and the price is a fraction of that of a butcher shop.

WASHINGTON BEEF COMPANY

573 Ninth Ave (at 41st St)
563-0200
Mon-Wed, Sat: 6:30-5:30; Thurs, Fri: 6:30-6:30

The amenities are totally lacking here, since Washington Beef treats each individual customer as a wholesaler. Because of the prices, good quality, and enormous selection, their average customer usually purchases as much as a small retail store would. Washington Beef claims to be the nation's largest meat distributor. The retail store is touted as operating on exactly the same rules as the wholesale operation, but they will also cut meat, sell by the pound rather than the side, and individually wrap it all up. Prices are guaranteed to be the city's lowest, and the quality is good. But there are disadvantages. Washington Beef is *huge.* As a result, the service is brusque and professional, offered on a "take it or leave it, there are others behind you" basis. An attempt to find guidance and recipe suggestions would be a joke. They will cut to order, but lines can be staggeringly long, and changing your mind or asking advice is strictly out of the question. To sum it up: the prices are fantastic, the quality good. If those are your main criteria, join the crowd.

YORKVILLE PACKING HOUSE
156 Second Ave (at 81st St)
628-5147
Mon-Sat: 7-7

Yorkville used to be a bastion of Eastern European ethnicity and culture before it became the Upper East Side swinging singles playground. Here and there, remnants of the previous Old World society remain, and within a four-block stretch on Second Avenue, there are three Hungarian butchers, each of whom offers the best in Hungarian provisions. Yorkville Packing House is patronized by Hungarian-speaking little old ladies in black, as well as some of the city's greatest gourmands. And the reason is simple: except for its neighbors, these prepared meats are available nowhere else in the city, and possibly not even elsewhere on the continent. The shop offers almost 40 different kinds of salami. And that's just for starters. Goose is a mainstay of Hungarian cuisine, so there is goose liverwurst, smoked goose, and goose liver. Fried bacon bits and bacon fried with paprika (another Hungarian staple) are other offerings. And ready for on-the-spot consumption are a selection of preserves, jams, jellies, prepared delicacies, and breads (Hungarian, natch! Try the potato or corn breads.) All of it is authentic and unique.

Mexican, Spanish

ANITA'S CHILI PARLOR
287 Columbus Ave (bet 73rd and 74th St)
595-4091
Sun-Thurs: noon-midnight; Fri, Sat: noon-1 a.m.

ROCKING HORSE CAFE
224 Columbus Ave (bet 70th and 71st St)
724-7816
Daily: noon-midnight

Anita rode to town on a rocking horse, carrying a platter of chili, and rounded up a heck of a crowd, partner. The chili parlor spawned the cafe, and both serve the greatest Mexican fare north of the border. The cuisine is authentic—so authentic that some of the help have the double distinction of being the only people in the place who can spell and/or pronounce what's on the menu while being unable to speak the same language as the clientele. Under those circumstances, a lot of pointing and grunting goes on. But it's all points and no grunts when the meals are served. Enchiladas, tacos and, of course, chili can be ordered to eat in or out, and either way makes for truly outstanding dining. Anita's was one of the pioneers on Columbus Avenue, and is certainly responsible for literally adding some spice and good taste to the neighborhood.

CASA MONEO
210 W 14th St
929-1644
Mon-Sat: 9-7; Sun: 11-5

Casa Moneo is actually two shops: the Casa is a food shop, and the Bazaar Moneo is a gift shop. Both offer the very best in Spanish and Latin American imports. Devotees of Mexican and Spanish food regard Casa Moneo as the very best source in the city and state. It has a collection of chilies, for example, that is unrivaled even in Mexico. The chilies come fresh, canned, stewed, and marinated in varieties that people never saw in their Mexican hometown. There is a similar array of sausages, cheeses, hot sauces, hams, and gourmet products. While Santiago Moneo, the manager, has a Mexican bias, every country in Latin America, and even Spain, is represented on Casa Moneo's shelves. There are also fresh vegetables and fruits flown up from the south, along with cheeses, meats, spices, and beans; in short, everything to make the most authentic Spanish meal in the city. For those who can't wait, light meals are served in the cafe. There is also a takeout department and catering service. Those who can pull themselves away from the table should browse in the Bazaar. There are perfumes, soaps, jewelry, records, tapes, and authentic clothing. All of it is great, but the peasant blouses and ponchos are positively super.

Middle Eastern

TASHJIAN'S
123 Lexington Ave (bet 28th and 29th St)
683-8458
Mon-Sat: 10-8

One of the oldest ethnic food stores in the city (founded over a century ago), Tashjian is Armenian in origin, but it's been in the melting pot long enough to encompass all of the Middle East. So, the shelves are jammed with all kinds of groceries and foodstuffs, and the counters display appetizers. There's even a catering service. Tashjian claims to be an importing business as well, and it would have to be to get some of the items it stocks. What is really amazing is that a century-old store has a proprietor named Viken Tashjian and a staff that still speaks with strong Armenian accents.

Noodles

YAT GAW MIN COMPANY
100 Reade St (at Chambers St)
233-7200
Mon-Fri: 8:30-4; Sat: 8:30-2

Yat Gaw Min bills itself as an egg noodle company and turns out noodles in all types of configurations and flavors. There is also a good selection of noodles that would be at home in the kitchens of other nationalities as well. Ingredients, incidentally, are the finest, and Yat Gaw Min attempts to use unadulterated products.

Nuts

AHA INTERNATIONAL FOOD COMPANY
165 Church St (at Reade St)
233-4592
Daily: 8-8

AHA is a Middle Eastern food shop, but it's the nuts that make the public go "Ah!" They are freshly roasted and simply sensational. Or as a staff member said, "We are nuts about nuts." Also check out the dried fruits and confections, though nothing compares with those nuts.

KADOURI IMPORT
51 Hester St (at Essex St)
677-5441
Sun-Fri: 9-5

Kadouri is a wholesale-retail store, operating out of burlap bags. Everything here is natural and healthful. The main staples are nuts and dried fruits. The almonds and their derivatives are especially good. Kadouri carries spices as well, but only the more popular varieties. Still, they are extremely fresh, and prices are wholesale, no matter how small the purchase.

Pasta

GOURMET PASTA
1470 Second Ave (at 77th St)
737-8750
Mon-Fri: 11-8:30; Sat: 11-7; Sun: noon-6

Gourmet Pasta is near the top of the list of Manhattan's trendy food shops. They seem to hedge their bets (and remain *au courant*) by offering the latest epicurian treats as well as pasta, but the pasta is in a class by itself. It is made fresh every day in a dozen configurations, and comes in spinach, tomato, egg, or whole wheat and the specialty pastas of herb, hot and spicy, and hearts of artichoke. (You read that right.) All of this is served with a choice of a dozen sauces, any one of which is quite remarkable. All the sauces are also salt and sugar free. Pasta suffers from an image problem, but Gourmet Pasta has set out to change all that by turning pasta into healthy, elegant fare. For nonbelievers, however, the shop also offers veal, chicken, and seafood entrees. With a bow to nouvelle cuisine, the desserts are highlighted by soufflés, tarts, and mousses. And those who eschew the pasta, seafood, and veal entrees can feast on escargot. Gourmet Pasta does catering as well. I'd assume that they get more calls for the latter entrees than the pasta. But in the store, it's just the opposite.

RAFFETTO'S CORPORATION
144 W Houston St (bet Sullivan and McDougal St)
777-1261
Tues-Sat: 8-6

You could go for pasta at a gourmet place or you could go straight to the source. Raffetto's is the source and has been since 1906. Since that time, they have made all kinds of pasta and stuffings. Though most of the business is wholesale, Raffetto's will dispense their ravioli, tortellini, manicotti, cannelloni, gnocchi, fettucine, and spinach fettucine to anyone, with no minimum order. Variations on the theme include Genoa-style ravioli with meat and spinach, Naple's style with cheese, and a nongeographic cheese-and-spinach ravioli. Prices also reflect the fact that this is indeed the source.

Pickles

GUSS PICKLES
35 Essex St (bet Grand and Hester St)
254-4477
Fulton Market
South Street Seaport (bet Front and Beekman St)
Daily: 10-10

In the first edition, I tried to chronicle the Lower East Side pickle business by focusing on the legends of the rivalry between Guss' and Hollander's pickles. In the second edition, having risen above such gossip (and having been inundated with comments from the locals, all of whom swore that only *they* knew the real story), we concentrated on the gastronomic differences and preferences of the two. Still, the pickle section remained one of the most commented on in the book, and we looked forward to reporting the latest developments for the third edition. Then, once again the Lower East Side pickle business soured the possibility of a clear report. That time, the unbelievable happened—Guss and Hollander became one business. Note my terms. They did not unite, they did not merge, and they certainly did not marry. For months after the consolidation, the two factions continued to wear their respective store-name T-shirts while working under the same roof. In any case, fully aware that whatever is said here invites the comments of the locals (I guess we can report on those in the fifth edition), here is my personal analysis of the situation.

The business that started with Guss and Hollander each dispensing pickles, tomatoes, sauerkraut, pickled peppers, and occasional watermelon rinds from barrels on the sidewalk has become one business that operates at Hollander's store. Pickles still come in sour and half sour, with a half-dozen gradations in between (there are those who say it's all the same anyway), and the business is still conducted out on the street with the "stock" taking up the interior of the store. One advantage Hollander always had is that beyond the barrels outside, customers could actually glimpse a semblance of order and even a refrigerator inside. Guss' place looked like a black hole. Guss has passed away; the legend remains, however. Except for the human interest in all of this background information, it's not terribly important. What is, however, is that this enterprise is still the best place in the world for fresh-from-the-barrel pickles. There are others on the block (the Pickle Man and Louis, to name two), but Guss is still the best.

Popcorn

KERNEL POPPINS
319 Sixth Ave (at W Third St)
989-6588
Sun-Thurs: noon-10; Fri, Sat: noon-1

In the last edition, we predicted that a host of popcorn purveyors would soon invade the city. Chalk one up for our powers of prediction, because that's exactly what has happened. There are so many popcorn parlors in the city these days that even purple popcorn doesn't prompt a second look. What does create second looks is quality, and since the day the shop opened, Kernel Poppins has received rave reviews. (Even the ushers at the Waverly movie theater next door pass up their own popcorn to line up for Kernel Poppins') The shop uses only natural ingredients and relies on a few flavors done well. The *Daily News* poll rated Kernel Poppins number one in the city, a fact that the owners take in stride, since their goal is to be a quality chain throughout the city. Our prediction is that they're going to make it.

Seafood

CATALANO'S FRESH FISH

1652 Second Ave (at 86th St)
628-9608
Mon-Fri: 9-7; Sat: 9-6

Add youth, consumer interest, and healthy eating to the ancient craft of the fishmonger, and you have Catalano's Fresh Fish market. Owner Joe Catalano is a rare blend of concern, knowledge, and youth. His customers—including many local restaurants—rely on him, as often as not, to select the best items for the dinner menu. And this he does with a careful eye toward health, price, and cookery. He feels strongly that a fish store should not be intimidating and that the only way to get new customers is to educate them. Catalano's also has a good selection of poached fish to order and some simply super salads. On cold, wintry days, don't miss the Manhattan clam chowder. Joe Catalano is too young to have made the recipe, but he surely deserves credit for adding the abundance of clam, ham chunks, and vegetables that float in his chowder.

CENTRAL FISH COMPANY

527 Ninth Ave (bet 39th and 40th St)
279-2317
Mon-Thurs: 7:30-6:30; Fri: 6:30-6:30; Sat: 7:30-5

Central doesn't look like much from the outside, but the stock is so vast that it's easier to list what is *not* available than what is. A very short list would include whatever seafood is hopelessly out of season. They have 35 different species in stock at any given time, including fresh imported sardines from Portugal and live carp. Guiding customers through this whale of a selection are some of the friendliest and most knowledgeable salespeople encountered anywhere. Louis and Anthony Riccoborno and Calogero Olivri are skillful guides, who also clean and filet fish. They stock fresh and frozen fish and seafood products. There are fish that even the most devoted seafood lover would have trouble identifying, and the prices are among the most reasonable in town.

CITARELLA FISH
2135 Broadway (at 75th St)
874-0383
Mon-Sat: 8:30-7; Sun: 10-6

I once won a bet by shopping here, when challenged to find the most esoteric seafood for sale in New York City. Citarella's selection includes everything! Prices are very reasonable and the selection vast, but they are not as informative as they might be, and when one is navigating amid bins of brook trout, Maryland croaker, and other living sea residents, a little direction would prove helpful. But try telling them you're looking for the most esoteric fish in town. They'll outdo themselves.

LEONARD'S FISH MARKET
1241 Third Ave (at 70th St)
744-2600
Mon-Fri: 8-6; Sat: 8-4

Leonard's, a family-owned business since 1905, is owned and run by John Leonard with the same exacting standards that the store has maintained throughout the years. This, too, is a neighborhood store that gears its selection to the neighborhood's menus. Thus, the better, smaller portioned seafoods are always in stock. There are sea trout, oysters, crabs, haddock, scampi, striped bass, halibut, salmon, live lobster, and squid. The latter is usually purchased by people who know what they are doing, but if they don't, John Leonard is happy to assist. He also runs daily specials on whatever happens to have been a good buy that day at the Fulton Market. This is not to say that Leonard's is a bargain establishment. Decidedly not. Leonard's is class all the way. And their takeout seafood department includes codfish cakes, deviled crabs and lobsters, and a super Manhattan clam chowder. Leonard's also carries a full range of imported appetizers. Yes, there is caviar, but you can also find filet mignon, smoked meats and fish, and canned delicacies. Barbecued poultry, cooked and prepared foods, and prime meats round out Leonard's selection.

MURRAY'S STURGEON SHOP
2429 Broadway (bet 89th and 90th St)
724-2650
Tues-Fri, Sun: 8-7; Sat: 8-8; Sun (July and August): 8 a.m.-2 p.m.

The answer to why Arthur Cutler is the owner of a place called Murray's Sturgeon Shop is that Cutler bought out Murray several years ago. That is of interest to every appetizer lover in New York, because Murray's was the definitive place to buy fancy and smoked fish. There was some apprehension when Cutler took over, but doubts were assuaged when Craig Claiborne, the *New York Times* gastronomist in residence, declared Murray's "my favorite purveyor of such things" after Cutler had operated the shop for just a year. (Claiborne's article described how he saved $1,290 by bringing his own dinner on a tourist-class round trip to Europe instead of flying first class. The dinner was catered by Murray's.) When Murray's is not winning accolades from the *Times*, it is dispensing the finest in appetizing products. There is sturgeon, Gaspe salmon, whitefish, kippered salmon, sable butterfish, pickled herring, schmaltz herring, and caviar. Quality is magnificent and prices fair, even if you're not flying across the Atlantic.

ROSEDALE FISH AND OYSTER MARKET
1129 Lexington Ave (at 79th St)
861-4323, 288-5013, 734-3767
Mon-Sat: 8-6

Rosedale has quality seafood in good supply at all times. In addition, there is a selection of takeout fish dishes and salads that are tasty, ususual, and noteworthy. They are not cheap. Their high quality is accompanied by equally high prices. According to many of the city's restaurants and caterers, they are the best fish source in New York.

SOUTH SEAS SEAFOOD
47 Wooster St
966-2340
Mon-Fri: 8-8
24-hour phone service

This is absolutely the number-one seafood place for selection, price, and quality. When you phone, ask for Mike Sirkus and tell him I sent you. They even deliver in Manhattan.

Spices

APHRODISIA
282 Bleecker St (at Seventh Ave)
989-6440
Mon-Sat: 11-7; Sun: 12-5; closed Sun in summer

Aphrodisia is stocked from floor to ceiling with every herb and spice that exists. All 700 of them are neatly displayed in easily visible glass jars. Some of the teas, potpourri, dried flowers, and oils are really not what one would expect. The general accent is on the occult and folk remedies, but all the ingredients for ethnic cooking can be found here. Prices depend upon the amount purchased and the scarcity of the spice. Aphrodisia conducts a large mail-order business via their catalog, available for a minimal fee.

MEADOWSWEET HERBAL APOTHECARY
77 E Fourth St (bet Second and Third Ave)
254-2870
Tues-Sat: 11-7; closed two weeks in Aug

Depending on how you look at it, Arcus Flynn's Meadowsweet Herbal Apothecary is otherwordly, a pacific respite, or more than a little bit weird. But you have to admit that Flynn is nothing if not a sincere believer, and the store is nothing if not unique. What Flynn believes in is the power of herbs and herbal medicine. In addition to all sorts of natural herbs, seasonings, and flowers, Meadowsweet dispenses its own mixtures, oils, ointments, medicines, and formulas to aid a variety of ailments from alcoholism to tranquilizer addiction. Flynn is very aware that herbists are not legally allowed to prescribe medicine, but nothing prohibits the sale of such items or prevents Flynn from recommending customers to literature and pointing out the possibilities of curative powers. This is the place to go for all kinds of natural herbs. Everything is displayed neatly in rows of glass jars. The store's motto is "The aroma alone is worth the visit," and that, along with the soothing music (Flynn admits to "an occasional Benny Goodman on a bright day") and "healing ambiance," make this an oasis in the city. And there are many who swear by the herbal remedies.

PETE'S SPICE AND EVERYTHING NICE
174 First Ave (bet 10th and 11th St)
254-8773
Mon-Sat: 10-7

Despite the name, Peter Garcea runs a fascinating shop that specializes in, naturally enough, spices. Inside, everything is serious business, because Garcea is serious about using herbs and spices for improving everyday life. To that end, he sells bean sprouts, rose hips, basil, nutmeg, and the whole range of spices. He has some exotic ones, but their low turnover does not warrant keeping large amounts in stock. The usual items he does stock are seaweed, kelp, sea salt, organic flours, dried fruits, bean sprouts, and teas.

SAINT REMY
818 Lexington Ave (bet 62nd and 63rd St)
759-8240
Mon-Sat: 10-6

The name is French, and this spice market is evocative of the best in French herb shops. In sharp contrast to the ethnic markets in other parts of the city, Saint Remy is an herb boutique. While it has its share of open bins and bags of fresh nuts, herbs, and plants, those on sale here are the kind a gourmet cook would need. (I asked for black poppy seeds and was told, "We have white only—from the opium fields of Turkey, but white.") Notice the sacks of herbs.

The stock is not enormous, and much depends on what is available in suitable quality. But what is there is of the best. Saint Remy also carries fabrics and cosmetics under the Saint Remy name, and they give advice on skin care and the use of herbs in cooking.

Swedish

NYBORG AND NELSON
153 E 53rd St (Citicorp Center)
223-0700
Mon-Fri: 11:30-9; Sat: noon-7; Sun: noon-6

This store stocks everything that a Scandinavian food emporium should, including authentic cheeses and meats. Owner Hans Boorge claims that most of his business is with Americans, but standards are maintained on a level to please the most finicky Swede. The store's specialty is Swedish, but the stock is broad enough to span all of Scandinavia. Try the Swedish cheeses; they are unrivaled. Thursday is customarily pea-soup day in Sweden, and the store keeps the tradition by selling its own version. There's enough food here to supply several smorgasbords (of any nationality): cheeses, fish, salads, breads, and meat, including Swedish meatballs. There are also imported housewares and gift packages. A store this big could exist only in New York, but once you're inside, you'd swear you were in Sweden.

V. Where To Find It: New York's Best Services

Animal Services

ANIMAL MEDICAL CENTER
510 E 62nd St (bet FDR Dr and York Ave)
838-8100
Daily: 24 hours

If your pet should become ill in New York, try the Animal Medical Center first. This nonprofit organization handles all kinds of veterinary work reasonably and competently. The care here is far better than almost anywhere else in the city. They suggest you call for an appointment. Emergency care costs more.

CANINE CASTLE
410 W 56th St
245-1291
Tues-Sat: 1:30-8

Anne Leone, Canine Castle's owner, has appeared on several TV shows espousing her methods of "dog grooming in a royal manor" and her expertise garnered from years of dog care. Her grooming of dogs and cats is impeccable. For tourists, Leone will waive the requirement of advance appointments. The shop also has a complete line of accessories for dogs and cats. Don't miss the extraordinary selection of collars.

FELINES OF DISTINCTION
552 Hudson St (bet Perry and 11th St)
675-9023
Mon-Sat: noon-6

Jerry Benisatto of Felines is a great guy. He understands cats and cat owners, and his business is run more as a club or co-op than a commercial operation. The store sells C.F.A. registered kittens and pedigreed cats; Abyssinian, Burmese, Himalayan, Persian, and Siamese are the specialties. Benisatto boasts that "we are known for selling healthy kittens." This accounts for a large percentage of the profits, but it is by no means the main business. Feline services are what the store prefers to sell. The open-membership discount club offers members 10 percent off on grooming and boarding services and 15 percent off on all dry goods. (Food and litter items are exempt.) With the discount, prices are very good, and the services are reputed to be excellent. They will groom cats or dogs, but they only board cats.

LE CHIEN DOG SALON
1461A First Ave (at 76th St)
861-8100
Mon-Fri: 8:30-7; Sat: 9-7

Le Chien is a sort of boarding and finishing school for dogs. In addition to boarding, there is a separate business that grooms and trains cats and canines, particularly poodles. The few dogs boarded here spend the day being groomed and fussed over (with periodic walks), and spend their evenings in large stalls. Most of the clients are either "students" being cured of bad habits, or dogs brought in for grooming. In addition to boarding and housebreaking, Le Chien offers a full line of dog and cat accessories. Lisa Gilford, Le Chien's president, handles her charges in the style of a headmistress at an exclusive boarding school.

MANHATTAN CAREER INSTITUTE
351 E 61st St (bet First and Second Ave)
593-1231
Mon-Fri: 8-9 by appointment

This school trains people as well as animals, and does a commendable job of educating both. Most of the students are immigrants training to become dog groomers, veterinary assistants, or pet-service shop managers. The bulk of the program is devoted to retraining pets. And since trainees need subjects to work with, pets volunteered as models get top-notch care at a fraction of the cost of regular pet salons. Current rates depend upon the size of the dog and condition of its coat. Full services include shampoos, cuts, baths, trims, and the clipping of nails and fur. Dogs are given show-dog cuts, if that's appropriate to the breed. The school also takes cats, and doesn't turn away any candidate, no matter how badly matted or ill-behaved.

WE KARE KENNELS
410 220th St (near Broadway)
567-2100
Daily: 9-6; summer: 9-6:30

Nat and Jan Koranhauser's motto—"If you care, send your pet to We Kare"—and *kute* name can be forgiven, since they really do spend as much time as they claim to with their animals. Care (not *kare*) here is first rate. The Koranhausers offer convenient services for tourists, including pickup and drop-off at home, office, hotel, and even airport. This is especially good for transferred or traveling executives. Furthermore, We Kare's policy is to follow the home schedule of feeding, walking, and bed times, rather than forcing pets to adjust to an institutional routine. They feel this practice makes the animals adjust better to their new home, and since We Kare also accepts long-term boarders, that's important. Grooming, training, and cat boarding are also available, and they sell dogs as well. Cats have a brand-new separate boarding facility.

Antiques Repair

MICHAEL J. DOTZEL AND SON
402 E 63rd St (at York Ave)
838-2890
Mon-Fri: 9:30-4:30

Dotzel specializes in repair and maintenance of antiques, so nothing will be done to your precious heirlooms that will hurt their intrinsic value. Dotzel won't touch modern pieces, or even inferior antiques, but if your antique is made out of metal and needs repair, he's the man for the job. He spends a lot of time and pays close attention to detail, and will hand-forge or personally hammer metal work, including brass. If an item has lost a part, he can re-create it. One thing is certain: when the job's finished, your piece will be as good as new. Dotzel also does stripping and replating, although he feels it isn't always good for an antique. He'll probably try to talk you out of it.

NOVAL'S ANTIQUES SERVICING
54 E 13th St (bet University and Broadway)
254-9479
Mon-Fri: 10-7; Sat: 10-6

Jimmy Noval can do almost anything. Correcting mistakes, doing simple electric work, and cleaning antiques, Noval spruces up items with a minimum of damage to the artist's original intent. The main business is what the name indicates—servicing—which includes making lamps from Aunt Minnie's ceramic coat tree, restoring hurricane lamps, and updating chandeliers. He says his main business is repairing and rewiring candelabras and chandeliers. Almost as much time is devoted to creating lighting fixtures for commercial and personal clients. Noval has an extensive inventory of authentic parts for period lighting fixtures, and he has such an extensive knowledge of the mechanics of these fixtures that if he can't fix the piece, he can create a new one. Much of this work is done for major galleries and interior decorators. Noval is also an accomplished restorer of artwork, particularly paintings. His expertise is so renowned he could probably make a go of it in that field alone.

THINGS ANTIQUE
483 Amsterdam Ave (at 83rd St)
873-4655
Daily: 10-6

Things Antique specializes in the sale of restored antiques. That makes them different from the run-of-the-mill antiques shop in that nothing delights them more than picking up some woebegone item and turning it into a gone-in-a-minute antique. The current specialty is trunks in all their manifestations, but chairs, tables, and other furniture are also handled. Since the store picks them up for a song (or for nothing), they are sold at very reasonable prices — much less than what an unrestored piece in good condition would usually go for. While doing this, Things Antique obviously became expert in restoration. They can strip, finish, stain, repair, cane, or weld antique furniture at the same reasonable prices and quality as their own pieces. With a healthy respect for things antique, this shop can do quality repairs without upsetting the value of the item.

Appraisals

GEM APPRAISERS LABORATORY
22 W 48th St (bet Fifth and Sixth Ave)
354-1122
Mon-Fri: 8:30-5; closed first two weeks of July

Leopold Woolf, who owns Gem Appraisers Laboratory Ltd., is also an officer and director of the Appraisers Association of America. As such, he is entrusted with the appraisals for major insurance companies, auction houses, banks, and the New York City Department of Consumer Affairs. In an area where it can't hurt to be too careful, this is a very safe bet. In addition to doing appraisals and consultations for estates, banks, insurance and tax purposes, Woolf also runs Gem Appraisers Laboratory Designs, which manufactures and designs jewelry. A better man would be hard to find.

Art Services

ART RESTORATION TECHNICAL INSTITUTE
71 W 23rd St
279-3073, 691-9767
Mon-Fri: 8:30-4 by appointment

Did you know that the newer a painting, or the more inexpertly framed, the sooner restoration is required? If you've learned this from experience, take solace in the knowledge that even the Mona

Lisa needs an occasional touch-up, and remember that your woes can end with a trip to the one place in the city that does nothing but restore artwork—the Art Restoration Technical Institute. They have been called upon to restore masterpieces from all periods, and their clients range from museum curators to families with heirlooms worth a fortune. There has never been a picture they did not deem worth restoring (under contract). But while they are not art snobs, they're too busy to bother with junk. And that works in your favor. Any painting restored here will be even more valuable when it comes out.

ELI WILNER FINE ART
305 E 76th St (bet First and Second Ave, #5A)
744-6521
Tues-Fri: 10-5

Eli Wilner offers art services with a unique personal touch. Five years as a framer and another year of working on art restoration taught him that most New Yorkers are loathe to even hang a picture themselves. So operating out of his home, Wilner and his crew of experts will position, group, and hang artwork. But even that is only a side specialty. The years of apprenticeship have made Wilner a master at period framing, which he accomplishes with genuine antique frames. He will enlarge or cut down a frame, and if the proper frame is not among his sizable collection of antique frames, he can locate any given size and period with advance notice. So the real specialty is period framing and restoration with genuine antiques. But there's got to be more than one relationship that has been saved by Wilner's professional picture hanger's decision on where the artwork should be hung—over *here*, not over there!

GUTTMANN PICTURE FRAME ASSOCIATES
180 E 73rd St (bet Lexington and Third Ave)
744-8600
Mon-Fri: 9-5

Though the Guttmanns have worked on frames for some of the nation's finest museums, including the Metropolitan, they stand apart from other first-class artisans in that they are not snobby or picky about what work they will take. They will restore, regild, or replace any type of picture frame, and while they are masters at doing the same for masterpieces, they are equally at home restoring or framing a Polaroid snapshot. Even better, the Guttmanns are not only willing to work on cheaper pieces, they are among the few experts who don't price themselves out of the market. And finally, when you bring a worn-out frame to them, they will graciously *and* gratuitously tell you exactly what it will cost to fix it. That's when their egalitarian attitude really comes to the fore.

JOEL ZAKOW
72 Greene St
226-6093
Mon-Sat: 9-6 by appointment

Don't bring the Rembrandt down to Joel Zakow without making an appointment and confirming it on the phone. Zakow just might be too busy working on the restoration of a painting belonging to a museum or destined for one of the Madison Avenue auction blocks. As the restorer in residence for the Museum of American Folk Art, Zakow is particularly adept with any folk artwork. But perhaps because he is not used to working exclusively with the old masters, Zakow seems more receptive to taking on works of greater sentimental than artistic value. This is not to say that the work is cheap; in fact, the opposite is usually true. If one owns a masterpiece, one takes care of it. It's the ancestor's portraits that usually hang forever without a cleaning. Zakow charges according to the work involved rather than the value of the artwork. For this reason, he offers free estimates and a frank appraisal of whether or not it's worth undertaking the work.

JULIUS LOWY FRAME AND RESTORING COMPANY
28 West End Ave
586-2050
Mon-Fri: 9-5

There are many firms in the city that specialize in art restoration and framing, but this is the definitive place for both of these services. Julius Lowy seems to have no space that isn't heaped with frames, and many look as though they've been there since the place opened 80 years ago. It's obvious that any kind of frame could be unearthed somewhere on their two floors. This means there is no framing job that Julius Lowy cannot do, and its clients include the Metropolitan Museum of Art and the White House. As a byproduct of having done some really odd jobs, a sideline was developed in art restoration, antique-frame reproduction, and frame rearrangement. (Rearrangement means enlarging or reducing existing frames to match new artwork.) All of this work is done impeccably. Prices are not as high as might be expected, and there are brand-new custom-made frames available.

READY FRAMES
14 W 45th St (bet Fifth and Sixth Ave)
719-2720
Mon-Fri: 10-6; Sat: 10-4

Framing pictures, prints, or needlework can often be as expensive as the work of art itself. There are a couple of solutions. Try a frame-it-yourself establishment or find a cheap custom-frame shop that sometimes discounts odd frames or rejects. Short of spending lots of money, those used to be the only options. But now Ready Frames has come up with a program that is all things to all people. They do custom framing at a discount, but do-it-yourselfers and those who can use stock frames can take advantage of the largest selection and variety of ready-made frames in the city. (Ready Frame is the most complete framing center in the area.) All are sold at up to 50 percent off. In addition to fully assembled frames, there are frames that can be put together for specific sizes and come equipped with glass and/or mats. The result is virtually indistinguishable from the expensive job. Ready Frame makes the best picture in town.

Babysitters

BABYSITTERS GUILD
60 E 42nd St (suite 912)
682-0227
Daily: 9-9

Established in 1940, the Babysitters Guild has high rates, but their reputation commends them. The Guild's reputation is based upon a thoroughly professional attitude. All of their sitters have passed rigorous scrutiny and only the most capable are sent out on jobs. There is a four-hour minimum here, but as members of the New York Convention and Visitor's Bureau, they will sometimes relax the rule for tourists.

BARNARD COLLEGE BABYSITTING SERVICE
606 W 120th St
280-2035
Mon-Fri: 10-4

Barnard College, the undergraduate women's college of Columbia University, has—counting instructors and graduate students—an unusually large number of kids following their parents around campus. To keep them out of their folks' hair, the Barnard Babysitting Service was started by the Office of Career Services. Barnard students become mother's helpers (usually, room and board are exchanged for babysitting services) and full-time or one-time babysitters who will do light housekeeping. Most of the young women prefer to have permanent babysitting arrangements, though.

C.A.S.H./STUDENT EMPLOYMENT OFFICE
21 Washington Pl (at Greene St, third floor)
New York University
598-2971
Mon-Fri: 9-5

NYU has always been known for its free and easy attitude (perhaps because of its Village location). Its babysitting service is no different, and it's certainly refreshing after the list of restrictions imposed elsewhere. At NYU, rates are reasonable, with no minimum fees. Rates are negotiated between parents and students. With such a large student body, there is usually someone willing to sit, even on short notice. No further commitment is necessary. C.A.S.H. combines all the former student employment offices, so this is also the place to hire student bartenders, tutors, housesitters, or odd jobbers.

STERN COLLEGE FOR WOMEN
245 Lexington Ave
340-7700
Mon-Thurs: 8:30-4; Fri: 8:30-12:30

They do not have sitters for Friday nights, and no weekend appointments can be made for same-day sitting (the college is open Monday through Friday only). But the United Nations puts these people near the top of their list of sitters for diplomats' children, and you should, too. The students are reliable, courteous, dependable, and very good with kids. Most are education majors.

Beauty Care and Consultation for Women

BORJA AND PAUL
805 Madison Ave (at 67th St)
734-0477
Mon-Sat: 10-5:30

Pierre Henri, formerly of Saks, is in residence here on Tuesday, Wednesday, and Thursday, from 8:30 to 3:30. Though the other operators are good, Pierre is exceptional. He has a long line of clients who follow him wherever he moves. Indeed, this shop relies on steady clients. The service is courteous and old-fashioned, while the styles they cut are stylish and up-to-date. "Our makeup girl does elegant, chic makeup to complement our hair coloring. *That*, by the way, is natural coloring. We're not into the punk-rock look," said one operator. The salon also does manicures, haircuts, setting, and pedicures—everything you'd expect from a traditional salon.

CLAIROL CONSUMER RESEARCH FORUM
345 Park Ave (bet 51st and 52nd St, second floor)
546-2707
Mon-Fri: 9-3 by appointment only

If you're female and want to be pampered, Clairol is the place for you. From the moment you step out of the elevator to the last stroke of your free treatment, you're made to feel that you're the most special person in the world. There are two Clairol programs.

The Consumer Research Forum is the best-known of the two, and takes volunteers on an appointment-only basis. Time-pressed visitors will find that the rules aren't inflexible, however. At the Forum, a volunteer washes her own hair, testing such hair-care products as shampoos, conditioners, and blow driers. Afterward, a staff member asks a series of questions, the volunteer's hair is styled, and she is then sent home with a bag full of complimentary Clairol products. The only thing that the Consumer Forum doesn't do is hair coloring, which is done at the Research and Development Center. Volunteers who want to take advantage of this program have to submit to a "patch test," and Clairol doesn't take everyone who applies for the program. If Clairol can use you, the Forum will call you, and you'll come in for a hair-coloring session, followed by a styling and drying treatment. Gratis, natch. Once you've been a participant, Clairol will continue to color your hair for free once a month, and doesn't mind if you want to test other products, as long as you're in the neighborhood. This is a company that really does care. In fact, consumers are invited to call a hot-line number with any questions they may have about hair care. For out-of-towners, the toll-free number is 800-223-5800; open from 8:30 a.m. to 8 p.m., Eastern Standard Time. In New York, the number is 644-2990, and you can call collect.

DAVID-DAINES' SALON
833 Madison Ave (bet 69th and 70th St)
535-1563
Mon, Tues, Fri, Sat: 9-5;
Wed, Thurs: 9-7 by appointment only

Daines' offers a full range of services, including cutting, styling, sets, manicures, pedicures, cosmetics, coloring, permanents, treatments, waxing, and beauty accessories. They, too, are at the vanguard of hair styling, and many of the newest trends can be discerned here first. They also have a hair-training session where apprentices, under the guidance of a teacher, cut volunteers' hair. The program takes place every Tuesday and Friday nights, beginning at 6 p.m. Since subjects are selected on a first-come, first-serve basis, it pays to get there early, although they are seldom overwhelmed with applicants. The operators prefer to do real cuts rather than trims and will set hair as well, if asked. And it's all free.

KENNETH
19 E 54th St (at Fifth Ave)
752-1800
Mon, Tues, Thurs, Fri: 9-6; Wed: 9-8:30

Kenneth rose to national prominence in the Kennedy years when he was *the* hairdresser to the White House. And unlike many other fads, Kenneth has endured and is much as he was in New York before the glare of fame. Quite simply, he is one of the best. Of course, chances of getting Kenneth himself to touch your hair are just about nil. For that matter, so are chances of getting anyone to look at you without an appointment made well in advance. But success hasn't gone totally to Kenneth's head (ahem!). They have been known to be very kind to visiting out-of-towners, and prices hardly match the address and reputation; there are many more expensive salons around and few first-rate ones that are cheaper. At Kenneth's, they do everything from leg waxing to hair dying, and there's even a downstairs boutique to peruse fashions while waiting for service. The shop is housed in a townhouse, and they are always fully booked and staffed. (The ratio sometimes seems to be 10 staff members to every customer.) Despite a clientele of political, social, and show-business names, they are as friendly as a salon that has a branch in plebian Macy's. And Kenneth does. Every woman should try the Kenneth experience at least once.

LESLIE BLANCHARD

19 E 62nd St (at Madison Ave)
421-4564
Tues, Wed, Fri, Sat: 9-5; Thurs: noon-8

The Private World of Leslie Blanchard (that's the shop's official name, not flowery writing) offers everything for beauty preparation. Blanchard does haircutting, styling, and makeup, and has been known to do complete make-overs. However, they really specialize in simple but perfectly executed, individual treatments. Blanchard is best know for his coloring techniques. Anyone in New York who wants the best uses Blanchard.

LOUIS-GUY D

41 E 57th St (at Madison Ave)
753-6078
Mon-Wed, Fri: 9-5; Thurs: 9-6

A first-class 57th Street salon, Louis-Guy D is most notable for owner and chief hair stylist Louis Gignac's attitude. Despite his location, Gignac firmly believes that every woman is entitled to, and should be able to get, the very best hair and beauty care. So several years ago, Louis-Guy D began offering a one-day make-over program at very reasonable rates. When the deluge of satisfied customers proved him right, Gignac then authored a book, *Everything You Need to Know to Have Great-Looking Hair,* for women unable to visit the shop. There is also a self-service area where customers are free to try and style their own hair with the assistance and advice of the regular stylists. The salon's philosophy is that women should be able to look their best with as little help as possible. It's a refreshing attitude, and Louis-Guy D deserves credit for it.

MAKE-UP CENTER
150 W 55th St (bet Sixth and Seventh Ave)
977-9494
Mon-Wed, Fri: 10-6; Thurs: 10-8; Sat: 10-5

The purveyors of On Stage cosmetics for over two decades, the Make-Up Center counts everyone from teenage girls to the rock group Kiss among its clientele. What makes that range interesting is the Center's credo that makeup should be natural and easy to apply and not wash away at night. "Well and good for the thirteen year olds," you say. "But Kiss?" The answer is simple. The Center is set up along parallel lines to serve stage stars, formal events (such as weddings), and the everyday folks. All of it is individually geared to customer and lifestyle and packaged with instructions on how to achieve the look at home. Private one-hour sessions that feature the latest makeup techniques are tailored to the customer for around $25. It may well be the best bargain in town, for in addition to the personalized expertise, the lesson is given with the expectation that the client won't be back for quite a while, and there's only minimal pressure for you to buy On Stage cosmetics.

NAILS DESIGN BY RELLY
1107 Lexington Ave (bet 77th and 78th St)
535-5333
Mon-Sat: 10-7

Surreptitiously take your malnutritioned nails to Nails Design for present and future transformations. Aurelia Papadumitru and her associates will create beautiful plastic or paper nail wrapping, all the while making sure you end up with healthy nails in the long run—your own. TLC is regularly administered to help a client maintain healthy nails. While you're there, you may want to try the body-waxing and eyelash-tinting services.

NARDI SALON
143 E 57th St (bet Lexington and Third Ave)
421-4810
Mon-Fri: 9:30-5:30; Sat: 9:30-4:30

Vincent and Fred Nardi wrote a book called *How to Do Your Hair Like a Pro,* and their five salons (this is the only one in Manhattan) prove they live up to that title. These are full-service salons: they handle the client from head (hair styling, cutting, perming, coloring, etc.) to toe (pedicures), with makeup (classes and demonstrations as well as application), waxing, and accessory products. The aim is a total look, but it is a look less known for its professional gloss than its ability to be *almost* re-created by the client at home. Nardi even has services for men and children as well. All of this is well worth paying for, but those who wish to avoid 57th Street prices can do so by attending the 5:30 p.m. classes on Tuesday and Wednesday evenings. Nardi runs a school of cosmetology in the Bronx (in association with its own line of cosmetics), so models at the Manhattan salon are most likely to be used solely for hair treatment.

SUGA
115 E 57th St (Galleria, near Lexington Ave)
421-4400
Mon, Tues, Thurs-Sat: 9-6; Wed: 9-8

Among professionals (people whose business it is to look good), Suga is one of the names most often dropped when hairdressers are discussed. There are two interesting aspects to this. For one, professional listeners (people whose business it is to know where certain people shop) realize that *no one* discloses the name of a good hairdresser! Even more intriguing, though, is that Suga, who is credited with inventing the Dorothy Hamill cut, is favored by customers with both long and short hair. Almost never does that happen. Suga not only does both, but has devotees who swear that no one does it better. Here, too, professionals come first, and the average customer may have a long wait.

VIDAL SASSOON
767 Fifth Ave (GM Bldg, bet 58th and 59th St)
535-9200
Tues, Wed: 5:30 p.m.

The name itself conjures up the image of elegance. And who wouldn't want to have the Sassoon touch, especially if it's cheap? Anyone interested in a $5 Sassoon cut is invited to appear at exactly 5:30 at the main salon on Tuesday or Wednesday afternoon. The inspection resembles nothing so much as a cattle call. Depending upon the day, either mobs of straggly-haired women or no one at all shows up. (There are no advance reservations.) The odds are overwhelming that you will not be selected. But then, you may be lucky enough to be chosen for the latest Sassoon cut, unrivaled personal attention, and incredible care—for a small fee. Incidentally, the choice is not made on the basis of personal appearance, but rather the look of the hair—its texture and length. Unchosen customers may not be happy to be sent away by a supervisor with, "Oh, no, no. All wrong!" ringing in their ears. Worse yet (for the "lucky" chosen ones) is hearing the same refrain *after* the cut. So be forewarned.

Bookbinding

CRAFT STUDENTS LEAGUE
Y.W.C.A. of the City of New York
610 Lexington Ave
755-4500

While even a firm believer in do-it-yourself projects would have to admit that there comes a time when the value of a book forces you to have the binding done professionally, it never hurts to have the knowledge that will enable you to understand what an expert is doing to your valuable property. In simple terms of selecting the best craftsman or preventing rip-offs, it is helpful, but in the case of something like bookbinding, there are even greater benefits. While no owner would personally volunteer to bind a rare book, a not-so-valuable book can be made better by a do-it-yourself job. The best way to become a bookbinding expert in this city is to sign up for Natalie Blatt's class at the Craft Students League. The course is offered days or evenings, and the fee is a deal. The student comes away with a working knowledge of bookbinding and some ability to do it personally. The school also offers dozens of other classes, which range from beginner to professional levels. Send for the free catalog, which explains what they've been doing since 1932.

FFOLIO 72
888 Madison Ave (at 72nd St)
879-0675
Mon-Fri: 10-6; Sat: 11:30-5

Muriel Glaser runs Ffolio 72 with the same artistic flair with which she used to run Bendel's stationery department. She binds books in the finest leather or suede, or she places them in a lucite slipcase. Bookbinding is an exact art, and Muriel Glaser makes it a creative art as well. Her prices are high, but bookbinding is an expensive proposition. Ffolio 72 also has a gift boutique (which again reflects Glaser's taste) and a large selection of imprinted writing papers, some of which are custom made. Ffolio 72 creates one of the best collections of stationery in the city. I know for sure, since I use Glaser's personalized correspondence cards.

LEO AND HERBERT WEITZ
1377 Lexington Ave (bet 90th and 91st St)
831-2213
Mon-Fri: 10-6; Sat: noon-3

Bookbinding is a fine art, and Leo and Herbert Weitz are masters at bookbinding. (Their business was founded in 1909.) The specialty here is high-quality bookbinding, and they will bind any books to order. Recently, they rebound the rare-book section of the New York State Medical Library and duplicated 16th-century binding for another client. Leo Weitz claims that their completed job for the latter was indistinguishable from the original 16th-century work because they used the same materials and techniques that the old masters used. Bookbinding is expensive, so it doesn't pay to use inferior materials. On the other hand, given the generally high prices, the Weitzes, using the finest leathers and materials to produce a magnificently bound book, do not overcharge.

NATIONAL EDITION AND LIBRARY BINDERY

244 W 49th St
246-4392
Mon-Fri: 8-4:45

It's not fancy, but National Edition is one of the few binding places that will accept small, individual orders from customers, as well as the large orders they usually receive from libraries. Their style is called "library binding." It is inexpensive, competent, and fast; hence it appeal to libraries. Books bound this way are guaranteed to last twice as long as more expensive bindings. This binding is *not,* however, particularly attractive or even convenient. Library-bound books do not lie flat (as any library reader will attest), and that can be very annoying. National Edition also does thesis, music-score, and document binding, as well as copying and indexing. This is a functional place.

TALAS DIVISION OF TECHNICAL LIBRARY SERVICE

213 W 35th St
736-7744
Mon-Fri: 9-11:30, 1-5

Talas has tools, supplies, equipment, and books for artists, restorers, collectors, bookbinders, museums, archives, libraries, and calligraphers, and offers the same to retail customers. Elaine Haas presides over a wealth of services for bibliophiles. Should a book be in need of repair, there is no better place to take it. After all, if Haas can supply professional book repairers, she certainly knows all there is to know. The attitude here is briskly professional.

Camping Equipment Repair

DOWN EAST
240 Lafayette St
925-2632
Mon-Wed, Fri: noon-6; Thurs: noon-7; Sat: 11 a.m.-2 p.m.
Closed Sat in July and Aug

The full name of this shop is Leon R. Greenman's Down East Outdoor Service Center, and owner Leon R. Greenman provides a phenomenal range of services to outdoor people. He started Down East as a service center for hiking, camping, and outdoor equipment. He has excellent credentials, having been the proprietor of another camping equipment store and a veteran of years of hiking, camping, and trailblazing. During those years, he came to appreciate the lack of service centers for repair of camping equipment, and when he was ready to run a store again, Down East was the result. This store is a godsend for campers. Greenman can do it all. The store offers specialized down dry-cleaning, guidebooks, hiking maps, and USGS Topo maps. Outdoor gear can be modified, repaired, and customized. Hiking boots (which even qualified shoemakers are *not* qualified to fix) can be repaired, sized, and resoled with Vibram. Leo Greenman's expertise in camping equipment repair has almost forced him to branch out into the repair, modification, and customizing of soft travel luggage (but not the sewing of vinyl), as well as the dry-cleaning, repair, patching, modification and recovering of down garments and sleeping paraphernalia. Down East also offers custom-made nylon gear. Another nice feature is Greenman's ability to do business by mail and parcel post.

Carpentry

ERIC GAATHJE
525 W 26th St
563-9317
Mon-Fri: 9:30-4:30

Eric Gaathje ran a carpentry business cum woodworking school until he was forced to move when his old location was demolished. Instead of merely relocating, Gaathje reappraised the entire operation and when he went back into business, he stressed those aspects of the business that most appealed to him. So, nowadays Gaathje is spending his time on custom cabinetry, particularly bookcases, wall units, tables, and even turnings and carvings. It's hard to see who enjoys the work more, the craftsmen who are executing it or the customer who has commissioned it. It doesn't really matter since the work is marvelous. But the most popular are Gaathje's picture-framing classes. Small groups of students are walked through every aspect of picture framing and taught how to turn out picture frames by themselves. Classes are held on the Upper East Side on flexible schedules. During the course, students learn the design and mechanics of frame making, including mitering and gluing of the frame, matting, gold-leafing, painting, staining, and distressing. Many of those talents can be used in other craftwork, and of course the cost of framing is slashed. Graduates can even become professional picture framers. For either business, this place comes highly recommended.

WOOD ART
226 E 83rd St (bet Second and Third Ave)
535-4190
Mon-Fri: 8:30-7; Sat: 9-5

Michael Legos' service and art stem from his talent with chisels (he owns more than 300), planes, and saws—all of which are used to create some of the most magnificent wood pieces anywhere. His craft is so rare that in all the years he has been in business here, he has never wanted for a commission. Much of the business is in sanding, varnishing, polishing, and otherwise repairing wood pieces, and most of those are real antiques. Religious bas-relief icons are almost permanent residents, as are Colonial headboards and more chandeliers than a castle could use. And that doesn't make a dent in the pile awaiting Legos' attention. All of it is wood of intricate and detailed design. Legos enjoys occasional trips into the 20th century as well. So, while he can reproduce any article down to its defects (people *like* worm-eaten antiques and slightly rocky chairs), his imagination really takes flight when he executes original designs ("Yours or mine," he says). Trained in design and drafting in his native Greece, Legos can build an exact model of the space shuttle one day, then turn around the next day and create a classic chandelier inhabited by forest friends hiding between the lights.

Chair Caning

CHAIRS CANED
133 W 72nd St (seventh floor)
724-4408
Thurs-Sat: 1-5

One fine day, I actually got to speak to the proprietor of Chairs Caned. I told him that he came highly recommended and that I would like to recommend him to others. He was very busy (as befits an expert practitioner of a dying art) and told me that he would get the information about his hours, rates, and other items to me soon. Unfortunately, I tried once a week for almost a year to reach him again. Two years later, he hasn't moved, and his phone hasn't been disconnected, so if you can track him down, he is *still* highly recommended.

VETERAN'S CANING SHOP
550 W 35th St
868-3244
Mon-Fri: 6:30-4; Sat: 9-1

Veteran's owner John Bausert has written a book about chair caning, and claims his shop is one of the oldest in the world. Certainly, his prices and craftsmanship are among the best in town, and Bausert believes in passing his knowledge along. Customers are encouraged to repair their own chairs, and if you want to try, the procedure is outlined in his book, and the necessary materials are sold in the shop. If you don't want to try (or have had disastrous results on your own), the shop will repair the chair on the premises or, for a slight charge, pick it up from your home. Since chair caning is such a specialized and limited industry, a company often has a monopoly in its neighborhood. So, it's remarkable that Bausert offers such services at such good prices. Equally remarkable are the stacks of cane—I've never seen so much. In addition to caning, Veteran's also stocks materials for chair and furniture repair; you will be encouraged to tackle these jobs, too.

WEST SIDE STRIPPER
73 W 82nd St
873-3616
Call for hours

Aside from a catchy name, West Side Stripper also boasts a host of desirable services. They undertake furniture restoration and furniture stripping, but what really keeps then in demand is their expert chair caning. I guess the reason that service is not featured in the nomenclature is that "West Side Chair Caner" just doesn't have the same ring to it.

Chimney Sweep

CHIMINEY CRICKET
319 W 11th St
691-0171
Daily: 24 hours by phone only

Even 10 years ago, WBFP's (real-estate ad lingo for woodburning fireplaces) were detriments rather than attractions in an apartment. At about that same time, Allayane Johnson had become a former actress and sometime writer looking for a full-time job. When a neighbor's flue needed cleaning, Johnson tried doing it. She eventually decided that chimney cleaning wasn't really any dirtier than show business, and Chiminey Cricket was born. In a way, Johnson hasn't completely left the theater. For one thing, her occupation is one that lends itself to fantasy. She has a great sense of humor and tells tales about her funny experiences as a chimney sweep. She carts her paraphernalia in a shopping cart on the subway, since "like most city people, I don't drive, and anyway I don't need a truck. I'm told that in pre-war Europe, sweeps traveled on bicycles." As for experiences—well, she was once called to clean the flue of a hotel room by a guest in the hotel. And then there was the time when atop a chimney on a roof, she suddenly realized from the heat on her derriere that the fireplace was in use! Johnson, who prefers being called by her professional name, Chiminey Cricket, is of the old school. She eschews fancy equipment and vacuums; instead she relies on telescoping rods and brushes. And she can afford to be picky. Most of her work is in the Village, because it is convenient and because downtown fireplaces are less likely to have been covered over. But she will go elsewhere in the city if her safety and transportation is assured. She doesn't like to go higher than six floors (which eliminates luxury high-rises) since her brushes can't be manipulated at great lengths. Besides, her rates are based on the distance between the fireplace and the roof, but the rates are very reasonable—better than a Broadway show — and there are discounts for neighbors or for several fireplaces on the same location. And finally, there is no charge for her fireplace advice or her own entertaining slices of city life.

China and Glassware Repair

CENTER ART STUDIO
149 W 57th St (bet Sixth and Seventh Ave, second floor)
247-3550
Mon-Fri: 10-6; weekends by appointment

Center Art boasts "fine art restoration and display since 1919," and the operative word is *fine.* This is not the place to take a ceramics-class mug or ashtray, but owners of really fine crystal, porcelain, china, or bronze art cite Center Art as the definitive place to go for repairs. The house specialty is restoration of antiquities, with an emphasis on Oriental bronzes and ceramics. But that is but a fraction of their work. Lansing Moore's staff can repair and/or restore porcelain, terra-cotta, pre-Columbian, Oriental, and European artwork, as well as mother-of-pearl inlay, tortoise shell, ivory, coral, jade, and other precious stones. And that's not all. Center Art will restore antique furniture and decorative objects using original materials where possible. Once the piece is restored, Center Art likes to see it displayed to its best advantage. So, they also design and install display bases and cases, and they will pack and crate articles for shipment. In short, they claim to be the oldest and most diverse art-restoration studio in the city, and with their clientele of galleries, dealers, and finicky collectors, no one disputes that title.

EARTHWORKS POTTERY/M. SIMONDS STUDIO

255 E 74th St (bet Second and Third Ave)
650-9337
Tues-Thurs: noon-7; Fri, Sat: noon-5:30 (Earthworks)
Thurs-Sat: 2-5:30 (M. Simonds)

Margaret Simonds ran the M. Simonds Studio for more than 15 years. It was the best place in New York for the restoration of fine-art objects. In 1979, she moved around the corner to share quarters with Earthworks, and the merger created a comprehensive shop that caters to stoneware, pottery, and porcelain pieces from the kiln to "beyond hope" stages. The Earthworks section of the business is both a retail shop and a pottery school. The front of the shop has a fine selection of one-of-a-kind porcelain and stoneware pieces made by local potters. (Great for gifts!) The shop also conducts ongoing classes in pottery making, taking advantage of the on-site studio equipment. During the later part of the week (note the hours), Ms. Simonds is in residence. Her specialty is the restoration of pottery, glass, porcelain, jade, cloisonné, clay, and fine-art objects. If the use of the word *restoration,* as opposed to *repair,* doesn't set the tone for this business, then the term *art objects* should. Everything is treated as a valued piece of artwork, and the repairs themselves are flawless. There is an emphasis on pottery and restorations. Simonds is definitely not the place to come to repair a chipped coffee cup or last week's class project from Earthworks. But if you have a damaged Grecian urn, wrap it up carefully and bring it here. Simonds is friendly, competent, and reliable.

GEM MONOGRAM

623 Broadway (at Houston St)
674-8960
Mon-Fri: 9-5

Gem Monogram works with glass (as opposed to crystal), and their specialty is the repair and monogramming of glassware. It appears that the monogramming of fine crystal is very difficult, and most places—Gem included—will not undertake the job. Rather, Gem concentrates on producing a fine, if cheaper than crystal, glass that is turned into a variety of products. Should their own, or anyone else's, glass break, Gem can probably fix it. Gem's specialty is the sale and repair of crystal chandeliers.

HESS REPAIRS
200 Park Ave S (at 17th St)
260-2255
Mon-Fri: 10:30-4; appointments necessary for later times

Hess bills itself as "repairers of the irrepareable" (sic), and despite their misspelling, it does a fantastic job on anything but furniture, electrical appliances, and mechanical devices. Their specialties include china, glass, handbags, ivory, jade, lamps, *objets d'art,* and virtually the entire run of the alphabet, including *x, y,* and *z,* which proprietor Bernice F. Hirsch says stand for "unusual items not otherwise listed." The important thing, however, is that Hess can usually restore an item so that the damage is unnoticeable. (Broken crystal stemware pieces that cannot be restored are reincarnated as crystal dinner bells.) One specialty—the replacement of blue glass liners for antique silver salt dishes—is said to be unique in the city. Hess accepts parcel post-insured shipments of items to be repaired. Upon receipt, they mail an estimate for restoration. Many of Hess' best customers are museums and antiques dealers who are attracted by their craftsmanship.

MR. FIXIT
1300 Madison Ave (at 92nd St)
369-7775
Mon-Fri: 9-6; Sat: 9-5

True to his name, Mr. Fixit can fix almost anything. Indeed, it would be hard to find something that this shop *cannot* fix, although the specialties appear to be housewares and objects in the mineral class. This includes repairs on jade, ivory, shells, glass, and china, as well as all types of metal work.

SANO STUDIO
767 Lexington Ave (at 60th St, room 403)
759-6131
Mon-Fri: 9-5:30, closed July

Mrs. J. Baran presides over this fourth-floor antiques repair shop, and she has an eye for excellence. That eye is focused on the quality of the workmanship and the quality of the goods brought here to be repaired. Both are only of the best. Sano's area of specialization is limited to repair of porcelain, pottery, ivory, and tortoise-shell works and antiques. While Hess repairs everything but the kitchen sink (and might repair that, too, if you could convince them that it's an antique), Sano concentrates on specific areas. As a result, both have their loyal adherents. Some customers like the idea of being able to bring a hodgepodge of broken items to one repair shop. Other customers, particularly those who repair only one item at a time, prefer the feeling of security you get with specialized service. Perhaps it's safer to say that it's a matter of opinion.

Clock and Watch Repair

CLOCKS AND THINGS
1001 Second Ave (at 53rd St)
755-8766
Mon-Fri: 10:-5:30; Sat: 11-5

Clock repair here refers to grandfather clocks and to antique timepieces left by your grandfather. Now if that's the category you're in, Joseph Fanelli is the person to see. He claims a specialty in the care of high-quality "investment type" timepieces. He also has one of the world's largest selections of rare and unusual carriage clocks. They are something to see, but by no means are they all the shop has ticking for it. There is about an equal split between sales and restoration, and Fanelli makes house calls, gives free estimates, and even rents out timepieces for special assignments. The next time an Agatha Christie movie is filmed in New York, you'll know where that antique clock on the mantel came from. And when it stops ticking, you know who'll repair it, for sure!

E. GREENBERG
400 Madison Ave (at 47th St, room 705)
759-6630
Mon-Thurs: 9-5; Fri: 9-2

There are hundreds of clocks inside this store, and those members of the staff who aren't selling timepieces are completely engaged in clock repair. They claim "complicated movements are our specialty," but the slogan is not limited to clocks. There is an interest in automations, including antique windup toys, music boxes, and magnificent dolls. They can competently repair any of these, and with great reluctance will occasionally sell a really good piece. E. Greenberg advertises "expert repair at reasonable rates." It's funny that they are the only shop to advertise as such since, while there's no quarrel with the quality of their work, the rates seem high.

SUTTON CLOCK SHOP
139 E 61st St (at Lexington Ave)
758-2260, 473-0196, 689-4596
Mon-Fri: 11-5

Sutton Clock Shop takes its name for Kay Sutton, not the nearby neighborhood of Sutton Place, but the service and selection is every bit as classy as that address. While Sutton's forte is the selling—and acquiring—of unusual timepieces, there is at least an equal interest in the maintenance and repair of antique clocks. (It appears that most timepiece merchants have to become expert at their repair if they enter the antiques business.) The business is about equally divided between the two, and Sutton's reputation is based upon the fine work evident in both. Some of the timepieces—even the contemporary ones—are truly outstanding, and there's a long list of satisfied customers endorsing their repair work.

Clothing Repair and Reweaving

MAGIC MENDERS
118 E 59th St
759-6453
Mon-Fri: 9-5

If you have an emergency with any of your clothing while you are in the vicinity of 59th Street, head over to Magic Menders. They will repair almost any type of wearing apparel, from monogrammed A's to zippers, on the spot. Of course, they prefer to be given some time in which to work, but their reputation rests on emergency repairs. Their vast repertoire includes panty-hose, glove, and umbrella mending and handbag or zipper repairs. And if you would like to keep Great Aunt Tilda's linens, although the monogram is all wrong, Magic Menders can fix that, too. Their mending really is invisible.

Delivery and Messenger Services

ARCHER SERVICES
855 Sixth Ave
563-7685
Daily: 24 hours

Archer can deliver anything from an envelope to a jet, but the main asset is that there is a 24-hour-a-day, seven-day-a-week courier service. That's for emergency messages, and Archer does it straightaway. They even have a "Lease-a-Man" service.

JIMINY SPLIT DELIVERY SERVICES
147 W 46th St
354-7373
Daily: 24 hours

Jiminy Split can hand-deliver a package from New York to Washington, D.C., in less than four hours. That's remarkably fast; the overnight service of Federal Express can't do that, and the U.S.

mail is not even in the running. (It once took three weeks for a package of mine to go from New York to Washington, D.C.—it went by way of Washington, North Carolina!) So, if you want a fast, reliable, and personal service, Jiminy Split can deliver anywhere within the continental U.S. as fast as a plane or train can deliver the messenger. (Rates include travel fare, plus delivery expense.) Within the city, rates depend upon distance traveled (the city is divided into zones) and how long delivery takes. There are several Jiminy Split branches around the city.

Doll Repair

NEW YORK DOLL HOSPITAL
787 Lexington Ave (bet 61st and 62nd St, second floor)
838-7527
Mon-Sat: 9:30-6; closed July and on Sat in Aug

The New York Doll Hospital has been fixing, mending, and restoring dolls to health since 1900. Owner Irving Chais has been operating in the cramped two-room hospital since 1947, when he took over from his grandfather who had begun fixing the dolls of his clients' children in his hair salon. Originally, the children wanted the dolls' hair done along with theirs. When the senior Chais obliged by keeping a supply of doll wigs, he discovered that he had a better business with the dolls than with the women. So, he abandoned the ladies and created the "hospital." Irving Chais came into the business one Christmas season when his father was ailing and needed help. Several flipped wigs later, Chais was the latest family member in the business, despite a lack of formal training and medical credentials. But he learned by experience. By now he has replaced antique fingers, reconstructed China heads and German rag dolls, and authentically restored antique dolls to within a month of accuracy on their birth dates. Chais doesn't collect dolls himself, and he thinks the Cabbage Patch doll looks like a pig. But he has a healthy respect for the affections of his customers, and no customer is told that it doesn't pay to repair a doll. If it is brought to the hospital, Chais assumes it has sentimental value to its owner, so he does his best to nurse it back to health and happiness.

Dry Cleaners, Laundries

MME. BLANCHEVOYE
75 E 130th St
368-7272
Mon-Fri: 7-4:30

Because of the shop's location, most of Mme. Blanchevoye's customers prefer to use the pickup and delivery service. Mme.

Blanchevoye offers hand laundering with exclusive hand finishing (actually, how could it be anything else?), and the specialty is the care and cleaning of fine and antique linens. The prices are on the high side, but at least Miss Evans (see "Laundry of Miss Evans") and Mme. Blanchevoye are competitive with each other, even though they share the same address.

CLEANTEX
2335 12th Ave (at 133rd St)
283-1200
Mon-Fri: 7-4

Cleantex specializes in drapery, slipcover, tapestry, and lampshade cleaning, with a free pickup and delivery service. It's an essential thing to offer since no one would go to this location laden with heavy draperies and slipcovers. Their reputation is the best, and they count museums and churches among their customers.

DUN RITE DRY CLEANERS
141 W 38th St (at Broadway)
221-9296
Mon-Fri: 8-5:25

If you're used to hometown prices, you'd better sit down when you get the bill from Dun Rite. No matter where your hometown is (including other parts of New York), this will seem high. Then again, such customers as Halston, Geoffrey Beene, and Oscar de la Renta know about the prices and *still* send their dirty clothing to be cleaned here, because they think that Dun Rite is the very best. Besides their reliability, they are known for fast service and for versatility, which enables them to clean any fabric. This is particularly important when you are dealing with designer clothing.

HALLAK CLEANERS
1239 Second Ave (at 65th St)
832-9015
Mon-Fri: 7-6:30; Sat: 8-3; closed on Sat in July and Aug and for first two weeks of Aug

Hallak is unusual on several counts. First, it is a 35-year-old family business run by Joe Hallak and his son, Jean Claude Hallak, which probably accounts for its exceptional pride and personal service. Second, its spotless reputation means that much of their work comes from referrals by designers of delicate fabrics and patterns as well as other dry cleaners who will not undertake high-risk tasks. Finally, Hallak pledges that no garment ever leaves the premises unwearable. So if there's a button missing, a hem hanging, or a zipper or seam ripped, the shop fixes it without being told. For me, that's the crowning touch, since there's not much worse than putting on a newly cleaned suit from the closet 10 minutes before a meeting and finding a button missing. (Surprisingly, Joe Hallak says that not every customer appreciates this service. Some won't pay for the labor, in which case Hallak chalks it up to a matter of *his* pride and does it gratis!) Hallak has had calls and customers from all over the world, and most of them agree with the man from San Francisco who wrote that "Hallak is the best dry cleaners in the country." Calvin Klein also thinks so. He uses Hallak for cleaning all of his suedes and leathers; he even seeks Hallak's advice when planning his designer show samples. He's not alone. Criscione, Lanvin, and Giorgio Armani do the same. So why not you?

LAUNDRY OF MISS EVANS
75 E 130th St
234-2334

As the name suggests, Miss Evans runs an establishment from a time gone by. Established in 1911, Miss Evans has hand-laundered and hand-ironed fine linens and clothing—with no markings—ever since. There are families whose heirloom linens are handed down from generation to generation, accompanied by Miss Evans' phone number. Since this plant is located in Harlem, Miss Evans picks up and delivers wherever the customers are. Prices are not cheap, but the best never is. I like the idea that *so* patrician is Miss Evans that its unmarked item is a status symbol.

LEATHERCRAFT PROCESS OF AMERICA
62 W 37th St
564-8980
Mon-Fri: 9-5; Sat: 10-1:45

Leathercraft is all things to all suedes, sheepskins, and leathers. They will clean, redye, reline, repair, and lengthen or shorten any suede or leather garment brought in. That includes boots, gloves, clothing, and handbags, as well as odd leather items. Because leather is extremely difficult to clean, the process can be painfully expensive. However, Leathercraft has a reputation to maintain (it dates back to 1938), and their prices have remained competitive.

PERRY PROCESS
1315 Third Ave (at 75th St) 1050 Sixth Ave
628-8300 730-0220
Mon-Fri: 8-6:30

Perry is one of the most reasonably priced dry cleaners in Manhattan. They also do alterations; in fact, they specialize in making repairs and dyeing knitted garments (Sixth Avenue branch only). This specialty makes this shop a favorite of the Madison Avenue Italian-knit boutique world, and they *still* don't raise their prices!

TIECRAFTERS
116 E 27th St (at Park Ave S)
867-7676
Mon-Fri: 9-5

Old ties never die or even fade away here, although they may be dyed, widened, straightened, or cleaned. Tiecrafters is dedicated to the philosophy that a tie can live forever, and they provide the services to make that possible. In addition to converting tie widths, they will restore soiled or spotted ties and clean and repair all kinds of neckwear. Perhaps most impressive is Andy Tarshis' willingness to discuss tie maintenance so that frequent visits to the shop won't be necessary. Tiecrafters offers several pamphlets on the subject, including one that tells how to de-spot a tie at home. Tiecrafters accepts business via parcel post, and their charge for cleaning a tie is reasonable. They also clean and restore antique and embroidered lace. Special free tip to gentlemen readers: if you roll your tie at night, wrinkles will be gone in time for that important meeting in the morning.

Eyeglasses Repair

DELL AND DELL
19 W 44th St (at Fifth Ave)
575-1686
Mon-Fri: 9-6; Sat: 9-1

If you desperately need Dell and Dell, you probably can't read this. But no need to worry. Their big advantage is that they do on-the-spot emergency repair on glasses even if they were purchased in Peoria! There are some exceptions (if the frames were trampled by an elephant at the circus, there might be a longer wait), but this is the place to go for eyeglasses emergencies in the city. They also repair binoculars. Of course, Dell and Dell won't mind if you stop by for regular optical needs.

Formal Wear Rentals

If you're in New York long enough to consider renting a tuxedo, you should consider buying one. There isn't that much difference in price, and the fit is better. (The only exception is that if you are in New York for just two days, and one of those two days is your niece's wedding.) There are many routes you can go. For totally serviceable, respectable tuxedos that you can buy off the rack at noon and wear at dinner, try Wallach's or any of the middle-range department stores. For elegant and suave formal wear, try André

Oliver, Paul Stuart, Madonna, or—my favorite—Saks. However, that can run into considerable money, and renting may suddenly seem like a better option. But not really. You can always try the thrift shops. Retail stores and manufacturers frequently give away large numbers of brand-new unsold formal suits to get a tax deduction and avoid a total loss. Look for this particularly after the rush of June weddings, graduations, and proms. You can pick up a brand-new suit for a song, and the sizing will be at least as good as at a rental shop. (The rental stores sometimes have seasonal sales to get rid of formerly rented garments.) Finally, if whimsy hits you, try the antique-clothing stores. Here, too, prices are rock bottom, and sometimes the fashions are so old they couldn't be more current (no matter how way-out you are, however, you really won't need a 1930s tuxedo!). Okay, okay. If you don't want to take my advice, here are some rental places.

A. T. HARRIS

47 E 44th St (bet Madison and Vanderbilt Ave, second floor)
682-6325
Mon-Wed, Fri: 8:30-6; Thurs: 8:30-7;
Sat: 10-3 by appointment

A. T. Harris has been in the business of outfitting gentlemen correctly since 1892. This store sells only current formal wear "of the better kind." So expect to find proper cutaways, tails, and tuxedos rather than iridescent disco wedding outfits. Shoes and accessories run in the same categories and are also readily available.

BALDWIN FORMALS

52 W 56th St (bet Fifth and Sixth Ave)
245-8190, 246-1782
Mon-Fri: 8:30-5:30; Sat: 10-1

Baldwin carries a full line of men's formal wear that ranges from tropical-weight dinner jackets to formal black tie and tails. It supplies head (top hats) to toe (shoes) coverage. The big virtue here is the same-day delivery, and it's free. On orders received before 5 p.m. weekdays and noon Saturdays, they guarantee same-day service. It's an offer you can't beat.

LORDAE FORMAL WEAR

Several locations (check telephone directory)
597-5100
Sun-Tues, Thurs, Fri: 11-8; Wed: 11-6; Sat: 10-5

Lordae is synonymous with rental wear in New York. With 20 branches throughout the city, they are accessible and draw on a wide stock that's made wider by their ability to send things from branch to branch. You also have the advantage of enabling members of a wedding party living in different boroughs to match ensembles without assembling en masse in one location. There is even an arrangement that gives the groom a free outfit, if enough members of the party rent from Lordae. The company prides itself on being trendy and modern. (I once overheard them ask what color the lady's gown was going to be so they could match the man's shirt and jacket with it.) If you like dinner jackets in all colors of the rainbow and want a place that has an excellent selection of what *you* want, Lordae should be first on your list. If, however, you are the conservative type, you will be shocked by what passes as formal garb here. Their black tuxedo selection is limited in both style and size, and the cutaway suit stock is paltry. Because of the size of the operation, however, styles are probably the most current and prices among the lowest in the city. If you want a teal-blue shirt to match your lady's gown, this may be the only place in the city that can oblige.

Fur Rentals

ABET RENT-A-FUR
307 Seventh Ave (at 28th St, room 2004)
989-5757
Mon-Fri: 9-6; Sat: 9-1; closed Sat in July and Aug

Abet rents some of the finest furs in New York. They have stoles, jackets, capes, and coats, and they will pick up and deliver as well. This is one rental that's worth the rent. Irving Shavelson of Abet also sells furs at a good savings.

Furniture Rentals

APARTMENT FURNITURE RENTALS
986 Third Ave (at 59th St)
751-1530
Mon-Sat: 9:30-6

Apartment Furniture Rentals claims that all of the furniture they rent is brand new. That being the case, it would be nice to know what they do with the stuff that is returned. But since I don't know, and I am going on the assumption that this is a short-term necessity, Apartment Furniture Rentals is a good bet. They well rent furnishings of any size, whether for a single room or a full apartment. The free decorator service helps, as does the immediate delivery and the rental-purchase plan. I would advise against the latter, though. While the furniture is good enough to rent, its price and quality wouldn't make it my first choice as a purchase.

CHURCHILL-WINCHESTER FURNITURE RENTALS
44 E 32nd St (at Park Ave)
535-3400
Mon-Fri: 9-7; Sun: 9-6

Say Churchill, and you think of staid old England, right? Well, *this* Churchill is starkly contemporary. They can fill any size order for business or residence, and offer free interior-decorating advice and a lease-purchase plan. Churchill has several floors of furniture, so a customer can simply select whatever is needed from stock or borrow from the loaner program until special orders are processed. Churchill can also offer a comprehensive package, including housewares and appliances if needed, and they specialize in executive locations (again, both corporately and personally). They will rent out anything from a single chair to entire homes and have done so for sports-team managers, executives on temporary assignment, and actors with tentative contracts. If modern is the look, Churchill is the choice.

INTERNATIONAL FURNITURE RENTALS
345 Park Ave (at 51st St)
421-0340
Mon-Fri: 9:30-5:30; Sat: 10-2

International Furniture Rentals has a small showroom, but claims to be the largest home and office furniture rental firm in the metropolitan area. The quality is very good—the kind of furniture you might actually buy yourself. There's no decorating service, but that's not a great loss since rental agencies seldom excel in the decorating area, anyway.

Furniture Repair and Restoration

ANTIQUE FURNITURE WORKROOM
225 E 24th St (at Third Ave)
683-0551
Mon-Fri: 8-4

William Olsen took over what may have been the definitive antiques-restoration firm in the city and made it even better. Antique Furniture Workroom was the traditional place of choice for French polishing, chair repair, and the restoration of woodwork. Olsen added services that were decidedly lacking, including antique-furniture restoration (with a specialty in American, English, Continental, and Oriental originals), fine French polishing, gold leafing, and caning. The cost of an antiques-restoration project is steep. However, Olsen's company has two big advantages. One is that they are reliable. Many an antique has lost all value after "help" from a restorer who didn't know what he was doing. The other plus is that estimates are given in the home.

MAX SCHNEIDER AND SON ANTIQUES

225 E 24th St
369-2065
Mon-Fri: 8-noon, 1-4 by appointment

Slightly more accessible than the Sack Conservation Company (see next entry) but no less competent or tony, Max Schneider is a family-run business that has restored New York's finest furniture for almost six decades. Certain trades seem to have family traits, and being selective about whom they will accept for customers appears to be the trait of quality furniture restorers. At Schneider, too, an appointment to view the furniture must be made and kept before they will deign to think about doing the actual work. But chances are better that the work will be accepted here because they are not restricted by period, time, or even original quality. In fact, they are not even restricted to wood; they do upholstery, wicker work, and even chair caning. If the dining-room chair needs a face-lift to fit your latest decorating motif, this is the place that can do it. The staff is also somewhat friendlier than Sack's

SACK CONSERVATION COMPANY

15 E 57th St (at Fifth Ave)
753-6562
Mon-Fri: 8-3:30 by appointment

Before you decide that Sack's is the place to get the old bean bag or the flour-sack sofa from the Sixties fixed, note the address and the particular hours when customers are allowed the honor of applying for an appointment to have furniture appraised. Obviously, this is a class act, and Sack is the proprietor's name rather than the kind of furniture he handles. Rumor has it that among those clients whose furniture has been deemed worthy of Sack's attention have been the White House and countless museums. So, if your sofa is valuable enough for such exclusive attention, this is the place to take it. There is a further caveat in that the firm deals only in Colonial furniture, although they will consider American items of the 1800s. The work is first-rate, if not cheap. But then, owners of such pieces probably aren't looking for cheap repairs, anyway.

Gift Wrapping

ANNIE WRAPPER
956 Lexington Ave (bet 69th and 70th St)
535-7903
Mon-Fri: 10-6; Sat: 11-5; closed Sat in summer

Anne Gerber has the sweepstakes for the most unique wrapping service in New York all wrapped up. Her package-wrapping talents have been applied to everything from 400 Christian Dior change purses given as favors for a benefit of the New York City Ballet to the live, on-camera wrapping of Chauncy Howell, one of the local news-show celebrities. In between, there have been thousands upon thousands of individual and group packages brought in by mothers, brides, birthday-party-goers, long-distance lovers, and corporations for the special touch that could even make 400 purses unique. These feats have been accomplished with the Annie Wrapper collection of over 250 ribbons, imported and unique papers, and more boxes, sequins, feathers, and cards than can be imagined. Anne Gerber aims to wrap each package with the recipient in mind (and sometimes with the giver literally and physically inside), and she draws on this huge collection to individualize each endeavor. Those who have a knack for wrapping can buy the papers and ribbons by the yard and do it themselves. Otherwise, Annie Wrapper can wrap and ship your object to you via UPS. Corporate gift wrapping is also available.

Haircuts

Children

F.A.O. SCHWARZ—BARBER SHOP
745 Fifth Ave (at 58th St)
644-9461
Fri, Sat: 10-5

F.A.O. Schwarz inherited the Best and Company haircutting shop, complete with barber poles. For an incredibly low price, Rudy Pecoraro and his staff will cut children's hair with the skill and care that Best and Company was known for. Smart parents take advantage of the cheapest and best haircuts in town by getting their own hair cut there, and some of them even manage to steer their children through F.A.O. Schwarz' three floors without purchasing a Schwarz toy. Take heart. It can be done!

KENNETH FOR KIDS

Macy's (at 34th St and Broadway, fifth floor)
594-1717
Mon, Thurs, Fri: 9:45-8:30; Tues, Wed, Sat: 9:45-5:30; Sun 10-5

Kenneth did Jackie O's hair when she was Jackie K., and for a reasonable fee (by New York standards), this salon inside Macy's will give your child's hair the Kenneth touch, too. Actually, the salon is the showpiece of the Macy's children's floor, and you can bet your pogo stick it is well done. The care and style are so good that many a smart mother has also sat in the custom-made seats. Kenneth has put a stop to that practice now, but any children's haircut here entitles an adult to a 20 percent discount downstairs at the store's regular salon.

MICHAELS'S CHILDREN'S HAIRCUTTING SALON

1263 Madison Ave (at 90th St)
289-9612
Mon-Sat: 9-5; closed Sat in July and Aug

A longtime New York tradition. Michael's drawing card has always been their rapport with children and the consistency of their personnel and style. Nick Di Sisto, the salon's owner, is living proof of this. He worked for Michael for years, and when Michael retired, Sisto bought him out. Many of the hairstylists have worked under both owners. Appointments are unheard of, and lollipops, seats shaped like toy cars, and comic books are *de rigueur*. This place is totally dedicated to children, but there is a sprinkling of mothers who get their hair cut at children's prices.

Family

ASTOR PLACE HAIR STYLISTS

2 Astor Place (at Broadway and Astor Place)
475-9854
Mon-Sat: 8-8; Sun: 9-6

Astor Place doesn't need its address listed here. Just follow the mob to the spot in Manhattan where getting a haircut is an entire *event* not unlike being admitted to the hallowed halls of the latest "in" nightspot. The personnel inside what was once a modest neighborhood barbershop don't even have to actually *do* anything to generate the crowds outside begging to get in. But they do give the trendiest, wildest, punkiest, and most unusual haircuts on the scene. The real reason to stand on the sidewalk is to see and be seen. How did this all get started? Well, it seems that the Vezza brothers inherited a barbershop from their father in the East Village at a time "when not even cops were getting haircuts." Enrico took note of the newly regentrified neighborhood's young trendies and their sleek haircuts and changed the name of the shop to "Hair Stylists." And that, folks, made history. Now, the shop is staffed with a resident manager, doorman (how may barbershops do you know of that need a doorman?), a loft, and an ever-increasing number of barbers. But for all the hullabaloo, Enrico and Frank Vezza operate this phenomenon as a family business in much the same way as Enrico Senior ran it in the 1940s. Prices are downright cheap (the top fee is $10), and they will just as happily cut a normal resident's hair as the next Andy Warhol cover girl. A haircut at this unique barbershop may be the cheapest, most fun-filled souvenir the city has to offer.

Men

ATLAS BARBER SCHOOL
44 Third Ave
475-1360
Mon-Fri: 9-9; Sat: 9-6

Atlas is the only barber school in the city. Haircuts here are as cheap as they come in the city, and senior students, under close supervision, work on customers. Custom grooming it's not, but for the price, it's excellent.

FEATURE TRIM
1108 Lexington Ave (bet 77th and 78th St)
650-9746
Tues-Sat: 10:30-7

Salvatore Andenocci started cutting hair when he was 12 years old. For 24 years, he cut hair in a shop in the East Sixties, but some years ago, escalating rent forced him to move further uptown. His clientele followed him, and for the last decade, he has operated a seven-chair shop at the Lexington Avenue location. All those years have given Andenocci expertise aplenty. He specializes in simple haircuts that need nothing more than a combing until the next trim. And despite a clientele that includes Rex Harrison, scores of prominent businessmen and politicians and "that sportscaster, what's his name?" Feature Trim is still reasonably priced and fairly unknown. Andenocci and his assistants offer five basic cuts. All follow the natural no-mess-no-fuss edict. Feature Trim was once named the top haircutting shop in the country by the now defunct *New York Herald Tribune*. As the hair-care ad says, "He's not getting older—he's getting better."

JAMES OF THE PLAZA

Plaza Hotel (at Fifth Ave and 59th St)
751-8380
Mon-Sat: 9-6

No genuine barbershop in New York is inexpensive, and the one at the Plaza is no exception. But if you want a really first-class trim, styling, manicure, or a combination thereof, there is no handier or better shop to visit. The location is right off the Plaza entrance, on the mezzanine. Ask for Marie to give you an extra-special manicure, and Emil is as fine a hair craftsman as there is in New York. Be sure to call for an appointment, as they have many regular customers. Tell them I sent you.

Handbag Repair

ARTBAG CREATIONS

735 Madison Ave (at 64th St)
744-2720
Mon-Fri: 9-5:45; Sat: 9-4; closed Sat in summer

Artbag will make, sell, or repair any type of handbag, and they will do it well. The range goes from mounting needlepoint bags to relining heirloom bridal bags, as well as leather, reptile (including some of the best lizard skins in the city), and beaded evening bags. Mssrs. Rosenberg, Moore, and Price are European craftsmen who modestly advertise themselves as "understanding, genteel, and good listeners. They know their business." Any of their customers could have been quoted as having said the same thing. Artbag is also known for its sense of style. It carries the latest and the best designs and frequently refashions old handbags into chic trend-setters. It isn't everyday that you come across men who know more about handbags than most women, but these gentlemen certainly do, and they keep up with the latest styles. Ask for Lou Rosenberg. I'm not alone in voting him one of the warmest and funniest people in the city.

MODERN LEATHER GOODS REPAIR SHOP

11 W 32nd St (bet Fifth and Sixth Ave, fifth floor)
279-3263
Mon-Thurs: 8:30-5:30; Fri: 8:30-5; Sat: 9-2

Modern Leather Goods does needlepoint mounting and handbag repairs, as well as luggage repair. Mr. Paul of Modern Leather claims that no job is impossible, and he respects the sentimental attachment many women feel for their bags. Indeed, many women would rather repair a bag than break in a new one. Modern Leather Goods will repair all types of handbags—including beaded and needlepoint ones—and leather goods. They also have facilities for cleaning leather and suede clothing, and they can make bags to order.

SUPERIOR REPAIR CENTER
133 Lexington Ave
889-7211
Mon-Fri: 9-6; Sat: 10-3; closed Sat in summer

Superior Repair Center is the first choice of Bergdorf's, Botticelli, Bloomingdale's, and Tiffany's for the repair of leather goods. With a recommendation like that, is anything else necessary? If it is, here's more. These people are expert at luggage and handbag mechanisms, so much so that they custom-make sample cases (with or without wheels) and can do the same for bags. They also repair or replace zippers, handbags, jackets, boots, and another specialty, instrument cases. Oh, yes, sporting equipment, too. They can fix tents, backpacks, and any of the myriad things that mud and rain can damage on camping equipment.

Health Clubs

With all the interest in physical fitness these days, there has been a corresponding growth in the number of health clubs, gymnasiums, and fitness centers. For the New York resident, membership in a club nearby is usually the most satisfactory way to be assured of availability of facilities. Note that some clubs are fly-by-night operations; you may not be able to get your money back if they go out of business. Also note that most clubs have constant come-on membership specials; so do not pay regular prices if you can help it. The New York Health and Racquet Clubs (24 E 13th St, 1433 York Ave, 20 E 50th St, 132 E 45th St, and 110 W 56th St) have generally good facilities, and are most convenient. A new one opens in the Wall Street area in 1986. The Vertical Club (330 E 61st St) is probably the classiest club; the Paris Health Club (752 West End Ave) is the handiest for Upper West Siders. Downtown, try the Apple Health and Sports Club (211 Thompson St and 88 Fulton St). Those staying at the Parker Meridien Hotel, the Vista International, or the Marriott Marquis will find excellent facilities in the hotels; memberships are also available for New York residents. Older midtown hotels do not generally have any health equipment. For those who just want a workout (unless you want to use Central Park) and pay a daily fee, try Natural Physique Center (104 Fourth Ave) or the Body Center (552 Sixth Ave). 21st Century Nautilus Center (220 E 57th St) will work out a special appointment for out-of-town visitors. When you finish your workout, rush over to Bloomingdale's and get some of Mrs. Field's chocolate chip cookies!

TENTH STREET BATHS

268 E 10th St (bet First Ave and Avenue A)
473-8806
Mon, Wed: 9-9; Tues, Thurs, Fri: 9-9;
Sat, Sun: 8:30-4:30

Way back in the old days, the city of New York set up public bathhouses, Turkish baths, and even swimming pools for the unwashed masses who didn't have proper facilities of their own. Over the decades, nearly all of them have closed, and most of the Turkish baths that remained have had reputations as sleazy meeting places. Through it all, the Tenth Street Baths *shvitzed* away with a steady clientele who understood that the Yiddish *shvitz* cured everything from sinus trouble to broken hearts; they were going for the healing vapors, *not* the company. Today, this Turkish-Russian bath is the last original such place in the city. For a while, it seemed as though the clientele was as old as the building, but the physical-fitness craze has brought about a resurgence of business. This place is still a deal, though. There is only a $10 fee, which includes towels but not the "platzka," a wacking broom made of oak leaves which, taken with soap and a hard scrubbing, knocks the *kishkas* out of the less hearty. So popular is the place that two days a week are "ladies days," and everyone I spoke to said that there has never been a visitor who hasn't become a regular.

Help for Hire

ACCURATE HOUSE AND WINDOW CLEANING COMPANY

230 E 93rd St
744-8644, 744-7020
Mon-Fri: 9-5

Lou Marchesi, Accurate's guiding spirit, is a stickler for "complete house cleaning" and operates a spic-and-span operation. He knows what New York wants in cleaning help. As a result, no request surprises him, and his staff will tackle almost any cleaning problem, including the all-time New York impossibility—windows. What is best about Accurate is their attitude. They don't come on as if they are doing you the biggest favor in the world by handling your dirt. Marchesi offers a free advisory service that covers not only what services are needed, but the proper way to do them. Moreover, Accurate is capable of repairing the cleaning errors of others, be they amateur or professional, as well as handling the big cleaning jobs that should be done several times a year. All workers are bonded and insured, and Marchesi vouches for their work.

COLUMBIA BARTENDING AGENCY
280-4536
Mon-Fri: 9-5

The Columbia Bartending Agency uses students so apt at bartending that one wonders what profession they could possibly do as well after college. The service has been around a long time, and there is no one better. Columbia also supplies waiters, waitresses, and hat checkers.

DIRTBUSTERS OF CLOSETS AND SPACES
31 W 16th St (bet Fifth and Sixth Ave)
242-1174
Mon-Fri: 9:30-4:30

Many a New York mother has probably had the thought at one time or another that the quickest way to strike it rich in New York would be to go into the procurement business, particularly the procurement of house-cleaning and child-care help. David Eason is not a New York mother, but he is a New York businessman who, while running a closet- and apartment-design shop called Closets and Spaces, reached the same conclusion. And so, Dirtbusters was born. Eason, a firm believer in the "personal touch," formed both of his businesses on the tenets of personal service and providing what is not usually available. Basically, Eason organized a corps of workers who clean apartments and residences for flat rates, usually two people working in three-hour sessions. But his staff, hours, and rates are flexible. Dirtbusters are bonded, and the service entitles clients to Eason's newsletters, which are models of his strict guidelines. Taking his cue from customer feedback and staff meetings, Eason now offers dog walking, servicemen recommendations, an advertising directory, floor waxing, party servers and cleaners, painters, floor sanders, and singing telegrams. But no, they don't do windows. What did you expect? Perfection?

EASY HOUSEKEEPING SERVICE
4898 Broadway
569-9203
Mon-Fri: 8-5:30

One day, John and Eleanor Ford of Ford Piano Supply were offered the Easy Housekeeping business previously owned by one of their neighbors. They barely knew the proper way to dust a piano, but when they realized that a dozen or so people relied upon Easy Housekeeping for steady employment, they decided to give it a try rather than leave their neighbor's employees stranded. That happened so long ago that John Ford can't give an exact date. The business has remained a small, friendly place, where people come before profits, particularly since the Ford's have never had much interest in Easy Housekeeping other than to keep the people who depend on it happy. The entire staff numbers less than 20, and the Fords know all of them personally. Most of the staff does day work and housekeeping, but party help can be obtained with a day's notice and a four-hour minimum.

GRADUATE BARTENDERS
558 Broome St
925-5995

These people are secretive about their organization, but they have good credentials. They have an unlisted number, and for rates that are rather reasonable, it's hard to believe that they are part-time professional bartenders who learned the trade while working their way through school. Still, they are reliable, and best of all, have been known to work on a week's notice and sometimes less. They also accept jobs outside Manhattan.

GREAT PERFORMANCES: ARTISTS AS WAITRESSES
125 Crosby St
219-2800
Daily: 9-5 phone orders only

Janet Lee and Liz Neumark are a flamenco dancer and photographer, respectively, who paid their bills between jobs by working as waitresses in a help-for-hire agency. Several years ago, they realized that they were far from the only artists in the city with that moonlighting talent, so they organized their own agency to supply New Yorkers with party help from the city's artistic community. Today, Lee and Neumark are still dancing and taking pictures, but only because they *make* time for it. Their agency—Great Performances: Artists as Waitresses, Inc.—has become a long-running hit with rave reviews. Perhaps because of their artistic backgrounds, every job is treated as a theatrical production and emerges as something special. Basically, the agency provides party planning and party help, but they work in conjunction with caterers and other specialists to create an entire event, if desired. Most of the staff is geared for waiting on tables, party clean-up, or bartending, because most struggling artists are most experienced in those areas (they hire no one without experience and references) and there's a greater demand for those services. Great Performances is still too young for any of their staff to have "made it" yet, but part of this agency's appeal is the possibility that 10 years from now you may be able to say: "Oh, yes. She served me dinner way back when."

LEND-A-HAND
200 W 72nd St (at Broadway)
362-8200
Mon-Fri: 9-5:30; Sat: 9-1; closed Sat in summer

Donald Eggena, Lend-A-Hand's owner and president, offers an enormous list of people and services available through his business. Some of the more exotic include fortune tellers, decoders, cat sitters, drama coaches, furniture painters, shampooers, upholsterers and refinishers, voice teachers, portrait artists, locksmiths, interpreters, and tarot-card readers. However, Eggena said: "We are better known for providing houseboys to clean apartments, bartenders and waiters for parties, catering, and babysitters, as well as help for home and offices."

LYNN AGENCY
2067 Broadway (bet 71st and 72nd St)
874-6130
Mon-Fri: 9-5; office closed sometime in Aug

Lynn is a venerable service organization. Their staff can supply any kind of help: bartenders, butlers, chauffeurs, cooks, companions, couples, governesses, maids, nursing aides, and housekeepers. There is also a party planning service; the agency can supply the help for any function, from a tête-à-tête to a formal corporate dinner. They are flexible, as well, in attitude and uniform. Owner Elaine Sandler (a licensed certified social worker and the mother of twins who knows of what she speaks) claims that Lynn's biggest virtue is its ability to mold its services to clients' needs. So, the butler can come formally dressed in tails or look like the prodigal son who was getting up anyway to answer the door. Why would anyone *hire* a butler to look like that? Who knows, but Lynn can supply it. They are also flexible in that they will serve outside Manhattan. Their rates are very reasonable, as these things go, and their experience with out-of-towners has led them to offer guides to the city to help make the entire stay—not just Lynn's immediate date—a pleasant one.

McMAID
127 E 59th St
371-5555
Daily: 24 hours

McMaid's biggest virtue is that they are on call anytime. Of course, a call for an immediate housekeeper at three a.m. Thanksgiving morning may not be greeted with an instant (or even polite) response, but McMaid can produce help in a remarkably short time. But they prefer to be known as a source for other than last-minute clean-ups. Indeed, they provide the standard maids, waiters, and bartenders as well. But still, it's hard to ignore that initial virtue, despite McMaid's policy of payment by cash. But even that, given enough notice and patronage, can be waived.

Home Installations

SABER'S HARDWARE ARNESTO
15 Avenue A (bet First and Second St)
473-6050, 473-6977
Mon-Fri: 9-7; Sat: 9-5

Marian Burros of *The New York Times* (and a good friend as well) recommends Saber's for general handiwork, bathroom fixtures, and particularly the installation of things like shower doors. She claims they are capable, efficient, and reasonable. Saber's, in turn, claims that Marian's is but one of many uptown households and stores that use its services. Both stores are general houseware emporiums with an emphasis on kitchen and bathroom fixtures. Ceramic tile, medicine cabinets, shower doors, kitchen cabinets, and hardware are house specialties. And they can install all of these items. The 15 Avenue A store has a good display of gates and locks as well. But where Saber's really shines is in service; as their motto says, "We hang the impossible." Mirrors and shower doors are a matter of course, locksmith emergencies are answered routinely, and they even stock and hang drapery hardware. Regular customers (and it isn't hard to become one) can get Saber's to do almost any kind of handiwork. And in this city—or perhaps this century—that's rare indeed. Think of Saber's, despite its location, as the city's general store and all-round handyman. Tell them Marian Burros sent you.

Hotels

Faithful readers of past editions will note that several hotels formerly listed have been removed, and a number of new listings have been added. I make a practice of checking each listing periodically, and I also pay close attention to reactions I receive from readers who follow my recommendations. One hotel (the Wales), which I thought was a very good value, was removed because of reports that the management there had a poor attitude when handling complaints.

A good hotel can really make your trip to New York, just as a bad one can ruin it. New York has nearly 100,000 hotel rooms in all kinds of styles and all kinds of locations. Price, for sure, is *not* a reliable guide. There are a number of large, impersonal, computerized operations that have absolutely no character and are not inexpensive. They are not included in this book. (Overpriced hotels, like the Carlyle, are also omitted.) I've tried to select places that offer something special in service, atmosphere, price, location, et cetera. And of course, remember that there are excellent week-end and season specials; the New York Sunday papers are the best source for finding them.

A few hotel hints:

1. Avoid placing telephone calls from your room. Service charges can be exorbitant.
2. Always lock your door at night. There is a special kind of inexpensive, portable alarm now available, which you can put on your doorknob.
3. Use the safe in the room, if available, or the safety deposit boxes in the hotel's offices.
4. Check the heating or air conditioning at once. If it doesn't work, your stay can be very unpleasant.
5. Allow yourself extra time to get a taxi at the hotel at dinner or theater time or when it is raining.
6. Room service in most hotels is expensive. Be sure to check the food prices and look for extra charges.
7. Make friends with the concierge, if there is one. He or she can make things a lot more comfortable and convenient for you.
8. After checking into your room, first examine the path to the nearest fire exit. Do not use elevators in case of fire.
9. Although hotels are convenient places to have breakfast, some of them have highly inflated breakfast menu prices. If you're on an expense account, it probably doesn't matter. If you're not, check out some of the breakfast suggestions listed elsewhere in this book. The food is better in many cases, and you'll save enough money to buy that extra gift for Aunt Martha.
10. Check with the doorman on approximate transportation times and charges to the airports. It may save you a major hassle or overcharge.

A room with a view of Central Park or the Manhattan skyline is an important consideration. Here are a few hotels that offer rooms with some of New York's best points of view:

American Stanhope, 995 Fifth Ave (Central Park)
Berkshire Place, Madison Ave at 52nd St (Skyline)
Helmsley Palace, 455 Madison Ave at 50th St (Skyline)
Marriott's Essex House, 160 Central Park S (Central Park)
Pierre, 2 E 61st St (Central Park)
Plaza, Fifth Ave at 59th St (Central Park)
Park Lane, 36 Central Park S (Central Park)
Vista International, 3 World Trade Center (New Jersey)
Waldorf Towers, Park Ave and 50th St (Skyline)

Luxury Suites

There are occasions when a simple hotel suite will not do, and it's time to pull out all the stops. Methinks that one of the suites at No. 1022 would do nicely, but if this exclusive *pied-à-terre*'s one-month rental minimum is excessive, there are several other units that various hotels pride themselves in keeping at the ready. Lately, it's become almost a matter of vanity as hotels vie with one another to offer the poshest suite. Here are a few:

Helmsley Palace (Madison Ave at 50th St, 888-7000) The triplex suites are queenly, just as you would expect from the renowned proprietress, Leona Helmsley. There are two-story, three-bedroom, and three-bath units with a spectacular view of the city, halfway to heaven. An elevator takes you to a solarium-type room with an outdoor patio. There is a dining room, full kitchen, baby grand piano, and palatial furnishings.

Marriott Marquis (1700 Broadway, 938-1900) In addition to dozens of regular suites, this magnificent new hotel offers three special units. The presidential and vice-presidential suites feature grand pianos, sky lounges, marble flooring, full kitchens and dining rooms, wet bars, and jacuzzi baths. At the very top of the hotel is the two-level J.W. Marriott suite; the upper level is encased in a glass-vaulted dome ceiling. Also included in this suite is a library with a working fireplace. The tab? Let's put it this way: one day's rent is almost equal to buying one copy of this book every day for a year.

Plaza (Fifth Avenue at 59th St, 759-3000) Perhaps because of the tradition of Eloise and her friends and various eccentrics all having established permanent residency at the Plaza Hotel, it does not emphasize the *super* luxurious suites as much as some of the other places in town. Nonetheless, the room of choice is one of the 87 high-ceilinged corner suites which offer more breathing space (and cocktail-party space) amid the Plaza's usually impeccable service. All are furnished with antique or good reproduction furniture, and it is not unusual to find an antique clock atop a fireplace's marble mantel. Most of the suites have magnificent views of Central Park, and there's always the chance Eloise will drop in!

St. Regis Hotel (Fifth Avenue at 55th St, 753-4500) The Presidential Suite at the St. Regis is a four-room, period-piece-decorated suite available at almost reasonable rates. The suite features a full kitchen and dining room and comes with automatic extra respect from the staff.

United Nations Plaza (One United Nations Plaza, 355-3400) The Ralph Bunche Suite basks in modern luxury as opposed to the Old World traditionalism of some of its peers. The bilevel masterpiece is full of mirrors and windows, all of which take advantage of the spectacular East River and United Nations' Gardens view. There are those who say this alone is worth the price; the ordinary view, looking east to Brooklyn and Queens, is anything but breathtaking. This suite manages to highlight the United Nations and its gardens and make it one of the best shows in town. The accommodations are ample enough to support a baby grand piano, spiral staircase, and spectacular glass-topped dining-room tables. Who says elegant has to be staid?

Waldorf Towers (100 E 57th St, 355-3000) The Waldorf Towers, the auxiliary to the Waldorf Astoria Hotel, houses the more permanent and notable guests. The Towers boasts a tradition that includes the hosting of every incumbent president since Herbert Hoover (who lived in the Towers until his death) and virtually every head of state who has visited New York. If the president is not in the city, the Royal Suite (42-R) might be available. *More* than fit for a queen, it can accommodate a reception for 100 or a sit-down dinner for 30. (Remember, this is a *hotel* room.) There are two bedrooms in this suite (more in some of the others) and a complete kitchen and dining room. The furniture is genuine antique, and the grand piano works. So do the views.

ALGONQUIN

59 W 44th St (bet Fifth and Sixth Ave)
840-6800
Moderate

The home of the famous Round Table, where Dorothy Parker, Harold Ross, Robert Benchley, and others sparred, the Algonquin—located in the heart of midtown Manhattan—is a hotel long favored by people involved in the arts. There are only 200 rooms, with family owner-management, a multilingual staff, and a lot of charm. Eating at the Algonquin is popular with visitors, for it's a place where one can see all sorts of interesting people, day or night. The lobby and lounge are famous as an after-theater spot for a drink or a supper buffet.

AMERICAN STANHOPE

995 Fifth Ave (at 81st St)
288-5800
Moderate to expensive

If the Metropolitan Museum is one of your main reasons for visiting New York, I'd suggest taking up residence at the Stanhope, located right across the street from the Met. The outside terrace is an attraction here, as well as a free morning limousine to take you downtown. The hotel has a very fine collection of American Empire furnishings and 19th-century art; the rooms have a tasteful noncommercial look; and the entire establishment is an example of what was best in early America. The service, although a bit haughty, is efficient. And you just can't beat that charming sidewalk cafe in the summertime!

BEEKMAN TOWER
3 Mitchell Pl
355-7300
Moderate

Beekman Tower is best known to those who frequent the Beekman Place area, but it is an excellent small hotel with comfortable rooms, which have recently been redone in a tasteful manner. Each room has a kitchenette, while some of the larger accommodations have full-size kitchens. There is a nice roof garden operation, Top of the Tower, which offers lunch (Monday through Friday) and a fine view.

EMPIRE
Broadway and 63rd St
265-7400
Inexpensive

Hotel Empire's main advantage is that it is close to Lincoln Center for the Performing Arts; the Coliseum is also nearby. Prices here are on the upper end of the inexpensive range, and the atmosphere is a little bit European. It is small enough to be friendly. Children under 14 can stay free of charge, if they share your room, and parking is free. For a family traveling by car, I'd recommend this one.

ESPLANADE
305 West End Ave
874-5000
Inexpensive to moderate

This hotel is ideal for someone wishing to stay on the Upper West Side and not far from Lincoln Center. The room rates are the same no matter how many share the room. As 75 percent of the hotel's rooms are used by permanent guests, I would suggest making reservations well in advance. The hotel is clean, kitchens include all the necessary essentials, like refrigerator and sink; and there is a color television in each room. There is *no* room service and not much food available close by. But if you're looking for a safe neighborhood and a really good value, try the Esplanade.

ESSEX HOUSE
160 Central Park S
247-0300
Moderately expensive

The view of Central Park is breathtaking, and the view inside Essex House isn't half-bad, either. The rooms are nicely appointed, but a bit on the snug side. The lobby is genteel and richly decorated with carpets and chairs you'd like for your parlor. The staff is on its toes, anxious to be of help when you need it and discreetly withdrawn when you don't. Try to get a room on one of the higher floors, in order to take advantage of the panorama. (You may find it so mesmerizing that you'll have difficulty tearing yourself away from the window!) These floors have been converted into the luxurious Essex Towers, with express elevators, private lobby, upgraded rooms, and a rooftop lounge. There is also a weekend-package deal.

GRAND HYATT
42nd St at the Grand Central Terminal
883-1234, 800-228-9000
Moderate to expensive

The gleaming glass-and-aluminum exterior of the Grand Hyatt is as cheerfully extravagant as the set of a Broadway musical, and the spacious lobby carries out the theme. A waterfall greets you as you enter. This kind of glossy grandeur isn't for those who like hotels with thick Persian rugs and antique furniture, but if you prefer space to ambiance, it's for you. The least expensive room is larger than those in comparably priced hotels. For a few dollars more, you can also get a sitting room that gives you enough space to host a small cocktail party. The top-of-the-line deal is the Regency Club. Amenities include complimentary Continental breakfast, wall-mounted hair dryers, and terry-cloth robes. The Grand Hyatt provides a babysitting service. There are also 32 rooms for handicapped guests. The security is top-notch. Guards are everywhere, keeping an unobtrusive eye on things, and an employee told me that every applicant for a Grand Hyatt job is carefully screened and given a polygraph test. Their Sunday brunch is the best in the city, and a hot buffet breakfast is available on weekdays. Many of the employees are part-time theatrical personnel.

HARLEY
212 E 42nd St (bet Second and Third Ave)
490-8900
Moderate

Harry Helmsley owns a lot of New York's prime real estate, and has branched out into the hotel business. (His wife is the official corporation president of the hotel division.) Although the Helmsleys own several hotels in town, the Harley is the first they designed from scratch. It is sleek and modern. Banquet facilities can accommodate from 15 to 300 people. Its East Side midtown location is close to Grand Central Station, although it's a bit off the track for other things. (It's a crosstown hike to the theater district.) And it's near the United Nations. Rooms are ample and new, and hotel personnel are under Mrs. Helmsley's eye; she's the lady who employs Larry Carroll as the doorman at the St. Moritz. (Obviously, she's a lady who can find quality help.)

HELMSLEY PALACE
455 Madison Ave
888-7000
Expensive

You've probably heard of the Helmsley Palace Hotel, located close to Saks Fifth Avenue, one block off of Fifth Avenue itself. It's enchanting in the evening! The public rooms are exceptionally attractive, encompassing the 100-year-old Villard Mansion, one of New York's legendary landmarks. The Villard House used to be the chancery office of the archdiocese of New York. There are no convention facilities here, although there are meeting rooms available. The Helmsley Palace has several hundred apartments and suites and even some triplex apartments. It's expensive, but rates have been brought down since the opening. If a good address and luxurious accommodations are what you're looking for, this is worth a try. An extra advantage here is that Leona Helmsley, the boss lady, is right on the job. She reminds me of my father, who even checked every week for dripping faucets and cracked fixtures in our store's washrooms. Mrs. Helmsley, like your author and his father, is a perfectionist, and the hotel sure shows it. This is New York's only AAA "5 diamond" award winner.

KITANO
66 Park Ave (at 38th St)
685-0022
Moderate

Hotel Kitano is the only Japanese-owned and -operated hotel in New York. The hotel features good service and typical Japanese hospitality. If you prefer to stay in the midtown area, this spot is attractive and reasonably priced. The restaurant features Japanese cuisine, and both Western- and Japanese-style modern accommodations are offered.

LOWELL
28 E 63rd St
838-1400
Moderate to expensive

With a good Upper East Side address and the added attraction of having a good restaurant nearby (the Post House), this small, quietly dignified hotel is a winner. Although its art-deco entrance might give another impression, the accommodations are modern and comfortable. Most of the rooms have private serving pantries, wood-burning fireplaces, built-in bookshelves, window seats, and even special terraces. If you're planning to spend a week shopping New York's Upper East Side and you want to stay in luxurious surroundings, take a room at the Lowell.

MADISON TOWERS
22 E 38th St
685-3700
Moderate

The Madison Towers in the Murray Hill area has been restored with an attractive and clean lobby, a very pleasant cocktail lounge, and good meeting facilities. Also available are a beauty shop, health club, some boutiques and Executive Tower floors, with lounges and extra-spacious guest rooms. The rooms in the main hotel are small and rather basic, but the location is good and the place has a friendly atmosphere.

MARRIOTT MARQUIS
1700 Broadway (at Times Square)
938-1900
Moderate to moderately expensive

The opening of this magnificent showplace in the center of Times Square in the summer of 1985 represented a major step in the rejuvenation of the area. Along with over 1800 rooms, huge meeting-and-convention facilities, and the largest hotel atrium in the world, guests can enjoy a 700-seat, three-story revolving restaurant and lounge at the top of the 50-story hotel, a revolving lounge overlooking Broadway on the eighth floor, a legitimate Broadway theater on the premises, a fully equipped health club, suites with walk-in wet bars and refrigerators, oversized rooms, and a sky lounge with personal computers. There are nine restaurants and lounges in all. A concierge level offers special amenities, including 24-hour room service. All rooms overlook Manhattan on the exterior and open directly to the atrium on the interior. One word describes this hotel: spectacular.

MILFORD PLAZA
270 W 45th St (bet Seventh and Eighth Ave)
869-3600
Inexpensive to moderate

"Between 10 p.m. and midnight, maybe a little after, there are no real problems on the street," confided a Milford Plaza bellboy. "But after that, the theater crowd thins out, and, listen, I don't go out on the street after that." Heed the man's words: the Milford Plaza's extraordinarily reasonable rates are offset by its proximity to seamy Eighth Avenue. If you are visiting New York for the first time, you'd be better off at a hotel in a safer neighborhood. If you're wise to the city, the Milford Plaza may strike you as an excellent bargain that's worth the extra precaution of taking a cab straight to the hotel's door. Rooms are small but clean; security is extremely tight. Late-night dining is available, and attractive economy packages are offered for individuals and groups.

MORGAN'S
237 Madison Ave (at 37th St)
686-0300
Moderate

If a downtown location and a "boutique" atmosphere are what you're looking for, this new hotel is it. The old Duane Hotel has been completely redone by a French designer, and the result is calm, comfort, and convenience. Twenty-four-hour room service is available, and room prices include breakfast.

NO. 1022
1022 Lexington Ave (at E 73rd St)
697-1536
Expensive

When is a hotel not a hotel? When it's the elegant *pied-à-terre*, consisting of three double suites and one single, known as No. 1022 for its address at 1022 Lexington Avenue. The select guests are treated to interiors by Jackie Onassis' designer, Georgina Fairholme, jacuzzis, maid, butler, laundry and airport service, a concierge and "room service" from the equally elegant and equally good Jack's Restaurant beneath them. Owner Edward Safdie gutted an 1870s building and then expanded its width to create these accommodations. The aim was to create the old-time flavor of an English country inn or European pension, and to that end, Fairholme was given free rein in gathering the appointments for each suite. So, in addition to quilt-covered four postered-beds, hand-painted silk pillows, tea services stored in country cabinets, and a microwave oven, each suite has its own kitchen fully equipped with crystal, china, and silver service. They are small, but with Jack's downstairs, probably no one eats in, anyway. If it sounds like it takes very little to get used to this style of living, that's just as well, since No. 1022 "rents" by the month and will only accept shorter reservations if space is available. And don't worry if you can't tear yourself away from the jacuzzi, or the temperature controlled shower, or the bed near the wood-burning fireplace, or the remote-controlled television and stereo system: the suites have telephone-answering machines (and private phone numbers to boot), and the staff will shop, clean, and launder as well. If you have to ask the price of all this luxury, don't bother. Console yourself with the thought that No. 1022 is probably booked, anyway.

PARK LANE
36 Central Park S
371-4000
Expensive

The Park Lane Hotel is expensive, but worth the price. It has a super location right on the park, a magnificent lobby, and 35 floors of truly elegant facilities. The 640 rooms and suites have large windows and a variety of superb views. All rooms have recently been redecorated. Special services include a nighttime butler service and 24-hour room service. The suites have two bathrooms and two color-television sets. If you want to splurge for a night or two, this is the place to pamper yourself.

PARKER MERIDIEN
119 W 56th St (at Sixth Ave)
245-5000
Expensive

This is a classic French beauty in midtown, complete with an in-house movie system and a health club with courts, track, and rooftop swimming pool. The rooms are very attractive, the service has a European flair (it is an Air France operation), and the lobby and the restaurants are elegant.

PICKWICK ARMS
230 E 51st St
355-0300
Inexpensive to moderate

Nothing fancy here, but if a good midtown location, clean accommodations and low rates are what you're looking for, forget about the small room size and the lack of private bathrooms for every room. This is an excellent find for young people and large families.

PIERRE
2 E 61st St (at Fifth Ave)
838-8000
Expensive

If price is no object, this one has to be right at the top of your list. It's a quiet, modest, luxurious place, with superb personal attention from the friendly staff. But it's a bit high priced, in my opinion, for the kind of accommodations you get. The location is good, right on Fifth Avenue, overlooking Central Park. The remodeled lobby area is very attractive, and the new Cafe Pierre, done in petite trianon style to the tune of $1,500,000, is magnificent. The personnel are well trained and will remember you on your second visit. Many of the units are occupied by permanent guests, and the hotel is a favorite of international travelers. It's a great spot for celebrity watching! P.S. No convention badges allowed.

PLAZA ATHÉNÉE

37 E 64th St
734-9100
Expensive

Those familiar with the famous Plaza Athénée in Paris will be interested in this reconstruction of the old Alrae Hotel, done with understated good taste. The lobby is charming and classy. The rooms are attractively furnished with pantry, individual wet bar, and two lines on each phone. Porthault bathrobes are also provided. There are 10 solariums at the top of the hotel, 10 roof terraces, and 10 private dining rooms in the higher floor suites. Le Regence Seafood restaurant is an added attraction and a superb place to eat. If price is no object and special niceties and excellent service are important to you (especially for older people), consider staying at the Plaza Athénée.

PLAZA HOTEL

Fifth Ave at 59th St
759-3000
Expensive

It can't be too unfair to have certain favorites, and I have to admit my favorite place to stay in New York is the Plaza Hotel for many reasons. Perhaps the most important is that I've been staying there since I was 10 years of age, and the place has many nostalgic memories. But for you, one of the big pluses is the excellent location, with horse-drawn carriages and Central Park on one side and the excitement of Fifth Avenue on the other. Inside, the ambiance is vintage New York, and Westin Hotels, who bought it some years ago, have spent millions bringing the Plaza back to its original condition. They are to be congratulated on a superb job. The place had been allowed to deteriorate under previous owners. Westin is now redoing every room of the hotel with emphasis on heating, air conditioning, and classy bathrooms. Under the modernization plan, each room will have designer period furniture and three telephones. Managing director Jeffrey Flowers serves up the Westin tradition that he learned overseas. He is in charge of people who are personally interested in making each one's stay at the Plaza an enjoyable one. Make no mistake—this is a busy place with hundreds of people coming in and out daily, but it's amazing that all the hotel people (bellboys, desk and mail information clerks) are well-schooled in friendliness. Look around the shops while you're there. Many interesting things can be seen at Shapero's; you can even pick up an extra copy of Gerry Frank's New York guidebook there! The Plaza is a New York landmark and tradition, and Westin Hotels prove that when it comes to innkeeping, they have the golden key.

PRINCE GEORGE

14 E 28th St
532-7800
Inexpensive

Many folks want to spend their hard-earned money on things other than a hotel room when they visit New York. If that's your strategy, you can't go wrong at the Prince George. It's within easy walking distance of the Merchandise Mart and a number of other major commercial buildings, and it's not too far from midtown. The rooms are comfortable but not fancy. (When it was built in 1904, it was one of the first luxury hotels in the city.) There is an attractive lobby bar, and a number of the rooms have been redone. The eating facilities are adequate and attractive, and I wouldn't hesitate to recommend this place as one of the best bets in New York.

RITZ-CARLTON

112 Central Park S
757-1900
Expensive

With a great new name (it used to be the Navarro) and a great location right on Central Park South, this hotel, owned by John Coleman, has been refurbished to the tune of $15 million and has been touted as one of New York's classier places to stay. Each guest room has several telephones, a complete bathroom with makeup light and heat lamps, and 24-hour room and valet service. The view from the rooms overlooking the park is breathtaking; ask for one. Unfortunately, the Jockey Club restaurant doesn't live up to its Washington, D.C., namesake.

SALISBURY

123 W 57th St
246-1300
Moderate

The Salisbury is clean and intimate, with just over 300 rooms, most of them with butler's pantries and refrigerators. The rooms are smallish but well appointed, all have safes, and the staff is particularly courteous and pleasant. Suites are large, comfortable, and reasonably priced. This is a favorite place for lady travelers. Bill Dadukian, the president, is one of the most accommodating guys in New York; he will personally make you feel welcome. If you want to be in the vicinity of Carnegie Hall and other midtown attractions, this is the place for you. If you should happen to wait until the last minute to make reservations, it might be a good idea to call here, as the Salisbury is not too well known to out-of-towners, and rooms are usually available.

SHERATON CENTRE
811 Seventh Ave (at 52nd St)
581-1000
Moderate to moderately expensive

A great location, a nationwide referral service, newly appointed guest rooms, and a wide selection of restaurants and lounges (with entertainment) add up to a very convenient and pleasant place to stay. The Sheraton Towers—the more expensive top floors—offer exclusive digs for the business or pleasure traveler. Amenities include terrycloth robes and butler service for breakfast. The Centre also has a wide selection of Big Apple package deals, and the price is right. While there, be sure to visit the newsstand. Tell the folks I sent you, and you'll get one of New York's biggest smiles.

SHERATON-RUSSELL
45 Park Ave (at 37th St)
685-7676
Moderate

An interesting area of Manhattan is historic Murray Hill, and the Sheraton-Russell fits right in. The manager is a charming lady, and her charm is apparent both in the guest rooms and in the public areas. They are decorated in good taste, with antiques, memorabilia, imported fabrics, and noninstitutional furniture. Some of the rooms even have fireplaces. The service goes along with the atmosphere—efficient and low-key. Even though it's a relatively small hotel, a concierge is available for service. All rooms are air conditioned, and each has color cable television with Home Box Office.

UNITED NATIONS PLAZA
1 United Nations Plaza
(bet First and Second Ave, at 44th St)
355-3400
Moderate to expensive

This is a very fashionable facility in the United Nations area, a gathering spot for the international set. The hotel is very modern, but done in good taste. It has a health club, and it features nicely appointed rooms and international-style service. The suites are particularly attractive. The 288 rooms and suites offer spectacular views, since they begin on the 28th floor.

VISTA INTERNATIONAL
3 World Trade Center
938-9100
Moderate to expensive

If business or other needs bring you to the lower end of Manhattan, I'd suggest you try the new Vista International, located right in the World Trade Center. As a matter of fact, you can go directly from the hotel into the shopping and office complex. This is the first major new hotel in Lower Manhattan in nearly 150 years, and it has a lot going for it: first-class restaurants, a handy business service center, and valet parking with a underground garage and airport pickup. The 20th and 21st floors are a club with special accommodations, including a concierge. There's also a well-equipped fitness center and rooftop swimming pool. The fitness center includes racquetball courts, a jogging track, sauna and steam bath, plus a fully equipped exercise facility. The hotel is operated by Hilton International, which, in my opinion, does a consistently good job.

WALDORF TOWERS
100 E 50th St
355-3100
Expensive

The Waldorf Towers, home to many celebrities and dignitaries (I once visited Herbert Hoover in his suite there), is completely separate from the hotel. Guests have their own entrance, elevators, registration desk, bell captain, and concierge. All rooms and suites, ranging from very comfortable to very deluxe, are above the 28th floor, with commanding views. This is A-1 for security and comfort. The Waldorf-Astoria hotel is a New York landmark. Their magnificent lobby, superb banquet facilities (the best service in New York), and specialty shops are top drawer.

WESTBURY
69th St and Madison Ave
535-2000
Moderate to expensive

Completely modernized from stem to stern, with closet safes and exceptionally tasteful décor in all rooms and suites, the Westbury is particularly suitable for the woman traveling alone or the businessman who wants quiet and comfort rather than big-city excitement. There is 24-hour room service, a greatly improved Polo Restaurant on the ground floor, and outstanding refurbished bathrooms. The top-of-the-line suites are some of the nicest in the city; they are of a manageable size, done in superb taste with every comfort without being ostentatious. Manager Pierre F. Constant presides over what seems more like a large guest house than a commercial hotel.

WESTPARK
308 W 58th St
246-6440
Inexpensive to moderate

For those attending a show or meeting at the Coliseum, the location of the Westpark is ideal, right on Columbus Circle. There is a restaurant and bar located off the lobby of the hotel; room service is available. I am particularly impressed with the small suites that represent some of the best values in New York; be sure to ask for one facing the park. The place is well kept, everything is clean, the rates are reasonable, and all is pleasant (though you could get claustrophobia in the small hallways).

WYNDHAM
42 W 58th St (at Fifth Ave)
753-3500
Moderate

This charming hotel is more like a large home where the owners rent out rooms. Many of the guests are folks who regularly make the Wyndham their Manhattan headquarters. The advantages are many: great location, individually decorated rooms and suites, complete privacy, individual attention, no business conventions. On the other hand, the hotel is always busy, and reservations for the newcomer could be difficult. No room service is available; however, there is a small restaurant, and the suites have kitchenettes.

Bed-and-Breakfast Lodging

B & B GROUP (NEW YORKERS AT HOME)
301 E 60th St
838-7015
Mon-Fri: 9-4

Although they have been popular in Europe for centuries and in existence for at least a decade in California, B & B's (Bed and Breakfasts) are just coming into prominence in New York. They are an economical way to get a unique view of how the natives live. New Yorkers at Home offers over 200 listings in Manhattan. Since most New Yorkers don't live adjacent to the Empire State Building or Bergdorf's (and those who do probably don't need to rent out rooms), most accommodations are in residential areas, not the usual haunts of the hotels. It's a good chance to see some really interesting neighborhoods (there are TriBeCa lofts and Central Park West co-ops listed) and meet fascinating people, and, of course, it's much cheaper than a hotel room. Most of all, it's personal. As one satisfied visitor said: "Would a hotel have told me I'd better take an umbrella and then give me one?" Reservations must be placed well in advance.

NEW WORLD BED & BREAKFAST
150 Fifth Ave (suite 711)
New York, NY 10011
675-5600

Ray Schill founded New World Bed & Breakfast in 1983 and has over 100 different rooms available in Manhattan. Schill is a go-getter, and odds are that he has increased his room inventory by the time you read this.

URBAN VENTURES
P.O. Box 426, New York, NY 10024
594-5650
Mon-Sat: 9-5

Mary McAulay and Frances Tesser founded this service, modeled after Britain's famous bed-and-breakfast rooms, because they felt something needed to be done about Manhattan's lack of reasonably priced lodging. After being carefully screened, 500 hosts, who live either in apartments, townhouses, brownstones, or lofts, signed up with Urban Ventures. Hosts range from older people living in big apartments to young hopeful artists; both groups need a little help with the rent, and are also friendly and interested in their guests. The spare bedrooms are on the Upper West Side and in the Village, with a smattering in midtown, on the East Side, in SoHo, TriBeCa, and even Brooklyn. Security is good—after all, this is someone's home—and the B & B's, as they are known, are concentrated in areas heavily populated by sons and daughters trying their wings in Manhattan. Hence, these rooms are convenient for visiting parents, since their child's apartment is rarely big enough to accommodate a visitor. Some apartments are even available for two nights to two months without hosts. The price is right, and this is a first-rate chance to get a sense of what it's really like to live in Manhattan.

Interior Decorators

NEW YORK CHAPTER OF THE AMERICAN SOCIETY OF INTERIOR DESIGNERS
421-8765
Mon-Fri: 9:30-5:30

This is not a decorating service; it's the credential-granting agency to which most ethical (and qualified) interior designers belong. For a phone call—during which you must specify your needs, taste, and, most important, budget—A.S.I.D. will recommend up to three members who would be suitable and available for the job. They are not snobbish and treat a $200 job just as seriously as a $5,000 one. Even if you don't go this route, be sure the decorator you *do* choose is A.S.I.D. affiliated.

PARSONS SCHOOL OF DESIGN
66 Fifth Ave (at 13th St)
741-8940
Mon-Fri: 9-5

Parsons, a division of the New School for Social Research, is one of the two top schools in the city for interior design. Marion Thunberg maintains a file of senior students (and some recent graduates), their areas of special interest, and their talents. Anyone who calls her is asked for the size of the project (it can go from a chair to a country mansion), the price range, and the sense of style desired. She then matches client with prospective decorator and gives the client a choice of names. Individual negotiations determine price and length of the job, but it is incredibly cheaper than what a not-so-recent student charges. The disadvantage is that most of these students don't have a decorator's card. On the other hand, they can probably borrow one. Even if they can't, the school should be first on your list if you merely want a consultation.

Jewelry Repair

B. HARRIS AND SONS
25 E 61st St (at Madison Ave)
755-6455
Mon-Sat: 10-5
Closed Sat in summer and last two weeks in Aug

William J. Harris' family started B. Harris and Sons in 1898, and since then, generations of customers have relied upon the family to repair their jewelry. The competence and courtesy displayed here hail from another era, and the classic jewelry available for sale and the ancient heirlooms awaiting repair show that this is a shop of the old school. The jewelry counter is limited to antique and fine contemporary jewelry. All of it is of timeless quality. East Side godparents have made visits there before the christening almost *de rigueur*, and the selection in baby and young children's jewelry reflects this unusual interest. Others use B. Harris as a prime source for repairs of all jewelry and timepieces. Harris himself (William J., that is) is particularly proud of the restoration they do on watches and clocks, be they antique, modern, or grandfather. (Do *not* bring the latter in without calling first. Usually they make house calls.) In addition, B. Harris deals frequently with estates; often the jewelry is not sold but merely modernized by the heirs. B. Harris can handle both jobs and, through the years, has learned to clean, repair, restore, and appraise old jewelry as well. They will also recut or repolish stones.

GOLDFIELD'S

229 E 53rd St (at Second Ave)
753-3750, 752-3892
Mon-Fri: 8:30-5:30

Despite appearances, jewelry is the one item Goldfield's does not sell. It does, however, repair jewelry, as well as lighters, electric shavers, and watches. Its forte is the repair of the latter items, particularly lighters, but Goldfield's also sells them as well. They are emphatic, however, about not selling jewelry. Jean Werner, the store's manager, usually lends a personal hand to the shop repairs, and she is extremely competent. As the days of cigarette lighters wane, so does the need for their repair. These days the shop is concentrating more and more on watch and jewelry repair.

RISSIN'S JEWELRY CLINIC

4 W 47th St
575-1098
Mon, Tues, Thurs: 9:30-4:15
Closed first two weeks of July and Christmas week

A few years ago, Joe Rissin was profiled in *The New York Times* as one of the few competent gemologists in the city. The resulting inundation of customers has made him shy of publicity, but he is still one of the best craftsmen around. Rissin is a jack-of-all-trades in the jewelry business. His chief virtue, though, is that he never turns down a customer, no matter how small or how ludicrous the request is. "A while ago, a lady asked me to fix a costume-jewelry pin. I charged her 80 cents for two rhinestones," Rissin said. "So I gave it to my wife to do. And then I checked it out. Last week, the lady came back with a paperbag full of 'some stuff' she wanted fixed. The repair bill alone came to $400, and some of the jewelry was priceless." It's easy to see why he never turns down an order. Aside from being the only place to repair your costume jewelry (though Rissin won't appreciate that description), the Jewelry Clinic also creates original works in jewelry. Two pairs of 14-carat-gold eyeglasses frames were Rissin's most whimsical creations. He also does antique-jewelry restoration work (much of it is for museums and other jewelers), alteration, and appraisals. The latter are done in his role as a gemologist rather than a jeweler, and the appraisal is clinically rather than monetarily correct. "No one can identify a stone from a price tag," says Rissin. "When I appraise, it is completely factual. Price is an opinion."

ZOHRAB DAVID KRIKORIAN

48 W 48th St (room 1409)
575-1262
By appointment only

Most of his work has been the creation of rare and original pieces for neighbors in the diamond district, but in his free time, Zohrab

David Krikorian will do the work he does wholesale for professionals for you, too. In addition to making jewelry, Krikorian will mend and fix broken jewelry, as only a professional craftsman who is also an artist can. He makes complicated repairs look easy, and has yet to encounter a job he can't handle. If he can't exactly match the stones in an antique earring, he'll redo the whole piece so it looks even better than before. That, too, is unusual for a craftsman who has a healthy respect for old things. He loves creating the latest, newest designs with traditional materials, and his prices are quite reasonable.

Lighting Fixtures Repair

ANTHONY BAZZA RESTORATIONS
315 E 62nd St
755-1179
Mon-Fri: 8-4; closed last week in July, first week in Aug

Anthony Bazza modestly claims that he is the best at repair and restoration of antique lighting, vases, candelabrum (sic), silver, and crystal. Humility aside, he's probably right. At least the White House and a score of museums think so. He is also not cheap—a fact that he also acknowledges openly. For example, he "will restore porcelain, *if* it is worth it." Unless the item is intrinsically valuable or of *great* (his emphasis) sentimental value, it is probably not worth Bazza's time. And if it's not worth his time, it can't be worth the client's money. His specialty is fine work done on fine works. Bazza has restored antique chandeliers, silver, crystal, and bronzes for many of the metropolitan area's historic homes. He has also mounted porcelain vases and remodeled or created table lamps (some from those same vases). And if you've got a theater-sized chandelier, Bazza will even pay a house call and clean it at home. To pay the bill, you may just have to open a box office, but he is indeed the best and worth every penny.

Luggage Repair and Cleaning

So the airline ruined your luggage again? It's going to be a long, drawn-out fight. If the luggage is expensive and you don't want to replace it, try Crouch and Fitzgerald. They're good on emergency repairs. (That is a problem in other leather repair-shop operations.) However, if the piece was mediocre to begin with, you're probably better off buying a new one at one of the places listed in this book under "Luggage." Unfortunately, whatever you decide, you'll have to save the evidence for the airline. Of course, real joy is toting around brand new or badly damaged old suitcases. Old-time bellhops continually ask me, "When did you get those leather Hartmann cases?" I've been using them for over 30 years.

CARNEGIE LUGGAGE
1388 Sixth Ave (bet 57th and 58th St)
586-8210
Mon-Fri: 8-6; Sat: 9-5

Carnegie is handy to most major midtown and Central Park hotels. Service can be fast, if you let them know you're in a hurry.

CROUCH AND FITZGERALD
400 Madison Ave (at 48th St)
753-1808, 753-2416
Mon-Sat: 9-6

Crouch and Fitzgerald is run along the lines of an exclusive Madison Avenue boutique. There is strict attention to detail and to the type of leather cases a Crouch and Fitzgerald customer would find essential to his lifestyle. Vice-president J. Wein emphasizes that the Crouch and Fitzgerald specialty is men's business cases in all sizes, but they are equally well known for the repair and cleaning of all leather luggage goods. Naturally, they repair their own merchandise best, but they will attempt to handle any item brought into the shop.

JOHN R. GERARDO
30 W 31st St (bet Broadway and Fifth Ave)
695-6955
Mon-Fri: 9-5:30; Sat: 10-2; closed Sat in July and Aug

Minus the glamour, Don Gerardo manages to dispense luggage and luggage repairs at John R. Gerardo that rival Crouch and Fitzgerald's. Gerardo's stock is a complete one. He carries all the standard brands in almost all kinds of luggage. There are sample cases, over-nighters, two suiters, and drawers with seemingly endless types and amounts of spare parts. There are zippers, handles, locks, and patches of fiber and material for emergency patching. Gerardo does quick, professional repairs competently.

Marble Works

NEW YORK MARBLE WORKS
1399 Park Ave (at 104th St)
534-2242
Mon-Fri: 8-4:30; closed July 1-10

Three generations of Louis Gleicher's family have run New York Marble Works since its inception in 1900. So, it's no surprise to learn that they know the marble business cold (sorry! couldn't resist) or that they are the first choice of the William Doyle galleries, Sotheby Parke Bernet, and North American Van Lines when it comes to marble repair. Gleicher will create and custom-design marble pieces and furniture for bathrooms, fireplaces, tables, and mantels. All of which can be made from the largest selection of floor-and-wall marble tiles in the country—a choice that includes more than 100 shades of marble. (I find it difficult to appreciate such "aid." Who can choose from 100 colors?) There are also bases for sculpture, custom-designed marble furniture, and a number of really outstanding gift items in marble. All of it, despite the size, can be shipped anywhere in the world.

PUCCIO EUROPEAN MARBLE AND ONYX
232 E 59th St (showroom on sixth floor; warehouse at 661 Driggs Ave, Brooklyn)
688-1351

Puccio's factory and warehouse are in Brooklyn, but they qualify for a listing since they do have a showroom in Manhattan, even though it is only open by appointment. Paul Puccio runs both as a showcase for his sculpture and furniture designs, which are both original and sleekly modern. It is almost incongruous to see an angular, free-flowing sculpture made of formal marble, when Roman busts on pedestals are what comes to mind. But John Puccio boasts that his tables are found in décors that are strictly modern and very chic. "We strive for plain but luxurious," he says. He succeeds, and the startling results are elegant. A project here takes up to two months for completion, but a commission is not even accepted (even though there is a ready-made line) if it is not received through a decorator or designer. Puccio is just not equipped to deal with retail orders, but a visit to the factory will enable you to see the line for yourself.

Massage

RON FILIPPI
758-7134
Daily

In a city known for every kind of massage, it is comforting to know that there are still some very reliable, capable, and thoroughly professional people. At the top of my list is Ron Filippi, who has had great experience as a sports trainer. Besides being a person who is especially interested in his clients, he gives an absolutely marvelous massage. I recommend him without reservation for both men and women.

Medical Services

CITY CENTER DRUGS AND SURGICALS

11 E 16th St (bet Broadway and Fifth Ave)
242-2725
Mon-Fri: 7:30-6; Sat: 9-3; closed Sat in Aug

This store consistently offers the best prices on prescription drugs and vitamins, and is equally well-known for its reliability. The service is so conscientious that the pharmacists will call, long-distance if necessary, to verify prescriptions. (And you know how most sales people react to the very *thought* of making a long-distance call.) City Center is owned by Alypan Corp., and will fill union prescriptions and honor other medical plans.

DOCTORS ON CALL

737-2333

This service has spread quickly throughout the metropolitan area and may go nationwide. It should succeed, for it answers a real need in the city. In the past, hotels always had staff doctors on call. Medical and dental associations arranged for doctors to cover the city during off hours, and, of course, hospital emergency rooms were open 24 hours a day. But private doctors have stopped making house calls, even to regular patients. Doctors on Call was created to take care of that problem. Though most calls are to people who don't have regular city doctors—patients are usually visitors—many calls are made on residents who for some reason need an in-house visit. The fee in Manhattan is about $50 (accurate at publication date), which covers the rising costs of parking and transportation, and most calls are completed within two hours of your phone call. All members of Doctors on Call are licensed, and if further tests or treatments are necessary, that can be arranged as well.

PORTNOW SURGICAL SUPPLIES

53 Delancey St (at Eldridge St)
226-1311
Mon-Thurs: 9-5; Fri: 9-2; Sun: 10-4

People in this neighborhood would say, "You shouldn't know from it," but for any kind of medical, surgical, or home nursing supplies, Portnow should be a first choice. Not only is the equipment modern and vast in selection, the prices are discounted, just as if there were many similar businesses on the block, even though there aren't. In fact, for the price, there probably isn't a better source in the city for surgical supplies, convalescent aids, wheelchairs, canes, crutches, walkers, trusses, belts, supporters, or surgical stockings. Portnow's own brand of therapeutic pantyhose comes in every size. The array of blood-pressure machines, ostoscopes, blood-sugar testers, and respiratory aids would make a hypochondriac happy. The healthy come for Portnow's exercise machines and bikes, as well as the best maternity pantyhose around. Most of all, these people know their stuff, just as you'd expect from a business established in 1898. Their immediate concern is the immediate relief of pain. Portnow aims to handle any medical situation with the best, most economical treatment. To your health, Portnow!

QUALITY CARE

25 W 43rd St
730-7077
Mon-Fri: 9-5 (office); daily on call: 24 hours

Quality Care is a nationwide organization dedicated to providing temporary health-care personnel on all levels. It was created to meet the changing needs of medical care: formerly, the sick were treated at home, but today they are sent to institutions, although that isn't always what patients want. So, there was a need for professionals who would work at a patient's home. Quality Care supplies registered and licensed practical nurses, home health aides, homemakers, companions (there's a term you don't see often outside 19th-century novels), physical occupation and speech therapists, and just about every other kind of home-care specialist imaginable. These professionals will adapt their program to special needs, such as kosher cooking, small rooming accommodations, or anything else, as well as providing health screening tests and guidance to clients. Here's hoping you won't need them, but it's nice to know that Quality Care is there and that a national organization is behind it.

UPJOHN HEALTH CARE SERVICES

90 Park Ave (bet 39th and 40th St)
972-3360
24 hours

Upjohn is a nationwide service that provides fully screened, bonded, supervised, and trained home health aides. The type of person sent and the subsequent bill depend upon the level of care needed, but they are capable of supplying registered nurses, licensed practical nurses, and live-in companions. The general idea is that they will supply complete home-nursing service as well as hospital support.

Messages

BALOOMS
147 Sullivan St
673-4007
Mon-Fri: 10-6; Sat: 12-6; Sun: available for parties

Balooms differs from most balloon services in that customers are not only invited, but requested to visit the office. That is because the Balooms office is a legitimate, albeit small, store that encourages browsing and spur-of-the-moment sales. While there are still skeptics who feel that *no one* impulsively buys a balloon, Balooms' sales prove otherwise. In addition to the standard balloon bouquet, there is party decorating and custom-designed or personalized bouquets with either names, logos, or even portraits on each balloon. Balooms will only deliver in Manhattan, but they will ship anywhere. They appreciate advance notice, and there are special discounts for caterers and hotels. As befits this lighthearted business, owners Marlyne Berger and Raymond Baglietto are delightful.

EASTERN ONION/LOONEY BALLOONS
39 W 14th St (room 301)
741-0006

Eastern Onion is in the New York messenger business in a new incarnation. Owner Stan Wilcox offers almost everything except the conventional telegram. Indeed, singing telegrams are as conventional as they get, but even they get pretty far-out when the singer is a professional dressed as a gorilla, Fairy Onion, or Mr. Macho (wonder if they use the same person for both characters?). There are also belly-grams and, of course, Looney Balloons. The latter is a bouquet of 24 multicolored balloons and one mylar balloon, delivered by a suitably dressed messenger. At press time, all of this costs about $30, but bear in mind that that is for only one mylar balloon.

TOY BALLOON CORPORATION
204 E 38th St
682-3803
Mon-Fri: 9-5

We shall leave the Toy Balloon under "Toys," but for the record, they must be mentioned here. Though they are still a wholesale operation, the Toy Balloon is not impervious to the balloon craze, which is good news for the average balloon buyer. The company's prices are still sensational—inflated mylar goes for $2, and the latex variety go for less than $9 a dozen. And there is no minimum order. But Peter Warny points out that his company's priorities are still geared to commercial accounts, and the smart customers are people who dispense with the retail frills and services and buy directly from the Toy Balloon. "Really smart bosses send messengers down to pick up balloons for National Secretaries Day," says Warny, who notes that the cost of the messenger, tip, and super bouquet was *still* less than the balloon-service operations. Once in a while, the Toy Balloon delivers. (They will ship any order). But if they don't deliver the actual order, they *do* deliver on service, quality, and price. The only drawback is that there is at least a three-week wait for personalized orders.

Metal Repair

RETINNING AND COPPER REPAIR
525 W 26th St (near 10th Ave)
244-4896
Mon-Fri: 9:30-6; closed Christmas to New Year's and last two weeks of Aug

Only in New York would a 75-year-old Italian retinning business be headed by a female woodworker in her thirties. Her name is Mary Ann Miles, and hers may be the only business of its kind in the city. Retinning and Copper Repair maintains a reputation as one of the best anywhere; the original business was founded on the same spot in 1916. When the second owner went bankrupt, Miles, who owned the woodworking business next door, bought it. Changing chisel for vat was not as easy as she supposed, but employees who had toiled through the two prior owners taught the current owner the business, and *voilà*, Miles became a retinning and copper expert. And expert she is. In addition to the retinning (which is basically what copper repair amounts to), Miles restores brass and copper antiques, designs and creates new copperware (almost all copper pots in use today are heirlooms), and sells restored copper pieces.

Movers

GRADUATE MOVERS
558 Broome St
925-5995

Though Graduate Movers started in the Columbia University area, they have matriculated to SoHo and are moving in the adult world. This address also houses a small moving supply store to help with moving needs. These are the same people who supply bartenders, party personnel, and general help for hire. They have expanded the business to include insured moving and storage. The same impeccable service characterizes this endeavor, and their rates are as competitive here as they are in the party line.

IKE BANKS
718-527-7505

Ike Banks probably breaks every rule for inclusion in this book. He's not bonded or licensed, nor is he a resident of Manhattan (he lives in Queens), but he never breaks anything, and I trust him more than anyone else listed here. He was first recommended to me by an appliance store, when a delicate and temperamental washing machine needed to be delivered. Since then, he has moved pianos, households, and dining rooms for friends. Several years ago, estimates for moving a nine-piece dining room ran from $100 to $300. Banks did it perfectly for $25. He will travel anywhere in the city, sometimes further, and will work odd hours (unless he's taking his nephew to a ball game). He's a super guy. The only complaint I have is that he's so careful that he can be very slow. It's a good thing he doesn't charge by the hour.

MOVING STORE
644 Amsterdam Ave
874-3800
Mon-Fri: 8:30-6; Sat: 9-2

Steve Fiore started West Side Movers in the kitchen of his studio apartment 15 years ago. Business was so good that he soon moved into a storefront. He was happy there until he realized the magnitude of requests he was getting from people who wanted to borrow or rent moving pads, ramps, dollies, and, most particularly, boxes of all sizes. A man who knows a good business opportunity when he sees it, Fiore moved into a brownstone storefront on Amsterdam Avenue to sell nothing but moving aids and paraphernalia. Fiore's business is unique in New York and, most probably, in the world. Most of his customers today are either box seekers or descendants of box seekers, so the main stock in trade is still boxes. They come in more sizes than it seems possible, including three different sizes just for mirrors. And since all of the items are built to the specifications of professional movers, they are *very* durable. While searching for a source to build crates, Fiore met carpenter Ed McLaughlin. McLaughlin built Fiore his crates and went on to help in the renovation of the brownstone. Today, West Side Movers takes up the first floor of the building, while McLaughlin occupies the basement.

WEST SIDE MOVERS
644 Amsterdam Ave
874-3800
Mon-Fri: 8-6; Sat: 9-3; closed Sat in July and Aug

We came to West Side Movers via their Moving Store. But such ecumenical and diverse groups as the Union Theological Seminary and Tiffany and Company came to West Side Movers by recommendation and have added their accolades to the file. A company with a subdivision that specializes in helping people move themselves has to be top-notch. West Side Movers pays particular attention to efficiency, promptness, care, and courtesy. Customer after customer has called their staff the most courteous they've dealt with; if you've ever had to move in a city you can understand why that consideration comes *before* concern over dents on the furniture to New Yorkers. *But* they don't dent the furniture, either!

Newspaper Delivery

LENOX HILL NEWSPAPER DELIVERY
502 E 74th St
879-1822

Lenox Hill Newspaper Delivery is an excellent door-to-door service. For a slight charge, they will deliver the New York papers, the *Christian Science Monitor*, the *Washington Post*, *Women's Wear Daily*, or the *Sunday Observer* to your door. They will also deliver any foreign publication available in New York, as well as most magazines. All of these, Lenox Hill claims, can be delivered "earlier than subscriptions reach your mailbox." For many people, that's worth the service charge.

Office Services

"WE TYPE IT!" CENTER KBM
60 W 39th St (at Sixth Ave)
354-6890
Mon-Fri: 8:30-5:30; Sat: 10-4

Trust the folks at KBM to be in touch with the typing needs of New Yorkers. For years they ran a center where people could rent typewriters. But when more and more clients began offering to pay KBM to do the typing for them, out went the rental cubicles and in came professional typists who can type anything from a letter in Yiddish at three in the morning (that's their line not mine) to a lengthy manuscript. KBM boasts the ability to do any job in record time, at record prices, in a record number of languages. When one checks out the competition, that seems to be true. "We Type It!" is especially geared to the needs of travelers and businessmen who may be far from a home office and in need of a fast, efficient typist. The center even offers stylistic and editorial assistance. It looks to me as if "We Type It!" has struck the right keys again.

WORLD-WIDE BUSINESS CENTRES
575 Madison Ave
486-1333, 605-0200, 1-800-847-4276
Mon-Fri: 9-5:30; Sat, Sun: 10-4

Alan Bain, a transplanted English lawyer, has created a highly profitable business that caters to business executives who need more than a hotel room to work from when visiting New York. The need for the business grew out of Bain's own frustrations in trying to put together a makeshift office, write and get out reports, answer telephones, and still attend to the matters that brought him to the city in the first place. The World-Wide Business Centres (there are other branches throughout the world) can house any business for any amount of time. Personnel, including typists, stenographers, administrative assistants, and clerks, can be hired by the hour. Desks, rooms, and even the conference suite can be rented on a daily, weekly, monthly, or quarterly basis. The daily rate includes a telephone switchboard, receptionist, and an office. None of these arrangements shows an indication that they are not permanent and, in fact, arrangements can be made to have a company listed in the lobby directory, on the mail drop, and in the phone service. Bain claims that the services most in demand by his business clients are the secretarial, telex and telephone facsimile services that allow the traveler to keep in touch with the home office. These services are available at night and weekends as well. Clients, incidentally, are carefully screened.

Party Rentals

SERVICE PARTY RENTAL
520 E 72nd St
288-7384
Mon-Fri: 8:30-5

These people have a nice range of quality party wares, with a good selection at the top of the line. They emphasize specialty items, such as champagne glasses and buckets, salmon poachers, silver, and stunning punch bowls.

Pen and Lighter Repair

AUTHORIZED REPAIR SERVICE
143 E 60th St (bet Lexington and Third Ave)
759-9765
Mon, Thurs: 9-6; Tues, Wed, Fri: 9-5

If a business' specialty is the repair of fountain pens and cigarette lighters in this day of disposable ball point pens and no-smoking campaigns, you wouldn't think it could be a viable concern. But you would think wrong. Morton Winston first started the business two decades ago, and it is still incredibly busy today—perhaps because it is almost without competition. Those who use fountain pens are devoted to them. Authorized Repair sells and services nearly every brand and the shop can refill lighters as well as all kinds of pens. (This means ball point and cartridges as well as fountain pens.) Authorized also sells, repairs, and services electric shavers. Tourists can even pick up 220 V appliances or adapter plugs, and the staff is well versed in the fine points of each brand.

FOUNTAIN PEN HOSPITAL
18 Vesey St
964-0580
Mon-Thurs: 8:30-5:30; Fri: 8:30-5

This establishment is one of the only places in town that repairs fountain pens. There used to be scores of such shops around town, but these kinds of pens have fallen out of flavor and popular use. So, now, the Fountain Pen Hospital sells and repairs pens of all types—and other writing implements as well. They are probably the most experienced shop around.

Personal Services

CATHERINE VAN ORMER
(Image Wardrobe Fashion Consultant)
238 Madison Ave (suite 2C)
532-4446

Catherine Van Ormer not only associates with diplomats, socialites, executives, and show-business personalities, she dresses them. In fact, she was named the fashion consultant to WCBS-TV's news reporters when she owned a boutique. As more and more people began demanding her fashion-shopping expertise, she closed the store and went into personal shopping full time. She is quite simply the best in the business. Most of her clients are people who have neither the time nor talent to put together a top-notch wardrobe, and they benefit from her close association with the city's top clothing designers. She scouts all of the lines and then shows the best to the client. Clothes can be purchased at Catherine's wholesale cost, which is roughly 50 percent less than retail, and the fashions reflect her eye for couture lines and natural fibers. The fee for all this is a mere pittance for those who simply must have this service. (There *are* those who simply can't keep all those cocktail parties straight.) Much like a decorator, Van Ormer charges 15 percent of the total amount purchased through her. By appointment only.

PASSPORT PLUS
663 Fifth Ave (sixth floor)
759-5540

You haven't experienced New York unless you've stood in the passport line at Rockefeller Center prior to summer vacation. Sometimes the line weaves through floors and staircases, and other times the day's work quota stops the line at 11 a.m., assuring the last "lucky" person of service by 5 p.m. Elise Gans was one such lucky person several years ago, and she decided to do something about it. She started Passport Plus, a service that takes the waiting out of obtaining a passport for the client. Gans' staff will do all the leg work involved in obtaining passports, visas, tickets, certificates, driver's licenses, and other documents. Auxiliary services include photo service and a pickup and delivery service currently available in Manhattan and Brooklyn. Fees are based on how quickly the item is required, but there are many (me included) who think it is worth virtually anything to get off those lines. Rockefeller Center is great, but not for 8 hours in one spot!

RESOURCES
2 Tudor City Pl
883-9119

In 1981, Barbara Peters started Resources to offer New Yorkers the proverbial "extra pair of hands." To her surprise, the business was an instant success, and 90 percent of it was spent organizing—that is, organizing everything from desk drawers to checkbooks to entire offices. Peters did it with aplomb, and business soon expanded (often for the same customers) into billing, administrative services, typing, writing, editing, insurance claims, and shopping. In addition, Resources personnel speak five languages, which has led to guiding, touring, and "gofering" for foreign visitors. A disproportionate amount of business is done with people who work at home; and most are inexpensive part-time, or even one-time, assignments. Rates are reasonable, with no job exceeding $30 an hour and straight typing going for $10 an hour, which may be the best rate in town. Short of sprouting another pair of arms, Resources is probably the best hope for harried, unorganized people.

SERVICES UNLIMITED
10 Rockefeller Plaza (at 48th St)
586-8880
Mon-Fri: 9-6:30
1 Penn Plaza (at 34th St)
695-3600
Mon-Fri: 9-5:30

There is nothing like waiting on line in New York (note that in this city one waits *on,* not *in,* a line), and David Alwadish decided to do something about it. In the beginning, Services Unlimited did things like stand on line to process drivers licenses and passport applications and to pay traffic tickets. Some people scoffed, but they weren't the ones who saved man hours for a fee that was less than what it would have cost the client to stand on line themselves—not to mention the cost of physical inconvenience. In fact, it proved so successful that Services Unlimited branched out into case work for attorneys and added an automobile leasing service. They are also expert in tracing duplicate documents and processing insurance claims. Their motto could be "Let Services Unlimited do the standing."

Photographic Services

A. A. IDENTIFICATION SERVICE
698 Third Ave (bet 43rd and 44th St)
682-5045
Mon-Fri: 9-5:45; Sat: 11-3

A.A.'s main virtue is its ability to do passport and identification photos competently and quickly while you wait. This is no small matter since many of the passport photo shops—particularly those close to passport offices—are totally unreliable. A.A. has a good reputation.

BACHRACH
48 E 50th St (bet Park and Madison Ave)
755-6233
Mon-Fri: 9:15-5; Sat: 10-4

If you have never heard of Bachrach, a quick glance at the society page of *The New York Times* will establish its credentials. Bachrach is *the* eminent photographer in New York, the United States, and possibly the world. For over a century, Bachrach has photographed the social events in its patrons' lives. Most visible are the bridal portraits that appear week after week in the newspapers, but there are also executive portraits, candids, and portraits of debutantes, children, and bridal parties. There are also family and oil-painting departments, all of which are handled with the same fine attention to detail. Bachrach does magnificent work, but the prices are magnificent, too. And some of their personnel make you feel they are doing *you* a favor—which doesn't really fit into today's ultracompetitive world. A little humility, please.

GENE BARRY ONE HOUR PHOTO
130 E 57th St (at Lexington Ave)
838-8316
Mon-Fri: 8-7; Sat: 10-6; Sun: noon-6
1282 Broadway (at 34th St)
695-1519
Mon-Fri: 7:30-7; Sat, Sun: 10-6

You don't have to wait days for snapshots. Gene Barry really can develop most photographs in one hour. The shop has a good reputation to back its claims.

PHOTOGRAPHICS UNLIMITED/ DIAL-A-DARKROOM
43 W 22nd St (bet Fifth and Sixth Ave)
255-9678
Mon-Fri: 9 a.m.-11 p.m.; Sat: 10-7; Sun: noon-7

Here's another only-in-New York idea. Photographics Unlimited offers photographers of limited physical means a full range of photographic equipment and a place to work on a rental basis. The shop has everything from the simplest equipment to an 8x10 Saltzman printer, including all manner of printing paper and film supplies, as well as a lab for on-the-spot developing for black and white and color. Ed Lee claims his center is a complete one for the most amateur or most advanced professional photographer, and he aims to prove it. Both studios and darkrooms can be rented, and both come with advice and suggestions from the darkroom's owner. It would be hard to describe all of the resources here. Whatever could be desired in a personally owned studio is available for rent at Lee's. And don't overlook the advantages of having company. Fellow photographers exchange advice, support, and encouragement.

PROFESSIONAL CAMERA REPAIR SERVICE
37 W 47th St (bet Fifth and Sixth Ave)
382-0511
Mon-Fri: 8:30-5

Marty Forscher started this service in 1946, and he and the business are still going strong. Not only do they repair all still cameras from 35 mm up, they also do work on movie cameras. If you're in a big hurry, they will oblige. Designing and building special camera equipment is an important part of their business.

Forscher was the inventor of the Polaroid film pack for the 35 mm camera; he's very much in focus, if you'll pardon the expression!

STAT STORE
148 Fifth Ave (bet 19th and 20th St)
929-0566
Mon-Fri: 9-6:30; Sat, Sun: 12-4; closed Sun in summer

In medical parlance, *stat* means faster than pronto. In photo jargon, *stat* is short for photostat, and it has come to mean virtually any copy. Either definition applies for the stat store, which specializes in copying and photographic developing for business and professionals, rapidly and competently. The Stat Store offers the following: stats, veloxes, films, murals, color, cibaprints, Xerox, polaprints, viewgraphs, white keys, transfers, and cibastats. What is all that stuff? Fortunately, the folks at the Stat Store know—as well as how to get it done quickly.

Plant Consultation

COUNCIL ON THE ENVIRONMENT OF NEW YORK CITY
51 Chambers St (room 228)
566-0990
Mon-Fri: 9-5

A little-known fact is that the city will loan tools and "how to" books free of charge to any group that can demonstrate a serious gardening interest. Loans are limited to one week, but the waiting list is not long, and for the "price," it makes sense to get on the list. Once on, you can rent the same tools several times a season, as long as it isn't concurrently and there is no one ahead of you on the list. Until this publication, almost no one knew of it, so the list was quite short. Incidentally, the number of tools available for loan is extensive enough to make a professional gardener envious. The Council prefers groups, but a group can be as few as four people.

Plumbers

KAPNAG HEATING AND PLUMBING
326 E 91st St
289-8847

As an out-of-towner, I'm not often in need of a Manhattan plumber, so there's a story behind how I learned that Kapnag is a really first-rate operation. A while ago, I was visiting a friend who was having a plumbing problem. She called Kapnag, but got no response. When she called a second time, Kapnag apologized profusely and came out immediately to fix it. There was even a follow-up call to make sure the problem had been completely corrected. Ask any New Yorker, and you'll learn what a rare virtue this story illustrates. Brett Neuhauser, Kapnag's president, has got to be the reason for all this kindness. When we first published this story, Neuhauser wrote to tell us that the sudden surge in sales was due to his mother "supplying the northeast region." May they both continue to thrive!

Postal Services

MAIL BOX
1742 Second Ave (bet 90th and 91st St)
289-5500
Mon-Fri: 8-8; Sat: 9-4

The Mail Box is based on the concept that the United States Postal Service is a good thing that can be made better. Actually, most of their initial business comes from people on the Upper East Side who could not wait for post-office boxes to become available in their neighborhood. And once they were customers, they realized the many additional advantages of the Mail Box. The boxes themselves are identical to those at the post office, and they afford the same privacy. However, the Mail Box leases on a month-to-month basis rather than the usual six-month lease offered by the post office, and the client's address is the Mail Box' address plus a suite or office number, which lends a more professional image to the client's mail. The Mail Box will also forward mail and features a phone-answering service. With a call-in service for mail checks and package acceptance (the post office will not accept UPS or other deliveries), the Mail Box creates the impression of a fully functioning office when only the Mail Box exists. Note, also, the hours. Where else can you get your mail at 8:00 in the evening?

Quilting Instruction

CRAFT STUDENTS LEAGUE
YWCA of the City of New York
610 Lexington Ave
755-2700

Because not many tools are needed to make a quilt, few stores are devoted solely to quilt-making. The best instruction is to be found in such schools as the Craft Students League. There are limited classes with an average of six meetings. During the course, each student works on a project and, depending upon proficiency, either starts or completes at least one quilt. The Craft Students

League also has any number of other excellent courses. All of them, while "crafty," are immensely practical as well. The bookbinding course is known for its professionalism (see "Bookbinding"). Send for a catalog to get a better idea of what they offer. You won't be disappointed.

Reweaving

FRENCH-AMERICAN REWEAVING COMPANY
37 W 57th St (at Fifth Ave, room 409)
753-1672
Mon-Fri: 9-6; Sat: 11-2

For more than 50 years, this company has been repairing and mending knit, lace, linen, silk, and wool fabrics with an almost invisible mending process that makes the new threads indiscernible from the originals. Even when an item is badly—and seemingly irreparably—damaged, French-American claims that if they can't weave the wound, they can at least repair it so that their work is the next best thing to invisible. Needless to say, one doesn't submit a $3 tie to these costly procedures. But if an item is worth saving, it's almost a sure thing that these people can pull it off.

Rug Cleaning

A. BESHAR AND COMPANY
49 E 53rd St (bet Park and Madison Ave, second floor)
758-1400
Mon-Sat: 9-5; closed Sat in summer

Lee Howard Beshar's family has run this carpet and Oriental rug business for three generations. Consequently, there is little he doesn't know or hasn't seen in the carpet business; he can handle any kind of request competently. His expertise and experience are the basis of the Besharizing Cleaning Process, which all floor coverings submitted for correction receive. Naturally, if a rug only needs cleaning, you're ahead of the game. Beshar does not make house calls; all carpets must be cleaned at the company's offices. This can be expensive, so if your carpet isn't very valuable, you might be better off buying a new one. Here, too, Beshar can come to the rescue with a large range of Oriental rugs and carpets. All are of good quality and value, and Beshar stands behind—and sometimes *on*—them all.

Schools

Cooking Schools

New Yorkers are conditioned to getting everything wholesale. So while they'll never give up Zabar's, Balducci's, Dean & DeLuca, or Sarabeth's Kitchen, many city residents become cooking school students who learn how to prepare all of their favorite dishes at home. In the New York style, there are cooking schools in every denomination, economic bracket, and ethnic persuasion. The New York Association of Cooking Teachers keeps a list of their members. Check out any instructor's credentials with them. The following schools are your best bets:

China Institute (125 E 65th St, 744-8181) Don't tell the China Institute that learning Chinese culture is only incidental to the hoards of students who sign up for the Chinese cooking classes at the School of Chinese Studies. They labor under the illusion that all students enroll for the purpose of the school—to study Chinese life. But we know better. They come for the most revered cooking lessons in the medium. Florence Lin's and Madame Li Ling Ai's courses at the Institute are as much a legend as the late James Beard's were.

Culinary Center of New York (100 Greenwich Ave, 255-4141) The Culinary Institute is up the Hudson River in Hyde Park. Serious students with an eye on professional kitchen work enroll there; it's less than two hours from the city. Within the city, the Culinary Center is the most professional establishment for amateur and less-than-totally-committed chefs.

French Culinary Institute (462 Broadway, 807-0936) This is a cooperative effort between the Paris Chamber of Commerce, which authorizes cooking schools in France, and Apex Technical Institute. The latter runs those incessant ads for computer training on TV, but that doesn't take away from the very impressive curriculum here. The goal is to create professional cooks capable of obtaining a job either here or back in France. (What other school can equip a student to cook in Paris?) This is not for dabblers.

Lydie Marshall (23 Eighth Ave, 675-7736) The professional kitchen downstairs in Lydie Marshall's townhouse is the site of some of the city's best French cuisine classes.

New School Culinary Arts Program (27 W 34th St, 947-7097) The New School is a New York institution—and that's not merely a pun. Improvement-minded New Yorkers enroll in the New School's continuing education for everything from "cinematology" courses with Robert Redford to a culinary-arts program that was so successful it outgrew the school building and now has its own quarters. Half the school is for professional restaurateurs. The other half teaches everything from "How to Boil Water" (a favorite among the newly single) to "Better Flambé."

Peter Kump's New York Cooking School (307 E 92nd St, 410-4601) Peter Kump's New York Cooking School is one of the best culinary trade sources in the city. They take weekend cooks as well as professional chefs, and the courses are geared accordingly. Kump is always trying to upgrade and improve the courses, and one innovation is his "An Insider's Gastronomic Guide to the Big Apple," which covers everything from where to eat to how to run a restaurant in New York. The program lasts three or four days and stuffs almost more than can be digested into that time frame. It starts with a special dinner at Cellar in the Sky, includes visits to the wholesale markets, and ends with champagne and caviar. It ain't cheap, but many of Kump's other courses are, and the expertise is worth the price.

Fashion Schools

FASHION INSTITUTE OF TECHNOLOGY

227 W 27th St
760-7642 (760-7654 placement)

What do Sal Cesarani, Jhane Barnes, Andrew Fezza, Bill Haire, Norma Kamali, and Calvin Klein have doubly in common? They are all F.I.T. graduates who have received the coveted Coty Award, the fashion industry's version of the Tony or Oscar. That's quite a record for a school which has celebrated its 40th birthday and which was founded to supply artisans to the garment center just up Seventh Avenue. But over the years, F.I.T. has become much more. Today, a partial list of the school's majors would include advertising display, jewelry, interior, textile, exhibit, and fashion design, illustration, photography, fine arts, cosmetics, fragrances and toiletries, fashion buying and merchandising, apparel production management, pattern making, fur design and marketing, and leather accessories. The faculty for all of these fields reflects the fact that F.I.T. is the worldwide premier institute serving the fashion industry and that students seriously interested in any of the above fields consider F.I.T. their first choice. F.I.T. students know their stuff, and the rest of the populace flocks to the area much as they go to Lincoln Center for culture or Columbia for intellectualism. F.I.T. maintains a student placement service which will match students' majors in the above fields with people looking for their talents. Those in interior design can help with everything from bathroom faucets to entire homes. So, call F.I.T., and ask for help. They offer a wide range of services, and all of their students are top-notch, since only one-quarter of the school's applicants are accepted. Their staff is superb, and their chief financial man, Fred Blatt, is one of the classiest guys in New York. There are also two other F.I.T. programs of interest to the general public. Every year in December, the school holds a fabric sale to benefit the scholarship fund. Donations come from alumni and friends in the industry who appreciate F.I.T.'s contributions. The result is some of the season's most spectacular fabrics at absurd prices. It shouldn't be missed. (Call 760-7701 for the date.) The other program is the Edward C. Blum Design Laboratory. This repository of the history of fashion is open to members and has over one million articles of clothing. It is incredible. The galleries at F.I.T. are open to the public and reflect some of the Blum collection. They stage periodic shows, almost all are furnished from the collection, and they are quite a show in themselves. (Call 760-7760 for information regarding exhibits.)

TOBE-COBURN SCHOOL FOR FASHION CAREERS
686 Broadway (bet Fourth and Great Jones St)
460-9600
Mon-Fri: 8:30-5:30

Tobe Coller Davis and Julia Coburn were two of the top names in the fashion industry when they jointly founded the Tobe-Coburn school in 1937 as a training ground for careers in fashion marketing and management. Tobe was a personal friend of mine, and I had the privilege of attending many of her spectacular fashion clinics when I was in the retail business. And what a treat it was to visit with her at her brownstone apartment. What an incredible person! Today, Ann Wareham and her crew are keeping up the outstanding, professional reputation of the great lady. Tobe-Coburn students receive an intensive two-year course in all aspects of the garment industry. Even the liberal arts courses are specifically oriented to industry application. Universal business skills courses stress advertising and public-relations writing, and the history courses deal with the history of retailing and merchandising, as well as fashion trends. Over the years, the school has established a better than 95 percent placement record and a reputation as one of the best schools for training in the merchandising, marketing, and management aspects of fashion. The school has co-op programs and internships with the top names in the business, and when the students graduate, they know the city as well as they know the inside of Seventh Avenue.

School Services for Consumers

The city is an educational center, and everyone can benefit from the schools in the city. There are plenty of apprentices who offer services at cut rates, and anyone can take courses and pick up training in useful skills. The following places were found from research on this book, and I'm sure there are many more.

Atlas Barber School (44 Third Ave, 475-1360) In a city where haircuts can cost $50, this is a real bargain.

Christine Valmay School (730 Fifth Ave, 581-1520) In the beauty services section, there are several schools listed that provide beauty services by students at vastly reduced prices. Christine Valmay is one such place. Studios and salons around town offer her elegant methods of facials, skin-care, and beauty techniques. Valmay also has a school for training students in her own special methods. Customers can receive the same carefully supervised services at a fraction of the cost. And there's no tipping.

Craft Students League (Y.W.C.A., 610 Lexington Ave, 755-4500) The Craft Student's League has a full range of courses, which range from bookbinding to quilt making. They are expert and very reasonable. The student learns a practical trade as well. There's metalwork, jewelry, ceramics, painting, drawing, woodworking, calligraphy, weaving, needlecrafts, sewing, and dressmaking.

Eric Gaathje Custom Cabinetry (525 W 26th St, 563-9137) Gaathje also runs cabinet-making and picture-framing classes, which are held on the Upper West Side at flexible hours.

High School of Fashion (255-1253) This city-run high school maintains a list of graduates and evening students who are adults and experts in fabric and dress making. Many of them are recent arrivals from other countries, who need American schooling in professions they had been working at in their native lands. Aside from earning money, they gain experience, exposure, and references. For the customer, it translates into a professional dressmaking job at an excellent price.

H. Roth & Sons—Lekvar by the Barrel (1577 First Ave, 734-1110, 535-2322) While there are those who would love to learn how to become an accomplished Hungarian cook, H. Roth's classes are in cake decorating. Maybe someone could talk them into branching out.

Juilliard School of Music (Lincoln Center, 799-5000, ext 313, Placement Office, Mon-Fri: 9-5) Juilliard, the renowned school of music and the arts, offers one of the very best deals in the city for music aficionados. Carefully screened students (to get into Juilliard, the best have already been chosen) are available for concerts and performances. The current rate is $40 to $50 an hour per musician, including everything from harpists to oboe soloists. But pianists are the most popular, and are capable of playing everything from classical piano to jazz to piano-bar cocktail hours.

Kree Institute of Electrolysis (1500 Broadway, 730-9700) It offers reasonable prices for clients who allow students to do the work, which is carefully supervised and a fraction of the cost of what the same student will charge when he becomes a graduate.

The Learning Annex (36 W 62nd St at Broadway, 956-8800) A smaller version of the New School, the Learning Annex offers adult-education courses interesting enough to lure people out of their homes after a work day. Two recent examples were David Mintz' "How to Create an Empire" course (Mintz is the genius behind Tofutti) and Michael Miele's (owner of that hot spot, Amsterdam) "How to Succeed in the Restaurant Business." There are many more, and the cost is less than dinner out in the respective lecturers' establishments. Come to think of it, it's proportional, too. Mintz' course is less expensive than Miele's. There's also "Buying a Co-op" and "How to Write for Cable TV," among other courses.

Manhattan Career Institute (351 E 61st St, 593-1231) There are many programs involving students here. The one I am familiar with is animal grooming by students at a fraction of what you'd pay elsewhere.

Metropolitan Museum of Art (Fifth Ave at 82nd St, 879-5500 membership office, ext 3753) The Met, as well as virtually every other museum in town, offers a series of classes for members and friends. Among the most renowned are the children's art classes, taught by Muriel Siberstein. From her parent-child workshops of the past 14 years, she has earned a reputation that almost matches that of the museum. She teaches children ages 3 to 5, one day a week (weekdays), in a variety of artwork. Other Met courses teach painting, sculpture, drawing, and sketching, with instructors for children aged five and up. Some, but not all, feature art-appreciation trips through the galleries. Most, however, offer hands-on experience in artistic media. Those courses are open for members only and are booked rapidly. They run on a semester basis, and March is not too early to book the September-to-December semester. The membership office has a brochure, which lists fees and a course schedule. Every Saturday and Sunday, the museum also hosts a gallery walk for children aged 5 to 12. Parents may or may not accompany students for the one-hour tour, and aside from the initial museum fee, thc gallery walk is free. Currently, the tours leave at 11 a.m. and 2:30 p.m. on Saturday and 11 a.m. on Sunday.

The New School for Social Research (66 W 12th St, 741-5600) The New School functions as a college and graduate school, although that would be news to most New Yorkers. It is better known for the tremendous variety of courses it offers to adults in the evenings and on weekends. Every fall, the New School's catalog signals the change of the seasons, and adults who have spent the summer relaxing "get serious" with a vengeance by enrolling in the New School's courses. The city's brightest luminaries staff the classes. The top people in every field teach all sorts of fascinating classes that are designed to entice tired, bored, and overworked New Yorkers in off hours. Filmmaking is a popular one, since it attracts stars and groupies. The instructor is Richard Brown, and he has had such guest lecturers as Robert Redford. But there are practical courses as well. "How to Get Organized" is always a favorite.

Scissors and Knife Sharpening

A. KOCHENDORFER MACHINERY
413 W Broadway (bet Prince and Spring St)
925-1435
Mon-Fri: 6:30-5; Sat: 8-4

West Broadway is in SoHo but you may never need to make the trek, for A. Kochendorfer offers free pickup and delivery on all orders in all boroughs. How he does it is hard to explain, since his prices are excellent. If you are in the Spring Street vicinity, repairs can be made while you wait, except during lunchtime.

Sewing Machine Repair

MILTON KESSLER
718-763-7897

More elusive than a needle in a haystack is an honest repairman, particularly one who makes house calls. Milton Kessler is one who is polite, thorough, and completely reliable. He is never home when you call, but he does get messages and can usually schedule an appointment within a week. In addition, he has a wealth of information on the care and maintenance of sewing machines in general, and he tells you how yours got into the shape that necessitated his visit in particular. On top of his honesty, promptness, and reliability, Kessler has rates that are dirt cheap. He's also one of New York's nicest people. And service runs in the family! Kessler's son, Terry (same phone number), runs a 24-hour locksmith service. He'll get you out of that locked room where you are sewing on the machine his father probably once fixed!

Shoe Repair

B. NELSON SHOE CORPORATION
1221 Sixth Ave (bet 47th and 48th St, McGraw-Hill Bldg, C-2 level)
869-3552
Mon-Fri: 7:30-5:15

If you haven't already explored the stores housed on the many levels of Rockefeller Center, perhaps a shoe in need of surgery will prompt you to visit one downstairs. A shoe repair shop located in a building frequented by tourists isn't usually a good bet, but B. Nelson receives a lot of work from people who work in Rockefeller Center, which is an indication of the store's good work. I recommend them highly. B. Nelson is one of the few people in the trade that can make custom alterations and adjustments as well as handmade shoes. They take great pride in refinishing shoes so that the old shoes are indistinguishable from new. Rates, notwithstanding the Rockefeller Center address, are remarkably reasonable. Recently, B. Nelson began making high style custom-made women's shoes. Prices are less than those at some high fashion salons, and the workmanship is super. If I can be forgiven a prediction, I think the old-fashioned shoemaker is going to turn from being a repair shop to becoming literally a shoemaker, and more and more are going to be creating shoes solely. I guess I also have to be forgiven a pun.

JIM'S SHOE REPAIR
50 E 59th St (bet Madison and Park Ave)
355-8259
Mon-Fri: 8-6; Sat: 8-4; closed Sat in summer

This operation offers first-rate shoe repairing and shining and shoe supplies. Shoe repair is a field that is rapidly losing its craftsmen, and Jim is one of the few who uphold the tradition. Jim's owner is Joseph E. Rocco who specializes in orthopedic work and boot alteration. But people still call him Jim.

MANHATTAN SHOE REPAIR
6 E 39th St 42 E 41 St
683-4210
Mon-Fri: 8-6

Manhattan Shoe Repair offers a large range of orthopedic and fashion repairs. In addition to the regular resoling and heel repairs, Manhattan does rebinding, vamp cutting, redyeing, and orthopedic work. Their motto is, "Work that lasts." That pun is theirs, not mine, but after 33 years in the business, Mr. Lucas is entitled to make jokes about his work.

Silver Repair and Replating

BRANDT & OPIS
145 W 45th St
245-9237
Mon-Fri: 8-3:30

Charles Opis can handle just about anything to do with silversmithing. For over 35 years, this shop has been replacing silver, doing gold and silver plating, repairing silver and brass, refinishing silver flatware, and taking monograms off of silver. They are trustworthy and experienced, and are able to handle mail orders.

THOME SILVERSMITHS
328 E 59th St (bet First and Second Ave)
758-0655
Mon-Fri: 8:30-5:30; Sat: 10-4

Thome Silversmiths have been handling Plaza Hotel patrons and their ilk for many years. The Plaza itself brings over serving pieces in need of touch-ups or replating, and this is sufficient recommendation for its customers. Thome cleans, repairs, and replates silver in addition to dealing in the buying and selling of some magnificent pieces. They have a real appreciation for the material, and it shows in everything they do. They claim to specialize in brass and copper polishing, and they also do restorations, silver and gold plating, pewter repair and cleaning, lacquering, and refining. Incidentally, *don't* attempt pewter repair yourself. Pewter is an alloy and must be handled delicately. Thome also specializes in brass. This company is one of the very few still in that business.

Stables

CLAREMONT RIDING ACADEMY
175 W 89th St (bet Amsterdam and Columbus Ave)
724-5100
Mon-Fri: 6 a.m.-10 p.m.; Sat, Sun: 6-6

Claremont, located at a certified national historic site, is the oldest continuously operating public stable in the country and the only one in New York. Nonriders will find a visit here enchanting, if only for a glimpse of traditional equestrian life in New York. Horse enthusiasts (like me) with no other riding option in the area will be happy to learn that Claremont is as finely and professionally run as if there were stables on every corner. The riding style is exclusively English (no Western style here), and that orientation is evident throughout the business. Claremont shows, buys, sells, boards, jumps, rents, and teaches horses, though not necessarily in that order, and even that is only a partial list. They claim specialties in dressage and hunt-seat equitation, but the average city rider knows them as the source for renting mounts to traverse Central Park's bridal paths. Claremont also runs two ongoing summer camps—one for children and one for adults—as well as an enviable riding program for handicapped children. Their two annual horse shows are well attended by spectators as well as riders, and the variety of mounts for hire would be amazing anywhere. That all of the horses are kept right on the premises in New York City is incredible. Claremont makes it possible for you to visit the Big Apple and come back telling the dude-ranch vacationers in your office that you went riding everyday, too—only you had better quality, better trained animals, and you did it *in* the city.

Stained Glass Repair

JACK CUSHEN STUDIO

110 W 17th St (bet Sixth and Seventh Ave)
675-6674
Mon-Sat: 8-5; Sun: by appointment only

Jack Cushen is an artist of another era. After serving an apprenticeship in Ohio, he moved to New York to take advantage of the demand for stained-glass windows in postwar churches. But the demand diminished drastically, so in order to stay in business, the studio went from working on new edifices to repairing windows and lamps. He also does occasional custom-made pieces. In fact, the industry has slowed so much that the union Cushen apprenticed for doesn't exist anymore, and he is the only person left in the city—and possibly the nation—with his expertise. While training to become a stained-glass craftsman, Cushen garnered expertise in a number of divergent areas. He can discourse on the difference in fund raising and church building of various denominations (Catholics put in windows while the building is going up and pay for them from a diocese fund; Protestants sell windows "In memorium" and often wait years to finish the project). He can also guide urban homesteaders into sound buildings and away from those which look good but are cheaply constructed, and he is a walking encyclopedia on the history of stained glass. (A bit of esoterica from the latter skill: there is no such thing as stained glass. What Cushen works with is *colored* glass. The color goes all the way through, not merely stained on top.) Finally, Cushen is still hanging in there for one reason. Though business is terrible now and he can hardly remember the last church commission he had, stained-glass making is an ancient craft that often undergoes resurgences of interest. One of the major renaissances occurred right after the Industrial Revolution in England. "As things got more and more industrialized," says Cushen, "people went back to home comforts, such as calligraphy, quilts, and stained glass." Cushen's wife does calligraphy; his neighbors sell quilts. And stained glass will probably be making a comeback any day now.

Tailors

MAL THE TAILOR
50 W 72nd St (near Columbus Ave)
799-6120
Mon-Sat: 9-6; closed Aug

Mal made his reputation doing theater and television costume alterations. Often, an outfit had to be altered overnight (in a tight-budgeted production) when there was a replacement for a departed star. Mal came to the rescue with aplomb, earning many a production chief's gratitude—as well as future business. The result is that Mal is probably *the* tailor to Broadway and local TV productions. But man does not live by TV alone, and Mal prefers to bill himself as a custom clothes-maker, as well as a specialist in leather alterations. He claims that he can execute almost any type of garment in leather, and the shop usually displays a few carefully crafted examples. He will happily make up suits, sport jackets, or slacks for new customers as well, and his creations usually sell for about half as much as off-the-rack garments.

SEBASTIAN TAILORS
767 Lexington Ave (at 60th St, room 404)
688-1244
Mon-Fri: 8:30-5:30; Sat: 9-4:30

Tailors are a peculiar breed in New York. In a city that is the home of the garment industry, most garment repairmen build their trade as either custom alteration and design specialists or dry cleaners who incidentally mend whatever bedraggled outfit has been brought in for cleaning. Sebastian Tailors is one of the few shops in the city that is exactly what it says it is—a tailor shop. Their custom alterations for men and women are quick, neat, and, wonder of wonders, reasonable. But, best of all, everything is accomplished without the normal ballyhoo most such New York establishments seem to regard as their due. Incidentally, Sebastian was recommended to me by another tailor who particularly praised their alterations. Praise from someone within the trade is the highest praise of all. And when the praise includes the less common skill of ladies' tailoring, it marks a place worth trying. I use him, and I think he's great.

SILLS OF CAMBRIDGE
588 Fifth Ave (bet 47th and 48th St)
355-2360
Mon-Sat: 9:30-5:30; closed Sat in July and Aug

Self-styled as a custom English tailor, Sills impeccably creates suits and jackets that are individually suited from start to finish.

With a wide selection of fabrics, styling, and design, no two suits are the same; all are custom-made. Sills is noted for excellent service and craftsmanship, and while there is no comparison to the off-the-rack variety, prices are not that much higher. For the ultimate luxury experience, try Sills.

Taxicabs, Limousines

All licensed taxis in New York are painted yellow and have a medallion affixed to their hoods. These medallion cabs are a limited number of very closely regulated taxis under the jurisdiction of the New York Taxi and Limousine Commission. By law, they are required to have a light on top of the roof. The light shows their own unique number if they are available for hire, or an "Off Duty" sign if they are not. Any yellow medallion cab must at all times display one of these two lights on the streets of New York. In exchange, these cabs are the only vehicles allowed to cruise for customers in the city. Other cab companies do exist, but they are either liveries (called "gypsy cabs" because they have no home and are basically illegal), limousines, airport transportation carriers, or call-for-hire cars. None of these is allowed to cruise, and all are supposed to have fixed meter costs identical to those of the medallion cabs. The limousine and airport transportation cars have a set fee. That is the law. In reality, there is a different story.

All of the jokes about getting a cab in the rain are true. In New York, you can't. In addition, almost every yellow cab has a prescribed area which—for financial or safety reasons and despite the law—it will not enter. If a cabbie refuses to take you to your destination, you can always copy down his number to report him, but it won't get you where you want to go. As one nonmedallion group has printed on the side of its cars: "We're not yellow. We go anywhere." That's a good rule of thumb. There are disadvantages, however. Gypsy cabs are neither government licensed nor inspected. The more ethical do have livery licenses but are subject to a much less rigorous inspection. Almost without exception, you will pay more than what is on the meter—assuming you get a cab with a meter. Gypsy cruising is patently illegal, and the evasive action taken to avoid prosecution makes gypsy riding somewhat inconvenient at the very least.

Radio taxis are another story. Here you call a number, and via two-way radio, a taxi is sent to meet you at your location. They, too, are not allowed to charge over the meter rate. If it sounds too good to be true, it is. Simple arithmetic shows that a company that has to pay for two-way radios, drivers at the ready, and the drive from their garage to you and from your destination back to the garage can't possibly have the same profit margin a cruising cab has. How is this made up? By an unofficial over-the-meter charge. No one will ask you for it, but if you don't pay it, don't expect to get a radio-dispatched taxi again. Also, radio-dispatched cars usually have some reservation as to where they will go. Since you have to call in advance and state your destination, it may be even more difficult to get one to take you where you want to go.

There are lots of limousine services in the Manhattan Yellow Pages, which helps keep prices down. These services, however, compensate for the stated low fees by tacking on little surcharges. When shopping around by phone, be sure to ask specifically about the following: Do they a have a car that suits your needs? A car which seats eight is great, but if it's only going to seat two, why pay for the larger car? Is there a minimum number of hours you must pay for? If so, does it start when you get in the car, when the chauffeur gets in the car, or when the chauffeur pulls up in front of your residence? Some companies have garages in Queens, and your are charged for the commuting time. Is there a reduced rate for several days? Is there a reduced rate for a prescribed tour, be it sightseeing, the airport, or dinner and a show? Is the chauffeur's tip included? You may be pleasantly surprised. Several businessmen have discovered that renting a limousine is comparable to renting a car.

Cars for hire of any kind are among the most tightly regulated businesses in New York. Any complaints should be sent to the New York City Taxi and Limousine Commission, 221 W 41st Street, New York City, NY 10036, (869-4110, ext 866 or 869), preferably with the taxi's number or, at the very least, its license-plate number. Again, this won't get you a ride, but it might offer some satisfaction and prevent its happening to someone else.

CAREY CADILLAC
41 E 42nd St (near Madison Ave)
937-3100 (reservations), 986-5566 (office)
24 hours

Carey is the grandfather of all the car-for-hire services. They advertise availability any hour, any day, anywhere, any weather, and their word is good. They are experts at disguising the rented look and having their cars appear to be privately owned. Disadvantage: they are not open to last-minute reservations.

COOPER CLASSICS
132 Perry St (bet Washington and Greenwich St)
929-0094
24 hours

When you own an ailing Rolls-Royce, it's nice to know that its status allows you to watch its repair work in progress, and you don't have to sit in a grimy waiting room glaring at the sign, "Insurance regulations forbid customers beyond this point." There is very little concerning Rolls-Royce or Bentley service that Elliot Cooper of Cooper Classics, Ltd., does not perform. Cooper has a complete rental and sales service, including a chauffeured limousine service with a star-studded clientele list. (There are even groupies who have tried to rent specific cars after certain pop idols have used them. If they can afford it, Elliot Cooper tries to oblige.) Cooper also runs a complete restoration service, and his Rolls-Royce-trained mechanics can handle any kind of body or mechanical work. Finally, Cooper Classics sells and rents Rolls-Royces and Bentleys. At any given time, there are a half-dozen classic models keeping company with the latest modern ones. Most of the current editions, though, are custom-ordered. If you have Rollsmania, this is the place to satisfy it, if only by renting for a day.

LONDON TOWNCARS
988-9700 (New York)
800-221-4009 (anywhere, toll free)

Television enthusiasts know that London Towncars supplies the chauffeured cars to the guest stars of most New York television shows. So, if nothing else, a London Towncar chauffeur can regale his passengers with tales of the celebrities he has driven. But there is more. London Towncars (which is affiliated with the parent company in London) rents all types of cars, including station wagons, which means they are more flexible and better able to handle different lifestyles. All of their cars are chauffeur-driven. They are available for any period of time, with a one-hour minimum.

TEL AVIV
343 E 21st St
505-0555, 800-222-9888

Tel Aviv comes highly recommended from several friends in Oregon who somehow connected with this New York car service. Most of Tel Aviv's cars are regular ones (i.e., not limousines), and the prices are not in the limousine class as well. Best of all, these people show up!

Television Rental

GRANADA T.V. RENTAL
416 Third Ave (at 29th St)
679-9600
1410 Sixth Ave (bet 57th and 58th St)
308-0901
1069 Third Ave (at 63rd St)
935-4410
Mon-Fri: 9-7; Sat: 9-6

These folks just may be in the vanguard of a way of life for the future. In a remarkably short time, they have successfully spread all over the metropolitan area with a concept that is surprisingly simple yet clever. To wit, Granada's founders felt that televisions, VCRs, stereos, and even washers and dryers had a rental market with people who were not the usual transients. They decided to tap the market of people who for either financial or technological reasons didn't own electronic items. To do this, they made it seem a virtue to "wait and rent" rather than invest thousands of dollars in items that very shortly might be obsolete. And they twist it further by saying that if you should be so pleased (as to want an obsolete piece), you can turn your rental agreement into a sales agreement after the first year. But the real attraction is that people can have televisions and VCRs without the hassle of owning, repairing, or moving such items or investing a large sum in them.

TELEVISION RENTAL COMPANY
118 E 28th St (suite 508)
683-2850
Mon-Fri: 9-6; Sat: 9-4

Ted Pappas runs a rental service that is fast, good, and efficient. He will rent televisions for long- or short-term periods, and will happily deliver the sets and pick them up. He also rents VCRs and other audio-visual aids. The prices are among the best in the city, and in a business like this, his solid reputation is a formidable recommendation in itself. Tell him I sent you.

Theater Tickets

In New York, theater tickets are more than admission to a show. They are signs of power, snobbery, love, and savvy, depending upon how they were obtained and who is going to use them. Only a hick would come to town without tickets and expect to see the show of his choice that evening. Ticket buyers in New York can be divided into two categories: those who have no particular show in mind and all the time in the world to wait for tickets, and those who are frantic for a particular show on a particular night.

Fortune is on the side of the former group; they are the ones who will get good prices and perhaps excellent seats as well. Unfortunately, almost all the city's potential theatergoers fall into the latter category. Several years ago, there was a major scandal involving scalpers—people who bought up vast quantities of tickets and resold them at highly inflated prices. The result was a law setting an absolute maximum *anyone* was allowed to charge above the stated ticket price. Reputable reservation centers operate under the maximum, which makes most of them excellent values. If you're really in a bind for tickets, and price is not important, check with Florence Read at the Pierre Hotel, Monday through Saturday, from 11 a.m. to 7 p.m. (757-5210). But there are still places where, for a steep price, you can get same-day tickets for sold-out performances. The most likely spots are in proximity to the theater's own box office. Someone is *always* standing there mumbling "tickets tonight, tickets tonight." But I emphatically do *not* recommend going that route.

CHARGIT
1501 Broadway
944-9300

TICKETRON
1350 Sixth Ave
977-9020 (information only)
947-5450
(for charges by phone)

These agencies work for the strict legal fee above the base ticket price. They do it with low overhead (Chargit doesn't have an office for customers at all; business is done by phone) and not by necessarily buying up blocks of tickets. When a request is made for a ticket, they call the theater's box office to see what is available. Sometimes they "broker" tickets as well, but if you are wondering what it is they are doing that you couldn't do yourself, you have only to stand in line in the rain at a box office to find out.

Ticketron has several locations throughout the city and will take phone reservations. If the show you want is not available, Ticketron will make other arrangements. Were you to do this on your own, you'd have to go from box office to box office and run up against another quirky, unwritten New York rule: no two box offices are ever open at the same time. Two hints: take along your charge card when you pick up your Chargit tickets, and be patient when you're calling Chargit. It takes them forever to answer the phone.

HIT SHOWS

300 W 43rd St (at Eighth Ave, room 602)
New York, NY 10036
581-4211
Mon-Fri: 9:30-3:30

"Twofers" are colored tickets that offer two seats for the price of one at specific performances of specific plays. One will *never* find twofers for the top plays. "Going on twofers" means that the show's end is imminent. This is not to say that some shows haven't bounced back from twofers or remained on them for years on end. However, given a choice, a producer will never let on that he is having trouble filling a house, and issuing twofers is tantamount to taking out a billboard to that effect over Times Square. Note that a show must be established before going on twofers. No one issues twofers to previews or flops. For the theatergoer, it can be a chance for excellent seats to a good show at half price. Frequently, twofer users sit next to people who have paid full price for their tickets. Twofers are distributed by Hit Shows at strategic places all over the city. Schools, universities, waiting rooms, hair salons, hotels, department stores, and barbershops are just a few of the places where they can be found, or try the Visitors and Convention Bureau at 2 Columbus Circle (397-8200) and the Information Center at 207 West 43rd Street. You can also send a stamped, self-addressed envelope, and they will let you know what is available. Please note also that using twofers requires a trip to the box office in person. Even so, it may not be possible to get same-day seats.

THEATER DEVELOPMENT FUND

1501 Broadway
221-0013 (requests taken 3 p.m.-5 p.m.)

If you live within driving distance, write to the Theater Development Fund (TDF) and request an application. Ostensibly for educators, the clergy, theater lovers, and students, the Fund will open its lists to almost anyone. It maintains several lists, each with a single area of interest—musical comedy, drama, religious, etc. Once on the list, the subscriber receives a mailing describing what is being offered, which performances are available, and what price the tickets are. The latter are almost ridiculously cheap, but personally, I've never made a performance. The ones I've been invited to have all been obscure plays, a run on its last legs, or a time I could not make. Some people swear by TDF, though. TDF also has a voucher system; for a flat fee, a subscriber receives five vouchers, each of which is good for a ticket worth a minimum amount at a subscribing theater. Most subscribing theaters are off-off-Broadway. (Off-Broadway, incidentally, refers to small theaters not geographically on the Great White Way. Off-off-Broadway is more avant-garde, more experimental, and off the beaten track, primarily Village-area theaters.) The plays are usually new. And for a play that could be the next *A Chorus Line* (which did take TDF orders when it was playing off-Broadway), it's the best buy in town.

TICKET WORLD

555 W 57th St (at 11th Ave, 11th floor)
888-9000 (for tickets), 702-3400 (Ticket World Office)
Mon-Fri: 9 a.m.-midnight; Sat, Sun: 9-9
Locations all over town in such stores as Kelly Film, Sam Goody Music Stores, and Drug Fair

Ticket World is an affiliate of the national company Ticket Masters, and this upstart from Detroit has made great inroads into what had been a virtual Ticketron monopoly of ticket counters in New York. Their entry into the field has forced Ticketron to automate and improve its facilities. (Ticket World has five times as many outlets as Ticketron, though Ticketron claims they have a "quality" location advantage.) Both companies are also engaged in price and service wars, the result of which can only be good for ticket buyers. So what is the advantage of one over the other? Well, if one wants tickets to Madison Square Garden, the New York Yankees, the Nassau Coliseum, Radio City, or the Nederlander Theaters (there are family ties there), Ticket World is the exclusive agent for them, aside from their own respective box offices. In some cases, Ticket World has a better selection than the box office, and many of the companies switched to Ticket World because they are more efficient. Ticket World seems to have done the impossible: They have taken on Ticketron and become a formidable opponent. Ticket buyers can only say "Bravo!" for the competition that is benefiting everyone.

TKTS—TIMES SQUARE THEATRE CENTER

Broadway (at 47th St)
354-5800
Mon-Sat: 3-8

Bryant Park (at 42nd St, bet Fifth and Sixth Ave)
382-2323
Daily: noon-7

LOWER MANHATTAN THEATRE CENTRE

2 World Trade Center (mezzanine)
Mon-Fri: 11-5:30; Sat: 11-3

The biggest problem for a Broadway show is a less than full house. First, every ticket not sold is a loss of money. Second, playing to a half-empty house is disconcerting to the performers. And finally, if the audience looks around and finds the show poorly attended, human nature will make them wonder what everyone else knows that they don't. Hence, the play loses its word-of-mouth business which, despite what Broadway media critics like to think, is responsible for the vast majority of customers. In addition, every show has a limited number of tickets that are held back for the producer, director, stars, critics, or VIPs who might be in town. Naturally, not all of these tickets can be used every night, and what is *not* used leaves an empty space in the audience and the show's profits.

Some years ago, TKTS was started to solve these problems. On the day of the performance, tickets are placed on sale on a space-available basis and sold first-come, first-served. All tickets are sold at half price, plus a small service charge. One never knows what is available until a blackboard list is posted outside the booth, but the first people in line have been known to get front-row-center tickets at half price to plays for which scalpers were charging triple the ticket amount. Since it is a day-to-day affair with no publicity, the stigma of twofers is lacking here, and producers will frequently unload held-back tickets which, before TKTS, would have been wasted. If the weather is bad, or it's the night before Christmas, the odds are excellent for your getting the show of your choice. The TKTS booth at Bryant Park only sells full-price tickets to Broadway shows. Its big advantage is that it offers discount tickets to such cultural events as ballet and concert performances. For off- and off-off-Broadway theater information, call ART/NY at 989-5257.

Translations

EURAMERICA TRANSLATIONS
257 Park Ave S
777-7878

New York is a multinational city, and Euramerica offers a full range of multilingual communication services. Their client list reads like the Fortune 500, and with good reason—most of them are Euramerica's customers. Their ability to provide accurate, quick service is on a par with the Indy 500. Euramerica can provide written translations in technical, advertising, legal, and commercial documents, as well as simultaneous oral translations. It is also set up to do artwork, graphics, and typesetting in any of 80 languages and alphabets. These people are truly masters who cannot be adequately described in writing. Suffice it to say that if the U.S. State Department can have a translator mistakenly tell a country that our president desires them obscenely, accurate translating is not an easy thing. Euramerica has had no such accidents.

Upholstering

RAY MURRAY
418 E 59th St
838-3752

Here's the good news: Ray Murray is a reliable, capable, talented re-upholsterer. Now, the bad news: it costs just as much to re-upholster your furniture as it does to replace it. Murray's specialty is creating custom-made furniture. Cheap it isn't, but the quality is superb. He can copy any design you want (including heirloom pieces or furniture from museum exhibits), but he specializes in classic, contemporary, and modern furniture. Big, overstuffed sofas are his forte. A seven-foot custom job runs under $1500, which isn't bad, compared to the cost of ready-made furniture. The reasonable prices disappear when Murray talks about re-upholstering. Even if the customer supplies the material, a recovered sofa won't be much less than $500. However, if you're redecorating and your furniture is generally in good condition, Murray can coordinate all the work, fabric, and patterns. He can make drapery and accessory pieces to match the recovered furniture, and the total cost will be substantially less than it would be to throw everything out and start from scratch.

Welding

AMEROM
54 W 22nd St (bet Fifth and Sixth Ave)
675-4828
Mon-Fri: 8:30-5

Florin Carmocanu is a Romanian artisan, whose metal workshop mainly focused on welding and cutting metal to size. Not terribly exciting or demanding of Carmocanu's considerable talent. But then word of his handiwork got out to loft dwellers, co-op remodelers, and interior decorators, and suddenly Amerom is one of the hottest places in town. And no wonder. Carmocanu is a genius with decorative metal, structural steel, and wrought-iron furniture and gates. His spiral staircases are awesome. Amerom can even replace original artwork and wrought-iron designs of old brownstones. As for the name, which doesn't exactly come tripping off the tongue, could be a combination of American and Romanian? Carmocanu isn't telling.

VI. Where To Buy It: New York's Best Department And Specialty Stores

Over 200 of the Best and the Worst Places to Shop in New York

An Exclusive List

Best values in women's apparel: Ben Farber (462 Seventh Ave)
Best selection of Broadway show recordings: Footlight Records (90 Third Ave)
Best values in housewares: Zabar's (2245 Broadway)
Best general bookstore: Doubleday (Fifth Ave at 57th St)
No personality: Gimbel's (Broadway at 33rd St)
Best men's clothing department in a department store: Saks Fifth Avenue (611 Fifth Ave)
Great selection of children's clothing: Little Bits (1186 Madison Ave)
Best china and glassware: B. Altman (Fifth Ave at 34th St)
Great discount shoes for men: Stapleton Shoe Company (68 Trinity Pl)
Best selection of lucite items: Lucidity (775 Madison Ave)
Best prices on books: Barnes and Noble (many locations)
Fun merchandise, automated saleshelp: F.A.O. Schwarz (745 Fifth Ave)
Best button selection: Tender Buttons (143 E 62nd St)
Glad to have you back: Abercrombie and Fitch (South St Seaport, 199 Water St)
Great store for gifty-nifties: A & D Mercantile (South St Seaport)
Outstanding prices on athletic gear: Modell's (109 E 42nd St)
Best selection of Oriental rugs: Momeni (36 E 31st St)

Best furs for women: H.B.A. Fur (333 Seventh Ave)
Best piece-goods store: Samuel Beckenstein (125 Orchard St)
Best camera store: Grand Central Camera (420 Lexington Ave)
Best umbrella shop: Uncle Sam (161 W 57th St, 7 E 46th St)
Best values in art supplies: Pearl Paint Company (308 Canal St)
Best handbag store: Fine and Klein (119 Orchard St)
Distasteful high-pressured selling: Custom Shop (many locations)
Best magazine selection: Eastern Newsstand (Pan Am Bldg)
Best Gucci bargains: Gucci on Seven (2 E 54th St)
Best women's coats prices: Rubin's Fashions (242 W 38th St)
Best for out-of-print records: Dayton's (824 Broadway)
Best gift suggestions: Made in America (1234 Madison Ave)
Rudest bookstore personnel: Gordon's (St Regis Hotel Bldg)
Best selection of men's clothing at attractive prices: Saint Laurie (897 Broadway)
Good taste: Macy's street floor
Poor taste: Lord and Taylor's street floor
Best organized drugstore: Zitomer's Pharmacy (998 Madison Ave)
Great prices on woolens: Raleigh Textiles (294 Eighth Ave)
Best selection of bathroom accessories: Elegant John (812 Lexington Ave)
Most promising place to find book and art treasures amid the confusion: J.N. Bartfield Art Galleries (45 W 57th St)
Salesmen who are only walking mannequins: Andre Oliver (34 E 57th St)
Best stock of men's hats: Young's Hats (139 Nassau St)
Best selection and prices on domestics: Ezra Cohen (307 Grand St)
Best for jade jewelry: Jim Chan (3 Elizabeth St)
Best sunglasses selection: Gruen Optika (1225 Lexington Ave)
Women's small-size footwear: Giordano's (1118 First Ave)
Great Italian shoes for kids: Nutter Jr. (301 E 76th St)
Great discount office furniture: Frank Eastern Company (599 Broadway)
Best for light bulbs: Just Bulbs (938 Broadway)
Real bargains of all kinds: Unredeemed Pledge Sales (64 Third Ave)
Best for artifacts: Jacques Carcanagues (119 Spring St)
Bargains in men's and women's shoes: Valentina Lima (187 E 93rd St)
Electronic values: The Wiz (17 Union Square, 1922 Third Ave)
Great wine accessories: Wine Wares (307½ E 53rd St)
Statue of Liberty memorabilia: Statue of Liberty Gallery (525 Hudson St)
Best maps: Hammond Map Store (57 W 43rd St)
Discount pet supplies: Petland (132 Nassau St)

Made-to-order sweaters (men's and women's): Gwen Byrne (23 Eighth Ave)
Really ridiculous prices for men's clothing: Bijan (60 E 11th St)
Best prices on used and reviewers' books: Strand Bookstore (828 Broadway)
Best pipes: Connoisseur Pipe Shop (51 W 46th St)
Discount children's wear: Magic Treehouse (376 Amsterdam Ave)
Unusual silver: Jean's Silversmiths (16 W 45th St)
Classic clothing for women: Vermont Classics (284 Columbus Ave)
Just another store: Bonwit Teller (Trump Tower)
Best garden tools: Zona (484 Broome St)
Best shoji screens: Katsura Studio (389 Broome St)
Unusual hardware: D.F. Sanders & Co. (111 Bowery)
Sexy lingerie: Samantha Jones (1391 Second Ave)
Best briefcases: Carry On Luggage (150 W 26th St)
Imported gifts (and dust): J. Finkelstein (95 Delancey St)
Best discount china and glass: Lanac Sales (73 Canal St)
Thrift store finds: Everybody's Thrift Shop (261 Park Ave S)
High-fashion rainwear: Norman Lawrence (417 Fifth Ave)
Discount wine and liquor: Wine and Liquor Outlet (1114 First Ave)
Most unattractive new store: Charivari (18 W 57th St)
Best hosiery values for determined shoppers: Jacob Young and Son (329 Grand St)
Most fun shopping: Orchard Street on Sunday
Most insulting attitude: Gucci (689 Fifth Ave)
Best handmade boots and shoes for men: E. Vogel Boots and Shoes (19 Howard St)
Best tobacco store: J.R. Tobacco (11 E 45th St)
Best antique clothes: Antique Boutique (712-714 Broadway)
Best furniture department: Bloomingdale's (Third Ave at 59th St)
Best custom-made millinery: Don Marshall (465 Park Ave)
Great prices on gifts: Jompole (330 Seventh Ave)
Best mystery books: Foul Play (10 Eighth Ave)
Shoe prices only for millionaires: Susan Bennis/Warren Edwards (440 Park Ave)
Great kayaks: Hans Klepper (35 Union Square)
Discount sneakers for men and women: Shoe City (133 Nassau St)
Best antique bags: Sylvia Pines Uniquities (1102 Lexington Ave)
Best gift wrapping: Annie Wrapper (956 Lexington Ave)
Most honest diamond merchant: Rennie Ellen (15 W 47th St)
Best silver and wedding gift prices: Rogers and Rosenthal (105 Canal St)
Best floor-covering store: ABC Carpets (881 Broadway)
Best opera records: Music Masters (25 W 43rd St)

Great plant selection: Farm & Garden Nursery (2 Sixth Ave)
Great unusual gifts: The Kibbutz Store (856 Lexington Ave)
Best outdoor wear: EMS—The Outdoor Specialists (18 W 61st St)
Fur salespeople you can trust: G. Michael Hennessy Furs (333 Seventh Ave)
Best oak furniture: Stork (505 Broome St)
Best posters: Poster America (138 W 18th St)
Best values in silverware/hollowware: Eastern Silver (54 Canal St)
"No class" operation: Boyd Chemists (655 Madison Ave)
Best lingerie values: Goldman and Cohen (54 Orchard St)
Best block to purchase horseback-riding equipment: Miller's (123 E 24th St) and H. Kauffman and Sons (139 E 24th St)
Getting sadder by the month: Hammacher Schlemmer (145 E 57th St)
Best bicycles: Gene's Bike Shop (242 E 79th St)
Great auto boutique: Cars (118 Spring St)
Best bears: Teddy's (120 Thompson St)
Housewares at great prices: Davpol Enterprises (267 Lafayette St)
Best tie prices: Heritage Neckwear Co. (194 Allen St)
Great wine-making supplies: Milan Home Wine and Beers (57 Spring St)
Best herbs: Meadowsweet Herbal Apothecary (77 E Fourth St)
Great needlepoint: 2 Needles (1266 Madison Ave)
Best women's trendy fashions: Betsey Johnson (several locations)
Best perfume selection: Warwick Chemists (1348 Sixth Ave)
Best pine furniture: Better Times Antiques (500 Amsterdam Ave)
Best fashion stationery: Ffolio 72 (888 Madison Ave)
Great photo supplies: Ben Ness (114 University Pl)
Best science fiction: Forbidden Planet (821 Broadway)
Great discount accessories: Bernard Krieger & Son (316 Grand St)
Best jeans: Alaska Fashions (41 Orchard St)
Savviest jewellers: Fortunoff (681 Fifth Ave)
Best selection of lighting fixtures: New York Gas Lighting Company (145 Bowery)
Unreliable women's clothing shopping: S & W (165 W 26th St)
Best marine supplies: Goldberg's Marine (12 W 37th St)
Best women's sportswear prices: M. Friedlich (196 Orchard St)
Best handmade items: Handmaiden (104 W 73rd St)
Best candles: The Candle Shop (118 Christopher St)
Best back issues of magazines: A & S Books (274 W 43rd St)
Best working woman's clothing store: Streets (2030 Broadway, 941 Lexington Ave)
Best home-accessory store: Carole Stupell (check for new address)
You need (1) patience, (2) a road map, (3) an extra pen to sign all the slips—otherwise it's a great store for men and boys: Barney's (111 Seventh Ave)

Great for watches: M.A.G. Time (168 Fifth Ave)
Best picture frames: Ready Frames (14 W 45th St)
Best business books: Caddylak (62 E 55th St)
Best silk clothing at reasonable prices: Royal Silk (79 Fifth Ave)
Great antiques: French Country Store (35 E 10th St)
Best display of South Pacific art: South Seas Gallery and Travel (353 Bleecker St)
Best women's small-size footwear: Giordano (1118 First Ave)
Best Japanese books, records, art: New York Kinokuniya Bookstore (10 W 49th St)
Best locks: Lacka (214 W 48th St)
Best uniforms: Dornan (653 11th Ave)
Great roller-skating items: Precision Skates (475 Second Ave)
Best handmade toys: Dinosaur Hill (302 E Ninth St)
Best Oriental chests: Min-Yea (79 Madison Ave)
Best jewelry in SoHo: Richard Erker (132 Thompson St)
Best bet for tall gal clothes: Shelly's Tall Girl Shops (13 E 41st St)
Best ski boots: Mountain New York (211 E 60th St)
Great custom kitchens: Regba Diran N.Y. (105 Madison Ave)
Best lampshades: Just Shades (21 Spring St)
Women's ready-to-wear at good prices: Miriam Rigler (62 W 56 St) and Lia's (150 E 50th St)
Best discounts on designer shoes: Designer Shoes (150 W 26th St)
Great fishing tackle: Orvis (355 Madison Ave)
Best unisex sportswear: J. Taverniti (260 W Broadway)
Best selection of unusual clothing: The Gallery of Wearable Art (480 W Broadway)
Best antique watches selection: Aaron Faber (666 Fifth Ave)
Best minerals and fossils display: Crystal Resources (130¼ E 65th St)
Best medical supplies and equipment: Portnow Surgical Supplies (53 Delancey St)
Best movie-star photos: Movie Star News (134 W 18th St)
Complete soccer supplies: Soccer Sport Supply (1745 First Ave)
Best ceiling fans: Modern Supply (19 Murray St)
Best zippers: A. Fiebusch (109 Hester St)
Superb tapestries: Lovelia Enterprises (356 E 41st St)
Best orchid plants: Robert Lester (280 W Fourth St)
Best discount wallpaper: Pintchik (278 Third Ave)
Great soft luggage: The Bag House (58 E Eighth St)
Best belts: Marchant (389 Fifth Ave)
Best musical instruments: Sam Ash Music Store (160 W 48th St)
Great custom fur hats: Lenore Marshall (333 Seventh Ave)
Best discount on family clothing: National Ladies Specialty (470 Seventh Ave)
Best soaps: Soap Opera (51 Grove St)

Best aprons: Apron and Bag Supply Company (47 Second Ave)
Best military books: Soldier Shop (1222 Madison Ave)
"Ladies of the Evening": Sixth Avenue at 58th St
Best war games: Compleat Strategist (11 E 33rd St, 320 W 57th St)
Best fashion jewelry: Back in Black (123 Prince St)
Best afghan imports: Nasraty Afghan Imports (215 W 10th St)
Great Victorian antiques: Somethin' Else (182 Ninth Ave)
Need some New York memorabilia to take back home?: Welcome to N.Y.C. (26 Carmine St)
Best international theater posters: Triton Gallery (323 W 45th St)
Best jukeboxes: Back Pages Antiques (125 Greene St)
Best selection of Bibles in every language: International Bible Society (45 E 46th St)
Great discount T-shirts: Eisner Bros. (76 Orchard St)
Best black-colored merchandise: Black Market (307 E Ninth St)
Best custom furniture: Navedo Woodcraft (179 E 119th St)
Best record selection: Tower Records (692 Broadway, 1961 Broadway)
Great canvas goods: Matera Canvas (5 Lispenard St)
Best handmade sweaters: Nicole (19 Fulton St)
Great cinema items: Cinemabilia (10 W 13th St)
Best Judaica: Hecker Corp. (605 Fifth Ave)
Best stamps: Subway Stamp Shop (111 Nassau St)
Great gadgets: Brookstone Co. (18 Fulton St and Herald Center)
Best small-size ready-to-wear clothes: Minishop (38 W 56th St)
Best antique wristwatches: William Scolnik (1001 Second Ave)
Want a vending machine?: CMG Vending (600 10th Ave)
Best source for used Steuben glassware: Lillian Nassau (220 E 57th St)
Best imported fabrics: Far Eastern Fabrics (171 Madison Ave)
Great tennis racquets: Feron's (55 E 44th St)
Best sci-fi gifts: Star Magic (743 Broadway)
Best videotapes: New Video (124 MacDougal, 90 University Pl)
Great fragrances: Scentsitivity (870½ Lexington Ave)
Best discount coats for men: L.S. Men's Clothing (23 W 45th St)
Best West Side complete pharmacy: Windsor Pharmacy (1419 Sixth Ave)
Best topiary trees: Green Thumb Flowers (22 E 65th St)
Perfume copies: Essential Products Company (90 Water St)
Best for Western boots: Lord John Bootery (428 Third Ave)
Best for contemporary furniture: Elements Gallery (90 Hudson St)
Best gold and diamond jewelry: M. Boner and Son (114 Fifth Ave)
Great discount shoes: Alys Hut (85 Hester St)
Great discounts on electronics: Annex Outlet (43 Warren St)
Best brand-name men's suits at discount: L.S. Men's Store (23 W 45th St)
Best selection of women's small sizes: Piaffe (841 Madison Ave)

Great ladies' discount sportswear: Giselle (143 Orchard St)
Best art-deco furniture: Designer Furniture (100 Wooster St)
Best office supplies: Menash (2305 Broadway)
Best selection of music of all publishers: Music Store at Carl Fischer (62 Cooper Square)
Great security devices: REM Security (27 E 20th St)
Best drums: Drummer's World (133 W 45th St)
Best selection of Loden coats: House of Loden (155 W 72nd St)
Best Oriental fabrics: Oriental Dress Co. (38 Mott St)
Best embroidery: Selected Things (226 Front St)
Best Spanish antiques: Cobweb (114 W Houston St)
Best Amari china: Bardith (901 Madison Ave)
Best Chinese goods: Chinese American Trading Co. (91 Mulberry St)
Best discount perfumes: Round House Fashions (41 Orchard St)
Best evening clothes: Lucille Chayt (484 Broome St)
When you want butterflies: Mariposa (128 Thompson St)
Most accommodating proprietor: Ed Feeley, Caddylak Systems (62 E 55th St)
Best all-around proprietor personality: Lou Rosenberg, Art Bag Creations (735 Madison Ave)

Animals, Fish, and Accessories

BEASTY FEAST
605 Hudson St
140 Ninth Ave (bet 18th and 19th St)
237 Bleecker St
243-3261
Mon-Fri: noon-7; Sat: 10-7

If the name intrigues you, the stock will intrigue you even more. Beasty Feast carries pet food and supplies at good discount prices, and the salespeople are thoughtful, friendly, and cooperative.

BIDE-A-WEE HOME ASSOCIATION
410 E 38th St
532-4455, 532-5884
Mon-Sat: 9-7; Sun: 9-5 (adoption)
Mon-Sat: 9:30-12:30, 2-3:30 (clinic)

Bide-A-Wee is the only shelter I know of in Manhattan that does not kill animals it can't place for adoption. For this alone, it deserves special mention. Dogs, cats, puppies, and kittens are available for adoption at nominal fees. Bide-A-Wee also has a veterinary clinic open to the public.

PETLAND DISCOUNTS
132 Nassau St
964-1821

1443 St. Nicholas Ave
795-5783

304 E 86th St
472-1655

7 E 14th St
675-4102

Mon-Fri: 9-8; Sat: 10-6:30; Sun: 11-5

The folks at the New York Aquarium recommend this chain of stores for fish and accessories. They also carry birds and discount food and accessories for all pets, including dogs and cats.

Antiques

ANTIQUARIUM, FINE ANCIENT ARTS GALLERY
1061 Madison Ave (bet 80th and 81st St)
734-9776
Tues-Sat: 10-5 and by appointment; closed Sat and Aug in summer

Antiquarium is a magnificent gallery for those who appreciate museum-quality antiquities and can afford to own them. This gallery specializes in Middle Eastern and classical items, with a particular emphasis on ancient glass, marble and stone statuary and reliefs, bronzes, pottery, and coins. Even the modern pieces, such as the Louise Parrish and Winifred Wager jewelry items, are created from authentic antique artifacts, expressly for the gallery. These are exact models of ancient motifs shown in "wearable art," and even these incorporate bona fide antiques. Virtually every ancient civilization is represented. Antiquarium is definitely not the place to take your three-year-old or the Merrill Lynch bull. On the other hand, you'll probably need Merrill Lynch's help to send a piece home.

COBWEB
116 W Houston St (bet Thompson and Sullivan St)
505-1558
Daily: noon-7 p.m.; closed Christmas week

Cobweb (what a great name for an antique shop!) is the only store in the New York area which imports country furniture directly from Spain. What is more impressive is their stunning selection of merchandise. A partial listing includes armoires, brass beds, tables, chairs, benches, trunks, chests, wooden bowls, earthen olive-oil urns, water jugs, and customized Turkish kilim coverings, the house specialty. All of these pieces are distinctive, original, and authentic. In addition, Cobweb offers customized refinishing of its own furniture. And it's obvious the stock doesn't stay around long enough to house spiders, let alone cobwebs.

DEPRESSION MODERN

150 Sullivan St (at W Houston St)
982-5699
Wed-Sun: noon-7

Michael Smith, the owner, stocks nothing made prior to 1929. Much of the merchandise is even more current. Though he handles art deco, he specializes in a style he himself named: Depression Modern. He says his stuff was never meant to end up in a museum. Ten years ago, his shop wouldn't have found a market, but today, the pieces are valued for their sleek, functional lines. And Smith is a real showman. You'd have to be, if a number of your customers looked at your prized items and said, "Hey, I threw *that* out years ago." He exhibits many of his pieces in complete room settings. He once created a "Club SoHo" to display his tables, chairs, Stork Club ashtrays, and Russel Wright china. The setting looked as if it were awaiting the arrival of Zelda and Scott Fitzgerald.

HYDE PARK ANTIQUES

836 Broadway (bet 12th and 13th St)
477-0033
Mon-Fri: 9-5; Sat: 10-3; closed Sat in summer

No, ducky. Hyde Park is not the ancestral home of FDR up the Hudson River. Well, maybe it is, but that's not the Hyde Park that Bernard Duffy and his son-in-law, Dick Ross, are referring to. *Their* Hyde Park is in merry old England, with the emphasis on old (the 18th-century period, to be exact), and those coming to find pictures of Fala will be vastly disappointed by the floor upon floor of fine English furniture that is crammed into this showroom-warehouse. But they are the only people who could possibly be disappointed. Managing director Craig Williams boasts that his store (warehouse?) has the largest inventory in the world of genuine period English furniture. And who's to argue? There is William and Mary (which I believe is pre-18th century), Regency, and other antique periods to accompany the furniture; there are accents, mirrors, paintings, and porcelains. And if all this isn't enough to make a Roundhead's head turn, Hyde Park maintains a fine workroom for restoring the furniture. It's enough to brag about from a soapbox in Hyde Park!

JAMES ROBINSON AND JAMES II

15 E 57th St
752-6166
Mon-Sat: 10-5; closed Sat in summer

Collectors and specialists in antiques (particularly silver from the 17th and 18th centuries) are familiar with James Robinson, and many of them have dealt with the store, if only by mail. James Robinson is the best at what it does, but be warned that what it does *not* do is run an establishment where tourists can pick up knickknacks. Even the Victorian period, which is best known for its knickknack style of decorating, is represented with only its finest, most silvery, and expensive pieces. James Robinson specializes in antique silver, jewelry, porcelains, and glass. What is not available in the store but existent, personnel will comb the world for. What is no longer in existence will be periodically reproduced in handmade silver. ("In fact," says Edward Munves, Jr., "we offer the only fully handmade silver flatware made today.") All of it is handmade in England, faithfully reproducing two dozen or so authentic patterns. If a piece missing from a collection is not from one of those patterns, they will make it to order, assuming it cannot be located on the world market. Nonsilver antiques in which the store specializes include 17th- through 19th-century English bone china and porcelain (many in complete services), jewelry, and glass—and none of it is inexpensive. On the sixth floor, the James II Gallery specializes in less expensive Victoriana. The gallery is proportionately less expensive, but even James II is designed more for the collector than the browser. The items of interest are the authentic furniture, gadgets, and games, as well as antique brass, china, ironstone, and glass and silver jewelry.

LE VIEUX MONDE

94 Charles St (at Bleecker St)
675-4990
Mon-Sat: 1-6

Carl L. Tendler, an informative and helpful man, owns and runs this shop in the Greenwich Village antiques area. He specializes in antique French country furniture, but he also has English household accessories. All of his works are guaranteed to be authentic, and his fine eye is evident in the quality of the furniture he displays. He is obviously confident about his prices and quality. In a gesture, the likes of which I encountered nowhere else in the city, he noted that "there are several other shops specializing in French country furniture within a one-block area." He then proceeded to name the competition, which is certainly generous of Mr. Tendler. But then, his works and prices can stand the comparison.

LITTLE ANTIQUE SHOP
44 E 11th St (at Broadway)
673-5173
Mon-Fri: 10-5; Sat: 10-2; closed Sat in July and Aug

In a neighborhood that is borderline Village and often referred to as Strand territory, the Little Antique Shop stands out as a gem. This small store specializes in Oriental antiques, and it apparently has no peers anywhere. There are fine delicate antiques, and the prices are equally fine. There are small accent pieces as well as large screens. All of them are quality pieces, and you'll never believe you found them on East 11th Street.

MAYA SCHAPER
152 E 70th St
734-9427
Mon-Sat: 10:30-6; closed Sat and Sun in summer

Maya Schaper has been all over town. She started with a store on the East Side (I think), opened a branch on the West Side that sold "Cheese and Antiques," closed the East Side store, and then most recently closed down the West Side store and reopened yet another outpost of antiques back on the East Side. Got that? It doesn't really matter, because through it all, Maya Schaper has consistently offered the best in French and English country antiques of a vaguely defined era. But the vintage doesn't matter as much as the atmosphere. The cheese and cuisine wasn't an out-of-place touch, because Schaper really sells moods and entire environments based on her antiques. The store delights in giving interior-decorating aids, be it furnishing one piece or a complete room.

PIERRE DEUX ANTIQUES
369 Bleecker St (at Charles St)
243-7740
Mon-Sat: 10-6; closed Sat in July and Aug

One of three Pierre Deux shops in Manhattan, this antiques shop is the father of its equally successful heirs. The second shop shares this address but not the phone number. (Theirs is 675-4054.) All of the shops specialize in 18th- and 19th-century French country furnishings, the only difference being the material used in the furnishings. Pierre Deux Fabrics (870 Madison Ave) is *the* source for country farm cloth and cloth products. The shops guarantee every piece, and the owners' many years in the business make them the city's experts in the field. Aside from that, these folks are friendly.

PLACE FOR ANTIQUES
993 Second Ave (bet 52nd and 53rd St)
308-4066
Mon-Sat: 10:30-5:30; Sun: 2-5

The word for the Place for Antiques is eclectic. Owner Shelia Nilva established the store with her late husband, and it evolved into a mecca for all sorts of odd antiques. Most of it revolves around, but is not limited to, photography. There are stereo viewers, prints, and daguerreotypes. For years, the store was the only source in the city for reliable daguerreotype restoration. In recent years, Shelia has gotten away from that. The antique furniture highlights twig-and-horn styles, and she opened a side business making gift baskets ("A Tisket A Tasket"). The baskets reflect the same eclectic taste as the furnishings in the Place. (It looks like an Adirondack hunting lodge in the Roaring Twenties.) As yet another odd sideline, they also rent props and antiques to movie and production companies.

SIDESHOW
184 Ninth Ave (bet 21st and 22nd St)
675-2212
Tues-Sat: 11-6:30
Closed last week of July and first week of Aug

Sideshow's owner, Henry Kaplan is a former soap-opera director, but he's left the soaps, and at Sideshow he wants to talk shop, not soap. This is understandable: his tiny store is crowded with antique kitchen implements, the rustic kind of things that grandmother threw out as soon as she could afford the newfangled inventions. Today, these items are antiques, irreplaceable, and on their way to becoming priceless. You can buy them for decorating your home, or for the original use. Old baking pans are very popular, particularly iron and steel ones. Most items come to the shop as graduates from Kaplan's private collection. He seems to know each piece personally.

URBAN ARCHAEOLOGY
137 Spring St (at Greene St)
431-6969
Mon-Fri: 10-6; Sat, Sun: noon-6; closed Sat, Sun in summer

Suddenly, people are collecting *anything* and calling it antique (or at least nostalgia). Nineteenth-century wall-to-wall townhouses (the heritage of New Yorkers) have come to be considered architectural artifacts. This, in turn, is a fancy name for the kinds of things that used to come tumbling off buildings as the wrecker's ball struck. Gil Shapiro, Leonard Schechter, and Alan Myers formed Urban Archaeology to offer the best of the trims and architecture of New York from the 1880s to the 1920s. Schechter admits being a stealthy scavenger before he became so well known. The fact that the wrecking companies now prefer to deal with him legitimately means that Urban Archaeology gets excellent artifacts. While the business specializes in house artifacts and anything salvageable from buildings of the period, he displays entire "mood" settings as well; Urban even rents out props and maintains an upstate farm that can be used as a backdrop by photographers and for advertisements. The SoHo shop is a wonder. There are entire walls of barbershops, ice cream parlors, saloons, and general stores, which look as if they are awaiting your order. Scattered about are barber poles, wooden Indians, music machines, old street lamps, pedestals, Tiffany glass, marble-stained glass, mantles, shutters, and even accessories. Bear in mind that Urban Archaeology's period is really late Victorian and Edwardian, albeit in America.

WAVES
32 E 13th St (bet University Pl and Fifth Ave)
989-9284
Tues-Sat: noon-6

The past lives on at Waves, and Bruce and Charlotte Mager try to make it last forever with their collection of vintage record players, radios, receivers, and televisions. Though the Magers are under 30 years old, they have scorned the electronic age in favor of the age of radio; their shop is a virtual shrine to the 1930s and before. Here you'll find the earliest radios (still operative) and their artifacts. There are even radio promotion pieces, such as a radio-shaped cigarette lighter and recording discs (as in crank-handled phonographs, not video recorders). Gramophones and anything dealing with the radio age are available, and Waves is capable of repairing privately owned instruments. Waves also rents its phonographs, telephones, neon clocks, and photographica (sic) for media shoots. They also make appraisals, and will help with any questions on repair, sale, or rental.

Appliances, Electronics

The discount appliance center is the Lower East Side. But the discount policy has been creeping uptown along with the attitude that no true New Yorker *ever* pays list price for an appliance or electrical equipment.

AUDIO SPEAKER TECHTRONICS
250 W Broadway (bet Walker and White St)
226-7781
11 Sixth Ave
925-8149
Mon-Fri: 9-5:30; Sat: 10-4

This is a city of professional audio people with a range of knowledge that ranges from expert to genius. Audio Speaker Techtronics is the largest speaker repair house in the area and, in fact, in the entire East. The large showroom displays as much of their merchandise as they can cram into the space. There are loud speakers, speaker systems, mixers, headphones, microphones, signal processors and effects, dividing networks, power amplifiers and equipment cases. The specialties are pro sound, commercial and high-end hi-fi. Audio Speaker Techtronics also repairs everything it sells, though it wasn't dubbed the "largest repair house" because of repairs on their own models. (Let's hope not.)

BERNIE'S DISCOUNT CENTER
821 Sixth Ave (bet 28th and 29th St)
564-8582, 564-8758
Mon-Fri: 9-5:30; Sat: 11-3:30; closed in July and Aug

Bernie is nowhere to be seen, but the *discount* in the store's name is certainly apt. If you want to get first-class treatment, ask for George Vargas. Bernie's was the first appliance dealer in the country to discount the 1000 RCA Selectavision video recorder *before* the machine officially came out and at a time when it was the most popular item in town. Among the things that Bernie's stocks are electrical appliances, TVs, videogames, phone machines, radios, tape recorders, and air conditioners. The discount on these items is better at some of the other stores mentioned here, but Bernie's is more conveniently located. Bernie's also services what it sells.

BONDY EXPORT COMPANY
40 Canal St
925-7785
Sun-Thurs: 10-6; Fri: 10-3

Bondy is typical of the Lower East Side appliances places. It's also one of my favorites. It is newer, cleaner, and better stocked than many of the others, and the wait never seems to be interminable. Bondy is family-run by the Feigelsteins, all of whom are very friendly (I have never heard a cross word), and they really do try to help. When I wanted a set of Corelle, they asked how old the recipient was. I couldn't understand why they needed that information until they told me which pattern was most popular with people of that specific age group. The stock includes all electrical appliances—major and small, many of which are available in 220 volts—cameras, components, dishes, and tableware. Bondy's prices are consistently low, and it is one place where I do not bother to comparison shop.

DEMBITZER BROS.
5 Essex St (at Canal St)
254-1310
Mon-Thurs: 10-6; Fri: 10-2; Sun: 10-4

Dembitzer was one of the first discount appliance stores on the Lower East Side, and it was so successful it spawned many imitators. This is good for the consumer. With a host of imitators now nearby, Dembitzer is constantly alert to keep the business it has garnered so far. Dembitzer's motto is, "If it plugs in, we have it," but even that doesn't do justice to the stock. Left out of that description are pens, luggage, soda makers, cameras, film, china, ad infinitum. Dembitzer also breaks the Lower East Side rudeness code. Between them, the brothers speak 8 or 11 languages (it depends on whom you ask). While they clearly don't have time to traffic with people who are "just looking" or comparing prices, they can be charming to real customers in any of those languages.

GREATER NEW YORK TRADING

81 Canal St (bet Eldridge and Allen St)
226-2808, 226-2809, 226-8850
Mon-Thurs: 10-6; Fri: 10-3; Sun 9:30-6

Perhaps influenced by its proximity to the Jewelry Exchange on the Lower East Side, the Greater New York Trading Corporation dabbles in fine housewares while selling appliances. In addition to the toasters, cameras, and refrigerators that almost everyone else carries, Greater New York stocks all types of china, silverware (even discontinued silver patterns), jewelry, and gifts. All are sold at good discounts. Despite the location and the fact that it carries brands and products not readily available elsewhere, prices are said to be wholesale. Even more than the prices, I liked the personnel's boast, "Every one of our staff smiles and is helpful." It matters to them, and that certainly matters to me. In this messy store, one can unearth great buys on crystal, china, and flatware, with name brands unavailable elsewhere on the Lower East Side.

KAUFMAN ELECTRICAL APPLIANCES

365 Grand St
260-6625, 475-8313
Mon-Sat: 9:30-7

This appliance shop has its own mystique. People who buy here once usually forsake the comparison-shopping game and remain loyal. Locals patronize Chaim Kaufman's shop exclusively, and his big virtue is that he will tell you which brand and model number really is the best. His forte is remodeled kitchens. Kaufman's is next door to Kossar's Bialystoker Bakery. If the wait gets too long (and it can, because Chaim Kaufman is virtually a one-man business), stop in there for the best bagels, bialys, and old-fashioned onion boards in New York. You'll come back refreshed and ready to take advantage of Kaufman's prices.

LYRIC HIGH FIDELITY

1221 Lexington Ave (bet 82nd and 83rd St)
535-5710
Mon-Sat: 10-6

Lyric is the place for sound fanatics who know what they're doing. As Lyric's Michael Kays says, they're not for beginners, but anyone who has the knowledge and necessasry cash can indulge his wildest audio fantasies at Lyric. Cash is as important as knowing the merchandise; you can part with between $1,000 and $60,000 in a morning's worth of shopping here. Lyric has been in business for over 20 years, selling equipment to people who want—and get—the best. Kay sniffs at names like Sony, which the average person considers to be top-of-the-line. Lyric carries only the best lines of each component, and the names of its suppliers are unknown to all but the most discriminating audiophiles. If that's you, this is your store.

METRO SEWING MACHINES
148 E 28th St
725-4770, 686-1180
Mon-Fri: 10-6; Sat: 10-5

The area around Lexington Avenue in the twenties is industrial sewing-machine country. Beneath dirty, grimy windows, a passerby may notice a display of sewing-machine motors, belts, or parts laid out for easy access by those within the shop. Few, if any, of these shops are open to the public. This is a shame, particularly when a New Yorker has to phone a repairman for a house call to adjust a bobbin at a higher fee than a new machine would cost on 28th Street. People who have been selling and repairing industrial machines for years on end can do wondrous things with a family machine whose main problem is probably neglect. One of the few businesses that fall into all these categories is Metro Sewing Machines. This specialty store has been in business for more than 20 years, and most of their service has been with home machines. It has one of the largest inventories and displays in the United States, and, most important, the personnel dote on sales and repairs for individual customers. What's more, this is an authorized service and sales center for every brand of sewing machine I can think of.

THOR EXPORT SALES COMPANY
1225 Broadway (room 608)
679-0077
Mon-Fri: 9:30-5

Visitors from abroad most often view the New York market as a place to pick up quality appliances at favorable rates. For many though, their native lands operate on 220 volt/50 cycle electricity, so the American products are of no use in their homes. While some of the Lower East Side stores carry dual-voltage and 220 appliances, Thor is the only store in the area (and possibly the continent) that deals exclusively with those appliances. Thor's name, in fact, is probably better known among the United Nations staff, airline crews, and visitors than it is among natives of the city. That's because the company has been catering to those people for over 40 years, while very few natives have a need for that type of wiring. (In fact, I had never heard of them. Enzo Borges, Thor's president, bought this book at the South Street Seaport and informed me that he thought his company should be included. He was right.) In any event, years of experience have made Thor the expert in the field. They help relocating executives, stateside folks sending gifts abroad, and of course tourists. For the latter, there are dual-voltage appliances, which can be used both before and after the trip.

UNCLE STEVE
343 Canal St (at Church St)
226-4010
Mon-Sat: 9:30-6; Sun: noon-5

So you're convinced that no one with any regard for his wallet would buy appliances, dishes, televisions, or cameras at retail? Good. But what if the Lower East Side mob scene turns you off? Well, you can try "appliances by phone" brokers, but those who have reliable businessmen behind their phone voices are few and far between. Perhaps the only store in the business that is both price competitive on the phone *and* in the store in Uncle Steve. Uncle Steve will quote prices over the phone (which few other discount appliance stores will do), but you should visit him at least once. Your *real* Uncle Steve probably couldn't give you a better price if he were in the business. In addition to top-notch service, he has great contacts who supply the store with almost any electrical item, along with super service. In survey after survey of discount appliance dealers in the city, Uncle Steve is consistently on top of the list. He almost always manages to deliver the best prices. If you have but one stop to make before you buy an appliance, make it Uncle Steve's. And if you're apprehensive of the whole scene, simply call him. His quote will probably amaze you.

Art Supplies

CHARRETTE
5 W 45th St (bet Fifth and Sixth Ave)
921-1122
Mon-Sat: 8:30-7; Sun: noon-5

215 Lexington Ave
683-8822
Mon-Fri: 8:30-8:30; Sat: 10-7; Sun: noon-5

This branch of a Massachusetts company is for serious architects, engineers, and draftsmen. The stock includes more than 36,000 different items, which means that a practitioner in any of these fields would be hard-put *not* to find what he wanted. The professional could get lost in the art, drafting, engineering, and architectural supplies; the neophyte is lost as soon as he crosses the threshold. Charrette offers quality supplies, professional atmosphere, and good advice. The amateur would be better off scanning the catalog before wandering in, but the professional will be pleased to find that this store has everything. With 36,000 different items, it should!

EASTERN ARTISTS
352 Park Ave S (bet 25th and 26th St, 11th floor)
725-5555
Mon-Fri: 9-6; Sat: 11-5; closed Sat in summer

Eastern Artists supplies the professionals, but they are happy to serve the amateur as well. Ad agencies, poster companies, and artists buy their supplies here, as much for the personalized service tailored to an artist's temperament as for the 20 to 50 percent discount on all supplies. Store manager Cam Mailo claims that there are more than 20,000 different items in stock. This is probably a conservative estimate. Everything imaginable that is available for the artist seems to be in stock here, and all of it is of exacting standards to please the fussiest of artists. What's more, most of it is designed for professionals and is, therefore, of top quality and dispensed by salespeople who are artists themselves.

LEE'S ART SHOP
220 W 57th St (near Broadway)
247-0110
Mon-Fri: 9-7; Sat: 9:30-6

Ricky of Lee's Art Shop claims that his store is the city's most complete art supply store. Indeed, his shop is loaded with all the materials for both the professional and amateur artist. There is even a separate section for architectural and drafting supplies. The staff is among the city's friendliest and is extremely knowledgeable. Their help is needed to guide the uneducated through the wealth of transfer types, lamps, silkscreens, art brushes, and chart types. All are available here in various qualities. A related specialty of which Lee's proudly boasts is same-day framing. They will frame amateur or professional art for home or office within the same business day. I was also impressed by the range of auxiliary services Lee's offers—mail order, catalogs, and free delivery.

PEARL PAINT COMPANY
308 Canal St (near Broadway)
431-7932
Mon-Sat: 9-5:30; Sun: 11-4:45; closed Sun in summer

With five floors and 25 clerks on duty at all times, this shop is to SoHo what Eastern Artists is to Madison Avenue. Discounts range from 20 to 50 percent on stock that supplies everything to the artist.

The atmosphere is somewhat bizarre, with all kinds of professional painters shopping the jam-packed floors for their respective specialties, but great care is taken to maintain the quality of everything sold. Surprisingly, the first floor is devoted to *house* painting—a field I had never associated with art supply houses. The other floors have separate sections devoted to such art specialties as drafting, silkscreening, etchings, carving, sculpting, batik, molding, casting, crafts, lithographs, pen art, and graphic arts. This company claims to be "one of the largest and most complete professional artist suppliers in the world."

SAM FLAX

15 Park Row
620-3030

25 E 28th St
620-3040

12 W 20th St
620-3038

747 Third Ave
620-3050

55 E 55th St
620-3060

Mon-Fri: 8:30-5:30; Sat: 10-5; closed Sat in Aug

Superlatives are as common as canvas in the art supply business, and Sam Flax is yet another who claims to be the biggest and the best in the field. Since no one is going to sit and count the paint brushes in stock, the question is moot, but Sam Flax does carry the full range of art and drafting supplies, drawing-studio furniture, and photographic products. There are also framing services at each store. The newest Sam Flax venture is the huge loftlike store at 12 West 20th Street, which is primarily devoted to furniture. The Flax brothers, Leonard and David, see this neighborhood as the up-and-coming creative district of the city, and they think artists, artisans, and professionals will be living as well as working in the neighborhood. So they stocked this store with basic functional furniture for that lifestyle, in a smashingly designed store that is the best model of what it is selling. The store is so large, though, that it can sport all that furniture and still stock all of the art supplies and paraphernalia of a traditional Flax store.

UTRECHT ART AND DRAFTING SUPPLIES

111 Fourth Ave (at 11th St)
777-5353
Mon-Sat: 9:30-6

We once mused about the name of this art supply outlet, and we received a letter from a reader who pointed out that Utrecht is a large city in Holland, with a long tradition of arts and crafts supply. Great, but we raised the question because this shop used to be called Utrecht *Linens*. In any case, little but the name has changed. Utrecht is a major manufacturer of paint and art and drafting supplies, with a large factory in Brooklyn. At this retail store, factory-fresh supplies are sold at factory discounts, and the Utrecht name stands behind every purchase. Quality is superb, as are the discounts.

Autographs

B. ALTMAN
Fifth Ave at 34th St
679-7800
Mon-Wed, Fri, Sat: 10-6; Thurs: 10-8

B. Altman, one of New York's better large department stores, harbors an eccentric delight in its autograph department. It is possibly the only department store in New York with such a department. Periodically, Altman's will take out an advertisement in *The New York Times*, announcing some unusual or special autographs. Altman's reputation is impeccable, and there is not the slightest chance that any autograph is not what it is represented to be. Autographs may be purchased by mail or phone, but it would be a shame to miss a visit to the store.

CHARLES HAMILTON AUTOGRAPHS
200 W 57th (suite 702)
245-7313
By appointment only

Charles Hamilton, the oldest autograph shop in the city, has marketed some unique autographs over the years. Much of the stock here is purchased from autograph collectors who instinctively turn to Charles Hamilton when they have something to sell. Charles Hamilton will offer expert appraisals, certifications, and advice at all times. The staff is totally objective in dealing with collectors, prospective sellers, and consignors. Charles Hamilton also markets documents, manuscripts, and signed rare books, and buys the same from current owners.

MRS. HENRY GERSHWIN MAZLEN & SONS —MEMORABILIA AMERICANA
1211 Ave I, Brooklyn
(718) 377-2759
Weekday evenings by appointment

Mrs. Mazlen has a large, unusual collection of autographs. Many of her pieces are attractively framed with interesting pictures. Since she is not located in Manhattan, give her a phone call and she will bring items of your choice to your location. You won't be sorry.

JAMES LOWE, AUTOGRAPHS
30 E 66th St (bet Madison and Park Ave, suite 907)
759-0775
Mon-Fri: 9-5

James Lowe is one of the most established autograph houses in the country. Catalogs, published several times a year, make a visit to the newly relocated gallery unnecessary, but in-person inspections are fascinating and invariably whet the appetite of most autograph collectors. There is no one specialty; the gallery seems to show whatever superior item is in stock, though there is a particular interest in historic, literary, and musical autographs, manuscripts, documents, and 19th-century photographs. The offerings range from autographed pictures of Buffalo Bill to three bars of an operatic score of Puccini's. Of course, there's much more in between. It all depends on what the buyer finds intriguing, and perhaps that explains why James Lowe prefers in-person visits.

Baskets

BE SEATED
66 Greenwich Ave (bet 11th St and Seventh Ave)
924-8444
Mon-Fri: 11-7; Sat: 11-6

In the beginning, Be Seated sold all kinds of chairs out of its tiny store in the Village. As time went by, the small store remained, but the chairs gave way to baskets of all shapes and sizes. Today, the store size is *still* unchanged, but now the baskets have been joined by rag and Turkish rugs, while the chairs have been crowded out. This explains why a store named Be Seated is a number-one spot for baskets. And there are baskets aplenty. They range from ancient antiques to modern palm-tree containers. All are elegant, and nothing would please Be Seated more than to have every household in the city own a half-dozen different baskets. To achieve that objective, the store specializes in unique baskets for unique uses. (When you have overloaded your space, you can't afford to fill it with trivia.) They recommend using baskets as decoration, containers (in kids' rooms, believe it or not), and for just about anything else you can imagine.

Bathroom Accessories

BATHS INTERNATIONAL
89 Fifth Ave (bet 16th and 17th St)
242-7158
Mon-Fri: 10-5:30

Now the transplanted Californian has lost his last excuse for not relocating to New York: his hot tub can be installed in the city! And that's not all. Baths International offers custom-designed whirlpools, spas, saunas, and exercise equipment, and space is no object. One of their brochures depicts a man and a woman emersed in a whirlpool bath aboard a personal jet plane. These catalogs are incredible. Just looking at them makes the studio apartment bathtub look like . . . well, a bathtub. Now you know who to contact for the best in bath furnishings.

ELEGANT JOHN
812 Lexington Ave (bet 62nd and 63rd St)
935-5800
Mon-Wed, Fri, Sat: 10-6; Thurs: 10-7

After getting over the initial awkwardness of entering a store that displays self-proclaimed "john seats" on its walls, you'll be amazed at the array of wallpaper, custom-made shower curtains, coordinated accessories, soap dishes, and, of course, seats, all sold with the aim of creating a bathroom that is every bit as comfortable, striking, and spacious as the rest of the house. Don't miss the Elegant John's attractive, unusually decorated rolls of toilet tissue. A friend even had me bring home some that comes in the shade of orchid!

SHERLE WAGNER INTERNATIONAL
60 E 57th St (at Park Ave)
758-3300
Mon-Fri: 9-5

If you thought the Elegant John was the definitive word on bathroom accessories, you ain't seen nothin' yet. Sherle Wagner takes a topic that even the Elegant John skirted, and places it in the most elegant location in the city, where it rubs elbows with silversmiths, art galleries, and exclusive antiques shops. However, the luxurious bathroom fixtures are almost works of art and are deserving of their 57th Street location. Fixtures come in every possible material, except ordinary chrome, and some are so striking that they make a glass display case seem like their natural setting. Prices are high, as might be expected. One warning! The displays are in the basement, and the world's slowest (almost) elevator gives you a good case of claustrophobia. Considering the prices they charge, you'd think they could afford to fix it after all these years.

Books

American Indian

BOB FEIN BOOKS
150 Fifth Ave (at 20th St, room 623)
807-0489
Mon-Sat: 11-5; closed Sat in summer

Bob Fein claims that his shop is the only one that's devoted to the literature of American Indians. Within this boundary, he also includes pre-Columbian art and Eskimos as subjects, and he has on hand more than 3,000 books and journals on those topics. Many of his items are out of print or one of a kind, and Fein is considered the primary source for such material. There is also a good percentage of what Fein terms "scholarly material," along with Smithsonian publications and reports. Most of the stock is unique and rare, and if any new literature is published about Fein's specialities, there's a very good chance that he'll have it first.

Architecture

URBAN CENTER BOOKS
457 Madison Ave (at 51st St)
935-3595
Mon-Sat: 10-6

Urban Center Books, the retail arm of the Municipal Art Society, practices what it preaches. The society was founded in 1892 to preserve the best of New York's historical architectural facades. That the society should be located in the north wing of the Villard Houses—historic homes that make up the base of the Helmsley Palace Hotel—is only fitting. And since most of the rooms in those buildings have been refurbished to resemble drawing rooms and libraries, it is equally appropriate that the society decided to retail publications on its interests in a suite that is a real library. If nothing else, a visit to Urban Center Books gives a visitor a chance to do some further exploration of the public rooms of the houses. Although only the physical amenities are left (wide doorways, parquet floors, painted ceilings), it is still a stunning look back into times gone by. The store itself naturally specializes in city architecture, history, and the city's physical plan. Publications on the topics of urban planning, design, and historic preservation are also prominent.

Art

E. WEYHE
794 Lexington Ave (at 62nd St)
838-5466
Mon-Fri: 9:30-5:15; Sat: 9:30-5

This bookstore dedicated to the subject of art has evolved from a small shop to a specialty store with an upstairs art gallery. Actually, it was only natural since Mr. Weyhe filled the small area with artists and art books (as well as their art) almost from its start in 1923. Over the years, Weyhe gave encouragement to scores of artists, and they reciprocated by giving him some of their paintings, tiles (note Rockwell Kent's offering on the brownstone), and sketches. Eventually, Weyhe was compelled to open the gallery to display the works of his patrons (and those he was patron to) and to prove that art literature is to be lived. Today, under the aegis of Weyhe's daughter and son-in-law, the store and the gallery continue the work Weyhe started. The bookstore carries literally everything related to art, architecture, or photography. A good part of the business also involves the purchase and resale of private art-book collections.

OCEANIC PRIMITIVE ARTS

88 E 10th St (near Third Ave, second floor)
982-8060
Fri, Sat: by appointment only

This is a magnificent bookstore and primitive-art gallery. Those who can afford it puruse, purchase, and take home primitive art from the gallery. Most customers, however, come to Oceanic to view the art and buy the various books dealing with the subjects that are on display. There are all types—current, out of print, and one of a kind. Some touch upon the anthropological aspects of the art as well. Once viewed, there's an innate urge to learn about the people who created this art. Armchair travelers will find this juxtaposition of art and anthropology particularly appealing. But Oceanic has universal appeal. Everybody should be able to find something of interest.

PRINTED MATTER

7 Lispenard St (one block south of Canal St, at W Broadway)
925-0325
Tues-Sat: 10-6

Lispenard Street is not exactly Broadway in terms of recognition. (Try getting directions from a New York native!) But find your way down here if you have any interest in contemporary art, and you'll find an artistic haven. Printed Matter is almost a misnomer since the store is the only one in the world devoted exclusively to artists' books. That's not books belonging to artists, or even art books, but rather a trade term for a portfolio of artworks in book form. The result is inexpensive, accessible art, which can span an entire artist's life, or a particular period or even one theme. The idea is carried further by Printed Matter's selection of periodicals and audioworks in a similar vein. Nearly all of the featured artists are contemporary, so just browsing through the store would bring you up-to-date on what is going on right now in the art world.

WITTENBORN ART BOOKS
1018 Madison Ave (bet 78th and 79th St)
288-1558
Mon-Sat: 10-5; closed Sat in summer

Possibly the ultimate art bookstore in the city, Wittenborn specializes in the arts, architecture, prints, archaeology, and fashion, and whenever fine-quality books on these topics are published, Wittenborn adds them to the stock. The staff makes a point of having it all—and having it all neatly catalogued as well. Not limited to only contemporary tomes, Wittenborn carries out-of-print, rare, and antiquarian volumes and foreign printings. If the topic and pictures meet Wittenborn's standards, it will carry the book, no matter what language it has been published in. Artfully done!

Business

CADDYLAK SYSTEMS BOOK CENTER
62 E 55th St (bet Park and Madison Ave)
935-9431
Mon-Fri: 10-6

Keep your eye on Ed Feeley. Not only is he personable and charming, he has one of the best noses for books in the business. He started the Complete Traveller and won our accolade for most accommodating proprietor in our last edition. Now he has opened Caddylak Systems Book Center, the first one-stop source for books, literature, and printed paraphernalia on business topics. Caddylak Systems is a Long Island firm that produces management aids, schedules, and boards for industry. This store was opened to showcase their work and offer business literature to people on their way up. Caddylak could have found no one better than Feeley as the epitome of the up-and-coming business success. He runs the business with an eye toward providing the unusual, specialized, and hard-to-find, and has managed to turn the book center into the best stop for business books. Say hello to Feeley. He won this edition's award again.

Children's

EEYORE'S BOOKS FOR CHILDREN
2252 Broadway (at 81st St)
362-0634
Mon-Sat: 10-6; Sun: 10:30-5
1066 Madison Ave (at 81st St)
988-3404
Mon-Sat: 10-6; Sun: noon-5

Joel Fram, Eeyore's proprietor, boasts that his is the only all-children's bookstore in Manhattan, and he runs it as if it were a child's haven. There are books for children of every age and interest, and there is even a corner where kids can sit or browse. The majority of the books are within the price range of a good allowance, and if it's an adult who is doing the purchasing, the unobtrusive staff offers guidance and suggestions. Eeyore's will order, at no additional charge, any book not in their extensive stock. The shop's highlight is its Sunday story sessions. Conducted by professional storytellers who pass out free refreshments and balloons along with their tales, these sessions are attended by standing-room-only crowds. Currently, the story sessions are held for kids aged 3 to 6 at 11 a.m. on the West Side and 12:30 on the East Side.

Comic

SUPERSNIPE COMIC BOOK EUPHORIUM

P.O. Box 1102, Gracie Station, 10028
879-9628
By appointment only

The ultimate comic book emporium, Supersnipe now deals only by phone and mail order. It is well worth your time, however, as their stock is unequaled.

Food

KITCHEN ARTS & LETTERS

1435 Lexington Ave (at 94th St)
876-5550
Mon: 1-6; Tues, Wed, Fri: 10-6:30; Thurs: 10-8;
Sat: 11-6; closed Sat and Aug in summer

Cookbooks traditionally top the best-seller lists in bookstores, and with the renewed interest in health, fitness, and natural foods, that rule of thumb is more operative than ever. So it should come as no surprise that Nachum Waxman's Kitchen Arts & Letters should be an immediate success as a store specializing in books, literature, photography, and original art about food and its preparation. Waxman claims that his store is the only one like it in the city and one of less than 10 in the country. Waxman is a former editor at Harper & Row and Crown publishers, who supervised several cookbook projects. Bitten with the urge to start a specialty bookshop, he discovered almost immediately that there was a huge demand for out-of-print and original cookbooks. So while the tiny shop stocks almost 3,000 titles as well as a gallery of photography and original art, much of the business is in finding out-of-print and "want listed" books. Waxman has become quite expert in the field, and by now he knows almost instantly what is in stock, what is available, and what can be found. Special topic mailings take the place of periodic catalogs, and Kitchen Arts & Letters seems to delight in the odd, esoteric, and unique in culinary literature.

Foreign

AFRO-AMERICAN BOOK CENTER
536 W 145th St (at Broadway)
234-3369
Mon, Wed, Fri, Sat: noon-7; Tues, Thurs: 3-7

Although the emphasis in this Harlem bookstore is on black Americans and their interests, it is an excellent source for books and materials about Africa. If the book in any way relates to black America, the chance is excellent that Afro-American carries it. Earl Hadley, the owner, is especially proud of the shop's children's books.

CHINA BOOKS AND PERIODICALS
125 Fifth Ave (bet 19th and 20th St)
677-2650
Mon-Fri: 10-6; Sat: 11-7; Sun: 12-5

This Oriental bookshop specializes in books and publications from the People's Republic of China. It's an excellent place for source material for a term paper or household decorating. There are handcrafted cards, bookmarks, papercuts, silk paintings, and posters—all imported. And oh, yes, the books—a full selection of English-language books cover all facets of China. The store specializes in "progressive literature from alternative book publishers and third world literature." I think this means their political viewpoint is not Republican.

KESHCARRIGAN BOOKSHOP
90 W Broadway (at Chambers St)
962-4237
Mon-Fri: 11-5; Sat: 12-5

Angela Carter runs this charming Irish bookstore, which serves cups of coffee and tea along with Irish literature. Carter claims that her store has the largest selection of books on Ireland in the country, and specializes in out-of-print and hard-to-find books on Irish topics. Any book not in stock can be ordered, and if the book is really difficult to find, Keshcarrigan will run a free search service for it. Even the simplest requests are delivered with a bit of Irish charm.

LIBRAIRIE DE FRANCE
and
LIBRERIA HISPANICA

610 Fifth Ave (bet 49th and 50th St)
581-8810
Mon-Fri: 9:30-6:15; Sat: 10-6:15

115 Fifth Ave (at 19th St)
673-7400
Mon-Fri: 9:30-6; Sat: 10-6

A short stroll through the Rockefeller Center promenade can bring you alongside the Librairie de France and Libreria Hispanica. Inside, you will find an interesting collection of French and Spanish newspapers, magazines, tourist guides, and light reading. But the real glory is downstairs, where more than one million French and Spanish books and records are in stock. If this isn't overwhelming enough, *all* of them are neatly catalogued and easily found. There isn't a topic on which at least several books in French or Spanish are not available, including a collection of books in Spanish about French literature and vice versa. A partial list of the available categories includes textbooks, dictionaries and encyclopedias, children's books and records, bilingual and bicultural educational recordings and tapes, games, posters, audiovisual aids, newspapers, magazines, and Haitian and African literature in French.

NEW YORK KINOKUNIYA BOOKSTORE

10 W 49th St (near Fifth Ave)
765-1461
Daily: 10-7

Kinokuniya is Japan's largest and most esteemed bookstore chain, and this is its first branch in New York. Located in Rockefeller Plaza, the store has two floors featuring books about Japan. The atmosphere is the closest thing New York has to Tokyo. The first floor boasts of 20,000 English-language books that leave no part of Japanese culture neglected. Art, cooking, travel, language, literature, history, business, economics, management techniques, martial arts—it's all here. The rest of the floor is rounded out with books on the same subjects in Japanese, and there are paperbacks on the second floor. Kinokuniya definitely has the largest collection of Japanese books in the city and possibly outside of Japan.

PARAGON BOOK GALLERY

2130 Broadway (at 74th St, mezzanine of Hotel Beacon)
496-2378
Mon-Sat: 10-5:45; closed Sat in July and Aug

Paragon has a full range of Oriental books and, in fact, is more of an Asian library and museum than a bookstore. Housed in a series of offices, each room is devoted to a different country, and all are presided over by Paragon's owner, who is always around to help. Most of the quarter of a million titles are catalogued and inventoried, and they include almost everything remotely connected with the Asian continent. A separate business here is reprinting out-of-date or translated Oriental books. The originals of those so transcribed can be found on Paragon's shelves. Besides translations of *Reader's Digest* and the like, there is a fine selection of rare and very old books.

RIVENDELL BOOKSHOP
169 St. Marks Pl (bet First and Avenue A)
533-2501
Mon-Sat: noon-7:30

Rivendell, which takes its name from the mythical town in J.R.P. Tolkien's *Lord of the Rings,* is rather magical itself. It survived a 500 percent rent hike at its old location and emerged bigger and better than before. Credit goes to Rivendell's new landlord, Ronald Shapiro, who owns a bookbinding firm; he thought the shop deserved a chance. Eileen Gordon, who started Rivendell as a shop focusing on books about Ireland and her native Scotland but ended up specializing in folklore, myths, and legends of the Middle Ages, refuses to speculate on the connection between Rivendell's name and her fortuitous second chance. Rivendell, you might remember, survived by becoming a source of light. Ahem.

RIZZOLI
31 W 57th St (at Fifth Ave)
223-0100
Mon-Fri: 9:30 a.m.-10 p.m.; Sat: 9:30 a.m.-7:30 p.m.

Rizzoli has been a fixture on the fine-books scene in the city for years. In 1984, the parent company bought Scribner's and took over the operation of the Scribner bookstore on Fifth Avenue. Rizzoli moved its own headquarters into the former Scribner building and its own bookstore to a newly renovated store on 57th Street. Rizzoli's has managed to retain the elegant atmosphere that made a patron feel he was browsing in a European library rather than shopping in midtown Manhattan. That was achieved in part by transferring the hand-carved marble doorway, some chandeliers, and the wood paneling. That should give you an idea of Rizzoli's ambiance. How many bookstores can boast of marble door sills, chandeliers, and cherrywood paneling? As for the books, titles lean heavily toward art, literature, photography, music, dance (particularly ballet), and foreign language. The store sells culture, albeit at full retail, but could you expect less from a place with those furnishings?

UNIVERSITY PLACE BOOK SHOP
821 Broadway (ninth floor)
254-5998
Mon-Fri: 10-5

In this out-of-the-way, dust-covered loft, Walter Goldwater may have collected the largest number of books on Africa and the West Indies in the world. After climbing up to its ninth-floor location, it is disconcerting to be greeted by piles and piles of books that seem to be arranged by chance, but there are some great finds here. The sales help are also friendly and very knowledgeable. The selection includes literature in more than 35 African dialects. Compensating for the fact that many African dialects have never been written down, University stocks 200 to 300 books about them as well; almost any subject or group is covered. In addition, University carries many old, rare, and out-of-print books on Africa and the West Indies. The newer books are those involved with current black America. Goldwater has been the proprietor for 45 years, and William French has been the manager for 20 years. They seem to know every book in the store—an amazing feat. The books they personally value the most are the early printed books (15th to 17th century) and the rare and out-of-print books on Africa, the West Indies, and Afro-Americans.

General

BARNES AND NOBLE

105 Fifth Ave	120 E 86th St
128 Fifth Ave	56 W Eighth St
600 Fifth Ave	1521 Broadway
175 W 57th St	750 Third Ave
1 Penn Plaza	2105 Broadway
999 Third Ave	38 Park Row

807-0099
Hours vary from store to store

Barnes and Noble is a mecca for college students in the metropolitan area, and many of the universities in the area have branches of Barnes and Noble on campus. Generations of New York students went through the college ritual of buying books from Barnes and Noble at the semester's beginning and selling them back after finals. A few years ago, this changed when Barnes and Noble was bought by a partnership whose members weren't of reading age when Barnes and Noble sold its first textbooks. The textbook division continues, but all types of other books are stocked as well, and all are discounted. Its particular specialty is one of the best discounts in town on any book on *The New York Times* best-seller list. As soon as a title makes the list, Barnes and Noble drastically discounts it and advertises that discount in the *Times*. There is an excellent assortment of all types of books, since Barnes and Noble has sources not available to smaller stores.

B. DALTON BOOKSELLER

666 Fifth Ave
247-1740
Mon-Fri: 8:30-8; Sat: 11-7:30; Sun: 12:30-6:30

109 E 42nd St
490-7501
Mon-Fri: 8 a.m.-9 p.m.; Sat: 9:30-6:30; Sun: noon-5

396 Sixth Ave
674-8780
Mon-Sat: 10-11:45; Sun: 12-7:45

170 Broadway
349-3560
Mon-Fri: 8-6:30

The B. Dalton shop on Fifth Avenue is one of the largest bookstores in the city, which befits the flagship for what is one of the largest and best bookselling operations in the nation. Books aren't just sold here—they are theatrically produced. Dalton has access to huge lots of remainders and reprints (due to its nationwide buying power). There are sections for children, technical books, special interest, and the arts. Dalton doesn't excel in any one particular area, but it should get an "A" for presentation. Their window displays are always must-sees for the latest in the publishing world.

BOOKWORM

368 Third Ave (bet 26th and 27th St)
696-5785
Mon-Sat: 10 a.m.-11 p.m.; Sun: 12-8

There's nothing wormy or moldy about this bookstore, and its late evening hours make this an optimal place for browsing. The piped-in music, which comes from classical cassette tapes (also for sale), only adds to the atmosphere, as do the homelike decorating touches. Bookworm emphasizes the small and homey and provides little extras in service. The store is recommended for its science-fiction selection; it's impressive. The store also offers hard-to-find European fashion and design magazines as well as foreign periodicals. And all of that is in addition to the usual bookstore fare—popular fiction and nonfiction—and a uniquely Bookworm specialty of stocking out-of-print books. This may be the best worm in the Big Apple.

DAUBER AND PINE
66 Fifth Ave (bet 12th and 13th St)
675-6340, 675-6341
Mon-Sat: 9-6

Dauber and Pine was founded by the father of the present owner, Murray Dauber, and the late Nathan Pine, who ran the store for nearly 60 years. In that time, the store earned a reputation as the definitive bookseller in New York. Always small (and none too clean), Dauber and Pine benefits from its size. There isn't a book and, according to *The New York Times,* hardly an American author who isn't personally known to the staff. When Pine retired in 1982, the manager of the Gotham Book Mart threw a party for him which was attended by the Gotham's Frances Steloff (herself 94 at the time), as well as people from as far away as Syria, who were faithful Dauber and Pine customers. And why would Gotham hold a party for what is probably its only competition? (No, *not* because Pine retired! The store is still in business.) Perhaps because between the two stores and their founders, there is a mutual respect and 130 years in the business. For book buyers, that translates into two great sources for all kinds of American literature. These proprietors knew the authors personally, and there is no better source for literature on or about them. Dauber and Pine, in particular, specializes in old, rare, and antiquarian books with an emphasis on American literature.

DOUBLEDAY BOOK SHOPS
724 Fifth Ave (at 57th St)
397-0550
Mon-Sat: 9:30-midnight; Sun: noon-5
673 Fifth Ave (at 53rd St)
953-4805
Mon-Sat: 9 a.m.-11 p.m.; Sun: 12:30-6:30
777 Third Ave (at 49th St)
953-4707
Mon-Fri: 9-6:30; Sat: noon-5
Citicorp Center (Third Ave at 53rd St)
953-4714
Mon-Fri: 9-9; Sat: 10-6; Sun: 12-6

Doubleday, the granddaddy of the Fifth Avenue bookstores, has it all. Between the four stores, there probably isn't a topic or title in the world that they don't stock (they are particularly proud of their back list), and the bigger stores probably stock the complete list by themselves. The two Fifth Avenue stores are the prototype of what a bookstore should be—particularly a bookstore in the city. The first floor of the 57th Street store is known for its selection of current and best-selling books. If a title is newly released, Doubleday's main section has it, often before the publication date. Other floors in the 57th Street store concentrate on art books, cookbooks, political issues, and back-listed publications, and that is only a partial list. But the quintessential bookstore relies heavily on its personnel, and it is in this area that this store really excels. It still gives service with a capital *S.* Manager Paul Kozlowski and his staff are true professionals. All stores reflect their neighborhoods. The other Fifth Avenue store, while smaller, carries a similarly extensive title list, with a selection on New York that must be the envy of the Visitors and Convention Bureau. The Third Avenue store is less for tourists than for homebodies, while the Citicorp branch blends perfectly with its locale. Philosophical works are basically nonexistent there, but gift books, coffee-table art books, and light fiction are runaway favorites. All Doubleday stores have a large selection of light reading: fiction, mysteries, self-improvement books, and cookbooks.

McGRAW-HILL BOOKSTORE

1221 Sixth Ave (bet 48th and 49th St)
512-4100
Mon-Sat: 10-5:45

This huge shop, located downstairs in the McGraw-Hill building at Rockefeller Center, is limited in fiction and general titles, but for anything published by McGraw-Hill or with a business, technical, or scientific bent, it is excellent. Prices are at list, but the wide selection of books would make any engineer happy. A fine, well-run, professional store.

METROPOLITAN BOOKSTORE

38 E 23rd St (at Madison Ave)
254-8609
Mon-Fri: 7:45-6; Sat: 9-5; closed Sat in July and August

Rockefeller University and the Morgan Library buy their books here, and that's a pretty good indication that Metropolitan is a bookstore worth looking into. And it is. Hyman Goor has run Metropolitan from the same location (across the street from the Metropolitan Life Building) for more than 40 years. They offer a flat discount of 20 percent on all books (including current paperbacks). Metropolitan also stocks an excellent selection of art books (a subspecialty) and publishers' overstocks. The latter are sold at 60 to 70 percent off the original publication price. This is a shop for bibliophiles. Someone is always browsing, and the timeless stance of a book browser makes all the shoppers look distinguished. Then again, this could be because many of the customers are judges and business executives.

STRAND BOOKSTORE
828 Broadway (at 12th St)
473-1452
159 John St (South St Seaport)
809-0875
Mon-Sat: 9:30-6:30; Sun: 11-5

The Strand is the best-known bookstore among "those who know" in New York. It is also one of the least expensive—a bargain hunter's paradise. Outside the shop, there are several tables of very old, very dirty books, which sell from 10 cents apiece to upward of three for 50 cents. Since no store would display anything of value outside the shop in that area, that should give you an idea of what those books are worth. The dim interior of the shop is equally unmemorable (unless some of the dust happens to land on your clothes), with the exception of a few choice tables at the front that offer reviewers' copies of current best-selling books for half the retail price. (Reviewers' copies are books sent to reviewers gratis by publishers. No reviewer can keep, let alone read, all the books he receives, so a lot are sold to the Strand. Many critics enter into yearly arrangements with the store as to the number of books received per year that will be sold for a flat fee.) An entire separate kingdom downstairs is known as the Underground Strand. Here, too, things are not at all pretentious. It is very easy to miss the staircase, but it leads down to a bibliophile's heaven. The Underground has nearly every popular printed book in recent memory and, more often than not, has a half-dozen copies stacked on the shelves. Prices average around a dollar or two per book, and it is thus possible to supply a high-school English class with hard-cover copies of a popular novel for less than school paperbacks. Many books are reviewers' copies that did not sell upstairs, but there are some used ones and some celebrity books as well. A special upstairs room is devoted to valuable and scarce volumes. The glory here is that if the book was ever in print, it is likely that the Strand has it in abundance *and* at reasonable prices. The Strand also operates a kiosk at Fifth Avenue and 60th Street in the summer, from 11 a.m. to 7 p.m.

WALDEN BOOKS
57 Broadway (at Exchange Pl)
269-1139
Mon-Fri: 8-6

My opinion of Walden Books is somewhat biased. It was while I was browsing there that I overheard someone specifically ask for my own book. That was enough to endear the store (or at least the literary taste of its clientele) to me, but the sheer size of its selection and stock makes it all the more exceptional. (In addition, ex-manager Michael Campbell comes from my hometown, Garden Home Oregon.) Walden Books has the largest collection in three fields—New York City, finance, and business—that I've ever seen. From the street, the store looks like a regular storefront. But inside, clever architectural design (engineering is another well-endowed section) has turned the store into a trilevel emporium. Each floor is subdivided by curving walls and cylindrical display areas, creating the feeling of several small bookstores. And each subdivision contains as good a selection as in any specialty bookstore. The selection is so vast that the fiction browsers on the main level may never know the upper level has what may be the best selection of science, technical, financial, and reference books in the city. Walden Books rivals B. Dalton as the nation's largest bookstore chain. As a result, it has access to remainders, classics, and hard-to-find titles. While the bargain tables of these books (mostly on the lower level) are super spots, this is strictly a retail operation, for the most part. The store has a new CompuCenter, which offers several hundred software titles as well as hands-on computer demonstrations.

Military

MILITARY BOOKMAN
29 E 93rd St
348-1280
Tues-Sat: 10:30-5:30

The inventory here is limited specifically to books of a military nature. There are rare, one-of-a-kind antique volumes on the shelves, alongside the military strategy of Moshe Dayan. The truly rare ones are not quite so accessible, but they are all available for sale. The specialty is out-of-print and rare books on military, naval, and aviation history. (Who else would differentiate between the three?) At any given time, there are about 10,000 such titles in stock. Topics run the gamut from Attila the Hun to atomic warfare. The Military Bookman also accepts mail and phone inquiries, maintains a want list, and has some of the city's nicest proprietors.

SOLDIER SHOP
1222 Madison Ave (bet 88th and 89th St)
535-6788
Mon-Fri: 10-6; Sat: 10-5; Sat: 10-3 in July and Aug

The military is a deadly serious business here. This is *not* for the little boy who likes to play soldier, since many of the books are extremely rare and valuable. The general specialty, however, is military in all of its ramifications, and as a result, the Soldier Shop stocks current as well as rare military books concerning history, battles, theory, and biography. A catalog that lists 166 pages of military history books, antique soldiers, arms, and armor is also available.

Mystery

FOUL PLAY

10 Eighth Ave (at 12th St)
675-5115
Mon-Sat: noon-10 p.m.; Sun: noon-6

If the urge to curl up with a good mystery grabs you some Sunday afternoon, Foul Play is the only place to satisfy it "between here and Philadelphia," says manager Patricia Smith, who also manages Wendell's next door (both are owned by Wendell Huston). Indeed, Foul Play is the only bookstore devoted totally to mystery and suspense novels that's open on Sunday. And other than a remarkable black-and-red neon interior design and simply super salespeople, it is interchangeable with the other stores of its ilk. But neither of these are distinctions to be taken lightly. While I was there, two men came in and took considerable time draping body and fingers over as much of the stock as possible. After a seemingly endless time (during which it seemed that the sole aim was to see how much a storekeeper would put up with), one of the men walked up to Smith and asked to see her collection of books on morning glories. Afterward, she explained that I had just witnessed something common enough to have a name in the trade! It's called the "Nairobi Journal Syndrome." It seems the object is to ask for something so esoteric that the inquisitor gets his jollies from stumping the poor merchant and making him feel inferior. Others have killed for less, but Smith simply smiled. You'll like her *and* Foul Play.

MURDER INK.®

271 W 87th St
362-8905
Mon-Wed, Fri, Sat: 1-7; Thurs: 1-10

Murder Ink. was the first mystery bookstore in the city. When Dillys Winn founded Murder Ink., she started not so much a bookstore as a way of life. Today, Carol Brener runs the store along much the same lines as Winn did, although she has added feminist accents. The store still claims to stock every murder or mystery book in print and several hundred selections no longer in print. You'll find some rare books and other artifacts, but the emphasis is really on good, entertaining books.

MYSTERIOUS BOOK SHOP

129 W 56th St
765-0900
Mon-Sat: 11-7

Otto Penzler is a monthly columnist for *Ellery Queen* magazine, a Baker Street Irregular, a Sherlock Holmes fan *extraordinaire* (an elementary deduction!), and the Mysterious Bookshop's owner. As a result, the shop is run as a friendly business, and biweekly parties and spontaneous conversations among customers are the norm. On the ground floor (literally: the shop is a few steps below street level), Mysterious stocks new hard-cover and paperback books that deal with any genre of mystery. ("But *not* science fiction. Science fiction is not mystery," said the store's manager.) Upstairs, via a winding circular staircase, the store branches out to the width of two buildings, and is stocked floor to ceiling with out-of-print, used, and rare books. Amazingly, they seem to know exactly what is in stock, and if it is not on the shelves, they will order it. (Assume that a book not in stock *has* to be old or rare. This store has *everything* else.) There is as much conversation as business conducted here, and you can continue the conversation at the store's next autographing party or lecture.

New York

CITYBOOKS
61 Chambers St (near Broadway)
566-1442
Mon-Fri: 10-5
1 Centre St (Municipal Bldg, room 2213)
566-2616
Mon-Fri: 8:30-5

It's obvious that Citybooks is a government agency. Not so obvious or well known is that these two outlets have access to more than 120 different official publications, all of which are dedicated to the motto "We help New Yorkers cope." While there are such clinkers as *Rules and Regulations Governing the Manufacture, Storage, Transportation, Delivery and Processing of Liquified Natural Gas,* most of the books are worthy of a city where one of its departments authored the basis for the famous Weight Watchers' Diet and still offers it free of charge. (Send a self-addressed stamped envelope for "Eat to Lose Weight," New York City Department of Health, 125 Worth Street, New York, NY 10013.) There are great publications describing the city's historical districts, listings of dental services, maps of services for senior citizens, and a five-volume set (one for each borough) listing services for senior citizens. Should you want to contact any of the city's 15,000 employees, the Centrex directory provides that information, while the authoritative city source is the Green Book, an official directory that lists all courts and agencies (complete with phone numbers) and still manages to remain pocket-size. By the way, they don't accept cash—just checks. That's city government!

NEW YORK BOUND BOOKSHOP
43 W 54th St (bet Fifth and Sixth Ave, fourth floor)
245-8503
Tues-Fri: 10-5:30; Sat: 12-5

Reviewers, says columnist George Will, have to express their bias, so it must be noted that much of this book was written with an "Anderson Esometric Map of Midtown Manhattan" as inspiration. And that map was purchased at the New York Bound Bookshop. The shop is as inspiring as the map. In it, Barbara Cohen and Linda Voorsanger have assembled a printed ode to New York. The older and more esoteric a view of New York a publication has, the more these ladies covet it and try to acquire it for their shop. The specialty is old, rare, out-of-print, and unusual ephemera (their word) relating to New York, but the real love is the city in general. History buffs will have a field day with the eyewitness accounts of early life in the Big Apple (a relatively recent term), but anyone can enjoy the Anderson map or one of the myriad other items. The map is a steal at $4; believe me, it's awesome. Check out the photographs or browse through the current catalog, but definitely visit. Old New York is alive and well at New York Bound.

Occult

SAMUEL WEISER
132 E 24th St (near Lexington Ave)
777-6363
Mon-Wed, Fri: 9-6; Thurs: 10-7; Sat: 9:30-5

For stocking all kinds of publications on metaphysics, religion, and the occult, Samuel Weiser has a worldwide reputation that is well deserved. The shop is clean, modern, and so well equipped that many of its customers have no idea that its selection includes the eeriest titles found anywhere. The specialties cover almost any topic that is otherworldly: witchcraft, astrology, alchemy, magic, mysticism, E.S.P., flying saucers, Zen, and herb medicine. These are explored in books, magazines, periodicals, and foreign publications. (Some of the best in the field seem to be printed in foreign languages. Many are translated and sold here in both versions.) Finally, Samuel Weiser is one of the most obliging shops in town. They maintain a waiting list for out-of-print titles, and when the title arrives (by whatever mystical means), they will ship it out anywhere in the world. It arrives in plain mailing wrappers, but, no, it is not delivered by broomstick or magic carpet!

Paperback

CLASSIC BOOK SHOP

1212 Sixth Ave (at 48th St)
221-2252
Mon-Fri: 8-8; Sat: 10-6; Sun: noon-5

Classic Book Shop is one of the few shops in New York that deals exclusively in paperbacks. It pursues the unusual, rare, and esoteric in paperback, and its selection is among the best. Although paperback at one time meant inexpensive, this is no longer always true. Classic has books that cost upward of $10. The 25-cent Pocketbook is a thing of the past. Classic's forte is paperback "backstock," and it claims to have the best collection in the midtown area.

Photography

PHOTOGRAPHER'S PLACE

133 Mercer St (at Prince St)
431-9358
Mon-Sat: 11-6; Sun: noon-5; mail order address:
P.O. Box 274, Prince St Station, New York, NY 10012

There is no doubt that photography is an art form to Harvey Zucker and Gene Bourne, the gentlemen who run A Photographer's Place. The shop is a temple to photographers, both past and present. It is *not* however, a supply shop. Rather, it pays homage to great pictures of various eras and the people who took them. The owners claim to be "the only photographic book shop in the city and perhaps the country." Their interest isn't so much in competing as in being the best they can be. It's a credo they feel is shared by every photographer, and the shop excels at offering inspiration, history, advice, and the latest in technological advances. There is a super catalog.

Poetry

PHOENIX BOOK SHOP

22 Jones St (bet Bleecker St and Seventh Ave)
675-2795
Daily: noon-7:30; closed Sat from May to Sept

Robert A. Wilson, Phoenix Book Shop's owner, likes to boast that his is "the leading avant-garde poetry shop in the country," and whose to argue with a man who displays a stuffed owl at full wing span over the doorway because he hasn't come across a real phoenix "yet"? There are no ashes here, which may explain why

Wilson still hasn't come across his phoenix. Rather, Wilson specializes not merely in poetry but in "rare and unusual literary treasures unavailable anywhere else." So while there is an emphasis on contemporary poetry, it's obvious that the fun is in unearthing lost finds. The smaller the press the more likely it is that Phoenix stocks it. There is also a good sampling and background in magazines and journals on literature and poetry.

Rare

ANTIQUARIAN BOOKSELLERS' CENTER
50 Rockefeller Plaza
246-2564
Mon-Fri: 10-5:30; closed in Aug

This shop was founded as a cooperative venture by more than 50 rare-book dealers. In addition to being a showroom, the center acts as an information clearing house and referral center for rare-book dealers nationwide. Browsers are welcome, and there is much to see—many of the books double as interior décor, since they are offset in glass cases. Prices start at a few dollars, so the neophyte needn't feel intimidated. This is the definitive place to go for an education in the world of rare books.

GOTHAM BOOK MART
41 W 47th St
719-4448
Mon-Fri: 9:30-6:30; Sat: 9:30-6

If you want a personal glimpse of one of New York's living legends, try to make the Gotham Book Mart around 2:00 any weekday afternoon. It is best to pretend you're browsing, but if you arrive much before 2:00, you won't have to pretend, since you will have become so absorbed in the fascinating collection of books that you may have forgotten that you really came to see Frances Steloff. At 97 or so, Steloff still lives atop the bookstore that she owned and ran for over 50 years. During that time, she was often the first and only supporter of such literary lights as Henry Miller, James Joyce, e.e. cummings, Gertrude Stein, W. H. Auden, Tennessee Williams, and Dylan Thomas, to name just a few. Steloff could never understand how a book could be banned, and particularly when the author was known to her, she did everything possible to publicize his works. To that end, she once smuggled 25 first editions of Miller's *Tropic of Cancer* into the country from Paris via Mexico. From such humble origins grew the Gotham's reputation as a rare-book center—rare not in terms of age so much as availability and early encouragement given to the author. When no one had Ezra Pound in stock, Steloff featured him in her advertisements. This small store also features books on the arts. They come in all sizes, ages, and values, and more than 1,000 different poets are represented. Because Steloff's first Gotham was located near the theater district, there's a heavy emphasis on drama and theater materials. As a shrine to the First Amendment, as a source for dramatic arts, and simply as a habit, the Gotham still packs in readers much as it did 50 years ago. Browsers are welcome, and if Steloff comes downstairs, she'll be glad to visit with you.

J. N. BARTFIELD ART GALLERIES
45 W 57th St (second floor)
753-1830
Mon-Fri: 10-5

Bartfield is a specialist in old and rare books, with an emphasis on old maps and Western prints. Much of its material is culled from estates and complete private libraries that have been sold. There are also paintings, bronzes, watercolors from the 19th century, and clutter and clutter and clutter.

PAGEANT PRINT AND BOOK SHOP
109 E Ninth St (bet Third and Fourth Ave)
674-5296
Mon-Sat: 10-6:30

This shop could be as old and rare as the stock it carries. A holdover from when the Cooper Square area was the rare and old-book capital of the world, it displays, and sometimes sells, antiquarian books, maps, prints, and first editions from the 15th to the 19th centuries. I would doubt that anyone inside the shop could readily tell me what year it is today, let alone the date, but then again the shop is as timeless as its attitude. Pageant carries virtually any kind of printed matter. There are etchings and early printed items, and it would require several days just to admire the prints. But remember this is a book and print shop, and the emphasis is on the former. In the old days, this would have been one of a dozen shops. Today, it may be one of the very few places left for an authentic rare-book-buying experience.

XIMENES RARE BOOKS
19 E 69th St
744-0226
Mon-Fri: 9:30-5:30 (appointment advisable)

In a profession whose proprietorship immediately calls to mind a stooped Dickensian character peering through a pince-nez in a paneled library, Stephen Weissman of Ximenes stands alone. Though young, he has an understanding and knowlege of rare books that would seemingly come only after years of burial under dusty volumes. Furthermore, Ximenes' collection is among the more affordable (prices start at about $50), and Weissman will happily discourse on his trade, if asked. Listen carefully, because he knows his stuff. Weissman's specialties are English-language first editions printed between 1500 and 1890. In that field, he is a primary source.

Religious

CALVARY BOOK SHOP
139 W 57th St
315-0230
Mon-Fri: 10-6; Sat: 11-5

Down the block from the Calvary Baptist Church, the Calvary Book Shop stocks a wide variety of nondenominational religious books, references, gift items, and articles.

INTERNATIONAL BIBLE SOCIETY
45 E 46th St (bet Madison and Vanderbilt Ave)
752-1822
Mon-Thurs: 9-5; Fri: 10-6

The Bible is the best-selling book of all time, and the New York International Bible Society sells it in nearly every written language. An added incentive for visiting this place is a chance to see Vanderbilt Avenue. It runs behind Grand Central Station, and many New York drivers swear that it has no purpose, except for making a trip around the station take triple driving time.

Royalty

ROYALTY BOOKSHOP
30 E 60th St (bet Madison and Park Ave, suite 803)
759-3351
By appointment

In the book world, *royalty* usually refers to the percentage the author receives on each book sold. But not here, where Dr. Wayne S. Swift has set up a contemporary archive on literature for and about the blue bloods among us. And the archive isn't limited to books. Visit Dr. Swift, and you'll also visit the national headquarters of the Royalty Collectors Association of North American (RCANA) and a source for autographs and literature (would you bow to a journal with scholarly articles and a newsletter called *Sceptre*?) on all aspects of royalty. Surprisingly, this is a very serious business, with large support in this country. Royalty Bookshop isn't into Charles and Diana T-shirts (although they have them) as much as commemorative and collectible items. The books are but a small part of the storehouse.

Science Fiction

FORBIDDEN PLANET

821 Broadway (at 12th St)
473-1576
Mon-Sat: 10-7; Sun: 11-6

227 E 59th St (near Third Ave)
751-4386
Mon-Sat: 10-9; Sun: 12-9

When Mike Luckman started a science-fiction book cum toy shop in his native London, he quickly discovered that a good percentage of his customers were Americans clamoring for a similar shop at home. So, Luckman obliged and opened a satellite store at 12th Street and Broadway, directly across the street from the Strand. With a location so close to a book giant like the Strand and in an area known as the black hole of New York merchandising, the shop had to be out of this world to succeed. And Forbidden Planet is. In fact, it has actually inspired pilgrimages to this shrine of science-fiction literature and artifacts. While most of the store is devoted to comic books and science-fiction publications, Luckman discovered in London that sci-fi devotees are not catholic in taste. First-edition collectors love Chewbacca face masks and bookends, and Darth Vadar fans browse through the vintage comic books and fantasy art. In between, there are enough toys and games to entertain the crew of *Star Trek*'s Enterprise during a trip to Saturn, and there is probably at least one copy of every science-fiction title ever written.

SCIENCE FICTION SHOP

56 Eighth Ave (at Horatio St, two blocks below 14th St)
741-0270
Mon-Fri: 11:30-7:30; Sat: 11-6; Sun: 12-6

Eleven years ago, Martin Last and Baird Searles decided to do something about the dearth of science-fiction stores in New York and open the aptly named Science Fiction Shop. Since Last and Searles are enthusiasts themselves, they knew what the average sci-fi book buyer wanted, and the store is geared accordingly. (Searles does some writing and reviewing himself.) So while there are now other special sci-fi stores, theirs is still the only one devoted totally to science-fiction literature. (The others dabble in games, tricks, and extraneous literature). As such, this is probably the definitive store. There are past and current (but not future) books and magazines in the field, and that includes rare and want-listed literature. Occasionally, the shop sponsors autograph parties and other activities to bring authors and readers together. This is a special place. It's definitely the first place to go for a view of the future.

Theater

ACTOR'S HERITAGE

262 W 44th St (bet Eighth Ave and Broadway)
944-7490
Mon-Fri: 10 a.m.-11 p.m. (closes earlier in winter)

An affiliate of Triton, the international theater-poster shop a block away, Actor's Heritage does for books, T-shirts, cards, and records what Triton does for posters. They claim to surpass every other store in the city in those areas, and I suppose that no one *outside* the city could attempt to match any of these stores. It certainly is worth browsing in, and Actor's Heritage also deserves a nod for being part of the effort to spruce up the Times Square area with interesting legitimate businesses.

APPLAUSE THEATER BOOKS

100 W 67th St (bet Broadway and Columbus Ave)
496-7511
Mon-Sat: 11-7; Sun: 1-6

Some years ago, bookstores with a specialty in theater wee so few and inept that the only really good one was the Drama Bookshop. But all that's changed, and if there could be a fad or "in thing" in bookstores, the style would be theater. Riding the crest of the wave is Applause Theater Books, and their business is the epitome of the trend. The folks here claim that a graph of their business would show an incredible rise in the last few years as people have become aware of theater literature. Applause also specializes in British plays and claims to have the complete playscript for every British play. A perk of their business is the necessity of traveling to England to check sources. We spoke to them right after they'd returned from one such trip.

DRAMA BOOKSHOP

723 Seventh Ave (bet 48th and 49th St, second floor)
944-0595
Mon, Tues, Thurs, Fri: 9:30-6; Wed: 9:30-8; Sat: 10:30-5

No drama is involved in guessing the chief subject of the books sold at the Drama Bookshop, where the selection may well be the largest assembled anywhere outside of the Library of Performing Arts at Lincoln Center. Nearly everything in the shop is confined to the written word. There are few recordings outside of original cast albums, tapes, or theater props, but if it was ever written down, it is available here. There are works on theater (both domestic and foreign), performers, scenery, props, makeup, lighting, staging, puppetry, magic, and all aspects of music and dance. One of the more scholarly undertakings is a quarterly listing of the latest available literature in entertainment, but the shop is best known for having the most complete selection of scores, libretti, arrangements, scripts, and plays in the world. While this store is not always the least expensive, you can believe it's the biggest.

RICHARD STODDARD—PERFORMING ARTS BOOKS

90 E 10th St (bet Third and Fourth Ave)
982-9440
Wed-Sat: 11-6; Sun: 1-6

Richard Stoddard runs a one-man operation dedicated to theater arts. But despite a Ph.D. from Yale in theater arts, over 10 years of experience as a performing-arts material collector and appraiser, and a specialist in rare and out-of-print books on the topic, Stoddard is determined to be considered an artist and not (in his words) "an expensive or hoity-toity" businessman. So, while there are extensive numbers of unique books, playbills, souvenir programs, original scenic and costume designs, and back issues of performing-arts magazines, Stoddard is especially proud of his case of paperback plays. They are within the financial reach of even the most impoverished of actors, and there is a similar table of bargain books. Stoddard's pride, however, is his collection of scene and costume designs. The sole agent for the estate of the late Jo Mielziner, the Broadway designer, he also has the plans for a half-dozen other set designers as well. In fact, this is the only shop in the country that sells such designs as a matter of course.

THEATREBOOKS

1576 Broadway (bet 47th and 48th St, room 312)
757-2834
Mon-Fri: 10:30-6; Sat: noon-5

Another example of the demand for theater literature, Theatrebooks is just what its name implies—a shop devoted to books on theater. Its specialty is esoteric literature on the topic. The only store in the city with a selection of out-of-print and used books on the performing arts, it is also the only store with a search service for books not in stock. But the staff is proudest of being, in their own words, "the most trivia-laden staff of any theater bookstore in town." And that proves the real love of theater here. Twofer theater tickets are available at the counter, and the staff couldn't be more helpful in discussing the current status of the Broadway theater. With their location and stock, they have an eye on it all.

Travel

COMPLETE TRAVELLER

199 Madison Ave (at 35th St)
685-9007
Mon-Fri: 9-7; Sat: 10-6; Sun: 12-5

Need a subway map of Paris? Or a road map of the Sudan? If anyone in New York has it, it's the Complete Traveller. This shop specializes in books, travel guides, and maps for the entire world. As hard as it is to imagine, there are few requests they can't fill on the spot, and none (unless it's for Christopher Columbus' navigation chart; he supposedly kept two logs) that can't be ordered. Many of the store's customers are professional travelers; the store is geared to their interests, featuring esoteric and hard-to-find aids. But the tourist, armchair traveler, and just plain browser will feel instantly at home as well.

TRAVELLER'S BOOKSTORE

22 W 52nd St (75 Rockefeller Plaza, bet Fifth and Sixth Ave, lobby of Warner Communications Bldg)
664-0995
Mon-Fri: 9-6

When Candance Olmsled and Jane Grossman opened their Traveller's Bookstore in Rockefeller Plaza, they practiced what they sold. Theirs may be the only bookstore in the city with two distinct addresses for one location, and what could be more fitting for a bookstore for people on the move? Recently, they've developed a catalog for those who can't travel to their address (addresses?) and who like to do their armchair shopping (and possibly traveling) at home. As in the store, the catalog arranges books geographically, and each area is represented with a selection of maps, guides, dictionaries, fiction and nonfiction both in and about the native tongue. The ladies have a very comprehensive selection, and there is hardly a travel area that they haven't covered in depth. Perhaps they've gained experience from trying to guide visitors to their single shop with double addresses!

Women's

WOMANBOOKS

201 W 92nd St (at Amsterdam Ave)
873-4121
Tues-Sat: 10-7; Sun: noon-6; closed Sun in summer

Yes, Betty Friedan, Gloria Steinem, and NOW literature can be found here, but you'll also find cookbooks, decorating books, and child-rearing literature. In fact, the catalog includes almost any topic that would interest women and even many men. Karyn London and the other founders met through the feminist movement and decided to start the store together, but over the years, Womanbooks has evolved into more of a community center than a feminist forum. Children are more than welcome. Neighborhood people, browsers, and tourists are among the people who drop in to enjoy the company and surroundings. Today, Womanbooks stocks most of the books found in a regular bookstore and has a clientele that includes both sexes. (The owners tell an anecdote about a male customer who thought that Womanbooks specialized in books with exotic pictures of women à la *Playboy*.) There is an entire wall of books by women writers. Jewelry, volumes on child-rearing, children's books, and records are also sold.

Butterflies

MARIPOSA
128 Thompson St (bet Prince and W Houston St)
505-5760
Tues-Sun: noon-7

Butterflies are free, but not at Mariposa, the Butterfly Gallery, where they are regarded as an art form and are displayed under panes of acrylic, like any other art medium. Butterflies are unique, and Mariposa (Spanish for butterfly) displays them separately, in panels and as parts of groups. (There are even butterfly farms, which breed and raise butterflies for their brief one-month lifespan under ideal conditions for creating this art.) I admit that sounds a little coldhearted, but Mariposa has to be seen to be appreciated. Besides, it would be impossible to appreciate so many beautiful specimens during their extremely fleeting lifetimes.

Buttons

GORDON BUTTON COMPANY
142 W 38th St
921-1684
Mon-Fri: 8:30-5:30; closed first week of July

Peter Gordon's collection of incidentally acquired, old, unusual, and antique buttons is extensive. I use Gordon, however, for its new buttons, since the enormous stock is used by all of the neighboring garment manufacturers. Gordon's quality, selection, and variety are that good. Belt buckles, components, chains, and brass rings are also sold here and at the same excellent discount that comes to the retail customer courtesy of the wholesale operation going on simultaneously. Courtesy is the "buyword" here. Most garment center manufacturers cannot be bothered with small retail customers, and it seems that their courtesy varies in direct proportion to the size of your order. But at Gordon, which also accepts mail orders, the size of the order seems to be irrelevant.

TENDER BUTTONS
143 E 62nd St
758-7004
Mon-Fri: 11-6; Sat: 11-5:30; closed Sat in July and Aug

Retail button stores can only *hope* to match the selection available here. Owners Diana Epstein and Millicent Safro have assembled one that is complete in variety as well as size. The highlights are buttons that reflect the whimsical nature of the owners; the Donald Duck, silver buckle, soda-pop bottle cap, and little animal buttons slated for children's clothing evoke smiles from the most serious visitors. My personal favorites were the tiny carrot-shaped buttons and the little wooden mice buttons. One antique wooden display cabinet shows off Tender Buttons' selection of natural, original buttons, many of them imported or made exclusively for them. Here are buttons of pearl, wood, horn, Indian bead, leather, ceramics, bone, ivory, pewter, and even precious stones that could outdazzle any outfit. The New England scrimshaw buttons are valuable today as artwork, and a good sample can cost as much as a painting. Some of these buttons, in fact, are so fine they should be mounted on black velvet and framed. There are also antique buttons, buckles, cuff links and the like for those who are so inclined. After a visit here, everyone seems to be so inclined, and you walk out suddenly conscious of the buttons all around you. None, though, are as fascinating as Tender Buttons'. Many unique pieces can be made (by Tender Buttons) into special cuff links—real conversation pieces for the lucky owner. As a cuff-link buff, I have purchased some of my best pieces from this shop.

Cameras

ALKIT CAMERA SHOP
866 Third Ave (bet 52nd and 53rd St)
832-2101
Mon-Fri: 8:30-6:30; Sat: 9-5

If you're professional enough to want to go where the photographers of the Elite and Ford modeling agencies go, Alkit is the shop for you. But come here even if you haven't the faintest idea which end of a camera to look into. Most establishments that deal with the real pros have little time for rank amateurs. Not so here. Nothing gives Edward Buchbinder, the store's manager, more pleasure than introducing the world of photography to a neophyte. And few stores are better equipped to do so. Alkit maintains a full line of cameras, film, and equipment, as well as stereos and TVs. The shop repairs and rents these items, and it also maintains a professional catalog of preferences for and gripes about particular models. The attitude is always briskly professional. Buchbinder hastened to point out that the stereo and TV line is not an extraneous frill: many of his best customers find it essential to work with one or both playing in the background.

BEN NESS CAMERA AND PHOTO STUDIO
114 University Pl (bet 12th and 13th St)
255-4270
Mon-Fri: 8:30-6; Sat: 10:30-5

Ben Ness is best-suited for professionals who know exactly what they want, because the very substantial discount creates a demand the saleshelp aren't always able to satisfy. But those who know what they want in photographic supplies will find them here. The shop bills itself as a "Kodak professional stock-house," and that is but a part of it. The store stocks everything from Matthew Brady's camera to prototypes not yet on the market. And remember *all* of this is discounted. For proof, ask for Ben Ness' price list. Special student discounts are also available.

BIG APPLE CAMERA AND SOUND
99 Chambers St (at Church St)
233-1865
Mon-Sat: 9-6; Sun: 11-5

Despite the "Sound" in Big Apple's name, the music to a customer's ears comes mostly via the prices and a small smattering of audio devices rather than stereo systems. Big Apple specializes in selling the best cameras for the best prices. And as if to prove it, they are not averse to phone or mail inquiries; they will even quote prices over the phone. Cameras and photographic equipment stocked by Big Apple represent all of the major names, and the staff will instruct customers on the merits of each of them.

47th STREET PHOTO
67 W 47th St and 115 W 45th St (bet Sixth Ave and Broadway)
260-4410*
Mon-Thurs: 9-6; Fri: 9-2; Sun: 10-4

You can't beat the prices on all kinds of cameras and photographic equipment at this bustling emporium. Watch their ads, and you'll save the price of a ticket to Hong Kong (but you'll miss the fun of haggling). *P.S. It's rather futile to phone them. Why they don't put in extra lines I don't know. They're missing more business than they realize.

HIRSCH PHOTO

699 Third Ave (at 44th St)
557-1150, 800-223-7957
Mon-Fri: 8:30-5:45; Sat: 10-4

Hirsch has suddenly become a big name in the camera business, perhaps because they advertise extensively. Although that much advertising usually boosts prices, Hirsch's are among the lowest in the city, and their selection is vast. They promise, "We offer service and honesty at very competitive prices." Unfortunately, in the camera business, those are attributes very hard to come by. This shop covers *all* aspects of photography, from developing to the repair of damaged cameras, and the staff is exceptionally capable of helping with any customer's problem. They also maintain a toll-free number for out-of-town orders and information, and have recently added industrial and audio-visual departments.

WILLOUGHBY'S CAMERA STORE

110 W 32nd St (bet Sixth and Seventh Ave)
564-1600
Mon-Wed, Fri: 9-7; Thurs: 9-8; Sat: 9-6:30; Sun: 10:30-5:30

This is the largest camera shop in New York. With a large stock, extensive clientele, and a good reputation. Willoughby's can handle almost any kind of camera order. For those in doubt, there is always the mail-order division. Write and ask for something really esoteric. It's my bet that Willoughby's can fill it without a problem. In addition to selling all kinds of cameras, Willoughby's also services them, supplies photographic equipment, recycles used cameras; and rents equipment at prices that, minus the hefty deposit, are quite reasonable. Renting is recommended, in fact, as the best way to see if a particular camera fits the purchaser's needs. This is truly a photograhic emporium *plus.*

Candles

CANDLE SHOP

118 Christopher St (bet Bleecker and Hudson St)
989-0148
Sun-Thurs: noon-8; Fri, Sat: noon-10

Thomas Alva Edison's inventions haven't made a flicker of an imprint on the folks at the Candle Shop. Rob Kilgallen has assembled a collection of beeswax, paraffin, and stearin candles in an assortment of sizes and colors for every possible need. In fact, it's positively illuminating to learn that candles are available in so many configurations and that there could be a demand for all of them. They even mailed very breakable pieces to me in Oregon with nary a scratch!

HOUSE OF CANDLES AND TALISMANS
99 Stanton St (at Orchard St)
982-2780
Mon, Wed-Sun: 10:30-4:30; Tues: 10-4

Most of the candles sold here are for religious use; mood and accent candles are almost a sideline. A.R.S. Manufacturing Company (House of Candles, etc., is another name) fills its stock with those priorities and obilgingly offers lists of candles associated with saints and other mystical connotations. (Colorado Red, for example, is a sign of love and affection, according to Psalm 142.) For secular use, there is a complete line of incense and an array of unusual candles.

Canvas

MATERA CANVAS PRODUCTS
5 Lispenard St (one block south of Canal St, off W Broadway)
966-9783
Mon-Fri: 10:30-5:30; closed Christmas week

John Matera is an expert with canvas. His store covers the canvas scene from the raw product to very elaborate finished items. And since he manufactures as well as sells all of the items, he has a firm hand on the quality of everything that the shop handles. Some of those items include custom-made tarps, boat covers, navy tops, and automobile covers, which are fairly large and simple, on to artists' canvases, tarpaulins, and even pool covers. Matera also turns out custom-made canvas products for items that require canvas and nylon materials. (One customer used it to repair the top of a rolltop desk. It works fine!) If the need is for canvas, particularly large pieces, this place should be your first choice.

China, Glassware

B. ALTMAN
Fifth Ave at 34th St
679-7800
Mon-Wed, Fri, Sat: 10-6; Thurs: 10-8

Two factors are to be considered here. Altman's is an affluent department store and caters to an affluent clientele. The merchandise is of fine quality, meant for formal use, and it must be special enough for an Altman's client to purchase it at Altman's instead of the neighborhood store. This principle guides Altman's quality control, and backed by Altman's solid (if somewhat stolid) reputation, it distinguishes Altman's housewares from that of lesser establishments. Its selection, too, is fantastic! The second factor is that Altman's can be quite reasonable, and when the exceptional quality of their merchandise is taken into account, its prices can be astounding. Altman's dinnerware and housewares sales should not be missed. At those sales, it is possible to pay less for top quality china and glassware than for bargain-basement quality elsewhere.

GLASS STORE
1242 Madison Ave
289-1970
Mon-Sat: 10-6

This is not the store for a boisterous child—or a rowdy adult, for that matter, particularly if the adult is enamored of glass and crystal and has no willpower to resist them. The Glass Store carries art glass from around the world, rounding out their showcases with rare jewelry, Baccarat, and Lalique French crystal. Not cheap. Not cheap at all! It is luxurious and in excellent taste. While some of it is quite expensive, there are also lower-priced paperweights, vases, and decorative glassware. This would be a good place to buy an extravagant gift.

HEMPSTEAD CHINA
27 William St (bet Wall St and Exchange Pl)
344-6970
Mon-Fri: 8:30-6

Nick Alleva is the manager of Hempstead China. Come here for a chance to see more than 1,000 patterns in stock, all of which are sold at big discount prices. Though china is obviously the specialty, Hempstead can set the entire table. Check out the glassware, flatware, and serving pieces. For those setting up a household, this may seem like a mirage. Aside from the vast selection of every possible style and manufacturer, the price couldn't be more right.

LANAC SALES
73 Canal St (at Allen St)
226-8925, 925-6422
Mon-Thurs: 10-6; Fri: 10-2; Sun: 9-5

Under new ownership and across Allen Street from the old store, Lanac is still a source for chinaware, cut glass, silverware, and gifts at discount prices. Lanac has a reputation for having excellent discounts on everything in stock, and that stock includes some of the finest domestic and imported tableware and crystal in the city. *Lanac,* incidentally, is *Canal* spelled backward—that's in case you get lost!

Christmas Decorations

FRANKEL ASSOCIATES
202 Fifth Ave
679-8388
Mon-Fri: 8:45-4:45

Some people are so organized that they are thinking about next year's Christmas decorations as soon as New Year's is over. In keeping with this book's concept that we want to be everything to everyone, I think I can help out those folks. There are some rules of the game here, though. Since this is *not* a retail store, and since they are *not* officially going to say they can help you, your best plan is to enter in a very low-key manner, give a big smile to an accommodating guy, Mr. Felix, and you're sure to walk out with some real finds at a great price. But please be discreet. Merry Christmas!

Clothing and Accessories

Antique

ANTIQUE BOUTIQUE
712-714 Broadway (at Washington Pl)
460-8830
Mon-Fri: 10:30-9; Sat: 10:30-10; Sun: noon-8

Despite the name, nothing at Antique Boutique is as antique as it is vintage. Translated, that means that this is the place to find recently recycled clothing, as opposed to a Victorian wedding gown. But that's the genre of what is fashionable in the Village. It is Village chic, the kind of fashion you'd find for weekday wear rather than dressing up for the cameras. The good news is that the prices reflect the fact that these clothes are not one-of-a-kind antiques, while at the same time, they are recent enough and/or fashionable enough to be in style today. Antique Boutique actually makes it easy to dress vintage. The selection is excellent; they claim to be the largest vintage-clothing store in the world. They seem to carry everything from argyle socks to suede jackets, and incredible sweaters in alpaca, mohair, and moth-free wools go for a small price. There are no rowboats full of cast-off Bowery raincoats, but rather rack upon rack of clothing designed, as they say, to make their customers legends in any time. The Antique Boutique has become so established that it now has branches in Macy's, West Hollywood, and Madison, Wisconsin. You can't get more Middle American than Madison.

BEST OF EVERYTHING
307 E 77th St (at Second Ave)
734-2492
Mon-Fri: 11:30-8; Sat: 11:30-6:30; Sun: noon-6

Meredith Fiel stresses that her sources of supply are largely estates and auctions, where she or a member of her staff can go over everything and make the best selection. Some of the stock goes back to the 1920s, and all of it surprisingly apropos for today. Prices for the original style are a fraction of those on tags hanging on modern copies in the department stores. Meredith says that the store specializes in antique dresses in "wearable" sizes (usually 3-14), styles, and condition on a wholesale and retail level. The Best of Everything also carries jewelry, accessories, skirts, and blouses from the 1920s to the 1950s. But the main business at the store is quasi-antique furniture, which is sold at prices Fiel challenges anyone to beat. The stock is changed weekly, and an eagle eye and white glove (usually Fiel's) maintains stock that is in virtually mint condition despite being from the 1919-1945 period. The furniture is usually English, American, and art deco in style, but Victorian has been known to appear as have some magnificent armoires, pottery, and the pink, green, and blue varieties of Depression glass. But most of all, check out the prices.

BRASCOMB & SCHWAB
148 Second Ave (bet 9th and 10th St)
777-5363
247 E 10th St (at First Ave)
254-3168
Daily: noon-7

Robert Brascomb and Thomas Schwab started their vintage-clothing store in the East Village when the neighborhood had little redeeming past and less future. But they stuck it out, and now they're right in the midst of the newest up-and-coming neighborhood. The main store at 148 Second Avenue offers vintage clothing for men and women, ranging from the Victorian age through the 1950s. Styles range from nightgowns to evening gowns and formal wear. (Some of the latter are more smashing than Brooks Brothers' latest offerings.) The second store concentrates on the Forties and Fifties eras and only carries daywear. If the offering looks familiar, it doesn't necessarily mean your circle wears dated fashions. Rather, you may have seen Brascomb & Schwab's line on Broadway, off-Broadway, or in television commercials. This is a prime source for wardrobe mistresses as well as people who dress vintage.

CIVILIAN CLOTHING
164 Ninth Ave (at 20th St)
243-9160
Daily: 1-7:30

Despite the fact that Civilian Clothing will probably be the number-one clothing shop in Manhattan in a few years (it has already been designated the best shop in Chelsea by the *Daily News*), the prices are incredibly reasonable. Civilian Clothing features what owner Gloria Venere terms "high drag" (vintage 1950s clothing), which was stored away in mint condition for 20 or 25 years. Almost nothing in the shop has ever been worn, but, boy, is it ever vintage! There are bold-colored sharkskin pants, girls' cotton Capris and pedal pushers (remember them?), pleated pants, seamed and pattered nylon stockings, bowling shirts, small-collared shirts, rayon socks, and evening wear that the store terms "straight out of *Grease,* only better." And this is the place to get all-cotton shirts and high-heeled, pointed-toe, T-strap shoes.

HARRIET LOVE
412 W Broadway (at Spring St)
966-2280
Tues-Sat: noon-7; Sun: 1-6

Harriet Love is a pioneer. Her shop was one of the first in SoHo and one of the very first to market antique clothing as a specialty. When all the uptown stores jumped onto the Victorian and Edwardian clothing bandwagon, Harriet Love moved on to the Thirties, Forties, Fifties, and the Hawaiian sport-shirt age. Now, it's the cat's pajamas of antique-clothes stores. You can be sure that she is always at the vanguard of what's new in "old," and she handles nothing but mint-condition clothing. The store claims that everything sold is one of a kind and that the stock changes weekly. The scarves range in length from long to longer to great-grandmother-length piano shawls. There are also silk blouses that are snatched up as quickly as they are put out, as well as an excellent collection of movie-star lingerie and antique liners. Almost everything (except the piano drapes) comes in small sizes.

PATRICIA FIELD
10 E Eighth St
254-1699
Mon-Sat: noon-8; Sun: noon-6

A description of Patricia Field is a little bit like the proverbial blind man's view of the elephant. One patron will tell you that Patricia Field is the trendiest place around for antique clothing.

Another will launch into a long-winded history of how Patricia Field started as a pants source during the jeans craze (before designer jeans, if you can remember that far back) and ended up as a chic downtown source for uptown fashions. Perhaps the most apt description was offered by one of Field's salespeople, who said, "We have a lot of old, a lot of new. You have to come down and see us to understand." Yes, go see, but even then I won't guarantee you'll understand. So chic and elegant a shop is not usually located in the Village. The lifestyle Field designs for seems to favor classy sportswear separates. But that doesn't preclude the very dressiest evening wear from both former and ultracurrent eras. For the most part, Patricia Field's line is modern—so modern, in fact, that it is often years ahead of what is being seen uptown. Experience has shown that Patricia Field (and she does much of the designing herself) can see into the future of fashion. Her lines are often copied and seen several seasons later elsewhere.

REMINISCENCE
74 Fifth Ave (near 13th St)
243-2292
Mon-Sat: 12-8; Sun: 1-6

Reminiscence has a clientele and wardrobe which would do any vintage-clothing store proud. Owner Stewart Richer, a former stockbroker, has an uncanny eye for recyclable clothing. While looking for used denim, he discovered excellent sources for stylish old clothing that no one wanted. Richer bought it all, as well as tons of army surplus, which he dyed outlandish colors. Suddenly, he was a hit, and the lines outside the store are proof that many people rely on Richer's taste to furnish a wardrobe. Reminiscence's old clothes are primarily 1920s through 1950s vintage, and there is enough variety in size and shape to please almost everyone. For the few who don't enjoy dressing like their parents once did, Richer has a full line of personally created new clothing. The look is youthful, and the prices are reasonable. Reminiscence's success forced a move from the original Village quarters to a new sprawling store near the Strand. (The Village seems to be creeping uptown!) The new store sports 16 (count 'em—16, and probably still not enough), dressing rooms, bright green walls adorned with neon signs and a 1950s atmosphere created in large parts by its clothing. As long as it's funky, nostalgic, a little offbeat, or all three, Reminiscence has it. That goes for ski pants (remember the ones with stirrups?), Hawaiian shirts, and vintage formal wear. It's the kind of stuff you reminisce about.

SCREAMING MIMI'S

100 W 83rd St (at Columbus Ave)
362-3158
66 W 84th St (shoes only)
799-0299
Mon-Sat: 11-7; Sun: noon-6; closed Sun in Aug

This is yet another chic, fashionable Upper West Side antique clothing boutique. So what makes this one different? Mainly owners Biff Chandler and Laura Wills, two ex-fashion coordinators, who outfit their shop and customers with whatever appeals to their personal sense of style. Screaming Mimi's features a "popular" (Biff's word) collection of men's and women's hats, women's lingerie, day and evening dresses, blouses, pants and skirts, and men's sportswear and formal wear. These date almost entirely from the Thirties, Forties, and Fifties. In addition, you'll find similarly "antiquedated" accessories, including neckwear and shoes. Normally, used shoes turn people off, but many of the shoes and most of the regular collection here have never been worn, and they sport original tags and labels to prove it. There's also a party-dress and tuxedo-rental section. And in addition to the spanking new "old" clothing, the distinctive features here have to be the attitude and guidance of the owners. There is no junk, and several customers rely completely upon Biff and Laura to select their wardrobes. The new branch at 66 W 84th Street is an exclusive Screaming Mimi's shoe salon.

TRASH AND VAUDEVILLE

4 St. Mark's Pl (bet Second and Third Ave)
982-3590, 777-1727
170-172 Spring St
226-0590
Mon-Thurs: noon-8; Fri: 11:30-8; Sat: 11-8; Sun: 1-6

This place is almost impossible to describe, since the stock changes almost constantly. What stock there is seems to have no boundaries. The store describes its stock as new and antique clothing, accessories, original designs, and vaudeville items. I was more impressed with the latter (at least, I could catalog *that*), but even the former items are loosely described at best. Antique clothing seems to mean 1950s rock & roll styles, although there are some older—much older—things. There are some real finds here, but perhaps because this is a wholesale as well as a retail business, the individual customer gets the feeling that someone who has been here before has escaped with the best values. Most recently, the store has concentrated on new "new" clothing from Europe.

UNIQUE CLOTHING WAREHOUSE

718 and 726 Broadway (at Eighth St)
674-1767
Mon-Sat: 10-9; Sun: 12-8
Also a branch in Macy's

Harvey Russack opened his Unique Clothing Warehouse in 1973 when SoHo wasn't SoHo, and his beyond-the-fringe clothing consisted of embroidered denims, military-surplus items, and other bygone fads that were merely memories on the fashion scene. Russack started with "antique" rather than the clothing the natives were wearing, and he has successfully worked through all of the latest trends in "creative dressing." So the store has seen vintage men's wear à la *The Sting* (Unique was one of the only sources for the style in the early days), military surplus, the Annie Hall look, surgeon's garb (remember that one?), high-tech, and, most recently, clothes dyed in fluorescent hues. Shopping Unique is, well, a unique experience. The store itself is as much an experience as the clothes, and one of the biggest mysteries in town is how Russack and his buyers seem to be able to predict the latest trends. There are those who have a clue. They claim Unique *makes* the trends, and that may be the answer. In any event, Unique is a bona fide success. A second Unique store has now taken over 26,000 feet of the old Wanamaker garage a few doors away. The current strategy is to use the new store to highlight the dyed goods as well as the more "fashion forward clothing."

Boys' and Girls'—General

CERUTTI

807 Madison Ave (at 67th St)
737-7540
Mon-Sat: 9-5:30; closed Sat in July

Cerutti can completely outfit a child from socks (no shoes) to hat, in a manner fit for a prince or princess. If its luxurious off-the-rack clothing doesn't appeal to your taste, this specialty shop will custom-design and coordinate an outfit for the lucky child. That will almost certainly *not* appeal to your pocketbook (without batting an eye, they can charge $250 for a dress), but the outfit can make the child almost ethereal. Sizes start at infant and go to teen, and the manufacturers are both American and European, but decidedly the best of both. Cerutti claims that its prices go from moderate to very expensive. If the prices don't turn you off, dressing your kids here can be somewhat akin to playing with dolls in your youth. The things are that special.

CHOCOLATE SOUP

946 Madison Ave (at 74th St)
861-2210
Mon-Sat: 10-6; Sun: 1-6

A unique type of children's clothing store, the Chocolate Soup specializes in handmade clothing and tops for children—"and some special things for adults." The atmosphere is warm and friendly and totally unlike the posh boutique ambiance one expects on Madison Avenue, perhaps because Chocolate Soup began as a small store in the Village. The imported and handmade clothing comes in sizes to fit infants and children up to 12 years old. Chocolate Soup also carries Danish school bags and unbreakable handmade toys. The something special for adults has got to be, at least in part, the great care the staff gives each customer.

GREENSTONE AND CIE

442 Columbus Ave (at 81st St)
580-4322
Mon-Fri: 11-7; Sat: 11-6; Sun: noon-6

Greenstone and Cie has been a family operation since 1919, and it has never been a secret to the likes of the children of Dustin Hoffman, Carly Simon, and Sammy Davis, Jr. A visit to the store makes it easy to see why. The Greenstones (the business is now run by grandchildren of the founder) offer primarily imported fashions for boys and girls, newborn to 16 years old. Most of it is unique in styling and certainly unique to the area. Moreover, there is a pricing policy that discounts everything, including outfits that are totally unavailable elsewhere at any price. Greenstone and Cie can coordinate an entire ensemble down to (but not including) the shoes.

KINDERSPORT OF ASPEN

1260 Madison Ave (at 90th St)
534-5600
Daily: 10-6; closed Aug

How New York! How chic! How typical! Where else would one find a shop founded in Park City, Utah (with a branch in Aspen, Colorado), specializing in exclusive top lines of European clothing, sports, and ski wear for children, but on Madison Avenue in New York? Did New York need an outfitter of ski equipment exclusively for children? Apparently. Kindersport has made a big splash. Stylish tots aged 2 to 16 snap up Kindersport's sweaters, ski suits, sportswear, and even party dresses. If not all of them end up on the ski slopes for which they are intended, at least they make knockout fashion statements. And if Junior really is off for a trip to Aspen or the Alps, have no fear that Kindersport can outfit even a size 4 at a moment's notice with Austrian skis and the best Italian ski boots. Price? The dearest. But then, what is it worth to have your two year old slide down the slopes in the finest togs?

LITTLE BITS OF NEW YORK
1186 Madison Ave (bet 86th and 87th St)
722-6139
Mon-Thurs: 10-7; Fri, Sat: 10-6

Lucky is the child who is under size 7 and whose parents wander into this very special shop. Most outfits here are originals, and each has its own unique features. Many include caps and pants in the same bright fabric as the outfit. Most ensembles are made for growth, which means that the cost of the garment has to be calculated on a "two years of use" scale, instead of the usual "one season" life expectancy. And they will last the two years! On that basis, the prices are quite good. Hand-knit sweaters are a specialty; sizes can be made to order.

R.G. CRUMBSNATCHER
254 Columbus Ave (bet 71st and 72nd St)
724-8681
Mon-Fri: 11-7; Sat: 11-6

This is no ordinary store—it claims to have other locations in Oz and Never Never Land, and who's to prove them wrong! It doesn't sell ordinary items, either. R.G. Crumbsnatcher snatches up the best in children's clothing, accessories, and toys that the world has to offer and makes them available to customers. R.G. Crumbsnatcher features the exotic and trendy in children's haberdashery. Many of the items are one-of-a-kind pieces, and the staff is great at translating both sizes and needs for inexperienced adult customers. Have you ever seen a grandfather shop for a child 3,000 miles away? "I think he's a six. No, seven. Big for his age? Maybe." R.G. Crumbsnatcher is expert at assembling wardrobes from such sketchy guidelines, and they do it with a flair that's almost, well, otherworldly.

RICE AND BRESKIN
323 Grand St (at Orchard St)
925-5515
Sun-Fri: 9-5

If the Lower East Side has a quality shop for children's clothing, Rice and Breskin is probably it. Wrapped in plastic, the merchandise includes good brand names at a 25 percent discount. They specialize in infant clothing and baby gifts. Despite its Lower East Side location, the saleshelp are charming, even motherly.

Boys' and Girls'—Used Clothing

BEST DRESSED KIDS

2741-A Broadway (bet 105th and 106th St)
222-3740
Mon-Sat: 10-6:30

Best Dressed Kids' owner Beth Thomas has had at least two brilliant ideas. One was opening a shop that stresses quality and style rather than location and sky-high prices; the second was her half-serious suggestions that those who need the status of buying high-class labels should first go to the big department stores and buy a shopping bag and then come to Best Dressed Kids to fill it. This shop sells previously owned (but not necessarily worn) clothing in excellent condition on a consignment basis. The labels are as good as they were the first time around, but the prices are fractions of the originals'. In fact, the prices are the only giveaway that this spanking clean bilevel shop is not the expensive boutique it appears to be. This youngster's haven is replete with a play area, toy boxes, an old-fashioned rocker, rocking horses, and an antique wicker baby doll carriage. In addition to the clothing, Best Dressed Kids retails used toys, books, footwear, maternity clothing, juvenile equipment, and the pride of the shop, a Dolls of the World collection. There are even dressing rooms (something lacking in some retail children's stores), and the atmosphere is created by a staff whose concerns are keeping prices down and children happy.

SECOND ACT CHILDREN'S WEAR

1046 Madison Ave (bet 79th and 80th St, upstairs)
988-2440
Tues-Sat: 10-5; summer: Mon-Fri: 10-4:30

The best buys here are the clothes that were bought and used for only one or two occasions, such as communion dresses, Easter outfits, and flower-girl gowns. Some of the other items don't seem worth the one-third-of-the-original-cost price tag, but everything is kept in A-1 condition. All clothing is washed and ironed or cleaned before it is put up for sale, and it is, indeed, in "like new" condition. Clothing is consigned to separate rooms according to sex, and within these rooms everything is sized in order. Sizes go from girls' infant to 14 and boys' infant to 18. In addition to clothing, there are ice skates, riding apparel, ski boots, books, and toys. Note the bulletin board that lists such larger items as carriages and cribs for sale.

WEST SIDE KIDS

498 Amsterdam Ave (at 84th St)
496-7282
Mon-Sat: 10-6

If this store is for New York kids, then 90 percent of the city's—indeed, the country's—kids can't afford to be one. Ostensibly a resale shop, West Side Kids has been known to turn down Florence Eiseman and Bloomingdale fashions because they weren't special enough. Everything sold here is squeaky fresh and at the height of kids' fashion. Nantucket Designs passes the test; Buster Brown does not. In fact, the only thing that distinguishes West Side Kids from a full-fledged retail shop is its prices. But even at a third of the original retail prices (with half of that going to the consignee), those prices are not much less than what Sears charges. The difference is quality. West Side Kids' clothing is high-quality outgrown—not outworn—merchandise. In addition to the clothing, there is a rapidly changing supply of recycled children's furniture and equipment, toys, games, and books, all in A-1 condition. Neighborhood craftsmen make exclusive-to-the-store hand-knitted outfits, as well as unique quilts and toys. And it is a neighborhood store. Alice Bergman and Lynn Stiles offer advice on neighborhood schools, stores, day care, and babysitters, and maintain a "want file" for customers seeking special items. Finally, this is also a source for exceptional maternity clothing.

Bridal Gowns

Congratulations! You've just gotten engaged, and you're looking for wedding attire in New York. That's the second smartest decision you've made recently, since wise bridal candidates come here from as far as the West Coast to buy the family's outfits at savings that make the airfare negligible. All the department stores have bridal salons, where custom-made gowns can be ordered. No one is better than any other in my opinion, since the prices for the same gown are identical, and all are ordered from the wedding-gown manufacturers in the garment district. Before we discuss that, be aware that sample gowns are often donated to the thrift shops, as are "once-worn gowns" by brides who have no further use for them. Indeed, the resale shops are a prime source for elegant new bridal attire, and that goes for formal wear for gentlemen, too.

In the garment center, there are two bridal buildings, one at *499 Seventh Avenue* and the other at *1385 Broadway.* With Macy's across the street, no one is going to admit that you can buy the same gowns the store is selling at wholesale in their buyers' office, but people have gotten into both buildings, and Saturday mornings at 1385 Broadway are more crowded than assembly-line catering halls. (I wouldn't attempt 499 Seventh Avenue unless you have the hide of an armadillo!) The rules are simple: Arrive early Saturday morning (it's mobbed by 9 o'clock), and ask the elevator operator for the business which is least crowded and best suits your needs. The 18th through 22nd floors are basically all wedding-gown floors, while the others carry outfits for the rest of the family as well. The really elegant bridal designers are not in this building, and most of the styles and price ranges are about the same in each showroom. (I won't be chauvinistic and say a white gown is a white gown is a white gown.) Discounts vary, so it doesn't hurt to know the market before sharpening your elbows, but one almost *has* to save money here, and several of the businesses that specialize in bridal-party attire can coordinate the entire party's uniforms for less than one gown would cost at Macy's. (Of course, we're not talking about outfitting the Brady Bunch.) Since most gowns have to made up (unless you get a fantastic buy on a sample, which has happened), it's not necessary to bring lots of cash on the first visit. After that visit, you'll claim the discount as your reward for braving the mob scenes.

Individual stores sometimes have excellent bridal frocks but no formal wear. Laura Ashley's white Victorian outfits come to mind. Some are specifically bridal costumes; most are not. And of course, if the wedding is in the Village or SoHo . . . well, brides have been known to get dressed in black leather down there. There are two dressmakers who will work with entire bridal parties. *Katy K* (814 Broadway, 254-2975) has dresses in stock from the Fifties and other eras and will also make garments from fabric supplied by the customer or will use their own. The company's prices are reasonable and whole weddings can be outfitted from bride to flower girl. Her styles tend to be funky. *Lu Ellen* (239 E 12th St, 982-4218) primarily creates garments to order from scratch. This too would be a good choice for a bridal party since they have made bridal gowns and are quite good at adapting specific patterns to specific needs.

One very petite bride was turned away from Franklin Simon's bridal salon and told that the dress that would fit her was a communion dress in the children's department. "And dear, it comes with the veil," said the saleslady snidely. And people wonder why they are out of business! Nevertheless, most bridal dresses do not come with the headpieces, though salons will usually sell them; the bridal-building companies do not. The wholesale market for that is 38th Street off Sixth Avenue, and while the market is diminished, there are still places that have them on hand or can make up headpieces, veils, and crowns to order. One of the best specialists in wedding accessories is *Paul's Veil & Net* (66 W 38th St, 391-3822). A couple of others are *Arden's* (1014 Sixth Ave, 391-6968) and *Max Millinery Center* (13 W 38th St, 221-8896). Since all three are virtually on the same block, comparison shopping is easy though not really necessary.

Dance Wear

CAPEZIO'S

755 Seventh Ave (at 50th St)
245-2130
Mon-Wed, Fri, Sat: 9:30-5:45; Thurs: 9:30-7:30
136 E 61st St
758-8833
Mon-Fri: 10:30-6
177 MacDougal
477-5634
Mon-Sat: noon-8

Capezio's is the definitive store for dance paraphernalia, and if first-timers display any sense of wonder about the shop, they are amazed not because New York can easily support several such fully equipped professional shops, but because Capezio is a name that's known worldwide. The Seventh Avenue store boasts that it is the largest dance/theater retail store in the world. It carries only dance wear and dance-related materials. Each store is separately owned, and reflects the style of its owner and its neighborhood. The most professionally oriented is Capezio's Seventh Avenue, but the most exciting is the Village shop. It even has a men's wear department.

FREED OF LONDON

108 W 57th St
489-1055
Mon-Wed, Fri, Sat: 10-5:45; Thurs: 10-7

Freed of London has landed on its toes in New York, and the venerable English establishment has brought along its tradition of supplying the best and finest in dance supplies. The style is definitely traditional, but there is virtually no piece of dance gear that Freed does not carry or cannot order. The store keeps leg warmers, leotards, shoes, skirts, and tutus in stock. A list of the shop's clientele reads like a who's who of stars who've danced in London (the store carries, as a matter of course, the complete line of regulation wear for the Royal Academy of Dancing). For those who can't stop in, there's a measuring chart and mail-order catalog available. Apparently, Freed was getting so many orders from New York that it was cheaper to open a store here than service them from abroad. For dancers, this store is a must. If you're simply a dance fan, this is where you'd be likely to spot your favorite dancer.

Handkerchiefs

VILLARI HANDKERCHIEF COMPANY

30 W 54th St (bet Fifth and Sixth Ave)
586-2991
Mon-Fri: 9-4

Whether its for a wedding, for dropping in front of a suitor, or for sobbing in front of the boss, a knockout handkerchief can come in handy. And Villari is the place to get it, as well as aprons, towels, and kerchiefs. Miss Lia Villari is as much an anachronism as her hand-embroidered, handmade linen handkerchiefs. Her store is a suite in the Dorset Hotel (which is also her home), and she operates as though everyone—gentlemen as well as ladies—still carries a monogrammed handkerchief in his or her pocket. Nearly everything Villari sells is handmade in the West Indies. (Villari claims that for "really rush jobs," she will *call* the workroom, which saves 10 days in delivery time. Does that give you the flavor of Villari?) There are also gentlemen's Irish linen handkerchiefs that can be personalized with a monogram or full name, as well as gift handkerchiefs for nearly every occasion. But Villari's specialties are wedding-party items. The embroidered items can list as little as initials and as much as the names and date of the entire wedding party. Miss Villari's newest item, in her own words, is "a special handkerchief for the bridegroom so that he can never forget the date of his wedding." She is one special lady!

Hosiery—Family

FOGAL

680 Madison Ave (bet 61st and 62nd St)
759-9782
Mon-Sat: 10-6

Before Fogal came to New York from Switzerland, the thought of a Madison Avenue boutique devoted to hosiery was, well, foreign. But since its opening in 1982, it's hard to imagine Manhattan without it. If it's new, fashionable, and different leg wear, Fogal has it. Plain hosiery comes in nearly 100 hues, at last count; the designs and patterns of the colors make the number of choices almost incalculable. You might say that Fogal's has a leg up on the competition, but there have never been any serious contenders. Just be warned that after visiting Fogal's, it will be impossible to ignore hosiery as part of your wardrobe again.

JACOB YOUNG AND SON

329 Grand St (at Orchard St)
925-9232
Sun-Fri: 9-5

If you are the type whose feelings are easily hurt, Jacob Young is a place to avoid. The "wholesale only" sign in the window means that retail business is not welcome. But ignore the sign. Jacob Young has hosiery for the entire family at unbelievable prices.

LOUIS CHOCK
74 Orchard St
473-1929
Sun-Thurs: 9-5; Fri: 9-1

It's hard to find a classification for this store. It seems to stock a little of everything, but perhaps the old-fashioned term "dry goods" sums up the stock sold here. Louis Chock sells dry goods for the home, school, and the entire family. There appears to be a subspecialty in hosiery and family underwear. Children's nightwear—which is only peripherally related to the underwear category—is available in a large choice of colors and sizes, and there is something in the hosiery section for every member of the family. Furthermore, everything in the store is sold at a discount that begins at 25 percent. Another plus: there is a larger discount on items bought in quantity. Louis Chock also has a mail-order department, offering a 25 to 30 percent discount on everything in stock. For a price list, send a self-addressed, stamped envelope to the store.

M. STEUER HOSIERY COMPANY
31 W 32nd St (near Fifth Ave)
563-0052
Mon-Fri: 7:45-5:20

By walking one block from Herald Square, hosiery wearers can save a bundle. Steuer is a wholesale operation that treats each retail customer as a wholesaler, no matter how small the order. They even speak a half-dozen languages—the better to welcome visitors to New York. There is a huge selection and large inventory of name brand hosiery, socks, pantyhose, and dance wear. Steuer has been known to fill unusual requests with aplomb.

R. C. SULTAN
55 Orchard St (at Grand St)
925-9650
Sun-Fri: 9-5

Sultan is a source on the Lower East Side for all manner of attire for the feet, except shoes. Better yet, it is a place that will quote prices by mail. Every major brand of hosiery is available with a discount that starts at 20 percent off retail and increases according to the number of pairs purchased. Next door at 47 Orchard Street, Sultan (966-3488) maintains a similar policy for lingerie and underwear. And while information and conversation are in very short supply, both Sultan stores seem to have a bit more "charm" than is usual on the Lower East Side.

VALUE HOSIERY CENTER

4225 Broadway
(bet 177th and 178th St)
795-1680

1653 Second Ave
(bet 85th and 86th St)
628-5140

4930 Broadway (at 207th St)
569-2250

255 W 23rd St
243-7243

Mon-Sat: 10-6

The specialty here is Danskin. Irregulars of Danskin leotards and clothing are sold for at least one-third less than in neighboring department stores. They are sold at the beginning of the season at prices that are not always matched by other stores at clearance sales. In addition, Value Hosiery lives up to its name with a complete line of hosiery for the entire family. Pantyhose comes in all sizes and qualities, the best buys being their own brands.

Jeans and Casual Wear—Family

ARNIE'S PLACE
37 Orchard St (at Hester St)
925-0513
Sun-Thurs: 8:30-5:30; Fri: 8:30-3:30

Arnie Goldstein runs a shop that proves that the Lower East Side is always changing in style, but is always the same when it comes to discount policy. For here, on the corner of two of the busiest Lower East Side streets, Arnie serenely sells the most sophisticated collection of jeans and denims. The collection is so top drawer, in fact, that many Madison Avenue shops don't have as good a selection of jeans, and what they do sell is more than twice the price. Arnie stocks jeans for men, women, and children in more than 20 different brands. Sizes range from toddler to embarrassingly large. Levi's are the main stock in trade, but everyone I could think of who has ever made jeans is represented. There are also shirt, skirt, and overall departments. Arnie's personnel have become expert in the fine nuances of size and shape among the various manufacturers. Translated, that means a better fitting for the customers and at a discount, to boot.

CANAL JEANS
504 Broadway (off Spring St)
226-1130
Daily: 10-8

304 Canal St (at Broadway)
431-8439
Daily: 10-7

From the moment you walk by the bins full of sweaters, you know Canal Jeans is not your ordinary store. And it's not. Canal

Jeans buys, sells, and wholesales the latest SoHo looks and has made itself a popular place. The look is certainly casual. Even their best *new* clothing stretches the meaning of sportswear, but if it's bomber jackets, brightly colored pants, tops, and outfits you want, this is the place to shop. A large percentage of the customers are Europeans who stock up on as many pairs of jeans as they can horde in their suitcases and backpacks. (If they buy enough, they can sell them back at home and make enough profit to pay for their trip.) Other clothing items include punk outfits, bins of junk clothes (don't bother—they're just that), and closeouts.

Judicial, Educational, and Religious Robes

BENTLEY AND SIMON
450 Seventh Ave
695-0554
Mon, Wed, Fri: 8:30-4:30 by appointment

Bentley and Simon is one of those "only in New York" institutions. In business since 1912, it supplies only one product—robes for judicial, educational, and religious use. They are probably *the* outfitter for judges across the country, up to and including the Supreme Court. But despite a long and unique reputation, ownership by the Oak Hall Cap and Gown Company of Roanoke, Virginia, and a Seventh Avenue address, Bentley and Simon is still run like a small, personal business. As for styles and selection, well, a robe is simply a black thing with pleats in the back, right? Well, sort of. While Bentley and Simon don't make robes in styles per se, they are quite convinced that their judicial robe's design is the ultimate one, and they make it in different sizes. Although clergymen (and women) have more of a choice, Bentley and Simon are convinced that *they* know the proper garment, so most clergymen usually end up relying upon their judgment. And as might be expected in a profession that has such a stodgy image, Bentley and Simon's reaction to the increasing number of women in the judiciary and clergy was barely perceptible. They simply made up smaller and shorter robes.

Leather

BARBARA SHAUM
13 E Seventh St
473-8132
Wed-Fri: 1-7; Sat: 1-6

Barbara Shaum does magical things with leather. The main stock is custom-made sandals, although there are some ready-made pairs available for emergencies. In addition, there are bags, belts (with handmade brass, nickel-silver, inlaid wood, and copper buckles), attaché cases, and briefcases. Everything is designed in the shop, and Barbara Shaum meticulously crafts each item, using only the finest materials. She's a wonder. As well as being a strong community activist, Shaum is the chairperson of the Lower East Side Business and Professional Association. Her aim is to safeguard the burgeoning East Village community.

NORTH BEACH LEATHER

772 Madison Ave (at 66th St)
772-0707
Mon-Fri: 10-7; Sat: 10-6; Sun: 1-6

If leather wear connotes home on the range or some sleazy bar on the Village waterfront, then you are obviously unaware that leather is the flip side of fur and can be just as elegant. North Beach Leather's locations are proof enough of that (with stores in Houston, Los Angeles, and San Francisco, to name but a few), and the fashions are further evidence. Madison Avenue isn't the place to look for an outfit to wear when cleaning the barn, and North Beach couldn't oblige, even if it wanted to. But if you need a leather ensemble for an outing in the Mercedes, then North Beach is the place to look. There is, of course, an emphasis on jackets, coats, and outerwear, but there are also suits and even skirts and dresses for women. Gloves and accessories are available as well. Their leather jackets and boots for men are just the thing to round out an outfit. But they aren't cheap.

SAN MICHEL LEATHER

396 Fifth Ave (at 36th St, second floor)
736-2000
Tues, Wed, Fri, Sat: 10-6; Mon, Thurs: 10-8;
Sun: 12-5; summer: Mon-Sat: 10-6

In the heart of Manhattan, less than one block from B. Altman's, San Michel manufacturers the finest in leather, suede, and sheepskin apparel for both men and women. There is also a small selection in boys' sizes. If what you want is not available, San Michel can make it up for you. They claim that every garment is sold at a price that is 40 to 60 percent less than elsewhere.

SOHO ZOO

176 Spring St (bet Broadway and Thompson St)
226-0915
Daily: noon-8

The animals who inhabit this zoo aren't alive now, but their hides and skins are sported on the backs of some of the most fashionable people in town. The basic medium at SoHo Zoo is leather. It comes custom-made or off-the-rack in pants, knickers, belts, jewelry, and of course, jackets. Many of the designs, which are unique to the store, are sold wholesale to other stores, and the work of up-and-coming local designers is also showcased. Some of the imported items are not necessarily leather, but they maintain the animal-kingdom motif by using the skins of other animals. Even belts are dyed to look like zebra, cheetah, or leopard for those who find regular leather boring. The store is small (as are most of the stores in the neighborhood), but these people know how to fashion leather, and they carry the very best. Buy one of these wildlife creations, and it could be the first time that being told your clothes look like they came from a zoo could be a compliment.

Maternity

LADY MADONNA

793 Madison Ave (at 67th St)
988-7173
Sat-Thurs: 10:30-6; Fri: 10:30-8

I'd like to reaffirm that I personally visited nearly every one of the stores listed in this book—even the maternity shops. I wasn't exactly a regular customer, but even so, my visits were pleasant and informative and not half as embarrassing as one might think. Okay, back to business. Lady Madonna started with the premise that most pregnant women were adults who would like to dress as adults, rather than as Raggedy Ann or Pollyanna. The idea took off beyond anyone's imagination. It was helped along by the rising number of women who combined careers with families and who, therefore, needed good, stylish clothing that was fashionable even in the advanced stages of pregnancy. Old-fashioned ideas fell by the wayside. One such idea was that a pregnant woman should be hidden, either by staying home or by being swathed in voluminous clothing. Another was that maternity clothes should be inexpensive, since no one looks good pregnant anyway and who wants to pay money for an outfit worn a maximum of five months? Lady Madonna banished these concepts once and for all by pricing their clothing just as fashionable, functional, nonmaternity clothing would be priced.

MANOLA MATERNITY

802 Lexington Ave (at 62nd St)
861-9772
Mon-Sat: 11-6

Manola is for the classy expectant mother who wants to look good more than she wants to look pregnant. So, the emphasis is on the same quality and style that the client would wear regularly, and there is a heavy emphasis on designer fashions *and* discount prices. If a style or size is not in stock, Manola can make or order it, and alterations can be done in less than three hours. Apparently, Manola has done such a good job of attracting and satisfying their customers that some found it difficult to stay away. So, Manola now stocks imported designer clothing for children that is sold at a discount as well. It's not a fantastic discount (15 percent at nonsale times), but it is easily the best wardrobe that Spain, France, Austria, England, Argentina, and the U.S. have to offer. And now the baby can be dressed as stylishly as the mother. Another plus: Manola's salespeople are helpful and knowledgeable.

Men's—General

ANDRE OLIVER
34 E 57th St (near Park Ave)
758-2233
Mon-Sat: 10-6

Andre Oliver pops up on more "best dressed" lists than any other store name in the city. Oliver is obviously doing something right, whether it's the high styles, fashion sense, or color-coordinated displays of sweaters, mufflers, shirts, and jackets. Indeed, many of the customers are women who rate this store number one for themselves as well as their male friends. Oliver's style is classical, luxurious, and upbeat. The emphasis is on casual elegance and timelessness, much like that of the better women's designers. And both women's designers and Oliver's strive to enhance the person wearing their clothing rather than their own name. Prices, to put it mildly, are not cheap. But you can do quite well by picking up one or two items that can change your whole wardrobe. This is class. But the attitude of the self-important saleshelp is not.

BARNEY'S
111 Seventh Ave (at 17th St)
929-9000
Mon-Fri: 10-9; Sat: 10-8

Walk into the masculine lobby of the "World's Largest Men's Store," and a hostess will direct you to the area of the store most likely to fulfill your needs. Her job is quite necessary, because Barney's aims—via separate "rooms" set aside for the purpose—to outfit every male to his exact size and taste. Rooms range from the traditional Madison House and English Room to very mod sportswear. In recent years, Barney's expanded to include a barbershop, tearoom, and Pub Club, as well as a women's section and a gift and home accessories shop. Prices are good and include free alterations. But the key here is hitting their sales. There is a big sale each season that's difficult to miss, since it lasts several weeks and is advertised extensively. The best buys are always to be had at the beginning of the sale, and being on Barney's mailing list will assure you of advance notice. Don't miss the warehouse sale, held somewhat less frequently, across the street at 106 Seventh Avenue. One word of caution: Barney's is *big,* so there are two major drawbacks. The place is poorly organized; without the aforementioned hostess, you'd never know where to look for what you want, and for that reason, you feel you aren't seeing everything. And the paperwork! Barney's seems to require as many forms for each sale as the federal government requires for an environmental impact statement! More people should tell them that they are losing many sales because of their antiquated administrative procedures. (I have, several times.) And even with all the red tape, they still managed to lose one of my friend's suits.

CAMOUFLAGE
141 Eighth Ave (at 17th St)
741-9118
Mon-Fri: noon-7; Sat: 11-6; Sun: 1-6 (Nov and Dec only)

In the heart of Chelsea, Camouflage looks like it would be better suited to the Village, while its fashions would be at home on Madison Avenue. It sells American designer clothing for men during hours more in keeping with the Village than the straight-laced nine-to-five neighborhood. It outfitted the new "gentrifiers" of the neighborhood long before it was a fashionable neighborhood. In short, Camouflage has never been just another store, and more often than not, it has managed to shine out of all proportion to its small size. If you've got patriotic tastes, this may be the store for you. If is one of the few shops that eschews foreign designers, selling only American clothing. Names such as Susan Horton, Perry Ellis, J. G. White, Alexander Julian, Garrick Anderson, and Jeffrey Banks are crammed into a tight space. Prices range from very reasonable (their chinos may be one of the best buys in the city) to good, considering those pricey designer names. But one of Camouflage's best virtues is the ability to dress its customer with a dignified but special appearance. There's nothing at Camouflage that would blend into the wallpaper.

DIMITRI COUTURE
110 Greene St (at Prince St, sixth floor)
431-1090
Mon-Sat: 10-6 by appointment
Closed two weeks in Aug

Dimitri's custom-make suits are worn by some of the best-dressed people anywhere, and the firm has a steady list of customers who call regularly from the West Coast and even Europe to have suits made up. But Dimitri doesn't like to do long-distance orders, because dimensions can change and the incorrect sizing "reflects badly on us." Besides, we all know that the beautiful people come to New York often enough to fit in a trip to Dimitri. And they do, they do! That's because Dimitri offers a powerful collection of suits for men (and women) in almost any imaginable unblended fabric, with a heavy emphasis on leather. (Even their business card is a thick swatch of leather.) Each suit is precisely made and stitched by hand under the direct supervision of one craftsman from start to finish. The process creates a suit that is timeless, elegant, and subtly states exactly what it is: a handmade, custom-made suit of quality. Prices are expensive, but the Old World service and excellent quality are well worth it.

HARRY ROTHMAN
111 Fifth Ave (at 18th St)
777-7400
Tues-Sat: 9:30-6; Mon, Thurs: 10-7

Across the street from Barnes and Noble, Harry Rothman's sign has long attracted book browsers who happened to look upward. Once the customer is inside, the shop has been able to hold him on its own. Brothers Harry and Jack Rothman run this discount suit business (which is larger than many hometown retail stores) on a personal basis. One or the other is always available, and they exude a friendly, homey touch. Their clothing is billed as custom quality at discount prices. Their radio ads used to say, "How does Harry Rothman do it?" The question was never satisfactorily answered. They are not, for example, manufacturers like so many of their neighbors. But do it, they do. Sizes range from 36 to 56 in regular, short, long, extra long, extra short, portly short, and portly. Every suit is sold at discount, usually in the vicinity of 40 percent, and quality is excellent. There is also an odd-lot suit collection, which has even greater savings on broken sizes and sample suits. The stock is not limited to suits, though. They also carry raincoats, all-weather coats, slacks (including jeans and hand-tailored gabardines), sports jackets, and leisure suits. In short, they carry everything any men's store does, but at a substantial discount.

IRVING BARON CLOTHES
343 Grand St (at Orchard St)
475-1718
Mon-Thurs, Sat, Sun: 9-6:30; summer: Sun-Fri: 9:30-6

Once inside, a customer at Irving Baron might think he's in a posh Fifth Avenue store. Such brand names as Groshire, Marzotto, Corneliani, Yves St. Laurent, Halston, Le Baron, Louis Roth, London Fog, Pierre Cardin, Countess Mara, Damon, and Calvin Klein are part of the stock that the staff says can outfit a man from top to bottom. (Shoes are an exception.) It is only when the bill is presented that the customer realizes that this is, indeed, a Lower East Side store, for the discount starts at 25 percent. Suits, sport jackets, pants, overcoats, raincoats, outerwear, shirts, sweaters, and ties are carried to suit men sized from 36 short to 50 long. The salespeople are excellent.

J. PRESS
16 E 44th St (bet Fifth and Madison Ave)
687-7642
Mon-Fri: 9:15-5:30; Sat: 9:15-5

As one of New York's classic, conservative men's stores, J. Press prides itself on its sense of timelessness. Its sales people, customers, and attitude have changed little from the time of J. Press to that of Richard Press today. Styles are impeccable and distinguished, if not *distinguishable.* Blazers are blue, and shirts are button-down and straight. Even in the days when button-down collars were out, Press was such a bastion of support for them that it went so far as to make them available in colors other than blue.

LESH CLOTHING
115 Fifth Ave (at 19th St, sixth floor)
255-6893
Mon-Fri: 9-6; Sat: 9-4; Sun: 10-3

Irving Lesh claims that his family business was one of the first, if not *the* first, wholesale men's clothing lofts. He has a certain pride in the bare-piped surroundings, and the quality of the suits, sports jackets, slacks and outerwear seem designed to prove that here the dollar goes to the merchandise rather than the décor. Lesh manufactures its own suits, and when the overhead (i.e., rent) gets to be too much, they move to another (read cheaper) loft. Consequently, it always pays to call before paying Lesh a visit. Speaking of overhead, that's where you'll find the merchandise. It literally hangs from the rafters and the pipe racks. Not incidentally, the selection of suits and their quality is great. Since Lesh has been manufacturing them since 1935, they adhere to the fine nuances of tailoring, fit, sizes, and design. And all of this for one low price. Everything in the warehouse goes for the same price, and that price is almost laughably cheap. The average customer invariably walks out with twice what he intended to buy—and for no more than he'd originally planned to spend.

LOUIS BARALL AND SON
58 Lispenard St (bet Canal St and Broadway)
226-6195
Mon-Fri: 9:30-6; Sat: 9:30-5; closed Sat in July and Aug

Although it has been in existence for almost 75 years and Louis Barall has been succeeded by Irving Barall, this store is one of the best-kept secrets in town. The only possible reason is that the savvy

Wall Street types who shop here have no desire to share the market with anyone else. Styles are conservative and traditional at best. But that doesn't mean old-fashioned or even out of season; it simply bypasses the ultratrendy. If your style runs to the tried and true, try Barall. Prices *begin* at one-third off list price and go down from there. Garments—all with recognizable names—come in first-quality or clearly marked irregulars, with the latter going for 50 percent off list price and more.

L.S. MEN'S CLOTHING
23 W 45th St (bet Fifth and Sixth Ave, second floor)
575-0933
Mon: 9-7; Tues-Fri: 9-6; Sun: 11-4

L. S. Bills itself as the "Executive Discount Shop," but I would go further and call them a must for the fashion-minded businessman. For one thing, their midtown location precludes a trip downtown to the Fifth Avenue-in-the-teens area that is the usual spot for finding men's discount clothing. Better still, as owner Israel Zuber puts it, "There are many stores selling $200 suits discounted, but we are one of the few that discount the $300 to $400 suits *and* are located in mid-Manhattan." The main attraction, though, is the tremendous styles and selection of the stock. Style is primarily executive class, and within that category, a man could almost outfit himself entirely at L. S. The natural and soft-shoulder designer suits are available in all sizes. This is one of the top spots for top names (Hickey Freeman is one). I would make it number one on the midtown shopping itinerary.

NAPOLEON-JOSEPHINE
762 Madison Ave (bet 65th and 66th St)
737-7701
Mon-Sat: 10-6:30

Trump Tower (Fifth Ave at 57th St)
759-1110
Mon-Sat: 10-6

Trump Plaza
1048 Third Ave (at 62nd St)
308-3000
Mon-Sat: 10-7

This is one of the number-one men's boutiques in the city—or anywhere, for that matter. The customer is emperor here, and what an empire he has! Napoleon has only the finest in haberdashery. The style is set by modern Italian designers; there's an extensive (and exclusive) line by Ermenegildo Zegna. Its superb quality and style are matched only by an incredibly personalized service that makes each person who enters the shop feel that he or she is someone special. Prices are in the if-you-have-to-ask-you-can't-afford-it class, but the merchandise and ambiance make them worthwhile. Napoleon-Josephine really does carry clothes fit for a king and his consort. Tell Denny I sent you.

PAN AM SPORTSWEAR AND MENSWEAR

50 Orchard St (at Grand St)
925-7032
Sun-Wed: 9:30-6; Thurs: 9:30-8:30; Fri: 9:30-3:30

With more stores like this, the Lower East Side could become synonymous with class as well as bargains. From the shiny glass windows (as opposed to the clutter of hangers that usually denotes an entrance) to the extremely fine stock, Pan Am is distinctive enough to be on Madison Avenue, except for its prices. They are nothing short of super! Adolfo, Armani, and Pierre Cardin are but a few of the names that adorn the racks in all their glory, but sans the excessive price tag (at least a third of the uptown price). What's more, styles are *au courant*; they often preview here first, and they're in classic good taste. There are no screaming purple parachute suits and no 1940s (or even last year's) lapels. Finally, the saleshelp are a major exception to the Lower East Side norm. They are prompt and courteous and, if anything, a little too quick to pounce on any customer who walks through the door. But at these prices, that's a minor annoyance. Besides, who ever heard of complaining of too much service on the Lower East Side?

PARKWAY NEW YORK

Astor Pl at Broadway
254-5449
Mon-Fri: 10-6; Sat: 10-5; Sun: 10-4

Parkway is where the best-dressed New Yorkers dress themselves. It carries every major brand, including Manhattan, Botany, and London Fog, at excellent prices, which already include sales tax. Quality is magnificent, and the styles are sometimes ahead of the department stores. Parkway is particularly noted for outerwear. The back of the store carries ladies' raincoats, primarily Misty Harbor. The discount there is about 30 percent.

PAUL STUART

Madison Ave at 45th St
682-0320
Mon-Fri: 8-6; Sat: 9-6

Paul Stuart is an elegant store, with elegant clothing for both men and women. Even the specialty—sportswear—is elegant, and Paul Stuart excels in a look that is at once casual and well dressed. A Paul Stuart customer never has the old-shirt-and-cut-off-blue-jeans look. The store claims to carry "all sizes with the exception of children's," but there is a scarcity at the extremes. The shirt, tie, slacks, and sports-jacket collections are particularly extensive. You'll find a good line of custom-made shirts as well. Although Paul Stuart does carry suits, the strong area in this store is the outerwear—sweaters, jackets, and the like. It's number one in the natural-shoulder league.

SAINT LAURIE
897 Broadway (at 20th St)
473-0100
Mon-Fri: 9-6; Thurs: 9-7:30; Sun: 12-5

Saint Laurie is an example of consumer power *par excellence*, proving that consumers who want top quality at low prices can get them when they demand it. A little history: Saint Laurie manufactures top-quality men's suits under its own and national brand names, and they are retailed from coast to coast. Some years ago, manufacturers in the area around Saint Laurie began to open their men's wear factories to the public. Prior to that time, few, if any, New Yorkers knew about this "men's wear garment district," but suddenly customers flocked to the area. Saint Laurie began to feel the pressure. At this point, Saint Laurie says that as an act of public service, it stopped selling retail in New York and opened its loft on a wholesale basis to the public. The more cynical view is that Saint Laurie's retail outlets did not like being undercut by the manufacturer so close to their own shops. The result was that Saint Laurie ceased selling to stores in New York; it now distributes its retail line entirely outside the city. Obviously, due to consumer pressure, they decided that business would be better if they relied solely on direct-to-the-public sales rather than wholesale trade in the city. Quality and selection (thousands and thousands of pieces) are superb, the more so because the entire business depends upon a satisfied customer. Sizes include 35 to 48, regular, short, long, and extra long. Saint Laurie also manufactures women's classic business suits. Made of 100 percent worsted wool, they're magnificent. This is a must stop for a man who only wants to go to one place to get a good suit or sports jacket at a reasonable price. Their new building now has a "living museum" demonstrating Saint Laurie's production of its clothing as well as a tour of the workrooms and an exhibit showing various suit styles over the years. Note: The tailor recommended by Saint Laurie (in their own building) is rude (he kept right on smoking after we asked him to stop) and disinterested. For tailoring, you can do much better elsewhere.

SAKS FIFTH AVENUE
611 Fifth Ave (bet 49th and 50th St)
753-4000
Mon-Wed, Fri, Sat: 10-6; Thurs: 10-8:30

Saks is one of New York's most elegant, classic stores and a personal favorite. Time is suspended here, and styles, while modish, are also classical. Saks is somewhat different from conventional department stores (although the style is spreading of late) in that it has almost autonomous departments, and there are sections within departments. Such departments as gifts, linens, and luggage, are actually located in separate stores that are often adjacent to the main store and accessible by street or by a circuitous route through the store. Men's wear is located on the sixth floor. In each section, only top-quality merchandise is sold, and the selection, personnel, and atmosphere are of an equally high level. No one in New York, with the possible exception of Barney's, has a better selection of quality suits and sports jackets for men. The tailor shop is excellent, and the fitters are among New York's best. This is undoubtedly New York's finest men's clothing operation in a department store. The selection is enormous, the fashions current, and the taste impeccable. The help are unusually professional, but if you want someone who will go that extra step for you, ask for Dennis Weiner. He's knowledgeable, courteous, not pushy, and a good friend.

TOBALDI VOMO
83 Rivington St (at Orchard St)
260-4330
Sun-Fri: 9-6

At opposite corners from Veetal, Tobaldi does for the male what the latter does for the female. Here, too, the image is sleek, expensive, and elegant, at a Lower East Side discount. (Be warned: prices are still high.) Virtually all of the items are Italian imports. The store is not large, but the clientele they aim for expects a small, intimate setting, and they get it. The stock includes magnificent shirts (check out the linen ones, but don't overlook the silk; both are made for Tobaldi's own label), leather jackets (as in suede leather, *not* motorcycle chic), and magnificent Italian suits, slacks, and sports jackets. There probably isn't a more elegant store on Madison Avenue (or in Milan), and while the prices will set your budget back, they are the best for the best merchandise. While this clothing is sometimes obtainable uptown in the best stores, it is not available at a discount.

Men's Coats

EISENBERG AND EISENBERG
149 Fifth Ave (at 21st St, 11th floor)
674-0300
Mon-Wed, Fri: 9-6; Thurs: 9-7; Sat: 9-5; Sun: 10-4

The Eisenberg and Eisenberg style is a classic one that dates from 1898, the year they opened. Although Eisenberg and Eisenberg has a loft in the men's wear garment district, it consistently offers top quality and good prices on suits, coats, and sportswear. E. and E. also stocks outerwear, slacks, name-brand raincoats, pure cashmere sports jackets, and 100 percent silk jackets. All are sold at considerable discounts, and alterations are free. London Fog coats are featured here, and no label is better known for wet weather needs.

NORMAN LAWRENCE
417 Fifth Ave (at 38th St, suite 1116)
889-3119
Mon-Sat: 10-4

The buzz about Norman Lawrence started years ago when he was known as Lawrence of London and specialized in ultrastylish rainwear at prices that, while still in the range of hundreds of dollars, were incredibly less expensive than his more established counterparts. Today, this is still true. The men's line includes fur-lined raincoats, luxurious ultrasuede overcoats, and raincoats in all fabrics and sizes. Women's wear includes raincoats of ultrasuede and silk, for which Norman Lawrence is famous, and a 15½ ounce silk poplin raincoat. Also, there is the hooded "signature coat" in a variety of materials and borders, and a made-to-order department. Prices are 20 percent off retail at all times, and more at sale times. Norman himself is a super salesman and a charming guy.

Men's Dress Shirts

PENN GARDEN GRAND SHIRT CORPORATION
58 Orchard St (at Grand St)
431-8464

BASSIN MENSWEAR
450 Seventh Ave (at 34th St)
244-7976

G&G INTERNATIONAL
62 Orchard St (bet Grand and Hester St)
431-4530
Sun-Wed, Fri: 9-6; Thurs: 9-8

And you thought the Lower East Side pickle business was inbred! It's got nothing on the local men's haberdashery dynasties, and these stores are probably the most typical of the breed. (Their neighbor on Orchard Street, Pan Am, seems to be establishing a horizontal empire designed to clothe every member of the family.) Penn Garden isn't that extensive yet, but give them time. Currently, there are three stores (there may be more masquerading under yet other names) devoted to men's wear. Each considers itself a distinct entity, to the point that the people at Penn Garden will not tell you to go across the street to G&G if you can't find what you want with them. (Tell you? Ha! They won't even give out the others' phone numbers!) Taken separately, however, each store is a gem, and the saleshelp can be charming. Bassin's, at the edge of the garment center, is where the men in the ladies fashion industry go for their shirts. These men know clothing, fashion, and styling, and if they shop here, everyone could safely follow suit.

SEEWALDT AND BAUMAN

565 Fifth Ave (at 46th St, 11th floor)
682-3958
Mon-Fri: 9-5; closed middle two weeks of Aug

One of the granddaddies of the custom-made-shirt business, Seewaldt and Bauman has been here since 1921, when Stanley Seewaldt's father started making shirts for the grandfathers of some of today's customers. The same care and quality that served their ancestors now ensure the loyalty of the current generation. The small store is crammed full of a variety of materials in various stages of shirt-making. What space isn't filled with fabric is filled with filing cabinets, which carry a history of shirt styles and measurements dating back to the beginning of the firm. If any 1920s customer were to call in an order for a shirt, Seewaldt and Bauman could make it up without batting an eye. They might insist that the customer come in for a new fitting, but they do that for every order. A week of heavy suppers could change any man's measurements, and 50 years is bound to do even more. The most popular material is 100 percent preshrunk cotton. (Seewaldt preshrinks it himself.) Most orders are filled within four to six weeks.

SHIRT PLAZA

1375 Broadway (bet 37th and 38th St)
221-9344

36 W 40th St (near Fifth Ave)
221-1959

Mon-Fri: 9-6; Sat: 10-5

Men's shirt stores are ample in New York, but finding a shirt for an ample man is not so easy. Shirt Plaza—particularly the 40th Street Store—specializes in solving this large problem. All of the shirts are ready to wear, but as a specialty store, Shirt Plaza is able to garner the best of the field. Add to that the selection in large and tall sizes, and it's an excellent bet for men who haven't much choice elsewhere. The diversity of the selection in big sizes filters down to regular sizes as well.

VICTORY SHIRT COMPANY
345 Madison Ave (at 44th St)
687-6375
Mon-Fri: 9-6; Sat: 9:30-5
10 Maiden Lane (bet Broadway and Nassau St)
349-7111
Mon-Fri: 9-6
96 Orchard St (bet Delancey and Broome St)
677-2020
Sun-Thurs: 9-5; Fri: 9-4

Victory operates three shops in different parts of town with one goal in mind: selling shirts—their own—that are guaranteed to be equal to, but less expensive than, national brands. And if their ads (which show two seemingly identical shirts side by side) don't convince you, a personal visit for a more substantial comparison probably will. So, for off-the-rack men's shirts, Victory should be a first choice if labels don't mean much to you. Victory manufactures as well as retails shirts for men and women. They have the facilities to taper, shorten, lengthen, alter, or monogram any shirt to individual specifications. They will also special-order unusual sizes, but a shop whose stock includes sizes 14 x 32 and 18½ x 36 doesn't have much call for that service. They also carry 100 percent cotton shirts and silk ties, as well as some men's accessories. But their own shirts are the big drawing card, and periodic sales make their prices even better.

Men's Extra Tall/Large

IMPERIAL WEAR
48 W 48th St
719-0290
Mon-Wed, Fri, Sat: 9-6; Thurs: 9-8

Among New York's specialty shops, several are devoted exclusively to clothing in extra-large and extra-tall sizes. The salespeople at this one are well trained in the problems that large men usually encounter, and quality is not sacrificed in garments that require more material. It is this, perhaps, that has guaranteed Imperial its clientele *and* kept them returning. Many stores cater to big men, but having a captive audience causes some stores to relax in their standards. The many regular customers who return to Imperial again and again prove that this is not the case here. The new line of designer fashions for big men is also a major attraction.

Men's Formal Wear

JACK AND COMPANY FORMAL WEAR
128 E 86th St
722-4609
Mon-Fri: 10-7; Sat: 10-4; closed Sat in July and Aug

Jack's will rent and sell men's ready-to-wear formal wear. They carry an excellent selection of sizes (nearly all) and names (After Six, Lord West, and Palm Beach), and they have a good reputation for service. In sales or rentals, Jack's can supply head-to-toe formal wear. The people here are excellent at matching outfits to customers, as well as knowing exactly what is socially required for any occasion.

Men's Furs

BROTHERS II
333 Seventh Ave (third floor)
695-8469
Mon-Fri: 9-6; Sat: 10-4

The thoroughly professional atmosphere and showroomlike inventory belie the fact that Brothers II really is what it tries so hard to appear to be: the best source for a man's fur coat at wholesale prices. The racks at Brothers II are shaggy with furs of all descriptions and in all sizes for both genders. Prices are wholesale but go up slightly if a garment has to be specially ordered. This shouldn't be necessary, though, since the off-the-rack selection is probably the most extensive and of the best quality in the city.

Men's Hats

FELTLY HATS
101 Delancey St (at Ludlow St)
473-1343
Daily: 9:30-5:30

Gene of Feltly boasts that the store carries every imported and domestic brand in hats and *almost* every size. Sizes range from 6½ inches to 7¾ inches; the styles range from golf caps to formal top hats. And everything is sold at discount prices. This is definitely one of the best places in town for men's hats.

JAY LORD HATTERS

30 W 39th St (bet Fifth and Sixth Ave)
221-8941
Mon-Fri: 10-6; Sat: 10-5; closed Sat in summer

One of the city's better ironies is that Burton Berinsky—who was the official photographer for the presidential campaign of Robert Kennedy (the brother of the president who did the most for the demise of the men's hat)—should end up proprietor of the only shop for custom-made men's hats in the city and possibly the nation. But the lack of competition does not diminish Jay Lord's quality. All of the hats—with the exception of the most formal top hats and the cloth caps—are made on the premises to fine exacting standards. Every possible style and color are available, and adjustments can be made on them. But if the brim isn't wide enough, the crown deep enough, or the size big enough, Jay Lord will custom-make it for the same under-$100 price that the ready-made ones go for. There is also an up-and-coming women's line; it started with the Annie Hall look and expanded from there. Nowadays, 25 percent of the business is devoted to feminine head styles. Whatever you're shopping for at Jay Lord's, be prepared for a lot of chatting with the friendly salesmen. Jay Lord also does a hefty business in hat renovation. As a sideline to that sideline, lesser repairs are also attempted, such as changing brims, primping feathers, and the general sprucing up of headgear.

KOREANA TRADING

43 W 29th St (near Broadway)
679-0420
Mon-Sat: 8-6; first Sun of month: 10-5

English is not the main mode of expression here, and small purchases are not welcomed with open arms, but if you have ready cash and the ability to express yourself in pantomime, Koreana Trading will sell you quality hats and gloves with courtesy and at prices not found at more conventional establishments. Koreana carries an excellent line of hats and gloves in leather and wool. They appear to be primarily an importing and distributing company, and they pass the wholesale price along to the retail customer with no loss of quality.

VAN DYCK HATTERS

90 Greenwich Ave
929-5696
Mon-Fri: 9-5:30; Sat: 10-4

The quintessential hatter, Van Dyck is the first choice for anything that has to do with men's hats in New York. Since 1940, Van Dyck has been known for the quality of its own brand, which it manufactures and sells. Prices and quality can't be beat, but should you not trust its brand (New Yorkers do), Van Dyck also discounts

Stetson and Borsalino hats at a minimum of 25 percent. No matter what the brand, Van Dyck can also clean, block, restyle, or reband any hat brought in, but they no longer "renovate" them.

YOUNG'S HATS
139 Nassau St
964-5693
Mon-Fri: 9-5:30; Sat: 10-3; closed Sat in summer

This small corner store in the City Hall area is unknown to tourists, but a mecca for savvy locals who know that Young's is a direct outlet for Stetson and Dobb hats. It isn't every store that boasts a selection of 10-gallon hats. Young's does, along with the usual varieties, and one whole wall is devoted to sporting caps. That is no small accomplishment, considering wall space is at such a premium that most of the stock is packed away. Indeed, Young's was able to offer a selection for a 7⁵/₈ inch head when few in the city could.

Men's Sport Shirts

HOWRON SPORTSWEAR
295 Grand St (bet Eldridge and Allen St)
226-4307
Sun-Fri: 9-5

Within a one-week period, three friends mentioned Howron, which was rather amazing since no one had ever mentioned this store to me before; in fact, it hadn't been in existence all that long. Howron was transformed from a typical Lower East Side shop into a fashionable boutique without sacrificing Lower East Side prices. My three friends were extolling Howron's virtues because of the store's Act III clothing for women, sport shirts for men, and an excellent collection of Spanish leather coats for both sexes. Howron also manages to carry Damon, Lee's, Stanley Blacker, and other top-notch men's and ladies' sportswear at almost laughable prices. Outfits can be put together for half their uptown cost and at prices that would purchase a much cheaper quality elsewhere. Add to all of this the fact that the saleshelp here are decidedly *not* Lower East Side caliber, and you see why Howron is a real find.

Men's Ties

COUNTESS MARA
110 E 57th St (near Park Ave)
751-5322
Mon-Fri: 9:30-5

Countess Mara is a men's store with a woman's name and a lady retail manager, Jessica Bennett. For the most part, it offers men's accessories: "Ties, shirts, robes, belts, etc., and all high class," says Bennett. (Their ties are world renown.) A word must be said about the saleshelp; they are excellent. The fact that they are extremely knowledgeable, helpful, and capable makes shopping here a good experience, even for men who hate to shop and women who don't know what they are shopping for. I know a senior citizen who wears smoking jackets the way most people wear sweaters (Peter Pushbottom did not convert him). The last smoking jacket he purchased was in 1947, and he hadn't been able to find one since. Countess Mara had them. There wasn't a large selection, but it was infinitely better than that of other stores. Not that Countess Mara deals in antique clothing. It doesn't: the stock is modern and sleek. But most of all, the clothing is comfortable, and a man can feel at ease, knowing that he is well dressed. Besides that, no tie ties better—or hangs better—than one from Countess Mara.

HERITAGE NECKWEAR
194 Allen St (at Houston St)
673-2570
Mon-Fri: 10-4:30; closed July 1-Aug 10

Richard Guerreiro took over what was one of my favorite stores in the city and made it even better. In the old days, the shop was dark, dank, and dirty. Nowadays, it positively gleams, and it is a joy to shop here. What enhances this joy is that Guerreiro considers himself a consumer and a comparison shopper. So he frequently scouts the department stores and specialty shops to make sure that his prices are at least 50 percent less. How does he do it? For starters, Heritage imports and/or manufactures the ties that are exclusively all silk; many are even handmade. It also helps that the overhead is low and that Guerreiro wholesales his items to the very stores he comparison-shops. The prices for pure silk ties at Heritage are at least half of those elsewhere. And they are magnificent. Guerreiro has rejuvenated what was already a fine shop.

Men's Underwear

UNDER WARES
1098 Third Ave (bet 64th and 65th St)
535-6006
Mon, Thurs: 10-9; Tues, Wed, Fri: 10-6:30;
Sat: 10-6; Sun: 12-5

Until quite recently, men's underwear was the stuff of slapstick comics, and the average man not only couldn't tell you what kind of underwear he wore, he probably didn't buy it himself or remember when or where it was purchased. All that changed when Calvin Klein came out with men's underwear that was snapped up by women for personal use, and it was abetted by Jim Palmer and other jocks' ads. These days a man's underwear is the basis of his fashion wardrobe. So it was probably inevitable that some bright soul would come up with a fashionable shop for fashionable underwear, and Ron Lee did. His Under Wares offers over 40 styles of briefs and boxer shorts. Purists who claim that briefs and shorts are by definition the two styles of bottom undergarments, will discover that Lee expands on those styles with variations in fabric (cottons and, yes, silk), colors, prints, and special designs. (Skintight pants get skintight briefs, pleated pants get pleated boxers, etc.) T-shirts are similarly represented. There are sleeveless, short sleeve, and hand-painted ones, and of course, there's hosiery and gift items. Lee's favorites are the "New York" boxer shorts. They make a great gift.

Men's Western Wear

BILLY MARTIN'S
812 Madison Ave (at 68th St)
861-3100
Mon-Sat: 10-6

In the event that you are one of the few who has no idea what the name Billy Martin means in New York, you are also one of the few who doesn't know why this store needs no further introduction. But even if you *do* know who Billy Martin is, it would not explain how the once-and-future manager of the New York Yankees ended up marketing Western wear on Madison Avenue. (He started with a store around the corner on 69th Street.) Well, even baseball managers have to do something in the off season, and apparently this is what Billy Martin does. His shop is crowded with all kinds of authentic Western wear. The walls are lined with buckskin and leather jackets. Bandanas drape the chairs, and cowboy hats are stacked on the floor. They must be made for well-paid cowboys, though, because these duds are well tooled, beautifully designed, and expensive. There are also such contemporary items as leather jackets, fur coats and hats, coyote parkas, and one of the best collections of boots (for men and women) in the city. And don't overlook (hard as it might be) the jewelry, including earrings, silver and exotic gemstone buckles and belt straps. As a source for Western wear, Billy Martin is a must. As a manager, well . . . a guy from Oregon shouldn't venture an opinion on that!

Men's and Women's Coats and Suits—Custom-Made

OTTO PERL
26 E 64th St (near Madison Ave)
838-8519
Mon-Fri: 8:30-5:30; Sat: 9-2
Closed Sat in summer; closed Aug

Otto and Susanne Perl cater to women who like the functional, highly fashionable tailored look that suits create. Although they can copy almost any kind of garment, the Perls are known for their coats, two-, three-, or four-piece suits, and mix-and-match combinations. Usually, this look is favored by busy executives, artists, or journalists who have to look very well dressed and haven't the time to spend hours dressing. Perl creates blazers (or suits) in a range of 2,000 different fabrics, but those in suede, leather, or a solid virgin wool are sensational. In addition to the women's garments, the Perls can design and create coats and suits for men, in the same broad range of fabrics. They promise fast service, expert tailoring, and moderate prices on everything they do.

Men's and Women's—General

BURBERRYS
9 E 57th St
371-5010
Mon-Wed, Fri, Sat: 9:30-6; Thurs: 9:30-7

Burberry's opened this four-storied shop on 57th Street late in 1978. Once inside, you could swear you were in the original London store. The mood is, in part, created by $600,000 worth of imported furnishings that Burberry's shipped from London. And the clothing styles are strictly British, to boot. The first two floors are dedicated exclusively to men's wear. The sizes range from extra short to extra long, and the store carries almost anything but socks. There are overcoats, topcoats, trenchcoats, raincoats, slacks, knitwear, sweaters, ties, scarves (a famous trademark in the Burberry plaid), and a new addition—luggage. Scotch House for ladies, on the third floor, is a temple of tartan and Scotch plaids, available in every possible style. (There is a similar section for men downstairs.) If you can't find the configuration you want, the fabric is sold by the yard. Women's wear, on the fourth floor, carries a parallel line to the men's wear. There are overcoats, trenchcoats, shirts, blouses, suits, and sportswear all with the British look.

CHARIVARI FOR MEN
2339 Broadway (at 85th St)
873-7242

CHARIVARI FOR WOMEN
2307 Broadway (bet 83rd and 84th St)
873-1424

CHARIVARI SPORT
2345 Broadway (at 85th St)
799-8650

CHARIVARI 72
257 Columbus Ave (at 72nd St)
787-7252

CHARIVARI WORKSHOP
441 Columbus Ave (at 80th St)
496-8700

CHARIVARI 57
18 W 57th St
Mon-Wed, Fri: 10:30-7; Thurs: 10:30-8; Sat: 10-6

When Selma Weiser opened the first Charivari (58 W 72nd St) over 18 years ago, no one—not even Weiser—envisioned that Charivari would spawn so many other stores, culminating in a mini-emporium with a showcase on 57th Street. But it has happened. And Charivari's success is the furthest thing from blind luck, since every bit of that success is due to Selma and her son Jon's hard work. Each store has a specialty, but all cater to a specific image—a modern, swinging, affluent, and sports-oriented lifestyle. The original store (58 W 72nd St) carries both men's and women's wear and still seems the most genuine Charivari. Everything from the *loud* music to the costumed salespeople (they don't know it) speaks attitude. Designer names abound, and no one checks prices. Sportier clothing, but no less posh, can be had at Charivari Sport. The Charivari Workshop is far from the usual work-clothes image, offering ultramodern designs from all over the world, with a particular emphasis on Japanese styles. The new Charivari on 57th Street is the culmination of all the other shops. There are exclusive selections from the rest of the shops, and it is all highlighted in an unattractive Japanese-designed shop (by architect Shigeru Uchida), featuring a Yohji Yamamoto boutique on the top floor of six floors of clothing from around the world. As a merchandising showcase, it is a disaster, in my opinion. Charivari summed up? It's unique. And keep an eye peeled. There are at least two other stores scheduled to open in the future.

CHASERIE SOHO

337A W Broadway (at Grand St)
219-1010
Sun-Thurs: 12-6; Fri, Sat: 12-7

If the high-fashion SoHo look is what you want but you haven't the confidence to carry it off, then Chaserie is the place for you. Owner Teresa Hyland believes that what her shop sells best is a sense of style, and cultivating customer confidence is her primary goal. So while her accessories are known for being the most unique in SoHo—and the duplex store is spectacular from an architectural standpoint—the real drawing card is exactly what Ms. Hyland says it is: the ability to help customers cultivate their own fashion statements, mostly in sportswear. To that end, Chaserie encourages new talented designers and showcases their work. The result is that the shop's customers are privy to bright unknown names, while wearing unique statement-making clothing that is in perfect taste. That image can be peeked at in *New York, Talk, The Village Voice,* and other magazines, where Chaserie has been known to style the fashion layouts. The personal Chaserie touch is available at the store.

DEALS

81 Worth St (bet Broadway and Church St)
966-0214
Mon-Wed, Fri: 8:30-6; Thurs: 8:30-8; Sat: 9-6; Sun: 10-5
142 W 72nd St (bet Broadway and Columbus Ave)
873-0790
Daily: 10-7

The frugal Brooks Brothers man or woman should check out the deal at Deals. While the emphasis is on traditional styles, the prices are anything but traditional. The smallish shops manage to stock shirts, pants, skirts, dresses, sweaters, sportswear, accessories, and shoes for men and women, and all of it is sold at 50 percent off regular price. And if that isn't enough, traditional doesn't mean staid here. Deals leans toward natural fibers and exalts designer, or if need be, brand names. Nothing sold is "off" in terms of style, quality, brand, or season. Deals is also very patriotic; each holiday brings a sale with even bigger reductions. All of which makes Deals a real find, and one of the few places where both men and women can do well.

MATSUDA NICOLE TOKYO

854 Madison Ave — 461 Park Ave
988-9514 — 935-6969
Mon-Sat: 10-6

Leave it to the Japanese to take the Madison Avenue boutique concept and do it one better. In this case, the boutique sells all kinds of clothing for men and women that's made in Japan. The styles are both traditional Japanese and contemporary international. But all of it reflects the Japanese eye for excellent quality and workmanship. Prices, given the Madison Avenue location, are not astronomical, and the styles are unique and interesting.

Outerwear—Family

DOWN IN THE VILLAGE

652 Broadway (at Bleecker St)
260-2330
Mon-Sat: 10-6; Sun: noon-5

For the name alone, this establishment is worthy of an award, but the store has even more going for it than that. As one of the best sources for down products in the city, they have a mastery of the field that is definitely unrivaled. Though Down in the Village sells winter outerwear (in sizes ranging from toddler to XXL) all year long, the store must be seen during its prime season, October to December, when there are an infinite number of down garments on display and an equal number available upon order. If you've ever tried to park a down coat in a cloakroom, you can imagine what this store looks like. But it's not all coats. There are accessories and "thinsulate" garments as well. Down in the Village even carries comforters, hats, vests, and an assortment of garments it's hard to believe actually do come in down.

HOUSE OF LODEN

155 W 72nd St (bet Broadway and Columbus Ave, fifth floor)
362-7443
Mon-Fri: 11-6 by appointment only
(may be closed in summer)

Getting in here was one of the most difficult experiences we encountered. English is at a premium; common courtesy and information are even scarcer. But it's worth the effort, because for some unfathomable reason, the original Loden coat's Austrian manufacturers decided to open a direct outlet in Manhattan—sort of. If you can figure out when they are open and snag an "appointment," you will be treated to a room full of the finest Austrian Lodenwool coats, car coats, wools, and capes for men and women. This outlet will custom-order exact sizes, fabrics, and designs. Better still, there is an incredible in-stock selection in sizes and designs. In a city where the top department and specialty stores have a very limited selection of the Loden coat, this is amazing and makes the hassle worth it. But remember, one way or another, a Loden coat will cost you—in either dignity or price.

MORLAND'S OF ENGLAND
1168 First Ave (at 64th St)
737-3443
Mon-Fri: 10-7; Sat: 10-6; Sun: 1-5

Morland's is known for its fine collection of sheepskin outerwear, but that isn't the only reason to shop here. They are an all-around winter-clothing store, with footwear, hats, boots, gloves, wool items, and sweaters. The latter collection is particularly outstanding. Morland's has exclusive distribution rights to Icelandic wool sweaters in many styles and designs, all of them show-stoppers. But first and foremost is the sheepskin. It comes in a huge selection of styles. And in terms of warmth, it's super.

Shoes—Children's

H&J SHOES
131 Orchard St
982-0840
Daily: 9-5

PECK AND CHASE
163 Orchard St
674-8860
Daily: 9-5:30

JULES HARVEY
132 Orchard St
475-4875
Daily: 9-5:30

These three stores have always had a reputation for discounting sneakers and casual shoes for the entire family, with an emphasis on children's shoes. All three stores are run much the same; the only reason to choose one over the other is to find the one you can squeeze into. The stores' proprietors don't seem to care which store you patronize, since all three are owned by the same people. It's as complicated and in-bred as the Lower East Side pickle and haberdashery businesses. Harvey Chase and Jules Peck are two real people. Combine their names in various forms, and you come out with H&J, Jules Harvey, and Peck and Chase. All three stores now offer 10 to 20 percent off on Adidas, Nike, Puma, Converse, and Pro-Keds adult athletic shoes. So join the crowds at any of the three stores. The prices are good.

RICHIE'S DISCOUNT CHILDREN'S SHOES
183 Avenue B (bet 11th and 12th St)
228-5442
Mon, Tues, Thurs-Sat: 10-5; Sun: 10-3

There is no sign on the building, and it's difficult to distinguish anything amid the dirty and boarded-up windows on the block, but if you can spot a window displaying shoes next to a movie marquee, Richie's will offer an experience your children's feet will never duplicate. Inside, the décor is probably as old as the surrounding environment outside, but the stock includes the very latest shoes, at a fraction of the prices anywhere else. Brands include Stride Rite, Blue Star, Jumping Jacks, and Keds sneakers, and the clincher is that the fit will be extraordinary. An inordinate amount of time is spent on each customer, and for each time a pair of shoes has been sold here, a pair has also *not* been sold. Reasons for the latter include the customer's being told that the child's old ones are still good. (Has that ever happened elsewhere?) Salesmen have even admitted that the quality desired just wasn't in stock or that Richie's would not sell a lesser quality to a customer. So, the drawback? The neighborhood. Though it is only two blocks from Stuyvesant Town, it is really bad. The filth alone is not something children should be exposed to. Gentrification hasn't quite reached this block of the East Village.

Shoes—Family

ALYS HUT II
85 Hester St (at Orchard St)
226-5555, 226-5475
Sun-Fri: 10-5; summer: Sun-Fri: 9:30-5:30

Aly's applies the East Side discount fashion code to shoes, boots, handbags, and men's imported footwear. They claim that there's always at least 20 percent off, more often it's 50 percent off, and at end-of-season sales, prices are slashed even further. And that discount goes for such shoe labels as Jacques Cohen, Golo, and Sandler of Boston to name but a few. The men's collection is even more exclusive since it relies entirely upon imports. And don't overlook the handbags. They're pretty special, too. Actually, though, it's hard to overlook anything since Aly's attitude, as exemplified by Mr. Pumilia, is "This is the best, and it's about time you discovered that fact."

LEACH-KALE
1261 Broadway (at 31st St, suite 815-816)
683-0571
Mon-Fri: 9-5

While some custom shoe craftsmen are determined to prove that their product can (and should be) owned by every man, Andre S. Feuerman of the Leach-Kale Company is not among them. Perhaps he has been burned too many times by the bargain hunter who thought that the gap between a high-class shoe salon's product and Leach-Kale's couldn't be as great as it is, or by customers who, prepared to shell out money, think at that price the shoe should cure all their orthopedic problems for life. Feuerman is careful to point out that this is not the case. The business has customers who have been loyal patrons for 25 to 30 years (Joan Crawford was one), and these are the people Feuerman would rather court. They have neither unrealistic expectations nor impossible dreams, but appreciate the quality item that Leach-Kale produces. Leach-Kale specializes in orthopedic work, which is probably why many of their customers come here and pay the price without batting an eye. They have no choice. Surprisingly, especially since Feuerman insists that "We are not a bargain-basement-type operation," prices are among the best in town. Shoes start at about $500 for the first pair, but some first orders, and all subsequent orders, can be substantially less. Still, this is not the spot to visit with an eye on the tab. A paradox, to be sure: this may be the cheapest such place in town, but they don't know it, don't want to know it, and you shouldn't let on that you know it, either. Just sail in like money is no object.

LESLIE'S BOOTERY

36 Orchard St
65 Orchard St
431-8556 (men's); 431-9196 (women's)
Sun-Thurs: 9:30-5:30; Fri: 9:30-4:30

Leslie's was recommended to me as a place to get top-brand designer shoes at a steady discount of 20 percent. At first glance, the women's shop doesn't seem to have much more than rather loud disco music and a few shoes on display, so I was sure that the information was wrong. A closer check, though, showed that there wasn't a shoe of less than designer status. Calvin Klein was but one of the names I saw, and prices were indeed 20 percent off and more. Leslie's is not the place for walking or "grandmother" shoes, but it should be number one on your list if you're into designer footwear. Prices for Leslie's shoes are comparable to department store prices for shoes of less distinguished origin. The men's store offers similar quality and prices in a somewhat better setting. Almost all the shoes are on display by brand name, and the selection is equally impressive in both quality and price. This store also carries lesser status, more functional women's shoes.

LORD JOHN BOOTERY

428 Third Ave (bet 29th and 30th St)
532-2579
Mon-Fri: 9:30-6:30; Sat: 9:30-5; closed Aug 10-20

John Kyriannis and three generations of his family have aimed to provide "quality and service first" for the 30-plus years they've operated Lord John Bootery. But despite the service (which is excellent) and the opportunity to see three generations working together *happily* under one roof, the real reason to shop here is their excellent selection of shoes and boots at some of the best prices in town. Although the ambiance of the shop doesn't reflect it, the quality of the footwear available is excellent. Dexter shoes and boots are discounted as a matter of course, as are Dan Post's. Both go for about 30 percent less than they do at spiffier shops. All of the footwear is of that quality. John calls it "dressy and/or imported." Snakeskin sandals are priced at less than $50 (that's for a pair!), as are evening shoes imported from Italy. The really smart Lord John patrons wait for the semiannual clearance sales, usually held in July and January.

MANUFACTURERS SHOE OUTLET
537 Broadway (bet Spring and Prince St)
966-4070
Mon-Fri: 8-6; Sat: 9-5; Sun: 10-5:30

The hours and phone number are nebulous, and the attitude is "go help yourself, don't bother me." But if a lack of amenities doesn't bother you, then run, don't walk, to this dirty store in SoHo. It carries a wide variety of shoes, slippers, hosiery, and socks, and the sizes range from infants' to large men's. And if that isn't inducement enough, there are such top brand names as Nunn Bush and Freeman sold at a discount. Finally, note the hours. If your son breaks a buckle at 8 a.m., or the heel falls off your shoes an hour before *the* business meeting, this is the place to go for a quick replacement at discount prices. They claim to keep these hours because "everyone else here does." Now you know another difference between SoHo and the Village!

PARADISE BOOTERY
1586 Broadway (bet 47th and 48th St)
974-9855
Mon-Sat: 10:30-7:30

Alex Kaufman supplies the shoes for almost every Broadway show, and that's probably how Elizabeth Taylor heard of him and why she ordered 12 pairs of the same shoe in different colors to augment her wardrobe. And she could have done the same thing for the current man in her life, because Kaufman custom-makes men's shoes as well. The prices are fabulous, and the workmanship is first quality. Paradise has custom-made shoes for less than $100, which is less than the department stores charge for some of their ready-made ones. There is also a large in-house stock that sells for less than half the custom-made rate. If you have difficulty with arithmetic, Kaufman's quality boots in stock sell for $30 a pair and up. The next time you leaf through a *Playbill,* check the wardrobe credits. Odds are you'll find Kaufman's or Paradise's name. Or you could just ask Liz!

SHOE CITY/SNEAKER CITY

133 Nassau St (at Beekman St)
732-3889
Mon-Fri: 8-6; Sat: 10-3

Shoe City (don't you like the name?) started as a place to get cut-rate, brand-name shoes for men. With such names as Bostonian, Dexter, Hanover, Herman, Massagic, Hush Puppies, and Timberland in good selection at excellent prices, it was no surprise that business was very good. So, Shoe City spawned Sneaker City, in the same building, with sneakers for the entire family and a smaller women's shoe department that offers the same quality and discounts for the distaff side. It's easy to do one-stop shopping here.

SUSAN BENNIS/WARREN EDWARDS

440 Park Ave (at 56th St)
755-4197
Mon-Fri: 10-6:30; Sat: 10-6

Once upon a time, Susan Bennis and Warren Edwards ran a very expensive, very exclusive shoe salon for men and women called Chelsea Cobbler. I was particulary struck by their Western-style boots, while their regular men's shoes and full line of women's footwear all boasted the same kid-leather softness, fine quality, and high-styled details. Several years later, they abandoned the footwear of others, renamed the shop after themselves, and devoted the entire store to creations designed by Bennis and Edwards and executed in their studio in Milan, Italy. The finished products grace the walls of their new New York store in an assortment of styles and materials that can only be called exotic and luxurious. Careful hand detail is given to all the work, and the materials used include nappa goat, antelope, wild boar, calf, iguana, python, and silk crepe de Chine. An affluent customer of any age can find an appealing shoe here.

TO BOOT

100 W 72nd St (at Columbus Ave)
724-8249
Mon-Fri: noon-8; Sat: 11-7; Sun: 1-6

Bergdorf Goodman
Fifth Ave at 57th St (second floor)
872-8883
Mon-Wed, Fri, Sat: 10-6; Thurs: 10-8

Tip the top of your 10-gallon hat to Al Martinez, who has to be one of New York's great mercantile geniuses. Martinez rode To Boot in from Texas to meet the Urban Cowboy fad of the Seventies by opening an authentic, genuine cowboy-boot store in the wilds of the Upper West Side. (Well, the Dakota is up there!). Detractors predicted that the craze wouldn't support To Boot, let alone the scores of imitators who hopped upon the wagon train, and they were right. But then, so was Martinez. To Boot spawned Clothes to Boot and then rustled up its own business by breaking into half a dozen successful sidelines. About the only thing all of the lines have in common with the traditional original showcasing of the top-of-the-line boots (such as those of Justin, Tony Lama, Dan Post, and Nocona) is that they are stylish, fashionable, and usually have some relationship to either footwear or western gear. And that fine sense of style is always evident.

T.O. DEY
509 Fifth Ave (at 43rd St)
682-4790
Mon-Fri: 9-5; Sat: 9-1

T.O. Dey is a fancy jack-of-all-trades operation. Though their specialty is custom-made shoes, they will also undertake any kind of repair on any kind of shoe. In fact, if you ask a New Yorker for the first name that comes to mind in custom-made shoes, odds are that the name will be T.O. Dey. They will create both men's and ladies' shoes, based on a plaster mold taken of the customer, and their styles are limited only by the customer's imagination. Probably because of the size of the operation. T.O. Dey's prices are slightly less than other custom boot-makers. They also do shoe repair, including difficult jobs that few others would undertake. (Perhaps because they deal with the project from start to finish, they are more familiar with remedies for shoe problems.) But they are not cheap. The attitude seems to be that the job should be done as thoroughly as possible, and naturally, that can be costly.

VOGEL BOOTS AND SHOES
19 Howard St (bet Broadway and Lafayette St)
925-2460
Mon-Fri: 8-4:30; Sat: 8-2
Closed Sat in summer and first two weeks of July

The Vogels—John, Hank, and Dean (who are the fourth generation to join this 100-year-old business)—happily fit and supply made-to-measure boots and shoes for any adult who can find the store. Howard is one of those streets that even native New Yorkers don't know exists. The many who *have* found it beat a path to the door for top-quality shoes and boots, personal advice, excellent fittings, and prices which, while not inexpensive, are reasonable for the service involved. The fit is not to be taken lightly, for made-to-measure shoes do *not* always fit properly. At Vogel, they do. Once you have a shoe pattern on record at Vogel, they will make up new shoes without a personal visit and ship anywhere. For top craftsmanship, this spot is top drawer. There are more than 600 Vogel dealers throughout the world, but this is the grandfather store, and the people here are super.

Shoes—Men's

ADLER SHOE SHOPS

6 E 46th St (at Fifth Ave)
687-8810
Mon-Sat: 9-6

Adler's is a chain of men's shoe stores in New York, featuring Weyenberg and Nunn-Bush brands. At this store, all of the rejects, unsalables (for whatever reason), and odd lots are sold at big reductions. Incidentally, after having checked out over 100 shoe stores, I still remember the staff here as having been exceptionally friendly and outstanding.

CHURCH ENGLISH SHOES

428 Madison Ave (at 49th St)
755-4313
Mon-Fri: 9-6; Sat: 9-5:30

Anglophiles have a ball here, not only because of the *veddy* British atmosphere, but for the pure artistry and Britishness of the shoes. Church has been selling British shoes for men since 1873, and since that date, it has been known for classic styles, superior workmanship, and fine leathers. The styles basically remain unchanged year after year, although one or two new designs are occasionally added as a concession to fashion. All are custom-fitted by shoe salesmen. If a style or size does not feel right, Church's will make up a customized special order at approximately $25 more than the regular price. The salesmen are superprofessional. Foot problems? This is the place for competent advice.

EGGERS AND SILK

102 Fulton St
227-0012
Mon-Fri: 9-5:30

The discount here during nonsale times is only 10 to 25 percent on men's shoes, but with the price of leather going up, every little bit helps. Eggers and Silk carries excellent brands of men's shoes. You'll find Bally, Freeman, Johnston and Murphy, and other shoes in current styles fitted correctly and well. Eggers and Silk also carries Church shoes at a 10 to 20 percent discount, which may well be the best part of the shop, since discounts of any kind on those shoes are hard to find. End-of-the-season sales make prices even better.

J. SHERMAN SHOES

121 Division St (bet Orchard and Ludlow St)
233-7898
Mon-Thurs: 8:30-4:30; Fri: 8:30-3; Sun: 8:30-4:30

Upholding the Lower East Side tradition, J. Sherman has excellent prices on its merchandise. But its shoes are nothing less than top-of-the-line quality. So here's the place to pick up Bally, Bruno Magli, Sandro, Moscoloni, French Shriner, Freeman, Paolo Terracini, Dexter, Bass, Zodiac, Timberland, Frye, Giorgio, Brutini, and other brand-name shoes for 20 to 60 percent off list price. J. Sherman claims they have the best buys on brand-name shoes in the city. They may be right.

STAPLETON SHOE COMPANY
68 Trinity Pl (at Rector St)
964-6329
Mon-Fri: 8-6

Their motto is "better shoes for less," but that doesn't begin to cover the superlatives that Stapleton deserves. Gather around, gentlemen, because here is the place to get Bally and a slew of other top shoe names at a discount. Stapleton is located on the same block as the Amex (American Stock Exchange). With the money saved here, there's enough left over to take a flyer in the stock market. There probably isn't a better source for quality shoes anywhere. And that's a free tip on the market!

Shoes—Women's

ANBAR SHOES
93 Reade St (bet Church and W Broadway)
227-0253
Mon-Fri: 8-5:30; Sat: 11-5; closed Sat in July and Aug

You can't judge a shoe store by its décor. As long as you walk out wearing the best shoe for your money, who cares what the store's windows look like? Certainly not the people at Anbar, who just may offer the best shoes in town for the best prices. Anbar, the fashionable sister to Shoe Steal, is the place to find top labels at prices that do not exceed $65. Those who never pay $65 for a pair of shoes may not be overly impressed by that statement, but perhaps the fact that people have paid more than two and three times that amount uptown makes Anbar more impressive. Names like Charles Jourdan, Ferragamo, Hernandez, Garolini, and Allure also make Anbar impressive. Prices for these brands and others are always discounted, often as much as 50 percent. Overlook the grubby décor. Anbar is a gold mine.

GIORDANO'S SHOES
1118 First Ave (at 61st St)
688-7195
Mon-Fri: 11-7; Sat: 11-6; Sun: 12-4

Susan Giordano has a very special clientele. In fact, if you're a woman whose shoe size is larger than 6½, you can't imagine how important this store is. On the other hand, if you're a woman with a shoe size in the $3^1/_2$ to $6^1/_2$ range, you have just justified the price of this book. Giordano stocks a fine selection in a tiny range of tiny sizes of women's shoes. While there are women with smaller sizes still, Giordano's range is nonexistent in regular shoe stores. (Occasionally 5Bs, a sample size, can be found in closeout shops.) Most women in this category shop in the children's shoe departments or have shoes custom-made, either of which can cramp your style. For these women, Giordano's is a godsend.

LACE UP SHOE SHOP
110 Orchard St (at Delancey St)
475-8040
Sun-Fri: 9-5:30

For years, Lace Up was an upstairs appendage to Fine and Klein. Today, however, the demand is such that Lace Up has come into its own. It has moved to the corner of Orchard and Delancey Streets; if you can't find *that* address, just look for a crowd of well-dressed women. Lace Up's stock features the best designer styles at the very best prices: Joan and David, Anne Klein, Bandolino, Charles Jourdan, Alberto D. Molina, and Yves St Laurent, among others. All shoes are discounted, and ultrafashionable pairs unavailable anywhere else can be found at Lace Up often in season. Discounts start at 15 percent.

MAUD FRIZON
49 E 57th St (near Park Ave)
980-1460
Mon-Sat: 10-6

This tiny shop is not for the faint of heart—or wallet. But if you have what it takes, you shouldn't miss it. Maud Frizon (who is a real person, alive and well and living in Paris) believes in quality and fashion. Her shoes, handmade in Venice, are personally designed for style and comfort. Her shops are located in places like Cannes, Paris, Milano—you get the idea. If you simply have to have the suede ("*Not* ultrasuede; we never use that," said the saleswoman), two-toned shoes with matching leather laces, they are available on the spot. But if the purple kid-leather boots would suit you better in a beige over-the-knee style, that can be arranged, too. In fact, almost anything Maud Frizon designs can be custom-made. Styles include both day and evening wear for men and women. This is not a store for mere window shopping, but if you want to own a truly beautiful shoe, Maud Frizon is the place to find it. You'll appreciate the unusual shoes and boots for men, as well. Maud Frizon shoes can also be found at several major specialty and department stores, such as Bergdorf's, Barney's, and Bloomingdales'.

PETER FOX SHOES

105 Thompson St (bet Prince and Spring St)
431-6359
Daily: noon-7

Peter Fox is the downtown trailblazer for women's shoes. Everything sold in the shop is exclusive, limited-edition designer footwear. Perhaps because of the store's location, Fox designs seem more adventurous than its uptown competitors, but then, no one ever accused Maud Frizon or Susan Bennis/ Warren Edwards of being staid. However, the look seems younger and more casual here than it does with other designers. For those looking for shoes to be seen in, Tanya Fox is the lady to see.

S & T SHOES

1405 Second Ave (at 73rd St)
861-9470
Mon, Tues, Thurs, Fri: 10-7; Wed, Sat: 10-6; Sun: 1-5:30
1043 Lexington Ave (at 75th St)
988-0722
Mon-Sat: 11-6

S&T is short on ambiance (unless ambiance includes dust, dirt, grime, and do-it-yourself sizing) but makes up for it with sensational prices on top designer and brand-name shoes. This bargain-basement company has some of New York's best shoe bargains for women, and at sale time it seems like the whole city is crowding into the store to cop the bargains. But it's well worth it. While S&T carries cheap yet stunning shoes, they're also offering them in unheard-of 4-narrow to 10-wide sizes—even AA to C widths. Many of their customers would pay any amount of money anywhere for a shoe that fits. Here they can find them in style, fashion, and comfort at a great price. The store on Lexington Avenue carries children's shoes at the same discount, but since the children's shoes are not designer styles, it's not so hectic there. Thank goodness. S&T's less-than-genteel atmosphere during the week before school starts would be intolerable.

SOLE OF ITALY

119 Orchard St (at Delancey St)
674-2662
Sun-Fri: 9:30-6

Sole of Italy is the soul mate to Fine and Klein, and it is fittingly located above the latter store. Fine and Klein carries classy handbags and attaché cases, and Sole of Italy offers the perfect complement in footwear. The selection is limited to those labels sold in the finest boutiques; the collection of so many brands and sizes in one spot is awesome. The Fine and Klein (or Lower East Side) discount policy also applies here, which makes Sole of Italy a contender as the sole source for fashionable footwear. Some name dropping is in order: Adige, Pierre Balmain, Jacques Cohen, Collette, Courreges, Caiman Mode, Xavier Danand, Delman, Charles Jourdan, Ted Lapidus, Madame Gres, Vitto Latvada, Menin, and J. B. Martin are just a few of the labels Sole of Italy carries. There are few places to find them all under one roof and virtually none that discounts them all.

TALL SIZE SHOES
3 W 35th St (at Fifth Ave)
736-2060
Mon-Wed, Fri, Sat: 9:30-6; Thurs: 9:30-7

Even with a captive market, Tall Size Shoes acts as if they are trying to match the competition on the next block. Their service is super, the saleshelp polite, and the selection outstanding. Of course, it's only the latter that interests you, if you're a woman who has a 9½ to 15 (yes, 15) shoe size, or a quadruple A to triple E width. Sizes like that usually only appear in the crossword puzzles, but here's a place that offers a selection in those sizes. Incidentally, this and the small-sizes shoe shops are the most requested names in this section. I guess that if you're unable to find suitable shoes on the rack, you can get pretty desperate. But the people here don't act as if they know that. Don't tell them!

Sporting Wear

FINALS
149 Mercer St (bet Houston and Prince St)
431-1414, 800-431-9111
Mon-Sat: 10-5:30; Sun: 11-5

This is the case of a catalog having a store rather than the other way around. For the last eight years, Finals has published a catalog offering competition swim and running wear to schools, clubs, and YMCAs across the country. In that time, they have garnered 75 percent of the market, in part because no one could match their "factory direct" prices and in part because a majority of the customers were located far from other sources for that equipment. After all, there aren't a lot of variations in a lycra competition bathing suit. Yet Finals offers it in pinstripe, solid, and accented colors, when it would be hard to find one at all elsewhere—not to mention coming up with enough to outfit an entire team. The business operated out of New York, and it finally decided to open an outlet store in SoHo. Prices are the same as those in the catalog, but they are so sensational that visitors should not feel that the only savings are the cost of postage and handling. An added fillip is the chance to comb through whatever outdated, discarded, or noncatalog merchandise might be around. But it's really not necessary, when you can get the finest apparel at true factory prices.

PLAYING FIELD
955 Third Ave (at 57th St)
One Herald Square (at Herald Center, fifth floor)
421-0003, 421-0005
Mon-Wed, Fri, Sat: 10-6; Thurs: 10-8; Sun: noon-6

The Playing Field offers sports enthusiasts and fans the chance to dress up and play in the real thing. Their jerseys, uniforms, and professional sports apparel are indistinguishable from that of the pro teams because they are the exact garments that the players wear on the field. The official brand names of the major league teams are sold in a variety of sizes and colors, and every professional sport is well represented. Those who wish to draft their wardrobe from a variety of sports can look like Pele (pre-retirement) one day and Reggie Jackson the next, thanks to the Playing Field. And best of all, since the professional stuff has been tested on the hard turf, amateur players are assured of the best selection of gear with an eye toward durability. Tennis, anyone?

Sweaters—Men's and Women's

A. PETER PUSHBOTTOM
1157 Second Ave (bet 60th and 61st St)
879-2600
Mon-Sat: 11-7

The striking name implies an even more striking stock of sweaters for both men and women in all sizes. Stores that specialize in one particular item are, I think, pretty much indigenous to New York, and A. Peter Pushbottom is an example of a typical New York store. The merchandise is sweaters, in shetlands, cashmeres, cottons, and almost any other weave imaginable. They come in small, medium, and large in women's sizes. Men's sizes come in small, medium, large, and extra large. They come as pullovers, cardigans, cowls, coats, vests, and almost any imaginable style in between. What is really sold here is the *idea* of sweaters. After a visit, it suddenly seems as if everyone is wearing sweaters, and A. Peter Pushbottom sweaters at that. Their sweaters are fantastic, and the prices the more so. The fact that Pushbottom manufactures its own sweaters is reflected in the prices. Look what a sweater did for Dan Rather.

GWEN BYRNE

23 Eighth Ave
924-3232
Mon-Sat: 11-6

Gwen Byrne came from South Africa 12 years ago, just in time for Perry Ellis and others to take sweaters out of the drawer where mothers put them and onto the backs of *haute couture* models. An avid knitter, she applauded this trend, but was less than enthralled with the *haute couture* prices. So, she opened a yarn gallery in the Village and began to dispense and sell yarn, knitting needles, and knitting instructions. Whether it was the fashion mood or the energy shortage, it was an instant success. "Surprisingly," says Gwen, "over half my customers are men. And straight men at that." But there are still those among us who will never wield a needle, so Byrne will do the knitting for us. There are dozens of samples around the room, and they are used to custom-create sweaters ordered by individual customers. Each is hand-knit by either Byrne or a carefully screened knitter. The prices for these are not low (we're talking hundreds of dollars), but it will make you rue the day you refused to learn to knit and/or threw out Aunt Minnie's birthday sweater. You'll also have a unique garment. Maybe that's what all those men realized—making your own is a tremendous bargain!

SWING LOW

1187 Second Ave (bet 62nd and 63rd St)
838-3314
Mon-Wed: 11-8; Fri, Sat: 11-7; Thurs: 11-9; Sun: 1-6

Swing Low takes its name from the hammocks that hang from the rafters of the shop (and which they occasionally sell), but it makes its profits from imported ethnic handcrafts. The stars of the show are the shawls, sweaters, and ponchos—primarily those from Ecuador and Bolivia—that are made of alpaca or wool and come in a rainbow of colors. Rounding out the limited collection are imported blouses, tunics, jewelry, sweater coats, woven shoulder bags, vests, and shirts for the whole family. Swing Low is as well known for its sales as its in-depth but limited stock. The two big sales are usually held well out of season (around Thanksgiving and Easter), but the prices are well worth waiting for. To be more accurate, the prices are so good that it's worth shoving through the mobs of loyal fans. Swing Low is a super place at any time of the year, though. The colors are vivid, the quality great, the styles unique, and the attitude is totally exemplified by those Yucatan hammocks: swinging, easy, and relaxed. Sharon Garfunkel of Swing Low will also take orders for custom-made sweaters, which can be created within two weeks.

Thrift Shops

ENCORE

1132 Madison Ave (bet 84th and 85th St, upstairs)
879-2850
Mon-Sat: 10:30-6; Sun: 12:30-6; closed Sun from July to mid-Aug

There are thrift shops, and then there are thrift shops. Encore is so chic and select that it prefers to be billed as a "resale shop of gently worn clothing," and when one sees the merchandise and the caliber of the clientele, Encore can be forgiven its conceit. For one thing, Encore is a consignment boutique, not a charity thrift shop. Its donors receive a portion of the sales price, and according to owner Carol Selig (who bought the store upon the death of Florence Barry, who founded the business 30 years ago), many of the donors are socialites and other luminaries who can't afford to be seen in the same outfit twice. So Selig can afford to be picky, and so can you. The fashions are up-to-date, and if Jackie O doesn't mind dropping off her better items here, why should a customer mind grabbing these top fashions at 50 to 70 percent off original retail prices? At any time, there are over 6,000 items in stock, and all of it sells. Prices range from reasonable to astronomical, but just think how much more they sold for originally! Encore may be the only way to go if you're going to appear on the pages of "W" four times in a week and want to look fresh each time. If the sheer savings don't appeal to you, then maybe you should be an Encore donor.

EVERYBODY'S THRIFT SHOP

261 Park Ave S
355-9263
Mon-Sat: 10-5; closed Sat in summer

This one is high on the list of both purchasers and patrons. Originally, it was organized to support the "Bundles for Britain" program during World War II; today, it survives as an umbrella organization for 12 charities. Knowing who supplies it, and when, is what makes the line form outside the store on Thursday mornings. One of New York's best department stores donates unsold merchandise, which is sold the day it arrives.

FOUR CHARITIES THRIFT SHOP

380 Second Ave (bet 21st and 22nd St)
674-1444
Tues-Sat: 10:30-5:30; closed last two weeks of Aug

The Four Charities are the Legal Aid Society, Goddard-Riverside Community Center, the Easter Seal Society, and the University Settlement Housing. These are noteworthy organizations. A top

New York department store donates new merchandise several times a year when the store clears its racks. The shop stocks new and nearly-new merchandise, with an emphasis on furniture and bric-a-brac in addition to clothing.

IRVINGTON HOUSE
1534 Second Ave (at 80th St)
879-4555
Mon, Tues, Thurs-Sat: 9:30-6; Wed: 9:30-8

If one can be snobbish about a thrift shop, this is the one to justify it. The quality of the clothing is superior to that of most New York retail stores. It resembles a little boutique, complete with a designer room at the back, where there are such names as Bill Blass, Pucci, Cardin, and Halston. Items *start* at $50, so while there are bargains, the prices aren't low. Still, even the front of the store offers incredible finds. Art collectors have come across a Utrillo and a Manet here, and many first editions are found by bibliophiles.

REPEAT PERFORMANCE
220 E 23rd St (bet Second and Third Ave)
684-5344
Mon-Sat: 10-5; closed Aug

Repeat Performance is run for the benefit of the New York City Opera, a cause near and dear to the hearts of wealthy donors and major department and specialty stores. So, while there are the usual thrift-shop furniture, jewelry, bric-a-brac, and occasional paintings, the strong suit here is brand-new, designer-name, often store-labeled clothing at ridiculously inexpensive prices.

SPENCE-CHAPIN CORNER SHOP
1424 Third Ave (bet 80th and 81st St)
737-8448
Mon-Sat: 10-5

Spence-Chapin is a nonprofit family-services organization that used to be primarily an adoption agency. In these times of scarce adoptions, the agency has branched out to include all kinds of family services and social work. The shop carries a little of everything, but that doesn't begin to do justice to the shop that the *New York Times* called the "Cadillac of thrift shops." Possibly the city's best selection of designer clothes is found in its tiny boutique room. Most of it is vintage—but not all—and the vintage merely adds to the charm. There is lesser quality clothing for everyone from infants (antique christening gowns—what more appropriate item from an adoption-agency shop?) to extra-large men's hunting jackets. The household goods and antiques are of quality more befitting an antiques store than a thrift shop, and there is furniture, artwork, and jewelry, as well. The boutique room's offerings go for around $200 each, but you can pick up odd belts or pieces elsewhere in the shop for as little as two for a dollar.

THRIFT SHOP EAST
1430 Third Ave (at 81st St)
744-5429, 5430
Mon-Sat: 10-5:45

Thrift Shop East is run for the benefit of WNET (New York's educational TV station) and the United Jewish Appeal/Federation of Jewish Philanthropies. As such, its donors are educated highbrows, whose tastes are reflected in the merchandise. In fact, the management takes great offense at the thought that this could be mistaken for a junk shop. They describe their clothing as "slightly used," the furniture as "antique" rather than secondhand, and the bric-a-brac as *objets d'art* and accessories rather than odds and ends. And that's no pretentious joke. They're absolutely right. This is the place to find slightly worn designer clothing that is in excellent condition and has been freshly cleaned. Some of it is even new, coming as donations from regular retail stores. The décor lives up to the shop's self-image and is virtually indistinguishable from that of a small posh retail store. Prices are *not* in the Salvation Army store category, but then neither is the merchandise.

TRISHOP QUALITY THRIFT SHOP
1689 First Ave
369-2410
Tues-Sat: 9:30-4:15; closed mid-July through mid-Aug

Trishop's proceeds benefit the Mental Health Association of New York and Bronx Counties. I mention this, because somehow this charitable organization has struck a particularly responsive chord with major department stores in the city. As a result, the shop's manager, Rose London, is able to boast that the shop's basic stock consists of mainly brand-new (some are a bit shopworn) ladies' dresses, coats, sportswear (including an extensive selection of sweaters), children's and men's wear, costume jewelry, and some household goods. There are frequent shipments of new merchandise. This is a thrift shop that also offers a double benefit. Besides contributing to the sponsoring agency, the shop provides a training and work-experience program. So, in addition to aiding a worthy cause and finding fantastic bargains, a purchase here helps support a unique program for aiding a segment of the population that is too often neglected.

T-Shirts—Family

EISNER BROS.
76 Orchard St (bet Grand and Delancey St)
800-426-7700 (National)
800-426-7900 (NY State)
Mon-Thurs: 9:30-6; Fri: 9:30-1; Sun: 9-5

Except for its tiny, cramped quarters and its adherence to the local practice of hanging merchandise from every available space on walls and ceilings, Eisner Bros. does not fit the usual Lower East Side shopkeeper's mold. Whereas its neighbors sell everything from handbags to shoes to designer clothes, Eisner Bros. specializes in T-shirts. They claim to have the biggest assortment of colors and sizes in the *world*, and easily half of their business is custom-ordered. So although every neighborhood seems to have at least one T-shirt store, this is the granddaddy of them all. There are sweatshirts, jogging suits, sport shirts (that's sports as in baseball, football, soccer, etc., *not* dress shirts with an open collar), nightshirts, and baseball caps and jackets. Sweatshirts have become popular, and this is the place to get them. There's a tremendous selection, and the magnificent discount doesn't hurt, either. Eisner Brothers is constantly upgrading their line. The latest additions are extra-large shirts in sizes up to 4X and a wide range of colors.

JOHNNY'S T-SHIRT CITY
182 Bleecker St (at MacDougal St)
777-0453
Daily: noon-11

This shop specializes in on-the-spot T-shirts, handmade clothes, and quick service. While you wait, a T-shirt can be made to order, with almost any slogan emblazoned on it. (They claim that they have never had to censor a shirt. Apparently, if someone is willing to pay for a shirt, he doesn't want something on it he'd be embarrassed to wear.) Sizes start from children's very small to extra, extra large, and there is always some suitable size in stock.

Umbrellas

ESSEX UMBRELLA
101 Essex St
674-3394
Sun-Fri: 9-5; Sat: noon-4:30

There are those who think that the only time to shop the Lower East Side is in the rain. With good reason, because it's infinitely less crowded during inclement weather. You might even get some attention from the clerks. But if you happen to get caught unprepared in the rain downtown, duck into Essex Umbrella. The selection is as good as that in any uptown store, but prices are always at least 25 percent lower. On top of that, they have some of the best designer umbrellas in town, in styles and quantity available nowhere else. (Why someone would *want* a designer umbrella is beyond me, but I suppose it works as well as the regular ones.) Essex also makes many of the umbrellas it sells, and repairs any brand. It should be your first stop, even if it's not raining.

UNCLE SAM
7 E 46th St
687-4780
Mon-Fri: 9-5:45; Sat: 10-5
161 W 57th St
247-7163
Mon-Fri: 9-5:45; Sat: 9-5

These shops are another example of specialty shops that make customers feel as though their merchandise is the only product sold in the city. A postcard sent to the West 57th Street address will elicit a copy of their catalog, which will convey the mood better than I can. But I'll try. Uncle Sam sells umbrellas, canes them, services them, recovers them, monograms them, and customizes them. The umbrellas come in sizes for little children up to and including triple-width beach umbrellas. In between, there are umbrellas for golfers, fashion models, travelers, showrooms, motion pictures, chauffeurs, and doormen. *All* are hand-carved, handsewn, and hand-assembled, which means that these stores are *not* the kind that sell $2 specials when it rains. But before I get to prices, I must mention that Uncle Sam also sells umbrella accessories. There is a heavy-duty canvas satchel designed to hold an umbrella and who knows what else. And there is my favorite: the shooting stick cane, which can be used as a regular cane or as a seat in emergencies. It is available in a regular or crook handle. Umbrella prices range from two-digit figures for a simple, slim, eight-inch umbrella with a wooden handle, to three-digit figures for some of the finer canes. All in all, Uncle Sam is an experience. There is no place like it anywhere else in the world. P.S. Ask to see the fold-up walking stick!

Uniforms

DORNAN
653 11th Ave (bet 47th and 48th St)
247-0937 (800-223-0363 outside New York State)
Mon-Wed, Fri: 8:30-4; Thurs: 8:30-6; closed from end of July to beginning of Aug

In 1925, Gabriel Piro began working at Dornan Inc., selling all types of uniforms. By 1949, Piro had bought the company and become the president and expert-in-residence on all manner of uniforms, but particularly those for chauffeurs. In 1976, Piro retired, and his son, Gabriel E. Piro, took over, and he too offers the best service and advice on uniform wear. Dornan can outfit—just to name a few—butlers, maids, beauticians, hospital workers, hotel doormen, bellboys and maids, bartenders, chefs, waiters and waitresses, housemen, ground crews, stewards, stewardesses, airline pilots, police, firemen, postal employees, doctors, nurses, technicians, patients, clergy, and even tennis players. But Piro's pride and joy are the chauffeur's uniforms. Dornan is the oldest and largest continuing supplier of garb for uniformed drivers, and the Piros are a wealth of information on their evolution.

Women's—General

ATELIER/55
101 W 55th St (at Sixth Ave)
245-3650
Mon-Fri: 10-7; Sat: 11-6

ATELIER/86
144 E 86th St
427-2211
Mon-Fri: 10:30-8; Sat: 11-7; Sun: 1-6; closed Sun in Aug

When a store down the street from ABC and Burlington calls itself a "small family kind of place," it may be a little hard to believe. But Atelier, an Italian store with great fashions from American designers, does just that. Indeed, Atelier even claims that the 86th Street store attracts browsers and tourist clientele, while the 55th Street shop has loyal and devoted customers who, with all of the midtown-Manhattan stores to choose from, pick their wardrobes from Atelier, season after season. The reason is simple. Price. Atelier's prices on any quality garment are excellent; nothing in the store is of less than designer-name quality; and at those locations, it's no wonder that hoards of customers have learned to shop for their wardrobes on their office breaks rather than during leisure time.

AZRIEL ALTMAN
182 Orchard St (near Houston St)
982-7722
Sun-Fri: 9-5
204 Fifth Ave (bet 25th and 26th St)
889-0782
Daily: 10-6

If you happen down Orchard Street on a hot summer weekday, you will quite possibly pass right by A. Altman and miss the gold mine inside. Certainly, the shabby exterior doesn't hint at the fine imported designer clothes inside. Customers used to coming on a Sunday and standing in lines that can stretch into the middle of Orchard Street never get a good look at the outside of the shop through the mobs. The crowds know what they are waiting for: top names in women's clothes all sold at a discount. Without going into superlatives, it's been documented that Altman's frequently gets top designer originals *before* the department and specialty stores do, and actually gets some designs that never appear elsewhere at all. When you consider that the merchandise is sold here first, and for a fraction of its retail cost, the only question is why there isn't a long line on weekdays, too. Everything has labels intact, and all of it is top quality. Altman's may well be the best store in the city for junior clothes. It is certainly worth waiting for, and that is a concession that I would grant nowhere else. Check out the fitting room. *Room*, did I say? It must be a unique experience! If you want to avoid the Lower East Side, shop Azriel Altman at 204 Fifth Avenue under the same management and tradition. New York visitors: this is an absolute must. Your savings on purchases here could equal the price of your airline ticket.

BEN FARBER
462 Seventh Ave (at 35th St, eighth floor)
736-0557, 800-223-6101
Mon-Wed, Fri: 10-6; Thurs: 10-8; Sat: 9-4

Diagonally opposite Macy's, Ben Farber is an emporium all its own. With prices half those of its neighbors', it makes one wonder why anyone would shop the department stores. Ben Farber is more a distributor than a jobber. Ostensibly, he does not welcome retail trade, but he has dressing rooms (not fancy) for the trade that isn't supposed to be there, and a neat setup of clothing on display. His stock runs the gamut of better women's wear. He has coats, dresses, suits, rainwear, outerwear, and sportswear in all sizes. Note that last. Very few of these lofts cater to *all* sizes, or in fact, to anything above size 12. Ben Farber carries 24½, though not in an enormous range. I say that he is a distributor because everything is first quality. Even *requesting* irregulars can't produce them, and both these factors, along with his propensity for top-quality clothing keep even his discount prices in the high range. Good clothing is not inexpensive, but it is only when one realizes what the same money will buy at Ben Farber's and at Macy's that the former appears as good as it is. If you have time for just one shopping stop, make it Ben Farber. Ask for manager Joe Halperin or the boss, Don Farber—he has served literally dozens of my friends.

BETSEY JOHNSON

248 Columbus Ave (bet 71st and 72nd St)
362-3364
130 Thompson St (bet Prince and Houston St)
420-0169
251 E 60th St (at Second Ave)
319-7699
Mon-Sat: 12-7; Sun: 12-6

In the 1970s, Betsey Johnson was *the* fashion designer. Her designs appeared everywhere, as did she and her personal life. As an outlet for those designs not sold to exclusive boutiques, Betsey helped found Betsey Bunky Nini, but her own pursuits led to modeling, more designing, and ultimately a store in SoHo. The SoHo store proved so successful that Betsey moved first to larger quarters and then up and across town, as well as into Betsey Johnson Boutiques in such department stores as Macy's. The Betsey Johnson style is such that she can meld those diverse areas of the city. While the style has always managed to be avant-garde, it has never been way-out. The outfits will always stand out but never be dated. Johnson believes in making her own statement, and each store seems unique despite the fact that over 500 outlets carry her line. But in her own stores, she is able to control what is shown and show the line in depth. Prices, incidentally, particularly at the SoHo store which started as an outlet, are bearable and wearable.

BETTER MADE COATS

270 W 38th St (at Eighth Ave, 12th floor)
944-0748
Mon-Fri: 9-5; Sat: 9-3

Better Made began as a manufacturer producing coats and suits for the better stores to sell under their own labels. Since its name did not appear on the garments, it also accepted individual customers of the "Sam sent me" genre. Through this trade, Better Made received an excellent following, and over the years has become more of a public operation. It has even advertised on occasion. The stock has expanded, and in addition to custom-made raincoats, suits, and designer coats, there are some dresses and sportswear. The house specialties are still made-to-order coats and suits (which, incidentally, *are* better made) and the designer coats they make under contract. Calvin Klein and Harve Bernard are but two of those names. Prices are not inexpensive. However, you can be quite sure that the same quality would retail for double elsewhere.

BRIDGEHAMPTON CLOTHES HORSE

1033 Lexington Ave
988-6757
Mon, Fri, Sat: 10-6; Tues-Thurs: 11-7

Bridgehampton—and its neighboring Hamptons—is quite simply *the* summer address for what seems like half of Manhattan's residents. Joan Zimmermann's shop reflects that relaxed and friendly atmosphere. Antiques, background music, silk-flower arrangement, and accessories complement a range of fashions that could appeal to a young urbanite, a career woman, or a city/country hostess. The New York store features after-five clothes, but there is an excellent selection of separates for daytime country life. Sizes are from 4 to 16, and alteration services are available. Bridgehampton Clothes Horse has been successful in its translation from country to city life. The shop recently added a wonderful collection of irresistible gift items to tempt its on-the-go clientele.

CRISCIONE
248 E 60th St (bet Second and Third Ave)
838-2843
Mon-Sat: 10:30-7

Joanie and Jeanne Criscione grew up in the Riverdale section of the Bronx with dreams of taking the New York fashion scene by storm. So, after high school, they attended the Parsons School of Design, and in 1975, along with their mother and an industrial sewing machine given to them by their father, they set up shop at home. In July 1977, while still supplying their designs to special boutiques, the Crisciones women opened their own boutique. Jeanne married and moved to Rio de Janeiro and opened her own Criscione boutique there. Mother Joan now supervises the New York boutique, with Joanie as the resident designer, consistently turning out seasonless flowing styles that are both modern and timeless. They follow the credo that good clothing requires luxury fabrics, so when a customer pays the price for that kind of quality it shouldn't be relegated to the back of the closet as passé after one season. The line includes separates, classic dresses, evening wear, and accessories. Though Criscione does accept some custom orders, nothing in the shop sells for more than a thousand dollars, and much is considerably less. The small shop also offers exquisite detail, personal attention, and an attitude that could make a browser feel like a princess. This may be the ultimate example of how to run a store in New York.

DIANNE B.
729 Madison Ave (at 64th St)
759-0988
Mon-Sat: 10-6

426 W Broadway (at Prince St)
226-6400
Daily: 11-8

If we had a trendy women's boutique section, Dianne B. would be the example *par excellence.* It is really unrivaled (except, perhaps, by its neighbor, Betsey Bunky Nini) and is always at the vanguard of fashion. Dianne B.'s designers' names are not the kind that roll trippingly off your tongue *now.* But they will be in a few years, and by then the boutique will have moved on to others. But all of them are young, vibrant, brilliant (with style and color), and French-inspired. Dianne herself is evident in everything. A former buyer for Bendel's, she is sure of her taste, and the store reflects that. Aside from being a super place to shop, Dianne B. is perhaps the one store in the city where a less assured customer doesn't have to be cautious in her purchases. (That is, if price is no object. This place is not inexpensive.) Nearly every issue of *New York* magazine, Wednesday's *New York Times,* and *Shop* tells of Dianne B.'s latest acquistions. There's a reason why the store merits such publicity, and you'll understand it best once you're inside. You don't have to buy anything, but you *must* see it. An outlet at 116 Wooster St (Comme De Garçons) features a line by Japanese designer Kawakubo.

ELLEN LANSBURGH'S THERAPY
799 Madison Ave (bet 67th and 68th St)
288-1182
Mon-Sat: 10-6:30

Ellen Lansburgh's Therapy is a well-defined style unto itself. It existed for five years in the ski-resort area of Aspen, Colorado, before setting up shop in New York, where it continues its policy of definitely knowing what it wants to be and what it wants its customers to be. One of the things it wants its customers to be is *up*—as in "up and *noticed.*" The woman who shops here may or may not avail herself of the wardrobe coordination or shopping services the store offers, but Ellen Lansburgh's Therapy is quite prepared to put together her "look." The customer then makes her choices based solely on pocketbook and closet size. Lansburgh designs many of the items herself, and up to 80 percent of the merchandise is designed exclusively for the store by young New York designers. (The image won't sell at all in Aspen; it is distinctly New York.) There is a really nice relationship between the designers and the store and between the store and its customers. All have their eye on one style of dressing.

EMPIRE LADIES APPAREL
1206 Second Ave (bet 63rd and 64th St)
752-7146
Mon-Fri: 11-7; Sat: 11-6; Sun: 11-5

There probably isn't a native New York woman who hasn't bought at least one outfit at a considerable discount. A good percentage probably buy everything that way, and many of those women swear by Empire and its counterparts. Empire is one of the definitive jobbers in the area. It is more than a factory outlet (it doesn't rely upon any one manufacturer), and yet it glories in the fact that it is less than a retail store. Amenities— such as gift wrapping, lay-aways, and just plain friendly salespeople—are sorely lacking. Instead of ambiance, the prices are cut, and the saleswomen's ideas of service are to whisper either the designer's name on the cut-out label, or to tell you how Jackie O just bought the same dress elsewhere for considerably more. And always, always, the emphasis is on how much you are saving rather than how it looks. A common phrase around here is, "I don't know—but for the price . . ."

FORMAN'S
82 Orchard St (bet Grand and Broome St)
228-2500
Sun-Thurs: 9-6; Fri: 9-4

Forman's bills itself as "the fashion oasis of the Lower East Side." While you can determine for yourself if that overstates the case just a bit, it is true that they have enjoyed a good reputaton for years and years. By Lower East Side standards, the store is enormous, a feat made possible as much by judicious use of all three floors as by a large physical plant. The store is laid out in such a way that a teenaged daughter, mother, and grandmother can all head for sections designed for their needs and not meet for hours. Even then, it might be at one of the dozen (do you believe it?) dressing rooms or the cash register. The teens are attracted by the top floor—I guess they can best climb the stairs. Denim reigns here, but so does casual sportswear, separates, and trendy outerwear. The main floor dazzles the customer with designer sportswear (Calvin Klein must have a direct line here) and such better-made separates as T. G. Hook and Evan Picone. The basement (excuse me, the lower level) is dedicated to young suburban-type separates and sportswear. Forman's made its reputation outfitting these images. Prices are the obligatory Lower East Side discount. Read that to mean *very* good.

GISELLE SPORTSWEAR
143 Orchard St (bet Delancey and Rivington St)
673-1900
Mon-Fri: 9-6; winter: Mon-Fri: 9-3

"High fashion" takes on new meaning at Giselle, where the higher the shopping floor, the higher the price. So in this three-floor emporium, the names range from mass-market designers like Calvin Klein to private boutique labels, the kind of stuff no one would believe came from the Lower East Side—not even the new, fashion-conscious Lower East Side. But it does, and Giselle is pulling out all stops to raise the fashion image of the area to new heights. Discounts run around 30 percent, and while that's not much of a dent in Perry Ellis, Anne Klein, or cashmere Fairbrook coats, the easing on the budget can allow for some third-floor purchases that would never be obtainable elsewhere. Giselle is a find. Even the saleshelp act more like lunchbreakers at Bonwit's than natives on Orchard Street.

HENRI BENDEL
10 W 57th St (at Fifth Ave)
247-1100
Mon-Wed, Fri, Sat: 10-6; Thurs: 10-8

Bendel's views itself as a small specialty shop, a description that totally belies the mystique and uniqueness of the store. If there were only one establishment that had to be selected for the title of what most typifies New York, Bendel's (never Henri—or worse, Henry—always Bendel's) would win hands-down. It has it all, in every category. The guiding spirit behind Bendel's is its president, Geraldine Stutz, who, in 20 years, turned what was a dowdy, money-losing shop into a store whose very name is synonymous with "in style." In the process, Stutz has become a major style-pacer and the longest-tenured store president in the city. Her number-one concern is maintaining the Bendel's image. Bendel's clothing is *not* for everyone, and they are proud of that fact. If the customer does not fit the Bendel's image, she will not fit Bendel's clothing. What is that image? For starters, small. The top size here is a 12, and a small 12 at that. In any size, there is no place for large hips, pot bellies, or over 25-inch waists. This immediately eliminates a large percentage of the female population (and generates a lot of envy). With those measurements, it is hard to look dowdy, but Bendel's prunes its clientele even further to ensure the purity of its look. The image is also young and very affluent.

HONEY BEE
7 E 53rd St (at Madison Ave)
688-3660
Mon-Wed, Fri: 10-6:30; Thurs: 10-8; Sat: 10-6
7 Hanover Square (at Water St)
269-8110
Mon-Fri: 8-6

Honey Bee is a different shop to different people. To many of the city's fashion models, it is a small, intimate shop with a good collection of desirable clothing easily accessible on a quick visit. To out-of-towners, particularly those from Missouri, this is the flagship of a catalog and local branch store, with modern but not far-out sportswear. To the rising class of executive women, it is a shop where you may call to have a few things set aside appropriate for a trip to Pittsburgh, and know that they will be both appropriate and ready whenever you get there. Primarily, though, Honey Bee relies on its ability to be "totally service oriented." Salespeople carry books that record likes, needs, and previous purchases of customers. Shopping via the catalog is encouraged, and long waits for either service or checkout are taboo. With all this service, prices could be unreasonable. They aren't. In fact, prices in the catalog designed to appeal to Middle America do not differ at all from what is offered in the heart of Manhattan. And styles that appear across the country are *au courant* enough for fashion models.

LA RUE DES REVES
139 Spring St
226-6736
Mon, Tues, Wed, Sat: noon-6:45; Thurs, Fri: noon-8:45; Sun: 1-5:45

This store has high-fashion, designer-label merchandise, and even the size of the store (it is currently SoHo's biggest) belies its area. Although most SoHo residents live in large lofts, neighborhood shops tend to be small. Not La Rue des Reves. It's big enough to house a grand piano—the better for music to shop by. And the emphasis is on a woman's complete wardrobe, from shoes to hats and for all times of the day. So, the businesswoman can find a stylish suit for the office and a strapless, backless evening pants set on opposite racks in the same store. What it all has in common is a sleek elegance that women dream about. And hence the store's French name.

LAURA ASHLEY
714 Madison Ave (bet 63rd and 64th St)
371-0606

398 Columbus Ave (at 79th St)
496-5151

4 Fulton St (at South St Seaport)
809-3555
Mon-Wed, Fri, Sat: 10-6; Thurs: 10-7

For Laura Ashley, time and space have stopped in an Edwardian English countryside. Twenty-odd years ago, in part to answer the growing blue-jean trend and in part because she was always enamored with the romantic turn-of-the-century dress styles, Ashley and her husband, Bernard, turned out their first dress on their kitchen table. In the years since, the style and fabric have come to be known as Laura Ashley classic, distinguishable in over 47 exclusive shops around the world. There are now three stores in Manhattan, with a fourth being completed on 57th Street. The dresses are always in a small print fabric, which seems to emerge from the mills looking well worn. (Laura Ashley Ltd. designs and produces its own fabric.) The fabric is then used in a few classic, simple designs that vary only slightly from year to year. It always follows a romantic Victorian-Edwardian theme. In summer, the fabrics are 100 percent cotton; in winter, a light woolen tweed. Except for the seasonal fabric switch, the clothing is timeless, in terms of style and wearability. In recent years, Laura Ashley expanded to include fabrics for home furnishings as well. There are wallpapers, curtains, upholstery, and even loose fabric available, as well as Laura Ashley dresses for children in sizes 2 to 7.

LE GRAND HOTEL/TALES OF HOFFMAN
471 W Broadway
475-7625
Winter: Tues-Fri: noon-7; Sat: noon-6:30; Sun: 1-5:30
Summer: Tues-Fri: noon-7; Sat: noon-6:30;
Sun: 2-5:30; closed Aug

Jackie Lewis started Le Grand Hotel many years ago in the Village (on St. Marks Place), and needed another name when she opened the shoe and boot boutique in front of her SoHo store. Hence, two separate businesses, one owner, one location today. Le Grand Hotel evokes casual elegance, and Lewis strives to maintain that image, albeit in modern—not period—clothing. Nearly everything is of the style Jackie Lewis herself would wear: well made, of natural fibers, and feminine. That covers everything from nightgowns to business dresses, from ultrafeminine smocked outfits to very formal evening wear. All of it bears Lewis' mark, since she has personally designed some of them, influenced others, and commissioned local designers to make the rest. It's the kind of stuff that would fit the Grand Hotel lifestyle at any time of day. Tales of Hoffman brings the best of shoes and boots to SoHo. They have Tony Lama cowboy boots, and the boots keep company with Joan & David pumps. In short, the elegant, the chic, and the best are sold here.

LILLIE RUBIN
22 W 57th St (at Fifth Ave)
757-0370
Mon-Sat: 9:30-6

On classy 57th Street, Lillie Rubin is an institution. However, since institutions age along with their clientele, economic necessity has made Lillie Rubin look for a place in a more modern world. The result is a cautious blending of the two, which does not always work. The older crowd, who patronized the shop for the couture and evening clothing, is put off by the bolts of fabric (original designer though it may be) heaped along one wall. The younger crowd is put off by the salespeople, who are at their side before the front door is closed, and the matronly look of what is on the racks. At its best, however, Lillie Rubin is a gem. The store's trademark is knockoffs of designer clothing—in the original fabric—for a fraction of the original's cost. Prices for the original fashions vary widely, depending upon the designer's line, fabric, and quality, and the copies reflect a similar diversity. So, some of the outfits are easily affordable by people who would otherwise have to settle for off-the-rack wardrobes. On the other hand, a Givenchy or Dior-like ensemble can still run the bill way up. A dressmaker may do just as well for you, though not in the original fabric and probably not with as much experience. There is also a good line of ready-to-wear, of Rubin's and others' design. Often, the salesclerk will take something off the rack and identify it as "Liz Claiborne-inspired," in case the customer isn't too swift at identifying lines. The younger (and slimmer) customer, however, will still probably go down the block to Bendel's.

THE LOFT
491 Seventh Ave (bet 36th and 37th St, 19th floor)
736-3399
Mon-Fri: 9:30-5; Sat: 9:30-4

The Loft offers top, top designer labels amassed because the Loft is in the same building and/or on the spot to pick up overruns and cancellations from manufacturers who never sell to jobbers as well as from those who do. There are some samples, some one of a kind, and a full wardrobe of garments from coats and suits to sportswear. (The Loft also carries some formal wear). Prices start at 30 percent off retail and climb. At the end of the season, it's even better, and the Loft (despite not being listed in any phone book under that name) has a semblance of wanting to do business. Many of these places make you feel slightly more important than a cockroach.

LONIA
55 W 55th St (bet Fifth and Sixth Ave)
757-2655
Mon-Fri: 10:30-7; Sat: 10:30-6

Linda Friedman, Lonia's owner, runs this trendy boutique with great taste and extreme confidence in that taste. If she likes an item, she buys it; if she can't find what she wants, she commissions it. As much as 50 percent of Lonia's merchandise bears the Lonia label. The shop carries everything for a woman's wardrobe. Demure (but sexy) lingerie is matched only by a chic collection of casual separates and sportswear, and in the winter you can throw on a Lonia Original coat or wrap. Friedman has a dozen designers working exclusively for her. Her forte is obviously merchandising and design. Part of the shop is devoted to Lonia shoes, which match the Lonia clothing, style, taste, and restraint.

LUCILLE'S

33 W 55th St (Hotel Shoreham, suite 2B)
245-7066
Mon-Sat: 11-5:30; closed July 1-Aug 15

Women who wear sizes 6 to 20 can save substantial sums on designer fashions at Lucille's, a shop that specializes in designer clothing of timeless nature at good discount prices. The best part of all—as if that were not enough—is Lucille herself, who presides over her beautifully organized emporium with incredible taste and style. Exactly where Lucille gets her merchandise is uncertain, but somehow she gets fantastic designer clothing in striking colors, patterns, and ensembles. And the labels are intact, unlike nearly every other designer outlet I can think of. Lucille also has an instinct for the needs of her customers. Most are middle-age, very well dressed, and classically fashionable rather than fad-conscious. So, Lucille's styles show a prejudice for the larger sizes. They start at 6, and the higher you go (including a very unusual designer 20), the more varied the selection is. Lucille's concern is shown in her selection of summer outfits with coordinating sweaters for air conditioning, jerseys that pack easily, and three-piece ensembles in striking patterns that can be interchanged for various occasions. Finally, don't miss Lucille's formal wear; her dressy outfits are really special. And did I mention that all of these fashions are sold at a 20 to 40 percent discount?

MEZZANINE BOUTIQUE

102 Orchard St (at Delancey St, upstairs)
505-1010
Sun-Thurs: 10-6; Fri: 10-3; summer: Sun-Fri: 10-3

Mezzanine Boutique is part of the new wave of shopping on the Lower East Side and exudes friendliness, amenities, dressing rooms (10—count 'em—10), and discounts with a vengeance. So while the shop offers the usual Lower East Side discounts on such names as John Anthony, Oleg Cassini, Emmanuelle Khan, Jerry Silverman, and Pauline Trigere, among others, do you know of another shop that offers such items at a 30 percent discount, along with a sitting area with color television for family and friends? Or one which will special-order and ship anywhere in the country for that discount? If this is the *new* Lower East Side, then lead on!

M. FRIEDLICH

196 Orchard St (bet Stanton and Houston St)
254-8899
Daily: 9:30-5:30; closed Tues in July and Aug

Another typical Lower East Side boutique, Friedlich has the usual fabulous finds in both quality and price as well as the usual abrasive service people. Starting with the good points, Friedlich stocks women's fine imported sportswear in sizes 3 to 14, a range that includes misses and juniors sizes and is somewhat limited on the larger sizes. What they do have, though, is striking. Mr. and Mrs. Friedlich claim that most of their things qualify as designer sportswear, and while I did not see that many names, there was no mistaking the quality of the goods. M. Friedlich seems to favor imports from France and Italy—perhaps because they are the best—but there is a healthy assortment of better-quality American sportswear as well. Another plus is Friedlich's selection of coats and outerwear, which consists of great designer coats and better-brand offerings from both Europe and America. Comparable stores do not usually stock sportswear and outerwear at one location. For either or both, it's well worth the trip. The only problem with a visit here is what one would facetiously call ambiance. There is none. Perhaps the saleshelp are always too swamped with customers, or perhaps handling all these good-looking things while wearing a smock gets to them. In any event, *surly* is a polite way to describe their behavior. Never, never ask a question, unless being yelled at in the midst of a horde of tightly packed people turns you on. And that is the final point. The fantastic buys at Friedlich's are not a secret, so the store is always crowded. Would anyone whose pet peeve is standing in line and begging people to take his money come here? You betcha! It's that good!

MIRIAM RIGLER
62 W 56th St (bet Fifth and Sixth Ave)
581-5519
Mon-Sat: 10-6; closed Sat in July and Aug

Miriam Rigler offers the quintessential ladies' dress shop. It seems to have it all—personal attention, expert alterations, wardrobe coordination, custom designing, and a large selection in everything from sportswear to evening gowns, in sizes from 4 to 20. Despite the location, all items are discounted, including specially ordered outfits that are not in stock. I don't think there is much more to say. This store meets all of my criteria for being one of the very best.

NATIONAL LADIES SPECIALTY
470 Seventh Ave (bet 35th and 36th St, second floor)
695-1350
Mon-Fri: 9-6; Sat: 9-4:30

Albert Feld and Nathan Schechter run this factory loft, which has more clothing for the entire family than many department stores. I tried to compile a list of the different items they carried, and it took two full pages. As a jobber, National Ladies Specialty benefits from its location, which is smack in the middle of the garment center. They are literally right on the spot, which means that when a manufacturer wants to unload a shipment in a hurry or needs cash, National Specialty is often the beneficiary. As a result, they carry virtually all of the top brands of every type of garment, and sell at a minimum of 20 percent less than retail. There are free alterations in ladies' dresses, coats, and raincoats.

NEW STORE
289 Seventh Ave (bet 26th and 27th St)
741-1077
Mon-Fri: 10-8; Sat, Sun: 10-6

Listen, when your nearby neighbor is the emporium (kingdom?) of S&W, and your almost-as-near neighbors are the most fashion-wise people in the city at the Fashion Institute of Technology, it takes a lot of guts, *savoir faire*, or confidence to open a discount clothing store at this location. But the people at New Store did. And it worked, because they did it well and continue to do so. What they are doing is offering designer and better women's clothing and shoes at a 30 to 70 percent discount. Wanda, at the New Store, brags that many of their labels can be found nowhere else in the city at any price, and they manage to keep everything up-to-date by running frequent sales that empty the store. (Check out *New York* magazine for the best notice of when these sales are held.) When the sale price is literally a fraction of the original price, it's the stuff legends are made of. Perhaps the fact that the store's name is most frequently heard in connection with those incredible bargains explains why so many people have gone out of their way to shop here.

ONE BLOCK OVER
131 W 35th St
564-7035
Mon-Wed, Sat: 9-6; Thurs, Fri: 9-7

It's unclear from the clientele here whether "one block over" refers to the store's proximity to Macy's or the garment center. In any event, there's a reason for all those customers. Most of this store's clothing consists of sportswear: jeans, denim skirts, velour or terry tops (dependent upon the season), sweaters, and an occasional smattering of shoes, bags, coats, and accessories. But what sportswear! Jordache, Sasson, and Diane von Furstenberg are just a few of the names sold here for at least 50 percent off. The prices are truly amazing. The beat is young, swift, and loud, and in no way helped by the persistent music. But this is a store for New Yorkers, patronized by New Yorkers. And if this description describes the way *you* dress, this place is another must.

PARIS FASHIONS
512 Seventh Ave (sixth floor)
382-1895, 1896
Mon-Fri: 10-4; Sat: 10-3; closed Sat in summer

I first heard of Paris Fashions several years ago as a name whispered among friends as a wholesale place you could get into. The stock was almost entirely coats, and they differed only in whether they were trimmed or untrimmed with fur. Those first visits were very sobering; saleshelp did not exist, and one walked away with whatever one tried on. Apparently, Paris Fashion was a manufacturer of women's coats that were sold almost entirely under designer or store labels. (A trend can be noted here. It appears that when manufacturers' names are not on the garments, they are more willing to open their lofts to the public.) However, as time went on, the amount of business done this way became extensive. As a result, Paris Fashion branched out and became a jobber as well, which means that today, in addition to coats and suits, there are also dresses, semi-formal wear, London Fog raincoats and sportswear. Quality is still excellent (jobbing implies overstock, *not* irregulars), and the price is wholesale. Alterations are available.

PETA LEWIS
1120 Lexington Ave (at 78th St)
744-7660
Mon-Sat: 11-7; Sun: noon-6

In addition to accolades for selection and quality, Peta Lewis deserves praise for its advertisements. It's been a long time since *any* store came out with anything like the copy Peta Lewis used to introduce itself to the New York scene. ("Eat your heart out, Loehman's" said one. "Bring this ad to us. We want to see how good our ad agency is," said another.) Today, their advertising still excels. Of course, it wouldn't help to find out that they had the greatest ad agency in the world if they didn't have the goods to back it up. But they do. This is a shop that is very sure of its image and knows exactly who its customers are. It carries high-quality, high-fashion merchandise at substantial discounts. (Loehman's, by the way, is perhaps the best-known store of that genre in the world. It doesn't have a Manhattan branch.) Peta Lewis' goal is to prove that the two can go hand-in-hand in Manhattan without a lowering of standards. So, while many other high-quality shops have "enormous" discounts that might reach 10 percent, Peta Lewis finds 50 percent not unreasonable, and sometimes sales carry it further. And while many discount stores shave prices at the expense of décor and accommodations or quality of merchandise, Peta Lewis looks like a private showroom for Fifth Avenue's most treasured customers. The names on the labels are nothing short of tops, and Peta Lewis won't carry the lesser lines of those who do have such things. This puts even their least expensive items on the high side. But the discounts are there, and rest assured that the *real* prices are even higher. And if you want to check out those ads, Peta Lewis has a file for you. That is, if they're not still on the wall, where they were proudly displayed.

ROYAL SILK
79 Fifth Ave (at 17th St)
243-5507
Mon, Wed, Fri, Sun: 10-6; Tues, Thurs: 10-9

Silk, so the legend goes, was discovered about 2600 B.C. when the Empress Hsi Ling Shi landed a cocoon, not so daintily, into the hot tea she was about to drink. The cocoon, affected by the hot tea, melded into silk fiber, and an industry was born. The legend holds, to this day, that silk is one of the world's most expensive fibers, and that it has been used historically by the very rich, very elegant, and very royal. (Cleopatra supposedly used a red silk number to seduce Mark Antony.) Even today, there aren't many women who have more than a handful of silk outfits in their closets. That is unless they shop at Royal Silk. This store, the brainchild of Prakash Melwani, delivers silk items made and imported from the Far East at prices that are as cheap (if not cheaper) than man-made fibers. Melwani is a young genius from India. He started Royal Silk with a single mail-order ad in 1978. He keeps his prices low by operating as his own middleman, contractor, and retailer. While mail order and catalogs are still a large part of the business, he hopes to open stores across the country. This one in Manhattan is the flagship and the first, aside from the outlet at company headquarters in Clifton, New Jersey. (The catalogs, incidentally, are as striking as the clothing. Martina Navratilova and Vanessa Williams have modeled Royal Silk separates.) The company still specializes in the silk separates that it offered in the first advertisement. While sizes go up to 20, and there are dresses, pants, and men's and children's wear lines, the store pushes blouses in 22 colors, with mix-and-match skirts and pants in a similar rainbow of colors.

RUBIN'S COATS AND SUITS
242 W 38th St
354-1534
Mon-Fri: 9:30-4:30; Sat: 9:30-3; Sun: by appointment

Rubin's is a garment center source for excellent quality suits, coats, jackets, and skirts. They claim a large selection of quality merchandise and a subspecialty in rainwear. The coats, other than the rainwear, consist of down, leather, Borgana, fake furs, and wool. Suits are beautifully executed in wools, and like the skirts, they come in sizes from teeny to well proportioned (*very* well proportioned). And prices are 40 percent less than elsewhere. Men's zip-out raincoats are also available.

RUTH BROOKS FASHIONS
1138 Third Ave (at 66th St)
744-5412
Mon-Sat: 10:30-6; summer: Mon-Sat: 10:30-5

Ruth Brooks is not only a real person, she is a person with great connections in the garment center, and she can usually be found in person in her store. The sleek, modern facade belies the fact that Brooks has some of the best Upper East Side ladies' fashions at the best Lower East Side prices. She specializes in designer sportswear, which means that there is an emphasis on suits and dressy sportswear: things done with ultrasuede, velvets, gabardines, and the like, rather than jean separates. The store claims that all garments are sold at 50 percent off the suggested manufacturer's retail price. There are only occasional sales, but even without them, Brooks probably offers the best prices in the city on what she carries.

S&W
Coats:
287 Seventh Ave (at 26th St)
Dresses and Sportswear:
165 W 26th St (at Seventh Ave)
Evening wear, Bags, Shoes, and Accessories:
165 W 26th St
924-6656
Sun: 10-6; Mon-Wed: 10-6:30; Thurs: 10-8; Fri: 10-4

S&W is actually three stores, and each location features a specialty, as indicated above. While it is unclear exactly what the source of supply is, it is a well-known fact that S&W is one of the best places in the city for ladies' clothing. Clothing orders include elegant—the suedes and leathers in the coats and suits are magnificent—and top-of-the-line garments only. Unlike so many of the other discount boutiques, S&W maintains a consistent level of quality. It is *not* the place to uncover the buy of the year. Everything is of the same quality; nothing is either more spectacular but damaged, or less spectacular but clean. Prices, incidentally, are not incidental. The discount is a minimum of 40 percent, but 40 percent off a $300 suede suit still takes a lot out of a working girl's budget. Two serious drawbacks: prices are not marked for the customer to read, and rudeness seems to be a way of life at S&W.

SPITZER'S CORNER STORE
101 Rivington St
477-4088
Mon-Fri: 9:30-6; Sun: 8:30-6
156 Orchard St
473-1515
Mon-Fri: 9:30-6; Sun: 8:30-6

Spitzer's has been on the corner of Rivington practically forever. The new store at 156 Orchard carries the same merchandise, but it is newer, brighter, and easier to shop in. That last is no small matter. Although Spitzer's is the first choice of many Lower East Side shoppers for ladies wear, it is not a pleasant store. My number-one pet peeve, ambiguous price tags, is the norm here, and while that is usually a sign that bargaining (called *haandling* down here) is expected, it's hard to bargain with people who never seem to be around when you need them (pet peeve #2). Next comes pet peeve #3: the merchandise at 101 Rivington is spread out over three rooms. You always have the feeling that you're missing something better in the next room. And with no saleshelp helping (see pet peeve #2), it's highly possible that feeling is correct. Why bother then? Because Spitzer's puts together the best selection for a woman's wardrobe at the best prices. That's even without *haandling*.

SUZUYA
220 E 60th (bet Second and Third Ave)
688-8835
Mon-Sat: 11-7

Don't even walk in here if you are not young, lithe, and female. But, ah, if you are, this is the place! Several years ago, the Suzuya Corporation, which is the largest women's clothing retailer in Japan, opened a local branch in Manhattan, and for indefinable reasons, named it Les Halles. Almost instantly it was on the map, particularly for professional models, but it wasn't until very recently that the corporation went international and changed all of its store names to Suzuya. Clothing sold here comes from all over the world, and reflects the buyer's tastes at their stores in Paris and Hong Kong, as well as New York. As a result, much of what is on the racks in Suzuya is available nowhere else, and much of that is manufactured under its own Suzuya New York label. The styles are young (very young!), flippant, and tiny. Suzuya claims that the size range is from 3/4 to 11/12. Few nonspecialty stores in New York go that low, or stop at 12. Suzuya does, and they are much better equipped on the smaller sizes. Colors are brilliant. None of that watercolor Japanese pastel. These colors are vibrant and reflected in styles that are in the vanguard of fashion. There is even a large accessory area that Suzuya calls a "store within a store." Miscellanies range from feather-trimmed anklets to rocket-ship pins to an ashtray shaped like a cowboy hat. None of it sounds very Japanese, and it isn't. In fact, the only thing "made in Japan" about Suzuya is the price. Its own things are almost ridiculously inexpensive.

TAMALA DESIGN WITH BAGEL
153 Prince St (at W Broadway)
473-0197
Mon-Wed: 10-6; Thurs, Fri: 10-8; Sat, Sun: 11-6

Aggie Markowitz of Casual Grace caterers has an interest in Tamala Design with Bagel as well, and although she is not the controlling partner, her fashion flair, presentation expertise, and love of SoHo are all evident here, as well as her way with fast food. Tamara Melcher designs the clothing exclusively for the store, one of SoHo's first, and all of it is hand-painted or made with hand-painted fabric and molded into casual yet elegant fashion. Much of it is sportswear or separates whose basic patterns appear over and over again with slight additions, flounces, or alterations. Despite the hand-painting, or perhaps because of the basic no-nonsense fabrics, prices and styles are downright economical. The lunch counter, though tiny, is operated with the same straightforward approach. Bagels abound along with coffee, sandwiches, and soda, all designed for quick pick-me-ups. Come to think of it, so is Tamala's clothing.

VERMONT CLASSICS
284 Columbus Ave (at 73rd St)
874-0480
Mon-Fri: 11-7:30

Located amid the classy quiche-and-cheese sidewalk cafes on the Upper West Side's Columbus Avenue, Vermont Classics has made a mark on the New York clothing scene. The store's philosophy is simple: simple country styles are the best, both in construction and style. So, the founders toured New England to find the best at-home craftsmen to supply the store with an array of sweaters, pillows, clothing, outerwear, and bed clothes. What they came up with is classic in style, yet distinctive. Take particular note of the handmade sweaters that come from the talented hands of Vermont residents..The wools and patterns are truly outstanding, and each is by definition one of a kind. The raw silk dresses are turned out by small platoons of sewers still stationed at their homes across the state. And although some of the clothing is machine-factory produced, there is no deviation from the fine lines and simple taste of the Green Mountain state. As odd as it sounds, a shop exalting Vermont comes off as natural on one of the trendiest streets in Manhattan.

YONSON PAK
107 Thompson St (bet Prince and Spring St)
431-1733
Tues, Wed, Fri-Sun: noon-7; Thurs: 12-9

Yonson Pak is one of the many designers who, having established herself in shops and departments stores uptown, has now opened a direct-sale boutique downtown. Her designs will still be available elsewhere, but much like her peers, Pak had the SoHo store designed (by Stephen McKay) to specifically highlight her style and designs. In this case, it works well since Pak's use of patterns has been termed "architectural" and "geometric." Her collections are usually designed for mix-and-match dressing and sport a maximum of two or three colors throughout the design, in an assortment of patterns and textures. The store isn't large, but the halogen bulbs and sculptural aluminum forms they highlight make the store light and airy, much like Pak's designs themselves. But since Pak knows that that style has been passé for a long time, her designs offer modern innovations on the theme, much as the sculptural steel offsets the passé Hollywood bulbs. Prices are quite reasonable for designer outfits, and the clothing is very wearable. Pak is functional as well as striking.

ZYNN FASHION
270 W 38th St (18th floor)
944-8686
Mon-Sat: 7:30-5 by appointment only; closed May

Zynn is a factory-loft contractor of women's coats and suits that will sell to the public at discount prices. Zynn is a family operation, albeit a big one, but the name to mumble here is Zynstein, *not* Zynn, although name mumbling is not necessary at all, and anyone there will answer to Zynn. Coats and suits are of excellent quality, and are available in all sizes. If the racks don't offer the selection you want in the size you want, Zynn will happily make up coats and suits to order. In fact, most of its sales are custom-made orders, based upon the models that hang on those racks. It is only the more wary customer who contents herself with the off-the-rack models. There is a price differential, but it isn't that great, and the glory of a made-to-order suit or coat more than offsets it.

Women's Accessories

APRON AND BAG SUPPLY COMPANY
47 Second Ave (bet Second and Third St)
673-0835
Mon-Fri: 8:30-4:30

Stanley Grodzki and his staff are not just standing around waiting for the customer who wants to buy one apron to match the kitchen wallpaper. The majority of their orders are for institutions, kitchen supply stores, linen services, or restaurants. If they are busy filling orders, they are not overly receptive to single orders. On the other hand, why should you pay department store—or even kitchen-supply store—prices, when you can buy the best aprons and bags around for wholesale prices? The aprons come in different colors and materials, but most are in the sturdy, professional line rather than hostess style. Laundry bags, too, are sturdy, mostly canvas or denim bags, sewn up in the familiar contours of laundry bags, school bags, or duffel bags. They are made to last.

COACH STORE
754 Madison Ave (at 65th St)
594-1581
Mon-Sat: 11-6

Coach bags, with their clean lines and excellent quality, are well known to women throughout the country, but even better known in Paris where the manufacturer has had a small but very popular store. It was only natural that Coach would open an outpost in New York as well. Besides, the bags are manufactured on West 34th Street. And that's the good news. The shop's opening was long awaited, particularly by Coach loyalists who have had to sift through meager selections of Coach bags in other shops. But perhaps the shop's layout and location are not conducive to the proper ambiance, for something prevents the store from meeting its potential. Prices befit Madison Avenue, or even Paris. There certainly is no sign that the factory is within walking distance. And the much anticipated selection simply isn't there. The walls are hung with pictures of the product rather than displays of actual Coach bags. While every color is available, there just aren't that many styles. In any event, a company that exalts quality and value shouldn't have saleshelp who try to outpace Gucci's. If you're treated like a second-class passenger, you should at least get a reduced fare. Coach *outlet*, where are you?

FINE AND KLEIN
119 Orchard St (at Delancey St)
674-6720
Sun-Fri: 9-5:30

Zsa Zsa Gabor gets her handbags from this one-of-a-kind Lower East Side establishment, and so can you. The selection is vast: one whole wall is devoted solely to black leather shoulder bags. The quality ranges from excellent to posh luxurious, and the clerks are helpful without being pushy. Fine and Klein is one of the few truly elegant stores on the Lower East Side, yet its discounts are characteristic of the neighborhood. Leather bags start at $15 and climb up—way up. But the higher the price, the bigger the discount. Don't expect to find an inexpensive bag here, but you will find excellent quality and the possibility of locating exactly what you want. In recent years, Fine and Klein added briefcases, wallets, belts, and other goods to its stock. Its collection of women's shoes is housed upstairs in a separate store, Sole of Italy (see "Shoes—Women"). Ask for my good friends, Julius Fine or Murray Klein, and tell them you read about their store here. More accommodating and knowledgeable people you won't find. This is, without a doubt, America's number-one handbag store.

FRED LEIGHTON

773 Madison Ave (at 66th St)
288-1872
Mon-Sat: 10-6

Murray Mondschein worked for Carole Stupell before branching out into the ownership of Fred Leighton. The crown jewel of the store is the collection of gems and antique jewelry. (Stupell says Mondschein is an authority in the field.) Certainly, its collection of latter-day antiques is hard to top. The collection includes Cartier, Fabergé, Lalique, Victorian snuff boxes, and a fabulous collection of art-deco ornaments. One can also find loose and "rare jewels of antique origin." All of it is just the thing to complete any outfit.

HYUK BAGS

39 W 29th St
685-5226, 685-5399
Mon-Fri: 8-6; Sat: 8-noon

Hyuk K. Kim runs an importing company exclusively dedicated to handbags. Importing and wholesaling companies are common in this area. What is uncommon is the courtesy and selection the company gives individual retail customers. Kim has a knack for making everyone seem a valued customer, and she does not take offense when a finicky lady picks through the entire stock in search of the quintessential handbag. But it shouldn't be too hard to find, within certain guidelines. Imported here usually refers to origins from points West rather than East. So rather than an "LV," expect to see a "Made in Hong Kong." Hyuk seems to import every type of handbag—leather, vinyl, canvas, and nylon. Most of this is your average, serviceable stuff. But there are a few stars in the line, and prices border on magnificent. Spoken English is at a premium here.

JACKIE ROGERS

787 Madison Ave (bet 66th and 67th St, second floor)
744-7303
Mon-Fri: 9:30-5; Sat: 10-4:30

The Jackie Rogers look is distinctive and special. You won't see yourself coming and going in a Jackie Rogers outfit. Yet this is another one of the sources many of New York's best dressed consistently use. Everything is distinctive and *right*. Styles are, for the most part, definitively current, and there are two or three sales a year. They are usually advertised in *New York* magazine. If you want to look like you just stepped out of a fashion magazine, don't miss J. R. The line here is designed by Jackie herself. Her accessories are outstanding.

J. S. SUAREZ
67 E 56th St (bet Madison and Park Ave)
759-9443
Mon-Fri: 9:30-6; Sat: 10-5:30

J. S. Suarez has been in business for over 40 years, and in that time, he has made his reputation by selling name-brand bags at a 30 to 50 percent discount, and twins of name-brand bags (and *big* names at that) at even better prices. For years, Suarez was the source for unlabeled Gucci bags that were identical to the real thing (naturally, since they came from the same factory), for less than half the price. And, unlike Gucci, Suarez doesn't close for lunch or have the most obnoxious clerks this side of Italy. In fact, Suarez' people, and Suarez himself, are downright pleasant. He discounts name brands as well as "fake" (read "unlabeled") Bottega Veneta, Celine of Paris, Chanel, Fendi, and Hermes items. Suarez takes it as a matter of course that you are *supposed* to deliver top quality, great service, good selection, and excellent prices to all customers. Someone should tell Gucci.

ROBERTA DI CAMERINO
645 Fifth Ave (at 51st St)
355-7600
Mon-Sat: 10-6

CLOSED

The store's location in the Rockefeller Center area on Fifth Avenue, as well as its attractive display, make this store look as if it is something special—and it is. Roberta di Camerino is an Italian designer with a unique style. Her style is reflected in day, sports, and evening wear and in handbags for women and accessories for men, including ties. All of them are exclusive to the shop, designed and made in Italy. (Warning: prices are sky-high.) The real specialty of the store is in the handbag area. The velvet ones rate as some of the finest in the world. The highlights of the fashion collection are made of leather or, at the very least, have leather trim. Roberta di Camerino's store is located in the ultra-exclusive Olympic Tower, in case you want an excuse to say that you've been there. In January, there is usually a 20 to 40-percent-off sale.

SYLVIA PINES—UNIQUITIES
1102 Lexington Ave (at 77th St)
744-5141
Mon, Thurs, Fri, Sat: 10-6; closed Sat in summer

Sylvia Pines presides over an emporium of what she calls "uniquities," and that's not an inappropriate name. For years, she has amassed antique, art-deco, and art-noveau purses, *objets d'art*, and jewelry. One never knows what can be unearthed here, but with the largest collection of antique purses in the country, Sylvia Pines has it in the bag. And if it is not the perfect bag, the shop's repair and restoration services can make it so. Those who don't come to view the purse uniquities come for the collection of jewelry of similar vintage, though the best selection is of the Victorian era. Time has stood still for Sylvia Pines, and the uniquities are easy to appreciate.

WELLINGTON LEATHER GOODS
155 W 23rd St (sixth floor)
691-0436
Mon, Tues, Thurs: 1-5

Roupen Barsoumian runs a business that supplies quality leather briefcases, underarm cases, flap cases, zipper and writing cases, wallets, and a limited number of better quality bags to the best department stores in the city. Years ago, he maintained a street-level showroom, and the staff got into the habit of treating individual customers as if they were as precious as Saks' buyers. When the showroom closed and Barsoumian consolidated his showroom and factory upstairs, no one told him to change his attitude toward retail customers, so if the hours he welcomes individuals to his wholesale showroom aren't convenient, the common man (or woman) is invited to arrange other hours. I'd visit Wellington just to witness this attitude in this city. But there's more. His merchandise bespeaks price because of the incredible workmanship and quality, and as Wellington's spokeswoman Miss Germaine Adil says, "No one else can afford to sell at these prices." And don't forget to ask to see the discontinued and closeout lines. And finally, thank them. Would that the rest of the city were like this!

Women's—Business

ALCOTT & ANDREWS
335 Madison Ave (at 44th St)
818-0606
Mon-Fri: 10-7; Sat: 10-6; Sun: 12-5

Now the female Madison Avenue executive can shop for a business suit on Madison Avenue. Alcott & Andrews has opened under the premise that the busy woman will pay to have good quality clothing that is stylish and flattering. The A & A shopper can also buy everything for her personal and professional life under one roof with the assurance that it is the best available. Formerly, she would pick up a suit in one store, a jogging outfit in another, and a cocktail dress in yet a third. And while that still may be desirable for reasons of price and selection, the store is built on the premise that their customer is too busy to bother with such inefficient shopping. There are obviously people who think it's worth paying retail here to shop in one location.

STREETS AND COMPANY
2030 Broadway (bet 69th and 70th St)
787-2626
941 Lexington (at 69th St)
517-9000
Mon-Fri: 11-8; Sat: 10-6;
Sun: noon-5 (Lexington store only)

Just as Seventh Avenue is finally waking up to the fact that women come in sizes larger than 12, the retail apparel industry has begun to notice that many women are working high-paying office jobs, not as secretaries but as executives. So, it was inevitable that the industry would begin to cater to these women, particularly since such jobs imply a hefty wad of spending money. The major department stores have opened "professional" sections in the women's departments, and several neighborhood stores have sprung up as well. All are in sharp contrast to the very fashionable, very visible, and usually very trendy style of the boutiques that cater to models, TV stars, and cosmetics demonstrators. One of the best of the new breed, if not the prototype of what *all* such stores should be, is Streets and Company. Where the old boutiques were bright and playful, Streets is staid, with just a touch of whimsy. In keeping with its customers' lifestyle, the store keeps businesswomen's hours. If your job keeps you *so* busy that even those hours don't fit a hectic schedule, the store will deliver to your home or office. Streets can outfit the complete businesswoman. There are suits galore, sweaters, skirts, more blouses than can be imagined, coats, and accessories (*business* accessories, such as attaché cases and large handbags). Also offered are custom alterations and shopping services, as well as delivery. Given the time, they can put together an entire wardrobe for the busy professional woman.

Women's Evening Wear

BASULI
33 E 72nd St
628-5663
Mon-Fri: 10:30-6; Sat: 11-5; closed Sat in summer

If your social life is a whirlwind, and even if you only go to one formal dinner a month, you may need a store like Basuli to help your wardrobe rise to the occasion. Barbara and Rosyln Goldberg run a store that sells the best in women's formal wear. Most of it is for "after five," but there are daytime dresses for formal wear, too. The Goldbergs have their own staff of designers, and commission their own designs to be executed to order. They have been in business long enough to know what is suitable and what their clients will be demanding. Most of Basuli's clientele have many social engagements and need a number of distinctive outfits. Basuli also has an exclusive line of wedding gowns and fashions to outfit an entire bridal party. And there is a new accessory department which incorporates the same elegance in one-of-a-kind jewelry, gifts, bags, belts, hats, and fur accessories.

JEFF KINT

117 W Broadway (bet Duane and Reade St)
431-8043
Tues-Sat: noon-1 a.m.

The latest show in town belongs to Jeff Kint, a designer who claims to have opened the city's first after-hours shopping place, as well as TriBeCa's first boutique. Even during regular business hours, things are anything but sedate at Jeff Kint, for during the day he works up the street at 211 West Broadway, designing and creating the clothing that the store will ultimately feature at night. Day or night, Jeff Kint merchandises his look—and you can bet money that a man who is open until one a.m. is not designing man-tailored business suits. Tunics abound, as do metallic threads, gold lamés, and the house specialty—hand-dyed one-of-a-kind fabrics. Almost all of it is expressly designed for evening wear, although Kint's frame of reference for evening are the trendy all-night places, such as his shop, rather than company dinners and opera benefits. And speaking of the shop, it's a sight to behold. It, too, was personally designed by Kint and looks like a 20th-century cross between late Pompeii and flooded Florence. Columns befitting Roman busts display Kint belts and ties. Dresses hang from marble pillars that move and swing, and the entire length of one wall has been painted with Adrian Willemse's murals, specifically made to look like they have poorly withstood the ravages of time.

LE GASPI

250 W 35th St
714-0187
Tues-Sat: 11-6; closed Sat in summer

Larry Le Gaspi started by designing and selling clothing that was considered outrageous even in the Village. When he was discovered by a very trendy clientele—primarily people whose aim in life is to make a daily splash in *Women's Wear Daily*—he forsook the Village and moved uptown. If his fashions were shocking in the Village, you can imagine how quietly they blend with the neighborhood *now*. But there are many people who need to have that kind of wardrobe, if only for their public appearances; for them, avoiding the trip downtown is a bonus. And yet, Le Gaspi has mellowed somewhat in making his move. While everything in the store is a Le Gaspi original and custom-made (but *not* made to order; there is a large selection of ready-to-wear items), some of it is the kind of stuff you'd wear to the kid's PTA meeting—if the PTA was for an experimental school in SoHo. But that is a tone-down for Le Gaspi. In addition to a daytime line and some really striking bathing suits (when was the last time you saw a unique bathing suit?), Le Gaspi's evening-wear collection is his most functional. Partly because evening wear seldom looks ordinary anyway, the formal wear here is striking. It is distinctive, well-styled, and very individual.

LUCILLE CHAYT
484 Broome St (at Wooster St)
219-8422
Tues-Sat: 11-7; Sun: 12-5

Lucille Chayt's styles are flowing, sophisticated, and elegant. Her location in SoHo has got to be for its proximity on the cutting edge of art rather than for access to a marketplace of formally dressed clientele. Chayt has made a name for herself with a wholesale line that sells in the most exclusive shops uptown and elsewhere. In SoHo, she joins other designers such as Betsey Johnson in devoting a shop to showcasing her styles. There are occasional informal "meet the designer" shows, complete with models.

Women's Furs

Women's furs in New York can be purchased at wholesale, retail, or boutique level. As with most other kinds of women's garments, the wholesale fur business has carefully prescribed physical boundaries and equally prescribed rules and regulations. Despite—or perhaps because—the fur district is on the periphery of the entire wholesale garment area, fur buying in New York is one of the easiest things to do on a wholesale level. The following are establishments that openly welcome retail customers with wholesale prices. It is possible to get very badly burned while buying furs; there are so many variables. Before buying a fur, visit as many of these stores as you can. Compare. Talk with the owners. Be sure you have confidence in the people you are dealing with.

BALENCIA FURS
208 W 29th St (ground floor)
244-0005
Mon-Fri: 9-4:30; Sat and Sun by appointment
Closed Sat and Sun in summer

The word is *fur,* the feeling is luxurious, and the price is right. Balencia is a factory and showroom that merchandises furs in all shapes and forms. However, the real drawing card is that, in a city whose wholesale houses are notorious for shutting the retail customer out, each customer here is greeted as if she were the most important person in the world (other establishments, please take note). The showroom is beautifully decorated (primarily to impress out-of-town wholesale buyers), but as if the décor isn't enough, a personal tour of the factory and vaults is offered. Along the way, the customer is invited to mention anything that is particularly appealing, and once back in the showroom, all of the "mentionables" are brought out for a second look. The stock includes everything furry from pillows, scarves, and hats to long and elegant stoles, gowns, and coats. The furs range from frankly fun to unrivaled ranch mink and sable. With all of that to choose from, Balencia complicates things more by offering any combination thereof. Fun fur pillows can be made up in sable or ranch mink, and coats can have the style copied in fun fur, and vice versa. If it is possible that nothing suits your taste, they will happily make garments to order.

G. MICHAEL HENNESSY FURS

333 Seventh Ave (bet 28th and 29th St, 10th floor)
695-7991
Mon-Fri: 9:30-5; by appointment on Sat

Michael Hennessy has spent virtually all of his business life with furs. He started as an international fur trader, switched sides of the counter by running a fur salon in Beverly Hills, and later spent time as the fur director of Bonwit Teller and president of Maximilian Furs. In 1982, he, his wife Rubye, and another partner (who was later bought out) founded this fur-manufacturing company in New York, and both Hennessys seemed to have finally established a cozy den in the fur business. (Incidentally, Rubye Graham Hennessy is a former editor of *Seventeen Magazine* and the *Philadelphia Inquirer.* Her input is as valuable to the fashion sense as Michael's expertise is to the fur part of the business.) Which brings us to Hennessy Furs today. The business manufactures high-quality designer furs for women, which are sold to top stores in this country as well as Japan and Europe. New Yorkers benefit because Hennessy also sells retail (with no covert razzmatazz), and the entire collection is available to the public. This means that prices are about wholesale for the same garments that appear in better fur salons around the world. At the annual sales in August and late winter, those prices are even better. The best prices are for the in-stock furs, particularly the house specialty, which is mink. Mrs. Hennessy's fashion style is evident throughout because nothing is standard. Most are highly styled or made of unusual furs: Tibetan lamb, tanuki, fox, fitch, sheared and longhaired beavers, sables, and several varieties of raccoon. In addition, sizes for the ready-made garments come in a greater range than would be expected.

HARRY KIRSHNER AND SON
307 Seventh Ave (bet 27th and 28th St)
243-4847
Mon-Fri: 9-6; Sat: 10-5
Closed first two weeks in Aug

This should be one of your first stops for any kind of fur product, from throw pillows to full-length mink coats. Matthew, of Harry Kirshner, runs an operation that covers every aspect of the fur business. They reline, clean, alter, or store any fur at rock-bottom prices. What's even better is that they are neither pushy or snobbish, which may make them the only place to take Aunt Minnie's tattered but beloved lamb stole. ("Out, out, out," other fur fashion experts would probably cry.) This is remarkable for a business whose principal occupation is making and selling fur coats to order. Harry Kirshner offers tours of its factory (don't bother dressing; a more skeletal operation would be hard to find), and if nothing available appeals to the customer, a staff member will sit down and try to draw a coat to specifications. Many times, however, the factory tour includes the collection of secondhand furs that the company has restored to perfect and fashionable condition. And many customers come in for a *new* fur and walk out with a slightly worn one, for a fraction of what they were prepared to spend. Harry Kirshner is the only place in New York that offers such a wide choice.

H.B.A. FUR
333 Seventh Ave (bet 28th and 29th St)
564-1080
Mon-Fri: 8:30-5; Sat (Oct-Jan): 9-1

H.B.A. was one of the first of the fur-industry garment lofts to open to the public. As a result, they are more experienced and better attuned to customer requests than some of their neighbors. The stock includes all kinds of furs, but there is a tendency to avoid trends and stick to more classic styles. As a result, this year's fads, while available, are not singled out as *the* only thing to wear. (Please note that Geoffrey Beene designs for H.B.A.) Rather, there's a good selection of timeless furs, which can be taken off the racks or made to order. Prices are wholesale. Harold Frishman (the *H* of the name) is a knowledgeable and absolutely honest man. Ask for him, and you will see one of New York's top fur collections at unbeatable prices. Tell him I sent you.

NEW YORKER FUR SHOP
822 Third Ave (bet 50th and 51st St)
355-5090
Mon-Fri: 9-6; Sat: 9-5
Closed Sat in July and Aug

The New Yorker Fur Shop, like the Ritz, deals in new and used furs, and will sell, store, repair, and clean them. Because of the number of people who must wear current fur styles, New York is an excellent market for used furs, and both the New Yorker and the Ritz do a brisk business. The Ritz is the better-known shop, partly because of an extensive advertising campaign, which is just fine with the New Yorker, since people who can't afford to be seen selling back a fur prefer to go to the New Yorker. Bernard Glassman, the store's owner, says that half of his stock is new, and since the New Yorker isn't quite as well known as a recycling center, both sellers and buyers of furs feel more comfortable here. The New Yorker also does alterations, and they encourage browsing. Some of their best sales are made that way.

RITZ THRIFT SHOP
107 W 57th St
265-4559
Mon-Sat: 9-6

Down the block and across the street from Carnegie Hall, the Ritz Thrift Shop is as much an institution as its neighbor. And its clientele is just as loyal. The Ritz Thrift Shop seems to have been in business forever, buying and selling used furs to smart shoppers who know a super source when they see one. And all those years of experience have made the management as knowledgeable and fashion-conscious as the finest retail operations. The Ritz buys used furs outright. Because they are not a consignment operation (and perhaps because they offer free repairs and storage for as long as their client owns the coat), they are very picky about what they will buy. So, if your coat is passé, damaged, or not very good to begin with, the Ritz won't be interested—unless your coat is so outdated it's "in." (1940s jackets and long-haired and silver-fox furs fall in this category. The Ritz can't get enough of them.) So, customers are offered an incredible array of modern, stylish furs at prices roughly one-third of what the fur cost originally. At that rate, it's understandable that a good portion of their business is with people who trade in their furs every two years or so. The Ritz is also contemporary enough to sell 1980s men's furs.

VEETAL FASHION FURS
86 Rivington St (at Orchard St)
877-1010
Daily: 9-6

Note Veetal's official name because they dabble in a little bit of everything. But that little bit is only of the very best, and the store resembles the very best hometown ladies' specialty shop with a very eye-catching exterior. But everything is discounted, and some (though not all) prices are sensational. Sensational also describes Veetal's image. The goal seems to be outfitting a woman for a classy formal social occasion from head to toe. So while there is some sportswear, the emphasis is on shoes, bags, jewelry, fine leathers, and dressy evening clothing. The leather and suede coordinates can't be overlooked, except perhaps amidst the glitter of the cocktail dresses. And the fur salon has its own separate section since there is so much available. Virtually every type of fur can be had in jacket or coat length. It's not easy to leave this place empty-handed, but the discount policy makes it less painful to stock up.

Women's Knitwear

JOAN AND LILO KNIT COUTURE

1258 Third Ave (bet 72nd and 73rd St)
861-8190
Mon-Sat: 10-5

If you think *knit* when someone says *couture*, then Joan and Lilo are your kind of people. Their store specializes in designer (domestic and imported) knit dresses, sportswear, and suits for women, in sizes 6 to 20. The look is understated sophistication, much the way Joan and Lilo dress themselves. One unique service Joan and Lilo offers is a personal tour of the store, beginning with meeting clients at their hotels. From there, a discreet inquiry into the customer's lifestyle and wardrobe needs will produce exactly the right style for each individual. Of course, it helps if that style is best expressed in designer knits, but with the "unsurpassed quality and elegance" that is the store's motto, it would be hard not to find something to suit you here.

Women's Large Sizes

ASHANTI

872 Lexington Ave (bet 65th and 66th St)
535-0740, 947-8239
Mon-Wed, Fri, Sat: 10-6; Thurs: 10-8

Its name is a throwback to the days when ethnic boutiques were popular in Manhattan, but Ashanti's current image couldn't be more in vogue. Today, Ashanti carries better dresses, clothing, and accessories solely for the "larger woman." What they can't buy, they have made to order. In fact, says Bill Michael, 75 percent of his merchandise is of Ashanti's own design and manufacturing. And, adds Sandra Michael, the craftsmen who work exclusively for Ashanti are often supplied with patterns as well as designs, since the field is so new. There is more to large sizes than letting out seams or sewing up caftans in polka-dot polyester. Now, for the first time, there are boutiques that take pride in themselves *and* their customers: stores run on the belief that big ladies deserve a positive, stylish fashion image. Ashanti will do alterations and ship anywhere. It may be the only place to carry classic, quality clothing up to size 24.

FORGOTTEN WOMAN
888 Lexington Ave (bet 65th and 66th St)
535-8848
Mon-Wed, Fri, Sat: 10-6; Thurs: 10-7:30

Nancye Radmin, a former partner in the Farmer's Daughter Boutique, was so appalled by the dearth of size 20 clothes that she opened her own boutique. The Forgotten Woman thus became the first store in New York devoted exclusively to the larger-size woman and, in the process, became a trailblazer for Seventh Avenue manufacturers as well. The selection was so small in the beginning that Nancye designed much of her own merchandise. (She still creates about 25 percent of what is sold.) Eventually, manufacturers followed her lead, and the Forgotten Woman now stocks everything from Diane von Furstenberg's wrap dress to bathing suits with coordinated skirts for cocktail wear. Better still, as a "forgotten woman" herself, Nancye knows what looks good, and what styles have become almost a uniform for large women. Banished, therefore, are polka dots, polyesters in general, and three-piece polyester pant suits in particular. Nicest of all, sizes at the Forgotten Woman range from 0-8. Even if she is really a 48, the Forgotten Woman is one place where the well-endowed woman can forget that she is the scourge of the marketplace and feel wanted—and definitely *not* forgotten.

Women's Lingerie and Underwear

A. W. KAUFMAN
73 Orchard St (bet Broome and Grand St)
226-1629
Sun-Thurs: 10-5; Fri: 10-2:30 p.m.

Kaufman handles only the finest in ladies' lingerie and lounge wear, at prices that are substantially less than what uptown stores charge. In fact, Kaufman's discounts are so good that top quality merchandise here is competitively priced with lesser quality available elsewhere. Kaufman's line includes good, quality practical wear, such as lounge wear, hostess gowns, pajamas, slips, bikini briefs, terry robes, quilted velour robes, and flannel gowns, plus some items, such as the pure silk underwear and hand-embroidered accessories, that are both luxurious and downright frivolous. However, frivolity here is not as expensive as elsewhere, and if you're going to indulge yourself, it's nice to know you can do it at a bargain price. And quality is so good at Kaufman's that everything might last forever.

BRIEF ESSENTIALS
1407 Broadway (bet 38th and 39th St)
921-8344
Mon-Fri: 8:30-5:30

You should shop here, if for no other reason than to be able to brag that you got your sensational lingerie at 1407 Broadway—that veritable bastion of inaccessibility in the wholesale garment center. No matter that the store is off the lobby and is a legitimate store (or even that 1407 is known for junior sportswear and the only thing junior about Brief Essentials' stock is the sizes); if you can buy anything in this building, you've arrived! Not incidentally, the selection is great, if only slightly risqué. "Sensuous lingerie for the sensual woman" is their boast, and you'd better believe that a women's lingerie store doing business in a building full of men who wholesale women's fashions has got to offer the best items in terms of quality, fashion, and price. The ladies' lingerie business has really taken off in the New York area. Brief Essentials is just one of the many lingerie specialty stores with cute names that have sprung up all over. No longer are undergarments limited to bras and girdles purchased in a department store. These intimate boutiques consider such items as camisoles, corsets, and nightwear essential. And all of it is made up in such luxury fibers as silk and satin and the more plebian, yet highly popular, 100 percent cotton.

CHARLES WEISS
38 Orchard St (at Hester St)
226-1717
Sun-Thurs: 9-5; Fri: 9-2

Confusing Mendel Weiss with Charles Weiss is easy. Both stores carry the same general merchandise, are located in the same general area, and have the same last name. What is the difference? Charles Weiss is the place to better Mendel Weiss' discount. This discount ranges from 20 percent (rare) to 70 percent (rarer). In addition, it is laid out and run more like a small-town boutique than the typical Lower East Side operation. Do take advantage of its location, though. Charles Weiss sells the top brand names in lingerie, lounge wear, and ladies' undergarments.

D&A MERCHANDISE COMPANY
22 Orchard St (bet Canal and Hester St)
925-4766
Sun-Thurs: 9-5; Fri: 9-3

Elliot Kivell claims that a good reason to shop at D&A is "my sweet adorable smile," but even he concedes that his mother is probably the only person who would make that the first reason to come here. Most people come because it is a one-stop place to get underwear for the entire family at a minimum 25 percent discount, while ladies are impressed by the large selection of bras, gowns, lingerie, and underwear. (There is also a bit of sportswear.) But smart shoppers come to D&A for the labels they carry. Dior robes, designer tennis wear, nightwear, and top-of-the-line lingerie at these discount prices would convince anyone to shop here, whether Elliot smiles or not. Besides, who ever heard of an Orchard Street merchant boasting that he smiles? Or that he even knows how to smile? Finally, for those who can't see that smile in person, D&A will order any merchandise not in stock and ship it anywhere in the country. Items in stock are described in a brief flyer available to anyone who sends them a self-addressed envelope. The same discounts apply. They're enough to make *you* smile at Elliot.

GOLDMAN AND COHEN
54 Orchard St
966-0737
Sun-Fri: 9-5:30

Goldman and Cohen specializes in name-brand underwear and lingerie for women at a great discount—up to 70 percent! The lines include almost anything that falls within those two categories, including swimwear and matching accessories. This is one of the best.

HARRY MITTMAN
91 Allen St (at Broome St)
226-1738
Sun-Thurs: 8:30-4:30; Fri: 8:30-2:30
Closed second week of Feb and Aug

Harry Mittman specializes in cotton goods. Although this is primarily a wholesale operation, the salespeople are friendly and knowledgeable. The line includes almost anything in cotton but highlights dusters, smocks, nightgowns, and housedresses in all sizes. Because of the discount, they claim there are no refunds, charges, checks, exchanges, or try-ons. If you wear a large size—Mittman goes up to 52—it may be worth it. Otherwise, try a store that is happier to receive your money.

IMKAR COMPANY (M. KARFIOL AND SON)
294 Grand St (bet Allen and Eldridge St)
925-2459
Sun-Thurs: 10-5; Fri: 9:30-2; Sun (summer): 10-3

Imkar carries pajamas, underwear, and shirts for both men and women, at about one-third off retail prices. I include it here because the store has a fine line of women's lingerie, including dusters, gowns, and jackets. Some of the lines include such brands as Model's Coat, Barbizon, Skimma, and Munsingwear.

MENDEL WEISS

91 Orchard St (at Broome St)
925-6815
Sun-Thurs: 9:30-5:30; Fri: 9:30-4

Ladies' undergarments and lounge wear are a specialty on the Lower East Side, and Mendel Weiss is one of the stalwarts of the tradition. The first floor is dedicated to undergarments, with all of the famous brands well represented at a 25 percent discount. Trained specialists are available to aid mastectomy fittings. Upstairs, a similar selection in quality and brand names can be found in lingerie and lounge wear. The selection and quality can't be beat. The discount can.

ROBERTA

1252 Madison Ave (at 90th St)
860-8366
Mon-Sat: 10-6; closed Sat in July and Aug
410 Columbus Ave (at 80th St)
362-7750
Mon-Sat: 11-7; Sun: 12-6

So you thought that nightwear was either for the Las Vegas showgirl crowd or the convent? So did most everyone until Roberta Liford opened her shop for lingerie and "night dressing," which strives to be all things to all women, but is decidedly *not* either a Fredricks of Hollywood or a corset shop. Roberta is dedicated to the premise that a woman is entitled to the same luxury, style, and designer status for bedtime that she wears for daytime. She does it well, too. Lingerie, lounge wear, leg wear, bras, body suits, robes, nightgowns, and slippers are tastefully offered in all sizes. Where possible, Roberta deals in designer or brand names or, at the very least, in quality, luxury goods. The silver, art-deco store boasts *very* mirrored dressing rooms, where special attention is given to fit. Roberta says: "We offer personal service and a relaxed atmosphere without the hassle of department stores, but we carry the best of what department stores offer." Believe her.

SAMANTHA JONES

1391 Second Ave (at 72nd St)
472-3091
Mon-Sat: noon-7

Samantha Jones is the owner-operator of her own namesake boutique, specializing in romantic lingerie. That's romantic as in glamorous and soft, not risqué and obscene. Silk, cottons, and wool fibers are used alone or in combinations in almost every outfit. Ribbons, bows, and lace abound, as do the exclusive Samantha Jones scents that permeate the tiny shop. Kimono robes, lacy nightgowns of Victorian styling, and satin lounging outfits add to the allure of the Samantha Jones boutique's mystique. It isn't cheap—wool undershirts go for $35—but it is romantic.

Women's Millinery

The area bounded by 36th Street and 40th Street and Fifth Avenue and Seventh Avenue is the millinery district of New York and quite possibly the millinery capital of the nation. Within that area, there is a further segregation. Bridal millinery establishments are lumped together in the thirties off Broadway and Sixth Avenue; fur hats are in the garment district; and feathers, sequins, and other hat accessories are relegated to the peripheral twenties.

ARDEN'S
1014 Sixth Ave (bet 37th and 38th St)
391-6968
Mon-Fri: 9:30-6; Sat: 10-5

Brides in Middle America are forced to purchase their head wear from local bridal shops. But New Yorkers and New York visitors can purchase *their* veils and tiaras from the very source that supplies the local shops—Arden's. A large percentage of Arden's business is the wholesaling of bridal headgear to bridal shops. But here is a shop that is just as happy to meet the needs of a single bride as it is to outfit all of a Reverend Moon bridal procession. Arden's draws on an enormous supply of feathers, beads, flowers, and veils to create the perfect piece, and they can do it to order. (Bring your favorite picture from a magazine, and Arden's will recreate it.) Nonbrides or former customers can purchase felt hats. Here, too, they can be custom-made or purchased ready-made. All this, and the prices are wholesale!

DON MARSHALL
465 Park Ave (suite 305)
758-1686
Mon-Sat: 10:30-5; closed Sat from April to Sept

Even in fashion-conscious New York, personal milliners are a rare breed. In fact, Don Marshall, the owner of Don Marshall (obviously), says that although he has been in business over 30 years, his is a dying art, and he can see the writing on the wall. "It's too bad," he says. "This is a beautiful profession. Years from now, people will look at these hats and be amazed at the care that was taken to make each piece." And he's right, although it shouldn't take years for Marshall's work to be appreciated; Princess Di has already given hats a new lease on life. All of Marshall's hats and clothing (often in matching ensembles) are custom-made.

Marshall says that while custom-made hats are rare, couture work is all but dead. A visit here is in order just for the experience. And bear in mind that while an order is a good thing in its own right, Marshall's work may very well be the last of its kind anywhere. So your purchase could well be an instant heirloom, while its quality and style will always keep it fashionable. Marshall, who has good reason to be a remote craftsman or even a fashion snob, is neither. He is one of the friendliest guys you'll ever meet.

I. J. HERMAN
15 W 38th St (at Fifth Ave)
221-8981
Mon-Fri: 9-5; Sat: 9-3

I. J. Herman is a wholesale and retail operation that welcomes individual customers. However, their specialty is everyday wear rather than bridal. The stock is short on white nylon net and long on feathers and flowers. Herman has hat materials and finished hats, and if neither appeals to you, he will make hats to order. In contrast to his neighbors, Herman is extremely friendly, and will execute a hat design that any customer desires, as long as it is paid for first. Some of the samples hanging in the store are perfect as is, and several had been used in magazine ads. Herman's is also a good source for feathers and artificial flowers, which will interest those who don't wear hats but do wear hair ornaments. Herman's does ladies' hat cleaning and blocking, and receives many assignments from other manufacturers who no longer bother with blocking.

MANNY'S MILLINERY SUPPLY COMPANY
63 W 38th St
840-2235
Mon-Fri: 9-5:15; Sat: 9-3:15

Manny's is another New York institution. It carries millinery supplies, and that's an understatement. There are drawers, row after row, built up against the walls, and each is dedicated to a particular aspect of head adornment. The section for ladies' hatbands alone takes up almost 100 boxes and runs the gamut from thin pearl lines to wide leather belts, Western style. The center of the store is lined with tables that display accumulated odds and ends, as well as several bins of larger items that don't fit in the wall drawers. Hat forms can be found here, but they are available on hat-tree stands in the front, too. The front, incidentally, also displays sample hats in no particular order. The same hat tree had an inexpensive, unadorned felt hat at its pinnacle, and a beaver hat was buried about three quarters of the way down. Manny's likes unadorned hats. They will help fix up any hat and play with interchangeable decorations for it. It isn't necessarily money-saving, but it's a lot of fun. Manny's also sells completed hats, closeouts, and samples, and will re-create an old hat, too.

MAX MILLINERY CENTER
13 W 38th St (at Fifth Ave)
221-8896
Mon-Fri: 9:30-5:30; Sat: 10-4

Max Millinery Center is typical of the shops specializing in bridal millinery. Every conceivable type of headgear for the bride is available, and some that are not so conceivable as well. Mention should be made of the fact that the entire area considers itself a "wholesale only" trading center; therefore, few, if any, of the items on display are meant to be sold. The designer (whether a professional or a one-time customer) gathers the necessary materials, and the whole thing is put together elsewhere. Some of the companies really are wholesale suppliers, and will not tarry with single retail customers. Some begrudgingly do, and a handful—such as Max—conduct wholesale and retail (albeit at wholesale prices) side by side. There are enough of the latter companies for the bride-to-be to be satisfied without having to face the humiliation of being thrown out of a place where she is not wanted. Prices, however, are slightly higher in wholesale-retail operations, particularly if the premises are a street-level walk-in location. In addition to millinery supplies, Max also carries notions, bridal accessories, and related materials. In an effort to cater to the retail customer, Max will make up hats to order. Max carries bridal veils and hats for the mother of the bride and the bridesmaid, as well as some ordinary hats. They also stock dress trimmings, feather bags, artificial flowers, and bridal favors. If you bring in a picture, Max' personnel can duplicate it exactly.

PAUL'S VEIL AND NET
66 W 38th St (near Fifth Ave)
391-3822
Mon-Fri: 8:30-4:30; Sat: 8-2:30

It is inconceivable that the mob scene here is being repeated up and down the block, and that even *that* is a mere fraction of the bridal business nationwide. Despite the competition of its neighbors (or perhaps because of it), Paul's would be a first-choice recommendation for any bride-to-be who wants to put together her own bridal headpiece. Although they deal in illusion (lace, that is), they are one of the few stores on the block that does not maintain the illusion that they are a wholesale-only outfit, doing the lowly retail customer a *big* favor by unbarring the doors to her. The staff at Paul's seems genuinely glad to see you—glad to share your joy and overjoyed to help you create a truly unique bridal veil or crown. The store stocks all the equipment needed for the rest of the bridal party, as well as unusual accessories, bridal supplies, and a great collection of imported headpieces created from flowers. The lucky bride will find the savings—and the outfit—extraordinary!

Women's Small Sizes

LE PICCOLE

132 W 88th St (bet Columbus and Amsterdam Ave)
877-1633 by appointment only

Le Piccole means "the small one" in Italian, and the name describes owner Jane Klein's physical size. By no means, however, is it apt for describing her sense of style and business. At five foot, one inch in height, Klein had long suffered the indignity of being relegated to the children's department (or even the boy's shop) at department stores, where she was shown layer upon layer of "Rebecca of Sunnybrook Farm" type clothing. After it became obvious that no one else could recognize a petite woman as an adult—in terms of fashion, anyway—Klein decided to do the job herself. To minimize the financial risk, she renovated a salon in her brownstone home. Then, she sought out designers and manufacturers who created clothing she could personally wear. The original collection could have come right from Klein's ideal closet, and the subsequent ones have been similarly inspired. Great pride is taken in the fact that manufacturers of petite clothing are neither sought out or represented. Instead, many of the designers are new, innovative, and exclusive to the store. Nearly all of them first design an outfit for style, and then they cut it small for Le Piccole.

MINISHOP BOUTIQUE

14 W 55th St (at Fifth Ave)
873-5787, 247-0697
Mon-Sat: 10-7; Sun: noon-5

In an age where political minorities are demanding equal rights, it was inevitable that *physical* minorities would demand equal rights in fashion. As a result, the last few years have seen the opening of shops for large-size women, pregnant women, working women, and, now, small-size women. Minishop is run as the small woman's refuge. The specialty is sportswear, and *small* means really tiny sizes. The top size is a 5, and women who have bought their garments for years in the children's section are overjoyed to find the abundance of styles and colors available in their real size. Free alterations are also offered, but some of the customers who have never owned a garment that has not had to be altered say that the perfect fit at Minishop is worth the whole trip.

PIAFFE
841 Madison Ave (at 70th St)
744-9911
Mon, Fri, Sat: 10-6; Tues, Wed, Thurs: 10-7; Sun: 12-5

Piaffe has built a large business catering to small women. While not the only shop for petite women in town, Piaffe was one of the first and has consistently maintained an image of high fashion for dainty women. Piaffe can furnish a perfectly proportioned complete wardrobe with such labels as Stanley Blacker or Liz Claiborne as well as its own designs. And all of it is available in lingerie, sportswear, business attire, and evening wear (both formal and at-home). Prices are not cheap, but they aren't Madison Avenue exorbitant, either, especially considering that the alternative to Piaffe and its peers is custom-made clothing. Piaffe's biggest size is 6, and it stocks down to a 0. (0?) There are free alterations, and they promise express service for visitors who need it.

Women's Tall Sizes

SHELLY'S TALL GIRLS SHOPS
13 E 41st St (near Fifth Ave)
697-1115
Mon-Wed, Fri, Sat: 9:30-6; Thurs: 9:30-7

Tall ladies don't have much of a choice when shopping for clothing, even in New York. So, it is a bonus when a store specializing in fashions for tall women offers a designer line *and* reasonable, if not discount, prices. And Shelly's does. Shelly stands for Sheldon, not Rochelle, and that's the name for the designer line of tall fashions carried exclusively in the shop. Actually, that line is the only such line carried anywhere in the country! And while those fashions are particularly exciting for women who have heretofore been letting hems down no matter what the fashion experts decree, there's more. The store offers a complete wardrobe in sizes 7 to 17 and 8 to 22: sweaters, dresses, tops, skirts, pants, and even coats. That's *complete.* Filling all those requirements is a tall order. Since they are virtually unique, Shelly's also maintains an extensive mail-order business. They will ship anywhere in the country.

Coins, Stamps

GIMBELS STAMP AND COIN DEPARTMENT
Broadway at 33rd St (sixth floor)
564-3300
Mon, Thurs, Fri: 10-8:30; Tues, Wed: 10-7; Sat: 10-6

Gimbels, surprisingly, has one of the best numismatic and philatelic departments in all of New York City. Actually, this may not be so surprising, since each department store strives to have something that will set it off from its competitors and attract customers. Years ago, Gimbels built up its hobby departments, and the reputation has been sustained to this day; even several subway arcades and 33rd Street windows display those arts. Incidentally, the entertainment section of the Sunday *New York Times* always has a page dedicated to coin and stamp collecting. I mention it here because even a glance will show that Gimbels is, at the very least, competitive with smaller, exclusive shops in those fields. In addition, frequent closeouts and sales that can be handled by mail are advertised on that page.

HARMER ROOKE NUMISMATISTS
3 E 57th St (sixth floor)
751-1900
Mon-Fri: 9:30-5; Sat: 10-2:30

Harmer Rooke is a virtual cornucopia of coins, antiquities, stamps, and autographs, all stocked to abundance and available in hundreds of different styles and price ranges. Nancy McGlashan, one of the managers, says: "In antiquities alone, we have thousands of items on display, priced from a few dollars to $10,000. We feature Greek, Roman, Judaic, Pre-Columbian, Egyptian, and Middle Eastern coins and artifacts." There are also collections of Oriental prints, porcelains, American antiques, and a very large autograph collection. Each collection can stand among its peers throughout the country. Taken together, under one roof, it is positively staggering. The personnel behind the counters seem very knowledgeable and helpful, even if you don't make a purchase. They are besieged these days by people seeking value estimates of their prized possessions. Some may not be as valuable as Uncle Tobias had indicated in his will.

STACKS RARE COINS
123 W 57th St (near Sixth Ave)
582-2580
Mon-Fri: 10-5

Stacks, established in 1858, is the country's oldest and largest rare-coin dealer. With a specialty in rare coins, medals, and paper money of interest to collectors, Stacks has a solid reputation for individual service, integrity, and knowledge of the field. In addition to the specific sales of rare coins and the walk-in business, Stacks runs 10 public auctions a year. A $20 subscription fee is necessary for admission to the auction audience, but it is money well spent in the pursuit of money, because the best of Stack's collection is shown at its auctions. Both neophyte and experienced numismatists will do well at Stacks.

SUBWAY STAMP SHOP
111 Nassau St (bet Ann and Beekman St)
227-8637, 800-221-9960
Mon-Fri: 9:30-5:30

For 50 years, Subway has operated a stamp and coin shop, offering discounts to collectors and bearing one of the most intriguing store names in the city. In that time, they have become the largest stamp and coin mail-order supply company in the world, and a look at their catalog (and, more importantly, their prices) will explain why. There is more numismatic paraphernalia than can be described, and the family-run business has been in the same hands since 1952. There are also reference books, stamps and stamp products, and a new-issue service. Collectors should send for the catalog. It's an eye opener. Noncollectors can suffice with a request for an explanation of the store's name.

Crafts

A&S GEM AND MINERAL COMPANY
611 Broadway (room 721)
777-6080, 777-6081
Mon-Fri: 9-4; Sat: 10 a.m.-1 pm

A&S has both precious and semiprecious gems, as well as minerals of all sizes and types. The showroom has five full counters of cut stones, and the wallcases display minerals that weigh from a fraction of an ounce to over 200 pounds. Anywhere one looks, various stones are on display, and the few spots that are stone-free are stocked with lapidary materials. A&S claims that it carries at least a sampling of every possible type of stone. There are pearls, cabochon and faceted stones, and stone beads. All of these can be cut, ground, or otherwise processed to order for jewelry makers or mineral collectors. In addition, note the antique jade collection (including some super pendants), the stone and ivory carvings, stone boxes, and agate clocks. Much of this is displayed as if to show what can be done with the raw materials.

Most of all, a word must be said about the attitude here. Perhaps because they are far off the beaten track (at least as far as crafts or jewelry making goes), each customer is treated as an honored guest. When owner Serg Del'Fava died, his wife Anna took over to maintain the tradition. As a result, this is one of the top sources for a very diverse group, which includes jewelers, jewelry craft shops, jewelry manufacturers, jewelry students, neophytes, stone collectors, and adolescent mineral collectors. Tourists are invited to browse, and with the collection of aforementioned antiques and jade, the wholesale prices, the friendly help, and the expert selection of raw stones, it's a rare customer who walks out empty-handed. In the event he does, A&S also has a catalog for ordering at home on a wholesale or resale level.

ADVENTURES IN CRAFTS STUDIO
1321 Madison Ave (at 93rd St)
410-9793
Tues-Sat: by appointment

Here is a store devoted exclusively to decoupage, a specialty that's as adventurous as one can get in crafts. Dee Davis, who owns the shop, is fascinated by decoupage and, if allowed to, can talk anyone else into a fascination for it, too. Once she's converted the customer, she has a regular client, since no other store in New York has such a wide selection of decoupage materials or classes. Purse frames alone are more numerous than can be counted, and there are papers, hardwares, prints, old prints, plexiglass, trims, borders, and backgrounds. A complete list would also include the branching out into "country look" crafts and supplies, wood-burning, stenciling, and craft-design books. The shop appeared on *TV Bloopers* as the quintessential store visited by comedian Robert Klein searching for "adventure" in New York. Dee's definition of adventure wasn't his, but the cameras stayed around long enough to show one of the crafts classes.

ALLCRAFT TOOL AND SUPPLY COMPANY
64 W 48th St (room 1401)
246-4740, 895-0686 (mail order)
Mon-Fri: 9-4:45

If there is a definitive jewelry-making supply store, Allcraft is it. Its reputation is so old and solid that even the name of its manager, Catherine Grant, is legendary. Allcraft's catalog (write: 100 Frank Road, Hicksville, New York 11801) is so all-inclusive that it's impossible to describe. There is a complete (and it *is* complete) line of tools and supplies for jewelry making, silversmithing, metal smithing, enameling on metal, lost wax casting, and much, much more. Out-of-towners usually deal with the mail-order catalog, but New Yorkers don't miss the opportunity to visit the gleaming cornucopia that is the New York office. Most of what is available at the New York branch is in the tool line, and a trip elsewhere is necessary for gems or stones. But Allcraft has some supplies—certainly enough to get anyone started—and going through the little bins of odd brushes and supplies is half the fun.

BELL YARN
75 Essex St (bet Broome and Delancey St)
674-1030
Sun-Fri: 8:30-5:45

But for the fact that Bell Yarn is almost an institution with a nationwide following (some actually make pilgrimages to the store at sale time), I would not be writing about them. First, the good news. Bell is devoted to all kinds of needlework and has a stock and inventory that would satisfy anyone. Needleworkers are among the pickiest of hobbyists, yet Bell manages to provide every customer with material to match even the most exacting standards. Any purchase entitles you to wait in line for one of the ladies who will give qualified, free instructions. If you haven't any ideas of your own, inspiration can be gathered from the completed projects that hang from the ceilings and walls. In addition, a substantial discount is offered on every item sold, and there is a brisk mail-order business. That was the good news. The bad can be summed up in one word: *attitude.* It is abrasive. The salespeople are all middle-aged, local women who share a common, loud rudeness. To get service at Bell Yarn, one *must* push. You can stand for hours waiting patiently, and you will be totally ignored until a more battle-scarred customer usurps your place. Should you complain, the best you can hope for is a dirty look. A more typical reaction is, "So what should *I* do about it?" The much-touted free lessons are unavailable to anyone who didn't purchase every part of the project right there on the premises.

CERAMIC SUPPLY OF N.Y. & N.J.

534 LaGuardia Pl (bet Bleecker and Third St)
475-7236
Mon-Fri: 9-6; Sat: 10-1; closed Sat in summer

Ceramic Supply runs the whole wheel of pottery. They have a school, they sell supplies, wholesale and retail pottery, and they hand-make pottery, all from the same location. These people eat and breathe pottery, and their enthusiasm shows through in all of their projects. There are even special programs for the handicapped for work with clay, molds, and wheels. If classes aren't convenient, Ceramic Supply has books and materials available for the self-starter. In short, one can do everything at this location from buying an ashtray to casting a mold, or buying the mold and cast themselves.

CLAYWORKS

332 E Ninth St (bet First and Second Ave)
677-8311
Sat: noon-6; hours vary on other days

Clayworks is a pottery cooperative established over a decade ago. Each of the partners spends an equal amount of time teaching pottery classes, running the shop, and working on her own creations in the back of the shop. Out front, their own completed works, along with those of other artists who strike their fancy, are available for sale. Perhaps because pottery in general seems reminiscent of the farm kitchen, or because the feminine touch is very evident, Clayworks exudes a down-home feeling. Helaine Sorgen explains that with the security of their own place and so many years of experience, she and her partners are not reluctant to "take chances" with their work. "We try different glaze combinations, styles, shapes, and techniques all the time. With no middleman, we don't have to stick to tried and proven styles." And it works! Most happy to share its avocation through lessons, classes, and merchandising, Clayworks is also a super source for gifts. Perhaps it's because the items are not expensive and are obviously created to be used. For whatever reason, its items are whimsical, functional, and definitely cheerful.

ELDER CRAFTSMEN
850 Lexington Ave (bet 64th and 65th St)
535-8030
Mon: 11-5:30; Tues-Fri: 10-5:30; Sat: 10-4;
closed Sat in July and Aug

The Elder Craftsmen is a shop that epitomizes all that is great about New York. It is strictly a nonprofit organization. Everything that is sold is certifiably handmade by a senior citizen who's at least 60 years old. Often in desperate need of both money and something to do, these talented people are able to satisfy both needs, keeping 65 percent of the purchase price for everything they make that is sold (the remaining money goes to operating expenses for the shop). High standards are met here, for senior citizens have seldom gone through life without knowing one almost-professional craft, and most of the work is of quality higher than that of comparable machine-made items.

ERICA WILSON
717 Madison Ave (second floor)
832-7290
Mon, Tues, Wed, Fri: 10-5:30; Thurs: 10-7; Sat: 10-5

Erica Wilson is a British émigré whose name is synonymous with needlework, particularly in New York. Somehow, between writing books, a syndicated needlework column (appearing in the New York *Daily News),* doing a series on public television, and 20-hour work days, Wilson manages to run the store that supplies everything any needlework enthusiast could require. This is a needleworkers' needlework shop, and while Wilson is seldom in attendance, the competent staff would make anyone but Wilson herself superfluous. The store's pride are the custom-made designs and the copyrighted Erica Wilson designs, which are marketed throughout the world. The shop also has the usual line of services—blocking, padding, mounting, classes, and finishing—but here they are unusual. Many of the students in Wilson's classes are instructors and owners in other needlework shops. Perhaps because this is the definitive shop, Erica Wilson is not inexpensive.

ETTI'S YARN BARN

305 E 85th St (near Second Ave)
772-3111
Mon-Sat: 11-6:30

Etti (Ester) Drogicki has taken the venerable, homey hobby of knitting and brought it into the computer age. Her Yarn Barn still sports comforting touches of sensual wools and handmade sweaters, but the personal instructions and cozy classes are achieved by way of a Touch & Tell Computer System that has automated the entire store and spews out individual instructions in less than two minutes. Actually, the idea is long overdue. (Of course, my perspective is that of a nonknitting gadget lover, but it really makes sense.) Once a customer decides upon the pattern and colors, a computer will fine-tune the individual adjustments to size and style (crew or boat neck, cable or chain stitch?). The machine does this with a precision and speed unmatched by human hands, which frees Etti to offer her guidance in the selection of patterns or the teaching of stitches. And she needs that time, since the store offers classes and instructions for every level of knitting. I predict that within five years, it will be hard to find a shop that has *not* followed Etti's lead.

GLASSMASTERS GUILD

27 W 23rd St (fourth floor)
924-2868
Mon-Wed, Fri: 11-5:30; Thurs: 11-6:30; Sat: 10-5

Glassmasters carries all of the necessary components for making stained-glass windows, as well as tools, instruction books, and a complete line of stained-glass reproductions that they make themselves. It was the latter that brought me to them originally, and some are breathtaking. However, once I was inside the store, I was bombarded with talk of their sale "for beginners," which was offering glass cathedrals and opalescents as well as kerosene and SP40 soldering irons at substantial discounts. I was intrigued by the large range of materials I had never heard of. It's a fascinating hobby. The gallery features the work of the leading glass stainers and blowers in the country. Great for gifts. Personally, I'm greatly enjoying a stained-glass eagle window made by a local craftsman in my home state. When the Oregon sun shines through, it is sensational.

HIRED HAND

1324 Lexington Ave (bet 88th and 89th St)
722-1355
Mon-Fri: 10:30-6:30; Sat: 10-5:30

Although they've been in business together for almost a decade, Tullah Kellman and Fran Stein feel that their shop has only taken off since the recent baby boom. "All the war babies are moving back to the city, and they all seem to be having their first babies in their thirties," says Tullah. So you think the Hired Hand supplies nannies and the like? You think wrong. Those hands are busy creating pillows, tote bags, address books, picture frames, oven mitts, potholders, placemats, quilts, and just about anything else one can think of as long as it's fabric-covered. The fabric is calico for the most part, but there are paisleys and patchworks as well. ("As long as they are not Laura Ashley's or Liberty. We tried them once, but this is a neighborhood store, not a Madison Avenue boutique. The prices asked for those fabrics just put them out of our range," says Tullah.) Instead, it is the item that counts here. Big sellers are the children's quilts (adult sizes are available on special order) and the soft-covered toys. The Hired Hand would be overjoyed if the hand you hired was your own, and to this end they supply all quilting materials, fabric by the yard ("We sell as much fabric that way as on finished products"), and free instructions.

LIGHTHOUSE CRAFT SHOP
111 E 59th St
355-2200
Mon-Fri: 9-5

Maria Rodin runs this shop in the Lighthouse Building, which exhibits and sells the work of blind craftsmen. The setup and arrangements are similar to the Elder Craftsmen; the blind craftsman benefits directly from each purchase, and all of the merchandise is strictly professional. The Lighthouse used to be known for its collection of brushes and its chair-caning and reweaving service. It still is. (Chair caning is done by appointment.) But among New Yorkers, the Lighthouse is best known for its annual celebrity sale. Each autumn, people start to line up hours before the shop opens to get first chance at goods donated by the likes of Jackie Onassis and Seventh Avenue manufacturers. The first year, much of the stuff was of celebrity value and little else. However, the following year, celebrities donated better items, and the trend has continued. Designer gowns, sterling silver for 12, handmade clothing, and even trips to Europe have been offered. Some out-of-towners ask the Lighthouse for its dates in advance, and then plan their vacation around it. The merchandise is sensational in terms of price, quality, and style. Nearly every great designer is represented, and prices run about one-fifth of the original retail.

LOVELIA ENTERPRISES
356 E 41st St (in Tudor City)
490-0930
Mon-Fri: 9:30-5 by appointment only

Lovelia F. Albright and her establishment are one of New York's great finds. From a shop in Tudor City, overlooking the U.N., she dispenses the finest European Gobelin and Aubusson machine-woven tapestries at a price that can be one-third that of any other place. The tapestries are exquisite, and a visit tempts the customer into wanting them all, even if tapestries are not his style. (It wasn't mine until Albright started explaining the mastery involved.) *Her* mastery involves coordinating the proper décor with the proper tapestry, and she successfully demonstrated to me that every home, no matter what the décor, would look better with a tapestry. Some of the designs are the ubiquitous unicorns cavorting in a medieval scene; others are more modern. They come in all sizes. There is also a very impressive catalog for mail order, and she is now an agent for a famous artist's limited-edition handwoven tapestries.

MADE IN AMERICA
1234 Madison Ave (bet 88th and 89th St)
289-1113
Mon-Fri: 10:30-6; Sat: 11-5:30

To Margie Dyer, old American quilts are not things to be dragged out of the attic for an extra covering when guests show up; they're works of art. With that in mind, she opened Made in America to exhibit, display, and sell quilts and other Americana. Whether viewed as objects of art or not, these quilts are something to behold. Each pattern is categorized according to style and origin, and despite their age, they are still vividly bright and clear. At any given time, there are over 300 quilts in stock, all with authenticated histories. Ages date from 150 years old on up to the Depression, and the stock is always changing. That makes the ability to talk about each quilt all the more amazing. Made in America also sells country antiques and various pieces of Americana. (*This* in a shop on Madison Avenue!) Here, too, even rusted weather vanes aren't cheap; in fact, the more rustic and "country," the higher the cost. It's almost as though prices are guided by distance, in terms of time *and* space, from the farm. If you appreciate American Country décor, this is the place to pick up some sensational pieces.

NEW YORK EXCHANGE FOR WOMAN'S WORK
660 Madison Ave (bet 60th and 61st St)
753-2330
Mon-Fri: 9:30-5; Sat: 10-5

Established as a place for down-at-the-heels gentlewomen to sell their handiworks without a loss of pride, the New York Exchange for Woman's Work has been around for almost 100 years, with little change in its philosophy. True, its suppliers now include men as well as women, and few, if any, rely upon their handiwork to keep the family nurse in her pension. But the crafts are still quality handiwork in a wide variety of areas. The Exchange will finish your needlepoint, but their own is so far superior it makes more sense to buy a piece from them and put yours back in the closet. In addition to the needlepoint, there are dolls, shawls, mittens, fabrics, and model furniture. In fact, its Madison Avenue window displays are as professional as any of its neighbors.

NEW YORK YARN CENTER
61 W 37th St (near Sixth Ave, second floor)
921-9293
Mon-Fri: 10-6; Sat: 10-5

When Harry Baltaxe, the Yarn Center's owner, retired after 35 years in the business, he took his shop with him. Midtown knitters were desolate until Melinda Marinoff, Baltaxe's former assistant, picked up the needles and reopened a smaller but cleaner New York Yarn Center a few blocks away. Rejoice, knitters! The same incredible selection—in terms of colors, fibers, and quality—is once again available in midtown. Marinoff boasts that her credo is "the most exciting yarns, all at affordable prices!" The house specialty is a wool/rayon-textured yarn designed especially for use in sweaters, skirts, and dresses. Known as Fairtex velveteen, it is created exclusively for the shop. There are also cotton, linen, rayon, silk, and Persian wools available. All of it is enticing even to nonknitters.

PERFORMERS OUTLET
222 E 85th St
249-8435
Mon-Sat: 11-6; closed July and Aug

All of the merchandise here is ostensibly done by performers of stage, screen, and television, who have time on their creative hands. In addition to being talented, these performers are often unemployed, or even when employed they are frequently left with large blocks of unpaid time. Therefore, Performers Outlet was started as a cooperative venture to market the nonshowbiz talents of show-business people. The concept has worked so well that several would-be performers have given up the lively arts to develop full-time crafts careers. Undoubtedly, the performing arts would have had large numbers of defectors anyway, but in any event, this has left its mark on Performers Outlet merchandise. Today, very little of it is of amateur quality. Most of the items are of a caliber comparable with any crafts boutique. What makes things different here is that performers can be more daring and creative than other artists, and this shows through in their work. Thus, an item bought here may be truly unusual. But do not expect to see a ceramic ashtray made by a big star. One exception is Rosey Grier's needlepoint, which does appear here from time to time. As a little bonus, hot tea and sherry are served to any customers who wish it.

S. A. BENDHEIM COMPANY

122 Hudson St
226-6370
Mon-Fri: 8:30-5; Sat: 9-1

Bendheim offers everything Glassmasters does for stained-glass workers and more, but the atmosphere is more professional, more spartan, and more serious. Whereas Glassmasters often holds a beginners' sale, S. A. Bendheim barely recognizes neophytes, assumes everyone knows what he wants, and will sell both wholesale and retail to the public. For all these reasons, its prices are usually better, too. It appeared to me that Bendheim was also able to supply the customer more thoroughly. Bendheim offered antique glasses as well as opalescent and cathedral glass. It seemed consistently to do better in each field—tools, books, and leads—but not being an expert, I really couldn't say for sure. On the other hand, Bendheim is the only company that deals in mail orders, so if you are an armchair shopper, you have no choice. They now have glass rods and powders for glass blowing.

SCHOOL PRODUCTS COMPANY

1201 Broadway (bet 28th and 29th St, third floor)
679-3516
Mon-Fri: 8:30-5; Sat: 10-2

You'll like this one. Despite its name, this company has nothing to do with schools. What it does do is weaving and bookbinding, and it sells all the paraphernalia associated with these occupations. This is the only place in the city that sells spinning wheels for use rather than conversation pieces. One can even be made from a kit. School Products has a quarterly sale on yarn, for which mail-order customers will be notified. Orders will be mailed anywhere in the country, so a customer can take advantage of this sale without ever leaving home. Ask to be put on the mailing list.

SCULPTURE HOUSE

38 E 30th St (near Park Ave)
679-7474
Mon-Fri: 8-6; Sat: 10-4

In 1918, Bruno F. Barrie's family established a small sculpture and pottery workshop in Manhattan. The business grew and grew, and today, after one move (further downtown), it offers everything necessary for the serious sculptor. Note the *serious*, because Sculpture House, while pleasant and informative, hasn't the time or the space to initiate neophyte sculptors. It is assumed that the customer knows exactly what he wants. Sculpture House offers 16 different types of clay bodies, 12 types of wood suitable for carving, tools for ceramics and pottery, and more than 1,000 wood-carving tools that the Barrie business manufactures itself. While sculpture normally implies ceramics and clay, Claire Brush said that 90 percent of the business is related to wood-carving. Sculpture House offers a wide variety of services as well. There are no formal classes, but every conceivable related book can be found here, and observers are welcome in the casting department.

SELECTED THINGS
226 Front St (bet Beekman St and Peck Slip)
964-6755
Mon-Fri: 11:30-6; Sat, Sun: 12-6; closed New Year's Day, Easter, Christmas

This was one of the first shops in the South Street Seaport area to merit a listing in its own right, and Selected Things combines all the virtues that would make it noteworthy in any location. Situated in an 1801 former icehouse on the edge of the Seaport in a historic landmark district, Selected Things specializes in embroidered items. That includes both things to be done at leisure as well as gifts that have already been completed. With a nod toward the neighborhood, there are antique and hand-painted baskets, old sewing equipment, scrimshaw, old laces and linens, and tons and tons of pieces to embroider for all ages. As for "something special," there are black walnut knitting needles, contemporary pattern books, and hard-to-find needle items. Besides operating an old-fashioned store, Selected Things may well be the only embroidery-oriented store in the city. And the attitude of Dorothy Jurczenia at the shop is as homey as the sampler that hung in Grandma's kitchen.

SUNRAY YARN
349 Grand St (bet Essex and Ludlow St)
475-0062
Sun-Fri: 9:30-5; closed one week in July and Dec

Sunray is another of the Lower East Side needlework shops with all of the stock and discounts that the location connotes. Fortunately, though, it lacks the indigenous nasty personnel. In addition to the best prices on DMC and precut rug yarns, Sunray also has yarns for knitting (hand and machine), needlepoint kits and components, stitchery, latch-hook and punch rugs, and crocheting. There is also a brisk business in custom pillow design and needlework framing.

SWEET NELLIE (A COUNTRY STORE)
1262 Madison Ave (at 90th St)
876-5775
Mon-Sat: 10-6; closed two weeks in Aug

Sweet Nellie resides amidst quilts of all kinds. Most are antique, but there are others that are custom-made or quite modern. To make the quilts feel cozy and at home, Sweet Nellie has outfitted the rest of the shop to go with them. (One of the aims of the store is to make an antique quilt blend with modern décor.) I think a quilt goes well with virtually anything, but Sweet Nellie has shelves of handmade crafts, contemporary folk art, handwoven scarves, grain-painted frames, band boxes (they're not on the wall shelves), mohair throws, wool blankets, pillows, woven blankets, pictorial hooked rugs, baskets, handwoven rugs, and selected country furniture to complement the quilts. The rugs are handwoven by four weavers, and all of the things evoke a country setting. Sweet girl, that Nell!

WOOLWORKS

838 Madison Ave (bet 69th and 70th St)
861-8700
Mon-Fri: 9-4:30

Blocking costs at Woolworks are near the top end of the spectrum, but at least the blocking is done by its own studio and not farmed out. It also has one of the largest selections of wools for needlepoint in the entire city. Woolworks really has an extraordinary selection of both colors and canvases, many of which are custom-designed. Should your great-grandmother have left you a canvas now in need of repair, Woolworks does a remarkable job of restitching by placing another needlepoint canvas behind the original and reworking all of the holes. It is wizardry to behold. Check out the hand-designed pillows by Inman Cook, Woolworks' owner.

Dance Items

BALLET SHOP

1887 Broadway (bet 62nd and 63rd St)
581-7990
Mon-Sat: 11-8

This shop is a mecca for ballet fans. While the name presupposes that one would be inundated with tutus and leotards, the store has only a few decorating the walls. The entire display area of the store is devoted to books, records, and other memorabilia. Much of the Ballet Shop's business is conducted via mail with dance enthusiasts all over the country. Available are new books, gift and novelty items, rare or out-of-print books, limited editions, albums, programs, posters, art, collectors' items, ballet and opera videotapes, and autographs of stars. I list it all only to show that truly there are no ballet supplies. But now you know where to get a Nureyev T-shirt—your choice of several poses.

Department Stores, Malls

When a city boasts of the ability to sell virtually anything on a wholesale or retail level to virtually anybody, general department stores are either superfluous or make their mark by being very distinctive. The scores of department stores that have folded bear testimony to the former, and the survivors give proof of the latter. In New York, a department store is much more than a site for all-in-one shopping. It can be a charity-ball hall, the backdrop to a movie, or a way of life. About the only thing it is *not* is mundane, and about the only assumption that cannot be made is that the stores and their images are interchangeable. Even when they share corporate parents (as A&S and Bloomingdale's do) and merchandise lines, each store strives hard to make its own statement. The average New Yorker may have accounts at every store that's listed here, but the odds are that several of them are in the inactive files and that several more are used solely on specific occasions, such as the Altman's silver cloth sale. Furthermore, the Bonwit-Teller shopper has probably not set foot in Alexander's in years, while the Bendel customer wouldn't take her mother to Lord and Taylor. It isn't price. Really it's not. It's knowing the image and what to expect where.

While we're on the subject of department stores, we should mention a new development on the Manhattan shopping scene: the vertical mall. The first large one was Trump Tower, a glitzy, extravagant multilevel series of too-small shops with too-high prices. There are indeed some classy units with beautiful merchandise, but they look more like boutique showrooms than actual stores. But go see the waterfall—and don't lean over the ledges!

The latest addition is at one of the busiest corners in Manhattan: Herald Square, at 34th and Broadway, between Macy's and Gimbels, on the site of the old Saks 34th Street store. Herald Center resembles a poorly executed second-class version of a modern Hong Kong indoor shopping mall, without the color and the bargains. It is a vast disappointment; I cannot understand why Stanley Marcus (of Neiman-Marcus fame) lent his name to its planning. Each of the nine levels is named after an area of New York. None have any relevance to the namesake areas, except for a carousel on the "Central Park" floor. Stores are mainly small and uninteresting, except for Brookstone (housewares) and a huge butcher shop on the lower level. (The latter is adjacent to a fine jewelry operation. This is modern merchandising?) Perhaps some of the new stores planning to open here will add some much needed excitement. The "United Nations" food fair on the top floor can't begin to compare with the second-floor food carnival at the South Street Seaport.

ALEXANDER'S
Lexington Ave at 58th St
593-0880
Mon-Sat: 10-9; Sun: noon-5

Alexander's exalts its image as the ultimate bargain basement for those who consider gathering bargains a status symbol. Its strong points are its sales (check the Sunday papers) on "label out" name brands and occasional designer copies in better dresses and furs. Alexander's was one of the last New York stores to feature line-for-line Paris copies, and is nothing if not democratic. Everyone is invited to push, shove, and stand in line for long lengths of time. There are few amenities, and getting checked out of the store can seem like an inquisition. There are guards, security checks, and credit checks at every turn—but never a salesperson! It is not a terribly clean store, either. Alexander's makes a virtue of narrow aisles, jammed floors, and merchandise that is literally heaped in piles everywhere. Despite all this, some people swear by Alexander's on the grounds that all of these disadvantages result in great savings. And it must be said that I've heard from at least a half-dozen retailers: "I stopped carrying that. I just couldn't undercut Alexander's."

B. ALTMAN
Fifth Ave at 34th St
689-7000
Mon-Wed, Fri, Sat: 10-6: Thurs: 10-8

B. Altman is like a staid, wealthy old lady who stays home to supervise a bevy of servants and sets the perfect table in the proper house. And so are her clients. People who shop Altman's seem to have done so forever, but I've never heard of the passionate Altman's fan, anymore than I've heard of a teenager who demands an Altman's card of his own. *Women's Wear Daily* termed the store "totally asleep," and that's an apt description. Its strong points are home-and-hearth items: china, glassware, antiques, housewares, Oriental rugs, traditional furniture, and gifts. Its silver cloth sale and celebrity autograph sections are outstanding, as is the largest selection of Waterford crystal in the world. But those aren't reasons enough to shop the store, and neither is the full retail price or the lack of interest in current styles. They stay in business due to those affluent old ladies. When they go, so will Altman's—unless it wakes up.

BERGDORF GOODMAN
Fifth Ave at 57th St
753-7300
Mon-Wed, Fri, Sat: 10-6; Thurs: 10-8

Bergdorf's is what Altman's could be if it had management that was as concerned and well presented as Bergdorf's is. (The Goodman family used to live above the store's top floor. Now that's a family tradition of really being on top of things!) So the store has gone from being a much-better-than-average carriage-trade retailer specializing in top-of-the-line and custom-made clothing to an airy, totally redecorated environment that features designer boutiques. Heavy on European cachet yet perhaps still the quintessential New York store, it's much better than its advertising would lead you to believe. Anyone who has entered Bergdorf Goodman lately is an instant fan. So why hasn't the store publicized its metamorphosis? It is the premiere place to watch European fashion enter the American market, and its fashion sense is close to perfection. Its new accent is ready-to-wear designer fashion: classy, correct, and very *au courant*. Bergdorf specializes in conceptual designer boutiques; Pasta & Cheese, Van Cleef & Arpel's jewelry section, and the Delman shoe salon are just a few of these stores within the store. This is a store that has tried to correct its faults, while working out a new image. And it has succeeded. Its new face, new escalators, and new boutiques are very classy. It is a Fifth Avenue store at its best. A word of warning: At clearance sale time, all dignity seems to fly out the newly expanded windows. They may have needed the extra room for the frenzy.

BLOOMINGDALE'S

1000 Third Ave (at 59th St)
355-5900
Mon, Thurs: 10-9; Tues, Wed, Fri, Sat: 10-6:30; Sun: noon-5

This is *it* when it comes to New York department stores. Bloomingdale's has become a way of life, and rightfully so. The buyers have guts and aren't afraid to take a forward position with new ideas in merchandising. Practically all the departments are filled with interesting items; prices are not inexpensive, yet the selection is vast. Particularly fine departments include cosmetics, women's apparel, and furniture. No place in Manhattan has a better selection of quality furniture, and the model rooms (which are changed regularly), although sometimes extreme and over-theatrical, offer great new ideas in home decorating. The "Main Course" housewares floor is great—a "don't miss" attraction. The men's clothing department is not the best; however, there's a tremendous selection of all men's accessories, with more ties than you'll see anywhere other than on Allen Street on the Lower East Side. Service, however, can be indifferent; there are so many customers that the average salesperson just doesn't care. Bloomindale's food section on the lower level used to be number one, but Macy's has stolen that show. In any case, don't miss a day at Bloomie's. You'll come away tired and bruised and broke, but it's worth it! Try it on a Saturday; nothing can compare with that mob scene.

BONWIT TELLER
4 E 57th St (bet Madison and Fifth Ave)
593-3333
Mon-Wed, Fri: 10-7; Thurs: 10-8; Sat: 10-6; Sun: 12-5

New Yorkers were bereft when Bonwit's closed its flagship store in deference to the building of the Trump Tower. When Trump Tower opened, there was a cooperative agreement with Bonwit's, and the violet shopping bags and very feminine department store are now back on the New York scene. It is not clear, however, that the wait was worth it, or that all that anguish was necessary. The representative Bonwit's customer has always been the rich maiden aunt who came in once a season to augment her sensible shoes and sweater collections. Those ladies haven't shopped on 57th Street for years, and they're not about to return now. On the other hand, the average Trump Tower patron doesn't need Bonwit's. With all those elegant shops under the same roof, who needs violets? (Is the "average" Trump Tower patron a contradiction in terms?) So what does Bonwit have to offer? Mostly safe, expensive lines that neither excite nor draw attention. The store seems to have been built around Trump Tower, which is no marvel of cozy merchandising in itself. As an appendage without a clear drawing card, there is even less to recommend Bonwit's now. Why don't they wake up and smell the violets?

GIMBELS
Broadway at 33rd St
564-3300
Mon, Thurs, Fri: 10-8:30; Tues, Wed: 10-7; Sat: 10-6; Sun: noon-6

GIMBELS EAST
Lexington at 86th St
348-2300
Mon-Sat: 10-9; Sun: noon-6

The old-time tradition had Macy's and Gimbels as the retailing giants—and main competitors—in New York. "Does Macy's tell Gimbels?" was more than an expression, and the retailing wars between the two neighbors were legendary. But time has not been kind to Gimbels. For years, it has been searching for an image. The new Gimbels East was an attempt to answer Bloomingdale's. It didn't. The basic identity problem remains. Gimbels is neither inexpensive enough to be a discount store, nor quality enough to be a status shop. It seems to be basically a middle-class operation, but the middle class does not shop Gimbels. It either shops higher or lower. Of late, Gimbels has been trying to match both those markets. There's an emphasis on designer and better names, and the store sponsors a lot of "midnight madness" sales that aim for discount prices on what would normally be a regular retail operation. Does it work? Maybe. The sales days are zoos, but the rest of the time you could roller skate through the store.

HENRI BENDEL
10 W 57th St
247-1100
Mon-Wed, Fri, Sat: 10-6; Thurs: 10-8

Bendel's is divided into small shops with unusual items and high prices. It is fun to look around, but you aren't going to fulfill all your shopping needs at this store. Ladies, however, will be amazed by the accessory items in the store's many interesting boutiques. Elegance describes this smart, sophisticated shop for the trim, young New Yorker. The place is unique, and a Bendel's label really spells "in." Lately, Bendel's has slowed down. There are too many unrelated concessions (you can even get your teeth polished in the store) and not enough emphasis on current good looks. One of the street-floor sections does have the best gadgets selection around.

LORD & TAYLOR
Fifth Ave at 38th St
391-3344
Mon-Wed, Fri, Sat: 10-6; Thurs: 10-8

Lord & Taylor and New York have been "going steady" since 1826, when the store first opened. The relationship was cemented when L&T opened the first retail store on Fifth Avenue in 1903. Through all those years, L&T has been known for a tradition of good quality merchandise at good quality prices. Of late, the image has become somewhat stodgy. The store today still doesn't hold a candle to the days when Dorothy Shaver was its director, but efforts are being made to update the image without losing the tradition that L&T stands for. They spent a lot of money redoing the first floor, but it is still terribly dark and unattractive, and the giftware is still the type that would most appeal to Aunt Mabel. (Forget men's wear. It, along with home accessories, isn't worth the walk across the floor.) Upstairs are the women's fashion floors. Here it is apparent why a Lord & Taylor shopping bag is a status symbol that still means something. All of the fashions are tastefully selected and displayed, and dressing rooms are the epitome of what they should be. One woman said, "Doors! Do you believe it? Not only no community dressing room, but *doors!*" The specialty departments for college wear, separates, women's sizes, and the individual boutiques are particularly good, and you'll find all of the best names at sizable prices. You pay for those dressing-room doors!

MACY'S

Herald Square (Broadway at 34th St)
695-4400
Mon, Thurs, Fri: 9:45-8:30; Tues, Wed: 9:45-6:45;
Sat: 9:45-6; Sun: noon-6

Although Macy's advertises itself as the "world's largest store," I really don't know if that is a fact in terms of square footage. Some say that Marshall Field's in Chicago is larger; anyway, it is a big place and a great New York tradition. Moreover, Macy's has dramatically upgraded itself in recent years. One can find a vast selection of medium-to-better goods at the flagship store. Particularly outstanding areas are the housewares, children's wear, juniors, accessories, and domestics. A must at Macy's is the Cellar, located on the lower level. This is undoubtedly New York's best and most interesting section for all kinds of foods, houseware items, tableware, stationery, and anything you want for a party. Even if you aren't hungry and even if you aren't planning to have grandmother over for dinner, drop in and take a look at this exceptionally well-merchandised floor. There's even a branch of P.J. Clarke's restaurant. By the way, if you're ever near the Herald Square store during Easter, don't miss the flower show; it is worth a special trip, even from Scio, Oregon. I respect Macy's for what they are doing these days to modernize not only their store but the whole area. They are spending a lot of money and doing it well. Macy's is proving that there is class even in bigness. The new first floor is magnificent. Macy's computer department is state-of-the-art. Macy's management—at the top in retailing—has created a very exciting and value-packed store. Macy's is so much an institution that the annual Thanksgiving Day parade (which I think may be the single most exciting event in the city) is locally called the "Macy's Day Parade," as if Macy's and not Thanksgiving is being celebrated. And sometimes it should be. The latest Macy's tactic is to add proven outlets to their own store. Witness David's Cookies, Laura Ashley, Ralph Lauren, Porthault and Pratesi lines, Gucci and Vitton luggage, and P.J. Clarke's—and that's only a few.

OHRBACH'S

5 W 34th St
695-4000
Mon-Wed, Fri: 10-6:45; Thurs: 10-8:30;
Sat: 10-6; Sun: noon-6

Ohrbach's is a small, department-store chain that consistently brings better women's fashions to the general public at downright low prices. The image is *very* fashion-conscious (almost all of the soap operas—where clothing must be *au courant* daily—clad their staffs at Ohrbach's), but sometimes quality is sacrificed in the interest of fast style. About 15 years ago, Ohrbach's was purchased by a European consortium, and the image changed subtly—so subtly that the average shopper may not have noticed it. But if you look for it, the signs are there. For one thing, quality in general has declined. Prices have not. Ohrbach's no longer carries anything in a downright inexpensive class and yet, with the exception of women's coats and suits (where they should be your number-one stop), there is nothing truly outstanding. No one area excels, but if medium quality at medium prices attracts you, then Ohrbach's is your store.

SAKS FIFTH AVENUE

611 Fifth Ave (bet 49th and 50th St)
753-4000
Mon-Wed, Fri, Sat: 10-6; Thurs: 10-8

The definitive New York store *par excellence,* Saks Fifth Avenue is nearly everything a specialty department store in a big city should be. This statement will probably shock most people who feel they know the New York department-store scene, and there isn't much I can do to alter their opinion, except to say that the department store is one area I feel I can evaluate extremely well. Its detractors say that Saks is overpriced. Well, Bloomingdale's is more so. They also claim that the Saks image is staid. But it's really a matter of Saks knowing what its customers want and never varying from that. And, most of all, they claim that the store is small—small in terms of selection and physical layout. Well, my answer to that is that the latest style in department stores is to divide them up into smaller emporiums, a style Saks has used since 1928.

Saks has a perfect image, in my book. The ready-to-wear departments are luxurious, the merchandise is fashion-plus, and the labels are world famous. One answer to the "high priced" argument is that the Saks sales knock prices down to *below* what the factory outlets boast of. The beauty shop is one of the best in New York, and Saks' clientele reads like a Who's Who. The men's clothing department is super, with one of the largest selections in the city. The service and selection will not be bettered anywhere. Saks also has some interesting shops for giftware, luggage, and linens. Like any business, some spots are better than others. But furs, cocktail dresses, handbags, perfumes, designer costume jewelry, millinery, designer boutiques, and women's shoes are highlights. And the redesigned floors and transportation system are signs that the store is always interested in updating its image and service. Very, very classy.

Display Accessories

NIEDERMAIER DISPLAY
435 Hudson St
675-1106
Mon-Fri: 9-5; closed Dec 20-Jan 2

Niedermaier first came to public attention as a place to purchase the accessories for decorating a SoHo loft in early Pompeii or late Pompeii/early Manhattan styles. Its primary claim to fame was as a display design company that would sell its pieces to retail customers as easily as to Macy's. Their main business is conducted in two semiannual trade shows, which present samples of all possible displays to the trade. The samples themselves are sold to anyone who asks for them during the sales (January 2nd to February 15th, June 15th to July 30th). The rest of the year, items can be ordered or bought directly off the floor of the showroom at somewhat higher prices. What items? Well, nearly anything for display for stores, designers, decorators, or photographers. Whimsical home decorators go for the contemporary models, such as plaster-of-Paris folded T-shirts, or a plaster bucket made to look like wicker, or more models of various parts of the human anatomy that can be counted. Feet alone come in male legs, female legs, or one left, right, petite, extra large, or flat. I kid you not. There is more. Kenny and John Samuels of Niedermaier will design and create any kind of display needed for background work. While their forte is plaster work, they say that is a mere fraction of their business. They also supply sculptures, graphics, and models of fiberglass; in short, anything needed for household display.

Domestics

In my family store, we had a classification called "Domestics." But so much more is encompassed when applying such a heading to a group of stores in Manhattan instead of merely a section of a department store. Here, the term covers everything from down quilts to placemats. (For quilts, see also "Crafts.") Basically, what the following have in common is that the materials are all used in the home, and they are *not* housewares. Again, I include shops in every price range. They all deliver value and assortment.

AD HOC SOFTWARES
410 W Broadway (at Spring St)
925-2652
Mon-Sat: 11:30-7; Sun: 11:30-6

Julia McFarlane and Judith Kress Auchincloss were so successful with their uptown Manhattan Ad Hoc that they varied the usual "branch" idea and created an offshoot in SoHo that deals with linens, blankets, and bed and bath accessories. Despite two locations that span vastly different lifestyles as well as great geographical distances, both stores sell sleek, modern household necessities for the Eighties household. The image is still high tech, but the softwares store is perfectly named since it supplies exactly that—soft textures for the computer age. So there are sleek sheets and chic exercise equipment alongside hot-tub bath towels and bathroom accessories. This is one soft spot.

CACHE-CACHE

758 Madison Ave (bet 65th and 66th St)
744-6886, 744-7060
Mon-Fri: 10-6; Sat: 11-5

The linens sold in this boutique are far from inexpensive, but their designs can be just the thing to enliven a table or a room. Cache-Cache handles the better name-brand linens and housewares, but the real attraction is its own brightly colored, usually floral fabrics, which appear in several different items and sizes. If they do not have what you want, it can be specially ordered. People occasionally do that, but I found the available selection almost overwhelming. Cache-Cache is the Tiffany of domestic shops in the city. As for prices, well, there's a reason why the name is pronounced *cash-cash.*

D. PORTHAULT

57 E 57th St (bet Madison and Park Ave)
688-1660
Mon, Sat: 10-5; Tues-Fri: 9:30-5:30

Porthault, the queen of linens for queens, needs no introduction. Custom-made linens are available in a range of 600 designs (or more, if you count custom-copied designs), several scores of colors, and weaves of superluxurious density. Surprisingly, they claim to have been the originators of the nonwhite and solid-color bedcovering fad. More surprisingly, the people here are absolutely charming. There is an understanding that not everyone can afford to outfit one bed at a cost of $2,000. While Porthault will not compromise quality, much of what they sell is created with the belief that it is a better buy in the long run. Indeed, Porthault sheets last forever. They are handed down from generation to generation, and since they are decidedly not all scalloped embroidered-edge white, they are as modern as they are timeless. Ensembles can include everything from handkerchiefs to valances, and all is coordinated, right down to the towels. The extremely high thread counts in the linens make them not only supersoft but extradurable. And Porthault can handle custom work of an intricate nature for odd-size beds, baths, showers, windows, and curtains. You won't be saving bundles of money, but you will be getting every bit of what you paid for.

EZRA COHEN

307 Grand St (at Allen St)
925-7800
Sun-Fri: 9-5

Ezra Cohen is the first of the Lower East Side linen and dry-goods stores you encounter when coming from Allen Street. While the entire street—on both sides—is lined with them, Ezra Cohen is still the only one you have to know. Its floors are stocked with the finest linens, bedspreads, quilts, and draperies at prices that, at the very least, match the department stores' sale prices. Quality is always top-notch, and at a time when bed linens have styles and fashions like clothing, Ezra Cohen not only has what's current, but what will become current. The first floor is dedicated primarily to linens, and most customers never go any farther, since the sensational prices and vast selection can even make up complete trousseaus. The second floor is dedicated to bed coverings, and note the use of the word. It used to display bedspreads by Nettlecreek and custom-made designs, but as the "unmade" bed motif has spread, it has adapted as well. Today, it has coverlet, comforter, and sheet ensembles and such hard-to-find items as sheets for water beds and throws and comforters for platform beds. There is also a great selection of pillows. The top floor supplies upholstery and heavier houseware fabrics, such as quilts, slipcovers, and coordinated heavy drapery; lighter drapery is on the first floor. Ezra Cohen has been a family business for as many generations as it has floors. The current generation—Bob and Dave Cohen—are great people, who are as well versed as their ancestors in selling the best for the least.

J. SCHACHTER'S

115 Allen St (at Delancey St)
533-1150
Mon-Thurs: 9-5; Fri: 9-2; Sun: 9-4

J. Schachter's is the foremost purveyor of quilts in the New York area and perhaps the entire continent. If your grandparents had a quilt, at one time in its life it probably had some connection with Schachter's. It was either purchased, restuffed, mended, or sewn anew there, but somewhere, at some point, almost all but those quilts in museums have been to Schachter's. In the days before the home-crafts and comforter craze in home decorating, Schachter's managed to do a good business. Today, when everyone owns not only quilted coverlets but down-filled jackets and hoods, Schachter's business is booming. This is the oldest quilting firm in New York, and Schachter's knows everything there is to know about quilts and their making. The talents of the staff are almost infinite.

They can make a quilt in any size and in one of four quilting patterns from any fabric given to them. (If you want to use *their* fabric, that, of course, is available as well.) A choice of fillings includes down, feathers, lamb's wool, or dacron (for the allergic), and if all that confuses you, Schachter's will happily supply guidance. Schachter's has a complete line of linens as well as quilts. When both lines are combined, entire bedrooms or bathrooms, from rugs to ceiling and wall covering, can be completely coordinated. Schachter, the definitive quilt authority, has quilt specialists on the staff. Ask for Jay Rosenfeld or Tony Felix. Miss Kay handles the custom-made-quilt orders.

MAX EILENBERG COMPANY
449 Broadway (bet Canal and Grand St)
925-4456
Mon-Fri: 9-5

This long, narrow establishment is not a retail store, but it is stacked to the rafters with linens that are sold to retail customers at wholesale prices. If you want it, they have it or will order it. Eilenberg is the distributor for Cannon, Bates, Fieldcrest, Burlington, Bill Blass, and just about every other linen line. Perhaps because it is not a retail store, it lacks the usual unpleasant attitude I find common in discount linen shops. Eilenberg is great about refunds.

PILLOW SALON
238 E 60th St
755-6154
Mon-Thurs: 10-6; Fri: 10-5; closed Sat, Sun

Pillows are king here. Pillow Salon's complete line of pillows changes constantly, but always involves uniquely custom-designed pillows. Pillow units range from foot-rest to wall-sofa sizes. The latter can also be created with the aid of Pillow Salon's own carpentry experts. There are decorative pillows, custom-made pillows, and pillow samples, all of which are available to the trade and the general public.

PRATESI LINENS
829 Madison Ave (at 69th St)
288-2315
Mon-Sat: 10-6

If you want the experience of feeling outclassed and outpriced while buying sheets and towels, don't miss Pratesi. This is not to say that the linens here are not elegant; they are. But shopping here is an experience that would discourage anyone. The locked door is opened by a salesperson who does not leave your elbow as long as you are anywhere on the tiny premises. This includes being escorted out the door. Our guardian barely spoke English and couldn't answer any questions, including "What are your hours?" Why bother, then? Well, simply because the linens sold here are probably the best in the world. Families hand them down for generations. The absolutely plain designs and colors make them classics, and they also survive redecorating maneuvers. Downstairs, Pratesi stocks bed linens: sheets, pillowcases, and the like. All are in natural fiber cloth (the upstairs maid can always do the ironing!), and none will fill your bedroom with a riot of color. This is all classic, understated stuff. Upstairs (via a silver ultramodern stairway), the store displays bathroom linens. The robes are magnificent—again in natural fibers, again plush, and again quietly understated. So are the price tags. Towels are made in Italy exclusively for Pratesi and are of a thickness and quality that has to be felt to be believed. New lines include wallpaper, baby Pratesi, lingerie, and Pratesi Kitchen accessories. None of it is cheap by any stretch of the imagination.

TIGER'S EYE
157 W 72nd St (bet Broadway and Columbus Ave)
496-8488
Mon-Wed, Fri: 10-7; Thurs: 10-8; Sun: 1-6;
closed Sun in summer

How the store with the largest selection of bath towels, shower curtains, rugs, and accessories in the metropolitan area came to be called Tiger's Eye ceases to be a mystery when one meets owner Rick Tieger (get it?) and realizes it is his eye that's responsible for the tantalizing selection of bed and bath furnishings in his store. This is a specialized shop that is too big to be a boutique and too specific to be a department store. Tieger has furnished Tiger's Eye with items appealing to the polyglot neighborhood. It's not a position easily filled. Residents range from affluent designers who are professionals in style and tastes to welfare families. In between, there are yuppies, working-class natives who knew Columbus Avenue when it was just another neighborhood street, and their offspring, who reflect all of those other backgrounds. Yet the eye of the Tiger sees that all of those needs can be met. There are totally coordinated bed and bath suites and off-sized towels and liners. Curtains and draperies range from custom made to calico cafe-window treatments. Pillows, rugs, and window furnishings can be custom-ordered and designed to match other accessories. In short, this is probably the definitive shop in the field, and they discount what they sell along with offering an unrivaled knowledge of the field. Besides, who would argue with a tiger?

Drugs, Cosmetics

BOYD CHEMISTS
655 Madison Ave (at 60th St)
838-6558, 838-5524
Mon-Fri: 8:30-7; Sat: 9:30-6; closed Sat in July and Aug

Boyd is a drugstore in a city full of drugstores, so it has to have something special to be worthy of mention. Naturally, it does. In addition to a complete drug and prescription service, Boyd carries a complete line of cosmetics, soaps, jewelry, and brushes. The latter range from the common to the esoteric: i.e., nail brushes and moustache combs in a variety of sizes and shapes. I started my retailing career in the drug department of the family store, and I do not hesitate to say that Boyd has one of the largest and most complete selections I have ever seen of drugs, cosmetics, and sundries. Try the Spanish soap; it's super! Just one drawback: many of the salespeople can be brusque, crude, pushy, and indifferent. Shopping in this store is not always a pleasant experience.

CARLTON PRESCRIPTION CENTER
469 Seventh Ave (bet 35th and 36th St)
279-1813
Mon-Fri: 7:30-6:30; Sat: 10-5

This center offers a full-fledged pharmacy, with discount drug prices, as well as similarly discounted prices on vitamins and health and beauty aids. The latter are particularly important here. Brand-name perfumes are discounted 15 to 40 percent at all times. Brand-name cosmetics start at a 15 percent discount, but most are at least 20 percent, and some go for a as much as 40 percent off. Ed Weinberg at Carlton is willing to guarantee his low prices will remain the same for months on end. Finally, despite the discount image, this store stresses service. They stock odd items of interest to tourists and out-of-towners.

CASWELL-MASSEY PHARMACY
518 Lexington Ave (at 48th St)
(branches at South St Seaport and Herald Square)
755-2254
Mon-Fri: 9-6; Sat: 10-6

George Washington's personally concocted shaving cream is just one of the thousands of apothecary and toiletry articles sold at the Caswell-Massey Pharmacy, which was established in 1752. The store smells like the garden of specialties it is. In addition to regular pharmaceutical items, Caswell-Massey has a full range of perfumes, colognes, and the ingredients for making them. The apothecary catalog lists articles that have been sold since 1752, plus new items designed for the "natural look." It is the latter, in fact, that has brought a resurgence of interest in the shop. Caswell-Massey is one of the few places that sells unadulterated linaments, oils, waxes, soaps, and folk remedies. It may well be the only store in New York to have them all under one roof. Caswell-Massey's mail-order catalog cannot do justice to the rare and unusual items. George Washington's shaving cream isn't all that good, but try asking for a special blend of the house's choice.

ESSENTIAL PRODUCTS COMPANY

90 Water St (bet Wall St and Hanover Square)
344-4288
Mon-Fri: 9-6

Essential Products has been manufacturing flavors and fragrances for about 90 years. In that time, they learned that an enormous percentage of the prices of colognes and perfumes go into advertising and packaging. And so, as almost everyone with a chemistry set has wanted to do, they set to work to see how closely they could duplicate expensive scents at cheaper prices. The result is the Naudet line of fragrances, which president Barry Striem claims are indistinguishable from the real name brands, except for packaging and price. While they won't raise the prices for anything (to give you an idea of how absurd the real thing it, Essential Products sells *all* perfumes and *all* men's colognes at the same prices), they will gift-wrap. Perhaps the biggest gift, though, is letting someone else in on this. It's got to be one of the best buys in town. If you send them a self-addressed stamped envelope, they will send you sample sachets. After that, orders of $14 or more can be handled by mail. There is also a money-back guarantee, but they guarantee you'll be satisfied.

KAUFMAN PHARMACY

557 Lexington Ave (at 50th St)
755-2266
Daily: 24 hours

I hope Kaufman's is one phone number in New York you will never need, but it's wonderful to know it's there. In addition to the usual drugstore operation—soda fountain, sundries, cigarettes, electrical goods, and traveling needs—Kaufman's has a prescription department that's always open. Should the awful nightmare of being ill in a New York City hotel room actually happen to you, it's nice to know a pharmacy is open and ready to deliver your prescription by cab. Bless them! Incidentally, should you need a doctor to write that prescription, check this book's 24-hour numbers.

ROUND HOUSE FASHIONS

41 Orchard St (bet Grand and Hester St)
966-5951
Sun-Fri: 9-5

On the wrong side of Orchard Street (that is, south of Delancey), Round House wouldn't be worth searching for if it weren't for its discount policy on perfumes. Primarily a merchant of ladies' sportswear (which is, for the most part, decent if unexceptional), Round House discounts brand-name perfumes at 20 percent and more. In a day when everyone from Sophia Loren to Ralph Lauren is naming a scent for themselves, quality perfumes at a discount are hard to find. And after a day of egocentric clothes shopping on the Lower East Side, a stop at Round House will supply you with a gift for those you overlooked.

SOAP OPERA

51 Grove St (bet Bleecker St and Seventh Ave)
929-7756
Mon-Sat: noon-7; Sun: noon-5; closed Sun in July and Aug
30 Rockefeller Plaza
245-5090
Mon-Fri:10-6

The Soap Opera calls itself a "bath boutique," but its specialty is really soaps and soap products rather than bathroom furnishings. There is a full range of over 400 natural and herbal soaps, as well as soap powders, bath oils, and bath additives. Some, in fact, are packaged so that they make great gifts. The scents are long-lasting without being sickly sweet, and add a pleasing aroma to any room. Soaps are sold loose out of wicker baskets, and some are medicinal as well as fragrant. There is a good selection of oatmeal soaps that are supposed to be excellent for the complexion.

WILLIAM PAHL

232 W 58th St (bet Broadway and Seventh Ave)
265-6083
Mon-Fri: 9-5:15

The myriad number of artists, models, actresses, and theatrical people whose professions depend upon beauty supplies and cosmetics all seem to name William Pahl as their primary source. And for good reason: not only does the store stock every conceivable type of cosmetic, appliance, and beauty aid, it's all sold at a discount, and most of it is professional quality. L'Oreal, for example, makes a hair mousse in two varieties, one for public consumption and the other for use by hairdressers and salons. The latter is not obtainable by the general public, but Pahl has it, and at a price less than that of the regular product elsewhere. They also know their products. When customers' livelihoods depend upon it, they'd better!

ZITOMER PHARMACY
998 Madison Ave (bet 77th and 78th St)
737-5560
Mon-Fri: 9-7:30; Sat: 9-6:30; Sun: 10-5; closed Sun in summer

Last but certainly not least, Zitomer's is everything that Boyd Chemists is and several things that it is not. It has an absolutely complete cosmetics and sundries department, a fine, reliable pharmacy, and even a well-equipped electronics department. As an experienced judge of two of those fields, I can tell you that theirs is one of the very best. What they do not have is Boyd's arrogant attitude and rude salespeople. Perhaps it's because Zitomer is a family-run store. Bernard or Regina Zitomer are usually on the premises, which is another of my tenets of good retailing practices.

Exporters

MAR COMPANY
10 W 30th St (at Broadway)
889-7840
Mon-Sat: 10-6

Mar handles clothing and electrical appliances for domestic and export use. The sleek, clean store resembles nothing so much as an airport duty-free shop, with glass counters displaying electrical merchandise and clothing hanging from racks in the back of the store. Mar handles name-brand appliances, including Philco, Sony, Zenith, Panasonic, G.E., Yashica, and Texas Instruments. Merchandise in the clothing section is indicative of the United States in general and New York in particular. There are shirts and suits by Pierre Cardin, London Fog raincoats, Manhattan shirts, Cannon and Fieldcrest linens, and Levi and Lee jeans. The styling for all of these is classic as opposed to ultramodern, but the most interesting aspect is walking in and seeing the American lifestyle displayed as if it were that of a quaint foreign country. You fell like a tourist in your native land!

Eyeglasses

COHEN'S FASHION OPTICAL
117 Orchard St
674-1986
Locations throughout the city

Cohen's is a chain of optical stores whose drawing card is the ability to have eyeglasses ready in one hour. While not the first (or only) store to do this, Cohen's does have one of the best reputations. Furthermore, anyone in Manhattan who is in desperate need of a new pair of glasses (and it happens more frequently than imagined) benefits from the convenient locations. Cohen's also has qualified people to conduct eye examinations and fill prescriptions for glasses and contact lenses. Designer frames and brand-name contact lenses are sold at discount prices.

GRUEN OPTIKA CORPORATION
1225 Lexington Ave (bet 82nd and 83rd St)
628-2493
GRUEN OPTIKA WEST
2382 Broadway
Mon-Fri: 9:30-6:30; Sat: 9:30-4:30; closed Sat in July and Aug

The trend in optical stores is toward larger and more industrial settings. Gruen bucks the tradition, and aside for opening a West Side branch in 1985, it boasts the same faces and personal quality care year after year. Gruen enjoys a reputation for excellent service, be it emergency fittings or one-day turnaround, and a super selection of specialty eyewear. Their sunglasses, sport spectacles, and party eyewear are particularly noteworthy. The atmosphere is summed up by the continuous music and availability of coffee and soda. It's plain to see that these people care.

LUGENE OPTICIANS
38 E 57th St
486-7500
660 Madison Ave (bet 60th and 61st St)
486-7525
987 Madison Ave (Hotel Carlyle)
486-7520
Mon-Fri: 9-5:30; Sat: 10-5:30

Lugene is the Tiffany of optical stores, specializing in exclusive custom-made frames and sunglasses and the very finest in eyeglasses work. Its stock includes solid-gold frames, genuine tortoiseshell frames, and exclusive imported frames and sunglasses. There is a parallel service in eyeglass cases, chains, and accessories. Everything is top quality and made of the finest possible materials. The frames are all in the luxury class, either by virtue of their fine materials and workmanship, or by the fact that they are imported or uniquely styled. Lugene is well known for its quality and service, and its frames are something special.

PILDES

111 Nassau St
227-9893

1010 Third Ave
421-1322

147 E 86th St
831-0362

Mon-Fri: 9:30-6:30; Sat: 10-5

Pildes is the only "while-you-wait" eyeglasses chain in New York with an impeccable reputation. The surroundings and décor (at least on Nassau Street) are primitive, but the frames, styles, and service are first class.

Fabrics, Trimmings

A. A. FEATHER COMPANY (GETTINGER FEATHER CORPORATION)

16 W 36th St (bet Fifth and Sixth Ave, eighth floor)
695-9470
Mon-Thurs: 10-5; Fri: 10-4; closed July 1-15

What if you've made a quilt and want to stuff it with feathers? A.A. has more feathers than a gaggle of geese, but be ready for a high bill. Feathers are hard to come by and thus *very* expensive. If feathers are what you want, though, this company has the largest selection in New York. And if you'd like to wear them, it has boas and trimmings as well.

A. FEIBUSCH—ZIPPERS

109 Hester St
226-3964
Mon-Fri: 9-5; Sun: 9-4; closed Sun in summer

Would you believe a large store dedicated entirely to zippers? Well, in New York, nothing is impossible. One of the many amusing aspects of my visit here was hearing the boast, "We have one of the biggest selections of zippers in the U.S.A." *One* of the biggest selections? It's as if they really think there are zipper stores throughout the country! Anyway, Feibusch has zippers in every size, style, and color, and if it is not in stock, they will make it to order. There isn't too much of a demand for that service, however, since there are 200 colors in stock, in an almost infinite selection of sizes and styles. Should you need the matching thread to sew in a zipper, Feibusch carries that as well. A selection of threads rivaling the amazing number of zippers is available in all varieties. Eddie Feibusch assured me that no purchase is too small or too large. When I saw one woman purchase tiny zippers for doll clothes, I wasn't sure if that meant physical or financial size. In both senses, he was right. And he gives each customer prompt, personal service.

ART MAX FABRICS
250 W 40th St
398-0755, 398-0754, 398-0756
Mon-Fri: 8:30-6; Sat: 9-5

The fabric wholesale district is conveniently adjacent to the garment district, and the usual retail-shopper traditions of that area apply here. Some stores welcome the retail customer, some don't, and some fluctuate with the market. Art Max is dedicated to the retail customer. Its three floors are filled to overflowing with outstanding fabrics for clothing. Notice that I didn't mention the person who sews at home, for while there are hundreds of fabrics for home stitchers, the really striking brocades, metallics, and laces require an experienced touch. It would be a shame for a novice to ruin such beautiful fabrics. The real specialty here, however, is bridal fabrics. When the fabrics mentioned above are made into gowns, the wedding party could rival a *Vogue* layout. There are even a dozen different types of nets for bridal veils and infinite combinations of heavier materials. Try to get a look at the fabrics in the basement, not so much for the fabrics as for the basement. It looks like the catacombs!

C&F FABRICS
250 W 39th St
354-9360
Mon-Fri: 9-6; Sat: 9-5

Anyone who has ever used a sewing machine and inquired about buying top fabrics at the best prices in New York has been directed here at one time or another. The amazing thing is that as the years go by, this shop gains more and more customers and loses none. This loyalty is maintained because of the devotion with which Charles Friedstern and his wife collect mill ends, remnants, and special deals from the leading Seventh Avenue manufacturers. There is hardly a designer original in a fashion show whose fabric cannot be purchased from the Friedsterns. In addition to American designer fabrics, there are European designer materials, imported woolens, and decorator and upholstery fabrics that make interior designers drool. Friedstern's criteria for stocking them (since space is at a premium and such fabrics are bulky) are standards of variety, uniqueness, and sheer beauty. Needless to say, all of these fabrics are sold here at rock-bottom prices. All of this makes decorators and dressmakers alike come back again and again.

CINDERELLA FLOWER AND FEATHER COMPANY
57 W 38th St
840-0644
Mon-Sat: 8-4:30

A few years back, in the midst of a particularly cold and dreary winter, Seventh Avenue fashions began to blossom with artificial flowers in every possible spot as the "in" look for spring. The department stores quickly got the message, and in just a few weeks, people were removing their fur-lined gloves to hand $10 over the counter for a single flower for their lapel. Many of these transactions were made along 34th Street or Fifth Avenue, and only a few wise New Yorkers walked an extra two blocks to the "trimmings district," where they could have bought the identical flower for 35 cents. There were even buyers of the $10 variety who *knew* of the district and assumed that they couldn't get in. Cinderella Flower and Feather Company is for them. Jonathan Wolff, Cinderella's president, brags that they have the country's largest selection of feather trimmings, decorations, craft supplies, and conversation pieces, as well as silk and other artificial flowers. "And," he adds, "since we're the importer, our prices are unbeatable." The imported artificial silk flowers are the mainstay of the business, but it is the amateur who is the heart of the business. Cinderella loves to pull out box after box of glitter, paste, beads, corsages, plumes, or flower clusters for the retail customer, but the glitter is in *their* eye when the customer is an enterprising bride. Many bridal headdresses, bouquets, and table centerpieces originated here, and Cinderella will be happy to show pictures of completed arrangements. A free catalog is also available.

FABRIC WAREHOUSE

406 Broadway (bet Canal and Walker St)
431-9510
Mon-Wed, Fri: 9-6; Thurs: 9-7:30; Sat, Sun: 10-5

Fabric Warehouse is a store that has three very full floors of every imaginable kind of fabric and trimming, and since all of it is sold at discount prices, it's one of the best places to buy fabrics. Some of the attractions include an extensive wool collection and such dressy fabrics as chiffon, crepe, silk, and satin. There's enough to equip a wedding *and* all the guests. But most amazing are the bargain spots, where remnants and odd pieces go for so little its laughable. Two dollars for silk brocade? Since the Fabric Warehouse isn't exactly in the heart of the city, they sell patterns, notions, trimmings, and yarn at the same low prices, with the same excellent selection, so that customers don't have to make several stops.

FAR EASTERN FABRICS

171 Madison Ave (at 33rd St)
683-2623
Mon-Fri: 9-5

Far Eastern Fabrics is a small company that imports and retails some of the world's lushest fabrics from some of the world's most exotic places. From India, there are cotton prints and madras cottons, and, if that's too plebian for your taste, brocades and silks. There are even silk saris and stoles. From China, there are more brocades and silks, but China also offers damasks and woven and Jacquard tussah silk. Indonesia is represented by batiks, weavings, and cotton sarongs. Japanese silk pongee is among the cheapest silk Far Eastern offers, while Thailand is represented with a selection of cotton prints and silk scarves and stoles. And to show that Far Eastern is really global in its intent to pick the finest and the best, there are striking wax and java print cottons from the Netherlands. Prices for these often unique fabrics are excellent, and there are discounts offered for trade orders.

GAMPEL SUPPLY

39 W 37th St (bet Fifth and Sixth Ave)
398-9222
Mon-Fri: 9-4:30

This is the kind of business New York does best—esoteric. The sole stock in trade here is beads, and they know more about them than you will ever need to know. Just make a request, and you'll find that they have it—cheap. While single beads go for a dollar each at a department store one block away, Gampel sells them by bulk for a fraction of that price. Though they prefer to deal in bulk and at wholesale, individual customers are treated as courteously as if they were institutions, and the wholesale prices remain the same for all. As for the stock, well, a visit to Gampel is an education. Never again will you take a bead for granted. They come in sizes, colors, and varieties that boggle the mind. Pearlized beads alone come in over 20 different guises, and they are used for everything from bathroom curtains to earrings and flowers. Since many of its customers are crafts people, Gampel diverges slightly from its specialty to sell a few craft supplies—for bead-related crafts only. They stock needles, cartwheels, cord and chains (in enough different styles to match each bead), threads, poly bags, and weaving and macramé materials. Mail orders have a $20 minimum, and you may have trouble making that. Not because there isn't enough of a variety, but because prices are so reasonable.

GURIAN FABRICS

276 Fifth Ave (at 30th St)
689-9696
Mon-Fri: 9-5

Gurian is a family business (run by Stephen and Eli Gurian) that specializes in decorative fabrics. Some of the fabrics are sensational, but what makes Gurian a place to seek out is its discount prices on those fabrics. Gurian stocks fabrics for upholstery, draperies, slipcovers, and bedspreads, many of them in decorator and designer styles. All are sold at good discounts. A separate specialty worthy of note is the hand-embroidered crewel work. Crewel work makes for magnificent decorating accents under any circumstances, but when displayed side by side with the fabrics that will be used for furniture and draperies, it is exquisite. Gurian's crewel work is good enough to be featured in decorating magazines.

HANDLOOM BATIK

214 Mulberry St (at Spring St)
925-9542
Wed-Sat: 11-7; Sun: 1-6; Mon, Tues: by appointment

Note the hours here since the limited time can be a problem for anyone who wants to see one of the best collections of batiks outside a crafts museum. Carol Berlin runs Handloom Batik with near reverence for her merchandise. All of the fabrics are handmade, and she is quick to show how each can be set off to its best advantage. Imported handwoven and hand-batiked fabrics (primarily from India and Indonesia) are sold by the yard as fabric, or made up as clothing, napkins, tablecloths, or handiwork. Handloom Batik will also use its own fabrics for custom-made shirts and other garments. In addition, there is a gift selection featuring handicrafts of wood, stone, brass, and paper from the aforementioned countries. Pillows, bed covers, curtains, and napkins can be custom-made from the store's 100 percent cotton ikat and cotton batik. Incidentally, Carol Berlin says that collection is the largest in the country.

HYMAN HENDLER AND SONS

67 W 38th St (at Fifth Ave)
840-8393
Mon-Fri: 9-5:30

Down the block from Cinderella Flower and Feather, in the middle of what may be the trimmings center of the world, Hyman Hendler is one of the neighborhood's oldest businesses (established in 1900) and probably the crown head of the ribbon business. Hendler does it all: he manufactures, wholesales, imports, and acts as a jobber for every ribbon imaginable. It's hard to believe that there really exists as many variations as are jammed into this store. But Hendler's people can quickly shift through all of them (it seems to be a common trait on this street) and come up with the perfect trim, even when the customer isn't sure of what she needs. Hendler advertises that he has a similarly extensive selection of velvets and silks. It's possible, but those miles and miles of ribbons are the real attraction.

INTERCOASTAL TEXTILE CORPORATION
480 Broadway (at Broome St)
925-9235
Mon-Thurs: 9-6; Fri: 9-5; closed first two weeks in July

Intercoastal is an eight-story shop that carries decorator fabrics at wholesale prices. You must buy ample amounts of a particular item and know what you want when you come. The employees are used to dealing with large department stores and decorators. Bloomcraft and Scalamandre are a couple of the name brands that can be found here.

LEATHER FACTS
247 W 38th St (bet Seventh and Eighth Ave)
382-2788
Mon-Fri: 9-5:30; Sat: 10-2; sometimes closed Sat in summer

Dressmakers, sewers, and craftsmen consider Leather Facts the best source for their leather materials outside of Iowa. (Don't laugh. Iowa is a great source for pigskin.) Here in the midst of midtown Manhattan, Leather Facts deals with leather, skins, suede, snake, and exotic hides as if it were so much fabric. In addition to the skins, the store also offers processed goods. They have some completed items as well as skins that have been embossed, perforated, finished, or even printed. There aren't many alternatives in this business, and even less in the area, so it's doubly nice that these materials won't skin your pocketbook.

LEW NOVIK
45 W 38th St (at Fifth Ave)
354-5046, 221-8960
Mon-Fri: 9-5:15; Sat: 9:30-2:30

Lew Novik takes advantage of its location at the intersection of the wholesale millinery and fabric districts and dispenses both products. The millinery is primarily bridal in nature, and there is an enormous selection of lace, veils, flowers, light flower hair sprays, and bridesmaid hats. The bridal mantillas and illusion veils are particularly noteworthy. Accompanying the bridal millinery is a good collection of bridal accessories and favors and good-looking fabrics for made-to-order gowns. The fabric department excels in bridal fabrics, and the lace collection is extensive. There is also a selection of metallic fabrics that shimmer even on the bolt. As gowns, they must be magnificient.

LIBERTY OF LONDON
229 E 60th St
888-1057
Mon-Fri: 11-7; Sat: 10-6 (except summer);
open Sun in Dec

Liberty of London is world famous for its small-print fabrics, which come in such natural fibers as cotton, silk, wool, and challis. Most of the prints boast paisleys or flowers, and the overall look is very British. The fabric is sold by the roll and is available in most widths and types (as long as they are natural fibers), as well as some cotton-linen weaves, glazed chintzes, and wool-cotton blends. Many of the Liberty fabrics are displayed in the gift area. These items include cosmetic bags, padded hangers, address books, aprons, stuffed toys, and ties. Particularly note the ties; they're distinctive.

PIERRE DEUX FABRICS AND ACCESSORIES

381 Bleecker St
675-4054
870 Madison Ave (at 71st St)
570-9343
Mon-Sat: 10-6

Pierre Deux used to be an antiques shop that specialized in French provincial furniture. As such, it was one of the best. A few years ago, this store branched out into fabrics and fabric accessories. Today, Pierre Deux is synonymous with imported fabrics, tapestries, bags, tablecloths, and the like, all sold with the same attitude that characterized the antiques shop. The extraordinary cotton fabrics and the various accessories made from them are the store's highlights. Business is so good that Pierre Deux is gaining a nationwide reputation. The bags here are as much, if not more, of a status symbol as those of French designers. They are selectively distributed to better stores around the country.

RALEIGH TEXTILES

294 Eighth Ave (at 25th St)
255-9591
Mon-Fri: 9-5

Raleigh, located on the street level of the Raleigh Building, is a wholesale-retail operation that distributes the finest wools and woolen fabrics. Its excellent prices, more befitting the wholesale than the retail aspects of the business, are enough to recommend them. But there's more. This very formal business is run according to all the clichés of the garment center and fabric businesses in the city. And yet David Sturnin, the man who runs Raleigh, is one of the most down-to-earth human beings anywhere. (When I introduced myself, his first response was, "You make money from this book?") He is funny, witty, and very knowledgeable. He could even name both senators from Oregon, even if he did pronounce it "Ore-e-gone," New York style. So, for style in woolens, particularly fine fabric, and good quality at wholesale prices, try Raleigh. And tell Sturnin that the guy from Oregon sent you.

SAMUEL BECKENSTEIN

125 Orchard St
130 Orchard St
475-4525
Sun-Fri: 9-5:30

Samuel Beckenstein began business as a pushcart peddler in 1918. When he prospered, he opened a store selling wools for men's garments. Over the years, he became the definitive source for good wools, especially imported ones. Today, three men of the third generation preside over the empire born on that pushcart, and the reputation is meticulously maintained. The main branch is still devoted to woolen fabrics for men's wear, but there are gabardines, polyesters, and others as well. Customers include large stores, private tailors, and individuals who want fabric for custom-made suits. The branch at 130 Orchard Street is now a full trimming and appliqué supply shop, while there are couture fabrics, Shetland woolens, home-decorating and upholstery fabrics, as well as some of the most fantastic brocades this side of Damascus at the main store. Beckenstein's has a section for home sewers, as well as a home-decorating department that will make up custom slipcovers and matching draperies. The quality fabric sold wholesale at Beckenstein's is not readily available elsewhere at any price. It's worth a trip to the Lower East Side just to see the selection.

SHERU ENTERPRISES

49 W 38th St (near Fifth Ave)
730-0766
Mon-Fri: 9-6; Sat: 9:30-5

Sheru is almost impossible to describe. If you're into hobbies, crafts, or do-it-yourself decorating. Sheru has what you need. If you are an incurable bargain hunter, Sheru will satisfy your wildest dreams. And if you are none of these things, Sheru will guide, teach, and instruct you. Officially, Sheru is a wholesaler of beads and trimmings. Its stockpile includes bases for clips, shoe clips, ear posts, trimmings, artificial flowers, cords, ribbons, notions, buttons, and stringing supplies. You will need help from the friendly personnel, because these treasures are thrown about, and without a guide, many may well be overlooked. Antiquated and unwanted things are stored in the basement in probably the most haphazard order in the entire city. Amazingly, Mr. I. Sherwin seems to know what's down there. For the most part, though, stick to the main floor. The sheer amount of beads alone is overwhelming. Any possible configuration is represented, and Sheru will sell to a retail customer in any quality. In addition, the personnel almost zealously offer free instructions, perhaps on the theory that a hooked customer will return. And these instructions are invaluable.

Sheru is *very* up on what is "in" at the moment and how to recreate it at a fraction of the cost. If nothing else, this is a great place to pick up some beads or original jewelry for gifts.

SILK SURPLUS

223 E 58th St (near Second Ave)
753-6511

1147 Madison Ave (at 85th St)
794-9373

Mon-Fri: 10-5; Sat: 11-4; closed Sat in summer

Silk Surplus stores in the New York area are direct outlets for the fine Scalamandre fabrics. At each store, Scalamandre is sold for a minimum of one-third less than retail prices, and there is a choice selection of other equally luxurious fabrics at similar savings. There are periodic sales even on fabrics already discounted, and once or twice a year, there is an incredible warehouse sale in Long Island City. Smart shoppers line up hours in advance for a chance at those bargains. Lest it appear that Silk Surplus is a run-of-the-mill fabric store, we hasten to add that everything is elegantly run. Each store has a personal manager, and each manager strives to maintain an establishment more like an exclusive boutique than a fabric store. It is felt that the fabrics merit this kind of attention, and they do. Silk Surplus has the qualities I most like to see in a shop: quality, service, *and* a good discount price.

TINSEL TRADING

47 W 38th St
730-1030
Mon-Fri: 10:30-5; Sat: noon-5; closed Sat in July and Aug

Time at Tinsel Trading stopped around 1933, and anyone who spends any time here could believe that (a) all the traffic outside is caused by Model T cars and (b) a couple of hundred yards of various trims are absolutely mandatory. A comment from the personnel at Tinsel Trading: "We're the only firm in the United States specializing in antique gold and silver metallics, and we have everything from a gold thread to lamé fabric." Tinsel Trading offers an array of tinsel threads, braids, fringes, cords, tassels, gimps, medallions, edging, banding, gauze lamés, bullions, tinsel fabrics, ribbons, soutache, trims, and galloons. (No, I didn't know what all of things these were. However, these people not only know what they are, but where to find them in assorted colors. A galloon, for example, is an appliqué used in 1920s decorating, and, incidentally, it is not inexpensive. With its original ribbon or lace trappings, it can cost up to $30.) All of these trimmings are genuine antiques, but aside from the intrinsic antique value, many of the customers buy them for the accent they lend to modern clothing.

(Look what it did for Michael Jackson!) The collection of military gold braids, sword knots, and epaulets are unexcelled anywhere in the city, and are eagerly snapped up by those interested in the paramilitary look. Similarly, costume designers and museums purchase the metallic threads and other trimmings to complete outfits that could not be reproduced with currently manufactured items.

Fans

MANHATTAN LIGHTING AND CEILING FAN COMPANY

620 Broadway (bet Bleecker and Houston St)
254-6720
Mon-Fri: 10-6:30; Sat: 11-6:30; Sun: 12-6:30

This store used to be called the New York Ceiling Fan until owner Roy Schneit realized that people searching for lighting equipment were passing right on by his shop in NoHo (his version of SoHo), even though he stocked both lights and fans. So, he changed the name, and today the business is about equally divided between those seeking track lighting and lamps and those looking for ceiling fans. While the lighting possibilities are almost infinite, the selection of fans are limited to the ceiling types. Many of them even manage to be combinations: ceiling fans sporting lighting globes. The store also has a good selection of floor lamps, track lighting, table lamps, and lite kites (sic). For the less adventurous, Schneit offers consultation and designing on lighting systems.

MODERN SUPPLY COMPANY

19 Murray St (bet Broadway and Church St)
267-0100
Mon-Fri: 10-6; Sat: noon-5

The name was not an anachronism when Modern Supply conducted business for 40 years at a site now usurped by the World Trade Center. Today, however, it's hard to reconcile *modern* with a store that sells fans and only fans. But Leo and Jean Herschman are not about to change their habits of 50 years, so they still maintain their business name and a firm conviction that fans are the best way to keep things cool and comfortable. From un-air-conditioned offices on the third floor, the Herschmans dispense all kinds of fans. The floors are overcrowded with fans, and they hang from the ceiling in abundant formations that resemble a *Casablanca* jungle. Incidentally, did you know that Casablanca is a fan brand name? Mrs. Herschman says you should never order a Casablanca fan, because that's what you'll get—the brand-name model that is nothing like the one in the classic Bogart movie. Instead, ask for "the kind in the movie."

Fireplace Accessories

EDWIN JACKSON
1156 Second Ave (bet 60th and 61st St)
759-8210
Mon-Fri: 10-6

New Yorkers have a thing for fireplaces, and Edwin Jackson caters to that infatuation. Just as New York fireplaces run the gamut from brownstone antique to ultramodern blackstone, Edwin Jackson's fireplaces and accessories range from antique bed warmers to a shiny, new set of tools that look like plexiglass and silver. (They're really chrome. Do you know what would happen to silver in front of a fireplace?) The expanded two-store shop also stocks salvaged marble and sandstone mantelpieces, antique andirons, and an incredible display of screens and tool kits. In the Victorian era, paper fans and screens were popular for blocking fireplaces when not in use. Jackson's collection of surviving pieces is great for modern decorating. Along one wall is a group of bed warmers. If New York winters get any colder and fuel any more expensive, there may well be a run on these! Edwin Jackson will also do custom orders on mantels, mantelpieces, and accessories. This is primarily a fireplace *accessory* source, however; neither advice nor information is given on how to put a fireplace in working order. Edwin Jackson, after all, has been in business over 100 years, and assumes every New Yorker who has a fireplace knows how to run it.

WILLIAM H. JACKSON
3 E 47th St (at Fifth Ave)
753-9400
Mon-Fri: 9-4:30

"WBFP" in the real-estate ads stands for "wood-burning fireplace," and they are the rage in New York. Fifteen years ago, magazine articles were devoted to "how to decorate around your fireplace"; now *The New York Times* describes the best way to clean your flue. William H. Jackson is reaping the harvest of this resurgence in fireplace usage. In business since 1827, it is professionally familiar with all the various types of fireplaces in the city. In fact, many of the fireplaces were originally installed by the company. William H. Jackson has hundreds of mantels on display in its showroom. The variety ranges from antique and antique reproductions (in wood or marble combinations) to stark modern. There are also andirons, fire sets, screens, and excellent advice on enjoying your own fireplace. Jackson does some repair work (removing and installing mantels is a specialty), but it is better known for fireplace paraphernalia. A handy item: a "Damper is open"/"Damper is closed" reversible hanging sign.

Firewood, Ice

DIAMOND ICE COMPANY
216 W 23rd St (near Seventh Ave)
675-4115
Mon-Sat: 7-7

The iceman cometh in the summer, but he bringeth firewood in the winter. In an average winter, few people need ice, particularly the immense chucks sold here, so William Strong supplements his business by selling bags of firewood. The 40-pound minimum order of ice discourages all but restaurants and hostesses of *very* large parties from buying ice here. But if you've got the facilities, Diamond will fill orders for up to 5,000 pounds of the cold stuff. They deliver. At that weight, they'd better.

Flags

ACE BANNER AND FLAG COMPANY
107 W 27th St
620-9111
Mon-Fri: 9-5

Rally 'round the flag, boys, and if you need a flag, bumper sticker, or I.D. patch, Ace is the place to go. Established in 1916, Ace prides itself on having the flag of every country in the world readily available; other flags can be ordered. They range from lapel pins to George Washington Bridge banner size. (For those who don't know, the largest flown flag in the world is the Stars and Stripes, which hangs from the New Jersey side of the bridge every holiday.) For those who are not flag-waving types, Ace also stocks banners, buttons, pins, patches, balloons, pennants, and trophies. If you're running for office (school or national), all of the campaign paraphernalia can be ordered with a promise of quick delivery. Carl Calo, Ace's owner, does not exist on flags and campaigns alone, however. A large part of his business consists of outfitting grand openings and personalizing such equipment as pens, boat flags, and trophies. If your boat already has a flag and you're not running for office (a lot of my friends do), you can always try the T-shirts here. There's a full line, and all are custom-printed.

Floor Coverings

ABC CARPETS
881 Broadway (at 19th St)

ABC RUGS
888 Broadway
677-6970
Mon-Sat: 9-6; Thurs: 9-8; Sun: 11-5;
closed Sun in summer

If you like the carpets at Madison Square Garden, the Doral Hotel, the Palace Theater, or ex-CBS chairman William Paley's suite, you can come down to ABC and buy the same thing for yourself at the same discount prices they paid. ABC has been in existence over 80 years. Starting as a pushcart business, it expanded to a wholesale source for decorators, then to a retail store, and finally to the block-wide establishment it is today. Along the way, it made a reputation as the best carpet place in town, when price is a consideration. Dave Landy, ABC's vice-president, claims that ABC has the largest floor-covering inventory in the world readily available. Every major mill is represented, and there are Oriental (primarily machine-made) and area rugs as well. But the emphasis, Landy says, is always on price. Which is why decorators and designers line up alongside large industrial buyers and the small retail customer to get some of the best carpet values in town. Make this your number-one stop.

CERAMICA MIA TILE
405 E 51st St
759-2339
Mon-Fri: 10-6; Sat: 10-5; closed Sat in July and Aug

Ceramica Mia is an elegant store dedicated to custom tile and tiling. Neatly displayed in the showroom are the finest in imported and domestic floor and wall tiles. Some are so fine that the thought of walking upon them seems absurd. Indeed, the showroom director mentioned that some people have spent thousands of dollars buying these tiles, only to cover them with rugs. All of the tiles sold here are ceramic, and Ceramica Mia will do custom installation of any ceramic tiles purchased in the store. Much of the best work is destined for framing fireplaces or the backboards of sinks. Even single tiles have become hot plates and trivets in homes where the owner could not resist the sheer beauty of what is available here. Ceramica Mia imports Italian tile and distributes Mexican, Japanese, and domestic floor and wall tiles. The tiles are then custom-installed by the store's own craftsmen.

COUNTRY FLOORS

300 E 61st St
758-7414
Mon-Fri: 9-6; Sat: 9-5; closed Sat in summer

Country Floors is one of New York's biggest success stories, probably because they are offering a magnificent product. Begun in 1964, in the tiny cramped basement under the owner's photography studio, Country Floors has grown to today's size, which includes four huge stores in New York, Philadelphia, Miami, and Westport, Connecticut, as well as spacious New York headquarters and 21 affiliated representative stores nationwide. Customers from across the country have learned that Country Floors carries the finest in floor and wall tile, and have sought them out. Their sources include a wide variety of styles, artisans, and prices from all over the world. All are unique, and a visit—or at least a look at their catalog—is really necessary to appreciate the fineness and intricacy of each design. Some of the more complex patterns are hard to imagine as a whole when one concentrates on the individual tiles. The only common denominator is that even the simplest solid-color tiles are beautiful. Worthy of mention as well is the Caracalla collection of bath accessories imported from Italy. All are made of porcelain, and their sleek modern lines are beautifully understated.

DESIGNED WOOD FLOORING CENTER

281 Lafayette St (bet Prince and Houston St)
925-6633
Mon-Fri: 9-5; Sat: by appointment

Twenty years ago, the epitome of good decorating was wall-to-wall carpeting. Even ten years ago, industrial carpeting covered floors, walls, and even seating in the most modern homes. But nowadays, bare floors are in, and people who can provide those floors and care for them are as successful as the "in" can be. So it's no wonder that Designed Wood Flooring Center is in demand. Conventional homes are installing, finishing, or refinishing wood floors, while D.W.F.'s neighbors in former lofts have to deal with industrial flooring totally unacceptable for residential use. With the latter customer, the store can lay subfloor preparations as well as some magnificent wooden floors. These people are experts, and the floors come in almost as many varieties and patterns as that old-time wall-to-wall carpeting. And don't worry about their expertise. Despite the fact that they will accept the smallest private job, they are the choice of several of the city's major museums and department stores as well as major showrooms and building lobbies From now on, I guess I'll think twice before I walk over a wood floor without noticing it.

DILDARIAN
595 Madison Ave (at 54th St)
288-4948
Mon-Fri: 10-5

Floor covering is almost a misnomer here. These are works of art, and Dildarian treats each antique rug as such. Most of the business is dedicated to the sale of antique Oriental and European rugs, sold by experts who can tell a rug's pedigree by what seems like a mere glance. (It is, in reality, *much* more involved than that!) Dildarian operates in association with Vigo-Sternberg Galleries of London, and together they cover a significant portion of the antique floor-covering market. (They also handle tapestries.) As a sideline, which is by no means insignificant, Dildarian hand-cleans and repairs carpets of the same quality they sell. (Forget your home-hooked rug!) All restorations must first be cleaned, and both operations are carefully executed by hand.

ELIZABETH EAKINS
1053 Lexington Ave (bet 74th and 75th St)
628-1950
Mon-Sat: 11-6

Collectors would certainly choose Elizabeth Eakin's shop as a first-class source for handmade braided rugs and runners. But lest that conjure up the image of Colonial maple furniture, be warned that this is not rag-rug quality. All of the braided rugs sold here are handwoven and dyed in the shop's own New Hampshire mill and are made solely from their own fine wools. Since they are made on a custom-ordered basis, rugs are available in almost any size and shape, one of 200 colors or tweeds, and patterns that range from traditional to the house favorite, the "watermelon" design. Wool and linen runners are similarly available to order, and those who can't accommodate braided rugs in their décor can have runners woven together to create area rugs. To complete the look, coordinated upholstery fabric is also available. And finally, they handle white porcelain and stoneware tile. Though not recommended for hallways or other heavy-traffic areas, they are as up-to-date as can be for current decorating styles.

HASTINGS TILE
201 E 57th St (at Third Ave)
755- 2710
Mon-Fri: 9-5; Sat: 10-5; closed Sat in July and Aug

Tile will never seem the same after a visit to the Hastings Tile showroom. They bill themselves as "one-stop shopping for bath and kitchen design," but they are really an entry card for stylish and magnificent decorating ideas. The I. Balacchi collection of bathroom fittings offers towel racks, mirrors, and glass holders that look like red cathode-ray rods. The Principe collection of the same items comes in gleaming high-tech brass or coated satin-chrome brass. The pieces look more like executive desk sets than bathtub fixtures. And then we come to the tiles; they're not just for floors. Hastings' tiles cover walls, cabinets, ceilings, and even windows. There are polka dots, stripes, patterns and even murals, all made of tile. (The Pannelli collection features hand-painted patterns that are ceramic works of art. Believe it!) The showroom itself is so distinctive that it was cited by *Interior Design* for its complex of circles and polygons, which create a "controlled maze" that is also a vast open display space. A customer couldn't help but be inspired by the designs and displays, and with Hastings' products, it would be hard not to have sleek and distinctive tiling.

MOMENI INTERNATIONAL
36 E 31st St
532-9577
Mon-Fri: 9-5 by appointment only

The people here will tell you that they are wholesale only, and they will do everything short of saying "don't come," but try it anyway. Those who do will be rewarded by what may be the single best source for Oriental rugs in the city, because Momeni is a direct importer. Since they don't suffer individual retail customers officially, their prices reflect the wholesale rather than retail business. That doesn't make it cheap (good Oriental rugs never are), but it does assure the very best quality and the best price. So, don't let the wholesale-only policy scare you. They're really pussycats. But *don't* tell them I said so.

PILLOWRY
1034A Lexington Ave (bet 73rd and 74th St)
628-3844
Mon-Fri: 11:30-5:30; Sat: by chance or appointment; closed Sat in summer

Sandwiched between two generations of New York guidebook writers (her mother wrote one for the 1964 World's Fair, and her son, Peter, wrote *A Kid's New York*), Marjorie Lawrence specializes in Oriental rugs, and kilims at her latest shop on Lexington Avenue, the Pillowry. How she came to sell kilims while her relatives sold books is another story, but Lawrence has been doing so since 1971, and she is the best in the business. The name of the shop comes from the pillows that are made of tapestries, old rugs, and old textiles on the premises. Customers can select fabric from the kilims, knotted rugs, and Oriental carpets lying around the shop, or they can have them made to order. Her fabrics are old and authentic from all parts of the world, and the Pillowry does expert rug restoration as well as pillow creations from old textiles, needle-points, and rugs. You might say Lawrence has the subject covered, and thank goodness she didn't join the family in the guidebook business. With her competence, she'd be tough competition!

Folk Art

LESLIE EISENBERG FOLK ART GALLERY
1187 Lexington Ave (bet 80th and 81st St)
628-5454
Tues-Sat: 11-5; closed Sat in summer

Now that quilts have their place beside 18th-century Limoges as items that are now venerated as antiques, it shouldn't be surprising to find anything that Leslie Eisenberg stocks being termed as either art or very valuable. Still, it is unsettling to find weather vanes, wood widdles, figureheads, and ship models treated as genuine art, and it's even more unsettling to see the price tag. But perhaps the Folk Art Galley is trying to tell us something, while it is performing the valuable service of preserving it all. All these items—plus the prison art, whirligigs, black folk art, sailor's handiwork, and more—are indeed worthy of being called art; they're the country's heritage in 19th- and 20-century crafts. Most of it is sculptural, and there are no reproductions. Most of its ilk was thrown out, but that is exactly what makes it so valuable today. Eisenberg treats these items with the respect and veneration their age and workmanship deserves. And much of it is available nowhere else.

Furniture and Accessories

ACCENTS & IMAGES
1020 Second Ave (at 54th St)
838-3431
Mon-Fri: 11-7; Sat: 11-6

The merchandise is almost incidental to the display, which has come to be known throughout the city as being innovative, fascinating, and brilliant. In fact, a visit to Accents & Images is now almost *de rigueur* for many New York itineraries, even though most of those who see it haven't the vaguest idea what it is they sell. Well, they sell decorating accents and accessories, and the prices are moderate. But what is really sold here is savvy and atmosphere. The two owners, Ron Prybycien and Christopher McCall, are young men with designer credentials who opted for a retail store whose design they could personally supervise. The result broke both new ground and decorating dogma. Nothing is permanent. Walls slide, floors platform, panels pop in and out, and almost every month, there is a different featured exhibit. Most of all, this is a store that teaches as it sells. Exhibits featured here are frequently reflected in department-store model rooms several months later.

AMERICAN COUNTRY STORE

969 Lexington Ave (at 70th St)
744-6705
Mon-Sat: 10-6

Wall-covering and interior-design stores cite the American Country source books as popular items. The wall-covering books frequently have potential customers lined up for them, and the book *American Country* is a best seller at both decorator shops and bookstores. No one is quite sure why, but if high-tech was the interior-design mood of the late '70s, the '80s may be the era of American Country. Now, New York has an American Country Store. Its purpose is to make the American Country look an easy one to achieve by even the laziest or most amateurish of decorators. The shop specializes in the entire look, but its emphasis is on the little touches that bring it all together. So, there are wall hangings, folk art, antique samplers, candlesticks, plates, spoon sets, and more cups and saucers than you can count. "But," you are saying, "antiques aren't cheap." And you're right. American Country makes it all affordable by using modern fabric accessories that just *look* old, as well as a collection of antique furniture reproductions that are the pride of the store. The latter is really what the shop is all about. In stock are reproductions of Colonial furniture that are as authentic in detail as they can be. They say that their artists recreate old designs, which are then executed by craftsmen familiar with old-time traditions and work. Because they are not genuine antiques, prices are much more reasonable, with no loss of quality.

APARTMENT LIVING

12 W 21st St
260-5050
Mon-Wed, Fri, Sat: 10-6; Thurs: 10-8; Sun: noon-5

Now, in what other city would there be a mammoth business with a name like Apartment Living? And where else would such a store, in addition to touting its specialization in multi-use furniture specifically designed for city apartments, have to offer substantial discounts to be noteworthy? Probably nowhere else, but for New York, it's perfect. Apartment Living does specialize in furnishings for apartments. Most, if not all, is the kind New Yorkers love: lots of drawers, shelves, and storage space in functional form. Periodically, this specialty store also picks up pleasing accessories so that apartment furnishing can become an almost one-stop job when done here. But the real drawing card is the 40 percent discount offered on almost all bedding. New York-style sofa and hide-a beds, as well as more universal mattresses and box-spring sets are available. Rumor has it that Apartment Living's prices are the best in town. If not, they're close.

ARISE FUTON MATTRESS COMPANY

37 Wooster St
925-0310

57 Greene St
988-7274

1296 Third Ave (at 74th St)
496-8410

Mon-Sat: 11-7; Sun: 1-5

Futons are thick sleeping mats popular in Japan. They look much like upholstered cushions with cotton batting and unbleached muslin casings. Arise claims to have introduced them in 1970, and success has been such that in a few years, no one will need a further introduction to them. There are four different styles currently available, ranging from the standard futon to the "Living Health Imperial" models. So, while the classic futon has all-cotton batting, Arise's other models incorporate cores of various fibers for greater resiliency. In addition, the adaptation to New York has been made with the introduction of folding futon beds and even convertible sofas. These don't pull out; they simply drape the furniture. Frames are also available, and with custom-made futons, it is possible to decorate almost any room futon-style. Even living-room tables can be covered or uncovered, depending upon need. Cover the Arise cube, and you have a chair, hassock, or sofa. Remove the pillow, and it becomes a coffee table or dining table.

AU CHAT BOTTE DECORATION

903 Madison Ave (bet 72nd and 73rd St)
772-3381
Mon-Sat: 10-6; summer: 11-5; closed Sat in summer

Au Chat Botte is known for the finest imported clothing and shoes for babies and children. Now, the perfectly dressed child can hang his overalls on the perfectly executed bedpost in a room that's color coordinated and designed by Au Chat Botte Decoration. This store is a source for wardrobes, cribs, toy chests, tea tables, bookcases, changing tables, high chairs, and various other baby furnishings. All are hand-finished and hand-painted by a Brittany artist, and most of the stock has to be ordered from samples on display. Immediate delivery is possible, but the store prefers to custom-make each item. And all of the furniture decorated in pastoral designs can be accessorized, padded, covered, or displayed with suitable domestic items. Bibs, changing pads, bassinet linings, towels, linens, quilts, and even doll accessories can be ordered and color-coordinated. When Au Chat Botte is finished with a baby and its room, it is apparent that they have dealt with an heir apparent—and his parents.

BACK PAGES ANTIQUES

125 Greene St
460-5998
Tues-Sat: 11-6; Sun: noon-6 (call first)

The specialty here is turn-of-the-century oak furniture, and owner Alan Luchnick has a personal pride in roll-top desks, although he displays only a select few. Most of the antiques on display are related to what I'd call a whimsical musical motif. Stashed amid the Tiffany lamps, brass beds, and oak bookcases are classic jukeboxes, antique Wurlitzers, player pianos, and—combining both of Alan Luchnick's interests—antique upright oak pianos. The overall feel of the shop is one of massive oak pieces—pianos, desks, and the like—in a period setting. If you need a chair for that desk or piano, Back Pages has that, too. The SoHo Gallery where Back Pages is located can be rented for parties and advertising photo shoots.

BLOOMINGDALE'S FURNITURE DEPARTMENT

1000 Third Ave (at 59th St)
705-2576
Mon-Thurs: 10-9; Tues, Wed, Fri, Sat: 10-6:30; Sun: noon-5

The furniture floor at Bloomingdale's is, without question, the finest and most tastefully displayed collection of furniture in the United States. The model rooms, trendy and eye-catching, are changed periodically to show off large pieces (many are imports) and accessories in unusual settings, and each change is a media event. While one will see everything (or nearly everything) of a quality nature on this floor, there are some drawbacks. First, the prices (especially in the accessories and antiques area) are inflated; second, the salesmen do not seem to take that necessary personal interest; and third, delivery time is ridiculously long.

BRASS BED FACTORY

3 W 35th St (at Fifth Ave)
594-8777
Mon-Wed, Fri: 10-6; Thurs: 10-7; Sat, Sun: noon-5

This store is only two and a half blocks from Macy's, but the prices are not in the same neighborhood. Samples are available in the showroom, or you can order a standard-sized bed, custom-made. The Brass Bed Factory has been doing this for years, and it has an excellent reputation. It manufactures and sells directly to the consumer more than 20 different styles of brass beds, available in all sizes. If this is not enough, they are open to custom orders as well. Most of the styles are replicas of original antiques, and to their credit, they work with heavy solid brass exclusively. I particularly appreciated the magnificient four-poster and canopied styles. They show off brass to its best advantage.

BRASS BY BEN KARPEN

212 E 51st St
755-3450
Mon-Fri: 9:15-5:30; Sat: 10-4; closed Sat in summer

If it's made of brass, Ben Karpen has it, and at a good discount, too. The specialty is furniture: headboards, tea carts, tables, and the like, but there is also a fair amount of accessories, serving pieces, and giftwares to complement the furniture. Ben Karpen does not deal in used or antique brass, as do most New York dealers. All of his current stock, even that which is custom-manufactured, is totally lacking the "early farmhouse" look of antique (and near antique) brass furniture. If it does look familiar, you probably spotted it in scenes for advertisments or television and films. Karpen does a good business in rentals to photographers and the like. If that is impressive, do not lose sight of the knickknack department. It is one of the best around, with incredibly reasonable prices. Check the big-name catalog prices, then check the same thing here.

CITY LIFE INTERIORS

15 W 19th St (bet Fifth and Sixth Ave)
620-8110

661 Amsterdam Ave (at 92nd St)
866-6119

Mon-Sat: 10-7; Sun: 12-5

The view of city life from City Life is an eclectic one. Most of the furnishings are modern, to say the least, if not ultramodern. The imported Italian halogen lighting pieces are beyond high tech; they positively gleam. Most of the furniture in the store blends well with the lighting. But I said eclectic. There are handmade quilts alongside leather couches, and middle-class sleep sofas adjacent to one-of-a-kind artists' works. In fact, the 19th Street store boasts 3,000 square feet of space and 18-foot ceilings and is run almost more as a gallery than a furniture store. There are showings of artists whose creations range from Alan Hewson's hand-painted venetian blinds to kilim rugs and pillows. And that doesn't cover it all. Add wall units, upholstered furniture, and the City Life custom-built furniture and beds for people who have trouble finding anything to match those lamps and track lighting. If the Statue of Liberty sculpture is still on display (priced at $900), it's hard to miss City Life.

DECORATORS WAREHOUSE

665 11th Ave (bet 48th and 49th St)
489-7575
Mon-Sat: 10-6; Sun: noon-5; closed Sat and Sun in July and Aug and first two weeks in July

Decorators Warehouse tells New Yorkers that it aims to be "the Loehmann's of the furniture business," and city residents need no further introduction. Those who have never heard of Loehmann's will learn from a visit to either establishment that the name is synonymous with merchants who obtain the very latest, most fashionably high-quality items as jobbers and then sell them to the public at prices commanded elsewhere for just average merchandise. Loehmann's is unequaled in the clothing field, and Decorators Warehouse is working on a similar reputation for furniture. It's not unusual to see complete model rooms reassembled on one floor and a display of dishes and soup tureens on another, while the third floor is unveiling the latest in decorator and designer furniture. All of it is sold at an excellent discount price, reflecting its origins from over 75 different decorator and designer sources. There are those who say that Decorators Warehouse has the best prices for furniture in town. And anyone who has seen the selection will agree that it is awesome. Just get there fast. The stock is constantly changing.

DEUTSCH

196 Lexington Ave (at 32nd St)
683-8746
Mon-Fri: 9-5; Sat: 10-4; closed Sat in summer

Deutsch leaves the customer with the impression that his business is totally incidental. I tried three times to find out whether they accepted credit cards. I couldn't even find anyone who openly admitted that Deutsch accepted retail business. Suffice it to say that commerce here depends upon whim. Primarily importers, Deutsch usually deigns to deal with the retail customer, but be prepared for a total about-face when things get busy. (You might try dropping the name of Roger Deutsch should that happen. Mr. Deutsch assured me that he will give personal service to all retail customers.) Deutsch's rattan and wicker furniture is among the finest in the city. All of it is imported, and there are no cheap weaves here. Since the business is primarily wholesale, and the normal retail frills are dispensed with, prices are among the city's lowest.

FOREMOST-ARTHUR

8 W 30th St (at Fifth Ave, 10th floor)
242-3354, 889-6347
Mon-Wed, Fri, Sat: 9-4; Thurs: 9-7

First, the good news. Decorators recommend Foremost to friends who want to avoid decorator commissions, because it's a good place to get good quality furniture at a 20 to 50 percent discount. Foremost has four floors full of furniture, laid out by floor and room plans, and the personnel are friendly, knowledgeable, and helpful. (Ask for Harold Leeds, Mr. Starr, or Mr. Gilbert.) The discount *and* that knowledge make this an excellent source. The not-so-good news is that the four floors constitute the entire stock. Foremost can't (or won't) order anything that's not on display, and you must have a pretty good idea of what you want and how much you're willing to pay for it. Comparison and window shopping are particularly difficult here, and though the values are indeed very good, it isn't obvious unless you've shopped around. So, make this one of your last stops.

FRANK EASTERN COMPANY
599 Broadway (at Houston St)
219-0007
Mon-Fri: 9-5: Sat: 10-2; closed Sat in summer

First things first. No, I'm not related to this particular Frank. (And I'm resisting the use of all the puns on the name that I've accumulated over the years!) For business supplies and furniture, however, Frank Eastern Company should be a first choice. They are capable of completely furnishing a business office or even corporate headquarters. Tables, desks, chairs, files, bookcases, partitions, module components, and waiting-room furniture adaptable for residential use are all available here. And that's a partial list. Dollies and carts, wall units, shelf units, lockers, safes, glass-enclosed bulletin boards, and refrigerator-bars still don't make a complete list of the stock. The stationery and printing departments include calculators, pens, pencils, strapping tape, cassette recorders, magazine racks, time clocks, copy papers, and enough computer paper to satisfy the government's demand for red tape. And all of it is always sold at a discount. Smart people, these Franks!

HOWARD KAPLAN—
FRENCH COUNTRY STORE
35 E 10th St
674-1000
Mon-Fri: 10-6

For years, Howard Kaplan was a purveyor of quality French-country antiques for a business that operated on a wholesale-retail basis, with corresponding prices for different customers. The dichotomy in prices and the inability to furnish complete settings eventually got to Kaplan, and he decided to do something about it. His solution was to open his own shop, which is totally dedicated to French-country styles at wholesale prices. The new shop carries everything from napkin rings and toothpick holders to massive chests and dining tables in the French-country motif. Some are antiques, some are newly manufactured, but all the items fit Kaplan's two criteria: prices that are rock-bottom (although not necessarily inexpensive, they are the least expensive around for that particular item), and a wide selection that covers every room in the house.

ISABEL BRASS FURNITURE
120 E 32nd St
689-3307, 800-221-8523
Mon-Sat: 10:30-6; Sun: noon-5

Ex-law student Joao Isabel began selling brass furniture (particularly brass beds) almost by accident. But his merchandise was so good that in a short time he became the primary source for brass furniture in the city. However, Joao developed two minor problems along with his fame. First, no one could pronounce his Portuguese name, Joao; and second, many customers thought Isabel was a woman. Joao Isabel incorporated himself and his business, so he can concentrate completely upon being the best brass craftsman in the city. *Perfection* is the key word here, and painstaking work goes into the custom-made brass beds which are manufactured at the factory (one of the few in Manhattan) and sold in the showroom. Mirrors are used so that the craftsman can see both the front and back of the headboard as he works. All items are handmade to order. Such care pays off, for customers can spend up to $3,000 for a bed. Isabel creates tables, mirrors, and vanities, as well. Isabel's partner, Cal Donly, offers advice on design, style, and adaptability of brass beds to décor and lifestyle. (One of his favorites is a bed frame with a low footboard, the better to view television.) The factory turns out only custom work and repairs. Styles range from faithful reproductions of old brasswork to totally modern designs. Fringes and details cost money, but Donly suggests that the emphasis should be on quality over style, if a choice has to be made. How to tell quality? Two ways: by weight and rattle. The heavier the weight, the better, since the heaviest beds are made of cast brass (as opposed to brass plate or spun brass). And good beds don't rattle. The catalog is available for a small fee, refundable with the first purchase.

JAMES ROY
15 E 32nd St (bet Fifth and Madison Ave)
679-2565
Mon-Sat: 9:30-5:15

James Roy advertises that his prices are a guaranteed one-third less than those of the regular manufacturer's list price, and they have the documentation to prove it. For that alone, they should be a first choice for furniture buyers, but there is more! James Roy manages to maintain that discount by maintaining minimal stock and having most of his sales specially ordered. That way customers don't have to pay for overhead or large showrooms of furniture. Rather, they are invited to sift through the catalogs of major manufacturers and/or come to James Roy with specific manufacturer's and model numbers. They will then order the furniture and/or give a quote that is at least that guaranteed one-third off. They will not quote prices on the phone, but are most gracious, with no hard sell, in person. The showroom catalogs cover virtually every type of furniture and bedding, and the company can arrange for upholstery as well. Chairs, for example, can be ordered with the customer-supplied fabric, special fabric, or standard fabric. It also helps that the staff will sift through all those catalogs for the choices most compatible with the customer's needs. And finally, the showroom does have some furniture which is new and for sale. There are some fabulous buys on that furniture, since James Roy gets it at a good price and passes the savings on to consumers. This is a find!

JENSEN-LEWIS

89 Seventh Ave (at 15th St)
929-4880
Mon-Wed, Fri, Sat: 10-7; Thurs: 10-8

Jensen-Lewis is a canvas specialist who manufactures almost anything in canvas, including casual canvas furniture. (It got its start doing the canvas awnings for the stores along Ladies Mile in Gay Nineties.) Once, one of the decorating magazines had a spread on a client who wished to re-create a beach scene in an apartment living room. While the idea really sounds far-fetched, it was executed beautifully, and part of the charm was the use of the old-fashioned wooden-frame canvas beach chairs. The delighted owner found them so comfortable he had to replace some of them with straight-back chairs (also canvas), because he found himself falling asleep at his own gatherings. Jensen-Lewis offers these chairs and more. There are hammocks, portable hassocks, folding chairs, directors' chairs, stadium chairs, awnings, canopies, and a wide variety of such canvas products as luggage. The latter is a particularly good line. A friend of mine who has a folding canvas chair has to fight off her kids, who try to steal it from her room. It is that comfortable!

KLEINSLEEP/CLEARANCE

176 Sixth Ave (bet Spring and Vandam St)
226-0900
Mon-Wed, Fri: 10-7; Sat: 10-6; Thurs: 10-9; Sun: noon-5

Kleinsleep is a chain of stores in the New York area specializing in bedding needs. They have an excellent selection, from sofa beds to platform water beds. At each store, the byword is *discount,* and at this downtown location, everything is reduced even further. This is the final resting place of Klein's floor samples, closeouts, weird no-sells, mismatches, and just plain mistakes. Since almost all of these pieces are going to be covered with linens, almost none of the mistakes matter in the least, and a trip down here is a must for anyone in need of a bed. They boast that all sizes and types of sleeping furniture are available, including brass headboards. In particular, they claim New York City's largest showing of inner-spring and foam platform mattresses. At the very least, this is a company that is experienced and knows what it's doing. The customer gets advice, expertise, and exceptional bargains. Shipping is additional, but considering the neighborhood, it is usually well worth it. It is against the New York City health code to sell a used bed. Therefore, the leftovers sold here are just that; they're not used.

LA MAISON DES BIBLIOTHÈQUES (DISNET CORPORATION)
150 E 56th St (bet Lexington and Third Ave)
308-0181, 800-221-1335
Mon-Wed: 10-6; Thurs, Fri: 10-8; Sat: 11-4

La Maison des Bibliothéques offers a number of beautiful ways to house books. The firm sells French-made bookcases that can be created in almost any type of bookcase configuration. Styles range from French country to sleek black to brushed aluminum melamine, and they can be manufactured as wall units, corner pieces, glassed-in shelves, or with a variety of options for holding drawers, doors, TVs, or stereos. Given a room's measurements, La Maison de Bibliothèques can custom-manufacture shelving to fit almost any space. The company can work from decorator's sketches and set up the pieces once they are delivered. The finished product is a fitting place to house books and other valuables and a fitting product from one of the nicest companies in town.

METROPOLIS
100 Wooster St (bet Prince and Spring St)
226-6117
Daily: 11-6

SoHo has embraced art deco, particularly furniture of that period, as its own style. Within three short blocks, any number of art-deco furniture stores can be found. (It's a subject for another essay as to why art deco, the style of the thirties, is alive and well on the floors of the SoHo of the Eighties.) Metropolis is one of the best of these establishments, in part because it has gone far beyond the mere selling of nouveau antiques. The staff carefully researched the period and tracked down books on the subject and even the surviving original designers. When they had learned as much as they felt they could, they began to manufacture and sell their own furniture based upon the classic styles of that era, as well as some authentic vintage pieces. Today, Metropolis offers a full in-house design service as well as furniture of their own or of art-deco origin. They bill themselves as the largest store dealing with American art deco and modern furniture. They probably are, and they are certainly the most knowledgeable.

NEW YORK FURNITURE CENTER
41 E 31st St (bet Park Ave S and Madison Ave)
679-8866
Mon-Sat: 9:30-5; Thurs: 9:30-8

The New York Furniture Center is a five-floor building, less than a block from the sanctimonious, impossible-to-get-into New York Furniture Exchange, and it takes full advantage of its location. The New York Furniture Exchange is *the* "to the trade" building (actually, buildings) in the country. Every major furniture manufacturing company has an office and showroom there, and no retail consumer can gain access. Adjacent to the official buildings, however, are hundreds of businesses dealing in fabrics, accessories, wall coverings, and furniture. The New York Furniture Center is only one, but it is the closest the average customer can come to the wholesale market and still receive basic retail amenities.

Its five floors are stocked with furniture for every room in the house, in nearly every style. There are bedrooms, dining rooms, living rooms, sofa beds, leather pieces, wall bedding systems, and accent pieces in modern, contemporary, French and Italian Provincial, traditional, Spanish, and early-American styles. Due to the abundant floor space, many sample settings are on display, unlike other furniture showrooms, where furniture must be selected from a book and custom-ordered. Furniture, incidentally, is usually "cut" only twice a year, and orders for a particular style can backlog up to six months before being manufactured. If no one selects a piece, it isn't manufactured at all, even if it is shown in the catalog. N.Y.F.C. avoids some of this problem—sometimes—by having an inventory that's substantial by industry standards. Thus, there's a good chance that there will be no waiting period at all, and if the piece selected is one of the samples received from other showrooms, delivery can be arranged for the same day. There is also a free decorating service by professional staff designers and a personal guarantee from Leonard Borg that prices are among the lowest. In fact, they suggest you shop elsewhere and compare. If they don't have a piece, they will fill special orders.

OOPS (ORIGINALS ON PERMANENT SALE)

528 LaGuardia Pl (bet Bleecker and Third St)
982-0586
Tues-Sun: 12-6

OOPS is no accident for the clever furniture shopper. It deals with the class of furniture normally only available to designers and architects but sold to the public due to some mishap that occurred on its way to wholesalers. It may be damaged, but it is just as likely to be overstock, a cancellation, discountinued stock, or a showroom sample. So the chances of getting a bedroom suite or livingroom conversation pit with matching end tables are small, but OOPS is a top-notch source for distinctive individual pieces and vastly reduced prices. Since they deal in designer pieces (they claim the majority of their furniture can be seen in the Museum of Modern Art Permanent Collection), it is possible to collect specific names or styles, if not specific suites. The stock is not limited to current manufacturers; in fact, a store specialty is finding originals or creating approved reproductions of recent trends, such as Eliel Saarinen's art deco. They are also quite frank about the item's origin and how it go to be at OOPS in the first place. So you don't have to worry about spending $700 for a chair and then discovering that original though it may be, it spent the last 20 years on a Hamptons sun porch supporting a heavy statue.

PARABLE'S TAIL

172 Ninth Ave (bet 20th and 21st St)
255-1457
Mon-Wed, Fri: 10-6; Thurs: 10-8; Sat, Sun: 11-5

This is one of my favorites, if only for the vast selection and the owner's touch of whimsy, which is reflected throughout the store and in the store's name. Inside the crowded store, it is possible to find beds, tables, couches, canopies, cribs, and almost anything else imaginable made of solid brass. The accent is on contemporary furniture, as opposed to the care and nurture of brass beds per se, and it is a difference worth noting. Brass furniture is respected here because it's old, well preserved, and valuable. This interesting store has the leading edge in design in brass. It may well be the only place to get antique cribs and canopies of brass.

ROYAL OAKSMITH

982 Second Ave (at 52nd St)
751-3376
Daily: 11-8

Part of this book was written on a roll-top desk, so a review of any shop that specializes in them can't be totally objective. (If nothing else, they are great for pigeonholing thousands of odd scraps of paper!) Stuart Sackin and Jerry Zacker at Royal Oaksmith Ltd. obviously share my appreciation of these antiques. Their shop is totally devoted to antique oak furniture in general and roll-top desks in particular. They also offer a decorating service to help with problems—no small matter when you're trying to work around a massive three-by-four-by-five-foot piece of furniture. But Zacker is expert at transporting and placing such pieces, and knows just what to do. It helps that he assumes 19th-century oak craftsmen were no stronger than 20th-century oak furniture owners, and that they made the more massive pieces with removable parts. Zacker knows just where to take them apart. The shop carries other oak pieces in addition to the desks, but the latter is really their specialty.

STORK

505 Broome St (at W Broadway)
925-9724
Tues-Sun: 12-7

Stork is best known as a showcase for the limited-edition sculptures of Michael Garman, who specializes in reproductions of antique pieces. That's all well and good, but this Stork brings more good tidings in the form of solid brass beds, custom upholstery, hand-carved wood, and handmade oak furniture. While the store makes no distinction among its divergent specialties, pay particular attention to the quality of the oak furniture, and note that the common theme is the artistic handwork intrinsic to all these items. There are obviously artisans working here, and the furnishings in particular are outstanding. I think Garman is merely mass-producing copies of artworks. That's my opinion, so I'm underwhelmed on his account.

WICKER GARDEN

1318 Madison Ave (at 93rd St)
410-7000
Mon-Sat: 10-5:30; closed Sat in July and Aug

Pamela Scurry may be the quintessential yuppie New Yorker. She owns a successful business, has a son and a daughter, an I.B.M. executive for a husband, and a penthouse apartment on Fifth Avenue that has been written up for two pages in *The New York Times*. And her business, the Wicker Garden, has garnered similar space as well as spawned additions that paralleled Scurry's own life. So while the Wicker Garden was established as a prime source for wicker furniture and accessories spotlighted in a Victorian garden setting, when Scurry needed furniture for her children, the Wicker Garden's Children was created. When her own children needed clothing to match their stunning antique bedroom suites, the Wicker Garden's Baby was born to outfit them and other such lucky children. There is a tendency toward Victorian era pieces, and perhaps for that reason the shop is one of the few survivors of the "Casablanca" style of decorating that was popular a few years back. The Wicker Garden didn't go in for bamboo chairs and ceiling fans then, and it doesn't now. Rather, the image is totally Victorian. Linens, lace, quilts, and decorative accessories reinforce the image. And if decorating assistance is needed, Scurry and her staff stand at the ready to help there, too.

WICKERY
342 Third Ave (at 25th St)
889-3669
Mon-Fri: 10:30-6:30; Sat: 10:30-6

The Wickery handles wicker, rattan furniture, and accessories in tortoise shell, rolled bamboo, burned bamboo, or rattan core. Sizes range from basket to hamper size, with prices ranging from pennies to hundreds of dollars. Wicker in general and rockers requiring enormous space are not the most practical furniture for a New York apartment. Yet New Yorkers adapt their lives to what they like. All the luxury apartment buildings were built in the last 30 years, and they're filled with furniture that belonged to the era of the houses they replaced. Not only that, but these antiques were *never* found in New York. New York destroyed its antiques. Wicker isn't any better. Wicker belonged on a country porch, but now they make it as living-room furniture.

WIM AND KAREN'S SCANDINAVIAN FURNITURE
319 E 53rd St
758-4207
Mon-Wed, Fri: 10-6; Thurs; 10-7:30; Sat: 10-5

Wim Sanson's collection of Scandinavian furniture is light, airy, and functional. Unlike most Scandinavian and modern imports, they look and feel solid, which make them a good investment. Wim and Karen import oak, teak, and rosewood furniture for every room in the house. Most of it is made in factories abroad, and what isn't is manufactured to closely supervised specifications. If you think that all Scandinavian furniture is blond Danish modern, Wim and Karen deserve your visit. Most noteworthy is the encouragement they have given native Scandinavian designers. Many of the styles sold here are unique and suited for life on both sides of the Atlantic. It is possible that the mobile New York lifestyle finds its most sympathetic counterpart in Scandinavia. The convenient wall units in particular seem to bear this out, but there are also bedroom suites and super leather furniture for living-room seating.

WOODEN FURNITURE
508 Canal St
431-7075
Mon-Fri: by appointment; Sat, Sun: 11-6

One of the newest furniture shops in TriBeCa is a throwback to an old religious group: the Shakers. Primarily noted for their functional, no-nonsense approach to life, the Shakers made their own furniture in line with their philosophy. They died out long before TriBeCa—and Shaker furniture—became chic, and long before Kipp and Margot Osborne were born. But the Osbornes' store is devoted to Shaker-style furniture. Each piece is custom-made, which lets the Osbornes select woods and colors (they primarily work in oak and walnut). They can add un-Shakerlike drawers and hidden compartments to their pieces, because each piece is made to customer specification. The Osbornes make furniture in all sizes and dimensions, though they like to stick to Shaker-like proportions. They will create almost any type of furniture within those guidelines, and prices are less than those of genuine Shaker relics. The only disadvantage is that the Osbornes have become very popular, and a commissioned work can take between three and four months for completion. The move to their own 1836 Federal Row House in 1982 gave them greater space for work and display purposes. As a result, the Osbornes find themselves creating more and more of their own pieces, although many are still Shaker inspired.

WOOSTER GALLERY
86 Wooster St (bet Spring and Broome St)
219-2190
Daily: noon-7

Here's another entry for art-deco row. Wooster Gallery specializes in original art-deco furnishings and accessories. This shop enables the customer to do one-stop shopping for the 1930s and 1940s eras. There is also original European and single-commissioned furniture, and much like a book shop, the gallery maintains a "want list" and will try to locate specific pieces.

ZONA
484 Broome St (bet Wooster and Broadway)
925-6750
Tues-Sat: 12-6; Sun: 12-5

While we witness the arrival of Tex Mex on the city's restaurant menus, Zona has arrived in SoHo with echoes of the Southwest in housewares and furniture. The store revolves around the furniture, but it is set off by the fine soleri bells, gardening tools, decorative terra cotta and "found objects." All are "imported" from the Southwest and display good taste and a melding of images. I wonder if there's a store in Texas that sells New York hide-a-beds and water.

Games—Adult

MANHATTAN CHESS CLUB
154 W 57th St (10th floor)
333-5888
Mon-Fri: 3-10; Sat, Sun: 2-10

From the location (the 10th floor of the Carnegie Hall building) to its age (founded in 1877) to its membership roster (several grandmasters), the Manhattan Chess Club tells you that this isn't the place for dilettantes. Serious chess is played here, and the atmosphere resembles that of a cathedral. But like any religion, the Manhattan Chess Club welcomes devotees and even tries to proselytize. There are classes on Monday evenings for intermediate players and on Tuesday evenings for novices, as well as Saturday lessons for children. Friday evenings are rapid tournament nights, while on Tuesday and Thursday evenings there are round-robin tournaments. If that schedule doesn't mate with your own, there are also impromptu matches and more formal tournaments. And for the chess groupie, the small admission charge enables you to see, and sometimes play, a grandmaster.

MARION & COMPANY
315 W 39th St (16th floor)
868-9155, 594-1848
Mon-Wed, Sat: 9-5; Thurs, Fri: 9-6

After 80 years, this shop is still a homey, family-run business, despite the fact that they have a virtual monopoly on the adult-games supply business in New York. The majority of that business is on the wholesale level. "We supply 12 gross of playing cards a week to an uptown club," says Eddie Weinstein. "The retail business has only taken off in the last few years, and of course it could never match that level. We maintain it because it's fun." And fun is what is marketed here. The main drawing card is still cards, which come in every imaginable size, shape, and color. A purchase can evoke a lecture on the subtle distinctions between playing cards used in foreign countries. (Aside from the somewhat commonly known differences in face card appearances, which go to curly-haired, straight-haired, and all-male characters—including the queen, who is, obviously, not called that—European cards are marked on all four corners, while the American are only marked on two. "Much harder on left-handed players," says Eddie.) Marion & Company also distributes backgammon sets, dominoes, chess pieces, chips, crap tables, and all sorts of dice. They purchased their own dice factory in Manhattan, but even with that, they are hard-pressed to keep up with the demand. Eddie feels that legalized gambling in New York is inevitable, but it won't have any effect on his business. They are already selling all that they possibly can, because their quality is high and their prices are incredibly low.

VILLAGE CHESS SHOP

230 Thompson St (bet Bleecker and Third St)
475-9580
Daily: noon-midnight

People who play chess in the Village can walk to the Village Chess Shop to play a game for about $1 an hour. And those who are searching for really unique chess pieces would be wise to patronize this shop. Chess sets are available at the Village Chess Shop in everything from nuts and bolts to ebony or onyx, with all kinds in between. Many of those boards can be flipped over for backgammon, and, in fact, Village Chess—its name notwithstanding—has an equal number of outstanding sets for that game as well. In short, the Village should be a first stop for the moving of chess pieces, whether its from one square to the other, or from their store to your home.

Gifts and Accessories

ADELE LEWIS

101 W 28th St (second floor)
594-5075
Mon-Fri: 8-5

This operation may be called a pottery specialty shop. Everything is neat, clean, and well organized, and each item appears to be something special. Adele Lewis, the firm's vice-president who on numerous visits was always helpful, claims the she has "the largest selection of baskets and pots to cover plant pots in the city." While that may or may not be true, it's really rather irrelevant, since almost anything selected would make a pleasant gift. In addition to the baskets and pots, there is a fine collection of one-of-a-kind decorative pieces for the home. Lewis weaves her way among them with an unerring instinct for exactly the right gift. Prices are high, but the service and selection more than make up for it. It is here that you can find one-of-a-kind wicker log holders, Mexican jugs in descending order, and rattan Poncho Villa figures. And that is just a start. Partly because of its location and its name, this is one of the city's biggest secrets.

A TISKET A TASKET

993 Second Ave (bet 52nd and 53rd St)
308-4066
Mon-Fri: 11-6; Sat: 11-5

Sheila Nilva has been the successful co-partner of the Place for Antiques for years. The word *eclectic* describes both her stock and lifestyle and goes a long way toward explaining the fact that although their antiques are something to behold, we had always listed the store for its services: prop rentals and the restoration of daguerreotypes. The latter Sheila deems "a fairly unprofitable hobby." Which may explain why Mrs. Nilva and Jo Mellzer opened A Tisket A Tasket as yet another side line at the Place for Antiques. (Maybe it should be renamed the Place for Eclectic Small Businesses.) In any event, she needn't worry about unprofitable hobbies any more. A Tisket A Tasket has taken off like a hot air balloon, a success in no small way due to the resources of its two owners. The baskets carry nothing perishable (unless specifically requested), but they are clever, whimsical, and truly elegant. Baskets can be made up for almost anyone for any occasion, and each is custom-made in four price ranges, which range from about $40 to over $100. Nilva and Mellzer are emphatic that the baskets are comprised of all new items, but that doesn't preclude antique picture frames, perfume bottles, or personal items from the beautifully wrapped baskets. My favorite? Well, I'm not alone in going for the "Zero Caloric Chocolate Basket." It is chock full of chocolate theme items, but not one item is edible!

BLACK MARKET

307 E Ninth St (bet First and Second Ave)
677-6266
Tues-Sat: 12-6:45; Sat: 2-6

If Only Hearts is for Valentine's Day, then Black Market is for Halloween or just-back-from-a-funeral tea time. That may seem a little harsh, but what can you say about a store that specializes in basic black? There are some accessories, some one-of-a-kind items, and enough merchandise of you-know-what color to fill a black hole. So if your family black sheep is blackmailing the pocketbook black and blue for some black tie, now you know where to outfit the blackguard.

BOUTIQUE PETIT LOUP

187 Columbus Ave (bet 68th and 69th St)
873-5358
Mon-Thurs: 11-9; Fri, Sat: 11-10; Sun: noon-7
Mon-Thurs: 11-10; Fri, Sat: 10-11; Sun: noon-7 (summer)

Boutique Petit Loup is the home of fantasies for the cosmopolitan child of any age. The French-titled store has a branch in Tokyo and a place in the whimsically decorated bedroom of the city child. But age is no barrier, for as manager Hidetaka Frove says, "Our business is making the world happy." If any store can do that, this is the one. It is an exclusive outlet for Petit Loup products (labeled "unpredictable" by the boutique staff), but there are all kinds of gifts as well. Soft sculptures hang from the walls, ceiling, and every available hook. There's a menagerie of animal figures and products. Coffee mugs with odd sayings, themes, designs, and dolls brighten up even the most casual browser's day. Airy, light, and whimsical, they all share the "making the world happy" motif. If that sounds too gooey, be assured it's not. I don't know anyone who wouldn't be amused by a Boutique Petit Loup gift.

BRASS LOFT
20 Greene St (off Canal St)
226-5467
Tues-Sun: 11-5:30; closed Sat and Sun in summer

Ruth and Gayle Hoffman run the Brass Loft, which can only be referred to as an entire world of brass. After a visit here, any other metal pales in comparison, and that isn't just due to the brightness of polished brass. Nearly everything in the shop is made of brass or copper, and many of the configurations are most unusual, if not unique. Brass fireplace equipment, screens, sconces, candlesticks, hurricane lamps, chandeliers, and planters (large and small) are just a few of Hoffman's items. In addition, Brass Loft will repair and polish almost any brass and copper item, and they even electrify vases for lamps. Completed, many of them are unusually striking. Bar rails, handrails, and carpet rods are custom-made for homes and restaurants. This is the best source in the city for brass gifts at any price, and the 40 percent discount doesn't hurt.

CAROLE STUPELL
61 E 57th St (near Madison Ave)
260-3100
Mon-Sat: 9:30-6

Carole Stupell employs several personal table coordinators, who are expert in coordinating settings and appointments for the table and home. The selection is truly superb, and coordinators are ever-present to guide the customer to the most striking possibilities. The showcase of designs spans the range from traditional to contemporary, with many original creations designed by Stupell. The coordinators weave their way among 400 china patterns, beautiful stemware, and a similar number of flatware and linen patterns. There is also a magnificent selection of French antiques, sterling, bronze sculptures, porcelains, bar ware, serving carts, crystal chandeliers, and paintings. Everything has the stamp of perfect taste, and if I am waxing ecstatic, it's because the quality, variety, and sheer beauty of the merchandise deserves such appreciation. I have been a customer of Carole Stupell for years; I'm hooked. It's the best accessory shop in town, but take along your thickest checkbook. Call first; the shop will be moving in winter '85.

CHERCHEZ
864 Lexington Ave (at 65th St)
737-8215
Mon-Sat: 11-6

Cherchez's world is timeless, or at least not of our time. The store is jammed with the sweet and exotic scents of dried flowers and herbs. There are scented drawer-lined papers, flower-bouquet room sprays, scented hangers, shoe stuffers, and hundreds of sachets for closet, bed, or bath. Don't overlook the antique clothing (with some magnificent Victorian lace items), the Liberty of London garments, the hand-loomed-in-Vermont mufflers, and the handmade lap robes from Wales. That such a small shop carries so much is amazing.

CHRISTOPHER'S ON COLUMBUS
454 Columbus Ave (at W 82nd St)
873-4668
Mon, Thurs: 11-10; Tues, Wed, Fri, Sat: 11-7; Sun: 12-6
Mon-Thurs: 10-10 (summer)

This place gets our vote for one of the best shop names in the city. It gets another vote for its merchandise. Browse through Christopher's for the best in gifts in a large variety of price ranges. There are silk floral arrangements, jewelry, china, crystal, collectibles, home-design accessories and furnishings, and some of the neatest apartment-warming gifts in town. Christopher's will also do floral arrangements. The theme is decidedly modern. None of it was ever seen on the Nina, the Pinta or the Santa Maria, but it would be at home with descendants of the Mayflower Compact.

CRYPTOGRAPHICS
11 E 41st St
661-2277
Mon-Fri: 8:30-5

Whether it's a bowling trophy or the Man of the Year award, Cryptographics can design a piece that will be exactly right. Their basic line is anything that has to do with awards, and that includes plaques, nameplates, badges, signs, executive gifts, trophies, premiums, lamination, and signs. Any of these can be personalized quickly on the premises, but given ample time, Crytographics can design outstanding pieces. The personalized gift items are just the thing for really unique presents.

CRYSTAL CLEAR IMPORTING COMPANY

55 Delancey St
925-8783
Sun-Thurs: 10-5

This tiny Lower East Side store imports some of the finest crystal in the country, and sells it directly to retail customers at importers' prices. Almost all the crystal is hand-cut and unbelievably fine. There is some crystal and metallic (particularly gold) giftware as well. Normally, to call gold "metallic" is belittling, but gold among all of Crystal Clear's sparkling crystal can only come off a dim second best—even at today's prices. Those importers' prices start 40 percent less than retail, and that alone makes Crystal Clear a super place to shop.

CRYSTAL RESOURCES

130¼ E 65th St
744-1171
Mon-Sat: 12-7

Note the address and the hours and finally the name, and you'll see why Crystal Resources is in the running for the title of one of the smallest businesses in the city. From a tiny store (130¼? This is an address?), Richard Berger sells minerals and fossils that range in price from a few pennies to priceless. Most items fall in the middle range, but it's a great shop to take children (*careful* children, that is), and the perfect place for collectors. Two downstairs "caves" of crystal are showrooms for highlighting giant pieces. Kids love it. It's even a nice spot for finding a unique momento of New York, though most of the stock is not indigenous to the city. Best of all, Berger is a devotee of both fossils and minerals, and even if there wasn't a great interest in them when a customer wandered in, it's a sure thing that interest will be much stronger upon departure. Crystal Resources makes this fun.

FLIGHTS OF FANCY

450 E 78th St (bet First and York Ave)
772-1302
Mon-Fri: noon-7; Sat, Sun: noon-5

Flights of Fancy's shop exudes charm, with its 1850 clapboard facade, soft music gently beckoning passers-by, and the Americana "treasures" Don Detrick has arranged in a Victorian parlor setting. Many of the gifts are handmade and exclusive to the shop, and the window display, which changes weekly, often showcases only one item in a line. That item is often so unusual and special that orders pour in from customers around the country. Prices range from $2 to $2,000, so there is something for every kind of gift giving. Some suggestions? It's hard to be specific since the stock is always changing. But there is a handmade American theme that runs through the selection, and the best sellers include Pet Portrait Dolls, jewelry, and home-accessory designs. (The Pet Portrait Dolls incorporate a photo of any pet on a doll resembling it, which is then dressed in historical or literary costume.) There are other dolls, toys, soft sculptures, and miniatures available on the premises or by customer order and the largest selection of one-of-a-kind gifts in the city.

GRADISCA
140 E 55th St (at Third Ave)
753-0468
Mon-Sat: 10-6:30

Gicilie Talbert Kanner is the daughter of Guila Talbert, who for many years ran the Talbert Boutique miniature store on Fifty-third Street. Gicilie started out on her own, with her mother's encouragement, and quickly established a reputation as a source for gifts and collector's items. (Her card lists over a dozen collection specialties, and ends with the boast that she is a source for "collection collectors.") Mostly, Gradisca concentrates on gift items, decorative accents, and crafts of a fine nature that befit a shop patronized by collectors for their own use. There is definitely a touch of whimsy (i.e., the term "collection collectors"), but everything is of fine quality. Gicilie has done so well, in fact, that her mother closed her shop and now offers her miniatures alongside her daughter's collector's items. Gradisca is the definitive source for decorated eggs, crystal, paperweights, decorative accents, and, of course, miniature frames, paintings, and mirrors. It also exudes the charm reflected by the Talberts.

HANDMAIDEN
104 W 73rd St (at Columbus Ave)
787-2864
Tues-Fri: noon-9; Sun: 1-6; closed Sun in July and Aug and last two weeks of Aug.

This handmaiden is crafty, sleek, and decidedly American. In short, the store specializes in handcrafted gift items by American artists. The stock, which by definition is always unique and always changing, can range from thimbles to king-sized quilts, and that doesn't begin to cover it. (Poor pun there!) This should be a number-one source for terrific gifts, but don't overlook it for home-decorating touches as well. Barbara Mundy and Georgian Hearn really strive to find the unusual and the special to stock their store.

HOTHOUSE
345 W Broadway (bet Grand and Broome St)
966-7978
Daily: 12-7

Hothouse's wares would be as suited in the Soho of London as in the SoHo of New York. Check out Hothouse's ceramics, glass, clocks, lights, teapots, and housewares for the latest in British technology and design. Most of the items are better suited for gifts than for home use, but in either SoHo, they're accustomed to the unusual.

HUBERT DES FORGES

1193 Lexington Ave (at 81st St)
744-1857
Mon-Fri: noon-7; Sat: noon-6

Hubert De Forges' line is ethereal. There is a disdain for function that doesn't look good. As a result, this a great place for hostess gifts. The specialty is tabletop and giftware accessories, and this store considers itself a kitchen *gift* shop rather than a kitchen supply shop. You might ask R. Oscar Moore, director of the Lexington Avenue store, for assistance, but there's no reason why you shouldn't be able to find *something* positively perfect by yourself. Moore is very knowledgeable, and he tries to keep the store stocked with a good, varied selection of gift and kitchenwares.

JENNY B. GOODE

1194 Lexington Ave (bet 81st and 82nd St)
794-2492
Mon-Fri: 10-6:30; Sat: 10-6

Jenny B. Goode appears on everybody's list as *the* place for special household gifts. It's a super store, and a super source for really unusual gifts items; in fact, it's the type of place where you're tempted to buy something for yourself. Stephen Nittolo keeps the store stocked in hand-knit sweaters, Isadora perfume, antique watches, and tons of china. The latter spans the traditional to the unheard-of. Send your favorite feminist a set of souvenir "Give Women the Vote" plates. Give an elegant hostess a place setting of two of the shop's exclusive *porcelain d'Auteuil:* it will make *la table*! There are also birthday gift materials, odd pieces of unique stationery, and porcelain trivets that look like potholders. (Don't drop them. Unlike potholders, they break.) Plus, there are more coffee and tea sets and aprons than you could count. This store has something for everyone. Jenny B. Goode could charm Scrooge.

J. FINKELSTEIN

95 Delancey St
475-1420, 674-9582
Sun-Fri: 9-5

Finkelstein is a Lower East Side store with all the customs and mores thereof, but the stock is something different. Ostensibly an importer, Finkelstein carries fine glass, china, furniture, and Chinese artwork. There are Louis IV reproductions and some magnificent ivory and jade imported pieces. The excellent quality and uniqueness of some of the pieces shouldn't scare you off; Finkelstein adheres to Lower East Side prices. That's very nice, since the stock is so unusual that they could get whatever they asked for it.

JOMPOLE COMPANY
330 Seventh Ave (at 29th St, third floor)
594-0440
Mon-Wed, Fri: 10-5; Thurs: 10-7; Sat: 10-3; closed Sat in summer

When the local bank offers an electric blanket to anyone depositing $500, or the boss gives every employee a clock radio for Christmas, or the academy gives every graduate a silver pin, odds are that it was bought here. Jompole is a dynamite company. They offer great service at super prices, and Irving Jompole and Shirley Smith are two of the friendliest, funniest people around. They bill themselves as suppliers of business gifts, sales incentives, premiums, and awards, and they claim to have supplied everything from lollipops and imprinted toothpicks to diamonds, color televisions, and Cadillacs. Their stock in trade is crystal, sterling silver, and china. There is no name they don't carry or can't get, and, of course, it is sold at a substantial discount. "Very nice," you say. "But I'm not a bank, employer, or school." No problem. Jompole provides the service to individuals at the same discount price. Jompole warns that everything is not always in stock (this is mostly a brokerage operation), but anything can be ordered. Customers are invited to call or come in to peruse the catalogs and place orders. Shipping is reasonable (sometimes free), and the prices may be the lowest in town.

MABEL'S
1046 Madison Ave (bet 79th and 80th St)
734-3263
Mon-Sat: 10-6; closed Sat in summer

Whimsy is what is on sale here, and owner Peaches Gore (Mabel is her black and white cat) vows that "making our very demanding clients giggle with delight over their discoveries is what we're all about." If you can visualize Madison Avenue types giggling in a store jam-packed full of handmade accessories for decorating body and home, then you have Mabel's. Mabel isn't the only animal in residence. Virtually everything is built around an animal or fantasy theme, and prices range from $20 to $2,000. Mabel inhabits a splendid world. There are cushions (made to order and made to recline on), handmade sweaters and rag rugs, elegant wallpapers, hand-tooled belts, and all kinds of hand and shoulder bags. And that doesn't cover it all. Check out the hanging mobiles, the vases designed like pets, and the personalized gifts. (You can order an ashtray in the shape of your cat or a china dish for Fido's supper.) Mabel leads a charmed life, and her namesake store is overwhelmingly charming.

M&H STOCKROOM
654 Madison Ave (bet 60th and 61st St)
752-6696
Tues, Wed: 10-6 (Hours may be expanded and/or appointments made for other days); closed Aug and from Christmas to mid-January

I suppose the name M&H Stockroom comes from a conglomeration of the owners' names (Duane Hampton and Louise Melhado) and the fact that the cozy room (Duane says, "*Cramped* is more like it") on the 21st floor of an office building with a magnificent view of Manhattan is jam-packed with every type of antique, gift, and knickknack that can find a space, stockroom style. But this is a stockroom befitting owners who have spent years in the decorating business as buyers, stylists, and contributors to *Vogue*, *Mademoiselle*, and *House and Garden* and as wife to Mark Hampton (that's Portland-born Duane). So there is an emphasis on antiques, particularly items with a bookish or literary theme. The limited hours reflect the fact that the ladies spend as much time on European buying trips and in scouting the markets in this country as they do retailing their wares. They must have received lessons on packing since what they cram into the store and still manage to accent and make attractive is amazing. Check out the boxes that appear to be other items (usually a book), the antique (genuine) and *faux* inkwells, match strikes, perfume bottles, decanters, bookends, candlesticks, pitchers, picture frames, vases, foot stools, needlepoint pillows, framed hand-colored prints of flora, fauna, and architecture, mirrors, library steps, bookcases, hanging shelves, and much much more.

ONLY HEARTS
281 Columbus Ave (at 73rd St)
724-5608
Mon-Sat: 11-7; Sun: noon-5

This is the most popular store around on Valentine's Day. It's just a bit too hearts and flowers for my taste the rest of the year, but with the romantic set, it's a real hit any time. When Helena and Jonathan Stuart opened Only Hearts, the title was apt—everything in the store was a heart or heart-shaped. However, they have since branched out into general "romanceabilia," which is perhaps best indicated by their best-selling antique Valentine's Day cards. That's right, *used*. Helena says it has something to do with old-time romantic love being a current feeling, but we won't go into *that*! In addition to the cards, Only Hearts is big on velvet and lace and things like that. If your taste runs to the romantic, this place is a must.

POTTERY WORLD
807 Sixth Ave (at 28th St)
242-2903
Mon-Fri: 7:30-5; Sat: 10-5

Pottery World claims to have the largest selection of planters, baskets, and pottery for plants in the city, and with a location in the wholesale flower market, they operate on a wholesale-resale basis as well. (This is supposed to mean wholesale prices for retail customers.) Owner Robert Lapidus claims that his years in the business has made him an expert in supplying the best planter and vase for any plant. With such a selection and such a location (he knows what is available to place both *in* the planter and *as* a planter), he really does have an excellent vantage point. If on the off chance that Pottery World does not have *the* piece, Lapidus will search for it, and he can usually locate most any type of planter. What is nice is that the customer usually hasn't the faintest idea that Lapidus' stock will not suffice. But Lapidus is secure and honest enough to know this at a glance, and if necessary, he'll send out for it. Any plant that needs a new home can find one here.

SEASHELL BOUTIQUE
208A Columbus Ave (bet 69th and 70th St)
595-3024
Mon-Fri: 12-9; Sat, Sun: 12-6

It was almost inevitable that cosmopolitan New York would support more than one seashell shop. Dorothy Young squeezed her tiny (three and a half feet wide) shop onto the scene along with Seashells Unlimited. But there are some differences. Seashell Boutique shares its very precious space with semiprecious stone jewelry, small gift items (*very* small), sterling jewelry, and other items in addition to shell objects. What they all have in common is their natural origins and their size. (A giant tortoise shell may make a natural coffee table, but there's no way Young could squeeze it into her shop. Or if she could, there'd be nothing else to sell!) In any event, people other than mere beachcombers will enjoy both seashell shops. This one should be noted specifically for its handcrafted jewelry.

SEASHELLS UNLIMITED
743 Broadway (Eighth St and Astor Pl)
532-8690
Mon-Sat: 11-6

Another of the stores that make New York great, Seashells

Unlimited, located in the shadow of Grand Central Station, has a better collection of shells than all of Cape Cod. More enchanting than the subject matter is its owner, Veronica Parker Johns, who rules Seashells Unlimited like a fiefdom. Her tiny shop is run without help, except during "my infrequent absences, when my friends will strive to please." Doesn't that conjure a vision of Ms. Parker Johns placing a call to a friend to "please watch my shells," while she goes beachcombing at low tide? Only a small percentage of the stock has been personally collected, however. The rest come from a variety of sources, and range from common-but-perfect oyster shells to rare corals. Prices, incidentally, are extremely reasonable. No matter how unusual the shell, the cost rarely exceeds $100, and most are in the $5-or-less range. Shells for jewelry can be had for pennies. Johns is a shell expert and the author of *She Sells Seashells*, a title indicative of the enchantment here. She will cheerfully discuss her merchandise with any customer and suggest ways in which her shells can be put to the best possible use.

SOINTU
20 E 69th St (at Madison Ave)
570-9449
Mon-Sat: 11-6

Kipp Trafton, Sointu's owner, is at the vanguard of retailing and of what he is retailing. The shop has won an A.I.A. award for its designer, Tod Williams, and it is winning accolades for its collection of modern designs as well. Sointu is pronounced *Soyn-too*, but it's most pronounced in its definition of modern. Trafton's shop could pass as a branch of the Museum of Modern Art's housewares collection, or at least what that collection will show in five years. Within the definition of modern, there are no boundaries. Home furnishings keep company with jewelry, small appliances, gifts, and tabletop accessories. What holds it all together is that it is sleekly modern and as *au courant* as can be. Sointu's business card reads "Harmony in modern design," and its things do blend beautifully. Every item makes a definite statement, and yet, when seen in the shop, it is a perfect blend.

STAR MAGIC
743 Broadway (Eighth St and Astor Pl)
228-7770
Mon-Sat: noon-9; Sun: noon-7

Step through Star Magic's door, and you step through a time warp into the future. For Star Magic—from its midnight-black ceiling with suspended galactic spheres to its spacecraft-like walls to the floor plan that duplicates the feeling of walking in space—is designed to make a visitor forget contemporary New York and enter into a timeless universe. The mood is inducement enough to pay a visit. Short of *Star Trek* reruns or signing up for the next space shuttle, this is the closest thing on earth to an actual voyage. Star Magic's theme is "Yesterday's magic is today's science," and that perhaps is the only way to describe the eclectic selection that owners Justin Moreau and Daniel Lanocca call "gifts of science and spirit." There are toys (in this case, literally for children of all ages) with a scientific bent and scientific items strictly for fun. There are books specifically chosen for their ability to make a reader "ponder the cosmos." Star Magic offers minerals and prisms, scientific instruments to explore the universe, and electronic music that is positively futuristic. Over and out.

WOLFMAN-GOLD & GOOD COMPANY
484 Broome St (at Wooster St)
431-1888
Daily: 11-6

This SoHo shop is described as a "marriage of contemporary and antique table settings," and that probably says it best. There are linens available by special order that would look classy in a Park Avenue penthouse, and a series of white-on-white tableware that would blend with the starkest loft in SoHo. Some of the tableware is imported from France and England; some is domestic. But all of it is elegant. The store also stocks baskets, cutlery, glasses, linens, doilies, and one of the best collections of cloth napkins in the city. The linens can be specially ordered, and Holophane light fixtures can be similarly ordered for the ultimate table setting. This is a first-choice source for an exquisite house gift.

Greeting Cards

GREETINGS
35 Christopher St (bet Sixth and Seventh Ave)
242-0424
Daily: 11-11

740 Madison Ave (at 64th St)
734-1865
Mon-Fri: 10-6:30; Sat: 10-6

These two stores, part of a small nationwide chain, claim to have the largest collection of contemporary greeting cards and gifts in the country, and one would be hard-pressed to prove them wrong. The sheer number of cards is mind-boggling, and the types and titles cover topics that Hallmark never thought of. "Congratulations on your divorce" is one wry example. Don't overlook the stationery department; it's really unique and well stocked with a collection of New York City memorabilia. It makes the " I love

New York'' campaign look malnourished. For any type of stationery, Greetings deserves a ''hello.''

UNTITLED
159 Prince St (at W Broadway)
982-2088
Daily: noon-7

The Metropolitan Museum and the Louvre each have approximately 1,500 art cards. Untitled, whose reputation is not nearly as well known, has 4,000-plus cards in stock at any given moment. Those cards include modern-art postcards, greeting cards, and note cards, many of which are unused or old cards. The postcards are filed as either pre- or post- 1945 and within those classifications by artists names. There are also postcards of famous photos and depictions of every possible type of art known. Some of these items are good for gags, and some are suitable for framing. And it's all neatly catalogued.

Housewares and Hardware

BLACK AND DECKER
50 W 23rd St (bet Fifth and Sixth Ave)
929-6450
Mon-Fri: 8:30-5:30; Sat: 10-3

Black and Decker is a name well known in power-tool circles. At this location, the company sells, services, and reconditions Black and Decker tools. If you already own such power tools, this is the place to bring them when they don't work, since the company knows its product better than anyone else. If you wish to purchase tools, this is also a good source. New tools are sold at a discount, while reconditioned items go for even better prices. And everything is sold with a one-year guarantee. This is a real find. Imagine buying a power saw on your trip to ultra-urban New York!

BRIDGE KITCHENWARE
214 E 52nd St
688-4220
Mon-Fri: 9-5:30; Sat: 10-5

Some people redecorate a kitchen in ''early restaurant,'' because the longer they shop, the more apparent it becomes that professional equipment is always the best to use. Kitchen utensils, unlike other tools, are easily adapted from professional to home use, and that extra quality has obvious advantages. For one thing, it is amazingly durable. Professional cooks make millions of omelets a year, so their omelet pans must be much more durable than those designed for private kitchens. Professional cooks make their living with expeditious, dependable, and reasonably priced equipment. They will gladly sacrifice a canary-yellow kettle for a silver one that heats more efficiently. And when they pause to reflect, homemakers feel the same way. Hence, the desire for an "early restaurant" decor. Bridge Kitchenware Corporation is one of several places that can fill the bill. They are unique-to-New York stores; they supply almost every restaurant and institution within 500 miles. Bridge carries bar equipment, cutlery, pastry equipment, molds, glassware, copperware, cast ironware, woodenware, flatware, stoneware, and kitchen gadgets. All goods are professional quality and excellent for the home gourmet. Be sure to see the line of imported copperware from France, as well as the professional knives and baking pans. After trying them, people use no other. The peppermill collection, while not abundant in choice, has several top-quality items designed for function rather than funkiness. Bridge takes its name from owner Fred Bridge, not from the nearby 59th Street Bridge.

BROADWAY PANHANDLER
520 Broadway (bet Spring and Broome St)
966-3434
Mon-Fri: 10:30-6, Sat: 11-5:30; closed Sat in summer

Over 8,000 different items of cutlery and cookware are available at this SoHo store. Broadway Panhandler made its reputation supplying restaurants and hotels, and it has *everything*.

CATHAY HARDWARE CORPORATION
49 Mott St (at Canal St)
962-6648
Thurs-Tues: 10-8

In the heart of Chinatown, this gem of a shop has been dispensing Chinese cooking items, utensils, hardware, and restaurant equipment since 1928. There's no more authentic place to get your wok, chopsticks, or eggroll roller, and prices and quality are geared for the professional. This is also a great place for an unusual housewarming or shower gift.

CK & L SURPLUS
307 Canal St (at Broadway)
966-1745
Mon-Sat: 9:15-5:45; Sun: 10-5:30

In New York, a shopping trip for hardware wouldn't mean a thing without a trip to Canal Street. And on Canal Street, CK & L is the oldest and best. Years ago, these very same Canal Street stores dealt in industrial and war surplus. With the passing demand for military supplies and an influx of electronics, the Canal Street surplus stores turned to areas best described as "hardware whatever." All of the stores do business the same way. Sawed-off cardboard boxes, containing an assortment of homogeneous but totally implausible merchandise are "displayed" in front. There could be a box full of round washers, mouse traps, electric sockets, telephone coils without terminals, or things that are totally unidentifiable. Al Lipton at CK & L says that sooner or later everything sells. It may be *years* later (it would be nice to know who buys some of this stuff), it might be a trade off (Al sells his garbage to his neighbor, while his neighbor sells *his* garbage to Al), or it might be someone who actually needs 400 left hinges. But it really doesn't matter. The junk in the front is there to draw the customer inside the store, where the *real* merchandise is sold. There are power tools, accessories, simple tools, plumbing and electrical goods, and supplies. The only connection that the inside of the store has with the outside is that everything sold comes from surplus stock. Thus, prices, even for the complete line of hardware, are much lower than retail ones uptown. When you see the place, you'll understand immediately why the overhead is so low.

CLOSET KING
113 W 10th St (bet Sixth and Greenwich Ave)
741-0027

430 E 72nd St (bet First and York Ave)
734-2178

880 Lexington Ave (bet 65th and 66th St)
288-7871

Mon-Sat: 10-6

Spend any time in New York, and you'll know that rarer than a parking space is a place to park yourself or your belongings. Living quarters in the city have always been notoriously tight, but with the current economy, people are staying put, and small apartments are being measured for every inch of usable space. Frequently, closets—if they exist at all—are the first things to go. They are reincarnated as nurseries, bars, bathrooms, eating areas, and even at-home offices. So, it was inevitable that there would be experts who would specialize in organizing closet space, and Don Constable and his Closet King staff do just that. The three stores specialize in redesigning closet interiors for those who have closets. The overall aim is to provide a maximum amount of storage space customized to the customer's needs. For the most part, they rely on a vinyl-covered shelving and open-wire basket system that creates an extremely efficient industrial look. But the real boon here is that since the three stores exist to sell components, they encourage " do it yourselfers." So, a customized system can be planned out and purchased here, but self-installed at a fraction of the cost a professional closet organizer would charge. Yes, such people exist. And they're not mothers!

CONRAN'S
2-8 Astor Pl (at Broadway)
505-1515

160 E 54th St (at Third Ave, Citicorp Center)
371-2225, 800-431-2718

Mon-Fri: 10-9; Sat: 10-7; Sun: noon-6

Terence Conran's enterprise is not new to the home-furnishings and housewares business. His Habitat stores exist across Europe, and the same operating style has been brought to the New York store. The look is young. The furniture is sleek, modern, clean of encumbering frills and decorative accents, comparatively inexpensive, and, most important, portable. A good percentage of Conran's line can be carried out of the store at the time of purchase, and that is one of its canons. Some of the furniture items are blatant copies of more expensive lines. They were originally created for the store and are simply assembled under one roof for the first time. Conran's also has fabrics, linens, lighting, bath accessories, and toys. The entire store can be billed as a housewares store, but there is a specific housewares section on the second floor. There are china, glass, cookbook, and cookery sections as well. Everything is displayed on long open shelves, warehouse style, but is neat and sleekly done. Many of the items are unique to the store. Simply pick what you want, load it into a shopping cart, and wheel it to the checkout counter; its almost entirely self-service.

DELBON
121 W 30th St (near Sixth Ave)
244-2297
Mon-Fri: 9-5:30; Sat: 10-3; closed Sat in summer

Once Richard DeVito starts on the subject of Delbon, it is hard to stop him. What follows is gleaned from his conversation. Delbon was established in 1840, which makes it the oldest shop of its kind in the country. Customers come to browse around the shop (and the grinding shop in the rear) and avail themselves of the service center, which sharpens and fixes all manner of cutlery. The main business, however, is the sale of cutlery. There are two lists here: the items for sale and the brand names available for each item. The former list is almost endless. It includes anything that cuts: scissors, shears, hunting knives (the largest selection in the city, DeVito asserts), Swiss Army knives, pocketknives, industrial sewing shears, and gourmet and camping knives. The second list includes every great name in imported and domestic cutlery. Some (but not all) are: Wiss, Dexter cutlery, Sabatier, F. A. Henckels, and Ed Wusthof. Every knife purchased is finished, honed, and adjusted individually for the customer. Delbon also accepts mail and phone orders.

D. F. SANDERS

386 W Broadway (bet Spring and Broome St)
925-9040
Mon-Sat: 11:30-7; Sun: 12-5:30

952 Madison Ave (corner 75th St)
879-6161
Mon-Sat: 10-6; Sun: 12-5

This is a hardware cum housewares store, but with its original location in SoHo, you know it can't be that easy—and it isn't. In addition to the usual (which in any other city would seem highly unusual) assortment of kitchenware, Sanders specializes in commercial and industrial products for home use. In fact, in much the same way that the SoHo neighborhood converted industrial lofts to home use, Sanders takes delight in offering the best industrial products for individuals. The store has been cited for its "furniture." Industrial shelving, butcher-block tables (meant for a butcher, not a suburban buffet), and shelving are solid substantial pieces and worthy additions to any home. Though high-tech as a decorating style may be on the wane, Sanders doesn't care. The store's emphasis is on the best the industrial world has to offer a homemaker, period.

GARRETT WADE

161 Sixth Ave (at Spring St)
807-1155
Mon-Fri: 9-5:30; Sat: 10-3

The Garrett Wade customer is a person who uses and appreciates fine wood working tools, for the store prides itself on offering only the best-made tools from all over the world. But there is another Garrett Wade customer. He patronizes the store because it sells kits for making magnificent reproductions of Shaker furniture. So, if you're reasonably handy and want the pride of workmanship *and* ownership, a Garrett Wade kit might be just the thing. (The rocking chairs, while not cheap, are magnificent.) The main business is the mail-order selling of the finest tools available. The catalog is almost more than all-encompassing. It doesn't just list every imaginable woodworking aid, it makes a point of explaining each piece's function and advantage over its peers. It reads like a "how to" guide. While some of the pieces are incomprehensible to a layman, Garrett Wade never accepts that supposition. They assume that anyone could put together their rocker, or, at the very least, appreciate the function of their lightweight spokeshave. And after a visit here, you may become a believer, too.

GRACIOUS HOME
1220 Third Ave (at 70th St)
535-2033
Mon-Sat: 9-7; Sun: 10:30-5:30

Gracious Home is the New Yorker's version of the local hardware store. So while there are nails and screws and odd coffee-pot tops, the cosmopolitan environment is reflected in cooking demonstrations, space-saving appliances (including major items such as stacked washers and dryers), paints, closet organizers, and dinnerware sets. And Gracious Home doesn't stop there. The urban gracious home can be outfitted with curtain rods, lighting systems, tape recorders, telephones, vacuum cleaners, wallcovering, Venetian blinds, and food-storage systems. The staff aims to make the store a one-stop supplier for everything except food and clothing, though there is some pet food and a couple of gourmet items to tide one over through any emergency. We originally came to Gracious Home for its knife sharpening, one of the many services the store supplies. Most work can be done while you wait, though valuable items might be sent out. This is one shop that will do its job graciously and competently.

HOFFRITZ
331 Madison Ave (at 43rd St)
697-7344
Mon-Sat: 9-6
Other locations including:
Penn Station (main terminal), Grand Central Station, 46 W 50th St, World Trade Center (shopping concourse)

Hoffritz is another New York institution. Its mainstay is cutlery, but its image is built upon an enormous selection of gifts, housewares, optics, clocks, radios, games, and gadgets. The selection of knives is unrivaled anywhere. A customer who walks into a Hoffritz store to ask for a cheese knife is offered a dozen different varieties, and this is true even in the small stores. But New Yorkers love Hoffritz most of all for its unusual gadgets. Cherry pitters, self-supported magnifying glasses, folding glasses, and portable barometers are just a small portion of what's available. Some are frivolous and some vital, but all Hoffritz things make great gifts and conversation pieces. People know that a gift from Hoffritz (superstitions about knives aside) will be valued and appreciated. No matter how strange, Hoffritz products are well-made and serve a definite use. One of the handiest items is folding scissors for pocket or handbag. And Hoffritz stores are handy, too; they are in just about every neighborhood.

MANHATTAN AD HOC

842 Lexington Ave (at 64th St)
752-5488
Tues-Fri: 10-6:30; Mon, Thurs: 10-7; Sat: 10-6

This housewares store has a motif familiar to anyone who's ever had anything to do with housekeeping and a chemistry laboratory. The principle is simply that many glass chemistry items are not only adaptable to kitchen functions, but in many cases are preferable. So, there are heat-resistant jars and beakers in various sizes that are good for use as anything from canisters to soap dispensers. I particularly like the stoppered bottles used as containers for grains, cereals, and flours. They are attractive, compact, and clear, enabling one to see at a glance how much remains of any item. Even more important, glass containers are highly recommended as being bug proof. But Ad Hoc's idea of using stoppered glass bottles for soap dispensing seems questionable. It would be too easy for it to slip through your hands and break. Julia McFarlane and Judith Kress are great. They proudly showed off the strictly functional, very professional restaurant supply items, and then capped it off by showing "our collection of a few select 'mad' favorite things." Ad Hoc and staff definitely have just the right touch of whimsy.

M. WOLCHONOK & SON

155 E 52nd St (bet Third and Lexington Ave)
755-2168, 755-0895
Mon-Fri: 9-6; Sat: 9-4; closed Sat in July and Aug

Wolchonok has been a family wholesale-retail business in the midtown area for over 50 years. In those years, the neighborhood has influenced their business and vice versa. So, while they could have been a general hardware store elsewhere, in Manhattan Wolchonok is the prime source in furniture hardware, particularly legs and replacement pieces. Their business card says, "legs, legs, legs." (I wonder if they get calls from people expecting the Rockettes.) If a given limb, as the Victorians would say, is not in stock, Wolchonok can make it to order. They do the same thing with towel bars, cafe curtain rods, brass switch plates, and decorator hardware. Speaking of the Victorians, the line of porcelain plumbing fixtures is authentically reproduced, while the other end of the bathroom spectrum features futuristic metal and lucite fixtures. And while "legs, legs, legs" are the business specialty, they can stand on an equally extensive line of casters, sockets, and glides. This may be one of the city's most esoteric shops (a furniture-leg replacement center!), but they are some of the nicest people, and they offer help and advice as if everyone were replacing their legs, legs, legs daily.

VAN WYCK DRAPERY HARDWARE SUPPLY
39 Eldridge St (near Canal St)
925-1300
Mon-Thurs: 8-5; Fri: 8-4; Sun: 9-4; closed Sun in summer

New York has four pages of listings in the yellow pages devoted solely to *retail* hardware stores, so to be singled out, a particular store has to be special. Van Wyck merits this distinction by virtue of its specialty in drapery hardware. Harold Lamm stocks all manner of drapery hardware, as well as supplies, urethane foam, and drapery trimmings. This is a particular boon to the new do-it-yourself drapery makers, since they can buy the materials in the neighboring fabric shops, pick up the hardware here, and set it all up with one shopping trip. Should the draperies be ready-made (and these, too, can be purchased at a discount from the neighboring stores on Grand Street), the same holds true. Even if the draperies were purchased elsewhere, the discount here makes a trip to the Lower East Side for hardware worthwhile.

W. G. LEMMON
755 Madison Ave (bet 65th and 66th St)
734-4400
Mon-Fri: 9-6; Sat: 9-5:30

W. G. Lemmon is a neighborhood housewares and hardware store that is totally aware of its location. Considering that the neighborhood is the Upper East Side in general and Madison Avenue in particular, W. G. Lemmon has to be just a bit special, and it is. While there is run-of-the-mill hardware and housewares here, and while there is nothing glamorous about a nail, W. G. Lemmon manages to make this home-supply store look like a housewares boutique and gift center. Pots and pans are striking in both appearance and use, and there are interesting, small-sized housewares. If you've ever searched for a two-cup tea kettle, you'll appreciate the feeling of walking in and finding several to choose from.

Imports

Something like 90 percent of all immigrants who came to the United States entered through the New York harbor. They left an indelible cultural stamp upon the city and created the world's largest ethnic population. In some cases, there are more people of a particular nationality in New York than in the home country. So naturally, there are legions of stores specializing in imports. To list them all is impossible. What follows are some of the most interesting and unusual ones.

Afghan

NUSRATY AFGHAN IMPORTS
215 W 10th St (at Bleecker St)
691-1012
Sat-Thurs: noon-9; Fri: noon-10

Abdul Nusraty has transformed a corner of the Village into a corner of Afghanistan that is fascinating and free of politics. There are magnificently embroidered native dresses and shirts displayed along side semiprecious stones mounted in jewelry or shown loosely. Another part of the store features carpets and rugs, while yet another shows antique silver and jewelry. Nusraty has an unerring eye; all of this is of the very best quality, and often it is unique as well. The business also operates on both a wholesale and retail level. Short of a trip to Afghanistan (something few are currently wont to do), Nusraty is probably the best source for Afghan goods on this continent.

Africa

FOLKLORICA
89 Fifth Ave (bet 16th and 17th St)
255-2525
Mon-Fri: 10-7; Sat: 11-6; Sun: 1-5

This quaint shop has moved to a new and larger location, which better accommodates its burgeoning stock and growing clientele. Originally a small shop specializing in African imports, Forklorica has been expanded by Pamela Levy and Jack Bregman to include an international selection of quality crafts and art, with a new emphasis on South American handiwork, as well as the original African products. There are such traditional crafts as baskets, rugs, dolls, tapestries, musical instruments, and artwork. The colors and tones of everything seem to blend perfectly, as if they scoured the world for those items that would look best in their shop.

Bermuda

BERMUDA SHOP
605 Madison Ave (bet 57th and 58th St)
355-0733
Mon-Sat: 10-6

Unless you've personally dodged the traffic on the "wrong" side of the road or shopped Front Street in Hamilton, it is impossible to understand how totally evocative this shop is of Bermuda. The only thing missing is the sparkling blue water and tourist boats! In addition to being a tourist attraction, Bermuda is also a shopping mecca. This shop on Madison Avenue, in the heart of Manhattan, successfully imports the Bermuda shopping experience to New York. Bermuda is British in outlook, and the best of its shopping is to be had in British imports. Shetland sweaters, tartan plaids, and British woolens are the mainstay of Bermudian shops. Here, sweaters for women are available in a flower bed of pastels. Styles include plain crew or turtleneck, cardigans or cable knits. No matter what the season, there is a good selection of cotton, linen, gabardine, and other summer-fabric resort wear, and, of course, the ever-present Bermuda shorts! Of course, the catch is that import costs and taxes have increased the price tag significantly, but if you want a Shetland sweater—even at double the cost—it is still more inexpensive than many local shops and *much* less than a trip to Bermuda.

Canada

ALASKA SHOP
31 E 74th St (near Madison Ave)
879-1782
Tues-Sat: 11-6

They don't exactly consider what they sell here to be Alaskan. Owners Nicholas Di Granni and Jack Bryan opened this New York branch of a Chicago gallery devoted to Eskimo art, and "Alaska" is just a title. Much of the work comes from Canada as well as Alaska, and the shop is also called the "Gallery of Eskimo Art," which is a more apt description. Connoisseurs of contemporary Eskimo art are not what you'd call legion, but there are enough to support the shops and their exhibits. Each show highlights a different aspect of Northern carving. Some of the artists are totally unknown (because most still reside in their original villages). Other artists have large followings, and *their* pieces can go for thousands of dollars. What is most surprising, at least to me, is that the style isn't primitive at all. These artists are members of the 20th century; their crafts may be rooted in century-old traditions, but they have been adapted to modern times.

Central and South Amercia

BACK FROM GUATEMALA
306 E Sixth St
228-9496
Mon-Sat: noon-11; Sun: 2-10

OZYMANDIAS
32 St. Mark's Pl
254-6206
Mon-Fri: 12:30-9:30; Sat: noon-9

If these weren't two of the most intriguing import stores, I'd patronize them just for their names. Joe Grunberg and Susan Kaufman are the owners and buyers, and their devotion to Guatemalan artifacts is obvious. They are hard at work every night, stocking and rearranging their merchandise, which includes ethnic clothing, wall hangings, and jewelry from Central and South America and from Asia as well. There are both exotic and classic styles of ethnic clothing. (Ms. Kaufman is a specialist in antique Tibetan jewelry.) Back From Guatelmala also has the city's best collection of cloisonné earrings from mainland China. And there's more: preshrunk cotton clothing, puppets, masks, handmade sweaters, and artifacts from 30 different countries. Back From Guatemala has contacts with 35 countries and hundreds of world travelers, so it offers the best. Grunberg and Kaufman are among the most charming of New York's store owners. Their other store, Ozymandias, specializes in body scents and organic lotions personally blended for customers, along with Oriental jewelry, clothing, and artifacts.

HACHA INTI

103 Sullivan St (bet Spring and Prince St)
226-3544
Tues-Sun: noon-8; closed last week in Jan

Bee Bantug, a Philippine-born former advertising worker, collected so many Central and South American Indian crafts and artifacts from her travels that her apartment eventually overflowed with them. Opening a store seemed to be the only solution to Bantug's quandary, so the tiny SoHo Hacha Inti shop was born. The name means "Sun God" in the Incan lanuguage, and Bantug seems to have collected evey type of handcrafted item in the traditions of Central and South America. There are some antiques, but most items are contemporary, and all are virtually one-of-a-kind since they're handmade. The stock includes silver jewelry, ceremonial dance masks, wearable and collectible folk weavings, baskets from the Philippines, musical instruments from the Andes, and ethnic clothing and accessories from all over the region. (The *huipils,* large overblouses, from Mexico are popular with nursing mothers.) Prices are very reasonable. Yarn paintings, which are original works of art, sell for under $100. Authentic *huaraches*—an Indian shoe widely copied unsuccessfully—are about $30. And the handmade silver jewelry is equally reasonable. The Sun God shines on one's pocketbook at Hacha Inti.

General

JACQUES CARCANAGUES

119 Spring St (at Greene St)
431-3116
Tues-Sun: 11-6

After a stint in the diplomatic service, Frenchman Jacques Carcanagues decided to assemble and sell the best of the world's artifacts that he had run across in his travels. So, while the store has no particular ethnic or historical persuasion, it is, in his own words, "a complete ethnic department store, not a museum." Afghan textiles and Near Eastern rugs are everywhere, as are more jewelry and pieces of pottery than can be counted. What it all has in common is that it *is* (despite protestations to the contrary) all of museum quality. It is also very appealing to SoHo shoppers. The business is divided between the retail operation in the front and the import-distribution business in the back. The overall effect is nothing so much as an Eastern market-place; all that is lacking are the water pipes and music. Actually, truth to tell, the water pipes are probably floating around the store somewhere as well. All in all, Jacques Carcanagues is an artifact specialist. What's fortunate is that he can indeed pick out what will look great in a home as well as a museum.

NOTO

245 W 72nd St (bet Broadway and West End Ave)
877-7562
Mon-Sat: 10-7

Bob Noto, who runs one of the first and best folk-art import shops in Manhattan, is a self-proclaimed chauvinist about New York City in general and the Upper West Side in particular. So, visitors to Noto have as equal a chance of having a conversation about the grandeur of the Dakota apartment building as one about the origins of a cloisonné necklace from Asia. But the most interesting conversation would be about Noto's travels and purchases. Since 1958, Noto has personally scoured the world for interesting and unusual artifacts. The stock is ever-changing, but it is all unusual and surprisingly *very* reasonable. There is nothing in the shop (at the moment) over $250, and many bracelets, beads, mirrors, and art items are in the $10 to $30 range. Chinese silk panels, for use on screens, are a steal at $20 apiece. Silver bracelets and earrings from Bali, English brass candlesticks, batiks, and Chinese jewelry are displayed alongside copies of antique European art accessories. All of the latter are recast from original (or exact copy) molds that enable Bob Noto to sell what appears to be antique pocket mirrors for under $10. (All prices quoted at press time.)

TIANGUIS FOLK ART

284 Columbus Ave (bet 73rd and 74th St)
799-7343
Mon-Sat: 11-8; Sun: noon-6

Owners Robbyn Yoffee and Fane Bloom are not particular about what country their stock comes from, but they are most particular about what their store stocks. Countries of origin include Mexico, Japan, Afghanistan, Bolivia, Brazil, Thailand, and just about any other exotic place one can think of. All are represented by what can best be described as ethnic crafts. There are textiles, blankets (the ones from South America are magnificent), old tapestries and weavings, baskets, (natives everywhere seem to work on baskets, and Tianguis carries the best), clothing (much of it made from the aforementioned textiles), and artwork. The house specialty is haori jackets from Japan. They make excellent gifts. The store's credo is that the merchandise should be useful, exotic, well made, and affordable. They carry it off well.

Himalayas

HIMALAYAN CRAFTS AND TOURS

1219 Lexington Ave (bet 82nd and 83rd St)
744-8892
Mon-Fri: 11-7; Sat: 11-6

There's more to the Himalayas than Mt. Everest and the Abominable Snowman, and that which is marketable is for sale here. Shozo and Yoko Miyahara preside over an emporium of imports from Pakistan, Nepal, Tibet, and Northern India—in short, any country that even remotely can claim contact with the Himalayan mountains. Despite the exotic tundra image this description evokes, many of the items are easily adaptable for city life. The hand-detailed boots are desired as much for their warmth as for their show-stopping fashion quality. The Tibetan rugs are similar conversation pieces. And, of course, the shop houses much more—batik paintings, art, statues, antiques, and incredibly attractive sweaters. True to its name, the shop also arranges tours of the home country; there is probably no one more knowledgeable on the subject anywhere outside the mountains. But the real attraction here are the boots and sweaters. Don't miss them. And if you run into the Abominable Snowman on your trip, at least you'll be properly dressed. (I was once charged sales tax on a handmade rug I purchased at the base of Mt. Everest!)

India

HANDBLOCK

487 Columbus Ave (bet 83rd and 84th St)
799-4342
Mon-Wed, Sat: 10-7; Thurs, Fri: 10-8; Sun: 11-6

Handblocking, an ancient art of India, is what gives this store both its name and its wares. The four partners divide their time between overseeing production in India and merchandising at this store and their other ones in Canada. Aside from an Indian-milieu, handblocked style, it's hard to describe all that the store offers. There are linens, placemats, napkins, tablecloths, bed cloths, dish towels, and lampshades, all created in India of cotton tinted in brilliant colors and handblocked in designs that range from traditional to custom-made modern. And there's more. Sweaters from Columbia hang alongside Indian-embroidered smock dresses, and both drape above wicker furniture that can be handblocked and coordinated to match previously acquired fabrics. And we haven't begun to mention the rugs (also Indian for the most part) and the weaving. The motif is casual Indian-style cotton, but the price is newly arrived New York. Perhaps because it's cotton, everything is imminently affordable. (Well, maybe not the sweaters). The rest of the clothing is not only reasonable but distinctive and highly fashionable. For all of these reasons, Handblock deserves a visit.

HIND INDIA COTTAGE EMPORIUM

1150 Broadway (at 27th St)
685-6943
Mon-Fri: 9:30-6:30; Sat: 11-5

Hind India Cottage Emporium features clothing, jewelry, handicrafts, footwear, and gifts imported directly from India. Moti R. Chani has a sharp eye for the finest details, and the saris and other Indian clothing he sells reflect that. The clothing is prized by both Indian nationals, as well as neighborhood residents for its sheer beauty. The garments, made completely of cotton and featuring many unique madras patterns, come in sizes small, medium, and large. Pay particular attention to the leather bags and jewelry.

Ireland

HASKIN'S SHAMROCK IRISH STORE

205 E 75th St (at Third Ave)
288-3918
Mon-Sat: 11-6

Walk around the corner from Third Avenue, and if you didn't

know better, you'd think you had wandered into an Irish candy store. Haskin's dispenses anything and everything Irish, from county maps to Irish hometown newspapers. Signs around the shop read, "Papers will not be held more than two weeks." Cathy (who owns the store with Tom) explained: "We get all the local papers for people who pay in advance. But they're always forgetting to pick them up. So, we're stacked high with the news of every little town and village in Ireland." Haskin's was started in 1923, and Cathy and Tom took it over several years ago. The change has not been for the better. The store is downright sloppy, and it is hard to spot, let alone unearth, the treasure troves that Haskin's was always noted for. Supposedly buried in there are Celtic crosses, tweed hats and caps, Irish linens, stationery, and other Irish paraphernalia. If you're not Irish (and having once tried to cross Fifth Avenue on St. Patrick's Day, I suspect everyone in New York is), the hand-knit sweaters and Waterford crystal are the reasons for shopping at Haskin's.

Israel

KIBBUTZ STORE
856 Lexington Ave (bet 64th and 65th St)
772-6644
Mon-Fri: 10-6; Sun: 1-5

A kibbutz is a collective settlement, usually agricultural, in Israel. The country has over 200, and 83 of them recently formed a collective group to merchandise the crafts, jewelry, linens, wall hangings, and products that its members create. Nearly everything is created by hand, and the standards for exporting to Lexington Avenue are extremely high. The second floor of the Kibbutz Store sports an art gallery which displays art, lithographs, paintings, photographs, and sculptures of museum quality. The lower floor boasts similar quality in baskets, jewelry, crafts, pottery, shawls, and wall hangings. And throughout the two floors, there is an emphasis on Israel's culture. There are records, books, background recordings, and even rotating art exhibits and classes in Hebrew, as well as religious and secular art objects. Above all, the spirit of the kibbutz has been captured on Lexington Avenue.

Italy

CAROSELLO MUSICALE COMPANY
119 Mulberry St (near Canal St)
925-7253
Daily: 11 a.m.-midnight

Every section of New York with a concentrated ethnic population has a group of stores that serve the specific needs of that nationality. Usually, the group will include a bakery and coffee shop, a bookstore, and an import shop featuring various items of the homeland, and there is often one shop devoted to a distinctive characteristic of that nationality as well. What, therefore, could be more natural than a shop in Little Italy dedicated to recordings and music? Certainly, it's an obvious conclusion for any opera fan. Carosello is primarily an Italian music shop specializing in Italian recordings, operas, and sheet music. But Carosello is also a bit more diversified. Little Italy is particularly famous for its bakeries and food shops. People have traveled hundreds of miles to feast in its cafes, and transplanted natives have sent across the continent for breads and rolls. (Lasagne apparently doesn't travel as well.) Because of this, there is a preponderance of food shops in the area and an absence of the other complementary shops normally to be found. Carosello takes up the slack by being a bookstore, import store, and gift shop as well as a record shop. Thus, one can find perfumes, Italian newspapers, magazines, and gifts as well as Caruso recordings. The atmosphere is informal—but proud—and frequently, the customers can be heard humming an aria while checking record labels. But even if you don't buy anything here, check out the espresso and breads at any of the neighboring cafes.

Japan

O-ZORA

238 E Sixth St (at Second Ave)
228-1325
Mon-Sat: 11-7

Jiro Tsuji was a woodworker and cabinetmaker in his native Japan. The latter skill was much more in demand than the former when he made the move to New York, but he never outgrew his healthy respect for Japanese woodworking and hand tools. When finding them became difficult, he and his wife, Eileen, opened their own shop in the East Village for dispensing them. They called the store O-Zora, which is Japanese for limitless (as in "the sky's the limit"), so while hand tools are the basis of the business, virtually anything Japanese can be uncovered in this tiny store. Tsuji had the right idea. The Japanese tools, which range from antique to power saws and drills, are prized for their design and quality and are often exclusive to the shop. Artisans seek out O-Zora, and amateurs are carefully instructed in the use of the tools, much as they are in the use of sushi and sashimi knives and traditional Japanese clothing. The Tsujis make periodic buying trips to Japan, and whatever strikes their fancy ends up on O-Zora's shelves. As for those shelves, they were created by Jiro Tsuji who still does cabinetmaking via his Japanese construction company, Taiku, which does traditional Japanese carpentry. So when he sells his tools, he knows of what he speaks. The current O-Zora best sellers are Japanese work clothes for both sexes. There are also traditional kimonos with companion *monpei* (cuffed, baggy, elastic waisted pants), children's toys, and some really unique gifts.

THINGS JAPANESE
1109 Lexington Ave (bet 77th and 78th St)
249-3591
Tues-Sat: 11-5

Things Japanese believes that the thing Japanese most in demand is prints. So while there are all sorts of Japanese art and crafts, it is the prints that they really prize. They know the field well and believe that the market for prints, while almost exhausted on the high-priced, established end, is only just beginning for newer or unknown artists. The store will help would-be collectors establish a grouping or decorators in finding just the right pieces to round out the décor. And to round out the print image, there are also original 18th- to 20th-century Japanese woodblock prints. O.K., O.K., you say, that's *still* prints, so be assured that there are porcelains, baskets, lacquers, and books as well. Prices range from $10 to several thousand dollars, and everything is accompanied by a certificate of authenticity. Things Japanese claims that you need to appreciate both the subject matter as well as the artistry in its things, and that's not a difficult task at all.

Mediterranean Area

MEDITERRANEAN SHOP
876 Madison Ave (at 72nd St)
879-3120
Mon-Fri: 10-5:30; Sat: 10-5; closed Sat in summer

This Madison Avenue shop specializes in imported dinnerware and tableware. Tableware here is a category broad enough to include desk tables, and it's a toss-up whether the hand-embroidered linens or the exclusive Florentine desk accessories are the bigger drawing card. A good rule of thumb is that if it rests on a table top and is imported from a Mediterranean country, the Mediterranean Shop will have it. And all of it seems to shimmer like the waters of its namesake. Pay particular attention to the embroidered linens (including down-filled pillows in sizes as large as floor cushions) and the imported hand-detailed dinnerware.

New Guinea

SOUTH SEAS GALLERY AND TRAVEL
353 Bleecker St (bet W 10th and Charles St)
741-2777, 741-3179, 741-3185
Mon-Sat: 10-6

Sava and Bella Maksic are inveterate travelers and unabashed lovers of the South Seas. To finance all those trips, they combined business with pleasure and opened a travel agency in the Village. But without bias, the Maksics will plan itineraries for anywhere in the world. Of course, their first love is the South Seas, as is obvious from their agency's name and décor. The walls are covered with all manner of folk art accumulated during trips to New Guinea. All of it is handmade by natives, and it includes artifacts, masks (and more masks), pottery, wooden wares, and religious objects and statutes. Most of it is contemporary (and thus reasonably priced), but some are one-of-a-kind handiworks from another time. Those who can't afford a trip to the South Seas can do well by visiting the South Seas Gallery, if for nothing else but a wall hanging. Odds are, however, that such a visit will only whet your appetite for a trip to the source. And you know where you can make the travel arrangements!

Persia

PERSIAN SHOP
534 Madison Ave (bet 54th and 55th St)
355-4643
Mon-Fri: 10-7; Sat: 11-6

Persia, of course, no longer exists (today, that area is, more or less, Iran), but the Mideastern mystique is strong enough at this shop to encompass the ancient kingdoms. Merchandise includes a representative sample of past and present Oriental jewelry, magnificent brocades—the kind that used to hang behind a sheik in his palace—gifts, and *objets d'art*. What seems to be a pattern in imports shops—native dress that can be adapted to chic urbanites—is available, too. In the Persian Shop, it takes the form of caftans and Bedouin dresses (in small, medium, and large sizes) that can be worn by either sex (the natives wear them that way).

The selection is marvelous, and the only thing missing is a water pipe. Actually, the Persian Shop has them, and authentic espresso makers, too. Men: check out the sensational ties.

Scandinavia

BUTIK STOCKHOLM

928 Madison Ave (bet 73rd and 74th St)
988-9441
Mon-Sat: 10-6

Several years ago, all things Swedish became fashionable. Everyting from clogs to wooden salad bowls to home saunas could be seen in model homes. Competition is fierce for the title of being the definitive source, since nearly every suburban shopping center and every other block in Manhattan—not to mention most department stores—has a Swedish products boutique. But Butik Stockholm may be the winner. There are imports from all the Scandinavian countries, fashion designs (which have now been copied into sheet designs), genuine Swedish wooden shoes, and hundreds of constantly changing accessories.

Scotland

SCOTTISH PRODUCTS

133 E 55th St
755-9656
Mon-Fri: 10:30-6; Sat: 10:30-5; closed Sat in summer

Mrs. K. Graeme Ramsay brags, "We are an old-fashioned Scottish shop, full-service style," and this Scottish oasis in the city dispenses the best of the old country with the full flavor and fervor of oldtime service. For natives, there are more hometown touches than could be enumerated here ("But *no* liquor," says Ramsay firmly), and for nonnatives, it's all of Scotland's best. Imports include bagpipes, kilts, skirts, jewelry, and tartan tams. These are the genuine articles, and the difference between what is sold here and what can be seen elsewhere is extraordinary. In addition, there are ties, souvenirs, travel rugs, and more bolts of tartan plaids than were probably ever assembled in Glasgow. Of course, this makes good Ramsay's boast that Scottish Products has the biggest and best selection of namesake products in this country. And everything is dispensed with a smile. She's right! This is the finest that Scotland has to offer.

South America

PUTUMAYO
857 Lexington Ave (bet 64th and 65th St)
734-3111
Mon-Wed, Fri, Sat: 11-7; Thurs: 11-8
339 Columbus Ave (at 76th St)
595-3441
Mon-Sat: noon-8; Sun: 1-7
147 Spring St
966-4458
Mon-Sat: 12-8; Sun: 12-6

The majority of the merchandise at Putumayo comes from South America, but there is a touch of Asia as well. The emphasis is on fashion from around the world, and there is a strong line of folk art, artifacts, and antiques. Putumayo displays an extensive collection of South American outerwear. For summer, there are cotton sundresses and wrap skirts: cool, comfortable, and practical.

Tibet

THE TIBET STORE
21 Cleveland Pl (bet Spring and Broome St, off Lafayette St)
925-6145
Mon-Fri: 12-6; Sat, Sun: 12-7

One of the best contenders for "I dare you to find this address," the Tibet Store has other geographical displacement problems as well. For one, what is a store specializing in Himalayan products doing in SoHo? (They claim they love the ethnic diversity.) They are two blocks from Chinatown and a similar distance from Little Italy, while being in the heart of New York '80s arty scene. For another, why is the store called *Tibet* when the boundaries for the merchandise is the Himalayas? And finally, virtually all of the items in the Tibet Store are handmade by Tibetan refugees living in Nepal. Maybe "The Refugees in Nepal Store" didn't fit the SoHo image. And not surprising virtually everything in the store fits the New York image very well. There is clothing that is beautifully designed and appliquéd, and most of it is handcrafted and virtually unique. In addition, there are Himalayan arts and crafts that depict local life and lore. (That's Tibetan, not SoHo life.) All of it blends well and is quite remarkable. What makes it even better is the attitude here. In addition to boosting Himalayan imports, Lupi Gilroy is also a New York supporter. The store positively beams with "I Love New York," and maybe that's why they can't seem to get a geographic handle on things!

Ukraine

ARKA
48 E Seventh St (at Second Ave)
473-3550
Mon-Sat: 10-6

There's a little bit of everything here, but all of it is flavored with a Ukrainian accent, which explains why Arka bills itself as the Ukrainian department store. Most of the locals, particularly the Ukrainian natives, stop in for the conversations, newspapers, and atomsphere. Those from further locales overlook the décor to gaze at the native crafts and artwork (decidedly *not* arts and crafts!), literature, music, records, and musical instruments. In the heart of the Ukrainian neighborhood (Surma is on the same block), Arka is distinctive in its selection of Ukrainian instruments, particularly the bandura. It looks like a large mandolin, sounds like a small harp, and is usually played by a Ukrainian in an embroidered shirt. These, too, are available here (the shirts, not the Ukrainian).

SURMA "THE UKRAINIAN SHOP"
11 E Seventh St (near Third Ave)
477-0729
Mon-Sat: 11-6

Since 1918, Surma has conducted business as the "general store of the Slavic community in New York City." My only quarrel with that description is why it should be limited to the city, since it seems capable of serving the entire hemisphere. More than a store, Surma is a bastion of Ukrainianism, and once inside, it is difficult to believe that you're in New York. Another quote sums it up: "Visit Surma and spend time in the old country." Fortunately, language is not much of a problem. The clothing here is ethnic opulence. There are dresses, vests, shirts, hand-tooled and soft-soled leather dancing shoes, hundreds of blouses, custom-made Cossak tunics and dresses, vests, and accessories. All are hand-embroidered with authentic detailing. For the home, there are accent pieces (including an entire section devoted to Ukrainian Easter egg decorating), imported brocaded linens, and Surma's own imported Ukrainian-style honey (very different and very good). Above all, Surma is known for its records, stationery, and books; not surprisingly, the business is also known as the Surma Book and Music Company. And particularly note the collection of paintings and the stationery, which features modern-day depictions of ancient Ukrainian glass painting. Surma has even published *A Guide to the Ukraine,* a listing of Ukrainian-related spots in New York.

Jewelry

BILL SCHIFRIN
4 W 47th St (National Jewelers Exchange, booth 86)
245-4269
Mon-Fri: 10-5

From a booth in the National Jewelers Exchange—better known for its diamond engagement rings than its plain wedding bands—Bill Schifrin presides over a collection of 1,873 unusual wedding bands. Prices range from a few dollars to several thousand dollars, depending upon the complexity of the work and the stones used. If you have the time, Bill Schifrin will tell you a story about each ring. If it's not about where it came from or how he got it, then it's a story about someone who bought a similar one recently. He's been doing this for over 30 years, and after all this time, you'd think he'd be cynical. He's not; he's "just cautious," and his stories and prices draw customers from all over the world. The selection isn't bad, either.

DETAIL ACCESSORIES
204 Spring St (at Sullivan St)
925-8982
Mon-Sat: noon-7; Sun: 1-6

In this tiny, stark shop in SoHo, Anthony Robinson has set up the American branch of his successful London jewelry shop, which is dedicated to the credo that jewelry and accessories as integral parts of fashion should not be priced out of the reach of the average person. So, instead of precious jewels, there are strands upon strands of electroplated (to rainbow tint) titanium and other industrial metals. The components are unusual and artistic; this is exclusive high-fashion designer jewelry with accessories, and a hefty proportion of it comes from England. That may change. For now, though, the only American SoHo influence is seen in the splashes of color and unorthodox use of metals.

FORTUNOFF
681 Fifth Ave (at 54th St)
758-6660
Mon-Wed, Fri, Sat: 10-6; Thurs: 10-8

The Manhattan store is the city branch of what is probably one of the best stores in the country devoted to quality merchandise. Each section is run by its own manager as a separate entity. Each has sales, clearances, and specials that are unique to its deparment. The only common link is a compelling elegance that causes people to become lost in the store for hours. Considering that the Fifth

Avenue store is about one-tenth the size of the suburban stores, it isn't all that easy to do. Prices on all items are sensational, and Fortunoff has a reputation for matching or beating any legitimately quoted price in town. Anything purchased here is a reminder of a store that has it all. A brief look at some of the departments must include the jewelry department, which has a jeweler in residence at all times. It also sells 14k, 18k, and 24k gold jewelry, precious and semiprecious stones, and name-brand watches. In housewares, there are no pots, only sterling, silver-plate, gold-electroplate, and stainless-steel flatware of good quality. For serving pieces, there is sterling, sliver-plate, pewter, gold-electroplate, and Victorian and Georgian holloware of both imported and domestic famous brands. The gift section has similar lines, but here the salespeople are specifically trained to help with the gift selection.

JAN SKALA
1 W 47th St
246-2942, 246-2814
Mon-Sat: 9:30-5

Jan Skala is located in the diamond district, that mysterious one-block area of Manhattan which purportedly handles every diamond imported into this country. The retail customer's place here is nebulous at best. First, there isn't a New Yorker alive who doesn't have a friend, relative, or connection in the diamond district. As a result, no self-respecting New Yorker ever blindly wandered into the district. Many have never been there at all, relying instead on whomever they know to bring home a selection. Of course, tourists don't have that "in," and in fact, if anyone suggests a contact to them, they should become suspicious. Rather, they warily approach 47th Street not quite sure what to expect and, hence, receive a mixed welcome. Jan Skala, a reliable, non-"tourist trap" diamond dealer, is not adverse to retail customers. Jan Skala is ostensibly wholesale only, but its ground-floor storefront is the first spot off Fifth Avenue to welcome retail customers. In addition to diamonds, there is a large selection of pocket watches, antique watches, and jewelry. The latter includes a good selection of Russian enamels, Fabergé eggs, and the like. Quite a sight to see, even if you don't buy.

MAX NASS
118 E 28th St (bet Park Ave S and Lexington Ave)
679-8154
Mon-Fri: 9:30-6; Sat: 9:30-4

The Shah family are jewelry artisans; Arati is the designer, and Parimal ("Perry") is the company president. Together, they make and sell handmade jewelry, as well as service, repair, and restore antique jewelry. As Max Nass, they deal in virtually any type of jewelry—antique (or merely old), silver, gold, and semiprecious. Two special sales every year bring their low prices down even lower. One lasts for the last three weeks in January; the other is for two weeks in June. In between, Arati will design pieces on whim or on commission. The necklaces are particularly impressive, and all of his work is unique and often one of a kind. The store also restrings and redesigns necklaces. I can only assume Max Nass is the name of a previous owner. He sure isn't Parimal S. Shah.

MYRON TOBACK
27 W 47th St (bet Fifth and Sixth Ave)
398-8300
Mon-Fri: 8:30-4; closed first two weeks in July and from Dec 25-Jan 1

You must meet Myron Toback. Ostensibly, he is an refiner of precious metals with a specialty in findings, plate and wire. Not very exciting or helpful to the average customer. But that's where you're wrong. Note the address. Toback is not only in the heart of the diamond district, he is a bona fide landlord of a new arcade that is crammed full of wholesale artisans of the jewelry trade, and taking their cue from Toback, they are open and friendly to individual retail customers. So note Toback as a source of gold, gold-filled, or silver chains sold by the foot at a wholesale price. And don't overlook the gold and silver earrings, beads, and other jewelry items at prices laughably less than that at establishments around the corner on Fifth Avenue. Even though most of the customers are professional jewelers or wholesale organizations, Toback is still simply charming to do-it-yourselfers, schools, and hobbyists. Toback delights in showing people how to bypass jewelry middlemen in putting together their own custom-made items.

OCINO
66 John St (bet Nassau and William St)
269-3636
Mon-Fri: 8:30-6

Ocino is a fantastic find, right in the middle of the financial district. At Ocino, there are diamonds, custom-made jewelry (both to individual customer specifications and corporate advertising or logo inscriptions), handmade jewelry, resetting and redesigning, top brand-name watches, and gold chains sold by weight for those who want to make their own jewelry. For the latter, Ocino claims the lowest prices in the city. Ocino calls itself the "quality store downtown" and offers tableware by Lenox, Royal Copenhagen,

Waterford, Kosja Boda—you get the idea. Despite having a virtual monopoly on those brands in the area, everything is sold at enough of a discount to be among the best priced anywhere in the city. And did I mention that custom-logo'd leather goods, luggage, and even chocolates (in dark or milk chocolate) are also available?

RENNIE ELLEN
15 W 47th St (room 401)
869-5525
Mon-Fri: 10-4:30 by appointment only

A trip to New York without meeting Rennie Ellen is a trip without experiencing what New York shopping is all about. For openers, she is a wholesaler offering the discounts that New York's wholesale businesses are famous for. Second, she deals in diamonds—the real thing—which are certainly knockout souvenirs to bring back from the city. Third, she is a woman who has made it. Not only was she the first woman diamond dealer in the male-dominated diamond district, but feminism has made her a world-renowned consumer advocate. Rennie Ellen personally spent so much time and effort to keep the diamond district straight and honest that she earned the title "Mayor of 47th Street." Finally, only a fool would negotiate a purchase in any wholesale area without knowing the merchant. This is particularly true when one is dealing with diamonds, since thousands of dollars depend upon quirks visible only to a jeweler's eye. In such a field, Rennie Ellen's reputation is impeccable, and every customer who actually makes it to the fourth floor without being waylaid becomes a lifelong referral service.

Does this sound too good to be true? Well, there's more. The human touch is also evident. The small office is crowded with thank-you notes and albums of photos from happy couples. All of this makes a visit interesting, even if you're not shopping. However, if you *are* shopping, here's the scoop. Rennie Ellen deals exclusively in diamond jewelry. There are pendants, wedding bands, engagement rings, and diamonds which, Ellen says, fit all sizes, shapes, and budgets. All sales are strictly confidential and are made under Rennie Ellen's personal supervision. Refunds (which are seldom requested) are made within five days, and every price is wholesale. All this, and she is totally trustworthy, too. One last warning: if you do come to the diamond district, do not let anyone detour you to another store. Shills abound and cannot be trusted.

RICHARD ERKER
132 Thompson St (bet Houston and Prince St)
420-1326
Wed-Sun: 1-8

Among the natives of SoHo, Richard Erker is the name of the most admired business. That admiration is inspired by both his artistry and the artfulness with which he runs his business. That business is, not incidentally, jewelry. But this is a SoHo business run SoHo style. So, everything Erker sells is one of a kind and truly unique, while still being comprised of modest SoHo-type materials and prices. Erker claims that although every item is an original, his prices are no higher than those for "regular" jewelry. And for that price, there is sensational style, quality, and fashion. (His work is admired by Elsa Peretti, whose own jewelry designs are recognized outside the neighborhood with considerable awe and even more considerable price tags.) In addition, there are fashion accessories in the same style. If that is a vague description, it is only because that with an everchanging stock of unique items, it's hard to pin Erker down. So, take the natives' word: Erker is the quintessential SoHo store.

ROBERT LEE MORRIS, ARTWEAR
409 W Broadway (bet Spring and Prince St)
431-9405
Tues-Sat: 11-6; Sun: noon-6

ARTWEAR
456 W Broadway
673-2000

ARTWEAR
AT&T Bldg (Madison Ave at 56th St)

Robert Lee Morris ran Artwear as a jewelry gallery slightly off Madison Avenue. Nobody noticed. So, he moved the entire show (and show it is) to SoHo, and suddenly Artwear is everywhere. The Robert Lee Morris gallery offers his work solely, while the original Artwear and the AT &T branch still showcases jewelry to be worn. The uptown department stores run window displays based upon Artwear's wares, the newspapers are forever reporting the latest Artwear features, and the fashion magazines are either borrowing Artwear artifacts or shooting on the premises. In case you haven't heard, what Artwear does is *big* news. Between periodic exhibitions of the latest in contemporary jewelry, Artwear sells the jewelry of various artists. Jewelry is a very loose way of describing it; the real emphasis is on *art*. Anything from a wrought-iron necklace to a gold body suit can be found draped on incomplete body sculptures (which are designed by Morris and are his own personal hallmark). Exact specifics are hard to give, because the exhibit changes almost weekly. Man Ray's golden lips can drape a plaster torso one week and be replaced by small enamel cluster pins the following week. Often, whole collections are put together for clients, and, just as often, the clients are other SoHo shops, which design clothing in coordination with Artwear, or vice versa. Prices are high, but everything sold here is unique, and the philosophy is reflected in the name. The merchandise is wearable *art*—with an accent on the trend-setting, talented artist. (Much of it is Morris' own.) While most of the jewelry is as functional as it is ornamental, everything Artwear sells is considered an investment. As any good artwork, it is assumed that anything sold here will only increase in value.

UNDERGROUND JEWELER
147 E 86th St
348-7866
Mon-Fri: 10-8; Sat: 10-7
175 E 86th St
369-0920
Mon-Sat: 10-8; Sun: 12-6

Subway arcades are neglected areas of commerce in New York (unlike in Vienna, for example), and with good reason. There is very little sold deep underground that could withstand the scrutiny of the light of the day. Furthermore, most shops whose sales depend upon bright, open displays that attract casual passers-by do not believe potential clientele exist in a subway. Most people do not intentionally shop in a subway arcade. There are two exceptions. The nut concessions are pretty universal, and depend almost entirely upon impulse buying. The Underground Jeweler is the other exception, and it's worth a trip to see why. It carries jewelry from 60 countries. Most is of a whimsical nature and not made of valuable metals or precious stones, but all is very attractive and definitely not of the costume-jewelry class. That sentence is an attempt to categorize rather than define it, since one of the Underground's specialities is gold with real stones. However, the stones are mostly birthstones, or of birthstone class (semiprecious), and gold settings are used primarily because they won't make your finger turn green. The African wood carvings—rings, gifts, and statues—are sensational, and some of the genuine folk jewelry is just great. Imagine row upon row of hand-worked silver pendants of international origins. This is not the place to go for an engagement ring, but it's a perfect spot for many other types of jewelry.

YLANG YLANG
806 Madison Ave (bet 67th and 68th St)
879-7028
Mon-Fri: 10:30-6:30; Sat: 10:30-6
324 Columbus Ave
496-0319
Mon-Fri: 11-7; Sat: 12-7; Sun: 12-6
Herald Center
1 Herald Square
(Center hours)

Take note of Ylang Ylang's addresses. If Madison Avenue, Columbus Avenue, and Herald Center doesn't serve notice that this is a store for the up and coming, then there's always the clue of the out-of-town addresses, such as Rodeo Drive and Bar Harbor. By now you should have gotten the idea. But don't discount the store because there are no discounts. On the contrary, Ylang Ylang may be playing a joke on all of us and flaunting the ostentatious in style. Its jewelry is custom-made; the louder, glitzier, and gawdier the better. The most valuable glow with semiprecious stones or heavy silver. Notice I didn't say "most expensive" rather than "most valuable." There's something for everyone here, and there are many worse ways to bejewel oneself at less than diamond prices. I just wish I didn't get the feeling the joke's on me. (Maybe all the pieces are made with bubblegum!)

Ladders

PUTNAM ROLLING LADDER COMPANY
32 Howard St (bet Canal St and Broadway)
226-5147
Mon-Fri: 8-4:30

This is a great esoteric shop on an esoteric street. (Our only other Howard Street entries are Vogel Boots and Minter's Ice Cream Kitchen, which are down the other side of the street.) What, you might ask, would anyone in New York do with those magnificent rolling ladders used in traditional formal libraries? And could there possibly be enough business to keep a place like this running all those years? The answer is that Putnam has been in existence since 1905, and in that time, there were, indeed, lean years. When SoHo became residential, though Putnam was literally in the right place at the right time. Clever New Yorkers turned to Putnam for designing access to their lofts—both in general and for sleeping lofts in particular. Here's a listing of the different ladders Putnam has: Rolling ladders, rolling work platforms, telephone ladders, portable automatic ladders (some are made for the terminal rooms of telephone exchanges), scaffold ladders, pulpit ladders, folding library ladders, library stools, aerial platforms, library carts with steps, steel warehouse ladders, safety ladders, electric step ladders for industrial use, mechanic's stepladder, Alpine, Crosby, Peerless, Durable, twin and dual-purpose step ladders, extension ladders, window cleaners' ladders, sectional ladders, shelf ladders, extension trestle ladders, and much, much more. Putnam is a step up.

Lighting Fixtures, Lamps, Accessories

BOWERY LIGHTING
132 Bowery (at Grand St)
966-4034, 966-2485
Daily: 9-5:30

Those stores on the Bowery that do not sell restaurant supplies, sell lighting fixtures. All are ostensibly wholesale only, and have a supply that runs the gamut from portable emergency lamps to huge chandeliers befitting movie-theater lobbies. Retail customers are expected to follow the same rules that are followed when shopping for housewares: to be unobtrusive and definite in selection. In exchange, customers receive an excellent selection of the best quality lighting fixtures at wholesale cost. Bowery Lighting Corporation is typical of the Bowery establishments and has an excellent reputation. Shopping for lighting fixtures in the Bowery should by no means be limited to one store, but if a vantage point is needed, this shop should be it.

HAREM LITES
139 Bowery (bet Grand and Broome St)
226-3042
Daily: 9-5

Harem is another Bowery fixture store, but their big distinction is that they were among the first to introduce track lighting for home use. As so often happens (and it seems to happen consistently in the Bowery), home decorating receives its best ideas from professional or industrial use. So it was with the track lighting, originally seen in television studios and art museums. Harem was one of the first businesses to realize how applicable track lighting was to the modern home. Today, they have years more experience than other stores in selling and installing track lighting in homes, not to mention the years of experience in lighting installation for industry. Harem also carries table and floor lamps. Prices are at least 25 percent less than those of retail stores, and Harem displays the advertisements to prove it.

JUST BULBS
938 Broadway (at 22nd St)
228-7820
Tues, Wed, Fri: 8-5; Mon, Thurs: 9-6

A really bright idea, Just Bulbs was the brainchild of Phil and Shirley Brooks after they put in many an hour at the family store, Superior Lamps, around the corner. Thinking that bulbs in all their myriad configurations would be a fascinating thing to retail exclusively, they opened Just Bulbs to do just that. While scoffers said they couldn't imagine a sillier idea, they are now eating their words and joining the patrons who line up to flip the switches that activate the bulbs on display. From a practical point of view, this is probably the only shop in the world that can supply certain types of bulbs. In addition to the obvious ones, Just Bulbs has a collection for use in old fixtures. The Brooks' boast that the store houses almost 3,000 different types of bulbs. It's hard to imagine half that many exist. The shop looks like an oversized stage dressing-room mirror, and everywhere you look, there are bulbs connected to switches that customers are invited to flick on and off.

JUST SHADES
21 Spring St
966-2757
Thurs-Tues: 9:30-4

This lighting fixture store features shades. As experts on shades, they are equally expert on the proper shade for the proper lamp and share their expertise with retail customers. Their experience encompasses the entire subject, and they carry only the finest shades. They have lampshades of silk, velvet, parchment, and just about any other material imaginable. Interestingly, they said their biggest peeve was customers who "neglect" (a polite way of putting it) to take the protective cellophane off their shades. They say that it is bad for the lamp, and the shade actually collects ruinous dust.

LOUIS MATTIA
980 Second Ave (bet 51st and 52nd St)
753-2176
Mon-Fri: 9-6

Few stores repair or stock parts for lamps. Louis Mattia does. In his crowded shop, he has enough spare parts to fix almost any lamp on the spot. Consequently, he is patronized by a wide variety of customers, from socialites who need a priceless heirloom repaired to other merchants who need quick repairs on slightly damaged merchandise for their customers. All of them receive prompt and courteous attention from one of the most knowledgeable staffs in New York.

MANHATTAN SALES COMPANY
17 E 16th St (bet Fifth Ave and Union Square)
242-8262
Mon-Fri: 9-4:30; Sat: noon-3

This is the place to go for Ledu adjustable desk lamps. The 35 percent discount here makes the retail price difficult to believe. If the Ledu name means nothing to you, ask around.

NEW YORK GAS LIGHTING COMPANY

148 Bowery (bet Grand and Broome St)
226-2840
Mon-Fri; 9-5; Sat, Sun: 10-5

The definitive source for gas fixtures and other items of that bygone era, New York Gas Lighting Company is mentioned repeatedly by decorators. Purists and antiques lovers use the store as a source for parts, authentic oil lamps, and chandeliers. Others shop here for artifacts, conversation pieces, and mood-setters. Either way, it's a nostalgic step into the past, which is especially enjoyable since everything is sold at up to 60 percent less than anywhere else. And what a selection! Be sure to go through all the rooms; the place is a smorgasbord of lighting fixtures.

TUDOR—ELECTRICAL SUPPLY COMPANY

222-26 E 46th St (bet Second and Third Ave)
867-7550
Mon-Thurs: 9-5; Fri: 9-4:30

Although you may feel like you need an engineering degree to enter Tudor Electrical, the staff is geared to explaining everything in stock to even the proverbial novice who doesn't know how to replace a light bulb. Light bulbs are the store's forte. No one has ever counted the varieties available, but they are catalogued by wattage, color, and use by a staff who can almost immediately pull out the best bulb for your needs. Many of the items are so unique that they require explanations, and the staff really knows its stuff. If Tudor stocks it, you can believe there's a reason for it. Quartz, tungsten, and halogen bulbs don't distort light, while incandescent and fluorescent lamps offer the best of both kinds of lighting for desk work. Energy-efficient bulbs come with vital instructions, which is a boon to people who feel that you need a degree to separate wattage from lumens from output. And better still, while discounting at least 20 percent off list price, Tudor Electrical Supply will guide a customer to the best bargains.

UNIQUE LAMP SHADES AND ACCESSORIES

323 Second Ave (bet 18th and 19th St)
260-4670
Mon-Fri: 9-5; Sat: 10-5

Juan and Perry preside over a collection of lighting instruments that seems truly unique and gives full credence to their name. As anyone who has ever tried to replace a simple lampshade knows, the choice is not simple. Often, the shade can cost more than the lamp, and a cheap or inappropriate shade can ruin the effect of an expensive lighting fixture. The range of choices can be staggering to the poor soul who has only come to replace a frayed shade. Juan and Perry are better than most shopkeepers at guidance to the right choices. When the job is well done, the lampshade will be unobtrusive. When done poorly, the mismatch can be very noticeable. Unique's shades are custom-made and measured. Most are also handmade, as are many of the lighting accessories.

UPLIFT
506 Hudson St
929-3632
Daily: 12:30-8

I haven't quite gotten the hang of what the name Uplift has to do with a store that mainly sells art-deco and Victorian lighting fixtures, but maybe it's because the bases of many of the pieces are figures of nude women in various poses of lifting things. Or maybe the view is uplifting. In any event, these figurines are of the art-deco and Victorian eras. So this is the place to go for turn-of-the-century illumination. It's also interesting that there are few if any pieces from other periods. The more modern ones sport characteristic geometric patterns and etchings, while the antiques are heavy on brass, stained glass, and elaborate detail. There are also accessories for lighting fixtures—lamps, wiring, bases, and shades (including glass shades for lamps suspended from the ceiling). I guess that's a form of "uplift," too.

Locks, Locksmiths

AAA LOCKSMITHS
44 W 46th St (at Sixth Ave)
840-3939
Mon-Fri: 8:30-6

You can learn a lot from trying to find a locksmith in New York. For one thing it's the profession that probably has the most full-page ads in the Manhattan Yellow Pages. For another, a company that answers "AAA" is *not* the place to call about a dead battery. And finally, the phone company and other advertising media list companies alphabetically. So in an industry that has little company loyalty or recommendations, three A's is an important edge. But it's for none of these reasons that I recommend AAA Locksmiths. Rather, it's because after nearly 50 years in the business (and that says a lot right there), they were committed enough to New York to buy and refurbish a building on 46th Street as their headquarters. (There's a fourth lesson to be learned from this. The renovations took twice as long as expected.) The new building, with its metal columns and reinforced concrete, looks substantial and safe, which is part of the idea. It also stands as a statement that AAA is literally on the spot to help with the safes, security needs, gates, and locks of the diamond district and other neighboring businesses. With such a firm commitment to the city, this is obviously not a fly-by-night operation, and that is yet another recommendation. And incidentally, despite some major industrial customers, they are very cordial to hapless locked-out New York residents.

NIGHT AND DAY LOCKSMITH
1335 Lexington Ave (at 89th St)
722-1017
Mon-Sat: 9-6 (24 hours for emergencies)

To be safe—just in case you're ever locked out—Night and Day is a number you should be carrying close to your heart. New Yorkers, even those who are in residence for a short time, become experts on locks and cylinders. Cocktail party conversation is frequently peppered with references to dead bolts, Medeco, and Segal, and if you haven't the vaguest idea what all the talk is about, you obviously don't live in the city. On the other hand, a city locksmith is about as professional an expert as there can be. He's got to be ahead of the current cocktail circuit fads (as well as the local burgler's latest expertise) and be able to offer fast, on-the-spot service for a variety of devices (no apartment has *one* lock) designed to keep people out. The most sophisticated are keyless, unpickable, or of unknown solution. Mena Sofat, Night and Day's owner, fulfills these rigid requirements. They also answer their phone 24 hours a day. Posted hours are for the sale of their own locks, window gates, and keys. If you buy your lock here, you can be sure they'll be willing to help you out (or *in*, as the case may be) when the time comes.

Lucite

LUCIDITY
775 Madison Ave (at 66th St)
861-7000
Mon-Fri: 10:30-6:30; Sat: 11-6; closed Sat in summer

Plexiglass is a must in modern décor, and Lucidity highlights its best aspects. You could walk out of here convinced that the world could be re-created in plexiglass. Just about anything imaginable comes in plexiglass and is sold here. There are more magazine racks and stands that could be counted, and they represent almost every style, except maybe Italian Provincial. Picture frames and many accessories come in a large range of colors, and if there's someone on your list who has "everything," this is one place to purchase something you can be sure he doesn't have yet. Lucite can be had for less in the lucite district downtown. But for a Madison Avenue shop, Lucidity's prices are not high at all, and it beats traveling downtown. Periodically, there are sales here that reduce the price sting even more. These are nice people to do business with.

PLASTIC PLACE
309 Canal St (bet Mercer St and Broadway)
226-2010
Mon-Fri: 8:30-5; Sat: 8:30-4

This large loft is dedicated to plastics, both the lucite and soft plastic variety. Primarily wholesalers, they will cut anything from cubes to wall coverings, free of charge. Some of their line includes waterproofing material, lucite cubes, and sheets of plastic. They are particularly accommodating to do-it-yourself customers.

PLEXI-CRAFT QUALITY PRODUCTS
514 W 24th St
924-3244
Mon-Fri: 9:30-5; Sat: 11-4

Plexi-Craft offers anything made of lucite and plexiglass at wholesale prices. If you can't find what you want among the pedestals, tables, chairs, shelves, and cubes, they will make it for you. The personnel are extremely helpful in pointing out the various styles in cocktail tables, shelves, magazine racks, and chairs.

Luggage

A TO Z
425 Fifth Ave (bet 38th and 39th St)
686-6905
Mon-Thurs: 9-7; Fri: 9-5; Sun: 11-5
708 Third Ave (bet 44th and 45th St)
867-5556
Mon-Fri: 9:15-6
26 Broadway (entrance at 3 Beaver St)
344-0900, 344-0901
Mon-Fri: 8:30-5:30
790 Seventh Ave (at 52nd St)
307-5013
Mon-Thurs: 9 a.m.-11 p.m.; Fri: 9-8; Sun: 10-6

A to Z has been operating as a small family business for over 40 years. It's been so successful that owner-proprietor Isaac Krepel has seen his original Brooklyn shop spawn four Manhattan branches, all patterned on the original. A to Z's business is luggage. They stock it, sell it, repair it, and deliver it all over the city. And the staff is conveniently multilingual. The drawing card is a 20 to 50 percent discount on everything the store stocks, and that includes *all* major brands of luggage. Did I mention the repair department? They've seen and repaired all kinds of luggage catastrophes, and if their unusually speedy repair service is not fast enough for your schedule, they will ship it to you. A to Z has a catalog and handles mail orders.

BETTINGER'S LUGGAGE SHOP

80 Rivington St
674-9411, 475-1690
Sun-Fri: 9:30-6

This tiny shop can be located by keeping an eye peeled for a mound of luggage heaped all over the sidewalk in front of the store. Inside, it is even more crowded, but, amazingly, the people who run Bettinger's can put their fingers on almost any type of luggage in only a few minutes. Their merchandise includes Samsonite, American Tourister, Ventura, and Christian Dior luggage, camp trunks, briefcases, and leather envelopes in both first quality and irregulars. The prices are probably the best in New York. In any event, they're at least 50 percent less than you'd pay uptown.

CARRY ON LUGGAGE

97 Orchard St (bet Broome and Delancey St)
226-4980
Sun-Fri: 9:45-5:45

If I had to pick the most asked-for type of store, it would be a good place for buying luggage, attaché cases, and briefcases at a good discount. That may come as a surprise, but it really is quite rational. Those items are naturals for almost any gift-giving occasion and are also things that people buy for themselves. There should be hundreds of places to choose from, but there aren't. Fortunately, however, there is Carry On Luggage. They have it all—style, quality, selection, and a discount pricing policy that *starts* at 30 percent. Samsonite, Lark, Skyway, Altas, Ventura, Verdi, and Rolfs are but a few of the manufacturers represented here, and they are supplemented by the presence of every designer name in luggage. (And there are a lot! Ralph Lauren, Diane von Furstenberg, Dior, Bill Blass, Anne Klein, and Gloria Vanderbilt, among them.) The selection ranges from attaché cases to leather cases and jewelry bags. You won't find anything less than the best.

T. ANTHONY

480 Park Ave (at 58th St)
750-9797
Mon-Fri: 9:30-6; Sat: 10-6

T. Anthony handles luxurious luggage of distinction. Anything purchased here will stand out in a crowd as being of really fine quality, and that is a distinction that T. Anthony customers expect and receive. A. Karl knows the stock implicitly and unhesitatingly recommends the right luggage and gifts for his customers; every person who comes into the store receives courteous attention. Luggage comes in sizes from small overnight bags to massive pieces that just fall short of being steamer trunks. (Actually, were this the day of ocean voyages, they would still carry those as well.) Gifts have a similar range. All are based on the leather luggage theme, but the wallets, key cases, and billfolds are distinctive gifts, individually or in matched sets. No discount prices here, but the quality and service are well-established New York traditions.

Magazines

BACK DATE MAGAZINES (A&S BOOK COMPANY)
274 W 43rd St (at Eighth Ave)
695-4897
Mon-Fri: 10-6

For some reason, the sleazy Times Square area has always had back-dated-periodicals shops, even before the ubiquitous porno places. Back Date, one of the best, is a source for back issues of nearly every possible periodical. The more respectable the magazine, the better the possibility of finding it. Prices for what was originally very cheap but is now hard to find are reasonable, though they often surprise people who once threw out the very issue they now seek. Back Date specializes in cinema, martial arts, wrestling, and art magazines. You can avoid the neighborhood altogether and shop by mail or phone.

Magic

FLOSSO AND HORNMANN MAGIC COMPANY
45 W 34th St (room 607)
279-6079
Mon-Fri: 10:30-5:30; Sat: 10:30-3:30

Harry Houdini got his tricks and kicks here, which is not surprising, since he was but one of a score of professional magicians who have owned this shop since its creation in 1856. Flosso and Hornmann is proof that magic is timeless, not only because its clientele spans all ages, but because the store seems unchanged since Houdini's time. In part, that's due to the dim light and dust, but mostly it's because the stock is so complete. It's hard to think of a trick that's *not* stocked here, and it's just as hard to find one that you haven't seen before. The staff, if asked, will show you what's new. You have to visit the store to understand how amazing that is. In addition to magic acts, the shop carries books, manuals, historical treatises, and photographs,and even creates stage sets. For its final act, ladies and gentlemen, it produces a professional magic catalog, *The Story of Magic* for $2. In addition to describing the shop's early history, it lists the highlights of the store's inventory from a "cigarette vanisher" (not a bad idea!) to the workshop plans for the Vanishing Dove or Vanishing Lady tricks. For amateurs, the best thing about the catalog is that many of the tricks are explained in detail. Don't tell a living soul!

LOUIS TANNEN
6 W 32nd St (fourth floor)
239-8383
Mon-Wed, Fri: 9-5:30; Thurs: 9-7; Sat: 9-3

Levitate upstairs to this jam-packed magic store, and Tony Spira (or any of the other helpful personnel) will cheerfully demonstrate the latest in magic. Unlike many such shops, this one welcomes amateurs, and there is a large stock of simple, inexpensive acts. In case they *do* leave the customer baffled, the staff will patiently explain them. There is also a series of mail-order catalogs that seem to be produced as rapidly as rabbits. All are annual *Catalogs of Magic* and contain the store's inventory—over 8,000 individual items and 350 books about magic. But unlike the store, the catalogs seems to be for people who know what they are doing.

MAGIC TOWNE HOUSE
1026 Third Ave (bet 60th and 61st St)
752-1165
Tues, Thurs, Fri-Sun: 1-6 (store); Sat, Sun: 1, 2:30, 4 by reservation (children's magic show); Fri, Sat: 8:30-midnight by reservation (adult show and buffet)

Truly a place for children of all ages, the Magic Towne House dispenses magician's props when it is not presenting professional prestidigitators to its select audiences. The townhouse (literally) is heaped with magical backgrounds. The majestic entrance includes a grand staircase garlanded with magic posters, mirrors (two-way and funhouse), and eerie dripping things. And yes, the staircases sport blood-red banisters. The second floor houses the retail magic shop and the children's birthday party area and theater. Note the hours; none of the Towne House's activities overlap. And yet, with all this going on, each entity is still treated as the center-stage activity. The shop is one of the best stocked in the city, and the salespeople are all practitioners of the art they sell. As often as not, magic tricks are sold along with personal instructions on how to work them. The children's theater offers formal 55-minute magic shows, complete with audience participation and live doves. It has proven so popular that parents clamored to have the Magic Towne House handle their children's birthday parties, and the Towne House obliged. For approximately $15 per guest, the Towne House will cater the entire party, including banners, party hats, personalized cake, ice cream, punch, prizes, and goody bags. The birthday kid can even participate in the magic show. Adults who are magic fans aren't overlooked, either. The third-floor lounge is the site of the cabaret that hosts the adult shows.

Maps

HAMMOND MAP STORE
57 W 43rd St (at Sixth Ave)
398-1222
Mon-Fri: 8:45-5:45

Without ever leaving your home, it is possible to see the world through the maps, charts, and travel paraphernalia that the Hammond Map Store makes available to the general public. The Hammond name is well known to school children who study the maps and globes. The store carries these, of course, but there is much more as well. An an official government agent for nautical and aeronautical charts, Hammond is the place for a really unique personalized gift (try a government survey or aeronautical chart of a hometown area or street), as well as a source for topographical maps for hiking or drilling. Globes come in many configurations, and detail maps take on new meaning when marketed by Hammond. In fact, the possibilities are so extensive that the mail-order catalogs are divided into more than a half-dozen topics.

Memorabilia

ANNA SOSENKO
76 W 82nd St (near Columbus Ave)
799-1357
Mon-Fri: 2-5 by appointment

In a tiny, crowded ground-level store on the West Side, Anna Sosenko sells and maintains a magnificent collection of autographs and personal memorabilia. Most of the collection is show-business oriented, and the better items are framed and displayed on the walls. There are also bins of "common" autographs and piles of not-so-famous or imperfect items. Sosenko herself is obviously a person who loves what she is doing. She will expound for hours on the joys of autograph collecting and tell you how to start a collection. (Never, she says, collect haphazardly. Pick a field, or a person in a field, and stick to that.) It doesn't have to be a tremendously expensive hobby. Sosenko can pull out scores of samples that are very reasonably priced. Even if you decide against collecting 50¢ autographs, visit Sosenko anyway. She and her store are fascinating.

CINEMABILIA
10 W 13th St (bet Fifth and Sixth Ave)
989-8519
Mon, Wed, Sat: 11-6:30; Tues, Thurs, Fri: 11-7

Ernest Burns, who's been running Cinemabilia for over 20 years, says that although he thinks he knows the field as well as anyone, new things crop up everyday, and it's still the most exciting job he knows. It's strange for a man to think that vintage movie momentos are the latest thing in town, but it sure helps the shopper who is looking for a particular item or just wants to browse. Burns adds a gusto to his store that can only be matched by the hype of a Hollywood premiere. He carries books, periodicals, graphics, stills, and ephemera relating to film. There are posters and magazines, photos, sheet music, clipping files, souvenir programs, shooting scripts (and the books made from those scripts), movie graphics, and just about anything even slightly connected with the movie business of any age. Cinemabilia's collection goes back to the teens, and out-of-print, rare or hard-to-find items are the shop's specialty. Finally, Burns requests that no customer take what is seen at face value. He claims that the catalogs and store displays are but the tip of the iceberg. The back issues of magazines, poster and still collections, and the extensive files are all out of sight for space reasons. So although Cinemabilia answers mail orders promptly, a visit is really in order. Send your regards to Hollywood.

MEMORY SHOP
109 E 12th St (off Fourth Ave)
473-2404
Daily: 11-6

This dirty basement is virtually a Hollywood archive. The Memory Shop claims to have one million posters, 500,000 press books, and over eight million photographs in stock. If it exists, it's buried here somewhere. Customers don't browse; they know exactly what they want, hand in the order, and the counter clerk gets it. This is probably because *only* the clerk could find it. If you have a fetish for *Casablanca* or some other old movie, this is the place for you. A free listing is sent on request if you write Memory Shop Bay, 365 Cooper Station, New York, New York 10003. The Memory Shop is especially eager to fill requests from libraries and film students.

MOVIE STAR NEWS
134 W 18th St (bet Sixth and Seventh Ave)
620-8160
Mon-Sat: 10-6

In what is becoming the movie memorabilia center of the city, Movie Star News claims to have the world's largest collection of movie photos. If you thought the heyday of movie stars was long gone, don't tell the folks here, because the stars, past and present, still shine brightly in this shop. But film buffs can't shine (or survive) on photos alone, so Movie Star News offers posters, press books, and other cinema publicity materials as well. The selection is arranged like a library, and the Kramers, who run Movie Star News, do a lot of research for magazines, newspapers, and the media. This is the closest thing to Hollywood on the East coast.

MYTHOLOGY UNLIMITED

370 Columbus Ave (bet 77th and 78th St)
874-0774
Mon-Fri: 10:30-9; Sat, Sun: 11-6

You have to see Mythology Unlimited to understand it. Whatever you fathom on one visit may be completely different on the next. But visit again you will, as do most of the city's celebrities and trend-setters. What they find can be anything from an autograph party for the author of a book on diners or Atlantic City, to a showing of artists' books from California, or an exhibit of stationery and assorted objects that can politely be described as weird. All of these are accompanied by wine, cheese, crackers or coffee served at open-house gatherings. In between such get togethers, there's the regular stock of tons of archaic postcards, pins, posters, ray guns, tin toys, thousands of personalized rubber stamps, screen prints, masks, toys, knickknacks, and throw pillows. And the shop's T-shirts may have developed the largest following in the city. Nearly every organization, shop, and individual within a 30-block radius cites Mythology as a source for T-shirts. This eclectic shop is a celebration of whimsy and pop art, right across the street from the castlelike Museum of Natural History.

ONE SHUBERT ALLEY

1 Shubert Alley (bet Broadway and Eighth Ave)
944-4133, 800-223-1320
Mon: 10:30-8:30; Tues-Sat: 10:30-11:30; Sun: noon-7

Shubert Alley is a narrow alleyway in the Broadway theater district that is often used as a shortcut between theaters. In the past few years, though, its value as real estate has been recognized and several enterprising establishments have sprung up on the alley. One Shubert Alley is the first attempt to transfer the mystique of the theater to daylight hours other than the Wednesday and weekend matinees. The shop stocks T-shirts, posters, buttons, and other paraphernalia from current Broadway and off-Broadway productions, while the shop itself has a décor that is frankly nostalgic. In addition, drinks and other light refreshments are available for browsing customers or thirsty theater patrons. There is a mail-order catalog as well.

PERFORMING ARTS SHOP

Metropolitan Opera House at Lincoln Center (downstairs)
877-1800
Mon-Fri: 10-8

This little-known shop on the lower level of the Metropolitan Opera House is an aria unto itself. Everything on sale has a tie to the performing arts, no matter how tenuous. (A Harbor Sweets chocolate called Metropolitan Mint, which merits inclusion by virtue of its name, and a "Tea for Two" teapot are two of the extremes.) But all of it is high quality, and all is done in good taste. (How could you be located beneath Marc Chagall's panels and sell salt-and-pepper shakers?) So, there are top-notch gifts—all with a performing-arts motif, an eniviable collection of printed matter that is so encompassing that there are rumors of an underground link to the Library of the Performing Arts one building over, and much more. Records and tapes are balanced by beach towels and Beethoven T-shirts. And if you want to check out that underground rumor, the Performing Arts Shop also arranges tours of Lincoln Center. They should start with better directions to their own shop.

SILVER SCREEN
35 E 28th St (bet Park and Madison Ave)
679-8130
Mon-Sat: noon-7

You'll have to seek it out, but if you collect movie (or rare theater) memorabilia, a trip to the Silver Screen will be well worth the trouble. Ken, Carol, and Irma run a shop that looks like the dreams of a 1950s teenager. The store is jammed with movie stills, posters, press books, movie magazines, and autographs of movie stars. And the photographs, in black and white or color, are everywhere. There is bound to be one of your favorite here, even if you've forgotten who you favorite *was*. The Silver Screen also carries a full line of Beatles artifacts, and many customers make a pilgramage just for that. The more cultured of their parents come to view the theatrical memorabilia. The original production pictures of Roaring Twenties musicals may well be unique, and some of the costume accessories worn by Broadway greats certainly are. The stock is always changing, and for those who can't make it in person, the Silver Screen maintains a mail-order department.

SPEAKEASY ANTIQUES
799 Broadway (bet 10th and 11th St)
533-2440
Tues-Sat: 10:30-6; Thurs: 10:30-7:
Closed Sat, Sun, and Mon in summer.

Despite the name, this store reflects owners Bob and Rita Brand's interest in show-business mementos rather than in genuine antiques. Their current pride is a collection of over 100 Beatlemania items (available through a mail-order catalog.) In addition, the store has early 20th-century posters, cigarette cases, signs, and the original 1954 Marilyn Monroe pinup calendars. Prices—maybe because these aren't real antiques—are incredibly reasonable. They buy, sell trade, and rent their specialties. There is also a vintage-clothing department.

WELCOME TO NEW YORK CITY

26 Carmine St (off Bleecker St and Sixth Ave)
242-6714
Mon-Fri: 11-8; Sat: 11-11; Sun: 1-6

Joe Coppa started Welcome to New York City in a shop on Front Street, near the South Street Seaport. But the shop proved so popular that Coppa had to weigh the advantages of being in a nostalgia-minded neighborhood against having enough room to house his purchases. He opted for the latter when he found a vacant store that happened to be in a part of Carmine Street that looks exactly as it did when it was built over 100 years ago. Being in the Village (probably the only other place in the city that can match the Seaport in old-fashioned ambiance) didn't hurt either. So, Coppa moved into the larger quarters. Coppa sells New York City memorabilia, so the city that he is welcoming you to is not the city you are visiting today. The store resembles a time-transported stationery shop. The most recent items are circa 1933, but most of the shop's materials date from 1760 to 1912. (More current New York City paraphernalia also complements Coppa's theme.) There are postcards, maps, posters, photographs, prints, and murals. Many are original, but the shop also offers copies.

Mirrors

SUNDIAL FABRICATORS

1491 First Ave (at 78th St)
734-0838, 873-8154
Mon-Fri: 8-5; Sat: 10-4

Sundial claims that they supply "decorative treatments of distinction," and anyone who has ever seen a cramped New York apartment suddenly expand with the use of a few strategic mirrors will understand how they can make that claim. Sundial deals with professional decorators as well as do-it-yourselfers, and both reap the benefit of the staff's years of experience. There are mirrors for home, office, and showrooms (their office is a factory showroom). In addition, Sundial will remodel, resilver, and move mirrors in need of those services. Sundial also designs custom window treatments, doors, blinds, shades, storm windows, room dividers, and more. The primary service here, however, is the decorating advice, which can be really helpful. Mirrors may be just the answer to your decorating problems.

Models and Model Trains

AMERICA'S HOBBY CENTER
146 W 22nd St
675-8922
Mon-Wed, Fri: 8:30-5:30; Thurs: 8:30-6:30; Sat: 8:30-3:30

Hobbies and models are a serious business here, but there's a lighthearted touch to remind everyone that hobbies are *fun*. It is evident everywhere in this shop, but nowhere more so than when the proprietor Marshall Winston introduces himself as the "known authority on vehicular hobbies." Winston's vehicular hobbies include model airplanes, boats, ships, trains, cars, radio-controlled materials, model books, tools and "everything for model builders." They also sell wholesale to dealers and by mail order to retail customers. In fact, they fill more orders by mail than at the store. Ask for the catalog for a good indication of what they have.

JAN'S HOBBY SHOP
1431A York Ave (at 76th St)
861-5075
Mon-Sat: 9-7; Sun: 11-5

When Fred Hutchins was young (he's now in this twenties), he passed the time by building models and dioramas, particularly those on historical themes. Eventually, it became economically viable for his parents to buy his favorite source of supply. Now, he runs the shop. So, while the front of the shop is still your run-of-the-mill hobby shop, the star of the show is clearly the grown-up Fred and his childhood hobby, and you can bet on Fred's ability to keep Jan's stocked with everything a serious model builder could possibly want. Jan's has a superb stock of plastic scale models, model war games, paints, books, brushes (and other paraphernalia), toys, planes, ships, and tank models. But in the meantime, Fred has gone professional. He creates models and dioramas to order for television, advertising, and private customers. In addition to his craft skills, he is also noted for his accurate historical detail. And there is yet a third business: showcase building. Because any hobbyist likes to show his wares, Fred builds custom-made wood and plexiglass showcases for that purpose. Incredibly, he even offers two-day service. He also has remote-controlled cars, ships, and tanks.

RED CABOOSE
16 W 45th St (bet Fifth and Sixth Ave, fourth floor)
575-0155
Mon-Sat: 11-7

At the Red Caboose, owner-operator Allan T. Spitz will tell you that 99 percent of his customers are not wide-eyed children, but sharp-eyed adults who are dead serious about model railroads.

Since these are the people Spitz serves, it is difficult for a Christmas-morning engineer to adequately describe his stock, but I'll try. The Red Caboose claims to have 90,000 items in stock. That includes a line of 2,000 hand-finished, imported brass locomotives *alone*. That doesn't begin to cover the tracks or track gauges available. (Spitz claims that the five basic sizes—1:22, 1:48, 1:87, 1:161, and 1:220, in a ratio of scale to life size—will allow a model railroader to build layouts sized to fit into a desk drawer or a basement.) The store also carries the city's largest model-ship selection, and HO and N gauge equipment. If there is a model-train district, it is probably located on the upper floors of the buildings on this block. For that reason, Spitz offers a 20 percent discount on all purchases over $10. "We are prepared to help even customers just off the street with a full line of services," says Spitz. "And we regularly send foreign and air-freight shipments to clients who deal with us by mail."

TRAIN SHOP
23 W 45th St (basement)
730-0409
Mon-Fri: 10-6; Sat: 10-5

The second major resident of model-train row, this shop differs from its fellow traveler only by its basement location and its insistence that it has *no* specialty. It merely stocks everything. The Train Shop's manager (engineer?) is Paul Schulhaus, who is about as knowledgeable as they come, and his assistant, Russ, sums up the stock by saying, "Look around. If you need help, just give us a holler." Now isn't that just the way they'd do it at the local station? To name *some* specifics, the shop claims to have at least 30,000 different model pieces in stock. What is not in stock can be ordered, but they do not maintain their own catalog. (They accept mail orders.) Walther's Catalog includes the Train Shop and lists the unique items they have. (One favorite is a train engine, complete with its own realistic sound system.) But the stock can in no way be described. It is simply incredible and an awful lot of fun! Prices are competitive with the store's neighbors, and where else would you find two such shops within hollering distance? Even Jim Evans of Union Pacific fame would get excited here.

Music and Musical Instruments

BLEECKER BOB'S GOLDEN OLDIES RECORD SHOP
118 W Third St (bet MacDougal and Sixth Ave)
475-9677
Daily: noon to 3 a.m.

Let us sing the praises of Bleecker Bob's, who is nothing if not perverse. (Name another store open til 3 a.m. on Christmas Day!)

For one thing, although there is a real Bob (Bob Plotnik, the owner), the store isn't on Bleecker Street. For another, Bleecker Bob is almost an institution to generations of New Yorkers who have sifted through the selection of virtually every rock record ever recorded. Yet what did *The New York Times* finally cite Bleecker Bob's for? "The archetypal punk-plus record store." Come on, folks! With a stock that includes all those old records, autograph parties for rock stars, and a boast that they can fill any wish list from their stock, Bleecker Bob's is obviously much more than a punk-rock store. It is also *the* gathering place in the wee hours of the morning in the Village (where that *ain't* the wee hours of the morning). But above all, it's one great source for out-of-print, obscure, and imported discs. And the saleshelp, who used to be rather weird, have toned down their act.

DAYTON'S
824 Broadway (at 12th St)
254-5084
Mon-Fri: 10-6; Sat: 10-5:30; Sun: noon-5

Located across the street from the Strand Book Store, Dayton's is to records what the Strand is to books. They both have the same sources—reviewers' copies and promotional materials—and they both pass on their savings to retail customers. Dayton's reviewers' copies go for a price much less than the list price. I am talking here of best sellers or "hit parade" material; lesser works are relegated to lesser stores. Dayton's own boast is that they specialize in long-playing phonograph records, particulary those that are out of print. Again, this applies solely to best-selling records in mint condition, which partly explains the high cost. Anyone can unearth an old record by an unknown group in any discount department store, but an unplayed copy of the Beatles' first hit? For that, you need Dayton's.

DETRICH PIANOS
211 W 58th St (near Broadway)
246-1766
Mon-Fri: 10-6; Sat: 10-5

Kalman Detrich fled Hungary for the United States many years ago, bringing his love and knowledge of pianos with him. His shop, within earshot of Carnegie Hall, ministers to any of the myriad needs the piano player might have. Detrich will tune, repair, polish, rent, buy, sell, and even buy back a piano with all the finesse of his Old World training. But his specialty is antique pianos. He lovingly restores them, and the few that he can't restore, he polishes to a gloss and sells as furniture rather than musical pieces. The small shop is jammed with the cream of whatever is being revitalized at the moment, and passers-by cannot help but understand Detrich's attitude when viewing the finished results. Detrich also has a sideline that he calls "gifts for musicians," and for music lovers, he stocks music boxes, books, and figurines. The music boxes are good enough to warrant a shop to themselves.

DRUMMER'S WORLD
133 W 45th St (bet Sixth and Seventh Ave)
840-3057
Mon-Fri: 10-6; Sat: 10-4

Rap, tap, tap! This is a great place, unless the patron is your teenager or upstairs neighbor. In any case, Barry Greenspon and his staff take great pride in guiding students as well as professionals through one of the most well-rounded percussion stores in the country. Indicative of the store's attitude is that that qualifying "one of" is Greenspon's own. He wouldn't want to steer anyone wrong, even though professional drummers would be hard-pressed to name another such store. Inside this drummer's paradise, you'll find everything from commonplace equipment to one-of-a-kind antiques and imports. All of the instruments are high-quality symphonic percussion items, and the customers receive the same attention whether they are members of an orchestra or kitchen-spoon rappers. For the latter, the store offers instructors, instruction, and how-to books. For the former, there are esoteric and even ethnic instruments for virtuosos who want to experiment. For drummers who are offered long trips away from home by their friends and families, Drummer's World has a catalog and will ship anywhere in the country. But jokes aside, this is a unique store that caters to professionals and neophytes with the same grace. Bang the drum slowly!

FOOTLIGHT RECORDS
90 Third Ave (bet 12th and 13th St)
533-1572
Mon-Fri: 11-7; Sat: 10-6; Sun: noon-5

A short walk from Dayton's, Footlight Records has the same passion for rare and odd records, but there's an emphasis on show tunes and jazz rather than a general hodgepodge or discounted current recordings. This is not to say that Ed McGrath and Gene Dingenary's prices aren't good. In fact, for many of the albums, their prices are the best around, but that is really the point—these records just *aren't* around elsewhere. If an original cast album was made of a Broadway show, Footlight has it. Often, its customers are the artists themselves, who haven't copies of their own performances! What is more impressive is the organization that enables the store's personnel to know almost at a glance what is and is not available. Not an easy task when the stock is constantly being sold and much of it is out-of-print or hard-to-find recordings.

There are show tunes, whole collections of '40s, '50s, and '60s artists, and probably every Big Band record ever made. Part of the fun here is to find the most esoteric titles in stock on each visit. Ask McGrath or Dingenary for their favorite contender for the title, and then try to beat it!

FORD PIANO SUPPLY COMPANY

4898 Broadway (bet 204th and 207th St)
569-9200
Mon-Fri: 8:30-5:30

John Ford's father was in the piano-repair business. When John Ford took over, the main suppliers for esoteric parts were all out of town, and he soon tired of daylong trips to pick up supplies. So, he began collecting odds and ends whenever he found them, and he soon had more piano parts than pianos in his shop. Along with the best collection of supplies for piano repairs, Ford also garnered a reputation as *the* place to go for piano tuners. So, Ford all but abandoned the buying and selling of instruments and concentrated on the rebuilding of pianos (often from scratch) and the supplying of piano parts. The Ford family can refinish, tune, rebuild, or adjust any kind of acoustic piano. They will custom-make covers and benches as well as pedals, and there is an array of piano-tuning tools, lamps, chairs, and coasters. The Fords will happily conduct tours of their piano-rebuilding factory, which is a sight to see. But for the most part, Ford's customers never come to the shop. When you're the only store in town supplying everything for pianos, most customers order by mail or telephone. The Fords also rent and tune pianos. They are truly a family business: they are awaiting the day when little John Ford III is old enough to join the family ranks.

FREE BEING RECORDS

129 Second Ave (bet St. Mark's Pl and Seventh St)
260-1774
Mon-Thurs: noon-10; Fri, Sat: noon-11; Sun: noon-9

Free Being is a little-known source for used recordings at rock-bottom prices. Andrea at Free Being guarantees the quality of any used record, and patrons at the store cited it as the best place in the city to purchase out-of-print discs, particularly rock and jazz. Free Being buys, sells, and imports LPs and 45s. The place could be better organized, but that's really part of its charm, along with the great finds.

JACK KAHN MUSIC COMPANY

158 W 55th St (near Sixth Ave)
581-9420
Mon-Sat: 10-6

Jack Kahn is *the* best place to buy a piano or organ in New York. For one thing, a piano should only be purchased from a dealer who not only has a reputation to preserve, but a service department that can handle any problems that might occur. For another, a piano is better purchased from a source with many brands. Jack Kahn meets both criteria and more. It has the largest selection of pianos in the country, in both names and sizes. (The 9′6″ grand piano is exclusive in the United States.) Craftsmen at Jack Kahn are capable of rebuilding, refinishing, and reconditioning a piano. All of their work is fully guaranteed, *and* they guarantee that their prices are the lowest anywhere. If anyone can purchase a piano or organ for less, Kahn's will refund the full price, plus an additional 10 percent within 30 days. In addition, every instrument sold has a ten-year performance guarantee.

JAZZ RECORD CENTER

133 W 72nd St (bet Broadway and Columbus Ave, room 404)
877-1836
Mon-Sat: 11-7; closed Sat in summer,
first week in July and first week in Aug

This is the only jazz specialty store in the city, and in its jam-packed spaces it features a listening area for "tryouts" of records. The bins include all kinds of recorded jazz, from the earliest days to the most modern. The house specialty is out-of-print jazz records, but there are books, posters, photographs, and periodicals on the topic, and some of them are vintage as well. Jazz Record Center also buys and sells collections, runs a search service, offers appraisals, and holds an annual jazz antique auction. What is most amazing is that all of this is run by one man, Frederick Cohen, a walking (beating?) jazz enthusiast. When Cohen goes to the post office to mail the auction catalog, the entire staff has just left and the store is closed. He therefore advises you to call first. The whole operation is really incredible! Here's a world-famous specialist on jazz history running a one-man show from a fourth-floor room in an old office building. And he's a charmer to boot!

JOSEPH PATELSON MUSIC HOUSE

160 W 56th St
582-5840
Mon-Sat: 9-6; closed Sat in summer

Behind Carnegie Hall, Joseph Patelson is the shop known to every student of music in the area. From little first-graders in need of theory books to artists from Carnegie Hall in need of an extra copy of sheet music, *everyone* stops here first because of the fabulous selection as well as excellent prices. The stock includes music scores, sheet music, music books, and orchestral and opera scores. All are neatly catalogued and displayed in open cabinets, and one can pore through the section of interest—whether it be piano music, chamber music, orchestral scores, opera scores, old popular songs, concerts, ethnic scores, or instrumental solos.

Nelson Sullivan and Daniel Patelson are models of informative and unobtrusive saleshelp. They are there for guidance, but never interfere with a customer combing the files. Sheet music, incidentally, is filed the way records are elsewhere. You flip through the files to find what you want, and bring it up to the counter to be checked out. There are some musical accessories as well. Joseph Patelson is an unofficial meeting house for the city's young artists. Word goes out that "We're looking for a violinist," and meetings are often arranged in the store.

JUAN OROZCO

155 Sixth Ave (at Spring St)
691-8620
Mon-Sat: 10-5:30

As the third generation of his famiy in the guitar business, Juan Orozco has a knowledge of guitars that is unmatched. Guitars are as much members of the family as bona fide relatives, and each instrument is treated with respectful care. Orozco manufactures and distributes classical and flamenco guitars. Their own guitar strings, sold under the Aranjuez label, are sold here exclusively as well. The quality is outstanding. Everything about the shop implies that you are dealing with Spanish craftsmen. The décor has strictly classical Spanish-tile, stucco walls, black wrought iron, and red accents, while the merchandise shows fine care and appraisal. Guitars here are not inexpensive, and the handmade ones border on magnificent, but they can be had for less than you'd expect. People who use guitars to earn their livelihood are Orozco's biggest customers.

LAST WOUND-UP

290 Columbus Ave (bet 73rd and 74th St)	1 Herald Center
787-3388	(fifth floor)
Daily: 10-8	Daily: 10-6

This super store is dedicated to any kind of object that can be wound up. Within that classification, things are divided into music boxes and windup toys, with a roughly equal division between the two, though owner Nathan Cohen harbors a slight prejudice for the music boxes. He makes many of the boxes in stock, and his avocation is helping customers make their own music boxes out of almost any suitable container. The Last Wound-Up also sells the components to do this. The completed boxes for sale go from valuable antiques to modern models. Many are from abroad, and several are encrusted with gems and gold. (The Victorian boxes in particular were endowed with as many different jewels as they could hold.) There are also fun boxes of no intrinsic value, except for the tunes they play, as well as boxes of almost priceless value made of crystal and gold. While Cohen believes every home should have several boxes, he is not unmindful that other items can be wound up as well. So, there are barking dogs and minstrels, windup toys, and who-knows-what-else lining the walls. Finally, don't forget that the original Edison phonographs were also operated by crank. So, the Last Wound Up has several of those. Despite the fact that nearly every family threw one of them out, they are quite valuable now.

MANNY'S
156 W 48th St (bet Sixth and Seventh Ave)
819-0576
Mon-Sat: 9-6

Manny's is a huge discount department store for musical instruments. "Everything for the Musician" is their motto, and it is borne out by a collection of musical equipment so esoteric that different salesmen are experts in different departments. One person could not possibly understand everything the store sells. There is an emphasis on modern music, as evidenced by the hundreds of autographed pictures of contemporary musicians and singers on the walls, and the huge collection of electronic instruments. Even the photos tend to be of the musicians who rely on electronic components rather than classical music. This does not, however, preclude classical instruments, and there is a good collection of them as well. The best part is that all of the musical instruments, accessories, electronic equipment, and supplies are sold at very good discount prices. If you're into electronic music, Manny's should be your first choice.

MUSIC MASTERS
25 W 43rd St (bet Fifth and Sixth Ave)
840-1958
Mon-Fri: 10-5:30; Sat: 10-3

In the heart of the theater district, Music Masters is a recording shop that carries a full stock of records and tapes, with a strong emphasis on Broadway show albums and an even better collection of opera recordings. (The Metropolitan Opera was a resident of this neighborhood in its pre-Lincoln Center days.) Music Masters claims to stock 98 percent of all classical recordings and the largest collection of opera and theater material on records and tapes. Their own line of records produces whatever recordings are necessary to fill the voids in their stock, and the house specialty is hard-to-find discs and tapes. Of course, few are hard to find *for them.* They have huge numbers of private-label recordings (aside from their own label) and a list that must be considered esoteric even to collectors. (You can get *Maria Callas—Live Performance of Arias from Aïda, Mexico City, 1952,* or *So Long 174th Street,* with Robert Morse and Kaye Ballard.) Music Masters also sells audio equipment and music boxes. This is a great place to browse and listen.

MUSIC STORE AT CARL FISCHER

62 Cooper Square (at Seventh St and Fourth Ave)
677-0821
Mon-Sat: 10-5:45

Outside the Carnegie Hall area, the Music Store at Carl Fischer offers the best selection of sheet music from all publishers and categories, including pop, jazz, folk, rock, and classical. Everything is reasonably priced, with real bargains to be found in the older music. (That's in terms of publication, not composition.) The store also has extended research facilities and background information for piano, vocal, instrumental, band, orchestral, and choral music. And that pretty much covers it all.

NOSTALGIA . . . AND ALL THAT JAZZ

217 Thompson St (bet Bleecker and W Third St)
420-1940
Mon-Thurs: 1-8; Fri: 1-9; Sat: 1-10; Sun: 1-7:30

Guess what they sell here! Time's up: the answer is—envelope please—nostalgia records and LPs, especially jazz records. Most of the recordings are of early radio programs, jazz programs, and soundtracks of old shows. There are a few vocal LPs, too. All are very reasonably priced. The shop has set up a sideline in photography, and Kim Deuel and Mort Alavi do a healthy business in the production, cataloging, and reproduction of photos. Nostalgia will reproduce any photograph, in any size or quantity, up to 30″ x 40″. They also have a good collection of posters, movie and jazz stills, and large (16″ x 20″) show-business photos, in black and white *and* color. Prices are excellent.

ORPHEUS REMARKABLE RECORDINGS

1047 Lexington Ave
737-6043
Mon-Sat: 10:30-6:30

Remarkable here means "not cheap," but none of Orpheus' remarkable recordings descend to the depths. The emphasis is on culture, and that's as in highbrow and not Culture Club, so look for the classics and performance recordings as opposed to popular tunes. Orpheus also has a good selection that is not bound by time. If the very best recording of *Aïda* was made in 1947, then that's the one they stock. If it was made last month, so much the better. And while the store is small, it is extremely well organized and there's nothing crammed away in the basement. That's too bad; I could think of some great puns to say about that.

RITA FORD
19 E 65th St (at Madison Ave)
535-6717
Mon-Sat: 9-5

Rita Ford collects antique music boxes, and in the process, she has become an expert in all aspects of the business. Her stock consists of old valuable music boxes, old not-so-valuable pieces, pieces in various state of disrepair (Rita Ford also does repairs), and pieces so thoroughly modern they can be manufactured to order. The main stock in trade is expertise; Rita Ford trades on her ability to know all there is to know about the music-box business. She is an acknowledged expert on various music-box scores, workings, and outer casings. Some of her pieces are rare, one-of-a-kind, perfect antiques and are priced accordingly. Somewhat more reasonable are the contemporary pieces based upon original antiques.

TOWER RECORDS
692 Broadway
(E Fourth St)
505-1500
Fourth St and Lafayette
(classical records)
505-1500
Daily: 9-midnight

TOWER VIDEO
1977 Broadway
(at 67th St)
496-2500
Daily: 9-midnight

Tower, the largest record-store chain on the West Coast, came to New York in 1983 with an overture that is still resounding. New York had never seen recordings merchandised like this, and the 15-hour days made even the largest such store on this coast crowded. (In fact, zoolike would describe it better. Bear in mind that this is the Village area. Some of the patrons and saleshelp look quite weird.) Surprisingly, even in those environs, the most popular of the nine departments was the classical records', so much so that the entire department set up housekeeping in an annex around the corner. There is still a small section in the main store, along with the largest selection imaginable of all manner of recordings. Music and record lovers will go wild here. How about an exercise record? In Spanish? Or a barking-dog recording for scaring burglars? Or perhaps some white noise to sleep by—even a recording of traffic and blaring horns for city folk who can't sleep on vacation without the sounds of home. It's all here and much, much more. Tower Video, uptown on the West Side, does the same number with video discs and equipment. It's almost a New York pastime to see who you can see checking out what. Prices, incidentally, are always good, and they can be truly sensational.

VINYL MANIA RECORDS

30 Carmine St
691-1720

52 Carmine St
929-1658

496 Hudson St
989-8858

329 Amsterdam Ave
496-5600

Mon, Tues, Wed, Sat: 11-7; Thurs, Fri: 11-1 a.m.

Vinyl Mania is the archives for the latest tunes. If that is a contradiction in terms, so is Vinyl Mania. The store professes to be expert at vinyl discs. To that end, they even publish their own "Vinylmania" newsletter and have an ample stock of used and "golden oldie" recordings. But the crowds really jam Vinyl Mania for the *new* releases. The shop at 52 Carmine Street specializes in disco, while its sister at 30 Carmine boasts rock music so new that both stores are frequented by DJs who want to get the newest recordings before their own stations do. The staff claims to be 12-inch dance-music specialists, and that "12 inch" refers to the discs, not the size of the dance step. Anyone in the store is as up on current music as you can get. Often, late-night revellers top off the morning by picking up new recordings on their way home. Remember, I told you they keep a strange standard of time in the Village.

Newspapers

HOTALINGS NEWS AGENCY

142 W 42nd St
840-1868
Mon-Sat: 7:30 a.m.-9:30 p.m.; Sun: 7:30 a.m.-8 p.m.

As every homesick out-of-towner should know, hometown newspapers can be picked up at Hotalings for the regular price, plus the cost of transportation. Newspapers are sold on the day of issue (or soon thereafter), and many non-natives keep in daily contact with their homes through these papers. However, as many a Hollywood movie will attest, Hotalings also carries back issues (thereby enabling the hero to learn that his adversary had ceased to exist months ago, so he could return home). Back issues are erratic at best, and the days of sending the secretary out for the papers from Peoria for the past six months probably never existed, but there is still a pretty ample selection here.

Pictures, Posters, Prints

ARGOSY BOOK STORE
116 E 59th St
753-4455
Mon-Fri: 9-6; Sat: 10-5; closed Sat in summer

The main stock in trade here is ostensibly books (the older and rarer the better), but knowledgeable browsers usually pass the books by in favor of the antique maps and prints. There is an excellent collection of early American paintings and prints (Currier and Ives, among others) and a combination of maps and prints that makes a marvelous decorating background. In fact, if a bookstore could be classified as a decorating accessory store, Argosy would qualify. The books are valued as much for their appearance and bindings as their age and rarity, and maps and prints are similarly rated. Argosy handles first editions and Americana garnered from estate sales, and will buy books from private sources. The specialties are antique prints, maps, and, surprisingly, medical books. Argosy will also restore paintings, particularly early American paintings and watercolors of primitive or historical nature. The personnel seem most impressed with their own knowledge and position. Some customers feel intimidated here. Too bad. Otherwise, it's a great place to browse and shop.

LEE'S STUDIO GALLERY
211 W 57th St (near Broadway)
265-5670
Mon-Sat: 10-7

Across the street from Lee's Art Shop, Lee's Studio Gallery serves as an inspiration for what can be done with the paraphernalia purchased at the former establishment. They boast of the largest selection of modern posters in the city, some of which are truly magnificent. And once the budding artist has made it, Lee's can furnish the new studio and home. There are some of the most marvelous lamps ever to shed light on the subject, including what they call the "most unique collection of high-tech lamps in the city." To go with those professional lamps are drafting and drawing furniture from all of the major manufacturers, though there is a particularly heavy accent on Italian design. And finally, perhaps incongruously, the simple tourist can simply leave the drafting tables behind and emerge from Lee's with a map of New York City. But even that isn't really simple. This is certainly the best collection of maps outside of a map specialty store, and it is sold along with Lee's advice. Whether Lee's personnel are asked for subway directions, decorating advice, or professional advice, they handle it with aplomb.

LUCIEN GOLDSCHMIDT

1117 Madison Ave (at 84th St)
879-0070
Mon-Fri: 10-6; Sat: 10-5; closed in Aug

Lucien Goldschmidt deals in fine prints of the masters, both old and modern, and his establishment seems dedicated to proving that drawings and prints can be as costly as original paintings. His stock is well worth the asking price, but customers in search of inexpensive prints should hunt elsewhere. Goldschmidt handles only the best. His stock is extensive, beginning with 16th- and 17th-century masters, including Durers and Rembrandts, and running through 20th-century Matisses and Picassos. Some of the very contemporary prints can be had for under a hundred dollars, but the average price tag is in the thousands.

OLD PRINT SHOP

150 Lexington Ave (bet 29th and 30th St)
686-2111, 683-3950
Mon-Sat: 9-4:30; closed Sat in summer

Strolling down Lexington Avenue and glancing at the Old Print Shop, one might think that time was suspended and New York was once again in the 19th century. Established in 1898, the shop exudes an old-fashioned charm that makes it appear timeless, and its stock only reinforces that impression. Kenneth M. Newman specializes in Americana. That includes original prints, paintings, town views, Currier and Ives prints, and original maps that reflect America as it was. Most of the nostalgic bicentennial pictures that adorned calendars and stationery were copies of prints found here. Historians, amateur and professional, have a field day in this shop, and often purchase things that simply strike their fancy, having nothing to do with their original request. Kenneth Newman also does custom framing—"correct period framing," he hastened to add—and prints in his frames are striking. Everything bought and sold here is original. (Newman also purchases estates and single items.) A great place.

POSTERAMERICA

138 W 18th St (bet Sixth and Seventh Ave)
206-0499
Tues-Fri: 11-7; Sat, Sun: noon-5

Jack Banning and Sandra Elm literally live for their art. In this case, their art is original posters circa 1870 to 1950, nearly all of which are lithographs. But ah, the setting! For 10 years, they ran Posteramerica as the oldest gallery in the country devoted to vintage poster art. When their gallery on Ninth Avenue proved too small, they found and renovated a former stable and carriage house that used to serve the department stores on Ladies Mile in the 1880s. Their new quarters sport a magnificent mahogany-and-glass storefront that would be at home on Ladies Mile itself, a huge well-appointed gallery and living quarters upstairs for Banning and Elm. As a result, it is hard to choose what to envy first—the excellent collection of American and European posters (with strong emphasis on film, World War I, and travel), the gallery that the owners renovated themselves, or their living quarters, which are convenient and elegant. Their renovations were paid for with profits from the gallery. So the posters are not of the stuff people used to give away (or maybe they once did but not nowadays). These days, Posteramerica is known for the brilliant graphics, sheer size, and magnitude of its pieces. It is also the exclusive agent for California designer David Lance Goines. And if the urge strikes you to see these lithographs during nonbusiness hours, the owners are just right upstairs and available by appointment.

TRITON GALLERY
323 W 45th St (bet Eighth and Ninth Ave)
765-2472
Mon-Sat: 10-6

Theater posters are the show here, and Triton presents them like no one else. The complete list of current Broadway posters is but a small part of what's available, and it's balanced by an almost equally complete range of older show posters from here and abroad. Show cards are a standard 14″ x 22″ size and seem to be the most readily available items. Posters range in size from 23″ x 46″ to 42″ x 84″ and are priced according to how rare, how old, and how much in demand they are. None of these criteria, incidentally, have much to do with the actual success of the show. Often, hundreds of posters were printed for shows that lasted less than a week and no one has a use for. At the same time, a hit like *Annie* has produced more posters than anyone could use, so its show cards cost no more than some of the totally obscure ones. Note that the collection is not limited to Broadway or even American plays, and some of the more interesting pieces are of plays from other times. Triton also does custom-framing, and much of the business is done via mail and phone orders. Even the catalog will give you a lift!

Plants, Flowers, Terrariums

AUDREY JOCELYN
(Flower Arranging School)
223 E 58th St (near Second Ave)
759-4266
By appointment

Audrey Jocelyn runs dual businesses at one location. While the front of the shop could pass as a regular florist, albeit with rather unusual arrangements, the back of the shop is a school for flower arranging. The school combines all of the desirable features of flower arranging with the attributes of using only real and natural flowers. Each arrangement will last almost indefinitely. Jocelyn's hand is heavy on the dried flowers, fruits, and imported grasses, and yet somehow there is an overall light and airy touch.

BILL'S FLOWER MARKET
816 Sixth Ave (at 28th St)
889-8154
Mon-Fri: 8-5

Bill's prices are those of the adjoining 28th Street distributors, and his service and attitude are that of the Sixth Avenue merchants. Bill and his people make up some of the best flower arrangements in the city. In addition, there is an excellent selection of plants and flowers in season.

DIANE LOVE
851 Madison Ave (bet 70th and 71st St)
879-6997
Mon-Sat: 10-5:30; closed Sat in July and Aug

Here, the flowers are made of cloth, and Diane Love creates arrangements for everything from boutonnieres to permanent centerpieces. All of them bear the indelible Love stamp—a light airiness that can be very attractive. Usually, improving upon nature is not a terribly successful idea, but Diane Love seems to borrow merely the forms and colors to create her own accent pieces. The cloth flowers are used in accessories for the home or fashion. Some arrangements can be used loosely (you dip into a basket and pick up an intriguing flower), or they can be worn formally. Diane Love also carries pottery, lacquer ware, antique accessories for the home, handbags, jewelry, and hundreds of different types of baskets. The latter are best used when displaying—what else?—flowers. Her silk flowers can't be beat anywhere, and Diane Love is a household name in interior-decorating accessories. The second floor has art-deco and Japanese furniture, contemporary crafts, clothing, and fashion accessories.

FANCY FLOWER BASKET
255 Eighth Ave (bet 22nd and 23rd St)
243-6305
Mon-Sat: 9:30-7; Sun: 10-4; closed Sun in July and Aug

This aptly named store is much more than your neighborhood florist. The store is a gem and a superb source for flowers and plants when it comes to the unusual and unique. Fancy Flower will live up to its name and create a gift basket of flowers worthy of a king. There are miniature carnations from Israel, Dutch lilies, and genuine sterling-silver roses imported from Holland. The *genuine,* incidentally, refers to the flower and not the mineral. The store manager claims that they may be the only source in the city for these flowers, which look as though they were created in silver but are guaranteed to have been grown in nurseries in Holland. You've got to see them!

FARM AND GARDEN NURSERY
2 Sixth Ave (bet White and Walker St)
431-3577
Daily: 9-6; Jan, Feb: Tues-Sun: 10-6

Don't miss this—it's one of New York's most unusual enterprises. First, a little background. The towering buildings in this neighborhood are the two spires of the World Trade Center. However, a decade or so ago, the surrounding area was made up of 50-year-old buildings housing government offices, while the site of the future WTC housed tiny and dirty electronics, job-lot, and gardening shops. When construction began on the World Trade Center, all of the small businesses were dislocated. Some retired. Many vanished. A few historic buildings were relocated to the new Independence Plaza several blocks away, and an even smaller handful reestablished their businesses in proximity to the old neighborhood. Those that relocated have done remarkably well. Of the garden centers, Farm and Garden Nursery was the only one to remain in the area. Thus, it is part of a long and honored tradition, and it has done its best to maintain it. F and G operates like a suburban nursery, dispensing grass seed, fruit trees, vegetables, and sprays, and yet its nursery is, in its own terms, an "outdoor lot," while its customers' lawns are usually six-foot terraces. Oblivious of this fact, F and G blissfully sells all manner of garden plants and trees under the assumption that they will grow anywhere. Usually, they do. In addition, one holdover from the old days is the prices. They are nearly wholesale.

GRASS ROOTS GARDEN
75 University Pl (at 11th St)
533-0380
Tues-Sat: 9-6

Larry Nathanson's grass-roots movement began about 10 years ago, when he turned his hobby into a full-time vocation. The possessor of a genuine green thumb, Nathanson couldn't understand why city pavement had to be an inhibiting factor for would-be urban farmers. So, he blithely set up his Grass Roots Garden, paying no mind to the boutique atmosphere or cutesy merchandising that marked the shops of his peers. Nathanson's shop could be said to be spartan, except that there is no space not crammed with a sprouting green plant. The overall credo is that plants are supposed to make one happy, and Nathanson strives to sell happy-making plants. The cityscape is still irrelevant to him. The business is evenly divided between indoor and outdoor plants, and no one here blinks an eye at the sale of a six-foot orange tree or a quarter-inch tall cactus. Somewhere in this city, it will make someone happy. And if having to prune and water plants infringes on your happiness, Grass Roots can handle that, too. In addition to soil, plants, lighting units, insecticides, fertilizers, gardening tools and equipment, and a consulting business to select the best plant for your purposes, Grass Roots makes house calls "all over town" and runs a plant maintenance service.

PUBLIC FLOWER MARKET
796 Sixth Ave (at 27th St)
684-2850
Daily: 9-6

The Public Flower Market is not *the* flower market, but it is open to the public. It specializes in supplying flowers to retail florists, as well as creating lavish floral decorations for its own retail sale. Most of the latter are destined for weddings or funerals which, while occupying opposite ends of the emotional spectrum, are pretty much the same thing to florists. Ordering in advance assures top quality, and Public Flower Market guarantees wholesale prices to retail customers at all times.

RENNY
27 E 62nd St
251 E 62nd St
371-5354
Mon-Fri: 9-6; Sat: 9-5

Renny is primarily a florist. He carries the necessary materials for centerpieces, bouquets, sprigs, and plain flower decorations. But Renny really specializes in party pieces, and he will use his plants to create any kind of party background. (The *Daily News* credited the shop with creating a sheik's tent, complete with props, for an Arabian Nights party.) The *Times* thought that Renny was super for live plants as well as the pots and paraphernalia for keeping them. (They were less impressed with Renny's prices.) Renny also runs a plant maintenance and landscaping service. Socialites go to Renny for his flowers and centerpieces. He can get the unusual and unique and make them seem elegantly casual. But best of all, three different ladies can use Renny's service and each feel that it is unique to *her*.

RIALTO FLORISTS
707 Lexington Ave (bet 57th and 58th St)
688-3234
Daily: 24 hours

A good place to know. Rialto is one of the few florists in New York that is always open and will make deliveries until midnight. Great for patching up late-night quarrels.

ROBERT LESTER
280 W Fourth St
675-3029
Tues-Fri: 8-9 a.m. by appointment only; closed Aug

Robert Lester sells orchid plants from the greenhouse on the roof of his townhouse. He has at least 1,500 different plants available at any one time, *and* he is extremely picky about when and to whom he sells his plants. Now, add to this the fact that the Manhattan phone directory lists a Robert Lester on 35th Street and you have . . . nothing. Thought I was going to say Nero Wolfe, right? Well, it's not even close. The Robert Lester on 35th Street is not *our* Robert Lester, and this Robert Lester is neither rotund nor a private investigator. What he is, however, is probably the best orchid purveyor around. Phone for an appointment (you must!) and see for yourself. Note: Lester has a similar passion for bamboo. He makes the growing of both of these temperamental tropical plants look easy, and he cheerfully instructs the skeptical in their care and feeding. In fact, despite his fussiness about customers, once he is assured that the plants will have a good home, Lester overwhelms the customer with information.

RONALDO MAIA
27 E 67th St
288-1049
Mon-Sat: 9:30-6; closed Sat in summer

Ronaldo Maia is a former student of Judith Garden, who was the definitive florist. Now retired, Judith Garden buys her flowers from Ronaldo Maia. This should give you an idea of how good his work is. His arrangements are nothing if not different. For one thing, Maia scorns the use of anything artificial. Thus, if the season is such that the only material to work with is one species of flower, he will find *the* perfect flower and encase it in a bud vase inside a larger glass container. With other moods or materials, his favorite modes of expression run more to moss-covered animals (the largest is 15 feet high, the smallest 10 inches, with prices similarly sized), baskets of mixed flowers, and special collections grouped by common characteristics (scent, shading, or origin). He does his best work when given free rein. Maia volunteers that he has the best and most fantastic there is to offer. From anyone else, that's boasting. From Ronaldo Maia, it's probably an understatement.

SOUTHFLOWER MARKET
181 Columbus Ave (at 68th St)
496-7100
Mon-Sat: 8-10; Sun: noon-8

1045 Second Ave
355-6800
Mon-Sat: 10-9; Sun: noon-5

Southflower Market is to florist shops what the self-service meat counter is to the neighborhood butcher. The brainchild of Jose Falconi, Southflower created a new era in flower purveying and became the chicest shop in town within the first two years of existence. The premise is that flowers should be displayed and sold much like any other commodity. So, at Southflower, flowers are sold individually and with price tags rather than as part of floral bouquets. Customers can place orders for the day's floral fix on a "prix-fixe" chart, or they can come in and select specific blooms themselves. Because there is less personalized service and more direct dealing with importers and sources, prices are supposed to be much less, too. Surprisingly, Southflower is enjoying incredible success without yet being imitated. However, for the Southflower method, you still must deal with Southflower. If you detect a note of exasperation there, you're right. For while the idea is unique and long overdue, Southflower won't be winning any points for courtesy, ambiance, or charm. The whole operation is run with as much warmth as the meat department at the A&P.

SURROUNDINGS
2295 Broadway (bet 82nd and 83rd St)
580-8982
Mon-Sat: 10-7; Sun: 11-6; closed Sun in summer

This plant and flower shop is as noteworthy for its exotic flower and fauna as it is for its famous clientele. Carly Simon, Estelle Parsons, and Diane Keaton are regulars, and what draws them to the shop are imported flowers from all over the world, crafts that include collector's items from the United States, and exotic plants that are ready to be taken home. The plants are definitely unusual. (If your house is going to be featured in a magazine, how can you have ordinary ivy growing beneath your window?) Surroundings also offers landscape architecture, plant maintenance, and buying services, as well as all the horticultural supplies and paraphernalia necessary for an exotic plant's long, healthy life. The flowers come from Europe and Africa, with lilacs, lilies, tulips and roses available year-round, and mimosa, heliconia, and anthirium representing the exotic end. Finally, each piece of pottery is unique. How could you put your mimosa in anything less?

TERRESTRIS
409 E 60th St
758-8181
Tues, Wed, Fri-Sun: 10-7; Mon, Thurs: 10-9

Terrestris prides itself on its interior design, service, maintenance, and consultation programs. Part of its scientific image is an exactness that includes charts, scales, and measuring devices for all plants sold here. Those at Terrestris claim they have plants from 4 inches to 18 feet, and all are guaranteed to grow. Its attitude is typified by its publications, most particularly the free *Indoor Plant Selection and Survival Guide,* which needs hours of perusal to be fully appreciated. Terrestris knows what it's doing.

Religious Arts

GRAND STERLING SILVER COMPANY

345 Grand St (bet Essex and Ludlow St)
674-6450
Sun-Thurs: 10:30-5:30

Ring the bell, and you will be admitted to a stunning collection of silver religious art. You'll also find almost anything from silver toothpick holders to baroque candelabras over six feet tall. Grand Sterling will also repair and resilver any silver item, be it religious or secular. They are manufacturers and importers of fine sterling hollowware, and silver is revered with a dedication unmatched elsewhere.

HOLY LAND ART COMPANY

160 Chambers St (W Broadway and Greenwich St)
962-2130
Mon-Thurs: 9-4:30; Fri: 9-4
Sat: 9-1 (bet Thanksgiving and Christmas)

Across the street from Cheese of All Nations, there's another world at Holy Land Art Company. The store offers all kinds of religious articles to churches and the public. On hand is everything from Bibles to altars, although the latter, along with custom-made statues of wood, bronze, and marble are usually specially ordered directly for churches rather than individuals. In December, Holy Land is anything but pastoral, as customers snap up creches, nativity scenes, and challices. There's a tremendous selection, and the prices are really good. The company says that its work for churches is evenly divided between new buildings and refurbishing and reconstruction. That's in contrast to Jack Cushen's feelings that there is virtually no new church construction.

MORIAH ART CRAFTS

699 Madison Ave (bet 62nd and 63rd St)
751-7090
Mon-Thurs: 9-5; Fri: 9-4

Peter and Michael Ehrenthal, a father-and-son team, run Moriah with a sense of timelessness that could place the shop anywhere in the last 200 years. It's only when you become aware of the heavy security measures that you know exactly what city you're in and what era. Otherwise, it could be anywhere at all, from a fine museum to a Mideastern farmers' market. The specialty is antique Judaic and ceremonial art, and it is doubtful that anyone else in the world knows the business as well. Members of the Appraisers Association of America, the Ehrenthals are acknowledged specialists in the field. They come across a tremendous selection of old items of Jewish interest, and usually have first choice as to what they wish to keep and sell.

STAVSKY HEBREW BOOKSTORE
147 Essex St
674-1289
Sun-Thurs: 9:30-5:30; Fri: 9:30-2; closed Sun in summer

This store supplies synagogues and schools with religious books and objects. While they will fill an order for 10 coloring books, they are more accustomed to outfitting complete congregations, and they do it well. Their prices are fair, and service is excellent. Stavsky has the best collection of Jewish books, records, and everyday religious objects of any store in the city. They're also responsive to constructive criticism. I said in a previous edition that they should get better lighting, and they did.

Rubber Items

ABC FOAM RUBBER
77 Allen St (at Grand St)
431-9485
Sun-Fri: 9-6; Sat: 10-3

ABC is also known as the Foam Rubber Center, which is confusing because they are a breakaway from the nearby Economy Foam Center, which goes by the name of Foam Center as well. In any event, both businesses have more sizes, configurations, and types of foam rubber than most people know exist. Whole pieces can be purchased on the spot, or they will cut to order while you wait. That one such business exists is incredible. That there are two in the same area is amazing. And both are doing quite well, thank you, except when asked about the other. Then, watch the foam fly!

CANAL RUBBER SUPPLY COMPANY
329 Canal St (at Greene St)
226-7339
Mon-Fri: 9-5; Sat: 9-4:30

"If it's made of rubber, we have it" is this company's motto, and that sums up the supply at this wholesale-retail operation. There are foam mattresses, holsters, cushions, pads, floor pillows, pillow foam, pads cut to size, hydraulic hoses, rubber tubing, and sponges. And there is much, much more. They are right. If it's made of rubber, Canal Rubber Supply has it.

Screens

TONEE CORPORATION
389 Broome St (at Mulberry St)
966-4213
Mon-Fri: 9-4:30; Sat: 10-4

The lovely screens that slide back and forth between rooms and between house and garden in Oriental settings are usually Shoji screens, and the genuine article is seldom available outside Asia. Some years ago, however, the natural connection between light, free-standing space dividers and studios, lofts, and even offices dawned on some Japanese merchants, and this outpost of Japanese construction came to SoHo, an area where it was especially needed. Though this is one of the few Shoji outlets anywhere—and may be the only one manned by authentic native craftsmen—Tonee is not limited solely to Shoji screens. For one thing, the screens are defined by use, size, style, and material. For another, the Fusuma screen is also available, though the only thing it has in common with the Shoji is that they are both screens. If that sounds like so much Japanese jibberish to you, perhaps it explains best why an expert such as Tonee is the perfect person to guide a customer through the maze of screens, tatami mats, and general construction that the company offers.

Signs

LET THERE BE NEON
38 White St
226-4883
Mon-Fri: 9-6

Though the image of neon is modern, it harks back to Georges Claudes' capture of it (from oxygen) in 1915. And while "the flashing neon sign" is perhaps the ultimate cliché in tackiness, Rudi Stern and Dan Chelsea have turned the neon light into a modern art form. So, Let There Be Neon operates as a gallery. At any given moment, there is an assemblage of sizes, shapes, functions, and designs to entice the browser. Though they all have a common neon base (with transformer in the base), that is all they have in common. Almost all of Let There Be Neon's sales are for custom-made, commissioned pieces. This is partly because customers seem to feel that if something is this unique, it should be *really* individual and not an item scores of people have examined on display. Partly too, though, the commissions are a tribute to the shop's creativity. Stern and Chelsea claim that even a rough sketch is enough for them to create a figurative (literal or abstract) sculpture within 10 days. Each project is proof that neon is a versatile and easily used art form. There's a glow about the place!

UNIVERSAL BULLETIN BOARD COMPANY

920 Broadway (at 21st St)
473-7426
Mon-Fri: 9-5

This thoroughly professional company provides businesses with directories, bulletin boards, engraved and cast signs, and chalkboards. Despite the fact that most of their customers are *big* clients, they are happy to deal with small, individual orders. They are truly universal, offering the best to all.

Silver

EASTERN SILVER COMPANY

54 Canal St (second floor)
226-5708
Sun-Thurs: 9:30-5; Fri: 9:30-1; closed first week of July

Ascend to the second floor, ring the bell, and you enter a wonderland of silver, from floor to ceiling. Not all of it is clean or polished, but it has the potential of becoming as beautiful as only silver can be. The stock includes virtually any product made of silver or pewter, and the amazing thing is that Robert Gelbstein seems to be able to put his hand on any desired item almost immediately. Eastern has a large collection of Jewish ceremonial silver and secular silver items, such as candlesticks and wine decanters. However, most of the collection would be perfect gracing any home. Prices are extremely reasonable, and the quality is A-1. This place is a real find.

ROGERS AND ROSENTHAL

105 Canal St
925-7557
Mon-Fri: 10-5

Rogers and Rosenthal are two big names in the elegant place-setting business, and while this store claims that it is just a coincidence and that *their* Rogers and Rosenthal are merely the founders' names, the shop's title is an excellent sign of what is inside. Rogers and Rosenthal has to be one of the very best places in the city, if not *the* best, for silver and china. A visit to verify this statement isn't even necessary, since nearly all their business is done by mail. ("Very slow delivery," they warn!) This shop features every major brand name, and an immediate 25 percent discount on every piece is an added bonus. They will send price lists upon request, and what isn't in stock will be ordered. They are very accommodating.

TIFFANY AND COMPANY
727 Fifth Ave (at 57th St)
755-8000
Mon-Sat: 10-5:30; closed Sat in July and Aug

What can you say about a store that's such an institution that it has appeared in plays, movies, books, and even slogans? Almost nothing, except that the store really isn't *that* formidable and can even be an exciting place to shop. For the curious, let's begin by stating that, yes, there really is a Tiffany Diamond, and it can be readily viewed on the first floor. That floor also houses the stationery and jewelry departments, and while browsing is welcome, salespeople are quick to approach lingering customers. The second floor houses clocks, sterling silver, flatware, bar accessories, centerpieces, and knickknack gifts. The third floor highlights table settings of china and crystal, and the settings are changed every month. Needless to say, all of those displays reflect the qualities and standards for which Tiffany has been noted for generations. However, the real surprise—and a fact not known to many New Yorkers—is that Tiffany has an excellent selection of reasonably priced items. Many items come emblazoned with the Tiffany name, wrapped in the famed Tiffany blue box, and at prices less than those of many neighborhood variety stores.

Sporting Goods

New Yorkers, who spend most of their week as sedentary creatures, head for the sports arenas after work and on weekends. Surprisingly large numbers of amateur sports participants own their own equipment, and a visit to any of the following stores would convince you that sporting equipment is a large, serious business in New York. I've divided them according to their specialty, and not every sport is listed. However, these stores do cover a wide range of activities and are the very best in their fields.

Bicycles and Accessories

Bicycles can be rented at the Loeb Boathouse for riding in Central Park. The boathouse is at the West 72nd Street Lake (east side), at approximately 74th Street. Considering the fact that the park roadways are closed to vehicular traffic on weekends (Sat: sunrise to 7:00 p.m.; Sun: sunrise to 10:30 p.m.), except during the winter, this may well be the least expensive entertainment and exercise in town. If you want to buy or rent a bike, try the following:

BICYCLE DISCOUNT HOUSE
351 E 14th St (near First Ave)
228-4344
Daily: 9-6:30

For some reason, Stuyvesant Town is bicycle country, and there are a half-dozen different bicycle stores within a three-block area. To be patronized by the locals, a bike shop here has to be special, and this one is. This bicycle house has an excellent reputation, but with so many other shops in the area, a little comparison shopping can't hurt. All bikes (Trek, Panasonic, Motobecane, and Ross) are discounted.

BICYCLES PLUS
1400 Third Ave (bet 79th and 80th St)
794-2979, 794-2201
Daily: 10-6; summer: 10-8

Bicycles Plus rents bikes for use in Central Park and elsewhere, but they don't need rental clients to draw in business. The store is owned by bicycle mechanics Jeff Loewi and Larry Nuffus, who know cycling upside-down and inside-out. Their bikes, which include B.M.X., triathalon, and racing bikes, are sold with a four-year guarantee. The salespeople are absolutely into their sport.

BICYCLE RENAISSANCE
505 Columbus Ave (bet 84th and 85th St)
724-2350
Mon-Fri: noon-6; Sat: 10-5; summer: 10-7 daily

Biking here is a way of life, just as health foods are to most of the staff. Among the services are the custom building of bikes and winter storage. Their mechanics aims for same-day service on all makes and models. As for brands—well, they are all here, with an accent on racing bikes. In stock are Fuji, Peugeot, Motobecane, and custom frames for Stronglight, Campagnolo, Ideale, and many others. I appreciate the fact that this was the only bike shop that did not pretend to have discount rates. And, in fact, its prices were exactly on par with the so-called discount stores.

PEDAL PUSHER BICYCLE SHOP
1306 Second Ave (bet 68th and 69th St)
288-5592
Daily: 9-6

Roger Bergman, the owner of this low-key shop, is knowledgeable without being pushy. If you *ask*, he will tell you, but otherwise, you are free to browse around. Pedal Pusher buys, sells, rents, and repairs bicycles of all kinds (although it rents only 3-speed and 10-speed bikes), and it organizes bicycle parties and lessons (including a Caribbean tour). Prices on bikes are competitive, but prices on accessories (at least the ones I comparison-shopped) are almost half those of other stores. This *may* be an accident, but even if prices are the same, I prefer the attitude here.

STUYVESANT BIKE SHOP
349 W 14th St
254-0289, 675-2161
Mon-Fri: 9:30-7; Sat: 10-6; Sun: noon-5

Salvatore Corso, the owner of Stuyvesant Bike Shop, lives and breathes cycling, and will proselytize to anyone willing to listen. Backing him up is a four-floor establishment dedicated to the world of cycling and brimming with bicycles, accessories, burglar alarms, scooters, tricycles, and the like. With all that space, Salvatore Corso is also willing to store bikes over the winter months. This shop, too, has an incalculable storehouse of spare parts, which enables it to attempt most repairs within 24 hours. Other items offered include tandems, triplets, adult tricycles, exercisers, 3-, 5-, 10-, and 15-speed bikes, children's bikes, and racing equipment.

Billiard Equipment

BLATT BILLIARD
809 Broadway (bet 11th and 12th St)
674-8855
Mon-Fri: 9-6; Sat: 9-4; closed Sat in summer

Blatt is home for a store outfitted from top to bottom with everything for billiards. There are also friendly pointers from a staff that seems at first glance to be all business.

Darts

DARTS UNLIMITED
30 E 20th St (bet Park Ave S and Broadway)
533-8684
Tues-Fri: 11-5:30; Sat: 11-4; closed Sat in Aug

Most towns have sporting goods shops, but few have even a department (or display) for darts. In New York, things are different. There's Darts Unlimited, an emporium dedicated solely to darts and darting equipment. The collection of darts, dartboards, accessories, and English darting equipment (England's pubs are where it all started, you know) makes you wonder why they are not more prominent in other sports stores. Indeed, it seems that playing darts is a neglected game in America. Which is a shame, since it's good not only for exercise but for channeling aggression!

Fishing Equipment

CAPITOL FISHING TACKLE COMPANY

218 W 23rd St (Chelsea Hotel, near Seventh Ave)
929-6132
Mon-Fri: 8-5:30; Sat: 9-4

Historical records show that 100 years ago, the 42nd Street Library and the adjacent Bryant Park were once a cemetery and later a reservoir, so distinct and countrified was their location in relationship to the rest of the city. Thus, it is somewhat possible that in 1897, when Capitol Fishing Tackle Company was established, its present location might have justified a store dedicated to fishing. Today, in the hustle and bustle of Chelsea, the store is totally incongruous and yet it is typical of New York. Where else would one find a fishing store so totally landlocked that a subway roars beneath it, and yet it offers bargains unmatched at seaport stores? Capital features a complete range of fishing tackle with such brand names as Penn, Garcia, and Daiwa at the lowest possible prices. There is a constantly changing selection of specials and closeouts that can only be described as fantastic. All of it is achieved by Capitol's buying up surplus inventories, bankrupt dealers, and liquidations. Almost nothing in the store was purchased at full wholesale, and those savings are passed on to the customer.

Game Tables

V. LORIA AND SONS

178 Bowery (bet Delancey and Kenmore St)
925-0300
Mon-Fri: 10:30-6; Sat: 10-4; closed Sat in summer

This family business, established in 1912, is a mecca for indoor sports enthusiasts. One can find a complete line of equipment. There are bowling and billiard items, pool tables and such pool supplies as cues and chalk, plaques, awards, and trophies—not to mention ping-pong, shuffleboard, poker tables, and a magnificent collection of pinball machines. When the family champion is triumphant, the winner's trophy can be ordered from Loria as well. It is impossible *not* to try out some of the equipment here, and Vernon and Roger Loria don't seem to mind.

General

CROSSROADS OF SPORT

36 W 44th St (bet Fifth and Sixth Ave)
764-8877
Mon-Fri: 10-5

Crossroads here seem to refer to intersecting country lanes, and the store personnel are quick to tell you that sports to them is decidedly not team sports. So, it's not surprising that the atmosphere at the oldest sporting art gallery and gift shop in North America is reminiscent of a hunting club library. And well it should. In addition to an admirable collection of books, artwork, prints, and paintings relating to the store's definition of sports, there is also a variety of tankards, serving pieces, and tableware decorated with sporting motifs. Many of the books are collector's items, as is the artwork (note particularly the 18th-century prints). Crossroads is a primary source for appraisals and purchase of sporting art, and they are accomplished enough to trace and find any items that they don't have in stock. If there's a bit of country gentlemen in you, stop by. It's the closest thing to the hunt club you'll find in the city.

EASTERN MOUNTAIN SPORTS (EMS)

20 W 61st St (at Broadway)
397-4860

611 Broadway (at Houston St)
505-9860

Mon, Tues, Wed: 10-7; Thurs, Fri: 10-8; Sat: 10-6; Sun: 12-5

Eastern Mountain Sports started in the mountains of New Hampshire at the height of the backpacking craze. When they moved over to Manhattan, they became the immediate favorites of *New York* Magazine, and their hiking gear, outdoor clothing, and useful gadgetry were highlighted in issue after issue. Despite their geographic origins, it's almost a natural connection. New York is cold (weatherwise, of course), and the residents are fanatics for anything that is compact and functional. What could be more functional than thermal clothing that fits in a pocket? So, EMS' camping grounds in New York were an immediate success. In fact, it was so successful that it spawned a branch in SoHo as well as in several suburban malls and became the flagship store for a European conglomerate. Despite it all, it's the place to go for authentic outdoor clothing and gear although prices can be bettered individually for almost every item. (I would try the American Youth Hostel stores for one.) Still, for one-stop shopping, it's an excellent source for authentic equipment, and the authentic stuff is of better quality and price than that of the department stores. Incidentally, EMS covers virtually *all* outdoor sports. That includes mountain climbing, backpacking, skiing, hiking, tenting, and camping. And there's much more.

FERON'S
55 E 44th St (at Madison Ave)
867-6350
Mon-Fri: 8:30-5:30; Sat: 10-4; closed Sat in summer

If you want your racquet strung by the official stringers of the U.S. Open, or if owning the finest tennis equipment is your racket, then Feron's is the only place to go. In addition to tennis racquets, there are sports clothes, sporting goods, and some of the finest equipment assembled anywhere. Feron's has a reputation for all of the above since 1919, and deserves its renown.

HERMAN'S
110 Nassau St
233-0733
Mon-Fri: 9-6; Sat: 9-5

135 W 42nd St
730-7400
Mon-Fri: 9:30-7; Sat: 9:30-6

845 Third Ave (at 51st St)
688-4603
Mon-Fri: 9:30-7; Sat: 9:30-6

39 W 34th St
279-8900
Mon-Fri: 9:30-7; Sat: 9:30-6:30; Sun: noon-5

With only a small selection of women's and children's gear, Herman's is almost no *her* and almost all *man*. Long before the running and physical-fitness craze, this chain of sporting goods shops was set up to equip men for the enjoyment of sports, and the more macho, outdoorsy, or competitive the sport, the better. There are woodsmen's vests, plaid flannel shirts, and camping equipment, but there is more emphasis on clothing than equipment. Herman's sold down vests and chamois cloth shirts as standard equipment before such garments ever appeared on the designer's drawing board. As for price—in general, you can do better. But there is a sale every week on something, and those prices can be good. Add the convenience of a vast selection of equipment for all types of sports, and you know why the Herman's chain is growing.

MODELL'S
280 Broadway
962-6200
Mon, Fri: 8:30-6:30; Sat: 8:30-5:30

200 Broadway
962-6204
Mon-Fri: 8:30-6:30; Sat: 9-4

243 W 42nd St
575-8111
Mon, Fri: 9-8:45; Tues, Wed, Thurs, Sat: 9-7:30

109 E 42nd St
661-5966
Mon-Thurs: 8:30-6:30; Fri: 8:30-7; Sat: 9:30-6

Modell's is an old New York family chain. Founded in 1889, it is still a family-run operation with a personal touch. The store specializes in men's wear (with a nod to the ladies when the look is fashionable), sporting goods, footwear, luggage, and sundries. The guiding philosophy is to sell these items as cheaply as possible, and that is achieved with the purchase of overruns and irregulars, as opposed to goods made of cheap materials. Prices are never high, and the quality is usually excellent. Modell's, for example, carries most brand-name sneakers at rock-bottom prices. Their shoes are often regulation navy lasts, and this is one of the few places outside the military to carry them. There are usually advertisements in the Sunday *Daily News.* Don't go expecting to find the definitive basketball shoes or high-quality riding boots. But for their prices (and attitude), Modell's is worth at least a brief stop.

PARAGON
867 Broadway (at 18th St)
255-8036
Mon-Wed, Fri, Sat: 9:30-6:30; Thurs: 9:30-7:30; Sun: 11-6

Imagine being allowed into the stockroom and warehouse of the world's largest sporting goods store, and you'll have a good idea of what shopping at Paragon is like. The store is vast, but amenities are limited. Shopping carts replace glass display cases, and all kinds of sporting goods are poised so precariously that they threaten to come tumbling down at any moment. The selection is broad enough to cover over two dozen different sports and outdo specialty shops in any of those activities. Paragon knows its stock cold. This is good, since warm-up jackets can be located in any one of a dozen places on three floors. If there's a hockey emblem on a jacket, it's found among the hockey sticks (available for ice, field, or street play). If it has red and blue stripes on it, you'll find it in the tennis section (available for men, women, and children). Or if it bears a fleet-foot emblem, you'll find it in either the running section or stashed with marathon equipment or gym mats. Paragon carries everything from exercisers to skating pompons. But what brings people to this store is not the vast selection or décor (ahem!) but the super prices. Paragon's regular prices are never higher than those of its competitors, but through closeouts and odd lots, there are at least a dozen super sales each day. You never know what they're going to be, but it's always worth checking into. In January and July, the store advertises storewide sales. If you like absolute bargain-basement frenzy, you'll be in your element. If you have a shred of dignity you'd like to keep at the expense of a great bargain, stay away—but you'll miss the best buys on sporting goods in the city.

RICHARD'S
233 W 42nd St (bet Seventh and Eighth Ave)
947-5018
Mon-Sat: 9-7:30

Aside from being near the Port Authority bus terminal, there's nothing positive that can be said about the neighborhood, but much can be said about Richard's stock. The store calls itself an aqua-lung and skin-diving center, but there's also all kinds of sporting goods and clothing. The clothes are of the army-navy-surplus variety. And in keeping with the low rent (and lowlife) of the area, everything in the store is discounted.

Horseback-Riding Equipment

H. KAUFFMAN AND SONS
139 E 24th St
684-6060
Mon-Sat: 9:30-6

Because of the life-sized wooden horse that guards Kauffman's entrance, you can't miss the store, but then, if you're into horses and horseback riding, Kauffman's would be worth any kind of search. Kauffman's handles the subject so well that no one ever thinks that one of the world's finest equestrian supply shops is not only located in the midst of one of the world's largest cities, but it is miles from the borough's only bridal paths. It is taken for granted that for the very best in riding equipment, Kauffman's is the place to go. This specialty store has literally everything for the horse and its rider. (It even manages to sell a goodly amount of hay!) There is a resident boot and saddle maker who is equally adept at English or Western styles. In addition to the saddles, bridles, and riding equipment, there is a good line of gifts for horse lovers. Ladies' side saddles, Kauffman told me, are about the only thing he doesn't stock. Being a horse fancier, I found this place a fascinating spot, and it's very well stocked.

MILLER'S
123 E 24th St
673-1400
Mon-Fri: 9-5:30; Sat: 9-4:30

Typically, New York just couldn't make do with only one world-famous equestrian equipment source, so Miller's offers the city its second on the same block. But this flagship is only a very small part of a large business. The Miller symbol (a vaulting horse with rider) is displayed in hundreds of shops across North America that carry all or part of the exclusive Miller line, and that line is so distinctive that it literally covers a rider and his horse from head to hoof. Sizes suit men, women, children, stallions, mares, and colts. (Though few colts are ridden, they do use reins and medallions.) The haberdashery offers proper riding gear and saddles. (The Hermes saddles are registry numbered and go for a mere $1,600 and up!) There are boots, helmets, riding shirts, plaques, and riding potpourri. That makes Miller's a good bet for those who have never ridden, as well as for the U.S. equestrian team. For horse lovers, this is a super place to find gifts for both horses and their owners.

Marine

GOLDBERG'S MARINE
12 W 37th St (at Fifth Ave)
594-6065
Mon-Wed, Fri: 9:30-5:45; Thurs: 9:30-6:45; Sat: 9:30-3

Goldberg's sells marine supplies as if it were situated in the middle of a New England seaport rather than the heart of Manhattan. The staff looks like a crew from a marina who just happened to berth in Manhattan, and they are as knowledgeable as they would be if that were the case. Some of the things they carry include marine electronics, sailboat fittings, big-game fishing tackle, life-saving gear, ropes, anchors, compasses, clothing, and books. Many of those items—the ropes and compasses, for example—are of professional quality, and Goldberg's is an excellent source for purchasing such items for dry-land purposes. Rubber suits are a star attraction, but there is also a line of clothes suitable for yacht owners. Landlubbers are treated kindly, since Goldberg's realizes that some of the gear is purchased for other purposes. (The fishing line is used in many crafts; artists buy it by the yard.) They are even kinder to genuine marine people and weekend sailors.

HANS KLEPPER CORPORATION

35 Union Square W (near Broadway and 17th St)
243-3428
Mon-Fri: 9:30-5:30; Sat (April-Aug): 10-4

Hurry down to Union Square to get your own inflatable boat. That means folding kayaks, rigid kayaks, canoes, and even sailboats. In fact, Hans Klepper considers itself New York's inflatable boat center, and as compact as its products may be, this is not a small business. Klepper has survival equipment (also, for the most part, inflatable), boating accessories, and more information than even the most avid enthusiast could absorb. Most remarkable, however, is that nearly all of the equipment is easily transported.

MANHATTAN MARINE AND ELECTRIC COMPANY

116 Chambers St
267-8756
Mon-Fri: 8:30-5

The store is landlocked, so you'll have to dock your rowboat, cabin cruiser, or naval destroyer elsewhere. But if that's a problem, Manhattan Marine not only produces a mail-order catalog (424 pages!), but maintains a cable address (Marmalec, New York) and a telex number (232881). They are used to filling orders from around the world for customers aware of their almost 80-year-old reputation as the world's best-stocked marine equipment store. It would be difficult to list even a tenth of the merchandise. There's clothing, gear (there's a big run on waterproof boots by New Yorkers in snowstorms), sophisticated and run-of-the-mill marine equipment, heavy equipment, generators, desalinators, sophisticated electronics, and anything imaginable for outfitting a floating craft. The catalog is fascinating. Check out the navigator's kits, engine controls, filter systems, portable cooking equipment, and even a centrifugal-action windshield cleaner. If all of this sounds meaningless to you, check out the plaque section (great for decorating) and the shoes and boots. The saleshelp are friendly, even to people who ask, "What *is* that?"

Outdoor Equipment

AMERICAN YOUTH HOSTEL EQUIPMENT STORE

75 Spring St (at Crosby St)
431-7100
Mon-Wed, Fri: 10-7; Thurs: 10-9; Sat: 10-5

One of the best-kept secrets in New York is the American Youth Hostel Equipment Store. Even calls to the American Youth Hostel organization fail to elicit any recognition that there might be a store downstairs. Depending upon the whims of the personnel, entire days, weeks, and possibly even months can go by without anyone manning the shop. This is particularly true in the winter. So, if you are making a trip down to Spring and Greene Street just to see the store, it is best to call first to see if it is open. Why, then, should anyone bother? Because the American Youth Hostel people are to bicycle travel what the AAA is to cars. They even have an emergency road service that ships parts to stranded cyclers. In short, they know the field cold. They know every mechanical thing there is to know about bikes; they know every trail there is to take; and they know the best way to accomplish anything regarding bike travel. The store, located in one corner of the ground floor of the hostel headquarters, sells a wide variety of A.Y.H.-approved camping outerwear and biking and backpacking equipment. There is a 64-page catalog offering everything from oiled wool mittens to down parkas to flashlights, not to mention all kinds of biking gear. (They even clean nylon and down garments.) If they've got it, it's the best. No matter what the season, though, their forte is planning tours for biking or skiing. There are tours of any length, but most are planned for weekend travelers. In the summer, there is probably a tour leaving every day of the week. The winter ski tours are less frequent.

HUDSON'S
97 Third Ave (bet 12th and 13th St)
473-7320
Mon-Sat: 9:30-6:45

Ostensibly an army-navy surplus store, Hudson's carries more camping equipment than any store I've ever seen. Everything imaginable is here, including the kitchen sink (well, if it's a *portable* camp sink). There are such unusual items as butane portable stoves large enough for an army (that's what they were made for), air blowers for tents, tents the size of A-frame summer homes, dehydrated foods, and Swiss army knives that do more than you could possibly want them to. To say the stock is extensive is an understatement. It takes 100 pages of the store's catalog just to describe what is available by mail order. Needless to say, prices are great; it *is* ostensibly surplus. Hudson's should be a serious camper's first stop.

TENTS AND TRAILS
21 Park Pl (bet Broadway and Church St)
227-1760
Mon-Wed, Fri: 9:30-6; Thurs: 9:30-7; Sat: 9:30-5:30

Located in the downtown canyons near City Hall and the World Trade Center, Tents and Trails is one of the best camping outfitters anywhere. Vivian and Lou Lipman run a shop that is exclusively dedicated to camping, and the salespeople are as experienced and enthusiastic about camping as the owners. They give excellent guidance and advice, much of it based on hard-won experience. Their boots, for example, are exclusively Fabiano, Asolo, and Merrel brands, since experience has proved them to be the best. And when salespeople are enthusiasts, they are as interested in making a convert as in making a sale, and that is exactly what happens here. No question is too silly or too simple. ("We make sure everything fits correctly and everyone leaves as a satisfied customer," says Lou.) The camping stock features brands like Trailwise, Northface, Lowe, Madden, Jansport, and Camp Trails. And there are backpacks, sleeping bags, tents, and down clothing, in addition to boots. Finally, Tents and Trails rents camping equipment on a first-come, first-serve basis. It is a super way to see if camping is for you, without a substantial investment. You may be sure that if you rent from these people, they will do everything possible to make sure the experience is repeated.

Running

FAST FEET
118 E 59th St (bet Park and Lexington Ave)
838-2564
Mon-Thurs: 10-6:30; Fri, Sat: 10-6

Jogging is running away with New York, and the New York Marathon is just one of a dozen manifestations of the craze that has become an integral part of the urban lifestyle. On the shopping scene, that means there are dozens of sports shoe shops. One of the best in terms of quality and attitude is Fast Feet. Unlike branches of some of the larger corporations, all of the saleshelp are literally family, according to owner Victor Favuzza. There is no one in the shop who is not a relative *and* a sports nut. The shop sells only the best of what these people would personally use. Fast Feet features Adidas footwear and apparel, because that is what Victor's family prefers. They also carry Converse, Brooks, and Tacchini (the latter for tennis apparel), and Frank Shorter running gear, in nearly all sizes for children and adults. They are exclusive distributors of Cima footwear, which creates hand-dyed athletic footwear in all colors. The Fast Feet people are eager to please. That means excellent advice on city sports. Fast Feet now highlights "Athletic Style," their method of highlighting specific concepts twice a month. One show might be devoted to 10 hues of all cotton Russell athletic football jerseys, while the next might be followed by displaying boxing outfits from Everlast. What it all proves is that this is a place that's fast on its feet when it comes to selling sportswear.

SUPER RUNNERS SHOP
1337 Lexington Ave (at 89th St)
369-6010
360 Amsterdam Ave (at 77th St)
787-7665
Herald Center (Central Park floor)
Mon-Wed, Fri: 10-7; Thurs: 10-9; Sat: 10-6; Sun: noon-4

Gary and Jane Muhrcke are runners, as is every member of their staff. And when they are *not* running, they are advising other runners at Super Shoe. The original store was located in Huntington, Long Island, and Gary or Jane would grab a handful of shoes whenever they ventured into Manhattan and would peddle them on the street to whoever ran by. Their reputation grew so fast that the handful became a van-full, the street a permanent spot, and then a legitimate store, and ultimately branches of that store. Although their prices have risen with the move, they are still probably the most knowledgeable and reasonable athletic shoe store around. Unlike many such stores, they do not stock one brand exclusively. The staff of Super Shoe really believes that each person has to be fitted individually, both in terms of sizing and need. What's more, if a mistake in sizing is made, they will cheerfully correct it, although they claim such mistakes are few and far between. Super Shoe stocks men's and women's sizes (a few children's, too) and a full range of paraphernalia for devotees. In fact, they consider themselves a running-equipment source.

Skates

PECK AND GOODIE
919 Eighth Ave (bet 54th and 55th St)
246-6123
Mon-Sat: 10:30-6

Roller skating is a popular means of summer transportation in Manhattan, so there are plenty of skate shops. But Peck and Goodie seems to have been in business forever, offering equipment to skaters who need the best with minimum fuss. Now, they are doing the same for the scores of people who have suddenly rediscovered skating. The store offers a complete stock of roller and ice skates and accessories. Boots, blades, brackets, and braces are available, along with expert advice. And with faddish skates costing a hundred dollars a pair or more, it's wise to go to an expert.

Skiing

SCANDINAVIAN SKI SHOP
40 W 57th St (near Sixth Ave)
757-8524
Mon-Wed, Fri: 9-5:30; Thurs: 9-6:45; Sat: 9-6

Despite its name, this shop is really an all-around sporting goods store with an emphasis on skiing and other winter sports. They have a full range of goods, from skis and skiwear to a complete department that offers repairs and ski advice as well as outfitting. The shop has also developed a good reputation for serving other, decidedly non-Scandinavian sports as well. It is capable of outfitting its customers in tennis, golf, and hiking gear as well as in skis, and its selection of competition swimwear rivals the namesake specialty. The store also carries exercise equipment, running gear, and water skis—in short, everything athletic.

Soccer

SOCCER SPORT SUPPLY COMPANY
1745 First Ave (bet 90th and 91st St)
427-6050
Mon-Fri: 10-6; Sat: 10-3

Max and Hermann Doss, the proprietors of this 50-year old soccer and rugby supply company, operate as if they were located in merry old England instead of New York. And, indeed, they are international; half the business is involved in importing and exporting equipment around the world. Soccer Sport garners the finest rugby and soccer equipment available and ships it to its customers. Visitors to the store have the advantage of choosing from the entire selection, as well as having guidance from a staff that knows the field perfectly.

Tennis

MASON'S TENNIS MART
911 Seventh Ave (bet 57th and 58th St)
757-5374
Mon-Sat: 10-6; Daily (during U.S. Open): 9-7

Look at the hours they keep here, and you know what matters to the Masons. They outfit for tennis, stock for it, play it, etc. In fact, as owner Mark Mason puts it: "We have everything but the courts, and if real estate wasn't so high, we'd have that, too." They carry the clothing lines of three tennis designers: Ellesse, Fila, and Tacchini, a selection Mason claims is unrivaled anywhere. And once you're looking good on the court, Mason can supply racquets, ball machines, bags, and any other tennis paraphernalia you could possibly think of. They even offer a same-day stringing service for the unfortunates who didn't bring three or four racquets to the U.S. Open. Prices are not cheap, except for the annual sale in January. If you want the best at reasonable prices, that's the time to get it. There are also free Ellesse and Tacchini catalogs.

Women's

SPORTING WOMAN
235 E 57th St
688-8228
110 W 48th St
997-8403
Mon-Wed, Fri, Sat: 10-7; Sun: noon-5; closed Sun in summer

Women are turning to sports and exercise in record numbers, and Matt Zale of the Athlete's Foot will be the first to tell you so. They know because the success of their women-only sporting goods shop has rivaled that of their Athlete's Foot chain, and everyone knows that its rise was meteoric. But maybe women were turned off by those stores' name. In any case, *this* store stocks all kinds of sporting goods, clothing, and equipment geared specifically to women. Function is stressed over style. Swimsuits, for example, belong in the lap pool rather than draped across a lap, and nearly all the clothes are made of cotton because cotton "breathes" and is more comfortable. All types of equipment are available here as well, everything from leg weights to aerobic dancing records. And don't forget that the store's origins are in the shoe business, so for women's sport shoes, Sporting Woman is probably unexcelled.

Stationery

DEMPSEY AND CARROLL
STATIONERS AND FINE ENGRAVERS
38 E 57th St (at Park Ave)
486-7509
Mon-Wed, Fri: 9-5:30; Thurs: 9-6:30; Sat: 10-5:30; closed Sat in July and Aug

Your stationery is literally your calling card to the world, your statement of who you are and what you stand for. Fine, you say: you'll get your formal stuff from Tiffany's and the more casual paper at Ffolio or one of the classy but personal establishments. Of course, the trendy are into pads of paper from Bloomie's, but none of this will really do much for your *image*. Dempsey and Carroll are formal stationers who have been in business in New York for over 100 years. For many years, they have been in residence at the 57th Street flagship store of Lugene, the opticians, with whom they are affiliated. (Perhaps they feel that after you give your vision a new look, you should work on the correspondence you are now able to see.) The less knowledgeable will continue to go to Tiffany's; the more secure, to the more liberal establishments. But the secure and totally correct correspondents name Dempsey and Carroll as their stationers, and visit frequently to see what the latest traditional trends are. You can be assured that any purchase here will be totally correct, and many families have had that assurance for so many years that they never visit the store. They just pick up the phone to reorder.

HUDSON ENVELOPE
33 W 17th St
691-3333
Mon-Fri: 6 a.m.-5 p.m.

Many years before *The Graduate*'s immortal "plastics" line, there was a similar sentiment in another play. The name of it escapes me, but the thought always impressed me. To wit: If one wishes to own a good business, manufacture envelopes. There is no home or business without dozens of envelopes, and they have to come from *somewhere*. Mike Jacobs' father-in-law obviously heeded that thought when he opened just such a business in Manhattan. When Jacobs joined him, little changed until that fateful day when he was offered a printer's overrun of black envelopes. "Black envelopes?" he said. "Who but an undertaker wants black envelopes?" But the price was good, and Jacobs quickly found out that seemingly *everyone* wanted black envelopes: "It really classes up your correspondence." While black became the best seller, other colors weren't far behind. Hudson Envelope specializes in just that—envelopes—and the best buys are in overruns of distinctive envelopes. More routine stationery needs can be matched with mix-and-match stationery and envelopes. Jacobs claims to supply almost all of the stationery-by-the-pound places in the metropolitan area, and the prices here are much less. They also do printing.

RITE STATIONERY
113 Ludlow St (at Delancey St)
477-0280, 477-1724
Daily: 8-5

Considering the company this shop is keeping, there should be a fence, hedge, or at the very least a warning separating Rite Stationery from its fellows in this category. While all these stores deal in paper and the accessories necessary for correspondence, a visit here is more inclined to make you put pen to paper for an angry letter of complaint than to invite friends for cocktails at eight. This is just about as far from Tiffany's and Fifth Avenue as you can get. This Lower East Side store's claim to fame is its proximity not to the Plaza Hotel, but to the Ludlow Street entrance to the Municipal Garage. So why, you ask, do we mention it? Because it takes all kinds to create mail, and there are many times when you really don't need formal engraved calling cards. They specialize in school stationery. If there's a preteenage girl on your shopping list, there is no better gift you can give her than a box of stationery. And here Rite Stationery shines. There is an advantage to being pushed, shoved, and ignored, and that advantage is that their prices are dirt cheap and the selection vast. A similar policy exists for the toys they carry. Again, I won't cite this as a source for your godson's christening gift, but to pick up items at the lower end of the scale, this should be a first choice. A word of warning: one battle-weary patron came out of here mumbling, "I hope, if you're going in there, you have skin like an armadillo!" On the other hand, they are no *less* friendly than any other Lower East Side establishment. Make this your last stop after a day of shopping downtown, and you won't even notice the treatment.

TIFFANY AND COMPANY
727 Fifth Ave (at 57th St)
755-8000
Mon-Sat: 10-5:30; closed Sat in summer

Still the definitive place to go for stationery, Tiffany's offers great selection at an assortment of prices. If you want it done first class, or even if you just want information on the proper kinds of stationery, this is *the* place.

Telephones

FONE BOOTH
12 E 53rd St (bet Fifth and Madison Ave)
751-8310
Mon-Wed, Fri, Sat: 10-6; Thurs: 10-8

Until fairly recently, New Yorkers had no choice but to rent their equipment from the phone company. What few outlets there were for procuring sub-rosa additional equipment were usually desguised as "communications experts" selling shortwave radios, dictation equipment, answering machines, and only parenthetically marketing extension phones, jacks, and plugs to customers who were obviously not employees of Ma Bell. Harvey Stuart ran one of these companies, but when private equipment became legal, his store was one of the first to come out of the closet and into the phone booth. His Fone Booth carries anything an average phone user could want and then some. All of it, of course, at great prices.

Besides jacks, extensions, answering machines, and cords, the Fone Booth has automatic dialers, wireless phones, and a set of push-button phones capable of tying into any telephone network in the world. Harvey Stuart himself is an authorized dealer of Record-a-Call and Code-a-Phone (an Oregon product, by the way), which means that his knowledge extends to repairs as well as sales.

Tobacco and Accessories

BARCLAY-REX
7 Maiden Lane (near Broadway)
962-3355
Mon-Fri: 8-6

This is a tobacco connoisseur's shop, and a specialty tobacco shop at that. The specialty is pipes (cigars are an anathema and cigarettes more so), and owner Vincent Nastri knows the field inside out. His shop is prepared to create a pipe from scratch, fill it with any imaginable type of tobacco (including a good house brand), repair it if it should break, and offer all sorts of advice on proper care and the blending of pipe tobacco. Nastri has a good reputation for prompt quality repairs and reasonable prices. If you have no sentimental attachment to the pipe, it might pay to buy a new irregular pipe that can be had for a surprisingly low price. As with most specialties, there are esoteric models available at astronomical prices. If you have upwards of $1,000 to send up in smoke, Nastri can come up with something really extraordinary.

BARNEY'S 42nd STREET
25 W 42nd St (near Fifth Ave)
354-1366
Mon-Fri: 8-6:30; Sat: 9-5

Barney's looks like just another drugstore from the street, but its forte is a tremendous line of discounted cigars, cigarettes, and tobacco. The discerning shopper can see evidence of the collection both from the street (the tobacco is sold in the back of the store) and from the unusual number of customers who patronize a store that ostensibly sells sundries. Barney's prices on tobacco are supposed to be the best in town; they certainly are the best in midtown.

INTERNATIONAL SMOKE SHOP
153 E 53rd St (Citicorp Center)
755-8339
Mon-Sat: 7-7

The Citicorp Center is one of the city's best tourist haunts, in part because its trilevel lobby is full of restaurants and other interesting shops that keep "tourist hours." Despite this (and despite an intense campaign to make the shopping area a mecca for browsing), the area can seem cold and impersonal. So even if it had no other virtues, Citicorp's International Smoke Shop would be noteworthy as a friendly oasis in an otherwise cold region. The International Smoke Shop's Richard Barnett is one of the truly great people in the city. He is courteous, helpful, insightful, and genuinely down-to-earth in a place that prides itself on sleekness and sophistication. I would recommend a visit here just to meet him. True to its name, the store stocks all kinds of tobacco and tobacco paraphernalia. But it also carries books, magazines (including foreign publications), gifts, New York souvenirs, and imported chocolate. In short, his stock would enable the visitor to spend a whole day in the Citicorp and keep himself amused, well-read, well-fed, and in reach of plenty of tobacco. What is amazing is that the shop stocks it all in a very limited space that is kept as neat as a pin. Barnett values the imported cigars and cigarettes, and you'll value his friendship.

J. R. TOBACCO
11 E 45th St (at Madison Ave)
869-8777
Mon-Fri: 7:45-6; Sat: 9-4

Lew Rothman claims to carry the world's largest selection of cigars at the world's lowest prices. His business is run on three levels: retail, wholesale, and mail order (there is a free 32-page catalog). And it seems as though nearly everyone in New York who smokes has had a Rothman tobacco product at one time or another. There are thousands of loyal customers who won't buy anything else. The cigars come in 3,000 different configurations, and J. R.'s is an exclusive distributor of eight different brand names. Mail orders are handled by La Vanda Rothman, and a trip through the catalog prior to a visit is a good idea, since it will give you a better orientation to what is available. Free tobacco mixtures are also given.

PIPEWORKS AT WILKE
400 Madison Ave (at 47th St)
664-0665, 755-1118
Mon-Fri: 9-5:45; Sat: 10-5; closed Sat in summer

Elliot Nachwalter started creating briar pipes in Stowe, Vermont, more than a decade ago. He then moved to New York and established Pipeworks as the outlet for his exclusive handmade, custom-designed pipes. Each pipe is created and worked at the shop (the only store in New York that does so), and Nachwalter can create a pipe from a customer's design as well as his own. Only Grecian Plateux, Corsican, or Algerian briar is used for each pipe, and each goes through a 130-step process between design and the finished product. Once a pipe is in hand, customers can return to Pipeworks for custom tobacco blends, antique pipes, or repairs. Chances are that it won't be a Pipeworks pipe that needs repair. Each is guaranteed for five years for most parts, and Nachwalter says they are created to last a lifetime.

TOBACCO CENTER
130 St. Mark's Pl (near Ave A)
674-2208
Mon-Fri: 9-6

This wholesale and retail operation was established in 1902, which makes it the oldest and largest such business in the city. Some of their blends have been sold continuously since the store opened, so great is their popularity, but they are not averse to creating new blends to complement changing lifestyles. For a while, they even carried a few blends for women who smoked pipes, but for the most part that has been discontinued. The wholesale-retail operation offers retail customers the best and freshest tobaccos and blends at almost wholesale prices.

TOBACCO PRODUCTS
137 Eighth Ave
989-3900
Mon-Fri: 7-6:30; Sat: 9-4

Albert Castellano, Tobacco Product's manager, takes great pride in his handmade cigars, and if you're a cigar smoker, you'll see why. His cigars are imported from South America, Mexico, and the Dominican Republic, and they're the most impressive things in the shop. Castellano also claims that nobody in the city has as wide a selection of meerschaum pipes as he. The shop carries an impressive range of tobacco accessories, but although the pipe racks, pipe cleaning devices, and lighters are great, nothing matches those handmade cigars.

Toys

B. SHACKMAN AND COMPANY
85 Fifth Ave (at 16th St)
989-5162
Mon-Fri: 9-5; Sat: 10-4

In the midst of the wholesale toy district, B. Shackman has been playing house since 1898. But their play is a very serious business devoted to the manufacturing, importing, and sales of toys, novelties, dollhouses, and miniatures. Though a large portion of their business is still on the wholesale level, this is obviously a business run by people who enjoy what they are doing. They are willing to take time to share their vocation with amateurs and single retail customers. This is one of the few such firms in the area to do so. Shackman carries a full line of the aforementioned specialties. However, the items of interest to retail customers are their imported dollhouses and miniatures and a striking collection of Victorian nostalgia. Again, this is not at all in keeping with its neighbors, but Shackman's excels in Victorian postcards, Christmas tree decorations, and the like. There are also antique dolls and contemporary stuffed toys.

COMPLEAT STRATEGIST
11 E 33rd St (at Fifth Ave)
685-3880
Mon-Wed, Fri, Sat: 10:30-6; Thurs: 10:30-9
320 W 57th St (bet Eighth and Ninth Ave)
582-1272
Mon-Sat: 11-8; Sun: noon-5

Several years ago, the Compleat Strategist was established as a fortress for military games and equipment. As the only such sanctuary in the city (possibly the country), it was an overwhelming success and was soon overrun with military strategists. As time went on, they branched out into science fiction, fantasy, and adventure games and books. And when this, too, seemed to capture the imagination of the public, the Compleat Strategist opened a second outpost on 57th Street. So today, people who are refighting the Civil War can browse alongside Dragon Masters at two locations in the city. The stock is more than ample for any military or Dungeon and Dragon addict, and the personnel are knowledgeable and friendly. This is adult games with no sneering or innuendo—unless you're playing the villain.

DOLLHOUSE ANTICS
1308 Madison Ave (bet 92nd and 93rd St)
876-2288
Mon-Sat: 10-5; closed Sat in summer

Dollhouse Antics is straight out of childhood dreams. Their official claim is that they are a shop dedicated to miniatures, but the shop is run more like a playroom, and any of the three owners always seems to be ready to join in the games. But dollhouse-making is serious business here. Ever heard of custom-made dollhouses? Or mouse houses? The most popular orders are for replicas of ancestral homes, and you can bet your made-to-order miniature needlepoint rug that these dollhouses aren't made for eager little children. Dollhouses come in kit form, but when money is no object (or if the fun of assembling it yourself wanes), the store will put it together for you. But be wary: like real houses, these models need to be furnished. If you can afford the scaled-down

Oriental rugs, custom upholstery, special wallpaper, lumber, electrical supplies, and made-to-order furniture, you'll eventually want to redecorate the whole house. After all, how can your dollhouse have passé wallpaper? (Unless you've re-created Tara or Monticello—and people have!) This store is a charmer. They welcome kids, despite the value and delicate nature of their wares, and they are just what the serious homemaker hobbyist needs in terms of supplies, aid, advice, and moral support.

ENCHANTED FOREST

85 Mercer St (bet Spring and Broome St)
925-6677
Tues-Sun: noon-7

The Enchanted Forest is one of the very few shops that physically and philosophically matches its name. The husband and wife team of owners, David Wallace and Peggy Sloane, hired theatrical set designer Matthew Jacobs to create an Enchanted Forest setting to back a collection of toys, whimsies, and artwork that is positively enchanting. The announced intention of the shop was that it should be a "gallery of beasts, books, and handmade toys celebrating the spirit of the animals, the old stories, and the child within," with an emphasis on *gallery*. And indeed, many of the pieces are artworks worthy of museums and are priced accordingly. Despite (or maybe because of) the wooden foot bridge, lifelike trees, and painted sky tin ceiling, there are sculptures priced in the hundreds of dollars that no child at any age would be comfortable playing with. (The Puss-in-Boots is a case in point. Bejeweled with a rose-petal in resin head, it goes for over a thousand dollars. It's breathtaking and beautiful, but who would buy it?) Offsetting that, however, are plastic squeeze toys, soft sculptured cats, and imported jars of soap, soap bubbles, and bubblebath. Even the collection of antique toys doesn't seem overpriced, but again, it's not something for a child. Virtually everything has an animal motif, and all of it is bound to enchant.

F.A.O. SCHWARZ

745 Fifth Ave (at 58th St)
644-9400
Mon-Sat: 10-6

A New York tradition that has spread to the suburbs with the advent of shopping-mall branches, F.A.O. Schwarz is the stuff children's dreams are made of. It is a world dedicated to children. Its floors are packed with the objects of children's fantasies, and those spots not jammed with the Rolls-Royces of toys (including miniature Rolls-Royces) are dedicated to children's services. There is a barber shop and a photographer's studio on the premises. It would be impossible to list all the toys available here. They range from antiques and miniatures (as in old toy soldiers) to modern working models of cars. In between, there are dolls, adult and children's games, books, records, preschool toys, trains, dollhouses of all sizes, intricacies, children's furniture (including the junior-executive chair), sporting goods, and the world-famous Steiff stuffed animals. But there is a major problem at F.A.O. Schwarz. Without a doubt, it has the most poorly trained, least knowledgeable, and most indifferent salespeople in New York. (And how can anyone be indifferent in a toy store?) Getting helped is just about next to impossible; many times you have to plead. And is there ever a company executive on the floor to witness this confusion? I've been in a hundred times and have never seen anyone who even looks like he or she is in charge. Great merchandise, yes. A well-run store, definitely no. I even sought out an executive and talked with him concerning service. His follow-through with me, as expected, was zero. My comments concerning the service here were even reprinted in *Forbes* magazine. But things still haven't changed.

GO FLY A KITE STORE
1201 Lexington Ave
472-2623
Mon-Sat: 10-5:45; Sun (seasonal): 12-4:45
153 E 53rd St (Citicorp Center)
308-1666
Mon-Fri: 10:30-7:30; Sat: 10:30-5:45; Sun: 12-5:45

Of course, New York has a store dedicated totally to kites, and of course it's a great one. It is run by Karen Schlesinger and Andrea Skwarek, who sell plastic Batman kites with the same zest as they sell scientifically designed, custom-made space-age gliders. Prices range from a dollar to $1,000 (for hang gliders). There are also kites for people's houses, such as mobiles and wall hangings. There are custom-made specialty kites, brilliantly colored fighter kites made of tissue papers, and a kite repair service. The lack of fanatacism and the presence of genuine devotion is most evident in the community programs that Go Fly a Kite sponsors. There are kite festivals, kite exhibitions, and even "kite-ins." One was held to repeal an ancient statute forbidding kites in Central Park. Go Fly a Kite also carries plush stuffed animals and fine porcelain dolls.

MANHATTAN DOLL HOSPITAL/DOLL HOUSE
176 Ninth Ave
989-5220
Sun-Fri: 10-4:30

Jenny and Herman Grunewald operate two compatible businesses from this single address. While Herman runs the Doll

House, which boasts the city's largest collection of dolls, dollhouses, and doll paraphernalia, Jenny runs the Manhattan Doll Hospital from the back of the shop and the basement. Before you feel sorry for poor Jenny, laboring away in the basement, know that she has one of the greatest jobs in the city. For the last 40 years, she has repaired, refurbished, and restored valued dolls and stuffed animals. The value is sometimes only in the eyes (and arms) of the beholder. Often Jenny's customers come to her cradling childhood toys that could be easily replaced at the corner store. But she understands that these customers are no more interested in replacing them than they'd be in replacing human friends. So she sits amid the biggest collection of wigs, eyes, and limbs for dolls imaginable, and day after day, she repairs and remodels dolls in need. Upstairs, her husband has all the things necessary to create a castlelike home for the newly restored princess, and if you already have the castle, Grunewald will sell you dolls to inhabit it. This is a super place with super people. However, organized they're not.

MUPPET STUFF

833 Lexington Ave (bet 63rd and 64th St)
980-8340
Mon-Sat: 10-6

In case there's a person alive who missed *Sesame Street*, the Muppet movies, *Fraggle Rock,* or the syndicated *Muppet Show*, the store devoted to all that stuff runs a continuous video at the back of the shop highlighting the Muppets' best appearances. I have to be honest, I didn't think that a shop dedicated to Fraggles, Doozers, Oscar the Grouch, and Miss Piggy would be very interesting, let alone have staying power. Then again, there were those who thought the same thing about the Muppet's theatrical adventures—and we were all wrong. The store is better than charming. In addition to having every possible bit of Muppet memorabilia, it has Muppet-inscribed items that are functional and useful in their own right. The painting smocks are among the best I've seen, and the Sesame Street learning toys truly teach. If nothing else—and there is much else—small items from the store (even postcards) make big hits with small-fry Muppet fans. They can be the crowning touch to a New York trip, and naturally, the store welcomes children. Getting them out of there is another matter. And you may be surprised. There are many adult Miss Piggy fans. The Muppets and Muppet Stuff have something for everyone.

ORCHARD TOY AND STATIONERY COMPANY

185 Orchard St (at Stanton St)
777-5133
Daily: 9-5

If this were anywhere else, it would simply be a well-stocked stationery store, the kind where you could quickly pick up balloons for a last-minute birthday party. But Orchard Street is not just any location, and no toy store could survive there unless it offered what every other store on Orchard Street offers: fantastic values. And of course, Orchard Toy and Stationery does. The fair-sized store is simply packed with toys. A child's cup would brim over, while his parents wallet would not have to. There is a flat discount of 10 to 25 percent, with much better prices on closeouts and out-of-season or dated items (such as *Charlie's Angels* dolls). This should be the number-one spot on a tour of Orchard Street, if for no other reason than that it will appease any child who has been dragged along on your shopping trip. He won't appreciate the prices, but you will—particularly on the "better" toys, such as Fisher-Price, which are discounted 20 percent.

SECOND CHILDHOOD
283 Bleecker St
989-6140
Mon-Sat: 11-6

Enchantment is the only word to describe this store, which deals in antique toys and childhood paraphernalia. The customer not only seems to go back in time to his childhood interests, but childhood in general seems to be a time suspended. The stock changes constantly, but all of it is authentic and in excellent condition. I saw wicker doll carriages, hoops (from both the Gay '90s and the 1950s), china dolls, and toys that stirred forgotten memories. No matter what the age, customers love this place. Prices range from 50 cents to over $1,000, so there is usually something for everyone. Wisely, browsing is encouraged, since the charm of these toys is that they really grow on you. The longer you stay, the more impossible it will be to leave without a reminder of your childhood.

SPIEGEL'S
105 Nassau St (at Ann St)
227-8400
Mon-Fri: 9-6; Sat: 10-5; closed Sat in summer

You wouldn't expect to find a good, competent place to buy toys, party goods, and sporting goods down here, but Spiegel's is here, and they would be top-notch in any location. The most advantageous point (aside from the lack of competition) is their discount prices, which are as good as those anywhere in the city. In addition, the selection is ample, the saleshelp excellent, and the supply amazing for a store of its size. Spiegel's would certainly be first choice in this area of town, but it may well be worth a trip from other parts of the city as well. Call first, and they will tell you if they have what you want.

TEDDY'S
120 Thompson St (at Prince St)
226-5013
Tues-Sat: noon-7; Sun: 1-7

The most popular toy in America is not the Cabbage Patch doll, it is not the home computer, and it is not even Go Bots and Transformers. No folks, the most popular current item is the Teddy Bear, and the fact that it is, while the Bible is still the best-selling book, proves the timelessness of traditional values. New Yorkers manifest this trend by having a store dedicated exclusively to Bibles, and so I suppose it was inevitable that there would be one for teddy bears, too. And there is. Teddy's, both corporately and stylewise, has arrived. This store in SoHo offers virtually anything with a teddy bear theme and, or course, the furry creatures themselves. (Did you know that they are named for Theodore Roosevelt who was once governor of New York?) So visit and enjoy the posters, music boxes, candles, and pins. It is a token of the attitude here that co-owner Maria Luchese invites everyone to come in and hug the bears "with no obligation." Smart lady. Who could resist!

TOY BALLOON
204 E 38th St
682-3803
Mon-Fri: 9-5

I wandered in here by accident, but you'll want to wander in on purpose. This is a serious adult business. Balloons are dealt with here in exactly the same manner that any business would deal with its product, but how *can* one be serious when the product is balloons? The Toy Balloon tries. Balloons are sold individually or in multitudes of up to 50,000. Types are so varied that there are graduations in diameter, thickness, style, and type. Sizes range from peewees to blimps, while shapes include dolls, rabbit heads, hearts, dachshunds (a personal favorite; they're often used to advertise hot dogs), and extra-elongated shapes. Most of the business is done for advertising campaigns, and the Toy Balloon will make up and sell personalized logos, styles, or two-colored messages. This specialty store also sells complete kits and everything the balloons require.

Typewriters

CENTRAL TYPEWRITER AND APPLIANCE COMPANY
42 E 33rd St
686-0930
Mon-Fri: 9-7; Sat: 10-4

In a city sometimes described as a jungle of typewriters, the selection of one typewriter store above all others implies that this one is pretty special. At first glance, Central Typewriter doesn't seem to be worthy of that description. The storefront is small and not terribly clean. There is no sign that the world has changed since the 1950s. The typewriters and adding machines on display are of dubious age (that's charitable) and condition. Apparently, all modern equipment is kept out of sight. While I was there, three people came in. None was a paying customer, but each received courteous care. As if this wasn't refreshing enough, the store turned out to be quite remarkable. Central wholesales, retails, repairs, rents, and sells all kinds of typewriters, business machines, and some appliances. They also stand behind their merchandise: "When we sell something to the customer, we take care of it." Most of Central's customers come because of recommendations (it's obvious that few are attracted by the decor). They are drawn by an excellent selection, the service record, and, best of all, the prices. Central's are among the city's lowest, and customers are invited to return with any problems, should they arise.

TYTELL TYPEWRITER COMPANY
116 Fulton St (bet William and Nassau St, second floor)
233-5333
Mon-Fri: 10:30-4 by appointment

Detective story readers know that a typewriter's keys are as individual and unique as fingerprints, and in New York, Martin and Pearl Tytell have made a name for themselves by identifying typeface for over 50 years. Today, the so-called "questioned document" service has become a major operation that requires the full-time expertise of Pearl and the Tytell's son, Peter, while Martin devotes his time to running the typewriter sales and repair business, with rentals on the side. Tytell's is the United Nations, the Smithsonian, and the Elaine's of the typewriter business. The typefaces you can choose from are as varied as the types on a printer's chart. If English isn't the lauguage you want, that's no problem. Martin Tytell will craft, by hand, a set of keys in any one of 145 languages. If you're in hurry, he's been farsighted enough to have made up foreign-language typewriters for such emergencies. In addition to typewriters for every language, he can make up keys of corporate logos, six-pitch double-case type (good for teleprompter reading), phonetic alphabets, stencil cutting, and jumbo type. There are over two million pieces of type in stock, as well as typewriters so old they're rented by movie studios for props. Tytell's list of clients reads like a who's who of those who use typewriters.

Variety, Novelty

BARGAIN SPOT
64 Third Ave (at 11th St)
674-1188
Mon-Sat: 8:30-5

In one of Cynthia Freeman's books, the heroine makes her money by starting out in a pawnshop. The Bargain Spot also started in a pawnshop, but in this case, it's the consumer who makes the money. Established in 1909, the Bargain Spot is also known worldwide as the Unredeemed Pledge Sales Company, and that name says it all. If something has been pledged and left, the Bargain Spot will purchase it and resell it. But the day of pawnshops in New York is long gone (at last count, I think there were less than 11), so no one could rely on that alone for business. Today, the company uses its base of pawnshop spoils to buy, rent, sell, and exchange a tremendous variety of items. About all they have in common is that they are items of value in good condition (or they would not have been pledged in the first place). The clientele is hard to believe (my office didn't believe it included me!), but all of them are obviously smart shoppers who know great bargains when they see them. At this aptly named shop, it's possible to buy everything from diamonds to typewriters to antiques, and if you call first, they will happily tell you what is in stock. Cynthia Freeman's protagonist isn't the only one to know a fortune can be made in pawnshop redemptions.

GORDON NOVELTY COMPANY
933 Broadway (at 22nd St)
254-8616
Mon-Fri: 9-4:30

Paper parasols (and for that matter, lace, rayon, and Chinese parasols), animal masks, half- and full-face masks, rubber masks, wigs, moustaches, sideburns, beards, Groucho Marx glasses, clicking teeth, noses, eye patches, tails, and various costumes all reside at Gordon Novelty. The store celebrates Halloween year-round, though it must be an absolute zoo on that holiday. (And I'm not referring to the two-dozen animal masks.) The practical joker could have a field day here with such fun items as break away bottles, buzzers, an invisible-dog leash, clown hats, and squirting boutonnieres. There are more balloons than one could count, and did I mention hats and disguises, puzzles, decorations, and party favors catalogued along thematic lines? Well, those are here as well. One can go really wild at Gordon's, and as might be expected, the personnel are helpful and enjoy a good joke—on you!

I. BUSS AND COMPANY
738 Broadway
242-3338
Mon-Sat: 10-7

Despite much time spent in New York, years in the retail business, and a few years in the military service, I never shopped in any army-navy surplus store until recently, which is unfortunate, since shopping in these stores can become a way of life. Of them, I. Buss is one of the best. The walls and shelves are heaped with all sorts of merchandise, related only in their design for use by the military. One section on a wall has backpacks favored by students, campers, and first graders in need of book bags. All are attracted to the bags' rugged durability, roominess, and low price. A second section has equally rugged blankets—great for overnight guests—at a fraction of Bloomie's prices, while a third nook stocks pants in all sizes and colors.The more obvious uniforms (with stripes down the side) are cheaper still. In addition,there are bins of insignia, army medals, pocketknives, surplus hats, cots, footwear, ponchos, and European sweaters. My appreciation for the store's merchandise is based upon the fact that all of it is more durable and often more adaptable than things sold for the same purpose in department stores. The tarpaulins, for example, are versatile and virtually indestructible.

JOB LOT TRADING COMPANY—
THE PUSHCART

140 Church St
962-4142
Mon-Sat: 8-5:30

80 Nassau St
398-9230
Mon-Fri: 7:45-6:15

412 Fifth Ave
398-9210
Mon-Sat: 8-6

After only a day in New York, even the most casual visitor becomes aware of black-and-white paper bags (depicting jam-packed pushcarts) being carried around in all sizes by all sorts of New Yorkers. Close examination would reveal that these bags all emanate from Job Lot Trading. Their reputation is citywide, if not larger, and that reputation is maintained in the City Hall area and on Fifth Avenue. Job Lot and the Pushcart were originally two separate stores that were dislocated by the World Trade Center. The locale was originally an area of odd-lot stores, electronic component shops, and garden nurseries. Of those original residents, only a few survived, and none survived as spectacularly as these two stores that merged (on different floors of the same store), took over a building, and, week after week, offer some of the best bargains in the city. Job Lot carries an odd number of consignments that are unsalable through normal retail channels for one reason or another. Those reasons range from overordering to bankruptcy, or from water and fire damage to government surplus. Job Lot Trading taps all of these sources and more (auctions, for instance) and offers whatever it can get to retail customers at incredible prices. In the original store, the main floor seems to specialize in hardware and housewares, while the lower level has permanent stocks of perfumes, colognes, toiletries, and toys. Absolutely everything is sold below wholesale. There is no telling what can turn up here. The stock changes constantly, so some people make weekly shopping trips.

KAUFMAN SURPLUS
319 W 42nd St (near Ninth Ave)
757-5670
Mon-Sat: 9:30-6

Kaufman has the same basic arrangement as I. Buss, but its business is larger and commands a better share of the market from suppliers and customers. The paramilitary look is king here, and smart fashion coordinators pick up chic accessories at less than cost prices. Kaufman's boasts that they carry "the odd" in military surplus. Trendy dressers, however, are not Kaufman's only customers. They have benefitted from the back-to-nature and backpacking revivals, and supply the professionals in both fields. Indeed, this merchandise is sturdy, durable, and originally designed for that use.

ODD JOB TRADING
7 E 40th St (bet Fifth and Madison Ave)
686-6825

66 W 48th St (bet Fifth and Sixth Ave)
575-0477

149 W 32nd St
564-7370

Mon-Thurs: 8-5:50; Fri: 8-4:30; Sun: 10-5

Another of the jobbers in the wake of Job Lot-The Pushcart, Odd Job has been around for a while and seems to consistently come up with good buys on quality merchandise. What differentiates Odd Job from the other half-dozen stores of its type is that its quality merchandise is more *au courant*. You never know what is going to turn up here; it can be anything from book racks to perfume, but it's always interesting. It's also the perfect place for gifts for the folks back home, where they'll never know how little they cost, unless you tell.

PINK PUSSY CAT BOUTIQUE
161 W Fourth St (at Sixth Ave)
243-0077
Daily: 10 a.m.-2 a.m.

This is a shop for men and women, gays and straights. Some of the sexually-oriented items are even suitable for polite company. Most are more suitable for people who know each other quite intimately. If you're looking for titillating merchandise, the Pink Pussy Cat offers it in a way that manages to be as discreet as it is bold. No one will snicker, but I wouldn't suggest bringing along your mother.

ROMANO
628 W 45th St (entrance on 12th Ave)
581-4248
Mon-Fri: 8-5:30; Sat: 8-4:30

Nomenclature is a problem here. Romano goes under at least two other names, Paris-Rome and Rome Outlet. Not terribly well known to New Yorkers, it is as patronized by visitors (especially foreign visitors) as the airports. Perhaps the various names come about from the confusion of customers seeking it out in dozens of languages. What do they know that natives don't? Simply that this part of town—best known for redeeming impounded cars and boarding the Circle Line tour boat—operates like a miniature Hong Kong. The only ships to speak of are the aforementioned Circle Line and cruise ships, but the neighborhood seems to think that crewmen and ship stevedors are docking everyday with money to spend for gifts back home. So, the stock is a hodgepodge of American—distinctly American—culture. Luggage, watches, Ray-ban sunglasses, bath towels, pens, cordless phones, electronic games, Fisher-Price toys, designer scarves and umbrellas, tennis rackets, china, and small electric appliances are all in stock at excellent discount prices. There has to be a reason to get legally parked car owners or landlubbers over here, and Samsonite at 50 percent off will do it. Nothing is sold at list price, and many of the items (watches in particular) are sold at the best prices in town.

Videotapes

NEW VIDEO

276 Third Ave
475-7400
Mon-Sat: 10-10; Sun: 2-9

44 Greenwich Ave
675-6600
Mon-Sat: 11-11; Sun: 2-9

90 University Pl
243-0400
Mon-Sat: 10-10; Sun: 2-9

Billed as *the* video store in the Village, New Video boasts of a large selection of cult and foreign films and obscure tapes, and operates much as a good bookstore would. New Video even does things like title searches, back lists, special orders, and out-of-print orders for video tapes and films. It is, indeed, the latest trend in media communication. *The New Video Times,* which resembles an early *Village Voice,* is a chronicle of the store's activities. Issues boast of the latest acquisitions and services ("Rent a Beta for only $9.95 a day"), while the various movies in stock are highlighted and reviewed. For any other industry, it would be odd to see a full-scale tabloid newspaper issuing from a store, but New Video is truly in the media biz. Here, the media is definitely the message, and they want everyone to get it. And to prove the point, this is one of the few video sources in the city that discounts as well. Ask for the copy of their *Times.* It gives the best view of what New Video is all about.

VIDEO BUFF

1221 Third Ave (bet 70th and 71st St)
744-2680
Mon-Sun: 9-9

Tim Rogan, Video Buff's co-owner, has appeared in this book as the owner of an antique limousine bought specifically to enable him to park illegally in all sorts of auspicious spots around town. Several years ago, the car blew up, and Rogan cast around for a new venture. Ever enterprising, he noted the city's new fascination with video recorders and joined Jacki Nafash in opening Video Buff. Today, Rogan would have a tougher time parking a car (apparently, parking enforcement agents also read this book), but he doesn't really care because he doesn't own one now. He could probably afford a new antique limo, though, from his store's profits. The reason for his success in that Video Buff perfectly gauges its market (even though it's a market that lesser prophets weren't sure even existed). Most of the business involves renting and selling movie cassettes. New movies are available at Video Buff almost as quickly as they appear in theaters, and they claim to have the city's best collection of classic and foreign films. You won't find every current movie available, but if it *is* available, Video Buff has it. For special occasions, the store also offers short-term rentals of recorders and players, through the majority of its business involves the leasing of cassettes. Double park your limo outside, and try them!

Wall Coverings

JANOVIC PLAZA
67th St and Third Ave
772-1400
Mon-Fri: 7:30-6:30; Sat: 8-5:45
159 W 72nd St
595-2500
Mon-Wed, Fri: 7:30-6:30; Thurs: 7:30-8; Sat: 9-5:45; Sun: 11-5

Once upon a time, the Janovics ran a neighborhood paint store. But when the neighborhood is in Manhattan, even a paint store (or at least one that hopes to succeed) can never be mundane. So, the image was brushed up, fashion and fads became evident in their wall coverings, and the business expanded across town. Today, the Janovics cover the Upper East and Upper West Sides, and those who shop for paint as they do for croissants, shop at Janovic. It's not really just the trendiness that makes Janovic such a success. While it helps, the updated image is still based on the old store's years of experience with New York wall problems (which one Janovic ad once likened to the Great Wall of China). So, not only can the personnel handle the latest Bloomingdale's model-room look, they can tell customers how to achieve it on tenement or 1890 row-house walls. As Janovic puts it: "We give technical as well as decorating advice to amateurs as well as professionals." And it's still a family business. Ask for Neil or Evan Janovic for the personal touch at their gaily colored wall-covering, bath, and fabric shops. They have some of the best discounts in town on vertical blinds.

MERIT-KAPLAN PAINTS
227 E 44th St (near Third Ave)
682-3585
Mon-Fri: 7-5:30

Lester Kaplan and Sanford Josephson run this neighborhood store in the heart of Manhattan as a wholesale painting source for retail customers. There are complete lines of Benjamin Moore, P.P.G., and Pratt and Lambert paints, and Kaplan boasts of his ability to get obscure items. In addition to their custom mixes and rock-bottom prices for all their paints, the closeout section is a gold mine of assorted paints in whatever colors happen to be around.

The two sources for this section are their own mismatches and unclaimed items or manufacturers' "goofs." Merit-Kaplan also has a wallpaper section with similar bargains (they will give a discount of 50 percent for any pattern they can get) and a power-tool section that offers one-third off list prices. On any of these things, it would be hard to do better.

PINTCHIK
278 Third Ave (at 22nd St)
982-6600, 777-3030
Tues, Wed, Fri: 8:30-7; Mon, Thurs: 8:30-8;
Sat: 9-6:30; Sun: 11-5

Discount wallpaper shops are few and far between in Manhattan, despite its reputation as the discount center of the world. But Pintchik is one such source. They discount paint and wall coverings, as well as the supplies that go with them. Two of the better wall coverings they carry are Laura Ashley and Marimeko patterns—by coincidence, two manufacturers that have large stores in Manhattan. Nonetheless, Pintchik can always beat even the manufacturer's prices, except during the rare clearance sales at the previously named stores. An advantage (besides price) is that unlike the fabric stores (and basically that is Laura Ashley's and Marimeko's trading card), Pintchik's staff is well-versed in the city's painting and wall-covering needs. They are very good at coming up with solutions to problem walls (and there probably isn't an apartment in the city without a problem wall), as well as making accommodations to city living. (Needless to say, white backgrounds don't go over very well with city soot.)

SHELIA'S WALLSTYLES DECORATING CENTER
273 Grand St (bet Eldridge and Forsyth St)
966-1663
Sun-Thurs: 9:30-5; Fri: 9:30-2

Grand Street is a strange place for a wallpaper store, since those locals who are into wall decorating almost universally use the paint-pattern-on-paint school of design. But Shelia opened her shop about a decade ago and proved so successful that she now has imitators. And why not? She took her cue from the retail motif of the Lower East Side and sells everything at a good discount. And then she located her store on a block that is quickly becoming the mecca for fashion-and-budget-conscious home decorators. The result is the very best in wall coverings, drapes, bedspreads, vertical and horizontal blinds, shades and coordinated accessories. In fact, despite its location, Shelia's was one of the first places to sport the totally coordinated look. Those who want a tissue box to match the boudoir can find it at Shelia's—and at a discount, to boot.

WALLPAPER MART
187 Lexington Ave (bet 31st and 32nd St)
889-4900
Mon-Wed, Fri: 10-6:30; Thurs: 10-7; Sat: 10-5

Wallpaper Mart has thousands of rolls of wall coverings in stock and on display inside its distinctively painted building. No paper is sold at retail, and discounts range from a mere 10 percent for some very current stylish patterns ordered from books, up to 30 percent off on others. Wallpaper Mart also offers an additional 10 percent off the marked price of any item in stock to anyone who shows a copy of this book. (Thanks!) All of the papers are current and in vogue, and if a pattern is not immediately available, Wallpaper Mart will order it. (The discount in that case is about 10 to 30 percent.) They now have a bath shop with vanities, sinks, and decorative plumbing.

Watches, Timepieces

E. NACK WATCH COMPANY
226 Canal St (bet Center and Baxter St)
925-5012
Mon-Sat: 10:30-6:30; closed July 4-12

E. Nack is, in reality, Ely Nackab and his son Raphael, but any way you spell it, this is the finest spot for quality watches at excellent prices. Nack is a wholesaler who will deal with the smallest retail sale anytime. The Seiko watch is a fraction of what it is even at Alexander's famous sales, and Nack's watches are current stock. Likewise, the Citizen sportswatch line is cheaper than the little wrist jobs at the five-and-dime, and kids' wristwatches can be had for under $5. Better watches are in stock or can be ordered, but I've never had anyone give a better time or price on a watch than E. Nack. Anytime, fellows!

FOTO ELECTRIC SUPPLY COMPANY
31 Essex St
673-5222
Sun-Thurs: 9-7; Fri: 9-2

Foto discounts Casio and Seiko watches at 40 percent off list price. This small Lower East Side shop makes you work for that discount, however. They don't accept mail or phone orders and prefer that you have the exact model in mind before they bestow their time upon you. On the other hand, you can save $100 by submitting to their "kindness."

M.A.G. TIME
168 Fifth Ave (at 22nd St)
929-8100
Mon-Fri: 9-5

The area down here is all business, and wholesale business at that, although it is beginning to be settled by gentrified loft dwellers. So, now is the time to take advantage of M.A.G. Time, which is the outlet for a large New York distributor of clocks, watches, and related electronics. It seems as though timepieces are an item that the city excels at discounting, but don't discount M.A.G. This is truly a great spot for superior timepieces at wholesale prices.

VII. "Where To" Extras

Auctions

CUSTOM HOUSE AUCTIONS
Public Stores, Sales and Seizure Section (room 114)
U.S. Customs House, New York, NY 10048
6 World Trade Center
466-5550

Unless you have an immediate use for 400 Korean wigs or 35 black shoes (all for left feet), this auction won't be very helpful, but its catalogs make great reading. And there probably isn't a more entertaining free show in town. The United States Custom Service holds approximately six auctions a year (one every two months). In the past, complete catalogs were sent months in advance to all who requested them, but a new policy changed that. Now the Customs Service will mail one inclusive notice of the next three upcoming sales. A postcard to the above address will get you information on the next sales (usually conducted on Thursday mornings at nine); for notice of each group of three sales, it is necessary to send a separate postcard. There seems to be no end to what people try to get through customs. Bird cages, clothing, eyelashes, furniture, industrial tools, and musical instruments are examples of the more typical items. The only disadvantage is that almost everything is sold in large lots and is of little interest to the average consumer. (There are exceptions. I was told that at a recent auction 80 percent of the merchandise was confiscated liquor.) Custom House Auctions use the paddle system: by leaving a refundable deposit a person may purchase a paddle through which all bids are made.

POLICE AUCTION
Property Clerk Division
1 Police Plaza (bet Chambers and Centre St)
406-1369 (recording), 374-4925 (Property Clerk's office)

Several times a year, the police hold auctions that, depending upon your point of view, are either exhilarating or depressing. Everything auctioned off is recovered contraband that couldn't be returned to rightful owners because it couldn't be identified, wasn't reported stolen, or the owner couldn't be located or refused to pay the fines (as is usually the case with cars). To attend the auction viewing (always held on Mondays) and see row after row of items that fit the immediate criteria of having been both stolen and unreturnable is an awesome experience. Giving New York's police department credit, assume that 50 percent of all reported stolen goods are returned. Thus, what one inspects at the police auction is a fraction of what is annually stolen. (I wonder if my stolen wallet ever showed up?) The selection of items will boggle the mind. There are enough impounded cars and motorcycles to require their own auction on Tuesdays of auction week. Wednesdays are set aside for "general merchandise," which has included bucket seats, radios, trunk lids, batteries, and radiators from cars, console color TVs, kitchen chairs, furniture, videogames, silver, stereos, jewelry, watches, baby seats, wheelchairs, and bicycles. Notification is made by a recording at 406-1369, which gives the date and time of the next auction. Additional information can be obtained by calling the property clerk's office or from advertisements in the previous Sunday's *New York Times*. Viewing is on Monday, and merchandise must be removed within 48 hours. The exhilarating part comes (if you don't mind profiting from other people's losses) with the fabulous buys. The bicycle and auto auctions are attended by professional buyers, so amateurs don't have much chance. But the rest of the auction offers great possibilities.

POST OFFICE AUCTION
Claims and Inquiry Clerk
33rd St and Eighth Ave (basement)
971-5171

If you've never been here, you must attend it once, even though it takes three days of your time. The Post Office auction is so huge that one day is required for viewing, one for the auction, and a third to pick up the merchandise. Each activity is totally separate, and even the date of the auction can't be predicted more than a month in advance. A call to the above number will give you the dates of the next auction and any additional information they might have. There is a catalog available at the viewing and auction, but it's not very helpful. "Lot number 36—books," for example, could be anything from a complete set of the Encyclopedia Britannica to 4,000 shopworn, water-logged books. Anything and everything can turn up, and what the postal service can handle (or mishandle) has no limit. Everything auctioned off here has been lost, damaged, or unclaimed in the mail. Items that have been auctioned off in the past include a Wallace sterling silver service for 12, Tiffany watches, console color TVs, clothing, baby carriages, candlesticks, and crates of assorted "things." Paddles at the auction cost $20, which is applied to a purchase or refunded if no purchase is made. Any sum of purchases over $300 must be covered immediately. Anything below that amount is payable before the auction is over. Here, too, beware the professionals. Barnes & Noble and job lotters attend these, and the closest the average shopper can get to it is when he sees it for sale in their stores.

Brown-Bagging It

Despite the cold image of impersonal, towering skyscrapers, New York, perhaps more than any other city in the world makes a point of offering oases of calm every few blocks. To find a bench where you can eat lunch, all any city resident has to do is walk to the nearest river or park. All are lined with benches and even picnic tables. (Trivia fact: The East River isn't a river. It's an estuary.) In addition, there are handfuls of ''vest pocket parks'' (one at 72nd St off Broadway has been used for weddings) and any number of corporate and public spaces. The latter is a political term created by zoning legislation. What it means to the pedestrian is a place to eat lunch in some of the swankiest buildings in town at no charge. There are also places where the public is allowed to sit but is not allowed to eat. I'll note them and list the parks and the public spaces. Incidentally, no one has the right to ask a person to move from any of these sites.

Parks

Bowling Green (Broadway and the Hudson River) This is similar to City Hall Park, except that the orators have a historic soap box here, and some of them seem to have been around since the Dutch played Ten Pins on the site. (And hence its name.) Peter Minuet supposedly bought Manhattan here for $24 worth of trinkets. Bowling Green sort of links up with Battery Park and Castle Clinton, and there's enough space to forget the buzz of the financial district a block away.

Bryant Park (42nd St, bet Fifth and Sixth Ave) Bryant Park was better off in its much earlier days as a cemetery. Since then, it has been a reservoir and the capital of all sorts of sleezy drug-related activities. But plans have been made to create a European Plaza out of the park, and perhaps by the time you read this, it will be in the works. What is most indicative of New York was the tremendous hullabaloo that arose when one of the plans called for limited access to the park. New Yorkers wouldn't stand for that. So if you haven't heard of great activities in Bryant, don't go. But even now, there are perfectly safe festivals there several times a year.

City Hall Park (Broadway and Park Row) Though this is a large, expansive green, it is surrounded on every side by insane traffic which hinders serenity. At lunchtime, it's not just the traffic that seems a little crazy. Listen to the haranguers and soap-box orators! Still, if you can get far enough away from both, or if you come during a non-lunch hour, it's not a bad place. The site has been everything from a burial ground to a prison to a poorhouse, so the Delacorte Fountain is definitely a change for the better. Catch this place sometime when city employees are not picketing and/or it's not lunchtime.

Grand Army Plaza (Fifth Ave and 59th St) If location is everything in real estate, this is one choice property. It's the front yard of the Plaza Hotel, the base of Central Park, and the staging area for horse-drawn hansom cabs, and it's just across the street from the G.M. Building. It's also been the scene for a score of movies from *The Way We Were* to *Arthur*. That's the good news. The bad news is that it's crowded, not terribly green, and that fountain is an invitation to every strolling troubador and lunatic who isn't at Bethesda fountain in Central Park. (What is it about fountains?) Watch your wallet, too.

Greenacre Park (E 51st St, bet Second and Third Ave) Abby Rockefeller donated this gem of a spot in 1971. The small (6,360 square foot) park, complete with a 25-foot-high artificial waterfall, has a three-tiered patio and trees. It's a sanctuary for brown-bagging office workers and others who happen by. Skip lunch hour if you want privacy. A little imagination evokes the feeling of the Rockefeller Center skating rink and restaurant, which is not surprising considering who the donor was.

Jeannette Park (Coentis Slip, Water and South St, next to 55 Water St) Real New Yorkers might know this as Jeannette Park, named for the ship that went down with all its passengers on a trip to the North Pole. Others know it as the site of the New York Vietnam Veterans Memorial. Ninety percent of the crowd hasn't heard of either name, but it's quickly become known as *the* place for the brown-baggers in the Wall Street area, and the Memorial is putting it on the map.

Paley Park (53rd St, bet Fifth and Madison Ave) The donor here was William Paley, the former chairman of CBS and the benefactor of the Museum of Broadcasting just up the block. Paley Park is more of a media event and is especially wild during lunch hours in good weather. The rest of the time it's just a nice place to be.

Stuyvesant Square Park (Second Ave, at E 17th St) Even if the nearby Union Square Park met my criteria of "vest pocketness" (hardly!), it wouldn't get a listing here because it's not the nicest or safest of places despite a recent overhauling. But Stuyvesant Park gets the overflow from Beth Israel Medical Center and Stuyvesant

Town, and in addition to occasional children playing there, it has a calm, serene country glow. A find!

Washington Square (West Fourth St) It's hard to miss this geographic and spiritual hub of the Village. It suffers from all of the ailments of the aforementioned parks, but due to its huge size and neighborhood, there is none of that urban pressure-cooker feeling. There are art shows almost year round and the usual grab bag of interesting characters. These folks, however, speak with a Village accent.

Water Club (East River and 30th St) This very, very elegant restaurant is built over a wharf and often has more going on outside than inside. At one point, the owner parked a barge filled with sand and beach umbrellas alongside it. In any event, barge or no barge, there is a small public park there. By the way, it is almost possible to walk the length of Manhattan along the river on the East Side.

Building Plazas

AT&T Building (550 Madison Ave) When this building was built, it was the subject of endless reviews. The critique of the facade of the upper floors still gets mixed reactions, but the public space there always receives raves, particularly since an out-of-court settlement created a communications museum in the shorter annex adjacent to the Chippendale-topped building. On ground level, an airy public space opens Madison Avenue to the side streets. Along the 56th Street side, it is possible to almost touch the equally gigantic (and equally new) I.B.M. Building's greenhouse at 57th Street and Madison. That, too, is a public space and one of the best in town. (Enjoy all that greenery under glass as the snow falls!) The I.B.M. link to 57th Street also links (via Bonwit Teller) with the Trump Tower atrium. Together, these three buildings offer the newest, largest, and best public space in town.

Channel Gardens at Rockefeller Center (Fifth Ave, bet 49th and 50th St) Lively, beautiful, and busy. No matter what the season, the grounds are alive with flowers and activities. And it can get *very* busy here.

Chase Manhattan Bank Plaza (1 Chase Plaza) Four trees, Isamu Noguchi's stone and water garden, and Dubuffet's sculpture crown this plaza. It ain't great, but it's the biggest expanse in the area.

Corning Glass Reflecting Pool (Fifth Ave, at 56th St) If you're thinking big Washington-D.C.-like reflecting pool, revise that thought downward fast. This runs the length of the building and is only a few feet wide. The windows in the Steuben Building are interesting, but you can't sit on their ledges on the outskirts of the pool as you're supposed to be able to do.

Crystal Pavilion (805 Third Ave, at 50th St) This version features two indoor waterfalls, a Hyatt-type glass elevator, much polished steel, and a charming green and sunny retreat nestled among its three levels, encased in glass and crystal (naturally!). The public is made welcome with cafes, shops, restrooms, and tables and chairs sprinkled throughout the complex. Never has the modern look been made so homey.

Dag Hammarskjold Plaza (47th St and Second Ave) Unless there is a demonstration protesting something at the United Nations across the street, this block-long plaza is an oasis. Physical amenities are not that fantastic—a waterfall that works only sporadically, several trees, and a stairway to an elevated patio—but the sheer size makes it almost impossible *not* to find a place to sit down. Several of the locals spend the day playing chess and checkers on the benches. And if the view gets boring, the United Nations Gardens are across First Avenue. Incidentally, the Gardens and the restroom downstairs in the main lounge of the U.N. are on international territory. You can say you left the country for lunch!

875 Third Avenue (bet 52nd and 53rd St) The presence of a cafe and coffee shop here sanctifies eating at the three floors of tables and chairs. The management seems friendly (though you have to ask for access to the locked restrooms), and perhaps because there are so many such places in the neighborhood, this isn't too crowded.

Exxon Park (49th St and Sixth Ave) This street-level plaza is crowded with up-and-coming business people at lunchtime. The fountain is refreshing and much better than the smaller sister plaza on the west side of the building. Rumor has it that you can have a "high" time here.

The Galleria (117 E 57th St, east of Park Ave) This is a political hot potato, but if you'd like to exert your rights (perhaps to blow off steam after a frustrating day), ask the doorman at the Galleria to escort you to the public space in the building. If he doesn't tell you there are no public restrooms, you will be led to a tiny, unobtrusive sitting area that looks like some tenant's retreat. It isn't. It's yours in exchange for some zoning concessions, and apparently they are required to offer free seats. But the Galleria management acts as though that's news to them.

New York Telephone Building (Sixth Ave, bet 41st and 42nd St) Ma Bell (or is it Baby Bell now?) provides benches, and there's the obligatory waterfall and snack bar. Not all the sales that go on here are of a legal nature, but the clientele is made up of young business people, so safety is not a problem.

Olympic Tower (641 Fifth Ave) Another "public-access private place" plaza. Here the daring Olympic Tower owners carried the idea of hiding public places to new heights. There are cafes (that shall remain nameless) in the public-access space, and the average browser is led to believe that the only way to sit down is to pay for a meal. Not true. But it may not be worth the hassle. Fie on you, Olympic Tower!

Park Avenue Atrium (Lexington Ave, at 45th and 46th St) The building takes up the entire block, and the public space is equally vast. It is divided between Charley O's and Luchow's Viennese Cafe, a skylight elevator, and enough potted trees to have made some poor forest very bare. It's all very green and dramatic, and although the trees take up space that could otherwise be used for seating, the presence of two cafes make eating here a welcome event.

Park Avenue Plaza (55 E 52nd St, off Park Ave) This elegant, stern arcade offers some tables and chairs and an equally elegant and stern cafe in its midst. Apparently, there have been complaints because there are notices throughout attesting to the public's right to use the facilities. Try to tell that to the waiter hovering over the elegantly set table at lunchtime, though. I'd rather brown-bag it elsewhere.

Police Plaza (Chambers and Lafayette St) This new police headquarters, which was poetically built on the site of the "Tenderloin"—the very worst district in historic New York—is a delight for the law abiding. The plaza offers sidewalk dining and food festivals in the summer and real peace all year long. And where would you be safer?

Seagram Building (Park Ave at 52nd St) This open plaza has some seating. This is from the old school, and there are no sneaky tricks to close it off from the public.

Time Life Building's American Plaza (Sixth Ave, bet 50th and 51st St) and the *McGraw-Hill Plaza* on the next block. Both offer water fountains and some eating capacity. The area is very popular at lunchtime, but it's much more relaxed the rest of the time.

Whitney Museum of American Art at Phillip Morris (120 Park Ave, at 42nd St) This building seems to confound even native New Yorkers. One young man arranged to meet his blind date at "the Whitney. You know where that is?" "Of course," she said. "I've lived here all my life." So, he went uptown to the Whitney Museum and waited three hours, while she went to 42nd Street and waited the same three hours downtown. Unlike a Hollywood movie, they never did meet. In any event, that explains why a museum is on this brown-bagging list. It doesn't? O.K. I'll try again. Phillip Morris' Sculpture Court is a two-floored windowed area with exhibits from the "other" Whitney Museum uptown. There are tables, chairs, benches, and even an espresso bar, all of which encourage browsing, eating, and even meeting in a large room with a view of the Grand Central Terminal.

Entertainment

EXTRAS AT THE OPERA

799-3100
(Ask for Head Super's office or
Bill McCourt, ext 2510)

Quick—do you know what a supernumerary is? Would you like to be one? A supernumerary is the term for extras used in productions of the Metropolitan and New York City operas. Both companies perform at Lincoln Center—the Met at its namesake opera house and the City opera across the plaza at the New York State theater. Both companies require scores of extras for their productions, and that's where the supernumeraries come in. They do not sing, but they have been known to do any number of other tasks from simply filling up crowd scenes to stilt-walking and juggling. Pay (which is not the reason any of the supernumeraries take the job) starts at a minimum of $10 for each rehearsal and/or performance and increases for special skills or longer appearances onstage. The driving motivation for most supernumeraries is not to be behind the scenes at an opera but to appear onstage. Appearing on Broadway or in the other arts requires union affiliation or special training. But virtually anyone can appear in a crowd in an opera, and it's an opportunity for all the hams in the city to say they've performed at Lincoln Center. Incidentally, supernumeraries are usually committed for the season, and "auditions" occur in the early fall. I was told to call in August for the following year's season. But occasionally an extra needs replacing. It doesn't hurt to try!

LIGHT OPERA OF MANHATTAN

334 E 74th St
861-2288, 535-6310

This small theater, rented by the opera company, offers great productions of light opera throughout the year at good prices. The main offerings are usually Gilbert and Sullivan, with two or three different plays offered consecutively in a single season. There is a tendency to repeat the more popular *Mikado* and *H.M.S. Pinafore* at the expense of other less known works, most probably because they sell more tickets. The theater also offers *The Student Prince* and other popular light operas. Notwithstanding the excellent performances, the biggest virtue has to be the prices. Standard seats are reasonably priced and close to the stage. Senior citizens, students, servicemen, and many other groups get a discount. For the price and the show, it's the best entertainment buy in town.

THE "NEW YORK EXPERIENCE"
McGraw-Hill Bldg (Sixth Ave at 49th St, lower plaza)
869-0345
Mon-Thurs: 11-7; Fri, Sat: 11-8; Sun: noon-8

Although *The New York Experience* has been around for years, few natives know of it. It is the tourists and visitors who have made this multiscreen film extravaganza such a hit that it has established permanent residence here. The hourly show uses 16 screens, 45 projectors, and a battery of special effects to depict historic and contemporary New York City. Admission includes an old-fashioned amusement arcade and a "Little Old New York" gallery. The show itself is fantastic. Don't miss it!

NEW YORK PHILHARMONIC OPEN REHEARSALS
Avery Fisher Hall, Lincoln Center (Broadway at 65th St)
874-2424
Day of scheduled performances

Most every Thursday morning in season, the New York Philharmonic holds open rehearsals that begin at 9:45 a.m. Tickets go on sale about a month in advance. A ticket is currently $3 (underwritten by Merrill Lynch) for any seat in the house, and the experience is priceless. Patrons include music buffs who like to stretch their entertainment dollar and enjoy listening to the variations in technique of different conductors during rehearsal, people who are unable to go out at night, and all kinds of classical music lovers. It's not guaranteed, but usually a concert program is played in full. Tickets may be purchased at the box office or by sending a self-addressed stamped envelope to the New York Philharmonic Open Rehearsals, Avery Fisher Hall, Lincoln Center, New York, NY 10023.

Flea Markets

Living in a crowded city like New York makes it rather impossible to hold a garage sale to clear out accumulated and unwanted junk. But ever-resourceful New Yorkers teamed with ever-short-of-money residents to set up flea markets. The analogy is not exact. For one thing, the city's flea markets are short on used toasters and lawn mowers and long on weekend entrepreneurs who are privy to excellent merchandise. Great care and organization go into their formation, and once started, they tend to be a formal, structured sort of chaos. The upshot for the consumer is that reputable flea markets are far more legitimate than those hawkers who sell watches and designer jeans from suitcases on the sidewalk. If a purchase is not up to snuff, the dealer will probably be there the following week, and his reputation is at stake. Add these two facts together, and it's obvious why flea marketing is a prime activity in New York. It's a great place to get good merchandise cheaply. Most of the city's flea markets are only open on weekends—and often for only one day at that. Business is somewhat seasonal, since the outdoor markets are obviously only open in good weather. But the indoor markets often operate year round, and the merchants driven indoors frequent as many as possible. Some of the established markets in the city are among the following:

Annex Antiques Fair and Flea Market (Sixth Ave, bet 25th and 26th Sts, 243-5343; Sun: 9-6, April to Nov) Annex's antiques are rumored to be first class. Having lasted more than 20 years, it is one of New York's oldest flea markets, and it still manages to pack in phenomenal crowds. Included in the crowds are astute professionals, and rumor has it that the real trading occurs hours before the market officially opens. The merchandise sold then is often resold both at Annex and at markets throughout the area. All manner of antiques can be found here, from clothing to tableware and silver, and almost all of it is antique quality.

Canal Street Market (335 Canal St; weekends, March to Dec, 226-7541). Joe Kaufmann has run this flea market in an erstwhile weekday parking lot for 12 years. Everything sold by the 50-odd dealers is old but not necessarily antique. This eliminates the designer jeans-bargain hunters and appeal is to the new-antique crowd. For a minimum investment in time and money, tomorrow's finds can be found in Kaufmann's lot today. Those who don't mind the lack of contemporary bargains find this a shining example of flea marketing.

East 67th Street Antiques, Flea and Farmers Market at P.S. 183 (67th St bet York and First Ave, 737-8888; Sat: 9-5, year round) From the professional to the P. T. A., this and Market I. S. 44 are run year round by parent-teacher associations to benefit school activities. Is this the modern age of rummage sale? Judging from the merchandise, it would seem so. There is a little bit of everything both old and new with some good prices in vintage clothing and art-deco antiques. The professionals seem to be elsewhere.

Market I. S. 44 (Columbus Ave at 76th St, 362-4089; Sun: 11-6) East Side, West Side, the story is much the same here. The difference seems to be that I. S. 44 is newer in origin and merchandise. Both, incidentally, have adjacent Farmers Markets in season. Out of season, they move indoors. Sure beats bingo! This is the biggie on the PTA circuit.

P.S. 41 (Greenwich Ave at 11st St, 752-8475; Sat: 11-6) Officially called the Saturday Village School Mart, this professionally run flea market carries a little bit of everything. Note the location. There's an emphasis on the arty and the experimental.

Walter's World Famous Greenwich Village Emporium (252 Bleecker St, Ave of the Americas and Seventh Ave, 255-0175; Thurs-Sun: 1-8 p.m.) Despite the grandiose name, Walter Bum's privately run flea market is cozy and specialized. Most of the 50 or so booths offer jewelry or antiques, and a fair number combine both interests by offering antique jewelry. There's also antique clothing, vintage records, and old timepieces—the kind of stuff you'd find at a quality garage sale.

Free Activities

So you stopped in Atlantic City on your way to New York, or the trip cost more that you had budgeted—all is not lost! New York has a wealth of free activities, and even institutions which normally charge fees, such as zoos and museums, understand that culture should be available to all. Therefore, most museum fees are "voluntary contributions," and the zoo has free-admission days. Throughout the year, the city has an official policy of sponsoring free activities. Some of the better ones are offered in the summer when the Shakespeare Festival plays in Central Park at the Delacorte Theatre, and the Kool Jazz Festival takes to the city piers, the Metropolitan Opera and Philharmonic perform in the city parks, and various mobile entertainment troupes turn side streets into community street fairs. Walking and browsing are always free, of course. A stroll through Macy's, Rockefeller Center, the United Nations grounds, or any of the many city parks can occupy an entire day and cost nothing. The new Battery Park Promenade is not well known, but it offers vistas which beat those that are charged for elsewhere. Similarly, there are dozens of little places to sit and "take a load off," and they don't cost a load to do it. Inland office buildings are required to offer public spaces, and adherence to the law varies greatly. A company such as Bristol Myers is very consumer oriented. (They even had the former consumer-affairs commissioner Bess Myerson on the payroll offering consumer information.) So they run consumer panels such as the Clairol Consumer Research Center, which pampers testers of their products and then sends them off with free samples to boot. This may be indicative of the industry in general. Many beauty establishments use volunteers to train their personnel or try new products. In addition to the ones listed under Beauty Services, several other companies run panels. Among them are:

Cardeaux's makeup counters in the two Gimbels stores, which offer a facial and makeup analysis as well as a makeover. There's no hard sell and it's free.

I Natural (737 Madison Ave, 734-0664) does the same thing. However, you need an appointment, which is easy to get, and the session is private. (Cardeaux, while not on the main thoroughfare, is still in the middle of Gimbels.) I Natural dispenses natural products—naturally.

Finally, *Revlon* (600 Madison Ave, 527-5878) runs a product-evaluation center similar to Clairol's, on its third floor. Here, too, you need an appointment. Incidentally, for years it was a New York rumor that Revlon would buy nails that were over an inch long. (Two inches? Fu Man Chu length? That part always changes.) Ask them.

Now that you've got a new look, it's time to try the theater. Yes, the theater. (Of course, the political theater such as the U.N., City Council meetings, and other events are always free.) Several places (particularly off-Broadway) offer free performances or have pay-as-you-wish policies. The Avaigh Theater (108 W 43rd St, 221-9088) offers a different lunch-hour play every two weeks. They start at 12:15 and last about an hour. There are even groupies who critique each show!

Weekends, the Greene Street Cafe (101 Greene St) previews the Double Image Theater's Playwright Workshop. Currently, performances are on Saturdays at 1 p.m., and the performance doesn't end with the curtain call. Afterward, everyone gathers around to discuss how the performance went, and the budding playwright director, producer, actors et al. are usually very interested in an intelligent new opinion. (They've heard each other's for weeks.) You could actually be the encouragement for the next Broadway star!

Juilliard is the renowned School of Music and the Arts located in New York. The school's graduates number among the top artists in the country, and the list of those wanting to go there is hundreds long. With a location that is part of the Lincoln Center complex, Juilliard uses the center to optimal advantage. Students study concerts and frequently perform as part of the official cast or on their own. For added exposure, on most Friday evenings Juilliard students and faculty give free concerts at Alice Tully Hall (Lincoln Center, 874-8515). Reservations are in order, but there are no reservations about the quality of the performances. These are first-rate musicians playing in Lincoln Center. And it's highly possible that the performer is a future superstar.

Free "shows" staged by local businesses are another option. On the intimate level, there's the tour of Schapiro's Winery (126 Rivington St, 475-7383), which is probably the only such tour open on Sunday, and reservations are not necessary. On a bigger scale, the Con Edison Conservation Center and Energy Museums are free, and most museums have free nights in addition to their "suggested" but not mandatory admission policies. Many of the "Discovering New York" tours I discussed at the beginning of the book are also free, but they require reservations. Another industrial tour is the Friday at 12:15 tour of *The New York Times* (229 W 43rd St, 556-1310) held during school months.

Here is a list of *some* of the city's other free attractions:

1. *American Stock Exchange* (78 Trinity Pl, 306-1000; Mon-Fri: 10-3:30) Offers a tour of the Exchange and several exhibits. The view is from an overhead gallery.

2. *Citicorp Center* (53rd St and Lexington Ave) One of the first of the public-access spaces, the multifloored atrium is so successful it is often forgotten that this is primarily a corporate headquarters. On the atrium floors, shops (the International Smoke Shop is one) ring a skylight-brightened center court. Throughout the year, during lunchtimes, evenings, and weekends, there are various programs and shows to enjoy from tableside, and Saturday is "Children's Day," with special shows.

3. *Federal Hall National Memorial* (25 Wall St, 264-8711; Mon-Fri: 9-5) The site of George Washington's inaugural address and the first United States Treasury (the still-intact vaults are awesome), this often overlooked site is modeled after the Parthenon and is the city's best example of Greek Revival architecture. It is administered by the National Park Service, and despite the incongruity of seeing those green uniforms down the block from Wall Street, they do a notable job. Throughout the year, there are programs and concerts at this and other federal parks in the area. In the Hall itself, there is an excellent film on Washington's New York and his inauguration, several museum-quality exhibits, and a second floor devoted to freedom of the press and the trial of Peter Zenger, because this was the site of his trial. Throughout the parks, people are cooperative and helpful. They even provided a place for a woman to nurse her baby.

4. *Federal Reserve Bank of New York* (33 Liberty St, 791-5000) Tours must be arranged a week in advance, but it's worth getting a glimpse of New York's version of Fort Knox. There are no samples.

5. *General Motors Exhibit* (767 Fifth Ave, 486-4518; Mon-Fri: 9-9; Sat: 10-6) Another corporate headquarters and public-access site, it has car exhibits, which can be very interesting, particularly at the beginning of the new-models season.

6. *Hallmark Gallery* (Fifth Ave at 46th St, 489-8320; Mon-Sat: 9:30-6) "When you care enough" to see cultural exhibits and programs. The Christmas cards and trees are a must.

7. *New York Stock Exchange* (20 Broad St, 623-5167; Mon-Fri: 10-3:30) Note that the Stock Exchange is *not* on Wall Street. Note,

too, that this tour has taken a slide downward in recent years. These days the trend is that everything is seen on a self-guided tour from a balcony overlooking the exchange floor. A film and audience-participation program was both boring and out of order when I was there on two trips a year apart. Nonetheless, there is something to be said for seeing the Stock Exchange, and perhaps a trip will inspire a future Exchange member to clean up the visitor's gallery.

8. *News Building Lobby* (220 42nd St, 949-3531; Mon-Fri: 9-5) *Superman* fans will recognize this place immediately. So will fans of scores of other movies. Non-film buffs can content themselves with a history of classic *News* front pages (the #1 being"Ford to City: Drop Dead," which probably cost Gerald Ford the election) and a huge revolving globe. For some reason, the rest of the floor is obsessed with meteorology, astronomical, and geographical activity. Wait...I just got it. "Look up in the sky...It's a bird, it's a plane..." Well, whatever it is, the News Lobby can tell you about it.

9. *Lincoln Center* (Broadway and 65th St) There are free rehearsals and free shows in the mall. The Crafts Fair at the end of June is noteworthy, and the Library for the Performing Arts can entertain the whole family for days.

10. *79th Street Boat Basin* (Riverside Park) A great relaxation site. People live here year round on their houseboats and yachts on the Hudson River. Here again, attitude is the byword. The waterfront (and of course the river itself) is public property.

11. *The United Nations* (First Ave and 45th St) It's possible to see all but the guided tours for free. The public sessions are open to the public, obviously, and it's usually just you and the reporters. But if there's a hot issue, there's a line.

Legal Holidays

On the following public legal holidays, museums, businesses, libraries, post offices, banks, most schools, and some stores and restaurants are closed:

January 1: New Year's Day
January 15: Martin Luther King's Birthday
February 12: Lincoln's Birthday
February (3rd Monday): George Washington's Birthday
May (last Monday): Memorial Day
July 4: Independence Day
September (1st Monday): Labor Day
October (2nd Monday): Columbus Day
November (Tuesday after 1st Monday): Election Day

November 11: Veteran's Day
November (4th Thursday): Thanksgiving Day
December 25: Christmas Day

Museums

New York is museum-mad; even retail stores often maintain small exhibits, and that doesn't begin to cover the hundreds of special-interest groups who maintain monuments to their own pasts. There are people who come to New York solely to tour its museums, and indeed there is no better city for enjoying them. The following are some of the city's better — and most interesting — museums.

ABIGAIL ADAMS SMITH HOUSE
421 E 61st St
Mon-Fri: 10-4

Abigail Adams was the daughter of John Adams, sister of John Quincy Adams, and wife of Colonel William S. Smith who bought and sold the 23-acre estate that was the site of this stone stable and coach house. In later days, the coach house was the home of the Towle family (Jeremiah Towle was one of the first commissioners of Central Park) and later an inn. The Colonial Dames of America, owners of the house, have worked hard at restoring and furnishing the house as a testimonial to Mrs. Smith, who probably never set foot in the building when it was a stable. There are some very interesting historical exhibits, and the house shows clear signs of each stage of its occupancy. And here's a trivia fact: Abigail's father referred to her mother as the formal "Mrs. Adams" even in his diary. No comment.

AMERICAN CRAFT MUSEUM
77 W 45th St
869-9422
Mon-Sat: 10-5
(reopens in 1986 at 44 W 53rd St)

There is an admission charge, and the fee is worth it for most of the changing exhibits, as well as the permanent exhibit of American crafts of the 20th century. Call to find what the current display is.

AMERICAN MUSEUM OF IMMIGRATION
Base of the Statue of Liberty
732-1236
Daily: 9-4 (opens summer 1986)

The best part about this museum is taking the Liberty Island boat to get there. But no one comes to the Statue of Liberty just to visit the free museum. On the other hand, many visitors *do* while away the hours there while waiting for their more hardy companions to climb the statue's staircase. And here's another trivia fact for you. The above number is in the 212 area code. But the concession stand which is a short walk away is officially in New Jersey's 201. And the folks in Brooklyn, Queens, and Staten Island were upset with 718!

AMERICAN MUSEUM OF NATURAL HISTORY
Central Park W at 79th St
873-4225
Sun-Tues, Thurs: 10-5; Wed, Fri, Sat: 10-9

The granddaddy of all the city's museums, it has something for everyone. To see everything—from the dinosaurs and enormous suspended whale (perennial children's favorites) to the Egyptian tombs and mummies—could take several days. The Hall of Asian Peoples, the Christmas exhibits, theme shows, and the openings of new collections inspire visitors to return again and again. Adjacent to the museum is the Hayden Planetarium (873-8828), another sure-fire hit with children. The main show (which includes a general introduction to the stars and a seasonal highlight) illuminates the night skies and includes a brief explanation of astronomy.There are also exhibits on space artifacts and simulated life-in-space segments. Both the Museum of Natural History and the Planetarium should be avoided during school hours, unless you want your experience in natural history to be limited to "Child Behavior Outside the Classroom."

BLACK MUSEUM OF FASHION
155 W 126th St (bet Lenox and Seventh Ave)
666-1320
Daily: noon-6 by appointment only

Located in a renovated brownstone, this museum was founded in late 1979 by Lois Alexander, who wrote her master's thesis on fashions designed and created by black people. The museum's display guides visitors through 250 garments, from the 1800s to the 1980s. A stitch-for-stitch duplicate of the gown worn by Mrs. Abraham Lincoln at her husband's inaugural ball is here. It's the creation of Barbara Ann Black, a teacher at the Harlem Institute for Fashion, which is next door to the museum. The original gown, now on display at the Smithsonian in Washington, D.C., was designed by a slave named Elizabeth Keckly, who literally sewed her way to freedom (she also clothed Mrs. Stephen Douglas and Mrs. Jefferson Davis). The collection also includes an authentic slave dress from Staunton, Virginia; the yellow dress which Rosa Parks had made and which she wore when she was arrested for refusing to give up her bus seat; and costumes created for the musicals *Timbuktu* and *The Wiz*.

CHILDREN'S MUSEUM OF MANHATTAN (G.A.M.E.)

314 W 54th St (bet Eighth and Ninth Ave)
765-5904
Wed-Sun: 1-5

G.A.M.E., as the Children's Museum of Manhattan was originally called, was the brainchild of Bette Korman, a kindergarten teacher, who felt that children needed "laboratories" to explore their unique world during nonschool hours. Originally, the program ("Growth through Art and Museum Experience") was housed in a storefront on West 86th Street, with most of its functions integrated with local schools. Within a very short time, however, those quarters were outgrown, and the museum (it is a museum only in the sense that it has exhibits) moved to West 54th Street, next to a police station. Today, the lower floor maintains changing exhibits relating to children's lives in the city. One exhibit dealt with the life cycle of the cockroach, while others featured crickets, frogs, and turtles in residence for the pleasure and education of children whose city residence usually precludes getting to know such creatures. Platforms, stairs, and bilevels abound; all are geared to helping the child explore while learning. The upper floors are devoted to miscellaneous projects and arts and crafts.

CLOISTERS

Fort Tryon Park
923-3700
Tues-Sat: 9:30-5:15 (March-Oct)
Tues-Sat: 9:30-4:45 (Nov-Feb)

Brought over, brick by brick, from Europe, the Cloisters is a reconstructed monastery in northern Manhattan. This branch of the Metropolitan Museum of Art is devoted exclusively to medieval art. The grounds are magnificent (try to catch the sunset over the Hudson), as are the displays. There are free public tours every Tuesday, Wednesday, and Thursday at 3 p.m. in spring, summer, and fall. During the winter, they are held Wednesday only, and there are medieval festivals or concerts held twice a year.

COOPER-HEWITT MUSEUM

Fifth Ave at 91st St
860-6868
Tues: 10-9; Wed-Sat: 10-5; Sun: noon-3

Housed in Andrew Carnegie's Fifth Avenue mansion in the heart of the Museum Mile, the Cooper-Hewitt is the Smithsonian's National Museum of Design. Its purpose is to exhibit American interior designs and decorative art. There are permanent collections of pottery, textiles, and wallpaper.

DOG MUSEUM OF AMERICA
51 Madison Ave (bet 26th and 27th St)
696-8350
Tues-Thurs, Sat: 10-5; Wed: 10-7

Four times a year, the Dog Museum mounts a new exhibition of canines in art and literature. Each exhibit is accompanied by catalogs and posters, and past themes have featured "Presidential Pets," "Four Centuries of People and their Dogs," and "Geraldine Rockefeller: The Woman and Her Legacy" (Are they insinuating that she was a dog?). There have been dog fashion shows (hosted by Sandy of *Annie* fame) to supplement the Pampered Pets exhibit, as well as hardcover books covering exhibits such as "The Dog Observed: Photographs 1844-1983." School and other groups are welcome, and this place is nothing to "arf" about. They are very serious about the position of dogs in life and art.

ENERGY MUSEUM
145 E 14th St
460-6244
Tues-Sat: 10-4

Donations are requested, but not demanded, for this program designed especially for children. I strongly recommened that you call first to ask about what is available, because school groups are a priority, as are ongoing projects with children from the local community.

FIRE DEPARTMENT MUSEUM
104 Duane St
570-4230
Mon-Fri: 9-4

What child isn't fascinated by antique fire engines? This museum has it all: fire trucks and fire-fighting equipment from every era of the city's history. Everything is interesting, and the personnel are usually sympathetic to children.

FORBES GALLERIES
62 Fifth Ave (at 12th St)
620-2200
Tues, Wed, Fri, Sat: 10-4; Thurs: group tours

Malcolm Forbes, the publisher extraordinaire, has amassed several collections in his lifetime. (His penchant for hot air ballooning is one of the few that couldn't be catalogued.) In 1985 he finally put it all together in a gallery specifically constructed on the ground floor of the *Forbes Magazine* building. The large exhibition space is divided amongst Forbes collections of toy boats, lead soldiers, and the works of the czar's jeweler, Peter Carl Faberge. Included in the latter are ten authentic "Faberge Eggs," each of which is valued at over $1 million. That sort of makes the rest of the collection pale, but it shouldn't. Forbes is a master at whimsy, and his collection is that of a man who could afford to fulfill his whims and share them with others. There are 500 toy boats (some are so incredible in detail that they look seaworthy), 1200 lead soldiers, and a room of 160 bowling and swimming trophies. This is the best museum collection in town, outside of a museum. And Mr. Forbes deserves a hearty round of applause for wanting to share it.

FRICK COLLECTION
1 E 70th St
288-0700
Tues-Sat: 10-6; Sun: 1-6
Children under 10 not admitted

The Frick collection is housed in the former home of Henry Clay Frick, whose interest was in 14th-century through 19th-century art. Though absolutely unreceptive to children, the collection offers help to any serious student of painting, sculpture, European antique furniture, enamel images, or European and Asian porcelain. This is a quiet, serious place off the tourist trail.

JEWISH MUSEUM
1109 Fifth Avenue (at 92nd St)
860-1888
Mon, Wed, Thurs: 12-5; Tues: 12-8; Fri: 11-3

Housed in an old Fifth Avenue mansion, the Jewish Museum has left most of the original house intact. And "you don't have to be Jewish" to enjoy this place. The gift shop is one of the best in New York. The permanent collection concentrates on paintings, graphics, and sculpture inspired by the Jewish experience, and an unparalleled showing of Judaica.

METROPOLITAN MUSEUM OF ART
Fifth Avenue at 82nd St
535-7710
Wed-Sun: 9:30-5:15; Tues: 9:30-8:45

Sometimes the lines are so long you need advance reservations to get in. Other times, there are more people lounging outside on the steps than there are inside the huge building. It really depends on what the featured exhibits are. (The Van Gogh show was a sellout.) If you've never been here, it deserves at least one day of your time. The art, for the most part, is classical; they leave the modern stuff to other places. Indeed, the Met is a venerable institution and handles itself accordingly. The new Lehman wing exhibits furniture and paintings as they were in the Lehman house. Other rooms exhibit genuine 18th- and 19th-century European rooms. Upstairs, there are countless masterpieces—so many that even the greatest philistine should have seen at least a dozen of them as reproductions at some time in his life. The basement is devoted to pottery and ceramics and a super collection of authentic Dutch tile ovens. They are often overlooked. And check out the great gift shop and the Costume Institute.

MUSEUM OF AMERICAN FOLK ART
125 W 55th St (bet Sixth and Seventh Ave)
245-8296
Wed-Sun: 10:30-5:30; Tues: 10:30-8

Not to be confused with the American Craft Museum, this newly renovated museum specializes in folk art as depicted in American culture. It has a heavy emphasis on how that folk art was seen through history, and it mounts several shows a year with sculpture, paintings, and even furniture. In between shows, the museum closes completely for a week or two to prepare for the next show. So call in advance. These people are downright folksy.

MUSEUM OF BROADCASTING
1 E 53rd St
752-7684
Tues: noon-8; Wed-Sat: noon-5

This museum is literally for children of all ages; the older the child, the more enjoyable the visit. It is a repository of all of television's finest hours. Almost everything in the archives is entertaining (I once witnessed three husky, beer-bellied viewers wearing headsets, heaving with laughter at a screen nobody else could see or hear). Children are warmly welcomed here, and the staff will recommend selections. There is no admission, but donations are suggested. And while there's not a reservation policy per se, it helps to call ahead or arrive early in the afternoon.

MUSEUM OF HOLOGRAPHY
11 Mercer St
925-0526
Wed-Sun: 12-6

Holography is a fairly new art form: it uses the space in front of and behind the traditional two-dimensional plane. (When R-2 D-2 beamed the 3-D vision of Princess Leia's plea for Luke Skywalker in *Star Wars,* that was a hologram.) This museum has a whole roomful of these images, which appear to be floating in space. While it's hard to think of holography as a bona fide art form, it is fun and interesting, especially to younger visitors.

MUSEUM OF MODERN ART
11 W 53rd St
708-9400
Fri-Tues: 11-6; Thurs: 11-9

A popular place, even among nonmuseum lovers, the Museum of Modern Art is much appreciated in New York for its efforts to be modern in attitude as well as acquisition. This is best exemplified by the sculpture garden, which is not only open to those who wish to sit and muse in peace, but is frequently the scene of free or inexpensive summer evening concerts. MOMA also sponsors film festivals and revivals that are unsurpassed by commercial theaters, and stocks its gift shop with magnificent items. The latter offers games for both children and adults, copies of various home furnishings on exhibit in the museum itself, and the best selection of posters in the city. For those who do not care to take the inexpensive decorating route with MOMA posters, the museum itself offers paintings for rent. Rates are very reasonable (albeit with substantial deposits). Among those who use this service are diplomats on short visits; art connoisseurs who would rather have limited access to great art than a lifetime with mass-produced prints; people who need experts to prescribe the limits of good art from which they can select; and people whose tastes constantly change. This last category includes roommates who have divergent tastes; they rent paintings alternate months as a compromise.

MUSEUM OF THE AMERICAN INDIAN

Broadway at 155th St
283-2420
Tues-Sat: 10-5; Sun: 1-5

This is the world's largest museum devoted to the culture of the Indians of the Western Hemisphere, and it has three floors of displays featuring basketry, costumes, wood-carving, bead and quill work, weapons, and other artifacts. There are even some personal belongings of such great native American men as Sitting Bull, Crazy Horse, and Red Cloud. A gift shop on the first floor, just a few steps from an enormous totem pole outside, offers unusual items, and, for scholars of the native American, there's a terrific selection of over 1,000 titles on the subject. Admission is nominal and even lower on Tuesdays. If you want to make a day of it, three major institutions are next door: the Hispanic Society of America, the American Geographical Society, and the American Numismatic Society. They may be moving out of the city. (It's a political tempest.)

MUSEUM OF THE AMERICAN PIANO

211 W 58th St
246-4646
Tues-Sat: noon-5

Chalk this one up as another example of unique New York! Hungarian-born Kalman Detrich of Detrich Pianos at the same address wasn't satisfied with his life's work of tuning, restoring, and finishing antique pianos, so he rented an additional small room to show off some of the magnificent models he works with daily. The resulting Museum of the American Piano is Detrich's brainchild, but he is not its only parent. Contributions have come from all over, and the cramped space is stocked full of unusual instruments and piano paraphernalia. Actually, any room that houses a circa World War II concrete grand piano would suddenly seem cramped. Incidentally, it was created to surmount the rationing of wood, and it doesn't work now. Detrich sees pianos undergoing a revival and hopes this museum will abet that interest. A visit will insure that hope, and with Steinway Hall on the next block, all of New York seems a recital stage!

MUSEUM OF THE CITY OF NEW YORK
Fifth Avenue at 103rd St
534-1672
Tues-Sat: 10-5; Sun and holidays: 1-5

This museum is off the tourist trail, but it is one the whole family can enjoy. It is run by New Yorkers for New Yorkers, but out-of-towners can enjoy it, too, especially the terrific gift shop. For natives, this place is a must. There are true-to-life exhibits of New York costumes, flower, and fauna. And there is a "please touch" room that is a replica of a New Amsterdam home. The old-time pictures are enough to surprise anyone who knows the city today, and the changing exhibits are fascinating for a Big Apple addict. This is also one of the few museums that welcomes children.

NEW YORK HISTORICAL SOCIETY
170 Central Park W (at 77th St)
873-3400
Tues-Fri: 11-5; Sat: 10-5; Sun: 1-5

This is the oldest museum in New York (founded in 1804), and it specializes in American and New York historical materials. The permanent collection includes 433 of John James Audubon's 435 original *Birds of America* watercolors, as well as Colonial silver, early-American toys, and arts and crafts. There also is a permanent exhibit of glass and lamps of Louis Comfort Tiffany. For scholars, there is a first-rate research library.

SOLOMON R. GUGGENHEIM MUSEUM
1071 Fifth Ave (at 89th St)
360-3500
Tues: 11-8; Wed-Sun: 11-5

The Guggenheim, a Frank Lloyd Wright building, is as sleekly modern as its collection of paintings. It was designed around a continuous ramp that some critics said looked like an inverted snail. Admirers maintain that the structure makes it easier to see and appreciate paintings without the stifling, formal atmosphere of most museums. Because of its radical design and its fine collection of modern paintings and rotating exhibits, the Guggenheim is a must on every museum-goer's list.

STEINWAY HALL
109 W 57th St (near Sixth Ave)
246-1100
Mon-Wed, Fri: 9-6; Thurs: 9-9; Sat: 9-5

Steinway Hall is the showroom and showcase for the Steinway Piano company, and the place is magnificent enough to be classified a museum and to have been used as the backdrop of several dozen movies. (The day I was there, Catherine Deneuve was filming. It also played such an important role in one Dick Van Dyke movie that an exact duplicate was erected in Hollywood.) And it's easy to see why. The newest Steinway pianos are displayed against a backdrop that boasts a ceiling often compared to the Sistine Chapel, marble columns, and an art collection unrivaled among museums in the city. With a patron's hand, Steinway invites all to view the artwork and, yes, even to try out the pianos. (The only proviso is that genuine artists selecting instruments for use in concerts come first. But then again, who would want to sit down and play in front of the Philharmonic's guest soloist?) Tours of the entire premises—which point out salient features that could be overlooked amid the abundance of art on display—can be arranged by merely asking the receptionist to show you the hall. One Oregonian termed it the best thing he saw in New York, and I can only add a "bravo" to Steinway for their taste and willingness to share these riches with us.

THEATER MUSEUM
Minskoff Arcade
1515 Broadway (between 44th and 45th St)
944-7161
Wed-Sat: noon-8; Sun: 1-5

Faced with an enormous collection of theater memorabilia, the folks at the Museum of the City of New York decided to bring it downtown to the theater district and display it in this minimuseum. While the parent museum should not be missed, theatergoers, or those with only a short time to browse, have much to gain from a stop at this branch. Helen Hayes can be seen in an exclusive interview filmed for the museum, and in addition to a changing exhibit that highlights costumes, props, playbills, posters, and souvenirs from New York theater's illustrious past, there is an excellent sound-and-light show. This is theater about the theater, and it's thoroughly enjoyable. Suggested donations are one dollar for adults and 50 cents for students and senior citizens.

THEODORE ROOSEVELT BIRTHPLACE

28 E 20th St (bet Broadway and Park Ave)
260-1616
Wed-Sun: 9-5

T.R. was a born-and-bred New Yorker with his official home, Sagamore Hill in Oyster Bay, Long Island. This brownstone was his birthplace and boyhood home while the family was in the city. Several years ago, it was completely renovated and restored and now the Victorian edifice reflects his interests and political career. This is another spot to try on New Yorkers. Bet they can't locate it!

Sights

BROADWAY

Matinees are on Wednesdays, Saturdays, and Sundays. For a big hit, you're better off making advance arrangements with the box office. For other shows, try TKTS at Duffy Square or 100 William Street; if you're patient enough to wait for bargain-priced tickets, you can get in to see the most popular shows. (Not always, though.) The William Street branch doesn't handle matinees, but it's quicker for evening performances. (If time's important, it pays to go downtown on the day of the performance and plan the day from there.) If money's no object, remember that although New York has a strict law against scalping, you can probably find someone ignoring it, and can get tickets for any show—at a stiff price.

CENTRAL PARK

59th St—110th St (bet Fifth Ave and Central Park W)
397-3156

Quite safe, really—if you use common sense. This means no solitary midnight strolls through the park, particularly if you're dripping with cash and expensive accessories. During daylight hours, there are enough people in the park to make it safe, and there's enough to do to keep you busy for three or four days. A 30-minute horse-and-carriage ride (legally set at a fixed rate, no matter what the driver says) is delightful, and shows off the park's highlights.

There are more playgrounds than you can count. All of them are modern, child-safe, and contain some of the most imaginative equipment available. New York's youth experts have these playgrounds catalogued by specialties. Two of the best are on the East Side: the Sand Playground (85th St) and the Estee Lauder Adventure Playground (a stone's throw from the zoo entrance on 71st St). On the West Side, the largest and most popular playground is at the 86th Street entrance; a smaller, equally popular one is at the 68th Street entrance. During the summer, the Heckster Water Playground is a cool oasis in the middle of the park (62nd St entrance).

The Central Park Zoo (64th to 70th St, off Fifth Ave, 360-8288) is being renovated and brought up to snuff. The Lehman Children's Zoo will remain as it is, as it should. It's a marvelous place for children, with better fairy-tale attractions and animals than many tourist parks. Admission to the children's zoo is moderate.

The merry-go-round, recently restored, is old-fashioned and charming. It's almost in the center of the park (62nd St entrance), and it's almost as wonderful to look at as it is to ride. It you happen to see any old photographs of the carousel, don't be surprised if it looks the same today as it did back then.

For almost 20 years, the lowlifes have claimed Bethesda Fountain as their own, but they usually only show up on weekends, and they're more, ah, colorful than dangerous. Part of a reclamation project is the establishment of a restaurant there. Next to the fountain are two boating lakes and a pond devoted to toy sailboats. Boats can be rented at the boathouse (E 72nd St entrance), or by calling 288-7707.

When temperatures drop, it's the season for the Wollman Memorial Skating Rink (off the E 64th entrance, 397-3158). Fees are nominal, and skaters aren't as showcased as they are at Rockefeller Center. (Your spills aren't so public!) Call first. It's been undergoing renovations for years and was supposed to reopen some time ago. Instead, there have been astronomical cost overruns and delays.

And at Fifth Avenue and 60th Street, children can ride in the pony carts while parents browse through the discount book kiosks—which is a good way to pass the time while waiting for one of the free concerts, puppet shows, plays, or competitions that abound in the park during the spring and summer.

CHINATOWN, LITTLE ITALY, THE LOWER EAST SIDE

The lines between these neighborhoods blur more as the years pass by. For local color and some of the purest Chinese meals this side of the Great Wall, visit Chinatown. For equally good Italian food, go to Little Italy, where cheeses, breads, and pastries are knockouts. If it's festival time, you're in luck: the streets will be overflowing with good things to eat. Hurry through the Bowery (travel on Grand Street, and you can avoid it altogether), and you're on the Lower East Side. *That*, folks, is an experience. If I had time for only one place in the city, the Lower East Side would be it. It resembles nothing so much as a crowded Old World bazaar, especially on Sundays, and the bargains are sensational. However, if shopping, pushing and shoving, and hordes of rude people bother you, stick to the city's more refined neighborhoods.

CON EDISON'S CONSERVATION CENTER

Chrysler Bldg (Lexington Ave at 42nd St)
599-3435
Tues-Sat: 10-5:30

One of the best aspects of this exhibit is the opportunity to see the Chrysler Building, one of New York's most outstanding art-deco edifices. The exhibit fascinates children and parents alike. Con Ed, as the company is colloquially known, is the power company of New York, and its exhibit explains how electricity works and offers hints on how to conserve energy.

EMPIRE STATE BUILDING

Fifth Ave at 34th St
736-3100
Daily: 9:30 a.m.-midnight

The view from the Empire State Building still challenges that of the World Trade Center, and remains the city's reigning landmark. (I bet you've never seen a salt or pepper shaker made in the likeness of the World Trade Center!) The staff here also seems more receptive to children, and even the most cynical pint-sized tourist won't be able to resist a stop at the Guinness World Records Exhibit (947-2339) on the concourse.

LINCOLN CENTER

Broadway at 66th St

It helps to have tickets to a concert here, but there's a lot to see and do even without having something specific in mind. Visit the library, where patrons are invited to listen to recordings and tapes on the first floor, and see everything written about music, dance, theater, and film in the collections on the third floor. (There's also a videotape collection, but you have to make reservations.) There are also backstage tours of Lincoln Center, and sometimes there are open rehearsals—but never, ever, of the New York City Ballet. (Sorry, ballet fans.)

ROCKEFELLER CENTER

Radio City Music Hall should not be missed. There are several seasonal shows, and the Radio City Rockettes and orchestra are New York institutions. Elsewhere in Rockefeller Center, there are tours of the complex and NBC's studios, as well as dining. And there are shopping arcades, travel agencies, and international offices. If you spend a day here, go to the Rainbow Room for dinner and dancing. Don't forget *The New York Experience* (869-0345) across the street in the McGraw-Hill Building (49th St and Sixth Ave).

STATEN ISLAND FERRY

Battery Park Ferry Slips

This is the biggest and best buy in town: the ferry ride from South Ferry to Staten Island. Twenty minutes each way (allow extra time for the turnaround), this ride is twice as long as the ferry trips to Ellis Island or the Statue of Liberty, and you'll pass both sites. Kids love the ferry ride, and adults do, too. It's particularly refreshing during the summer, although in the autumn and spring, a stiff, salty breeze can be quite invigorating.

STATUE OF LIBERTY and ELLIS ISLAND

Battery Park Ferry Slips

The only way to get to the Statue of Liberty is via the Miss Liberty boats. And you *have* to see the statue if you're a tourist. But remember that the climb up the circular staircase inside Miss Liberty is tedious and tiring, especially for children, who tend to be unimpressed by the view from the statue's crown. Also, the statue is undergoing renovation in preparation for the celebration of its centennial, so it may be closed. An alternative that's more popular with the younger generation is Ellis Island. If your ancestors sailed to American and landed in New York, it's likely they entered by way of Ellis Island. (''Likely, '' because not all immigrants did: the well-heeled and well-connected bypassed it.) Today, the park is run by the National Park Service as a monument to U. S. immigration policies. (Ellis Island hasn't been used for immigration screenings for nearly 40 years.) While the place is in disrepair (some of the buildings are dangerously rundown), it's an educational experience. The ride to the island on the National Monument Ferry (269-5755) gives you a breathtaking vista of Manhattan.

THE UNITED NATIONS

42nd St at First Ave

Depending on the political climate, this can be a real snooze or quite enthralling. Free tickets to council meetings are distributed before sessions, and there are guided tours of the complex. Visit the cafeteria for a good (but not inexpensive) lunch; the gift shop sells unique gifts. Don't expect a warm welcome for you or your toddler. Security is tight, and those under five years of age are not allowed on tours.

WORLD TRADE CENTER

2 World Trade Center

466-7377 (observation deck)

The view from the 107th floor is phenomenal; it absolutely defies description. But lines can be *very* long. I suggest that if you're downtown anyway, you should combine this with the other sights of the neighborhood. The Commodities Exchange Center, the U.S.

Customs House, Windows on the World, and the Big Kitchen are all in the Center proper and are interesting to children. Just down the street is the New York Stock Exchange (20 Broad St, 623-5168), where there's a free tour from 10 to 4 weekdays. The South Street Seaport (Fulton and South St) is a bit of a hike from here, but it's worth the effort. So is the Fire Department Museum (104 Duane St, 570-4230), open weekdays from 9 to 4.

Special Telephone Numbers

EMERGENCY SERVICES

AAA Highway Conditions 594-0700
AAA Road Service 695-8311
Addict Assistance 222-8866
Ambulance 911
Arson Hotline 566-7340
Babysitters Association 865-9348
Babysitters' Guild 682-0227
Child-Care (part-time) 879-4343
Child Health Stations 349-2255
Crime Victims Hotline 577-7777
Day Care Council of New York 398-0380
Day Care (NYC Health Dept.) 334-7813
Emergency Dental Service 679-3966
Emergency Medical Service 879-1000
Eye Clinics 690-1875
Fire 911
Gas and Steam Leaks (Con-Edison) 683-8830
Immunizations 566-7103
New York Women Against Rape 777-4000
Parents League of New York 737-7385
Poisoning .... 340-4494 or 764-7667
Police 911
To locate nearest police precinct 374-5000
Police Rape Hotline 732-7706
Pre-School Association of the West Side (city-wide info on nearest child-care center) 222-0104
School Health (information on health services for children) 566-7082
Sleepline 882-7800
Suicide Prevention 532-2400

TRANSPORTATION

TRAINS

Amtrak 736-4545
JFK Express 858-7272

Long Island Railroad 739-4200
Metro North.................................... 532-4900
New Jersey Transit .... (201) 762-5100
PATH Train 732-8920
PATH Train (Newark Airport) 466-7649
Staten Island Rapid Transit.................... 447-8601
Subways .... (718) 330-1234

BUSES

Carey Bus Transportation (to airports)............ 632-0500
Continental Trailways 730-7460
George Washington Bus Terminal 564-1114
Greyhound Bus 635-0800
NYC Buses............................ (718) 330-1234
Port Authority Bus Terminal 564-8484

TAXIS

All City Radio Taxi 796-1111
Minute Men 899-5600
NYC Taxi & Limousine Commission
(lost property and complaints) 825-0420

AIR TRAVEL

Manhattan Air Terminal
(information and tickets for all major airlines) 986-0888
JFK Airport....................................... 656-4520
LaGuardia Airport 476-5000
Newark Airport......................... (201) 961-2000

ENTERTAINMENT

Big Apple Report (current events in NYC)............ 976-2323
City Park Information 472-1003
Free Daily Events in the City (recording) 755-4100
Jazzline 463-0200
Madison Square Garden (sports events) 564-4400
New York Convention & Visitors Bureau.............. 397-8222
New York Public Library General Information......... 340-0849
Sportsphone 976-1313
WNCN Concertline (for classical music)............... 921-9129

OTHER

City Phone (General Information).................... 675-0900
Customs 466-5550
Stock Market Reports 976-4141
Time of Day...................................... 976-1616
Weather 976-1212

Weather

New York weather can be very cold or very warm, but the climate does not impair the many activities in the city. The temperature has gone as low as 5° and as high as 105°. The temperate times are in April, May, September, and October. This chart gives you some idea of what you might expect during various times of the year in New York. If you'd like a current report on the weather, call 976-1212.

	Ave. Max. Temp.	**Ave. Min. Temp.**	**Ave. Precip.**
January	39° (4)	26° (-3)	2.71 in.
February	40° (4)	27° (-3)	2.92
March	48° (9)	34° (1)	3.73
April	61° (16)	44° (7)	3.30
May	71° (22)	53° (12)	3.47
June	81° (27)	63° (18)	2.96
July	85° (29)	68° (20)	3.68
August	83° (28)	66° (19)	4.01
September	77° (25)	60° (16)	3.27
October	67° (19)	51° (11)	2.85
November	54° (12)	41° (5)	3.76
December	41° (5)	30° (-1)	3.53

INDEX

B

D

G

H

I

J

K

L

N

O

P

S

T

U

V

W

X

Y

Z